Waiter, the check, please.—Herr Ober, bitte zahlen.

Where is there a good hotel?—Wo ist hier ein gutes Hotel'?

How do I get to the station?—Wie komme ich zum Bahnhof?

I'm sick.—Ich bin krank.

I need a doctor.—Ich brauche einen Arzt.

I want to send a telegram.—Ich möchte gern ein Telegramm' schicken.

Where can I change money?—Wo kann ich hier Geld wechseln?

Do you accept travelers checks?—Nehmen Sie Reiseschecks?

Right away.—Sofort'.

Help!—Hilfe!

Come in.—Herein'.

Hello (on telephone).—Hier . . . (say your name).

Stop.—Halt.

Hurry.—Schnell.

To the right.—Rechts.

To the left.—Links.

Straight ahead.—Gera'de aus.

Signs

Vorsicht—Caution	Raucher—For smokers
Achtung—Watch out	Nichtraucher—
Ausgang—Exit	For non-smokers
Eingang—Entrance	Rauchen verboten—
Halt—Stop	No smoking
Geschlossen—Closed	Kein Zutritt—
Geöffnet—Open	No admittance
Langsam—Slow	Damen (or) Frauen—
Verboten—Prohibited	Women
Gesperrt—Road closed	Herren (or) Männer—
Einbahnstraße—	Men
One way street	Abort—Toilet

The Random House German Vest Pocket Dictionary

GERMAN – ENGLISH

ENGLISH – GERMAN

By Jenni Karding Moulton

*Under the General Editorship of
Professor* William G. Moulton
Princeton University

RANDOM  HOUSE

NEW YORK

Abbreviations

abbr.	abbreviation	*intr.*	intransitive
adj.	adjective	*jur.*	juridical
adv.	adverb	*m.*	masculine
arch.	architecture	*math.*	mathematics
art.	article	*med.*	medicine
bot.	botany	*mil.*	military
chem.	chemistry	*n.*	noun
comm.	commercial	*naut.*	nautical
conj.	conjunction	*nt.*	neuter
cpds.	compounds	*num.*	number
eccles.	ecclesiastical	*pl.*	plural
econ.	economics	*pol.*	politics
elec.	electricity	*pred.*	predicate
f.	feminine	*prep.*	preposition
fam.	familiar	*pron.*	pronoun
fig.	figuratively	*sg.*	singular
geogr.	geography	*tech.*	technical
geom.	geometry	*tr.*	transitive
gov't.	government	*typogr.*	typography
gram.	grammar	*vb.*	verb
interj.	interjection	*zool.*	zoology

Concise Pronunciation Guide

Consonants

b Usually like English *b*: **Bett, graben.** But when final or before *s* or *t*, like English *p*: **das Grab, des Grabs, er gräbt.**

c In foreign words only. Before *a, o, u*, like English *k*: **Café'.** Before *ä, e, i* in words borrowed from Latin, like English *ts*: **Cicero;** otherwise usually with the foreign pronunciation.

ch After *a, o, u, au*, a scraping sound like Scottish *ch* in *loch*, made between the back of the tongue and the roof of the mouth: **Dach, Loch, Buch, auch.** In other positions, much like English *h* in *hue*: **Dächer, Löcher, Bücher, ich, manch, welch, durch.** In words borrowed from Greek or Latin, initial *ch* before *a, o, u, l, r* is like English *k*: **Charak'ter, Chor, Christ.** In words borrowed from French it is like German *sch*: **Chance.**

chs As a fixed combination, like English *ks*: **der Dachs,** *the badger.* But when the *s* is an ending, like German *ch* plus *s*: **des Dachs,** genitive of **das Dach,** *the roof.*

ck As in English: **backen, Stock.**

d Usually like English *d*: **Ding, Rede.** But when final or before *s*, like English *t*: **das Band, des Bands.**

dt Like English *tt*: **Stadt** just like **statt.**

f As in English: **Feuer, Ofen, Schaf.**

g Usually like English *g* in *get*: **Geld, schlagen, Könige, reinigen.** But when final or before *s* or *t*, like English *k*: **der Schlag, des Schlags, er schlägt.** However, *ig* when final or before *s* or *t* is like German *ich*: **der König, des Königs, er reinigt.** In words borrowed from French, *g* before *e* is like English *z* in *azure*: **Loge.**

h As in English: **hier.** But after vowels it is only a sign of vowel length, and is not pronounced: **gehen, Bahn, Kuh.**

j Like English *y*: **Jahr.** In a few words borrowed from French, like English *z* in *azure*: **Journal'.**

k As in English: **kennen, Haken, buk.**

l Not the "dark *l*" of English *mill, bill,* but the "bright *l*" of English *million, billion*: **lang, fallen, hell.**

m As in English: **mehr, kommen, dumm.**

n As in English: **neu, kennen, kann.**

ng Always like English *ng* in *singer*, never like English *ng* + *g* in *finger*. German **Finger, Hunger.**

p As in English: **Post, Rippe, Tip.**

pf Like English *pf* in *cupful*: **Kopf, Apfel, Pfund.**

ph As in English: **Philosophie'.**

qu Like English *kv*: **Quelle, Aqua'rium.**

r When followed by a vowel, either a gargled sound made between the back of the tongue and the roof of the mouth, or (less commonly) a quick flip of the tongue tip against the gum ridge: **Ring, Haare, bessere.** When not followed by a vowel,

iii

Consonants

r	a sound much like the *ah* of English *yeah*, or the *a* of *sofa:* **Haar, besser.**	
s	Usually like English *z* in *zebra*, or *s* in *rose:* **sie, Rose.** But when final or before a consonant, like English *s* in *this:* **das, Wespe, Liste, Maske.**	
sch	Like English *sh* in *ship*, but with the lips rounded: **Schiff, waschen, Tisch.**	
sp } **st** }	At the beginning of a word, like *sch* + *p*, *sch* + *t:* **Spiel, Stahl.**	
ss } **ß** }	Like English *ss* in *miss*. *ss* is written only after a short vowel when another vowel follows: **müssen.** Otherwise ß is written: finally **muß**, before a consonant **mußte**, or after a long vowel **Muße.**	
t	As in English: **tun, bitter, Blatt.**	
th	Always like *t:* **Thea'ter;** never like English *th.*	
tion	Pronounced *tsyohn:* **Nation', Aktion'.**	
tsch	Like *t* + *sch:* **deutsch.**	
tz	Like English *ts:* **sitzen, Platz.**	
v	In German words, like English *f:* **Vater, Frevel.** In foreign words, like English *v:* **Novem'ber, Moti've;** but finally and before *s*, like *f* again: **das Motiv', des Motivs'.**	
w	Like English *v:* **Wagen, Löwe.**	
x	As in English: **Hexe.**	
z	Always like English *ts:* **zehn, Kreuz, Salz.**	

Short vowels

a	Satz	Between English *o* in *hot* and *u* in *hut.*
ä } **e** }	Sätze } setze }	Like English *e* in *set.*
i	sitze	Like English *i* in *sit.*
o	Stock	Like English *o* in *gonna*, or the "New England short *o*" in *coat, road;* shorter than English *o* in *cost.*
ö	Stöcke	Tongue position as for short *e*, lips rounded as for short *o.*
u	Busch	Like English *u* in *bush.*
ü } **y** }	Büsche } mystisch }	Tongue position as for short *i*, lips rounded as for short *u.*

Unaccented short e

e	beginne	Like English *e* in *begin, pocket.*

Long vowels

a } **ah** } **aa** }	Tal } Zahl } Saal }	Like English *a* in *father.*
ä } **äh** }	Täler } zählen }	In elevated speech, like English *ai* in *fair;* otherwise just like German long *e.*
e } **eh** } **ee** }	wer } mehr } Meer }	Like English *ey* in *they*, but with no glide toward a *y* sound.
i } **ih** } **ie** }	mir } ihr } Bier }	Like English *i* in *machine*, but with no glide toward a *y* sound.

iv

long vowels

o	Ton		Like English *ow* is *slow*, but with no
oh	Sohn	}	glide toward a *w* sound.
oo	Boot		
ö	Töne	}	Tongue position as for long *e*, lips round-
öh	Söhne		ed as for long *o*.
u	Hut	}	Like English *u* in *rule*, but with no
uh	Kuh		glide toward a *w* sound.
ü	Hüte		Tongue position as for long *i*, lips round-
üh	Kühe	}	ed as for long *u*.
y	Typ		

Diphthongs

ei	Seite	}	Like English *i* in *side*. Also spelled *ey*,
ai	Saite		*ay* in names: *Meyer, Bayern*.
au	Haut		Like English *ou* in *out*.
eu	heute	}	Like English *oi* in *oil*.
äu	Häute		

The spelling of vowel length	**Short**	**Long**
An accented vowel is always short when followed by a doubled consonant letter, but nearly always long when followed by a single consonant letter.	schlaff	Schlaf
	wenn	wen
	still	Stil
	offen	Ofen
	öffnen	Öfen
Note that	Butter	Puter
	dünne	Düne
ck counts as the doubled form of **k:**	hacken	Haken
tz counts as the doubled form of **z:**	putzen	duzen
ss counts as the doubled form of **ß:**	Masse	Maße
Vowels are always long when followed by (unpronounced) **h:**	wann	Wahn
	stelle	stehle
	irre	ihre
	Wonne	wohne
	gönne	Söhne
	Rum	Ruhm
	dünn	kühn
Vowels are always long when they are written double:	Stadt	Staat
	Bett	Beet
	Gott	Boot
In this respect, **ie** counts as the doubled form of **i:**	bitte	biete

German Accentuation

Most German words are accented on the first syllable: **Mo'nate, ar'beitete, Düsenkampfflugzeuge**. However, the prefixes **be-, emp-, ent-, er-, ge-, ver-, zer-** are never accented: **befeh'len, der Befehl', empfan'gen, der Empfang'**, etc. Other prefixes are usually accented in nouns: **der Un'terricht**, but unaccented in verbs: **unterrich'ten**. Foreign words are often accented on a syllable other than the first: **Hotel', Muse'um, Photographie'**.

Note particularly the accentuation of such forms as **übertre′ten, ich übertre′te** *I overstep*, where **über** is a prefix; but **ü′bertreten, ich trete . . . über** *I step over* where **über** is a separate word, despite the fact that **ü′bertreten** is spelled without a space. These two types will be distinguished in this dictionary by writing **übertre′-ten** but **über·treten**.

German spelling does not indicate the place of the accent. In this dictionary, accent will be marked when it falls on a syllable other than the first: **Befehl′, unterrich′ten, Photographie′**. Where it is not marked, the accent is on the first syllable: **Monate, arbeitete, Düsenkampf-flugzeuge, Unterricht, über·treten**.

Nouns

This listing ↓	means this ↓
Wagen, -	plural is **Wagen**.
Vater, ⸚	plural is **Väter**.
Tisch, -e	plural is **Tische**.
Sohn, ⸚e	plural is **Söhne**.
Bild, -er	plural is **Bilder**.
Haus, ⸚er	plural is **Häuser**.
Auge, -n	plural is **Augen**.
Ohr, -en	plural is **Ohren**.
Hotel′, -s	plural is **Hotels′**.
Muse′um, -e′en	plural is **Muse′en**.
Doktor, -o′ren	plural is **Dokto′ren**.
Kopie′, -i′en	plural is **Kopi′en**, with three syllables.
Kuß, ⸚sse	final **ß** changes to medial **ss** because the **ü** is short.
Fuß, ⸚e	final **ß** kept in all forms because the **ü** is long.
Junge, -n, -n	nominative singular is **Junge,** all other forms are **Jungen**.
Name(n), -	declined like **Wagen** (above), except that nominative singular is **Name**.
Beamt′ -	takes adjective endings: **ein Beamter, der Beamte, zwei Beamte, die zwei Beamten**.
Milch	has no plural.
Leute, *n.pl.*	has no singular.

From almost any German noun meaning some kind of man or boy, a noun meaning the corresponding woman or girl can be formed by adding **-in**: **der Arbeiter** *worker* (*man or boy*), **die Arbeiterin** *worker* (*woman or girl*); **der Russe** *Russian* (*man or boy*), **die Russin** *Russian* (*woman or girl*). Such feminine nouns will not usually be listed in this dictionary, unless they involve some sort of irregularity: **der Franzo′se,** *Frenchman*, **die Franzö′sin** *Frenchwoman* (irregular because of the umlaut).

Adjectives

Most German adjectives can also be used, without ending, as adverbs: **schlecht** *bad, badly*. The few which never occur without ending as adverbs are listed with a following hyphen: **link-** *left*, **ober-** *upper*, **zweit-** *second*. (The corresponding adverbs are **links** *to the left*, **oben** *above*, **zweitens** *secondly*.)

Adjectives which take umlaut in the comparative and superlative are listed as follows: **lang** (ʺ), i.e., the comparative and superlative are **länger, längst-**.

Limiting or determining adjectives are listed in the nominative singular masculine, with an indication of the nominative singular neuter and feminine: **der, das, die, dieser, -es, -e; ein, -, -e.**

Descriptive adjectives take the following endings:

| | Strong endings | | | | Weak endings | | | |
	masc.	neut.	fem.	pl.	masc.	neut.	fem.	pl.
nom.	-er	-es	-e	-e	-e	-e	-e	-en
acc.	-en	-es	-e	-e	-en	-e	-e	-en
dat.	-em	-em	-er	-en	-en	-en	-en	-en
gen.	-en	-en	-er	-en	-en	-en	-en	-en

Weak endings are used if the adjective is preceded by an inflected form of a limiting (determining) adjective; strong endings are used otherwise.

Verbs

Regular weak verbs are listed simply in the infinitive: **machen**. If a verb is used with a separable prefix (accented adverb), this is indicated by a raised dot: **auf·machen** (i.e., the infinitive is **aufmachen**, the present **ich mache . . . auf**, the past **ich machte . . . auf**, the past participle **aufgemacht**). An asterisk after a verb refers to the following lists of irregular weak and strong verbs. The sign † means that a verb takes the auxiliary verb **sein**; the sign ‡ means that a verb can take either **sein** or **haben**.

Irregular weak verbs

Infinitive	3rd sg. present	Past	Subjunctive	Past participle
haben	hat	hatte	hätte	gehabt
bringen	bringt	brachte	brächte	gebracht
denken	denkt	dachte	dächte	gedacht
dünken	dünkt, deucht	dünkte, deuchte	dünkte, deuchte	gedünkt, gedeucht
brennen	brennt	brannte	brennte	gebrannt
kennen	kennt	kannte	kennte	gekannt
nennen	nennt	nannte	nennte	genannt
†rennen	rennt	rannte	rennte	gerannt
senden	sendet	sandte	sendete	gesandt
wenden	wendet	wandte	wendete	gewandt
dürfen	darf	durfte	dürfte	gedurft

Infinitive	3rd sg. present	Past	Subjunctive	Past participle
können	kann	konnte	könnte	gekonnt
mögen	mag	mochte	mche	gemocht
müssen	muß	mußte	müßte	gemußt
sollen	soll	sollte	sollte	gesollt
wollen	will	wollte	wollte	gewollt
wissen	weiß	wußte	wüßte	gewußt

Strong verbs

If a derived or compound verb is not listed, its forms may be found by consulting the simple verb. The sign + means that a regular weak form is also used.

Infinitive	3rd sg. present	Past	Subjunctive	Past participle
backen	bäckt	+buk	+büke	gebacken
befehlen	befiehlt	befahl	beföhle	befohlen
beginnen	beginnt	begann	begönne, begänne	begonnen
beißen	beißt	biß	bisse	gebissen
bergen	birgt	barg	bärge	geborgen
†bersten	birst	barst	bärste	geborsten
bewegen	bewegt	bewog	bewöge	bewogen
‡biegen	biegt	bog	böge	gebogen
bieten	bietet	bot	böte	geboten
binden	bindet	band	bände	gebunden
bitten	bittet	bat	bäte	gebeten
blasen	bläst	blies	bliese	geblasen
†bleiben	bleibt	blieb	bliebe	geblieben
braten	brät	briet	briete	gebraten
brechen	bricht	brach	bräch	gebrochen
dingen	dingt	+dang	+dänge	+gedungen
dreschen	drischt	drosch, drasch	drösche, dräsche	gedroschen
†dringen	dringt	drang	dränge	gedrungen
†erbleichen	erbleicht	+erblich	+erbliche	+erblichen
erlöschen	erlischt	erlosch	erlösche	erloschen
essen	ißt	aß	äße	gegessen
‡fahren	fährt	fuhr	führe	gefahren
†fallen	fällt	fiel	fiele	gefallen
fangen	fängt	fing	finge	gefangen
fechten	ficht	focht	föchte	gefochten
finden	findet	fand	fände	gefunden
flechten	flicht	flocht	flöchte	geflochten
‡fliegen	fliegt	flog	flöge	geflogen
†fliehen	flieht	floh	flöhe	geflohen
†fließen	fließt	floß	flösse	geflossen
fressen	frißt	fraß	fräße	gefressen
frieren	friert	fror	fröre	gefroren
gären	gärt	+gor	+göre	+gegoren
gebären	gebiert	gebar	gebäre	geboren
geben	gibt	gab	gäbe	gegeben
†gedeihen	gedeiht	gedieh	gediehe	gediehen

Infinitive	3rd sg. present	Past	Subjunctive	Past participle
†gehen	geht	ging	ginge	gegangen
†gelingen	gelingt	gelang	gelänge	gelungen
gelten	gilt	galt	gölte, gälte	gegolten
†genesen	genest	genas	genäse	genesen
genießen	genießt	genoß	genösse	genossen
†geschehen	geschieht	geschah	geschähe	geschehen
gewinnen	gewinnt	gewann	gewönne, gewänne	gewonnen
gießen	gießt	goß	gösse	gegossen
gleichen	gleicht	glich	gliche	geglichen
†gleiten	gleitet	glitt	glitte	geglitten
glimmen	glimmt	†glomm	†glömme	†geglommen
graben	gräbt	grub	grübe	gegraben
greifen	greift	griff	griffe	gegriffen
halten	hält	hielt	hielte	gehalten
hängen	hängt	hing	hinge	gehangen
hauen	haut	†hieb	†hiebe	gehauen
heben	hebt	hob, hub	höbe, hübe	gehoben
heißen	heißt	hieß	hieße	geheißen
helfen	hilft	half	hülfe, hälfe	geholfen
klimmen	klimmt	†klomm	†klömme	†geklommen
klingen	klingt	klang	klänge	geklungen
kneifen	kneift	kniff	kniffe	gekniffen
†kommen	kommt	kam	käme	gekommen
†kriechen	kriecht	kroch	kröche	gekrochen
laden	lädst	lud	lüde	geladen
lassen	läßt	ließ	ließe	gelassen
†laufen	läuft	lief	liefe	gelaufen
leiden	leidet	litt	litte	gelitten
leihen	leiht	lieh	liehe	geliehen
lesen	liest	las	läse	gelesen
liegen	liegt	lag	läge	gelegen
lügen	lügt	log	löge	gelogen
meiden	meidet	mied	miede	gemieden
melken	†milkt	†molk	†mölke	†gemolken
messen	mißt	maß	mäße	gemessen
mißlingen	mißlingt	mißlang	mißlänge	mißlungen
nehmen	nimmt	nahm	nähme	genommen
pfeifen	pfeift	pfiff	pfiffe	gepfiffen
preisen	preist	pries	priese	gepriesen
quellen	quillt	quoll	quölle	gequollen
raten	rät	riet	riete	geraten
reiben	reibt	rieb	riebe	gerieben
‡reißen	reißt	riß	risse	gerissen
‡reiten	reitet	ritt	ritte	geritten
riechen	riecht	roch	röche	gerochen
ringen	ringt	rang	ränge	gerungen
rinnen	rinnt	rann	ränne, rönne	geronnen
rufen	ruft	rief	riefe	gerufen
saufen	säuft	soff	söffe	gesoffen
saugen	saugt	†sog	†söge	†gesogen

ix

Infinitive	3rd sg. present	Past	Subjunctive	Past participle
schaffen	schafft	schuf	schüfe	geschaffen
schallen	schallt	+scholl	+schölle	geschallt
‡scheiden	scheidet	schied	schiede	geschieden
scheinen	scheint	schien	schiene	geschienen
schelten	schilt	schalt	schölte	gescholten
scheren	schert	+schor	+schöre	+geschoren
schieben	schiebt	schob	schöbe	geschoben
schießen	schießt	schoß	schösse	geschossen
schinden	schindet	schund	schünde	geschunden
schlafen	schläft	schlief	schliefe	geschlafen
schlagen	schlägt	schlug	schlüge	geschlagen
‡schleichen	schleicht	schlich	schliche	geschlichen
schleifen	schleift	schliff	schliffe	geschliffen
schließen	schließt	schloß	schlösse	geschlossen
schlingen	schlingt	schlang	schlänge	geschlungen
schmeißen	schmeißt	schmiß	schmisse	geschmissen
schmeizen	schmilzt	schmolz	schmölze	geschmolzen
schnauben	schnaubt	+schnob	+schnöbe	+geschnoben
schneiden	schneidet	schnitt	schnitte	geschnitten
schrecken	schrickt	schrak	schräke	geschrocken
schreiben	schreibt	schrieb	schriebe	geschrieben
schreien	schreit	schrie	schriee	geschrie(e)n
‡schreiten	schreitet	schritt	schritte	geschritten
schweigen	schweigt	schwieg	schwiege	geschwiegen
schwellen	schwillt	schwoll	schwölle	geschwollen
‡schwimmen	schwimmt	schwamm	schwömme, schwämme	geschwommen
‡schwinden	schwindet	schwand	schwände	geschwunden
schwingen	schwingt	schwang	schwänge	geschwungen
schwören	schwört	+schwur, schwor	+schwüre	+geschworen
sehen	sieht	sah	sähe	gesehen
sein	ist	war	wäre	gewesen
sieden	siedet	+sott	+sötte	+gesotten
singen	singt	sang	sänge	gesungen
‡sinken	sinkt	sank	sänke	gesunken
sinnen	sinnt	sann	sänne, sönne	gesonnen
sitzen	sitzt	saß	säße	gesessen
speien	speit	spie	spiee	gespie(e)n
spinnen	spinnt	spann	spönne, spänne	gesponnen
spleißen	spleißt	spliß	splisse	gesplissen
sprechen	spricht	sprach	spräche	gesprochen
sprießen	sprießt	sproß	sprösse	gesprossen
‡springen	springt	sprang	spränge	gesprungen
stechen	sticht	stach	stäche	gestochen
stecken	steckt	+stak	+stäke	gesteck
stehen	steht	stand	stände, stünde	gestanden
stehlen	stiehlt	stahl	stähle, stöhle	gestohlen
‡steigen	steigt	stieg	stiege	gestiegen
‡sterben	stirbt	starb	stürbe	gestorben
‡stieben	stiebt	+stob	+stöbe	+gestoben

x

Infinitive	3rd sg. present	Past	Subjunctive	Past participle
stinken	stinkt	stank	stänke	gestunken
‡stoßen	stößt	stieß	stieße	gestoßen
streichen	streicht	strich	striche	gestrichen
streiten	streitet	stritt	stritte	gestritten
tragen	trägt	trug	trüge	getragen
treffen	trifft	traf	träfe	getroffen
‡treiben	treibt	trieb	triebe	getrieben
‡treten	tritt	trat	träte	getreten
trinken	trinkt	trank	tränke	getrunken
trügen	trügt	trog	tröge	getrogen
tun	tut	tat	täte	getan
verbleichen	verbleicht	verblich	verbliche	verblichen
verderben	verdirbt	verdarb	verdürbe	verdorben
verdrießen	verdrießt	verdroß	verdrösse	verdrossen
vergessen	vergißt	vergaß	vergäße	vergessen
verlieren	verliert	verlor	verlöre	verloren
†wachsen	wächst	wuchs	wüchse	gewachsen
wägen	wägt	wog	wöge	gewogen
waschen	wäscht	wusch	wüsche	gewaschen
weben	webt	+wob	+wöbe	+gewoben
weichen	weicht	wich	wiche	gewichen
weisen	weist	wies	wiese	gewiesen
werben	wirbt	warb	würbe	geworben
†werden	wird	wurde, (ward)	würde	geworden
werfen	wirft	warf	würfe	geworfen
wiegen	wiegt	wog	wöge	gewogen
winden	windet	wand	wände	gewunden
wringen	wringt	wrang	wränge	gewrungen
zeihen	zeiht	zieh	ziehe	geziehen
‡ziehen	zieht	zog	zöge	gezogen
zwingen	zwingt	zwang	zwänge	gezwungen

The German
Vest Pocket Dictionary
GERMAN - ENGLISH

A

Aachen, *n.nt.* Aachen, Aix-la-Chapelle.

Aal, -e, *n.m.* eel.

ab, *adv.* down; off; **(ab Berlin)** leaving Berlin; **(ab heute)** from today on.

ab·ändern, *vb.* revise.

Abänderung, -en, *n.f.* variation, revision.

Abart, -en, *n.f.* variety, species.

Abbau, *n.m.* working; reduction, razing.

ab·bauen, *vb.* raze; mine.

Abbild, -er *n.nt.* image, effigy.

ab·blenden, *vb.* dim (headlights).

ab·brechen*, *vb.* break off; cease, stop.

Abbruch, ⁻e, *n.m.* breaking off; cessation; damage.

ab·danken, *vb.* abdicate.

Abdankung, -en, *n.f.* abdication.

Abdruck, -e, *n.m.* (printed) impression, copy.

Abdruck, ⁻e, *n.m.* impress, mark, cast.

Abend, -e, *n.m.* evening; **(zu A. essen)** dine, have dinner.

Abendbrot, -e, *n.nt.* supper.

Abenddämmerung, -en, *n.f.* dusk.

Abendessen, -, *n.nt.* dinner, supper.

Abendland, *n.nt.* Occident.

abendländisch, *adj.* occidental.

abendlich, *adj.* evening.

Abendmahl, -e, *n.nt.* Holy Communion, Lord's Supper.

abends, *adv.* in the evening.

Abenteuer, -, *n.nt.* adventure.

abenteuerlich, *adj.* adventurous.

Abenteurer, -, *n.m.* adventurer.

aber, *conj.* but.

Aberglaube(n), -, *n.m.* superstition.

abergläubisch, *adj.* superstitious.

abermals, *adv.* once again.

Abessi′nien, *n.nt.* Abyssinia.

ab·fahren*, *vb.* leave, depart.

Abfahrt, -en, *n.f.* departure.

Abfall, ⁻e, *n.m.* slope; decrease; defection; rubbish.

ab·fallen*, *vb.* fall off; decrease; revolt.

abfällig, *adj.* precipitous; derogatory.

ab·fangen*, *vb.* intercept.

ab·fassen, *vb.* draw up, compose.

ab·fertigen, *vb.* take care of, expedite.

ab·feuern, *vb.* discharge (gun).

ab·finden*, *vb.* **(sich a. mit)** put up with.

Abfluß, ⁻sse, *n.m.* drain(age), outlet.

ab·führen, *vb.* lead off.

Abführmittel, -, *n.nt.* laxative.

Abgabe, -n, *n.f.* levy.

ab·geben*, *vb.* hand over; check (baggage); cast (vote).

abgebrüht, *adj.* hard-boiled.

abgedroschen, *adj.* trite.

abgelegen, *adj.* remote.

abgemacht, *adj.* settled, agreed.

abgeneigt, *adj.* averse, disinclined.

abgenutzt, *adj.* worn-out.

Abgeordnet-, *n.m.&f.* representative, deputy.

abgeschieden, *adj.* separated, secluded; departed.

abgesehen von, *prep.* aside from.

ab·gewinnen*, *vb.* gain from.

Abgott, ⁻er, *n.m.* idol.

Abgötterei′, -en, *n.f.* idolatry.

Abgrenzung, -en, *n.f.* demarcation.

Abgrund, ⸚e, *n.m.* abyss, precipice.

ab-halten*, *vb.* hold off, restrain, deter.

abhan′den, *adv.* missing; **(a. kommen*)** get lost.

Abhandlung, -en, *n.f.* treatise.

Abhang, ⸚e, *n.m.* slope.

ab-hängen*, *vb.* depend.

abhängig, *adj.* dependent.

Abhängigkeit, *n.f.* dependence.

ab-härten, *vb.* harden.

ab-helfen*, *vb.* remedy.

Abhilfe, -n, *n.f.* remedy, relief.

abhold, *adj.* averse, disinclined.

ab-holen, *vb.* go and get, pick up, call for.

ab-hören, *vb.* listen to, monitor.

Abitur′,-e, *n.nt.* final examination at end of secondary school; high school degree.

Abkehr, *n.f.* turning away.

Abkomme, -n, -n, *n.m.* descendant, offspring.

Abkommen, -, *n.nt.* convention; agreement.

Abkömmling, -e, *n.m.* offspring, descendant; derivative.

ab-kühlen, *vb.* cool off.

ab-kürzen, *vb.* abbreviate, abridge.

Abkürzung, -en, *n.f.* abbreviation; abridgment.

ab-laden*, *vb.* unload.

Ablage, -n, *n.f.* depot, place of deposit.

Ablaß, ⸚sse, *n.m.* letting off, drainage; (*eccles.*) indulgence.

ab-lassen*, *vb.* let off, drain; desist.

Ablativ, -e, *n.m.* ablative.

Ablauf, *n.m.* running off, expiration.

ab-laufen*, *vb.* run off, expire.

Ablaut, -e, *n.m.* ablaut

(vowel alteration, as in **singen, sang, gesungen**).

ab-legen, *vb.* discard, take off.

ab-lehnen, *vb.* decline, reject.

Ablehnung, -en, *n.f.* rejection.

ab-leiten, *vb.* derive.

Ableitung, -en, *n.f.* derivation.

ab-lenken, *vb.* divert, distract.

Ablenkung, -en, *n.f.* diversion, distraction.

ab-leugnen, *vb.* deny, disavow.

Ableugnung, -en, *n.f.* denial, disavowal.

ab-liefern, *vb.* deliver.

Ablieferung, -en, *n.f.* delivery.

ab-lösen, *vb.* relieve.

Ablösung, -en, *n.f.* relief.

Abmarsch, ⸚e, *n.m.* marching off, departure.

ab-melden, *vb.* report the departure of.

ab-mühen, *vb.* **(sich a.)** toil.

Abnahme, -n, *n.f.* decrease.

abnehmbar, *adj.* removable.

ab-nehmen*, *vb.* (*tr.*) take off, remove; (*intr.*) decrease, lose weight.

Abnehmer, -, *n.m.* purchaser.

Abneigung, -en, *n.f.* antipathy, dislike, aversion.

abnorm′, *adj.* abnormal.

ab-nötigen, *vb.* force from.

ab-nutzen, *vb.* wear (something) out.

Abnutzung, *n.f.* wearing out.

Abonnement′, -s, *n.nt.* subscription.

abonnie′ren, *vb.* subscribe.

Abordnung, -en, *n.f.* delegation.

Abort, -e, *n.m.* toilet.

Abort′, -e, *n.m.* abortion.

ab-rackern, *vb.* **(sich a.)** drudge.

ab-raten*, *vb.* dissuade.

ab-räumen, *vb.* clear off.

ab-rechnen, *vb.* settle accounts.

Abrechnung, -en, *n.f.* settlement of accounts.

Abrede, -n, *n.f.* **(in A. stellen)** deny.

Abreise, -n, *n.f.* departure.

ab·reisen, *vb.* depart.

ab·reißen*, *vb.* tear off; demolish.

Abriß, -sse. *n.m.* outline, summary.

ab·rüsten, *vb.* disarm.

Abrüstung, -en, *n.f.* disarmament.

Absage, -n, *n.f.* refusal (of an invitation), calling off.

ab·sagen, *vb.* decline, revoke.

Absatz, ⁻e, *n.m.* paragraph; heel; landing; sale, market.

ab·schaben, *vb.* scrape off, abrade.

ab·schaffen*, *vb.* abolish.

Abschaffung, -en, *n.f.* abolition.

ab·schätzen, *vb.* appraise, estimate.

Abschätzung, -en, *n.f.* appraisal, estimate.

Abschaum, *n.m.* dregs.

Abscheu, -e, *n.m.* abhorrence, loathing.

abscheu·lich, *adj.* abominable, detestable.

Abschied, -e, *n.m.* departure, leave, farewell.

Abschlag, ⁻e, *n.m.* chips; repulse; refusal.

ab·schlagen*, *vb.* chip off; repel; refuse.

abschlägig, *adj.* negative, refusing.

ab·schleifen*, *vb.* grind off, abrade.

ab·schließen*, *vb.* lock up, close off; conclude.

Abschluß, ⁻sse, *n.m.* conclusion.

ab·schneiden*, *vb.* cut off.

Abschnitt, -e, *n.m.* section.

ab·schrecken, *vb.* frighten off.

abschreckend, *adj.* forbidding.

Abschreckungsmittel, -, *n.nt.* deterrent.

ab·schreiben*, *vb.* copy.

Abschrift, -en, *n.f.* copy.

abschüssig, *adj.* precipitous.

ab·schweifen, *vb.* digress.

ab·schwören*, *vb.* abjure.

Abschwörung, -en, *n.f.* abjuration.

absehbar, *adj.* foreseeable.

ab·sehen*, *vb.* look away; see from; **(a. von)** give up; **(auf mich abgesehen)** aimed at me; **(ist abzusehen)** can be seen.

abseits, *adv.* aside, apart.

ab·senden, *vb.* send off, mail.

Absender, -, *n.m.* sender.

Absendung, -en, *n.f.* send.

ab·setzen, *vb.* set off, set down, depose.

Absicht, -en, *n.f.* intent, purpose; **(mit A.)** on purpose.

absichtlich, *adj.* intentional.

absolut', *adj.* absolute.

absolvie'ren, *vb.* absolve; complete; finish (school); pass (an examination).

abson'derlich, *adj.* peculiar.

ab·sondern, *vb.* separate, detach; secrete.

absorbie'ren, *vb.* absorb.

Absorbie'rungsmittel, -, *n.nt.* absorbent.

Absorption', -en, *n.f.* absorption.

ab·spannen, *vb.* loosen (tension), relax.

ab·spielen, *vb.* **(sich a.)** occur, take place.

ab·splittern, *vb.* chip.

Absprache, -n, *n.f.* agreement.

ab·sprechen*, *vb.* deny.

ab·springen*, *vb.* jump down, bail out (of a plane).

Absprung, *n.m.* jump down, parachute jump; digression.

ab·stammen, *vb.* be descended.

Abstammung, -en, *n.f.* descent, ancestry; derivation.

Abstand, ⁻e, *n.m.* distance, interval; **(von etwas A. nehmen*)** renounce.

ab·statten, *vb.* grant; **(einen besuch a.)** pay a visit.

ab·stauben, *vb.* dust.

Abstecher, -, *n.m.* digression, side trip.

ab·stehen*, *vb.* stand off, stick out.

ab·steigen*, *vb.* descend, dismount; put up at (an inn).

ab·stellen, *vb.* put away; turn off.

ab·stempeln, *vb.* stamp, cancel.

ab·sterben*, *vb.* die out.

Abstieg, -e, *n.m.* descent.

ab·sti men, *vb.* vote.

Abstimmung, -en, *n.f.* vote, plebiscite.

abstinent', *adj.* abstinent.

Abstinenz', *n.f.* abstinence.

ab·stoßen*, *vb.* knock off, repel, repulse.

abstoßend, *adj.* repulsive.

abstrahie'ren, *vb.* abstract.

abstrakt', *adj.* abstract.

Abstraktion', -en, *n.f.* abstraction.

ab·streifen, *vb.* strip.

Abstufung, -en, *n.f.* gradation.

ab·stumpfen, *vb.* become dull, blunt; make dull, blunt.

Absturz, ⸗e, *n.m.* fall, crash.

ab·stürzen, *vb.* fall, crash.

absurd', *adj.* absurd.

Abszeß', -sse, *n.m.* abscess.

Abtei', -en, *n.f.* abbey.

Abteil, -e, *n.nt.* compartment.

Abtei'lung, -en, *n.f.* division, section.

ab·tragen*, *vb.* wear out.

ab·treiben*, *vb.* drive off; cause an abortion.

Abtreibung, -en, *n.f.* abortion.

ab·trennen, *vb.* detach.

ab·treten*, *vb.* cede.

Abtretung, -en, *n.f.* withdrawal, cession, surrender.

Abtritt, -e, *n.nt.* departure, exit; latrine.

ab·tun*, *vb.* put aside, settle.

ab·wägen*, *vb.* weigh out, consider.

ab·wandeln, *vb.* change, inflect.

ab·wandern, *vb.* depart, migrate.

ab·warten, *vb.* wait (to see what will happen), bide one's time.

abwärts, *adv.* downwards.

ab·waschen*, *vb.* wash off.

Abwaschung, -en, *n.f.* ablution.

ab·wechseln, *vb.* alternate, take turns.

abwechselnd, *adj.* alternate.

Abwechs(e)lung, -en, *n.f.* change, alternation.

Abweg, -e, *n.m.* wrong way, devious path; (**auf A. e gera'ten***) go astray.

abwegig, *adj.* errant.

Abwehr, *n.f.* warding off, defense.

Abwehrdienst, -e, *n.m.* counterintelligence service.

ab·wehren, *vb.* ward off, prevent.

ab·weichen*, *vb.* deviate, depart.

Abweichung, -en, *n.f.* deviation, departure.

ab·weisen*, *vb.* send away, repulse.

ab·wenden*, *vb.* turn away, deflect, avert.

ab·werfen*, *vb.* throw down, shed.

ab·werten, *vb.* devaluate.

Abwertung, -en, *n.f.* devaluation.

abwesend, *adj.* absent.

Abwesend-, *n.m.&f.* absent person, absentee.

Abwesenheit, -en, *n.f.* absence.

ab·wickeln, *vb.* unwind.

ab·winken, *vb.* gesture "no".

Abwurf, ⸗, *n.m.* throwing down; thing thrown down.

ab·zahlen, *vb.* pay off.

ab·zählen, *vb.* count off.

ab·zapfen, *vb.* draw off, tap.

ab·zehren, *vb.* waste away, consume.

Abzeichen, -, *n.nt.* badge, medal, insignia.

ab·ziehen*, *vb.* (*tr.*) draw off, subtract, deduct; (*intr.*) march off.

Abzug, ⸗e, *n.m.* marching off, departure; drawing off, subtraction, drain; print; trig-ger.

ab-zwingen*, *vb.* force away from, extort.

Acetylen', *n.nt.* acetylene.

ach, *interj.* oh.

Achat', **-e**, *n.m.* agate.

Achse, **-n**, *n.f.* axis, axle.

Achsel, **-n**, *n.f.* shoulder.

acht, *num.* eight.

acht-, *adj.* eighth.

Acht, *n.f.* attention, care; **(sich in a. nehmen*)** watch out, be on one's guard; **(außer acht lassen*)** pay no attention to, neglect.

Achtel, **-**, *n.nt.* eighth; **(ein a.)** one-eighth.

achten, *vb.* respect; **(a. auf)** pay attention to.

ächten, *vb.* outlaw, ostracise.

achtern, *adv.* aft.

acht-geben*, *vb.* watch out, pay attention.

acht-haben*, *vb.* watch out, pay attention.

achtlos, *adj.* heedless.

achtsam, *adj.* attentive.

Achtung, *n.f.* attention, regard, esteem; **(A.!)** watch out! attention!

achtzehn, *num.* eighteen.

achtzehnt-, *adj.* eighteenth.

achtzig, *num.* eighty.

achtzigst-, *adj.* eightieth.

Achtzigstel, -, *n.nt.* eight-ieth; **(ein A.)** one-eightieth.

ächzen, *vb.* groan, moan.

Acker, **ꞌꞌ**, *n.m.* field.

Ackerbau, *n.m.* farming.

addie'ren, *vb.* add.

ade', *interj.* adieu.

Adel, *n.m.* nobility.

Ader, **-n**, *n.f.* vein.

adieu, *interj.* adieu.

Adjektiv, **-e**, *n.nt.* adjective.

adjekti'visch, *adj.* adjec-tival.

Adjutant', **-en**, **-en**, *n.m.* ad-jutant, aide, aide-de-camp.

Adler, **-**, *n.m.* eagle.

Adler-, *cpds.* aquiline.

adlig, *adj.* noble.

Adlig-, *n.m.&f.* nobleman, -woman.

Admiral', **-e**, *n.m.* admiral.

Admiralität', **-en**, *n.f.* ad-miralty.

adoptie'ren, *vb.* adopt.

Adoption', **-en**, *n.f.* adoption.

Adres'se, **-n**, *n.f.* address.

adressie'ren, *vb.* address.

adrett', *adj.* trim, smart.

Advent', **-e**, *n.m.* Advent, each of the four Sundays before Christmas.

Adverb', **-ien**, *n.nt.* adverb.

adverbial', *adj.* adverbial.

Advokat', **-en**, **-en**, *n.m.* law-yer.

Aeronau'tik, *n.f.* aeronau-tics.

Affä're, **-n**, *n.f.* affair, love affair.

Affe, **-n**, **-n**, *n.m.* ape, mon-key.

Affekt', **-e**, *n.m.* affect.

affektiert', *adj.* affectea.

Affektiert'heit, **-en**, *n.f.* af-fectation.

äffen, *vb.* ape, mock.

Affix', **-e**, *n.nt.* affix.

Affront', **-s**, *n.m.* affront, snub.

Afrika, *n.nt.* Africa.

Afrika'ner, **-**, *n.m.* African.

afrika'nisch, *adj.* African.

AG, *abbr.* (= Aktiengesell-schaft) company.

Agent', **-en**, **-en**, *n.m.* agent.

Agentur', **-en**, *n.f.* agency.

Aggression', **-en**, *n.f.*aggres-sion.

aggressiv', *adj.* aggressive.

agie'ren, *vb.* act.

Agno'stiker, **-**, *n.m.* agnos-tic.

agno'stisch, *adj.* agnostic.

Ägyp'ten, *n.nt.* Egypt.

Ägyp'ter, **-**, *n.m* Egyptian.

ägyp'tisch, *adj.* Egyptian.

Ahn, **-en**, *n.m.* ancestor.

Ahne, **-n**, *n.f.* ancestress.

ähneln, *vb.* resemble.

ahnen, *vb.* have any idea (that something will hap-pen); forebode.

ähnlich, *adj.* similar.

Ähnlichkeit, **-en**, *n.f.* simi-larity.

Ahnung, **-en**, *n.f.* forebod-ing; hunch; **(ich habe keine A.)** I have no idea.

ahnungslos, *adj.* unsuspecting.

ahnungsvoll, *adj.* ominous.

Ahorn, -e, *n.m.* maple tree.

Ähre, -n, *n.f.* ear (of grain).

Akademie', -i'en, *n.f.* academy.

akade'misch, *adj.* academic.

Aka'zie, -n, *n.f.* acacia.

Akkord', -e, *n.m.* chord.

akkreditie'ren, *vb.* accredit.

Akkumula'tor, -to'ren, *n.m.* battery.

Akkusativ, -e, *n.m.* accusative.

Akne, -n, *n.f.* acne.

Akrobat', -en, -en, *n.m.* acrobat.

Akt, -e, *n.m.* act; nude (drawing).

Akte, -n, *n.f.* document, dossier, file.

Aktenmappe, -n, *n.f.* brief case.

Aktie, -n, *n.f.* share (of stock).

Aktiengesellschaft, -en, *n.f.* corporation, stock company.

Aktion', -en, *n.f.* action, undertaking.

Aktionär', -e, *n.m.* stockholder.

aktiv', *adj.* active.

aktivie'ren, *vb.* activate.

Aktivie'rung, -en, *n.f.* activation.

aktuell', *adj.* topical.

Aku'stik, *n.f.* acoustics.

aku'stisch, *adj.* acoustic.

akut', *adj.* acute.

Akzent', -e, *n.m.* accent.

akzentuie'ren, *vb.* accentuate.

Alarm', -e, *n.m.* alarm, alert.

alarmie'ren, *vb.* alarm, alert.

Alaun', -e, *n.m.* alum.

albern, *adj.* silly.

Albi'no, -s, *n.m.* albino.

Album, *n.nt.* album.

Alchimie', *n.f.* alchemy.

Alchimist', -en, -en, *n.m.* alchemist.

Alge, -n, *n.f.* alga.

Algebra, *n.f.* algebra.

algebra'isch, *adj.* algebraic.

alias, *adv.* alias.

Alibi, -s, *n.nt.* alibi.

Aliment', -e, *n.nt.* alimony.

Alka'li, -en, *n.nt.* alkali.

alka'lisch, *adj.* alkaline.

Alkohol, -e, *n.m.* alcohol.

Alkoho'liker, -, *n.m.* alcoholic.

alkoho'lisch, *adj.* alcoholic.

Alko'ven, -, *n.m.* alcove.

All, *n.nt.* universe.

all; **aller**, -es, -e, *pron.&* *adj.* all.

Allee', -e'en, *n.f.* avenue.

Allegorie', -i'en, *n.f.* allegory.

allein', **1.** *adv.* alone. **2.** *conj.* but.

allei'nig, *adj.* sole, only.

allemal, *adv.* always; **(ein für a.)** once and for all.

allenfalls, *adv.* in any case.

allenthal'ben, *adv.* everywhere.

aller-, *cpds.* of all; **allerbest'**, best of all; etc.

allerart, *adv.* all sorts of.

allerdings', *adv.* certainly, to be sure, indeed.

Allergie', -i'en, *n.f.* allergy.

allerhand, *adv.* all sorts of; **(das ist ja a.)** that's tremendous, that's the limit.

allerlei, *adv.* all sorts of.

alles, *pron.* everything.

allesamt, *adv.* altogether.

allgemein, *adj.* general, common; **(im a. en)** generally, in general.

Allgemein'heit, -en, *n.f.* generality, general public.

Allianz', -en, *n.f.* alliance.

Alliga'tor, -o'ren, *n.m.* alligator.

alliie'ren, *vb.* ally.

Alliiert'-, *n.m.&f.* ally.

alljähr'lich, *adj.* annual.

allmäch'tig, *adj.* almighty, omnipotent.

allmäh'lich, *adj.* gradual.

allmo'natlich, *adj.* monthly.

allnächt'lich, *adj.* nightly.

Alltag, -e, *n.m.* weekday, tedium.

alltäg'lich, *adj.* daily, routine.

allzu, *adv.* all too.

Almanach, -e, *n.m.* almanac.

Almosen, -, *n.nt.* alms.

Alpdruck, ‥e, *n.m.* nightmare.

Alpen, *n.pl.* Alps.

Alphabet', -e, *n.nt.* alphabet.

alphabe'tisch, *adj.* alphabetical.

alphabetisie'ren, *vb.* alphabetize.

als, *conj.* as, when; than.

alsbald', *adv.* immediately.

alsdann', *adv.* thereupon.

also, *adv.* so, thus, and so, hence, therefore.

alt, *adj.* old.

Alt, -e, *n.m.* alto.

Altar', ‥e, *n.m.* altar.

Altar'diener, -, *n.m.* acolyte.

Alter, -, *n.nt.* age.

altern, *vb.* age.

alternativ', *adj.* alternative.

Alternati've, -n, *n.f.* alternative.

Altertum, -ümer, *n.nt.* antiquity.

altertümlich, *adj.* archaic.

Altertumskunde, *n.f.* archaeology.

Ältest-, *n.m.* elder.

alther'gebracht, *adj.* traditional.

Altjahrsa'bend, -e, *n.m.* New Year's Eve.

altklug, ‥, *adj.* precocious.

ältlich, *adj.* elderly.

altmodisch, *adj.* old-fashioned.

Altruis'mus, *n.m.* altruism.

Altstimme, -n, *n.f.* alto.

Alumi'nium, *n.nt.* aluminum.

Amalgam', -e, *n.nt.* amalgam.

amalgamie'ren, *vb.* amalgamate.

Amateur', -e, *n.m.* amateur.

Amboß, -sse, *n.m.* anvil.

ambulant', *adj.* ambulatory.

Ameise, -n, *n.f.* ant.

Ame'rika, *n.nt.* America.

Amerika'ner, -, *n.m.* American.

amerika'nisch, *adj.* American.

Amethyst', -e, *n.m.* amethyst.

Ammoniak, *n.nt.* ammonia.

Amnestie', -i'en, *n.f.* amnesty.

Amö'be, -n, *n.f.* amoeba.

amoralisch, *adj.* amoral.

amortisie'ren, *vb.* amortize.

Ampere, -, (*pron.* **Ampär'**) *n.nt.* ampere.

amphi'bisch, *adj.* amphibious.

amputie'ren, *vb.* amputate.

Amputiert'-, *n.m.&f.* amputee.

Amt, ‥er, *n.nt.* office.

amtie'ren, *vb.* officiate.

amtlich, *adj.* official.

Amtseinführung, -en, *n.f.* inauguration.

Amtstratsch, *n.m.* grapevine, gossip.

Amtsschimmel, *n.m.* red tape.

amüsie'ren, *vb.* amuse; **(sich a.)** have a good time.

an, *prep.* at, on, to.

Anachronis'mus, -men, *n.m.* anachronism.

analog', *adj.* analogous.

Analogie', -i'en, *n.f.* analogy.

analo'gisch, *adj.* analogical.

Analphabet', -en, -en, *n.m.* illiterate.

Analphabe'tentum, *n.nt.* illiteracy.

Analy'se, -n, *n.f.* analysis.

analysie'ren, *vb.* analyze.

Analy'tiker, -, *n.m.* analyst.

analy'tisch, *adj.* analytic (al).

Anarchie', -i'en, *n.f.* anarchy.

Anästhesie', *n.f.* anesthesia.

Anatomie', -i'en, *n.f.* anatomy.

Anbau, -ten, *n.m.* cultivation; addition (to a house).

Anbeginn, *n.m.* origin.

anbei', *adv.* inclosed, herewith.

an-beten, *vb.* worship, adore.

Anbetracht, *n.m.* **(in A.)** in view of.

Anbetung, -en, *n.f.* adoration.

an-bieten*, *vb.* offer.

Anblick, -e, *n.m.* sight, view, appearance.
an·brechen*, *vb.* **(der Tag bricht an)** day breaks, dawns.
Anbruch, ⸚e, *n.m.* beginning, (day)break, (night)fall.
Andacht, -en, *n.f.* devotion.
andächtig, *adj.* devout.
andauernd, *adj.* continual.
Andenken, -, *n.nt.* memory, dememorial, souvenir.
ander-, *adj.* other, different.
and(e)rerseits, *adv.* on the other hand.
ändern, *vb.* change, alter.
anders, *adv.* otherwise, else.
anderswie, *adv.* otherwise.
anderswo, *adv.* elsewhere.
Änderung, -en, *n.f.* change, alteration.
anderthalb, *num.* one and a half.
an·deuten, *vb.* indicate, imply.
Andeutung, -en, *n.f.* indication, implication.
Andrang, *n.m.* rush, crowd.
an·drehen, *vb.* turn on.
an·eignen, *vb.* seize, appropriate.
Aneignung, -en, *n.f.* seizure, appropriation.
aneinan'der, *adv.* to one another, together.
Anekdo'te, -n, *n.f.* anecdote.
an·ekeln, *vb.* disgust.
an·erkennen* (*or* **anerkennen***), *vb.* acknowledge.
anerkennenswert, *adj.* creditable.
Anerkennung, -en, *n.f.* acknowledgment, recognition.
an·fahren*, *vb.* drive up against, collide with, hit; speak sharply to.
Anfall, ⸚e, *n.m.* attack.
an·fallen*, *vb.* fall upon, attack.
Anfang, ⸚e, *n.m.* beginning.
an·fangen*, *vb.* begin.
Anfänger, -, *n.m.* beginner.
anfänglich, *adj.* initial.
anfangs, *adv.* in the beginning.
an·fassen, *vb.* take hold of, grasp.
an·fechten*, *vb.* assail.
an·fertigen, *vb.* prepare, manufacture.
an·feuchten, *vb.* moisten.
an·feuern, *vb.* fire, incite, inspire.
an·flehen, *vb.* beseech.
an·fliegen*, *vb.* fly at.
Anflug, ⸚e, *n.m.* approach flight, slight attack, touch.
an·fordern, *vb.* claim, demand.
Anfrage, -n, *n.f.* inquiry, application.
an·freunden, *vb.* **(sich a. mit)** befriend.
an·führen, *vb.* lead on; allege; cite; dupe.
Anführung, -en, *n.f.* leadership; quotation, allegation.
Anführungsstrich, -e, *n.m.* quotation mark.
Anführungszeichen, *n.nt.* quotation mark.
Angabe, -n, *n.f.* fact cited, statement, assertion; (*pl.*) data.
an·geben*, *vb.* cite as a fact, state, assert; brag, boast.
Angeber, -, *n.m.* boaster.
Angeberei', -en, *n.f.* boast, boastfulness.
angeberisch, *adj.* boastful.
angeblich, *adj.* as stated, alleged.
angeboren, *adj.* innate, congenital.
Angebot, -e, *n.nt.* bid, offer.
angebracht, *adj.* proper.
angeheiratet, *adj.* related by marriage.
an·gehen*, *vb.* concern.
angehend, *adj.* beginning, incipient.
an·gehören, *vb.* belong to.
angehörig, *adj.* belonging to.
Angehörig-, *n.m.&f.* dependent.
Angeklagt-, *n.m.&f.* accused, defendant.
Angel, -n, *n.f.* hinge, axis; fishing tackle.
angelegen, *adj.* important, of concern.
Angelegenheit, -en, *n.f.* matter, concern, affair.

angelehnt, *adj.* leaned against, ajar.

angeln, *vb.* fish, angle.

angemessen, *adj.* adequate, appropriate, suitable.

angenehm, *adj.* pleasant, agreeable.

angesehen, *adj.* respected, respectable.

Angesicht, -er, *n.nt.* face.

Angestellt-, *n.m.&f.* employee.

angewandt, *adj.* applied.

an-gewöhnen, *vb.* accustom to.

Angewohnheit, -en, *n.f.* habit, custom.

an-gleichen*, *vb.* assimilate, adjust.

Angleichung, -en, *n.f.* assimilation.

an-gliedern, *vb.* affiliate.

Angliederung, -en, *n.f.* affiliation.

Angler, -, *n.m.* fisherman.

angreifbar, *adj.* assailable.

an-greifen*, *vb.* attack, assault.

Angreifer, -, *n.m.* attacker, aggressor.

an-grenzen, *vb.* abut, border on.

angrenzend, *adj.* contiguous.

Angriff, -e, *n.m.* attack, aggression.

Angriffslust, *n.f.* aggressiveness.

Angst, ⁒e, *n.f.* fear; **(A. haben*, A. sein*)** be afraid.

ängstigen, *vb.* frighten.

ängstlich, *adj.* timid, anxious.

an-haben*, *vb.* have on, wear.

Anhalt, -e, *n.m.* hold; basis.

an-halten*, *vb.* (tr.) stop, arrest; (intr.) last, continue.

anhaltend, *adj.* lasting.

Anhaltspunkt, -e, *n.m.* point of reference, basis, clue.

Anhang, ⁒e, *n.m.* appendix; adherents.

Anhänger, -, *n.m.* follower; pendant; trailer.

an-häufen, *vb.* amass, accumulate.

Anhäufung, -en, *n.f.* accumulation.

an-heften, *vb.* affix, attach.

anheim'-stellen, *vb.* submit.

Anhieb, -e, *n.m.* first stroke; **(auf A.)** right away, right off the bat.

an-hören, *vb.* listen to.

Anilin', *n.nt.* aniline.

Ankauf, ⁒e, *n.m.* purchase.

an-kaufen, *vb.* buy.

Anker, -, *n.m.* anchor.

Ankerplatz, ⁒e, *n.m.* anchorage.

an-ketten, *vb.* chain.

Anklage, -n, *n.f.* accusation, indictment, impeachment.

an-klagen, *vb.* accuse, indict, impeach.

Ankläger, -, *n.m.* accuser, plaintiff.

an-klammern, *vb.* fasten (with a clamp); **(sich a.)** cling.

an-kommen*, *vb.* arrive; **(a. auf)** depend upon.

an-kündigen, *vb.* announce.

Ankunft, ⁒e, *n.f.* arrival.

an-kurbeln, *vo.* crank up, get started.

Anlage, -n, *n.f.* arrangement, disposition, investment; inclosure; (pl.) grounds.

an-langen, *vb.* (tr.) concern; (intr.) arrive.

Anlaß, ⁒sse, *n.m.* cause, motivating factor.

an-lassen*, *vb.* leave on; start.

Anlasser, -, *n.m.* starter.

anläßlich, *prep.* on the occasion of.

Anlauf, ⁒e, *n.m.* start, warm-up; attack.

an-laufen*, *vb.* run at, make for; swell, rise.

an-legen, *vb.* put on; invest; land.

an-lehnen, *vb.* lean against, leave ajar.

Anleihe, -n, *n.f.* loan.

an-leiten, *vb.* lead to, instruct.

Anleitung, -en, *n.f.* instruction.

an-lernen, *vb.* train.

an·machen, *vb.* fix, attach, turn on.

an·maßen, *vb.* assume, presume.

anmaßend, *adj.* arrogant, presumptuous.

Anmaßung, -en, *n.f.* arrogance, presumption.

an·melden, *vb.* announce.

Anmeldung, -en, *n.f.* announcement, report, registration.

an·merken, *vb.* note.

Anmerkung, -en, *n.f.* (foot)note.

Anmut, *n.f.* grace, charm.

anmutig, *adj.* graceful.

an·nähern, *vb.* approach.

annähernd, *adj.* approximate.

Annäherung, -en, *n.f.* approach, approximation.

Annahme, -n, *n.f.* acceptance, adoption; assumption, supposition.

annehmbar, *adj.* acceptable.

an·nehmen*, *vb.* accept, assume, suppose, infer.

Annehmlichkeit, -en, *n.f.* pleasure, agreeableness.

Annonce', -n, *n.f.* advertisement.

annoncie'ren, *vb.* advertise.

annullie'ren, *vb.* annul.

Anomalie', -i'en, *n.f.* anomaly.

anonym', *adj.* anonymous.

an·ordnen, *vb.* order, arrange.

Anordnung, -en, *n.f.* order, arrangement.

an·packen, *vb.* grab hold of, get started with.

an·passen, *vb.* adapt, fit, try on; (**sich a.**) conform.

Anpassung, -en, *n.f.* adaptation.

anpassungsfähig, *adj.* adaptable, adaptive.

Anprall, *n.m.* collision, impact.

an·preisen*, *vb.* praise, recommend.

Anprobe, -n, *n.f.* fitting.

Anrecht, -e, *n.n.t* right, claim.

Anrede, -n, *n.f.* address, speech.

an·reden, *vb.* speak to, accost.

an·regen, *vb.* stimulate, incite.

Anregung, -en, *n.f.* stimulation; suggestion.

Anreiz, -e, *n.m.* stimulus, incentive.

an·reizen, *vb.* incite.

Anruf, -e, *n.m.* appeal, (telephone) call.

an·rufen*, *vb.* appeal to, invoke; call up.

Anrufung, *n.f.* invocation.

an·rühren, *vb.* touch; (cooking) mix.

an·sagen, *vb.* announce.

Ansager, -, *n.m.* announcer.

an·sammeln, *vb.* amass; (**sich a.**) congregate, gather.

Ansammlung, -en, *n.f.* collection, backlog.

ansässig, *adj.* resident.

Ansatz, -e, *n.m.* start; estimate; charge; added piece.

an·schaffen, *vb.* get, obtain.

Anschaffung, -en, *n.f.* acquisition.

an·schauen, *vb.* look at.

anschaulich, *adj.* graphic, clear.

Anschauung, -en, *n.f.* view, opinion.

Anschein, -e, *n.m.* appearance.

anscheinend, *adj.* apparent.

Anschlag, -e, *n.m.* stroke; poster; estimate; plot.

an·schlagen*, *vb.* (*tr.*) strike, affix, fasten, post; estimate; (*intr.*) work, start to function.

an·schließen*, *vb.* fasten with a lock, adjoin; (**sich a.**) join; fit tight.

Anschluß, -sse, *n.m.* connection, annexation.

an·schnallen, *vb.* buckle on.

an·schneiden*, *vb.* start cutting.

an·schreiben*, *vb.* write down, score, charge.

Anschrift, -en, *n.f.* address.

an-sehen*, *vb.* look at.

Ansehen, *n.nt.* reputation, repute.

ansehnlich, *adj.* handsome; considerable, notable.

an-setzen, *vb.* fix, affix; set, schedule; estimate.

Ansicht, -en, *n.f.* view, opinion.

an-siedeln, *vb.* settle, colonize.

an-spannen, *vb.* stretch, strain; harness.

Anspannung, -en, *n.f.* strain, tension.

an-spielen, *vb.* start to play; allude.

Anspielung, -en, *n.f.* allusion.

an-spornen, *vb.* spur on.

Ansprache, -n, *n.f.* pronunciation; talk.

an-sprechen*, *vb.* address, accost.

ansprechend, *adj.* attractive.

Anspruch, ⸚e, *n.m.* claim; (**A. machen auf**) lay claim to; (**in A. nehmen***) require, take up.

anspruchslos, *adj.* unassuming.

anspruchsvoll, *adj.* pretentious.

an-stacheln, *vb.* goad, incite.

Anstalt, -en, *n.f.* arrangement, institution.

Anstand, *n.m.* propriety; objection.

anständig, *adj.* decent.

Anständigkeit, -en, *n.f.* decency.

anstatt', *adv.* instead of.

an-stecken, *vb.* pin on, put on; light, set fire to; infect.

ansteckend, *adj.* contagious.

Ansteckung, -en, *n.f.* contagion.

an-stehen*, *vb.* line up, stand in line.

an-steigen*, *vb.* rise.

an-stellen, *vb.* place; hire, employ.

Anstellung, -en, *n.f.* employment.

Anstieg, -e, *n.m.* rise.

an-stiften, *vb.* incite, instigate.

an-stimmen, *vb.* intone, tune up.

Anstoß, ⸚e, *n.m.* shock; impetus; offense.

an-stoßen*, *vb.* knock, bump against, nudge; offend; clink glasses.

anstoßend, *adj.* adjoining.

anstößig, *adj.* offensive.

an-streben, *vb.* strive for.

an-streichen*, *vb.* paint; underline; mark.

an-strengen, *vb.* strain; (**sich a.**) exert oneself, try hard.

anstrengend, *adj.* strenuous.

Anstrengung, -en, *n.f.* effort, exertion.

Anstrich, -e, *n.m.* coat of paint; appearance; touch.

Ansturm, ⸚e, *n.m.* assault, run (on a bank).

Antark'tis, *n.f.* Antarctic.

antark'tisch, *adj.* antarctic.

Anteil, -e, *n.m.* share.

Anten'ne, -n, *n.f.* antenna.

antik', *adj.* antique.

Anti'ke, *n.f.* antiquity, classical times.

Antilo'pe, -n, *n.f.* antelope.

Antimon', *n.nt.* antimony.

Antipathie', -i'en, *n.f.* antipathy.

Antiquar', -e, *n.m.* secondhand bookdealer, antique dealer.

Antiquariat', -e, *n.nt.* second-hand bookstore.

antiqua'risch, *adj.* secondhand.

antisep'tisch, *adj.* antiseptic.

antisozial', *adj.* antisocial.

Antlitz, -e, *n.nt.* countenance.

Antrag, ⸚e, *n.m.* offer, proposal, motion.

an-treffen*, *vb.* meet up with.

an-treiben*, *vb.* drive on, propel, incite.

an-treten*, *vb.* enter into (office), start out on, step forward.

Antrieb, -e, *n.m.* impulse, impetus, force.

Antritt, -e, *n.m.* entrance into, start.

an·tun*, *vb.* put on, inflict, cause.

Antwort, -en, *n.f.* answer.

antworten, *vb.* answer.

an·vertrauen, *vb.* entrust; **(sich a.)** confide.

an·wachsen*, *vb.* grow, increase.

Anwalt, ⁀e, *n.m.* attorney, advocate.

Anwärter, -, *n.m.* applicant, aspirant.

an·weisen*, *vb.* instruct, direct; assign.

Anweisung , -en, *n.f.* instruction, assignment; money order.

anwendbar, *adj.* applicable.

an·wenden*, *vb.* apply, use.

Anwendung, -en, *n.f.* application, use.

anwesend, *adj.* present.

Anwesenheit, -, *n.f.* presence.

Anwurf, ⁀e, *n.m.* slur.

Anzahl, -, *n.f.* quantity, number.

an·zahlen, *vb.* make a down payment.

Anzahlung, -en, *n.f.* down payment.

an·zapfen, *vb.* tap.

Anzeichen, -, *n.nt.* sign, symptom.

an·zeichnen, *vb.* mark, note.

Anzeige, -n, *n.f.* notice, advertisement; denunciation.

an·zeigen, *vb.* announce, advertise; denounce.

Anzeiger, -, *n.m.* advertiser; informer.

an·ziehen*, *vb.* draw along, attract; put on, dress; rise.

anziehend, *adj.* attractive.

Anziehungskraft, ⁀e, *n.f.* attraction; **(A. der Erde)** gravity.

Anzug, ⁀e, *n.m.* suit; approach.

an·zünden, *vb.* ignite, light.

an·zweifeln, *vb.* doubt, question.

apart, *adj.* out of the ordinary.

Apathie', -i'en, *n.f.* apathy.

apa'thisch, *adj.* apathetic.

Apfel, ⁀, *n.m.* apple.

Apfelmus, *n.nt.* applesauce.

Apfelsi'ne, -n, *n.f.* orange.

apoplek'tisch, *adj.* apoplectic.

Apos'tel, -, *n.m.* apostle.

aposto'lisch, *adj.* apostolic.

Apothe'ke, -n, *n.f.* pharmacy.

Apothe'ker, -, *n.m.* pharmacist.

Apparat', -e, *n.m.* apparatus.

appellie'ren, *vb.* appeal.

Appetit', -e, *n.m.* appetite.

appetit'lich, *adj.* appetizing, inviting.

applaudie'ren, *vb.* applaud.

Applaus', *n.m.* applause.

Apriko'se, -n, *n.f.* apricot.

April', *n.m.* April.

Aquarell', -e, *n.nt.* watercolor.

Aqua'rium, -ien, *n.nt.* aquarium.

Äqua'tor, *n.m.* equator.

äquatorial', *adj.* equatorial.

Araber, -, *n.m.* Arab.

ara'bisch, *adj.* Arabic, Arabian.

Arbeit, -en, *n.f.* work.

arbeiten, *vb.* work.

Arbeiter, -, *n.m.* worker, workman, laborer.

Arbeiterschaft, *n.f.* labor.

Arbeitge'ber, -, *n.m.* employer.

arbeitslos, *adj.* unemployed.

Arbeitslosigkeit, -, *n.f.* unemployment.

Arbeitszimmer, -, *n.nt.* study.

Archäologie', *n.f.* archaeology.

Archipel', -e, *n.m.* archipelago.

Architekt', -en, -en, *n.m.* architect.

architekto'nisch, *adj.* architectural.

Architektur', -en, *n.f.* architecture.

Archiv', -e, *n.nt.* archives.

Are'na, -nen, *n.f.* arena.

arg, *adj.* bad.

Argenti'nien, *n.nt.* Argentina.

Ärger, *n.m.* anger, annoyance, bother.

ärgerlich, *adj.* angry; annoying.

ärgern, *vb.* annoy, make angry, bother; **(sich ä.)** be angry.

Ärgernis, -se, *n.nt.* nuisance.

Arglist, *n.f.* guile.

arglos, *adj.* harmless, unsuspecting.

Argument', -e, *n.nt.* argument.

argumentie'ren, *vb.* argue.

Argwohn, *n.m.* suspicion.

argwöhnisch, *adj.* suspicious.

Arie, -n, *n.f.* aria.

Aristokrat', -en, -en, *n.m.* aristocrat.

Aristokratie', -i'en, *n.f.* aristocracy.

aristokra'tisch, *adj.* aristocratic.

Arithmetik, *n.f.* arithmetic.

Arka'de, -n, *n.f.* arcade.

arktisch, *adj.* arctic.

Arm, -e, *n.m.* arm.

arm, *v.* *adj.* poor.

Arm-, *n.m.&f.* pauper.

Armband, ᵛer, *n.nt.* bracelet.

Armbanduhr, -en, *n.f.* wristwatch.

Armee', -me'en, *n.f.* army.

Ärmel, -, *n.m.* sleeve.

Armleuchter, -, *n.m.* candelabrum.

armselig, *adj.* beggarly, miserable.

Armut, *n.f.* poverty, destitution.

Aro'ma, -s, *n.nt.* aroma.

arrangie'ren, *vb.* arrange.

arrogant', *adj.* arrogant.

Arroganz', -en, *n.f* arrogance.

Arsen', *n.nt.* arsenic.

Art, -en, *n.f.* kind, sort, species; way, manner; **(A. und Weise)** way.

Arte'rie, -ien, *n.f.* artery.

Arthri'tis, *n.f.* arthritis.

artig, *adj.* good, well-behaved.

Arti'kel, -, *n.m.* item, article.

artikulie'ren, *vb.* articulate.

Artillerie', -i'en, *n.f.* artillery.

Artischo'cke, -n, *n.f.* artichoke.

Arzt, ᵛe, *n.m.* physician, doctor; **(praktischer A.)** general practitioner.

ärztlich, *adj.* medical.

As, -se, *n.nt.* ace.

Asbest', -e, *n.m.* asbestos.

Asche, -n, *n.f.* ash; **(glühende A.)** embers.

Asch(en)becher, -, *n.m.* ash tray.

aschgrau, *adj.* ashen.

Asiat', -en, -en, *n.m.* Asiatic.

asia'tisch, *adj.* Asiatic.

Asien, *n.nt.* Asia.

Asket', -en, -en, *n.m.* ascetic.

aske'tisch, *adj.* ascetic.

Asphalt', -e, *n.m.* asphalt.

Aspirin', *n.nt.* aspirin.

assimilie'ren, *vb.* assimilate.

Assistent', -en, -en, *n.m.* assistant.

assoziie'ren, *vb.* associate.

Ast, ᵛe, *n.m.* branch.

ästhe'tisch, *adj.* aesthetic.

Asthma, *n.nt.* asthma.

Astigmatis'mus, -men, *n.m.* astigmatism.

Astrologie', -i'en, *n.f.* astrology.

Astronomie', -i'en, *n.f.* astronomy.

Asyl', -e, *n.nt.* asylum.

Atelier', -s, *n.nt.* studio.

Atem, -, *n.m.* breath.

atemlos, *adj.* breathless.

Atempause, -n, *n.f.* respite.

Atheist', -en, -en, *n.m.* atheist.

Äther, *n.m.* ether.

äthe'risch, *adj.* ethereal.

Athlet', -en, -en, *n.m.* athlete.

athle'tisch, *adj.* athletic.

Atlan'tik, *n.m.* Atlantic Ocean.

atlan'tisch, *adj.* Atlantic.

Atlas, -lan'ten, *n.m.* atlas.

atmen, *vb.* breathe.

Atmen, *n.nt.* breathing.

Atmosphä´re, -n, *n.f.* atmosphere.

atmosphä´risch, *adj.* atmospheric.

Atmung, *n.f.* respiration.

Atom´, -e *n.nt.* atom.

atomar´, *adj.* atomic.

atomisie´ren, *vb.* atomize.

Attaché´, -s, *n.m.* attaché.

Attentat´, -e *n.nt.* attempt on someone's life.

Attentä´ter, -, -, *n.m.* assassin.

Attest´, -e, *n.nt.* certificate.

ätzen,*vb.* etch; *(med.)* cauterize.

au, *interj.* ouch.

auch, *adv.* also, too; **(a. nicht)** not . . . either; **(a. jetzt)** even now.

Audienz´, -en, *n.f.* audience.

Audito´rium, -rien, *n.nt.* auditorium.

auf, *prep.* on, onto.

auf·atmen, *vb.* breathe a sigh of relief.

Aufbau, *n.m.* erection, construction; structure.

auf·bauen, *vb.* erect.

auf·blasen, *vb.* inflate.

auf·brechen, *vb.* break open; start out.

auf·decken, *vb.* uncover, unearth.

auf·drängen, *vb.* obtrude; **(sich a.)** obtrude.

aufdringlich, *adj.* obtrusive, importunate.

aufeinan´derfolgend, *adj.* successive, consecutive.

Aufenthalt, *n.m.* stay.

auf·erlegen, *vb.* impose.

Auferstehung, *n.f.* resurrection.

auf·fallen, *vb.* be conspicuous.

auffällig, *adj.* noticeable, conspicuous, flashy.

Auffälligkeit, -en, *n.f.* conspicuousness, flashiness.

auf·fangen, *vb.* catch; intercept.

auf·fassen, *vb.* conceive, interpret.

Auffassung, -en, *n.f.* conception, interpretation.

auf·flammen, *vb.* flash, flare up.

auf·fordern, *vb.* ask, invite, summon.

Aufforderung, -en, *n.f.* invitation, summons.

auf·frischen, *vb.* refresh.

auf·führen, *vb.* list; *(theater)* perform.

Aufführung, -en, *n.f.* performance.

Aufgabe, -n, *n.f.* task, assignment; *(school)* lesson.

Aufgang, -e, *n.m.* rise.

auf·geben, *vb.* give up, abandon; *(luggage)* check through; *(food)* serve; *(jur.)* waive.

Aufgebot, -e, *n.nt.* banns.

aufgebracht, *adj.* angry, provoked.

auf·gehen, *vb.* (sun etc.) rise; *(math.)* leave no remainder; *(fig.)* beabsorbed in.

auf·halten, *vb.* hold open; stop, detain; **(sich a.)** stay.

auf·hängen, *vb.* suspend; hang.

auf·heben, *vb.* revoke, nullify; **(zeitweilig a.)** suspend.

Aufheben, *n.nt.* ado, fuss.

Aufhebung, -en, *n.f.* revocation, abolition.

auf·heitern, *vb.* cheer up.

auf·hören, *vb.* stop, quit.

Aufhören, *n.nt.* cessation.

auf·klären, *vb.* enlighten; **(sich a.)** clear.

Aufklärung, *n.f.* enlightenment.

auf·kommen, *vb.* come into use; **(a. für)** be responsible for.

Auflage, -n, *n.f.* printing, circulation.

Auflauf, -e, *n.m.* crowd, mob; soufflé.

auf·lösen, *vb.* dissolve.

Auflösung, -en, *n.f.* dissolution.

auf·machen, *vb.* open; **(sich a.)** set out for.

Aufmachung, -en, *n.f.* make-up.

aufmerksam, *adj.* attentive, polite; alert.

Aufmerksamkeit, -en, *n.f.* attention, attentiveness.

auf·muntern, *vb.* cheer up.

Aufnahme, -n, *n.f.* reception; (photo) shot; (phonograph, tape) recording.

auf·nehmen*, *vb.* take in; (phonograph, tape) record; film, photograph.

auf·opfern, *vb.* (**sich a.**) sacrifice oneself.

auf·passen, *vb.* pay attention, look out for.

auf·raffen, *vb.* (**sich a.**) bestir oneself.

auf·räumen, *vb.* put in order; (**mit etwas a.**) debunk.

aufrecht, *adj.* upright.

aufrecht·erhalten*, *vb.* maintain, uphold.

Aufrechterhaltung, *n.f.* maintenance.

auf·regen, *vb.* excite, agitate; (**sich a.**) get excited.

Aufregung, -en, *n.f.* excitement.

aufreibend, *adj.* exhausting.

auf·reihen, *vb.* string.

auf·reißen*, *vb.* tear open.

auf·richten, *vb.* erect.

aufrichtig, *adj.* sincere, heartfelt.

Aufruf, -e, *n.m.* proclamation.

Aufruhr, *n.m.* riot; (**in A. geraten***) riot.

aufrührerisch, *adj.* insurgent; inflammatory.

auf·sagen, *vb.* recite.

aufsässig, *adj.* rebellious.

Aufsatz, ̈-e, *n.m.* essay.

auf·saugen, *vb.* suck up, absorb.

auf·schieben*, *vb.* postpone, delay, procrastinate.

Aufschlag, ̈-e, *n.m.* surtax; (trousers, sleeve) cuff.

auf·schlagen*, *vb.* open; hit the ground.

auf·schließen*, *vb.* unlock.

Aufschluß, ̈sse, *n.m.* information.

aufschlußreich, *adj.* informative.

Aufschnitt, *n.m.* cut; (**kalter A.**) cold cuts.

Aufschrift, -en, *n.f.* inscription; address.

Aufschub, *n.m.* postponement, stay.

Aufschwung, *n.m.* upward swing, boost.

auf·sehen*, *vb.* look up.

Aufsehen, *n.nt.* sensation.

aufsehenerregend, *adj.* spectacular.

auf·setzen, *vb.* put on.

Aufsicht, *n.f.* supervision.

auf·speichern, *vb.* store up.

auf·springen*, *vb.* leap up; fly open; (skin) chap.

Aufstand, ̈-e, *n.m.* uprising, insurrection.

aufständisch, *adj.* insurgent.

Aufständisch-, *n.m.* insurgent.

auf·stapeln, *vb.* stack.

auf·stehen*, *vb.* get up, rise, arise.

auf·steigen*, *vb.* mount, ascend, rise.

auf·stellen, *vb.* put up; nominate.

Aufstieg, -e, *n.m.* ascent, advancement.

auf·suchen, *vb.* look up; seek.

auf·tauchen, *vb.* emerge.

Auftrag, ̈-e, *n.m.* instruction, order.

auf·tragen*, *vb.* instruct, assign; lay on; wear out; (food) serve up.

auf·treiben*, *vb.* raise.

auf·trennen, *vb.* rip.

auf·treten*, *vb.* appear; act.

Auftreten, *n.nt.* appearance; (**sicheres A.**) poise.

auf·wachen, *vb.* awake.

Aufwand, *n.m.* expenditure; display.

auf·warten, *vb.* wait upon; wait up.

aufwärts, *adv.* upward(s).

auf·wecken, *vb.* wake up.

auf·wenden*, *vb.* expend.

auf·wiegen, *vb.* balance.

auf·zählen, *vb.* enumerate; itemize.

auf·zeichnen, *vb.* record.

auf·ziehen*, *vb.* draw open;

(watch) wind; (knitting) unravel; (child) rear.

Aufzug, ⁻e, *n.m.* lift, hoist, elevator; procession; (theater) act.

auf·zwingen*, *vb.* force upon.

Auge, -n, *n.nt.* eye; **(blaues A.)** black eye.

Augenarzt, ⁻e, *n.m.* oculist.

Augenblick, -e, *n.m.* moment, instant.

augenblicklich, *adj.* momentary, instant.

Augenbraue, -n, *n.f.* eyebrow.

Augenglas, ⁻er, *n.nt.* eyeglass.

Augenhöhle, -n, *n.f.* socket.

Augenlid, -er, *n.nt.* eyelid.

Augenschein, *n.m.* evidence.

augenscheinlich, *adj.* ostensible.

Augensicht, *n.f.* eyesight.

Augenwimper, -n, *n.f.* eyelash.

August', *n.m.* August.

aus, *prep.* out of, from.

aus·arbeiten, *vb.* elaborate.

aus·arten, *vb.* degenerate.

aus·atmen, *vb.* exhale.

aus·bessern, *vb.* repair, mend.

aus·beuten, *vb.* exploit.

aus·bilden, *vb.* educate, train.

aus·bleiben*, *vb.* stay out; fail to materialize.

Ausblick, -e, *n.m.* outlook; view.

aus·brechen*, *vb.* erupt.

aus·breiten, *vb.* spread, expand.

aus·brennen*, *vb.* burn out; (*med.*) cauterize.

Ausbruch, ⁻e, *n.m.* outbreak, outburst, eruption.

aus·brüten, *vb.* hatch.

aus·buchten, *vb.* (**sich a.**) bulge.

Ausdauer, *n.f.* endurance, stamina.

ausdauernd, *adj.* enduring.

aus·dehnen, *vb.* expand, extend; prolong; (**sich a.**) distend, dilate.

Ausdehnung, -en, *n.f.* expanse, expansion.

aus·denken*, *vb.* think up, invent.

aus·drehen, *vb.* turn out.

Ausdruck, ⁻e, *n.m.* expression, term.

aus·drücken, *vb.* express, phrase.

ausdrücklich, *adj.* explicit.

ausdrucksvoll, *adj.* expressive.

auseinan'der, *adv.* apart, asunder.

auseinan'der·gehen*, *vb.* part; diverge.

auseinan'der·nehmen*, *vb.* take apart.

auseinan'der·reißen*, *vb.* tear apart, disrupt.

auserlesen, *adj.* choice.

aus·fallen*, *vb.* fall out, not take place.

Ausflug, ⁻e, *n.m.* excursion, outing.

aus·fragen, *vb.* interrogate, quiz.

Ausfuhr, *n.f.* export.

aus·führen, *vb.* carry out, execute; export.

ausführend, *adj.* executive.

ausführlich, *adj.* detailed, explicit.

Ausführung, -en, *n.f.* execution; statement.

aus·füllen, *vb.* fill out.

Ausgabe, -n, *n.f.* expense, expenditure; issuance; edition.

Ausgang, ⁻e, *n.m.* exit; end.

aus·geben*, *vb.* give out; spend, expend; issue; (**sich a. für**) pose as.

ausgefallen, *adj.* rare; odd.

aus·gehen*, *vb.* go out; date.

ausgelassen, *adj.* hilarious.

ausgenommen, *adj.* except for.

ausgestorben, *adj.* extinct.

ausgesucht, *adj.* select.

ausgezeichnet, *adj.* excellent.

aus·gleichen*, *vb.* balance, adjust.

aus·gleiten*, *vb.* slip.

Ausguß, ⁻sse, *n.m.* sink.

aus·halten*, *vb.* hold out; bear.

aus·händigen, vb. hand out, over.

Aushilfe, **-n**, n.f. assistance; stopgap.

aus·hungern, vb. starve out.

aus·kleiden, vb. undress.

aus·kommen*, vb. get along (with).

Auskommen, n.nt. livelihood.

Auskunft, **⸚e**, n.f. information.

aus·lachen, vb. laugh at.

aus·laden*, vb. unload.

Auslage, **-n**, n.f. outlay; display.

Ausland, n.nt. foreign country; **(im A.)** abroad.

Ausländer, **-**, n.m. foreigner, alien.

ausländisch, adj. foreign, alien.

aus·lassen*, vb. leave out; let out.

aus·legen, vb. lay out; interpret; (money) advance.

Auslegung, **-en**, n.f. interpretation.

Auslese, **-n**, n.f. selection.

aus·liefern, vb. extradite.

aus·löschen, vb. extinguish, efface.

aus·lösen, vb. release, unleash.

Ausmaß, **-e**, n.nt. dimension.

Ausnahme, **-n**, n.f. exception.

aus·nutzen, vb. utilize; exploit.

aus·packen vb. unpack.

aus·pressen, vb. squeeze.

Auspuff, **-e**, n.m. exhaust.

aus·radieren, vb. erase, obliterate.

aus·rangieren, vb. scrap.

aus·rechnen, vb. figure out.

aus·reichen, vb. suffice.

aus·reißen*, vb. run away, bolt.

aus·renken, vb. dislocate.

aus·richten, vb. align; execute; deliver (a message).

aus·rotten, vb. exterminate, eradicate.

Ausruf, **-e**, n.m. exclamation.

aus·rufen*, vb. proclaim, exclaim.

Ausrufungszeichen, **-**, n.nt. exclamation point.

aus·ruhen, vb. rest.

ausruhsam, adj. restful.

aus·rüsten, vb. equip.

Aussage, **-n**, n.f. statement; testimony.

aus·sagen, vb. testify.

Aussatz, n.m. leprosy.

aus·schalten, vb. eliminate; (elec.) disconnect.

Ausschalter, **-**, n.m. (elec.) cutout.

aus·scheiden*, vb. eliminate; (med.) secrete; retire, withdraw.

Ausscheidung, **-en**, n.f. elimination.

aus·schelten*, vb. berate.

aus·schimpfen, vb. scold, bawl out.

Ausschlag, **⸚e**, n.m. (med.) rash; **(den A. geben*)** clinch the matter.

aus·schlafen*, vb. sleep as long as one wants to.

aus·schließen*, vb. shut out, exclude.

ausschließlich, adj. exclusive.

Ausschluß, n.m. exclusion.

aus·schmücken, vb. embellish.

Ausschnitt, **-e**, n.m. section; clipping; neck (of dress).

aus·schöpfen, vb. bail out (water), exhaust.

Ausschuß, **⸚sse**, n.m. committee, board.

aus·schweifen, vb. go far afield; dissipate.

aus·sehen*, vb. look, appear.

außen, adv. outside; **(nach a.)** outward.

Außenbezirk, **-e**, n.m. outskirts.

Außenseite, **-n**, n.f. outside.

Außenwe t, n.f. outside.

außer, prep. beside(s), except; out of; **(a. sich)** beside oneself.

äußer-, adj. exterior, external.

außerdem, adv. besides.

außergewöhnlich, adj. extraordinary.

äußerlich, adj. outward.

äußern, vb. utter.

außerordentlich, adv. exceedingly.

äußerst-, adj. extreme.

äußerst, adv. extremely.

Äußerst-, n.nt. extremity.

außerstan'de, adv. unable.

Äußerung, -en, n.f. utterance.

aus-setzen, vb. set out; expose, subject.

Aussetzung, -en, n.f. exposure.

Aussicht, -en, n.f. view; prospect.

aus-speien*, vb. disgorge.

Aussprache, -n, n.f. pronunciation.

aus-sprechen*, vb. enunciate, pronounce; **(falsch a.)** mispronounce.

aus-spucken, vb. spit (out).

aus-spülen, vb. rinse.

Ausstand, -e, n.m. strike.

aus-statten, vb. equip, endow.

Ausstattung, -en, n.f. equipment, décor.

aus-stehen*, vb. bear, stand.

aus-steigen*, vb. get out.

aus-stellen, vb. show, exhibit; issue.

Ausstellung, -en, n.f. exhibit, exhibition.

aus-sterben*, vb. die out.

Aussterben, n.nt. extinction.

aus-stoßen*, vb. expel.

aus-strahlen, vb. radiate.

Ausstrahlung, -en, n.f. radiation.

aus-streichen*, vb. delete.

aus-strömen, vb. emanate.

aus-suchen, vb. choose, select.

Austausch, n.m. exchange.

austauschbar, adj. exchangeable.

aus-tauschen, vb. exchange.

aus-teilen, vb. distribute.

Auster, -n, n.f. oyster.

aus-tilgen, vb. expunge.

aus-tragen*, vb. deliver.

aus-treiben*, vb. drive out, exorcise.

aus-treten*, vb. step out; resign; secede.

aus-üben, vb. exercise, practice.

Ausübung, -en, n.f. exercise, practice.

Ausverkauf, n.m. sale.

Auswahl, -en, n.f. choice, selection, assortment.

aus-wählen, vb. select, pick.

aus-walzen, vb. roll out, laminate.

Auswanderer, -, n.m. emigrant.

aus-wandern, vb. emigrate.

auswärtig, adj. external.

Ausweg, -e, n.m. way out, escape.

aus-weichen*, vb. evade, dodge.

ausweichend, adj. evasive.

Ausweis, -e, n.m. pass, identification.

aus-weisen*, vb. evict; **(sich a.)** identify oneself.

Ausweisung, -en, n.f. eviction.

auswendig, adj. by heart; **(a. lernen)** memorize.

aus-werten, vb. evaluate; reclaim.

Auswertung, -en, n.f. evaluation; reclamation.

aus-wickeln, vb. unwrap.

aus-wirken, vb. work out; **(sich a.)** have an effect.

Auswirkung, -en, n.f. effect, impact.

aus-wischen, vb. wipe out.

Auswuchs, -e, n.m. protuberance, excrescence.

aus-zahlen, vb. pay out.

aus-zeichnen, vb. distinguish; **(sich a.)** excel.

aus-ziehen*, vb. move out; (clothes) take off; **(sich a.)** undress.

Auszug, -e, n.m. exodus; excerpt, extract.

authen'tisch, adj. authentic.

Auto, -s, n.nt. auto.

Autobahn, -en, n.f. superhighway.

Autobus, -se, n.m. bus.

Autogramm', -e, *n.nt.* autograph.

Automat', -en, -en, *n.m.* automat; automaton.

automa'tisch, *adj.* automatic.

autonom', *adj.* autonomous.

autoritär', *adj.* authoritarian.

Autorität', -en, *n.f.* authority.

Axt, ⸚e, *n.f.* axe.

azur'blau, *adj.* azure.

B

Baby, -s, *n.nt.* baby.

Bach, ⸚e, *n.m.* brook.

Backe, -n, *n.f.* cheek, jowl.

backen*, *vb.* bake.

Bäcker, -, *n.m.* baker.

Bäckerei', -en, *n.f.* bakery, pastry shop.

Backpflaume, -n, *n.f.* prune.

Backstein, -e, *n.m.* brick.

Bad, ⸚er, *n.nt.* bath.

Badeanstalt, -en, *n.f.* public bath.

Badeanzug, ⸚e, *n.m.* bathing suit.

Bademantel, ⸚, *n.m.* bathrobe.

baden, *vb.* bathe.

Badeort, -e, *n.m.* bathing resort.

Badewanne, -n, *n.f.* bathtub.

Badezimmer, -. *n, nt.* bathroom.

Bahn, -en, *n.f.* path, course.

Bahnhof, ⸚e, *n.m.* station.

Bahnsteig, -e, *n.m.* platform.

Bahre, -n, *n.f.* bier.

Bajonett', -e, *n.nt.* bayonet.

Bakte'rie, -n, *n.f.* germ.

Bakte'rium, -rien, *n.nt.* bacterium.

balancie'ren, *vb.* balance.

bald, *adv.* soon, shortly.

Balken, -, *n.m.* beam.

Balkon', -s, *or* -e, *n.m.* balcony.

Ball, ⸚e, *n.m.* ball.

ballen, *vb.* (fist) clench.

Balleri'na, -nen, *n.f.* ballerina.

Ballon', -s, *n.m.* balloon.

Balsam, -e, *n.m.* balsam, balm.

balsamie'ren, *vb.* embalm.

Bambus, -se, *n.m.* bamboo.

banal', *adj.* banal.

Bana'ne, -n, *n.f.* banana.

Band, -e, *n.nt.* bond, tie.

Band, ⸚e, *n.m.* (book) volume.

Band, ⸚er, *n.nt.* band, ribbon, tape.

Bande, -n, *n.f.* band, gang.

bändigen, *vb.* tame.

Bandit', -en, -en, *n.m.* bandit, desperado.

bang(e), *adj.* afraid.

Bank, ⸚e, *n.f.* bench.

Bank, -en, *n.f.* bank.

Bankgeschäft, -e, *n.nt.* banking; banking firm.

Bankier's, -s, *n.m.* banker.

bankrott', *adj.* bankrupt.

Bankrott', -e, *n.m.* bankruptcy.

Bann, -e, *n.m.* ban; (eccles.) excommunication.

bannen, *vb.* banish, outlaw.

Banner, -, *n.nt.* banner.

bar, *adj.* cash.

Bar, -s, *n.f.* bar.

Bär, -en, -en, *n.m.* bear; (Grosser B.) Big Dipper.

Barbar', -en, -en, *n.m.* barbarian.

Barbarei', -en, *n.f.* barbarism.

barba'risch, *adj.* barbarian, barbarous.

barfuß, *adj.* barefoot.

Bargeld, -er, *n.nt.* cash.

Bariton, -e, *n.m.* baritone.

Barium, *n.nt.* barium.

Barke, -n, *n.f.* bark.

barm her'zig, *adj.* merciful.

Barmixer, -, *n.m.* bartender.

barock', *adj.* baroque.

Barome'ter, -, *n.nt.* barometer.

barome'trisch, *adj.* barometric.

Baron', -e,⸗ *n.m.* baron.

Barones'se, -n, *n.f.* baroness.

Barrika'de, -n, *n.f.* barricade.

Bart, ⸚e, *n.m.* beard.

Barthaar, -e, *n.nt.* whisker.

bärtig, *adj.* bearded.

bartlos, *adj.* beardless.

Barzahlung, -en, *n.f.* cash payment.

Baseball-Spiel, -e, *n.nt.* baseball.

basie'ren, *vb.* base.

Basis, -sen, *n.f.* basis.

Baß, ⸚sse, *n.m.* bass.

Bastard, -e, *n.m.* bastard.

Bataillon', -e, *n.nt.* battalion.

Batterie', -i'en, *n.f.* battery.

Batist', -e, *n.m.* cambric, batiste.

Bau, -ten, *n.m.* construction; building; structure.

Bauch, ⸚e, *n.m.* belly.

bauen, *vb.* build, construct.

Bauer, -n, *n.m.* farmer, peasant; (chess) pawn.

Bauernhaus, ⸚er, *n.nt.* farmhouse.

Bauernhof, ⸚e, *n.m.* farmyard.

baufällig, *adj.* dilapidated.

Baukunst, *n.f.* architecture.

Baum, -e, *n.m.* tree.

bäumen, *vb.* (**sich b.**) rear.

baumeln, *vb.* dangle; (**b. lassen***) dangle.

Baumeister, -, *n.m.* builder.

Baumstamm, ⸚e, *n.m.* log.

Baumwolle, *n.f.* cotton.

bauschig, *adj.* baggy.

Bauunternehmer, -, *n.m.* contractor.

Bazar', -e, *n.m.* bazaar.

Bazil'lus, -len, *n.m.* bacillus.

beab'sichtigen, *vb.* intend.

beach'ten, *vb.* notice, pay attention to.

beach'tenswert, *adj.* noteworthy.

beacht'lich, *adj.* remarkable.

Beach'tung, -en, *n.f.* notice, consideration.

Beamt'-, *n.m.* official.

bean'spruchen, *vb.* lay claim to.

bean'standen, *vb.* object to.

bean'tragen, *vb.* propose, move.

beant'worten, *vb.* answer.

bear'beiten, *vb.* work; adapt; handle, process.

beauf'sichtigen, *vb.* supervise.

beauf'tragen, *vb.* commission.

Beauf'tragt-, *n.m.* commissioner.

bebau'en, *vb.* till; build on.

beben, *vb.* quake, tremble.

Becher, -, *n.m.* beaker, goblet.

Becken, -, *n.nt.* basin; pelvis.

Bedacht', *n.m.* deliberation, care.

bedäch'tig, *adj.* cautious, deliberate.

bedan'ken, *vb.* (**sich bei jemandem für etwas b.**) thank someone for something.

Bedarf', *n.m.* need, demand.

bedau'erlich, *adj.* regrettable.

bedau'ern, *vb.* regret.

Bedau'ern, *n.nt.* regret.

bede'cken, *vb.* cover over.

beden'ken*, *vb.* bear in mind.

Beden'ken, -, *n.nt.* compunction, misgiving.

bedeu'ten, *vb.* mean, signify.

bedeu'tend, *adj.* significant, important.

Bedeu'tung, -en, *n.f.* significance, meaning.

bedeu'tungslos, *adj.* insignificant.

bedie'nen, *vb.* serve, wait on; operate (machine); follow suit (cards); (**sich b.**) help oneself.

Bedie'ner, -, *n.m.* operator (of a machine).

Bedient'-, *n.m.&f.* servant, attendant.

Bedie'nung, *n.f.* service.

bedingt', *adj.* conditional, qualified.

Bedin'gung, -en, *n.f.* condition.

bedin'gungslos, adj. unconditional.

bedrän'gen, vb. beset.

bedro'hen, vb. menace, threaten.

bedrü'cken, vb. oppress.

bedür'fen*, vb. have need of.

bedrü'ckend, adj. oppressive.

Bedürf'nis, -se, n.nt. need, requirement.

Bedürf'nisanstalt, -en, n.f. comfort station.

bedürf'tig, adj. indigent, needy; in need of.

Beefsteak, -s, n.nt. beefsteak.

beeh'ren, vb. honor.

beei'len vb. (sich b.) hurry.

beein'drucken, vb. impress.

beein'flussen, vb. influence.

beein'trächtigen, vb. impair.

been'den, vb. end, finish.

been'digen, vb. end, finish.

beer'digen, vb. inter, bury.

Beer'digung, -en, n.f. funeral.

Beere, -n, n.f. berry.

befä'higen, vb. enable, qualify.

befahr'bar, adj. passable.

befal'len*, vb. fall upon, attack.

befan'gen, adj. embarrassed.

befas'sen, vb. touch; (sich b. mit) take up, attend to, deal with.

Befehl', -e, n.m. command, order.

befeh'len*, vb. command, order.

Befehls'haber, -, n.m. commander.

befes'tigen, vb. fasten, fortify, confirm.

befeuch'ten, vb. moisten.

befin'den*, vb. find, deem; (sich b.) be located, feel.

befle'cken, vb. stain.

beflei'ßigen, vb. (sich b.) endeavor, take pains.

befol'gen, vb. follow, observe, obey.

beför'dern, vb. advance, promote, transport.

Beför'derungsmittel, -, n.nt. conveyance.

befra'gen, vb. question, interrogate.

befrei'en, vb. liberate, exempt.

Befrei'ung, -en, n.f. liberation, release.

befrem'den, vb. appear strange to, alienate.

befreun'den, vb. befriend; (sich b. mit) make friends with.

befrie'digen, vb. satisfy.

befrie'digend, adj. satisfactory.

Befrie'digung, -en, n.f. satisfaction.

befruch'ten, vb. fertilize, fructify.

Befug'nis, -se, n.f. authority.

befugt', adj. authorized.

befüh'len, vb. feel, finger.

Befund', n.m. finding(s).

befürch'ten, vb. fear.

befür'worten, vb. advocate, recommend.

begabt', adj. gifted.

Bega'bung, -en, n.f. talent.

bege'ben*, vb. (sich b.) betake oneself; occur.

begeg'nen, vb. meet, encounter.

Begeg'nung, -en, n.f. meeting, encounter.

bege'hen*, vb. commit.

begeh'ren, vb. desire, covet.

begeis'tern, vb. inspire.

begeis'tert, adj. enthusiastic.

Begeis'terung, n.f. enthusiasm.

Begier'de, -n, n.f. desire, lust.

begie'rig, adj. eager, desirous.

begie'ßen*, vb. water.

Beginn', n.m. beginning.

begin'nen*, vb. begin.

Begin'nen, n.nt. inception.

beglau'bigen, vb. certify, accredit.

Beglau'bigungsschreiben, -, n.nt. credentials.

beglei'chen*, vb. settle.

beglei'ten, vb. accompany.

beglei'tend, adj. concomitant.

Beglei'ter, -, *n.m.* companion, escort; accompanist.

Beglei'tung, -en, *n.f.* accompaniment.

beglück'wünschen, *vb.* congratulate.

begna'digen, *vb.* pardon.

begnü'gen, *vb.* **(sich b. mit)** content oneself with.

begra'ben*, *vb.* bury.

Begräb'nis, -se, *n.nt.* burial, funeral.

begrei'fen*, *vb.* comprehend.

begreif'lich, *adj.* understandable.

begren'zen, *vb.* limit.

Begren'zung, -en, *n.f.* limitation.

Begriff', -e, *n.m.* concept; **(im B. sein)** be about to.

begrün'den, *vb.* establish; justify.

begrü'ßen, *vb.* greet.

Begrü'ßung, -en, *n.f.* greeting, salutation.

begün'stigen, *vb.* favor, support.

Begün'stigung, -en, *n.f.* favoritism, encouragement.

behä'big, *adj.* portly.

beha'gen, *vb.* please.

Beha'gen, *n.nt.* comfort, pleasure.

behag'lich, *adj.* comfortable, pleasant.

behal'ten*, *vb.* keep.

Behäl'ter, -, *n.m.* container.

behan'deln, *vb.* treat.

Behand'lung, -en, *n.f.* treatment.

Behang', "e, *n.m.* drapery.

behar'ren, *vb.* persevere, insist.

beharr'lich, *adj.* constant, persistent.

Beharr'lichkeit, *n.f.* perseverance.

behaup'ten, *vb.* assert, maintain; allege.

Behaup'tung, -en, *n.f.* assertion.

behe'ben*, *vb.* remove.

Behelf', -e, *n.m.* expedient, makeshift.

behel'fen*, *vb.* **(sich b. mit)** make do with.

behel'ligen, *vb.* bother.

behen'd(e), *adj.* nimble, agile.

beher'bergen, *vb.* shelter, lodge.

beherr'schen, *vb.* rule, govern; control, master; dominate.

Beherr'schung, *n.f.* rule, mastery.

beher'zigen, *vb.* take to heart.

beherzt, *adj.* courageous, game.

behilf'lich, *adj.* helpful.

behin'dern, *vb.* impede.

Behin'derung, -en, *n.f.* impediment.

Behör'de, -n, *n.f.* governing office, authority.

Behuf', -e, *n.m.* purpose; benefit.

behufs', *prep.* for the purpose of.

behü'ten, *vb.* guard, protect, keep from; **(Gott behüte)** God forbid.

behut'sam, *adj.* cautious.

bei, *prep.* at, near, by; in connection with; **(b. mir)** at my house, on my person.

bei-behalten*, *vb.* retain.

Beibehaltung, -en, *n.f.* retention.

Beiblatt, "er, *n.nt.* supplement.

bei-bringen*, *vb.* bring forward; **(jemandem etwas b.)** make something clear to someone, teach someone something.

Beichte, -n, *n.f.* confession.

beichten, *vb.* confess.

Beichtstuhl, "e, *n.m.* confessional.

Beichtvater, ", *n.m.* confessor.

beide, *adj.&pron.* both.

Beifall, "e, *n.m.* applause.

Beifallsruf, -e, *n.m.* cheer.

bei-fügen, *vb.* add, enclose, attach, include.

Beifügung, -en, *n.f.* attachment.

Beihilfe, -n, *n.f.* assistance.

bei-kommen*, *vb.* get at.

Beil, -e, *n.nt.* hatchet.

Beilage, -n, n.f. enclosure; supplement.

beiläufig, adj. incidental.

bei·legen, vb. add, attach to, inclose.

Beileid, n.nt. condolence.

bei·messen*, vb. attribute.

Beimessung, -en, n.f. attribution.

Beimischung, -en, n.f. admixture.

Bein, -e, n.nt. leg.

beinahe, adv. almost.

bei·ordnen, vb. adjoin, co-ordinate.

bei·pflichten, vb. agree with.

beir'ren, vb. confuse.

beisam'men, adv. together.

Beisein, n.nt. presence.

beisei'te, adv. aside, apart.

Beispiel, -e, n.nt. example.

beispiellos, adj. unheard of.

beißen*, vb. bite.

beißend, adj. biting, acrid.

Beistand, -̈e, n.m. assistance.

bei·stehen*, vb. assist.

bei·stimmen, vb. agree.

Beitrag, -̈e, n.m. contribution.

bei·tragen*, vb. contribute.

Beiträger, -, n.m. contributor.

bei·treten*, vb. join.

Beitritt, -e, n.m. joining.

bei·wohnen, vb. attend, witness.

Beiwort, -̈e, n.nt. epithet.

Beize, n.f. corrosion, stain.

beizei'ten, adv. in good time.

beizen, vb. corrode, stain.

bejah'en, vb. affirm, say yes to.

bejahrt, adj. aged.

bejam'mern, vb. deplore.

bejam'mernswert, adj. deplorable.

bekäm'pfen, vb. combat.

bekannt', adj. well-known; acquainted.

Bekannt'-, n.m.&f. acquaintance.

bekannt'·geben*, vb. make known, announce.

bekannt'lich, adv. as is well known.

bekannt'·machen, vb. acquaint, make known.

Bekannt'machung, -en, n.f. proclamation.

Bekannt'schaft, -en, n.f. acquaintance.

bekeh'ren, vb. convert.

beken'nen*, vb. confess.

Bekennt'nis, -se, n.nt. confession.

bekla'gen, vb. deplore, lament; **(sich b. über)** complain about.

bekla'genswert, adj. deplorable, lamentable.

Beklagt'-, n.m.&f. accused, defendant.

beklei'den, vb. clothe, cover; fill (a position).

Beklei'dung, -en, n.f. clothing, covering.

beklem'men*, vb. oppress.

Beklom'menheit, n.f. anxiety.

bekom'men*, vb. get, obtain, receive; agree with, suit.

bekös'tigen, vb. feed, board.

bekräf'tigen, vb. confirm, corroborate.

beküm'mern, vb. grieve, distress.

Beküm'mernis, -se, n.f. grief, distress.

bekun'den, vb. manifest.

bela'den*, vb. load, burden.

Belag', -̈e, n.m. covering, surface; (food) spread.

bela'gern, vb. besiege.

Bela'gerung, -en, n.f. siege.

Belang', -e, n.m. importance.

belan'gen, vb. concern; sue.

belang'los, adj. unimportant, irrelevant.

belang'reich, adj. important, relevant.

belas'ten, vb. load, burden, strain; incriminate.

beläs'tigen, vb. annoy, bother, molest.

Belas'tung, -en, n.f. strain; inconvenience; incrimination.

belau'fen*, vb. **(sich b. auf)** amount to.

bele'ben, vb. animate, enliven.

Beleg', **-e**, *n.m.* proof, evidence, documentation.

bele'gen, *vb.* attest; reserve (seat); sign up for (academic subject).

belegt', *adj.* (**b. es Brot**) sandwich.

beleh'ren, *vb.* teach.

belei'digen, *vb.* insult.

Belei'digung, -en, *n.f.* insult.

beleuch'ten, *vb.* illuminate.

Beleuch'tung, -en, *n.f.* illumination.

Belgien, *n.nt.* Belgium.

Belgier, -, *n.m.* Belgian.

belgisch, *adj.* Belgian.

belich'ten, *vb.* expose.

Belich'tung, -en, *n.f.* exposure.

belie'ben, *vb.* please; (**wie beliebt?**) I beg your pardon?

Belie'ben, *n.nt.* pleasure, discretion; (**nach B.**) as you please.

belie'big, *adj.* any (you wish); (**eine b.e Zahl**) any number you want.

beliebt', *adj.* popular.

Beliebt'heit, *n.f.* popularity.

bellen, *vb.* bark.

beloh'nen, *vb.* reward.

Beloh'nung, -en, *n.f.* reward.

belü'gen*, *vb.* lie to.

belus'tigen, *vb.* amuse, entertain.

bema'len, *vb.* paint up.

beman'nen, *vb.* man.

bemerk'bar, *adj.* noticeable, perceptible.

bemer'ken, *vb.* notice; remark.

bemer'kenswert, *adj.* notable.

Bemer'kung, -en, *n.f.* remark.

bemü'hen, *vb.* trouble; (**sich b.**) take pains, try hard.

benach'bart, *adj.* neighboring.

benach'richtigen, *vb.* notify.

Benach'richtigung, -en, *n.f.* notification.

benach'teiligen, *vb.* put at a disadvantage, handicap.

beneh'men*, *vb.* take away; (**sich b.**) behave.

Beneh'men, *n.nt.* behavior.

benei'den, *vb.* envy.

benei'denswert, *adj.* enviable.

benom'men, *adj.* groggy, confused.

benö'tigen, *vb.* need.

benut'zen, *vb.* use.

Benut'zung, -en, *n.f.* use.

Benzin', *n.nt.* gas, gasoline.

beob'achten, *vb.* observe.

Beob'achtung, -en, *n.f.* observation.

bequem', *adj.* comfortable, convenient.

Bequem'lichkeit, -en, *n.f.* comfort.

bera'ten*, *vb.* advise; (**sich b.**) deliberate.

Bera'ter, -, *n.m.* adviser, consultant.

berau'ben, *vb.* rob, deprive of.

Berau'bung, -en, *n.f.* deprivation.

berau'schen, *vb.* intoxicate.

bere'chenbar, *adj.* calculable.

berech'nen, *vb.* calculate, compute.

berech'nend, *adj.* calculating.

Berech'nung, -en, *n.f.* calculation, computation.

berech'tigen, *vb.* justify, entitle.

Berech'tigung, -en, *n.f.* justification.

bere'den, *vb.* persuade.

Bered'samkeit, *n.f.* eloquence.

beredt', *adj.* eloquent.

Bereich', -e, *n.m.* domain, scope.

berei'chern, *vb.* enrich.

berei'sen, *vb.* tour.

bereit', *adj.* ready, prepared.

berei'ten, *vb.* make ready, prepare.

bereits', *adv.* already.

bereit'willig, *adj.* willing (to oblige).

bereu'en, *vb.* repent, regret.

Berg, -e, *n.m.* mountain.

bergab', *adv.* downhill.

bergan', adv. uphill.

Bergarbeiter, -, n.m. miner.

bergauf', adv. uphill.

Bergbau, n.m. mining.

Bergkette, -n, n.f. mountain range.

Bergsteiger, -, n.m. mountain climber.

Bergung, n.f. salvage.

Bergwerk, -e, n.nt. mine.

Bericht', -e, n.m. report.

berich'ten, vb. report.

Bericht'erstatter, -, n.m. reporter.

berich'tigen, vb. correct.

Berich'tigung, -en, n.f. correction.

bersten*, vb. burst.

berüch'tigt, adj. notorious.

berück'sichtigen, vb. consider, take into consideration; allow for.

Beruf', -e, n.m. profession.

beru'fen*, vb. call, appoint; **(sich b. auf)** refer to, appeal to.

berufs'mäßig, adj. professional.

Beru'fung, -en, n.f. summons, appointment; appeal.

beru'hen, vb. rest, be based.

beru'higen, vb. quiet, calm.

Beru'higungsmittel, -, n.nt. sedative.

berühmt', adj. famous.

Berühmt'heit, -en, n.f. celebrity.

berüh'ren, vb. touch.

Berüh'rung, -en, n.f. touch.

besa'gen, vb. say, indicate, mean.

besagt', adj. (afore)said.

besänf'tigen, vb. soften, soothe.

Besatz', ¨e, n.m. border, trimming, facing.

Besat'zung, -en, n.f. occupying forces; crew.

beschä'digen, vb. damage.

Beschä'digung, -en, n.f. damage.

beschaf'fen, vb. get, obtain, procure; provide.

beschaf'fen, adj. constituted; **(so b.)** of such a nature.

Beschaf'fenheit, -en, n.f. nature, quality.

beschäf'tigen, vb. employ, occupy, keep busy.

beschäf'tigt, adj. busy, engaged.

Beschäf'tigung, -en, n.f. occupation, employment.

beschä'men, vb. shame.

beschämt', adj. ashamed.

beschat'ten, vb. shade.

beschau'en, vb. look at, contemplate.

beschau'lich, adj. contemplative.

Bescheid', -e, n.m. answer, decision; information; **(B. geben*)** let know; **(B. wissen* über)** know all about.

beschei'den*, vb. allot, apportion; inform.

beschei'den, adj. modest.

Beschei'denheit, n.f. modesty.

beschei'nigen, vb. certify.

Beschei'nigung, -en, n.f. certificate, certification.

beschen'ken, vb. **(b. mit)** make a present of.

beschie'ßen*, vb. shoot at, shell, bombard.

Beschie'ßung, -en, n.f. bombardment.

beschimp'fen, vb. abuse, insult.

Beschimp'fung, -en, n.f. abuse, insult.

beschir'men, vb. protect.

Beschlag', ¨e, n.m. metal fitting, coating, condensation; **(in B. nehmen*)** confiscate.

beschla'gen*, vb. cover with, coat, mount; **(sich b.)** become coated, tarnish.

beschla'gen, adj. experienced, proficient.

Beschlag'nahme, -n, n.f. seizure, confiscation.

beschlag'nahmen, vb. seize, confiscate.

beschleu'nigen, vb. quicken, accelerate.

beschlie'ßen*, vb. finish, conclude, decide, make up one's mind.

Beschluß', -sse, *n.m.* decision, conclusion.

beschmie'ren, *vb.* smear, spread on.

beschmut'zen, *vb.* make dirty, soil.

beschnei'den*, *vb.* cut off, clip, circumcise.

beschö'nigen, *vb.* make pretty, gloss over, excuse.

beschrän'ken, *vb.* limit.

beschränkt', *adj.* limited, of limited abilities.

Beschrän'kung, -en, *n.f.* limitation.

beschrei'ben*, *vb.* describe.

Beschrei'bung, -en, *n.f.* description.

beschul'digen, *vb.* blame, accuse, incriminate.

Beschul'digung, -en, *n.f.* incrimination.

beschüt'zen, *vb.* protect.

Beschwer'de, -n, *n.f.* complaint, burden, trouble.

beschwe'ren, *vb.* burden; **(sich bei jemandem über etwas b.)** complain to someone about something.

beschwer'lich, *adj.* burdensome.

beschwich'tigen, *vb.* appease, soothe.

Beschwich'tigung, -en, *n.f.* appeasement.

beschwipst', *adj.* tight.

beschwö'ren*, *vb.* swear to; implore.

Beschwö'rung, -en, *n.f.* swearing by oath; entreaty; exorcism.

besei'tigen, *vb.* remove.

Besei'tigung, *n.f.* removal.

Besen, -, *n.m.* broom.

beses'sen, *adj.* mad, possessed.

beset'zen, *vb.* occupy, fill; trim.

Beset'zung, *n.f.* occupation.

besich'tigen, *vb.* view, inspect, look around in.

Besich'tigung, -en, *n.f.* view, inspection, sight-seeing.

besie'deln, *vb.* settle, colonize.

Besie'd(e)lung, -en, *n.f.* settlement, colonization.

besie'geln, *vb.* seal.

besie'gen, *vb.* defeat.

besin'nen*, *vb.* (sich b.) remember, think over; **(sich anders b.)** change one's mind.

Besin'nung, -en *n.f.* consideration, recollection; senses, consciousness.

besin'nungslos, *adj.* senseless, unconscious.

Besitz', *n.m.* possession, property.

besit'zen*, *vb.* possess, own.

Besit'zer, -, *n.m.* proprietor.

besitz'gierig, *adj.* possessive.

Besit'zung, -en, *n.f.* possession.

besof'fen, *adj.* drunk.

besoh'len, *vb.* sole.

beson'der-, *adj.* special.

Beson'derheit, -en, *n.f.* peculiarity.

beson'ders, *adv.* especially.

beson'nen, *adj.* thoughtful, cautious.

besor'gen, *vb.* take care of, get.

Besorg'nis, -se, *n.f.* apprehension, anxiety.

besorgt', *adj.* anxious, worried.

Besor'gung, -en, *n.f.* management, care; errand.

bespöt'teln, *vb.* ridicule.

bespre'chen*, *vb.* discuss, talk over.

Bespre'chung, -en, *n.f.* discussion, review, conference.

besprit'zen, *vb.* spatter.

besser, *adj.* better.

bessern, *vb.* make better, improve.

Besserung, -en, *n.f.* amelioration, improvement; **(gute B.!)** I hope you get well soon.

best-, *adj.* best.

Bestand', -̈e, *n.m.* duration, stability; supply, stock.

bestän'dig, *adj.* steady, stable, constant.

Bestand'teil, -e, *n.m.* constituent, ingredient.

bestär'ken, *vb.* strengthen.

bestä'tigen, vb. confirm, acknowledge, verify.

Bestä'tigung, -en, n.f confirmation, verification.

bestat'ten, vb. bury.

Bestat'tung, -en, n.f. burial.

beste'chen*, vb. bribe.

beste'chend, adj. attractive, tempting.

Beste'chung, -en, n.f. bribery, graft, corruption.

Besteck', -e, n.nt. set of implements; knife, fork, and spoon.

beste'hen*, vb. exist; (test) undergo, pass; **(b. auf)** insist on; **(b. aus)** consist of.

Beste'hen, n.nt. existence; insistence.

besteh'len*, vb. steal from, rob.

bestei'gen*, vb. climb up, ascend; mount; go on board.

bastel'len, vb. order; send for; give a message; appoint; till.

Bestel'lung, -en, n.f. order; message; appointment; cultivation.

bestens, adv. very well.

besteu'ern, vb. tax.

Besteu'erung, -en, n.f. taxation.

Bestie, -n, n.f. beast.

bestimm'bar, adj. definable, ascertainable, assignable.

bestim'men, vb. determine, decide, specify, designate, destine, dispose.

bestimmt', adj. definite.

Bestim'mungsort, -e, n.m. destination.

bestra'fen, vb. punish.

bestrah'len, vb. irradiate, treat with rays.

bestre'ben, (sich b.) vb. strive.

Bestre'bung, -en, n.f. effort.

bestreit'bar, adj. disputable.

bestrei'ten*, vb. contest dispute, deny.

bestri'cken, vb. entangle, ensnare, captivate, charm.

bestür'men, vb. storm, attack, implore.

bestürzt', adj. dismayed.

Bestür'zung, -en, n.f. dismay.

Besuch', -e, n.m. visit; call; visitor, company; attendance.

besu'chen, vb. visit, attend.

Besu'cher, -, n.m. visitor.

betagt', adj. aged.

betä'tigen, vb. operate; show; **(sich b.)** be active.

betäu'ben, vb. stun, deafen, stupefy.

betäu'bend, adj. stupefying; narcotic, anesthetic.

Bete, -n, n.f. beet.

betei'ligen, vb. cause to share in; **(sich b.)** take part.

Betei'ligung, -en, n.f. participation.

beten, vb. pray.

beteu'ern, vb. assert, swear.

Beteu'erung, -en, n.f. assertion.

beti'teln, vb. entitle.

Beton', -s, n.m. concrete.

beto'nen, vb. stress.

Beto'nung, -en, n.f. stress.

betö'ren, vb. infatuate.

Betracht', n.m. consideration.

betrach'ten, vb. look at, consider, observe, contemplate.

beträcht'lich, adj. considerable.

Betrach'tung, -en, n.f. consideration, contemplation.

Betrag', -e, n.m. amount, sum.

betra'gen*, vb. amount to; **(sich b.)** behave.

Betra'gen, n.nt. behavior.

betrau'ern, vb. mourn for, deplore.

Betreff', n.m. **(in B.)** in regard to.

betref'fen*, vb. affect, concern.

betreffs', prep. in regard to.

betrei'ben*, vb. carry on.

betre'ten*, vb. step upon, enter.

betreu'en, vb. take care of.

Betrieb', -e, n.m. works, management, activity; **(in B.)** running.

betrin'ken*, *vb.* **(sich b.)** get drunk.

betrof'fen, *adj.* taken aback; affected.

betrü'ben, *vb.* grieve.

Betrüb'nis, -se, *n.f.* grief.

Betrug', *n.m.* deceit, deception, fraud.

betrü'gen*, *vb.* deceive, cheat.

betrü'gerisch, *adj.* deceitful, crooked.

betrun'ken, *adj.* drunk, drunken.

Bett, -en, *n.nt.* bed.

Bettdecke, -n, *n.f.* bedspread.

betteln, *vb.* beg.

Bettler, -, *n.m.* beggar.

Bettplatz, ⸚e, *n.m.* berth.

Bettzeug, *n.nt.* bedding, bedclothes.

beugen, *vb.* bend.

Beugung, -en, *n.f.* bend; inflection.

Beule, -n, *n.f.* swelling, bump, lump.

beun'ruhigen, *vb.* disturb, agitate.

Beun'ruhigung, -en, *n.f.* alarm, agitation.

beur'kunden, *vb.* authenticate.

beur'lauben, *vb.* give leave (of absence) to.

beur'teilen, *vb.* judge.

Beute, -n, *n.f.* booty, loot.

Beutel, -, *n.m.* bag, purse, pouch.

Bevöl'kerung, -en, *n.f.* population.

bevoll'mächtigen, *vb.* authorize, give full power to.

Bevoll'mächtigung, -en, *n.f.* authorization.

bevor', *conj.* before.

bevor'-stehen*, *be* about to happen, be in store for.

bevor'stehend, *adj.* imminent.

bevor'zugen, *vb.* favor.

bewa'chen, *vb.* guard, watch.

bewaff'nen, *vb.* arm.

Bewaff'nung, -en, *n.f.* armament.

bewah'ren, *vb.* keep, preserve.

bewäh'ren, *vb.* **(sich b.)** prove itself.

Bewah'rung, -en, *n.f.* conservation.

bewäl'tigen, *vb.* overcome, master.

bewan'dert, *adj.* **(b. in)** experienced in, conversant with.

bewe'gen*, *vb.* induce.

bewe'gen, *vb.* move.

Bewe'grund, ⸚e, *n.m.* motive.

beweg'lich, *adj.* movable, active.

Bewe'gung, -en, *n.f.* movement, motion, exercise.

bewe'gungslos, *adj.* motionless.

bewei'nen, *vb.* bewail, deplore.

Beweis', -e, *n.m.* proof, evidence.

bewei'sen*, *vb.* prove, demonstrate.

bewer'ben*, *vb.* **(sich b. um)** apply for.

Bewer'ber, -, *n.m.* applicant, contestant, suitor.

Bewer'bung, -en, *n.f.* application.

bewer'ten, *vb.* evaluate, grade.

bewil'ligen, *vb.* approve, appropriate.

Bewil'ligung, -en, *n.f.* approval, appropriation.

bewir'ken, *vb.* cause, effect.

bewir'ten, *vb.* be host to, entertain.

bewohn'bar, *adj.* habitable.

bewoh'nen, *vb.* inhabit.

Bewoh'ner, -, *n.m.* inhabitant, occupant.

bewölkt', *adj.* cloudy.

bewun'dern, *vb.* admire.

bewun'dernswert, *adj.* admirable.

Bewun'derung, *n.f.* admiration.

bewußt', *adj.* conscious, aware.

bewußt'los, *adj.* unconscious.

Bewußt'sein, *n.nt.* consciousness; **(bei B.)** conscious.

bezah'len, vb. pay.

Bezah'lung, -en, n.f. pay, payment.

bezau'bern, vb. bewitch, enchant.

bezeich'nen, vb. mark, designate, signify.

bezeich'nend, adj. characteristic.

Bezeich'nung, -en, n.f. designation.

bezeu'gen, vb. testify, attest.

bezie'hen*, vb. cover with, upholster, put on clean sheets; move into; draw (pay); **(sich b.)** cloud over; **(sich b. auf)** refer to.

Bezie'hung, -en, n.f. reference, relation; pull, drag.

Bezirk', -e, n.m. district.

Bezug', -e, n.m. cover(ing), case; supply; reference.

Bezug'nahme, n.f. reference.

bezwe'cken, vb. have as one's purpose, aim at.

bezwei'feln, vb. doubt.

Bibel, -n, n.f. Bible.

Biber, -, n.m. beaver.

Bibliothek', -en, n.f. library.

Bibliothekar', -e, n.m. librarian.

Bibliotheka'rin, -nen, n.f. librarian.

biblisch, adj. Biblical.

bieder, adj. upright, bourgeois.

biegen*, vb. bend; **(sich b.)** buckle.

biegsam, adj. flexible, pliable.

Biegung, -en, n.f. bend.

Biene, -n, n.f. bee.

Bier, -e, n.nt. beer.

Bierlokal, -e, n.nt. tavern, pub.

Biest, -er, n.nt. beast; brute.

bieten*, vb. bid, offer.

Bieter, -, n.m. bidder.

bifokal', adj. bifocal.

Bigamie', n.f. bigamy.

bigott', adj. bigoted.

Bild, -er, n.nt. picture, painting.

bilden, vb. form.

bildend, adj. educational, formative.

Bildhauer, -, n.m. sculptor.

bildhauern, vb. sculpture.

bildlich, adj. figurative.

Bildung, n.f. learning, education, refinement.

Billard, -e, n.nt. billiards.

Billett', -e, n.nt. ticket.

billig, adj. cheap; equitable.

billigen, vb. approve.

Billigkeit, -en, n.f. cheapness; justness.

Billion', -en, n.f. billion.

Binde, -n, n.f. bandage; **(Damenbinde)** sanitary napkin.

binden*, vb. tie; bind.

bindend, adj. binding.

Bindestrich, -e, n.m. hyphen.

Bindfaden, -, n.m. string.

Bindung, -en, n.f. tie, bond; (ski) binding; (fig.) obligation.

binnen, prep. within.

Binnenland, -er, n.nt. inland.

Biographie', -i'en, n.f. biography.

biogra'phisch, adj. biographical.

biolo'gisch, adj. biological.

Biologie', -i'en, n.f. biology.

Birke, -n, n.f. birch.

Birne, -n, n.f. pear.

bis, adv.&prep. till, until.

Bischof, -e, n.m. bishop.

bisher', adv. hitherto.

Biskuit', -e, n.nt. biscuit.

Bissen, -, n.m. bite, mouthful.

Bißchen, -, n.nt. bit; **(ein b.)** a bit, a little.

bitte, interj. please; you are welcome.

Bitte, -n, n.f. request, plea.

bitten*, vb. ask, request; beg.

bitter, adj. bitter.

bizarr', adj. bizarre, freak.

Bizeps, -e, n.m. biceps.

blähen, vb. bloat, puff up.

Blama'ge, -n, n.f. disgrace.

blamie'ren, vb. disgrace.

blank, adj. bright, shining; (without money) broke.

Blase, -n, *n.f.* bubble; bladder; blister.

Blasebalg, ̈-e, *n.m.* bellows.

blasen*, *vb.* blow.

blaß, *adj.* pale.

Blässe, *n.f.* paleness.

Blatt, ̈-er, *n.nt.* leaf.

Blattern, *n.pl.* smallpox.

blau, *adj.* blue.

Blaubeere, -n, *n.f.* blueberry.

Blech, *n.nt.* tin.

Blei, *n.nt.* lead.

bleiben*, *vb.* stay, remain.

bleich, *adj.* pale; (**b. werden**) blanch.

bleichen, *vb.* bleach.

bleiern, *adj.* leaden.

Bleistift, -e, *n.m.* pencil.

blenden, *vb.* blind, dazzle.

Blick, -e, *n.m.* look, glance.

blicken, *vb.* look, glance.

blind, *adj.* blind.

Blinddarm, ̈-e, *n.m.* appendix.

Blinddarmentzündung, -en, *n.f.* appendicitis.

Blindheit, -en, *n.f.* blindness.

blinken, *vb.* blink.

Blinklicht, -er, *n.nt.* blinker.

blinzeln, *vb.* blink; wink.

Blitz, -e, *n.m.* lightning.

blitzen, *vb.* flash, lighten.

blitzsauber, *adj.* immaculate.

Block, -s, *n.m.* bloc; block; (paper) pad.

Blocka/de, -n, *n.f.* blockade.

blockie/ren, *vb.* block; (account) freeze.

blöde, *adj.* stupid, dumb.

Blödsinn, *n.m.* idiocy, nonsense.

blödsinnig, *adj.* idiotic.

blond, *adj.* blond.

bloß, 1. *adj.* bare. **2.** *adv.* only, merely.

Blöße, -n, *n.f.* nakedness; (*fig.*) weak spot.

Bloßstellung, -en, *n.f* exposure.

Bluff, -s, *n.m.* bluff.

bluffen, *vb.* bluff.

blühen, *vb.* bloom; flourish.

blühend, *adj.* prosperous.

Blume, -n, *n.f.* flower.

Blumengeschäft, -e, *n.nt.* flower shop.

Blumenhändler, -, *n.m.* florist.

Blumenkol, -e, *n.m.* cauliflower.

Blumenstrauß, ̈-e, *n.m.* bouquet.

blumig, *adj.* flowery.

Bluse, -n, *n.f.* blouse.

Blut, *n.nt.* blood.

blutarm, *adj.* anemic; (*fig.*) penniless.

Blutarmut, *n.f* anemia.

Blutdruck, -e, *n.m.* blood pressure.

Blüte, -n, *n.f.* bloom, blossom; (*fig.*) prime.

bluten, *vb.* bleed.

blütenreich, *adj.* florid.

Bluterguß, -̈sse, *n.m.* hemorrhage.

Bluterkrankheit, *n.f.* hemophilia.

Bluthund, -e, *n.m.* bloodhound.

blutig, *adj.* bloody.

blutlos, *adj.* bloodless.

blutunterlaufen, *adj.* bloodshot.

Blutvergiftung, -en, *n.f.* blood poisoning.

Blutvergießen, *n.nt.* bloodshed.

Bock, ̈-e, *n.m.* buck.

bockig, *adj.* obstinate.

Bockwurst, ̈-e, *n.f.* sausage.

Boden, ̈-, *n.m.* ground, soil, bottom, floor; attic; (**Grund und B.**) real estate.

bodenlos, *adj.* bottomless.

Bodensatz, *n.m.* dregs.

Bö, -en, *n.f.* squall.

Bogen, ̈-, *n.m.* arch; bow; (paper) sheet.

Bogenschießen, *n.nt.* archery.

Bogenschütze, -n, -n, *n.m.* archer.

Böhme, -n, -n, *n.m.* Bohemian.

Böhmen, *n.nt.* Bohemia.

böhmisch, *adj.* Bohemian.

Bohne, -n, *n.f.* bean; (**grüne B.**) string bean.

bohren, *vb.* bore, drill.

Bohrer, -, *n.m.* drill.

Boli'vien, *n.nt.* Bolivia.

Bollwerk, -e, *n.nt.* bulwark.

bombardie'ren, *vb.* bombard.

Bombe, -n, *n.f.* bomb, bombshell.

bomben, *vb.* bomb.

Bombenflugzeug, -e, *n.nt.* bomber.

bombensicher, *adj.* bombproof.

Boot, -e, *n.nt.* boat.

Bord, -e, *n.nt.* shelf; board; **(an B.) aboard; (an B. gehen)** board.

Bordell', -e, *n.nt.* brothel.

Bordstein, -e, *n.m.* curb, curbstone.

borgen, *vb.* borrow.

borniert', *adj.* stupid.

Börse, -n, *n.f.* purse; stock exchange.

Borste, -n, *n.f.* bristle.

Borte, -n, *n.f.* trimming, braid.

bösartig, *adj.* malicious; (*med.*) malignant.

Böschung, -en, *n.f.* bank, embankment.

böse, *adj.* bad, evil; angry mad.

Bös-, *n.nt.* evil.

Bösewicht, -e, *n.m.* scoundrel.

boshaft, *adj.* malicious.

Bosheit, -en, *n.f.* malice.

böswillig, *adj.* malevolent.

bota'nisch, *adj.* botanical.

Bota'nik, *n.f.* botany.

Bote, -n, -n, *n.m.* messenger.

Botschaft, -en, *n.f.* message; embassy.

Botschafter, -, *n.m.* ambassador.

Bouillon', -s, *n.f.* consommé.

boxen, *vb.* box, spar.

Boxen, *n.nt.* boxing.

Boxkampf, -e, *n.m.* boxing match.

Boykott', -e, *n.m.* boycott.

boykottie'ren, *vb.* boycott.

Brand, -e, *n.m.* conflagration; blight.

branden, *vb.* surge.

brandmarken, *vb.* brand.

Brandstifter, -, *n.m.* arsonist.

Brandstiftung, -en, *n.f.* arson.

Brandung, -en, *n.f.* surf, breakers.

Branntwein, -e, *n.m.* brandy.

Brasi'lien, *n.nt.* Brazil.

braten*, *vb.* roast, fry.

Braten, -, *n.m.* roast.

Bratpfanne, -n, *n.f.* fryingpan, griddle.

Bratrost, -e, *n.m.* oven rack; broiler.

Bratsche, -n, *n.f.* viola.

Bräu, *n.nt.* brew.

Brauch, -e, *n.m.* custom, usage.

brauchbar, *adj.* useful.

brauchen, *vb.* need, require; use.

brauen, *vb.* brew.

Brauer, -, *n.m.* brewer.

Brauerei', -en, *n.f.* brewery.

braun, *adj.* brown.

bräunen, *vb.* brown; tan.

brausen, *vb.* roar.

Braut, -e, *n.f.* bride.

Brautführer, -, *n.m.* usher (at a wedding).

Bräutigam, -e, *n.m.* bridegroom.

Brautjungfer, -n, *n.f.* bridesmaid.

Bravour', *n.f.* bravado.

brav, *adj.* upright; (of children) good.

brechen*, *vb.* break; (*med.*) fracture.

Brechmittel, -, *n.nt.* emetic.

Brei, -e, *n.m.* pap; (*fig.*) pulp.

breit, *adj.* broad, wide.

Breite, -n, *n.f.* breadth, width; latitude.

Bremse, -n, *n.f.* brake; gadfly.

bremsen, *vb.* brake, put on the brake.

brennbar, *adj.* combustible.

brennen*, *vb.* burn, scorch.

brennend, *adj.* burning; fervid.

Brenner, -, *n.m.* burner.

Brennholz, *n.nt.* firewood.

Brennpunkt, -e, *n.m.* focus.

Brennstoff, -e, n.m. fuel.

brenzlich, adj. risky, precarious.

Brett, -er, n.nt. board, plank.

Bretterbude, -n, n.f. shack.

Brezel, -n, n.f. pretzel.

Briga'de, -n, n.f. brigade.

Brief, -e, n.m. letter.

Briefkasten, ⁎, n.m. mailbox.

Briefmarke, -n, n.f. stamp.

Briefpapier, n.nt. stationery.

Brieftasche, -n, n.f. wallet, billfold.

Briefträger, -, n.m. postman.

Briefumschlag, ⁎e, n.m. envelope.

Briefwechsel, n.m. correspondence.

Brille, -n, n.f. spectacles, glasses.

bringen*, vb. bring; take.

Brise, -n, n.f. breeze.

Britan'nien, n.nt. Britain.

Brite, -n, -n, n.m. Briton.

britisch, adj. British.

Brocken, -, n.m crumb.

Brombeere, -n, n.f. blackberry.

bronchial', adj. bronchial.

Bronchi'tis, n.f. bronchitis.

Bronze, -n, n.f. bronze.

Brosche, -n, n.f. brooch.

Broschü're, -n, n.f. pamphlet, booklet.

Brot, -e, n.nt. bread; (**beleg'tes B.**) sandwich.

Brötchen, -, n.nt. roll, bun.

Bruch, ⁎e, n.m. break, breach, fracture; hernia; (fig.) violation.

brüchig, adj. brittle.

Bruchrechnung, n.f. fractions.

Bruchstück, -e, n.nt. fragment.

Bruchteil, -e, n.m. fraction.

Brücke, -n, n.f. bridge.

Bruder, ⁎, n.m. brother.

brüderlich, adj brotherly, fraternal.

Brüderschaft, -en, n.f. fraternity.

Brühe, -n, n.f. broth.

brühen, vb. scald.

brüllen, vb. yell, bellow, howl.

brummen, vb. hum, buzz; grumble.

Brünet'te, -n, n.f. brunette.

Brunnen, -, n.m. well, fountain.

brünstig, adj. fervent.

brüsk, adj. brusque.

Brust, ⁎e, n.f. breast, chest.

brüsten vb. (**sich b.**) boast.

Brut, -en, n.f. brood.

brutal', adj. brutal.

Brutalität', -en, n.f. brutality.

brüten, vb. brood.

brutto, adj. gross.

Bube, -n, -n, n.m. boy; (cards) jack.

Buch, ⁎er, n.nt. book.

Buchbinder, -, n.m. bookbinder.

Buchbinderei', -ei'en, n.f. bookbindery.

Buche, -n, n.f. beech.

Bücherei', -en, n.f. library.

Bücherschrank, ⁎e, n.m. bookcase.

Buchführung, -en, n.f. accounting, bookkeeping.

Buchhalter, -, n.m. accountant, bookkeeper.

Buchhändler, -, n.m. bookseller.

Buchhandlung, -en, n.f. bookstore.

Büchse, -n, n.f. can.

Büchsenöffner, -, n.m. can-opener.

Buchstabe(n), -(or -n, -n), n.m. letter (of the alphabet).

buchstabie'ren, vb. spell; (**falsch b.**) misspell.

buchstäblich, adj. literal.

Bucht, -en, n.f. bay.

Buchweizen, n.m. buckwheat.

Buckel, -, n.m. hump, protuberance; hunchback.

buckelig, adj. hunchbacked.

bücken, vb. (**sich b.**) bend down, stoop.

Bude, -n, n.f. booth, stall, stand.

Büfett', -s, n.nt. buffet.

Büffel, -, n.m. buffalo.

Bug, -e, n.m. bow.

Bügeleisen, -, *n.nt.* flatiron.
bügeln, *vb.* iron, press.
Bühne, -n, *n.f.* stage.
Bühnenausstattung, -en, *n.f.* scenery.
Bulldogge, -n, *n.f.* bulldog.
Bulle, -n, -n, *n.m.* bull.
Bummel, -, *n.m.* spree.
bummeln, *vb.* gallivant.
Bund, -e, *n.m.* league, federation.
Bund, -e, *n.m.* bunch, bundle.
Bündel, -, *n.nt.* bundle.
Bundes-, *cpds.* federal.
Bundesbahn, *n.f.* West German Federal Railway.
Bundeskanzler, *n.m.* chancellor of Western Germany.
Bundesrat, *n.m.* upper house of West German parliament.
bundesstaatlich, *adj.* federal.
Bundestag, *n.m.* lower house of West German parliament.
Bündnis, -se, *n.nt.* alliance.
bunt, *adj.* colorful; varicolored, motley.
Bürde, -n, *n.f.* burden.
Bürge, -n, -n, *n.m.* sponsor, guarantor.
Bürger, -, *n.m.* citizen.
bürgerlich, *adj.* civil; bourgeois.
Bürgermeister, -, *n.m.* mayor.
Bürgerschaft, *n.f.* citizenry.
Bürgersteig, -e, *n.m.* sidewalk.
Burgfriede(n), -n, *n.m.* truce.
Bürgschaft, -en, *n.f.* guaranty, bond, bail.
Burgun'der, -, *n.m.* burgundy (wine).
Büro', -s, *n.nt.* office, bureau.
Bursche, -n, -n, *n.m.* chap, fellow.
Bürste, -n, *n.f.* brush.
bürsten, *vb.* brush.
Bus, -se, *n.m.* bus.
Busch, -e, *n.m.* bush, shrub.
Büschel, -, *n.nt.* bunch.
buschig, *adj.* bushy.
Busen, -, *n.m.* bosom.
Buße, -n, *n.f.* atonement, penitence; fine, penalty.

büßen, *vb.* do penance, atone for.
Büste, -n, *n.f.* bust.
Büstenhalter, -, *n.m.* brassiere.
Butter, *n.f.* butter.
Butterblume, -n, *n.f.* buttercup.
Butterbrot, -e, *n.nt.* slice of bread and butter.
Buttermilch, *n.f.* buttermilk.
buttern, *vb.* churn.

C

Café', -s, *n.nt.* café.
Cellist', -en, -en, *n.m.* cellist.
Cello, -s, *n.nt.* cello.
Charme, *n.m.* charm.
Chance, -n, *n.f.* opportunity, odds.
chao'tisch, *adj.* chaotic.
Charak'ter, -e're, *n.m.* character.
charakterisie'ren, *vb.* characterize.
charakteris'tisch, *adj.* characteristic.
Chauffeur', -e, *n.m.* chauffeur.
Chaussee', -e'en, *n.f.* highway.
Chef, -s, *n.m.* chef; boss.
Chemie', *n.f.* chemistry.
Chemika'lien, *n.pl.* chemicals.
Chemiker, -, *n.m.* chemist.
chemisch, *adj.* chemical.
Chiffre, -n, *n.f.* cipher.
China, *n.nt.* China.
Chine'se, -n, -n, *n.m.* Chinese.
chine'sisch, *adj.* Chinese.
Chinin', *n.nt.* quinine.
Chiroprak'tiker, -, *n.m.* chiropractor.
Chirurg', -en, -en, *n.f.* surgeon.
Chirurgie', *n.f.* surgery.
Chlor, -s, *n.nt.* chlorine.

Chloroform', *n.nt.* chloroform.

Clown, -s, *n.m.* clown.

Cholera, *n.f.* cholera.

chole'risch, *adj.* choleric.

Chor, -s, *n.m.* choir; chorus.

Chorgang, ⁓e, *n.m.* aisle.

Chorsänger, -, *n.m.* chorister.

Crème, -s, *n.f.* cream.

Christ, -en, -en, *n.m.* Christian.

Christenheit, *n.f.* Christendom.

Christentum, *n.nt.* Christianity.

christlich, *adj.* Christian.

Christus, *n.m.* Christ.

Chrom, *n.nt.* chrome, chromium.

Chronik, -en, *n.f.* chronicle.

chronisch, *adj.* chronic.

Chronologie', -i'en, *n.f.* chronology.

chronolo'gisch, *adj.* chronological.

Chrysanthe'me, -n, *n.f.* chrysanthemum.

Cocktail, -s, *n.m.* cocktail.

College, -s, *n.nt.* college.

Couch, -es, *n.f.* couch.

Coupon', -s, *n.m.* coupon.

Cousin', -s, *n.m.* (male) cousin.

Cousi'ne, -n, *n.f.* (female) cousin.

Cowboy, -s, *n.m.* cowboy.

D

da, 1. *conj.* because, since, as. 2. *adv.* there; here; then.

dabei', *adv.* near it; present; in so doing, at the same time.

Dach, ⁓er, *n.nt.* roof.

Dachrinne, -n, *n.f.* eaves.

Dachstube, -n, *n.f.* garret.

Dachtraufe, -n, *n.f.* gutter.

dadurch, *adv.* thereby.

dage'gen, *adv.* against it; on the other hand.

daher, *adv.* therefore, hence.

dahin, *adv.* (to) there.

dafür, *adv.* for that; instead.

dahin'ter, *adv.* behind it.

damals, *adv.* then, at that time.

Dame, -n, *n.f.* lady.

Damebrett, -er, *n.nt.* checkerboard.

Damenhut, ⁓e, *n.m.* lady's hat.

Damenunterwäsche, *n.f.* lingerie.

Damespiel, -e, *n.nt.* checkers.

damit', 1. *conj.* in order that. 2. *adv.* with it, with them, at that.

Damm, ⁓e, *n.m.* dam, causeway, levee.

dämmern, *vb.* dawn.

Dämmerung, -en, *n.f.* twilight.

Dämon, -o'nen, *n.m.* demon.

Dampf, ⁓e, *n.m.* steam, vapor fume.

Dampfboot, -e, *n.nt.* steamboat.

dampfen, *vb.* steam.

dämpfen, *vb.* muffle; (cooking) steam.

Dampfer, -, *n.m.* steamship.

Däne, -n, -n, *n.m.* Dane.

Dänemark, *n.nt.* Denmark.

dänisch, *adj.* Danish.

dank, *prep.* owing to.

Dank, *n.m.* thanks.

dankbar, *adj.* thankful, grateful.

Dankbarkeit, -en, *n.f.* gratitude.

danken, *vb.* thank.

dann, *adv.* then, after that.

darauf, *adv.* on it, on them; after that, thereupon.

dar·bieten*, *vb.* present.

Darbietung, -en, *n.f.* presentation; entertainment.

dar·legen, *vb.* state.

Darlegung, -en, *n.f.* exposé, exposition.

Darlehen, -, *n.nt.* loan.

Darm, ⁓e, *n.m.* intestine.

dar·stellen, *vb.* represent, constitute; present; portray.

Darstellung, -en, *n.f.* presentation; representation,

depiction; **(graphische D.)** diagram.

Dasein, *n.nt.* existence.

daß, *conj.* that.

datie'ren, *vb.* date.

Dattel, -n, *n.f.* date.

Datum, -ten, *n.nt.* date.

Dauer, *n.f.* duration, length.

dauerhaft, *adj.* durable, lasting.

Dauerhaftigkeit, *n.f.* durability.

dauern, *vb.* last, continue; take (a while).

dauernd, *adj.* lasting, continual.

Dauerwelle, -n, *n.f.* permanent wave.

Daumen, -, *n.m.* thumb

Daune, -n, *n.f.* down.

dazu', *adv.* in addition.

dazwi'schen·kommen*, *vb.* intervene.

dazwi'schen·treten*, *vb.* intercede.

Dazwi'schentreten, *n.nt.* intervention.

Deba'kel, -, *n.nt.* debacle.

Debat'te, -n, *n.f.* debate.

debattie'ren, *vb.* debate.

Debet, -s, *n.nt.* debit.

Debüt', -s, *n.nt.* debut.

Debütan'tin, -nen, *n.f.* debutante.

Deck, -s, *n.nt.* deck.

Decke, -n, *n.f.* cover; blanket; ceiling.

Deckel, -n, *n.m.* lid.

decken, *vb.* cover; **(sich d.)** coincide, jibe.

Deckung, -en, *n.f.* cover(ing); collateral.

Defekt', -e, *n.m.* defect.

defekt', *adj.* defective.

Defensi've, -n, *n.f.* defensive.

Definition', -en, *n.f.* definition.

definitiv', *adj.* definite; definitive.

Defizit, -e, *n.nt.* deficit.

Deflation', -en, *n.f.* deflation.

Degen, -, *n.m.* sword; epée.

Degeneration', *n.f.* degeneration.

degeneriert', *adj.* degenerate.

degradie'ren, *vb.* demote.

dehnen, *vb.* stretch, expand; drawl.

Dehnung, -en, *n.f.* stretch(ing), expansion.

Deich, -e, *n.m.* dike.

Dekan', -e, *n.m.* dean.

Deklamation', -en, *n.f.* declamation.

deklamie'ren, *vb.* declaim.

deklarie'ren, *vb.* declare.

Deklination', -en, *n.f.* declension.

deklinie'ren, *vb.* decline.

Dekorateur', -e, *n.m.* decorator.

dekorativ', *adj.* decorative, ornamental.

dekorie'ren, *vb.* decorate.

Dekret', -e, *n.nt.* decree.

Delegation', -en, *n.f.* delegation.

delegie'ren, *vb.* delegate.

Delegiert', -, *n.m.&f.* delegate.

delikat', *adj.* delicate, dainty.

Delikates'se, -n, *n.f.* delicacy.

Deli'rium, -rien, *n.nt.* delirium.

Demago'ge, -n, -n, *n.m.* demagogue.

demgemäß, *adv.* accordingly.

demnächst', *adv.* shortly, soon.

demobilisie'ren, *vb.* demobilize.

Demobilisie'rung, -en, *n.f.* demobilization.

Demokrat', -en, -en, *n.m.* democrat.

Demokratie', -n, *n.f.* democracy.

demokra'tisch, *adj.* democratic.

demolie'ren, *vb.* wreck.

demoralisie'ren, *vb.* demoralize.

demonstrativ', *adj.* demonstrative.

demonstrie'ren, *vb.* demonstrate.

Demut, *n.f.* humility.

demütig, *adj.* humble.

demütigen, *vb.* humiliate.

Demütigung, -en, *n.f.* humiliation.

demzufolge, *adv.* accordingly; consequently.

denkbar, *adj.* imaginable.

denken*, *vb.* think, reason.

Denker, -, *n.m.* thinker.

Denkmal, ¨er, *n.nt.* monument, memorial.

Denkungsart, *n.f.* mode of thinking, mentality.

denkwürdig, *adj.* memorable.

denn, 1. *conj.* for. **2.** *adv.* do tell me; I wonder.

dennoch, *adv.* still, yet, nevertheless.

denunzie'ren, *vb.* denounce, inform.

Deportation', -en, *n.f.* deportation.

deportie'ren, *vb.* deport.

Depot', -s, *n.nt.* depot.

Depression', -en, *n.f.* depression.

deprimie'ren, *vb.* depress.

der, das, die, 1. *art.&adj.* the, that. **2.** *pron.* he, she, it, they; that one. **3.** *rel. pron.* who, which, that.

derart, 1. *adj.* such, of such a kind. **2.** *adv.* in such a way.

derb, *adj.* coarse; stout; earthy.

dermaßen, *adv.* to such a degree, in such a manner.

Deserteur', -e, *n.m.* deserter.

Desertion', -en, *n.f.* desertion.

deshalb, *adv.* therefore, hence.

desinfizie'ren, *vb.* disinfect.

desodorisie'ren, *vb.* deodorize.

Despot', -en, -en, *n.m.* despot.

despo'tisch, *adj.* despotic.

Destillation', -en, *n.f.* distillation.

destillie'ren, *vb.* distill.

desto, *adv.* **(d. besser)** so much the better; **(je mehr, d. besser)** the more the better.

deswegen, *adv.* therefore, that's why.

Detail', -s, *n.nt.* detail.

Detektiv', -e, *n.m.* detective.

deuten, *vb.* interpret; point.

deutlich, *adj.* clear, distinct.

deutsch, *adj.* German.

Deutsch-, *n.m.&f.* German.

Deutschland, *n.nt.* Germany.

Deutung, -en, *n.f.* interpretation.

Dezem'ber, -, *n.m.* December.

dezentralisie'ren, *vb.* decentralize.

Dezimal'-, *cpds.* decimal.

dezimie'ren, *vb.* decimate.

Diagno'se, -n, *n.f.* diagnosis.

diagnostizie'ren, *vb.* diagnose.

diagonal', *adj.* diagonal.

Diagramm', -e, *n.nt.* graph.

Dialekt', -e, *n.m.* dialect.

Dialog', -e, *n.m.* dialogue.

Diamant', -en, *n.m.* diamond.

diametral', *adj.* diametrical.

Diät', -en, *n.f.* diet.

diät'gemäß, *adj.* dietary.

dicht, *adj.* dense, thick; tight.

Dichte, -n, *n.f.* density.

Dichter, -, *n.m.* poet.

dichterisch, *adj.* poetic.

Dichtheit, *n.f.* thickness.

Dichtung, -en, *n.f.* poetry; (*tech.*) packing, gasket.

dick, *adj.* thick, fat, stout.

Dicke, *n.f.* thickness.

dicken, *vb.* thicken.

Dickicht, *n.nt.* thicket, brush.

dicklich, *adj.* chubby.

Dieb, -e, *n.m.* thief, robber.

Diebstahl, ¨e, *n.m.* theft, larceny.

Diele, -n, *n.f.* hall, hallway.

dienen, *vb.* serve.

Diener, -, *n.m.* valet, butler.

Dienerschaft, -en, *n.f.* servant.

Dienst, -e, *n.m.* service.

Dienstag, -e, *n.m.* Tuesday.

dienstbeflissen, *adj.* assiduous; officious.

Dienstmädchen, -, *nt.* maid.

Dienstpflicht, *n.f.* compulsory military service, draft.

Dienstvorschrift, -en, *n.f.* regulation.

Dieselmotor, -en, *n.m.* diesel engine.

dieser, -es, -e, *pron.& adj.* this.

differential', *adj.* differential.

differenzie'ren, *vb.* differentiate.

Diktat', -e, *n.nt.* dictation.

Dikta'tor, -o'ren, *n.m.* dictator.

diktato'risch, *adj.* dictatorial.

Diktatur', -en, *n.f.* dictatorship.

diktie'ren, *vb.* dictate.

Dilem'ma, -s, *n.nt.* dilemma, predicament.

Dill, *n.m.* dill.

Dilettant', -en, -en, *n.m.* dilettante.

Ding, -e, *n.nt.* thing.

dingen*, *vb.* hire.

Diphtherie', *n.f.* diphtheria.

Diplom', -e, *n.nt.* diploma.

Diplomat', -en, -en, *n.m.* diplomat.

Diplomatie', *n.f.* diplomacy.

diploma'tisch, *adj.* diplomatic.

direkt', *adj.* direct; downright.

Direkti've, -n, *n.f.* directive.

Direk'tor, -o'ren, *n.m.* director.

Direkto'rium, -ien, *n.nt.* directorate, directory.

Dirigent', -en, -en, *n.m.* conductor.

dirigie'ren, *vb.* conduct.

Diskont', -e, *n.m.* discount.

Diskont'satz, -e, *n.m.* interest rate.

diskret', *adj.* discreet.

Diskretion', *n.f.* discretion.

diskriminie'ren, *vb.* discriminate.

Diskriminie'rung, -en, *n.f.* discrimination.

Diskussion', -en, *n.f.* discussion.

diskutie'ren, *vb.* discuss.

disqualifizie'ren, *vb.* disqualify.

Dissertation', -en, *n.f.* dissertation.

Diszi'plin', *n.f.* discipline.

disziplinie'ren, *vb.* discipline.

Di'va, -s, *n.f.* diva.

divers', *adj.* miscellaneous.

Division', -en, *n.f.* division.

D-Mark, -, *n.f.* (= deutsche Mark) mark, West German mark.

doch, 1. *conj.* yet. **2.** *adv.* yet; indeed; oh yes.

Docht, -e, *n.m.* wick.

Dock, -s, *n.nt.* dock.

docken, *vb.* dock.

Dogma, -men, *n.nt.* dogma.

dogma'tisch, *adj.* dogmatic.

Doktor, -o'ren, *n.m.* doctor.

Doktorat', -e, *n.nt.* doctorate.

doktrinär', *adj.* doctrinaire.

Dokument', -e, *n.nt.* document.

dokumenta'risch, *adj.* documentary.

dokumentie'ren, *vb.* document, authenticate.

Dolch, -e, *n.m.* dagger.

Dollar, -s, *n.m.* dollar.

dolmetschen, *vb.* interpret.

Dolmetscher, -, *n.m.* interpreter.

Dom, -e, *n.m.* cathedral, dome.

Domi'nion, -s, *n.nt.* dominion.

Donau, *n.f.* Danube.

Donner, -, *n.m.* thunder.

donnern, *vb.* thunder.

Donnerstag, -e, *n.m.* Thursday.

Donnerwetter, *n.nt.* (zum D.) confound it!; (what) in thunder.

Doppel-, *cpds.* double, dual.

Doppelgänger, -, *n.m.* double.

doppelkohlensaur, *adj.* (d. es Natron) bicarbonate of soda.

Doppelpunkt, -e, *n.m.* colon.

doppelt, *adj.* double.

Dorf, ⁀er, *n.nt.* village.

Dorn, -en, *n.m.* thorn.

dörren, *vb.* dry, parch.

dort, *adv.* there.

Dose, -n, *n.f.* (small) box, can.

dösen, *vb.* doze.

Dosie'rung, -en, *n.f.* dosage.

Dosis, -sen, *n.f.* dose.

Drache, -n, -n, *n.m.* dragon.

Draht, ⁻e, *n.m.* wire.

Drahtaufnahmegerät, -e, *n.nt.* wire recorder.

drahtlos, *adj.* wireless.

drall, *adj.* buxom.

Drama, -men, *n.nt.* drama.

Drama'tiker, -, *n.m.* dramatist.

drama'tisch, *adj.* dramatic.

dramatisie'ren, *vb.* dramatize.

Drang, ⁻e, *n.m.* urge.

drängeln, *vb.* crowd.

drängen, *vb.* urge, press.

Drangsal, -e, *n.f.* distress.

drapie'ren, *vb.* drape.

drastisch, *adj.* drastic.

draußen, *adv.* outside.

Dreck, *n.m.* dirt, mud.

dreckig, *adj.* filthy.

drehen, *vb.* turn; make (a movie).

Drehpunkt, -e, *n.m.* pivot, fulcrum.

Drehung, -en, *n.f.* turning.

drei, *num.* three.

Dreieck, -e, *n.nt.* triangle.

dreifach, *adj.* triple.

dreifältig, *adj.* threefold.

dreimal, *adv.* thrice, three times.

dreißig, *num.* thirty.

dreißigst-, *adj.* thirtieth.

Dreißigstel, -, *n.nt.* thirtieth; **(ein d.)** one-thirtieth.

dreist, *adj.* bold; fresh; nervy.

dreizehn, *num.* thirteen.

dreschen*, *vb.* thresh, thrash.

Drill, *n.m.* drill.

Drillbohrer, -, *n.m.* drill.

dringen*, *vb.* force one's way, penetrate; insist.

dringend, *adj.* urgent.

dringlich, *adj.* pressing.

Dringlichkeit, *n.f.* urgency.

drinnen, *adv.* inside.

dritt-, *adj.* third.

Drittel, -, *n.nt.* third; **(ein d.)** one-third.

drittens, *adv.* in the third place, thirdly.

drittletzt, *adj.* third from last.

Droge, -n, *n.f.* drug

Drogerie', -i'en, *n.f.* drug store.

Drogist, -en, *n.m.* druggist.

drohen, *vb.* threaten.

dröhnen, *vb.* sound, boom, roar.

Drohung, -en, *n.f.* threat.

drollig, *adj.* droll, funny.

Droschke, -n, *n.f.* hack, cab.

Drossel, -n, *n.f.* thrush.

drosseln, *vb.* throttle, cut down.

drüben, *adv.* over there.

Druck, -e, *n.m.* print(ing), impression.

Druck, ⁻e, *n.m.* pressure.

drucken, *vb.* print.

Drucken, *n.nt.* printing.

drücken, *vb.* press, squeeze; oppress; **(sich d.)** get out of work, shirk.

drückend, *adj.* pressing, oppressive.

Druckerpresse, -n, *n.f.* printing-press.

drunter, *adv.* underneath.

Drüse, -n, *n.f.* gland.

Dschungel, -, *n.m.* or *nt.* (-n *f.*), jungle.

du, *pron.* you (familiar); thou.

ducken, *vb.* **(sich d.)** duck.

Duell', -e, *n.nt.* duel.

Duett', -e, *n.nt.* duet.

Duft, ⁻e, *n.m.* fragrance.

duftig, *adj.* fragrant.

dulden, *vb.* tolerate.

duldsam, *adj.* tolerant.

Duldsamkeit, *n.f.* tolerance.

dumm*, *adj.* stupid, dumb.

Dummheit, -en, *n.f.* stupidity.

Dummkopf, ⁻e, *n.m.* dullard, idiot.

dumpf, *adj.* dull, musty.

Düne, -n, *n.f.* dune.

Dung, *n.m.* dung.

düngen, *vb.* fertilize.

Dünger, *n.m.* fertilizer, manure.

dunkel, *adj.* dark; obscure.

Dunkel, *n.nt.* dark(ness).

Dünkel, *n.m.* pretension.

dünken*, *vb.* seem; **(mich dünkt)** methinks.

dünn, *adj.* thin.

Dunst, -e, *n.m.* haze, vapor.

dunsten, *vb.* steam, fume.

dünsten, *vb.* steam, stew.

dunstig, *adj.* hazy.

Duplikat', -e, *n.nt.* duplicate.

Dur, *n.nt.* major; **(A-Dur)** A-major.

durch, *prep.* through; by means of.

durchaus', *adv.* entirely, by all means.

durchblät'tern, *vb.* leaf through.

Durchblick, -e, *n.m.* view (through something).

durch·blicken, *vb.* look through; be visible.

durchbli'cken, *vb.* see through, discern.

durchboh'ren, *vb.* pierce.

Durchbruch, -e, *n.m.* break-through.

durchdacht', *adj.* thought out.

durch·drehen, *vb.* panic.

durch·dringen*, *vb.* force one's way through, penetrate.

durchdrin'gen*, *vb.* permeate, impregnate.

durcheinan'der, *adv.* through one another; all mixed up.

Durcheinan'der, *n.nt.* confusion, turmoil, mess.

Durchfahrt, -en, *n.f.* passage, transit.

Durchfall, *n.m.* diarrhea.

durch·fallen*, *vb.* fail (a test).

durchführbar, *adj.* practicable.

durch·führen, *vb.* carry out.

Durchgang, -e, *n.m.* passage through; passageway; **(D. gesperrt!)** closed to traffic.

durch·gehen*, *vb.* go through; bolt, run away.

durchgehend, *adj.* nonstop.

durch·helfen*, *vb.* help

through; **(sich d.)** get along somehow.

durch·kreuzen, *vb.* cross out.

durchkreu'zen, *vb.* cross, intersect; thwart.

durch·leuchten, *vb.* shine through.

durchleuch'ten, *vb.* illuminate, irradiate, X-ray.

durchlö'chern, *vb.* perforate, puncture.

Durchlö'cherung, -en, *n.f.* perforation.

Durchmesser, -, *n.m.* diameter.

durchnäs'sen, *vb.* drench, soak.

Durchreise, -n, *n.f.* journey through; **(auf der D.)** passing through.

durch·schauen, *vb.* look through.

durchschau'en, *vb.* see through, understand.

durch·schneiden*, *vb.* cut in two.

durchschnei'den*, *vb.* cut, bisect, intersect.

Durchschnitt, -e, *n.m.* average.

durchschnittlich, *adj.* average.

durch·sehen*, *vb.* see through.

durchse'hen*, *vb.* look over, scrutinize; revise.

durch·setzen, *vb.* put through, get accepted.

durchset'zen, *vb.* intersperse, permeate.

Durchsicht, *n.f.* view; perusal.

durchsichtig, *adj.* transparent.

durch·sickern, *vb.* leak through, seep through.

durch·stechen*, *vb.* stick through.

durchste'chen*, *vb.* puncture, pierce.

durchsu'chen, *vb.* search.

Durchsu'chung, -en, *n.f.* search.

durchwüh'len, *vb.* ransack.

dürfen*, *vb.* be permitted, may.

dürftig, *adj.* meager.

dürr, *adj.* dry, barren.

Dürre, -n, *n.f.* drought, barrenness.

Durst, *n.m.* thirst.

dürsten, *vb.* thirst.

durstig, *adj.* thirsty.

Dusche, -n, *n.f.* shower.

Düse, -n, *n.f.* nozzle, jet.

Dusel, *n.m.* good luck.

duselig, *adj.* dizzy; stupid.

Düsenflugzeug, -e, *n.nt.* jet plane.

Düsenkampfflugzeug, *n.nt.* jet fighter plane.

düster, *adj.* gloomy.

Düsterheit, *n.f.* gloom.

Dutzend, -e, *n.nt.* dozen.

duzen, *vb.* call a person *du.*

Dyna'mik, *n.f.* dynamics.

dyna'misch, *adj.* dynamic.

Dynamit', *n.nt.* dynamite.

Dyna'mo, -s, *n.m.* dynamo.

Dynastie', -i'en, *n.f.* dynasty.

D-Zug, ⸚e, *n.m.* (= Durchgangszug) train with corridors in the cars; express train.

E

Ebbe, *n.f.* low tide.

ebben, *vb.* ebb.

eben, *adj.* even, level.

eben, *adv.* just; exactly.

Ebene, -n, *n.f.* plain, level ground; plane.

ebenfalls, *adv.* likewise.

ebenso, *adv.* likewise; (e. groß) just as big.

ebnen, *vb.* level, make smooth.

echt, *adj.* genuine.

Echtheit, -en, *n.f.* authenticity, genuineness.

Echo, -s, *n.nt.* echo.

Ecke, -n, *n.f.* corner.

eckig, *adj.* angular.

edel, *adj.* noble.

Edelstein, -e, *n.m.* jewel.

Efeu, *n.m.* ivy.

egal', *adj.* equal; **(es ist mir e.)** I don't care, it makes no difference to me.

Egois'mus, *n.m.* egoism.

Egoist', -en, -en, *n.m.* egotist.

Egotis'mus, *n.m.* egotism.

ehe, *conj.* before.

Ehe, -n, *n.f.* marriage, matrimony.

Ehebrecher, -, *n.m.* adulterer.

Ehebrecherin, -nen, *n.f.* adulteress.

Ehebruch, ⸚e, *n.m.* adultery.

ehedem, *adv.* formerly.

Ehefrau, -en, *n.f.* wife.

Ehegatte, -n, -n, *n.m.* spouse; husband.

Ehegattin, -nen, *n.f.* wife.

Eheleute, *n.pl.* married people.

ehelich, *adj.* marital; legitimate.

ehelos, *adj.* celibate.

Ehelosigkeit, *n.f.* celibacy.

ehemalig, *adj.* former.

ehemals, *adv.* formerly.

Ehemann, ⸚er, *n.m.* husband.

Ehepaar, -e, *n.nt.* married couple.

eher, *adv.* sooner, earlier; rather.

ehern, *adj.* brazen, brass.

Ehescheidung, -en, *n.f.* divorce.

Ehestand, *n.m.* matrimony.

ehrbar, *adj.* honorable.

Ehre, -n, *n.f.* honor.

ehren, *vb.* honor.

ehrenamtlich, *adj.* honorary, unpaid.

Ehrengast, ⸚e, *n.m.* guest of honor.

Ehrenplatz, ⸚e, *n.m.* place of honor.

ehrenvoll, *adj.* honorable.

ehrenwert, *adj.* worthy.

ehrerbietig, *adj.* respectful.

Ehrerbietung, -en, *n.f.* reverence, obeisance.

Ehrfurcht, *n.f.* awe, respect, reverence.

Ehrgeiz, *n.m.* ambition.

ehrgeizig, *adj.* ambitious.

ehrlich, *adj.* honest, sincere.

Ehrlichkeit, -en, n.f. honesty.

ehrlos, adj. dishonorable.

Ehrlosigkeit, n.f. dishonor.

ehrsam, adj. honest, respectable.

Ehrsamkeit, n.f. respectability.

Ehrung, -en, n.f. tribute.

ehrwürdig, adj. reverend, venerable.

Ei, -er, n.nt. egg.

Eiche, -n, n.f. oak.

Eichhörnchen, -, n.nt. squirrel.

Eid, -e, n.m. oath.

Eidam, -e, n.m. son-in-law.

eidesstattlich, adj. under oath; **(e.e Erklä'rung)** affidavit.

Eidgenosse, -n, -n, n.m. confederate.

Eidgenossenschaft, -en, n.f. confederation; **(Schweizerische E.)** Swiss Confederation.

eidgenössisch, adj. federal; Swiss.

Eifer, n.m. zeal, eagerness.

Eifersucht, n.f. jealousy.

eifersüchtig, adj. jealous.

eifrig, adj. zealous, eager, ardent.

Eigelb, n.nt. yolk.

eigen, adj. own; typical of.

Eigenart, -en, n.f. peculiarity, inherent nature.

eigenartig, adj. peculiar.

Eigenheit, -en, n.f. peculiarity.

eigenmächtig, adj. arbitrary.

Eigenname(n), -, n.m. proper name.

Eigennutz, n.m. selfishness.

eigennützig, adj. selfish.

Eigenschaft, -en, n.f. quality.

Eigenschaftswort, "er, n.nt. adjective.

Eigensinn, n.m. obstinacy, willfulness.

eigensinnig, adj. obstinate, willful.

eigentlich, 1. adj. actual. **2.** adv. as a matter of fact.

Eigentum, n.nt. property.

Eigentümer, -, n.m. owner.

eignen, vb. **(sich e.)** be suited.

Eilbote, -n, -n, n.m. special delivery messenger; **(per E.n)** by special delivery.

Eilbrief, -e, n.m. special delivery letter.

Eile, n.f. haste, hurry.

eilen, vb. hurry.

eilig, adj. hasty, urgent.

Eilpost, n.f. special delivery.

Eimer, -, n.m. pail.

ein, -, -e, art.&adj. a, an; (stressed) one.

einan'der, pron. one another, each other.

ein-äschern, vb. cremate.

Einäscherung, -en, n.f. cremation.

ein-atmen, vb. inhale.

Einbahn-, cpds. one-way.

ein-behalten*, vb. binding.

ein-bauen, vb. install.

ein-behalten*, vb. withhold.

ein-berufen*, vb. summon, convoke.

ein-bilden, vb. **(sich e.)** imagine.

Einbildung, -en, n.f. imagination; conceit.

ein-binden*, vb. bind.

Einblick, -e, n.m. insight.

Einbrecher, -, n.m. burglar.

ein-bringen*, vb. yield.

Einbruch, "e, n.m. burglary.

Einbuchtung, -en, n.f. dent; bay.

ein-bürgern, vb. naturalize.

Einbuße, n.f. forfeiture.

ein-büßen, vb. forfeit.

ein-dämmen, vb. dam.

eindeutig, adj. clear, unequivocal.

ein-drängen, vb. **(sich e.)** encroach upon.

ein-dringen*, vb. penetrate, intrude, invade.

Eindringling, -e, n.m. intruder.

Eindruck, "e, n.m. impression.

eindrucksvoll, adj. impressive.

ein-engen, vb. hem in.

einer, -es, -e, pron. one, a person; one thing.

einerlei', *adj.* of one kind; **(es ist mir e.)** it's all the same to me.

einerseits, *adv.* on the one hand.

einfach, *adj.* simple, plain.

Einfachheit, *n.f.* simplicity.

Einfahrt, -en, *n.f.* gateway, entrance.

Einfall, -e, *n.m.* collapse; bright idea.

ein·fallen*, *vb.* fall in; invade; occur to.

einfältig, *adj.* simple.

ein·fassen, *vb.* edge, trim.

ein·finden*, *vb.* **(sich e.)** present oneself, show up.

ein·flößen, *vb.* instill with.

Einfluß, -sse, *n.m.* influence.

einflußreich, *adj.* influential.

ein·fordern, *vb.* demand, reclaim.

einförmig, *adj.* uniform.

ein·fügen, *vb.* insert; **(sich e.)** adapt oneself.

Einfuhr, *n.f.* import, importation.

ein·führen, *vb.* import, induct.

Einführung, -en, *n.f.* induction; introduction.

Eingabe, -n, *n.f.* petition.

Eingang, -e, *n.m.* entrance.

ein·geben*, *vb.* give; inspire.

eingebildet, *adj.* conceited.

eingeboren, *adj.* native, indigenous.

Eingeborenn-, *n.m.&f.* native.

Eingebung, -en, *n.f.* inspiration.

eingedenk, *adj.* mindful.

eingefleischt, *adj.* inveterate.

ein·gehen*, *vb.* enter; shrink; cease, perish.

eingehend, *adj.* detailed, thorough.

Eingemacht-, *n.nt.* preserves.

eingenommen, *adj.* partial, prejudiced.

Eingesessen-, *n.m.&f.* inhabitant.

Eingeständnis, -se, *n.nt.* confession, admission.

ein·gestehen*, *vb.* confess, admit.

Eingeweide, *n.pl.* intestines.

ein·gewöhnen, *vb.* acclimate.

ein·graben*, *vb.* bury.

ein·greifen*, *vb.* interfere.

Eingriff, -e, *n.m.* intervention.

ein·halten*, *vb.* check, stop; observe, keep.

ein·händigen, *vb.* hand in.

einheimisch, *adj.* native.

Einheimisch-, *n.m.&f.* native.

Einheit, -en, *n.f.* unit.

einheitlich, *adj.* uniform.

einher', *adv.* along.

ein·holen, *vb.* gather; overtake.

ein·hüllen, *vb.* wrap up, enfold.

einig, *adj.* united, agreed.

einige, *pron.&adj.* some, several.

einigen, *vb.* unite; **(sich e.)** agree.

einigermaßen, *adv.* to some extent.

Einigkeit, *n.f.* unity.

ein·impfen, *vb.* inoculate.

ein·kassieren, *vb.* collect.

Einkauf, -e, *n.m.* purchase.

ein·kaufen, *vb.* purchase.

ein·kehren, *vb.* put up (at an inn).

ein·kerkern, *vb.* incarcerate.

ein·klammern, *vb.* bracket; put in parentheses.

Einklang, -e, *n.m.* harmony.

ein·kleiden, *vb.* clothe.

ein·klemmen, *vb.* wedge in.

Einkommen, -, *n.nt.* income.

Einkommensteuer, -n, *n.f.* income tax.

ein·kreisen, *vb.* encircle.

Einkünfte, *n.pl.* revenue.

ein·laden*, *vb.* invite.

Einladung, -en, *n.f.* invitation.

Einlage, -n, *n.f.* inclosure, filling; deposit.

Einlaß, -sse, *n.m.* admission, entrance.

ein·laufen*, *vb.* enter; shrink.

ein·legen, vb. insert; deposit; pickle.

ein·leiten, vb. introduce.

einleitend, adj. introductory.

Einleitung, -en, n.f. introduction.

ein·leuchten, vb. make sense.

einleuchtend, adj. plausible.

ein·lösen, vb. redeem.

Einlösung, -en, n.f. redemption.

ein·machen, vb. preserve, can.

einmal, adv. once; **(auf e.)** all of a sudden; **(noch e.)** once again; **(nicht e.)** not even.

einmalig, adj. occurring only once, single, unique.

Einmarsch, ⸗e, n.m. marching into, entry.

ein·mauern, vb. wall in.

ein·mengen, vb. mix in; **(sich e.)** interfere.

ein·mischen, vb. mix in; **(sich e.)** intervene, meddle.

Einmischung, -en, n.f. intervention.

Einnahme, -n, n.f. receipt; capture.

ein·nehmen*, vb. take; captivate.

Einöde, n.f. desolate place, solitude.

ein·ordnen, vb. arrange, file.

ein·packen, vb. pack up, wrap up.

ein·pflanzen, vb. plant.

ein·prägen, vb. impress.

ein·rahmen, vb. frame.

ein·räumen, vb. concede.

ein·rechnen, vb. include, allow for.

Einrede, -n, n.f. objection.

ein·reden, vb. talk into, persuade.

ein·reihen, vb. arrange.

ein·reißen*, vb. tear down.

ein·richten, vb. furnish, arrange, establish.

Einrichtung, -en, n.f. arrangement, institution.

ein·rücken, vb. move in; indent.

eins, num. one.

einsam, adj. lone(ly), lonesome.

Einsamkeit, n.f. loneliness, solitude.

ein·sammeln, vb. gather in.

Einsatz, ⸗e, n.m. inset; stake (in betting); (mil.) sortie.

ein·schalten, vb. switch on, shift into, tune in.

ein·schärfen, vb. inculcate.

ein·schätzen, vb. assess, estimate.

ein·schiffen, vb. embark.

ein·schlafen*, vb. go to sleep.

Einschlag, ⸗e, n.m. impact; envelope.

ein·schlagen*, vb. drive in; strike, break; take.

einschlägig, adj. pertinent, relevant.

ein·schließen*, vb. lock up, in; enclose, include, involve.

einschliesslich, adj. inclusive.

ein·schmeicheln, vb. **(sich e.)** insinuate oneself.

ein·schnappen, vb. snap shut; get annoyed.

Einschnitt, -e, n.m. cut, notch, segment.

ein·schränken, vb. limit, restrict.

Einschränkung, -en, n.f. restriction.

Einschreibebrief, -e, n.m. registered letter.

ein·schreiben*, vb. inscribe; register.

ein·schüchtern, vb. intimidate.

Einschüchterung, -en, n.f. intimidation.

ein·segnen, vb. consecrate, confirm.

ein·sehen*, vb. look into, realize.

ein·seifen, vb. soap, lather.

einseitig, adj. one-sided.

ein·setzen, vb. set in; appoint; install.

Einsicht, -en, n.f. insight; inspection.

Einsiedler, -, n.m. hermit.

ein·spannen, vb. stretch; harness, enlist.

ein·sperren, vb. lock up, imprison.

ein·spritzen, *vb.* inject.

Einspritzung, -en, *n.f.* injection.

Einspruch, ⁼e, *n.m.* protest. **(E. erhe′ben*)** to protest.

einst, *adv.* once, one day.

ein·stecken, *vb.* put in one's pocket.

ein·stehen*, *vb.* **(e. für)** stand up for, take the place of.

ein·steigen*, *vb.* get in; **(e.!)** all aboard!

ein·stellen, *vb.* put in, tune in, engage; stop, suspend.

Einstellung, -en, *n.f.* attitude; adjustment; suspension.

ein·stimmen, *vb.* chime in, join in, agree.

einstimmig, *adj.* unanimous.

Einstimmigkeit, *n.f.* unanimity.

ein·studieren, *vb.* practice, rehearse.

Einsturz, ⁼e, *n.m.* collapse.

einstweilen, *adv.* in the meantime.

ein·tauchen, *vb.* dip.

ein·tauschen, *vb.* exchange, swap.

ein·teilen, *vb.* divide, arrange, classify.

Einteilung, -en, *n.f.* classification.

eintönig, *adj.* monotonous.

Eintracht, *n.f.* harmony, concord.

ein·tragen*, *vb.* register, enter, record; bring in.

einträglich, *adj.* profitable.

Eintragung, -en, *n.f.* entry.

ein·treffen*, *vb.* arrive, happen.

ein·treten*, *vb.* enter.

Eintritt, -e, *n.m.* entry; beginning.

Eintrittskarte, -n, *n.f.* ticket of admission.

ein·üben, *vb.* practice.

ein(·)verleiben, *vb.* incorporate, annex.

Einvernehmen, -, *n.nt.* accord.

Einverständnis, -se, *n.nt.* agreement.

Einwand, ⁼e, *n.m.* objection.

Einwanderer, -, *n.m.* immigrant.

ein·wandern, *vb.* immigrate.

Einwanderung, -en, *n.f.* immigration.

einwandfrei, *adj.* sound, unobjectionable.

ein·wechseln, *vb.* change, cash.

ein·weichen, *vb.* soak.

ein·weihen, *vb.* consecrate, initiate.

Einweihung, -en, *n.f.* consecration, inauguration.

ein·wenden*, *vb.* object, interject.

ein·werfen*, *vb.* throw in; object, interject.

ein·wickeln, *vb.* wrap up.

ein·willigen, *vb.* consent.

Einwilligung, -en, *n.f.* consent, approval.

Einwirkung, -en, *n.f.* influence.

Einwohner, -, *n.m.* inhabitant, resident.

Einwurf, ⁼e, *n.m.* slot; objection.

ein·zahlen, *vb.* pay in, deposit.

Einzahlung, -en, *n.f.* deposit.

Einzäunung, -en, *n.f.* enclosure.

ein·zeichnen, *vb.* inscribe.

Einzelheit, -en, *n.f.* detail.

einzeln, *adj.* single, individual.

ein·ziehen*, *vb. (tr.)* pull in, furl, seize, draft; *(intr.)* move in, march in.

einzig, *adj.* only, sole, single.

einzigartig, *adj.* unique.

Einzug, ⁼e, *n.m.* entry.

ein·zwängen, *vb.* force in, squeeze in.

Eis, *n.nt.* ice.

Eisberg, -e, *n.m.* iceberg.

Eisen, -, *n.nt.* iron.

Eisenbahn, -en, *n.f.* railroad.

Eisenbahnwagen, -, *n.m.* railroad coach.

Eisenwaren, *n.pl.* hardware.

eisern, *adj.* iron.

eisig, *adj.* icy.

Eisregen, *n.m.* sleet.

Eisschrank, ⁀e, *n.m.* ice-box, refrigerator.

eitel, *adj.* vain.

Eitelkeit, *n.f.* vanity.

Eiter, *n.m.* pus.

Eiterbeule, -n, *n.f.* abscess.

Eitergeschwulst, ⁀e, *n.f.* abscess.

Eiweiß, *n.nt.* white of egg.

Ekel, *n.m.* disgust.

ekelerregend, *adj.* nauseous.

ekelhaft, *adj.* disgusting.

ekeln, *vb.* arouse disgust; **(sich e. vor)** be disgusted by.

Ekstase, -n, *n.f.* ecstasy.

ekstaʹtisch, *adj.* ecstatic.

Ekzem, -e, *n.nt.* eczema.

elasʹtisch, *adj.* elastic.

Elefant, -en -en, *n.m.* elephant.

elegant, *adj.* elegant, chic, smart.

Eleganz, *n.f.* elegance.

elektrifizieʹren, *vb.* electrify.

Elekʹtriker, -, *n.m.* electrician.

elekʹtrisch, *adj.* electric.

Elektrizitätʹ, *n.f.* electricity.

Elektron, -oʹnen, *n.nt.* electron.

Elektroʹnenwissenschaft, *n.f.* electronics.

Elementʹ, -e, *n.nt.* element.

elementarʹ, *adj.* elemental, elementary.

Elend, *n.nt.* misery.

elend, *adj.* miserable, wretched; sick.

elf, *num.* eleven.

Elfenbein, *n.nt.* ivory.

elftʹ-, *adj.* eleventh.

Elftel, -, *n.nt.* eleventh; **(ein e.)** one-eleventh.

Eliʹte, *n.f.* elite.

Elixier, -e, *n.nt.* elixir.

Ellbogen, -, *n.m.* elbow.

Elle, -, *n.f.* ell, yard.

Elsaß, *n.nt.* Alsace.

elterlich, *adj.* parental.

Eltern, *n.pl.* parents.

Emaiʹlle, *n.f.* enamel.

emanzipieʹren, *vb.* emancipate.

Embargʹo, -s, *n.nt.* embargo.

Emblemʹ, -e, *n.nt.* emblem.

Embryo, -s, *n.m.* embryo.

Empfangʹ, ⁀e, *n.m.* reception.

empfanʹgen*, *vb.* receive; conceive (child).

Empfänʹger, -, -, *n.m.* receiver, recipient, addressee.

empfängʹlich, *adj.* susceptible.

empfehʹlen*, *vb.* recommend, commend.

empfehʹlenswert, *adj.* (re)commendable.

Empfehʹlung, -en, *n.f.* recommendation.

empfinʹden*, *vb.* feel, sense.

empfindʹlich, *adj.* sensitive.

empfindʹsam, *adj.* sentimental.

Empfinʹdung, -en, *n.f.* feeling, sensation.

empfinʹdungslos, *adj.* insensitive.

emporʹ, *adv.* upward, aloft.

empöʹren, *vb.* make indignant; **(sich e.)** be furious; rebel.

emporʹ-ragen, *vb.* rise up, tower.

emporʹ-schwingen*, *vb.* **(sich e.)** soar upward.

Empöʹrung, -en, *n.f.* indignation; rebellion.

emsig, *adj.* busy, industrious.

Emulsionʹ, -en, *n.f.* emulsion.

Ende, -n, *n.nt.* end.

enden, *vb.* end.

endgültig, *adj.* definitive, conclusive, final.

endigen, *vb.* end.

endlich, 1. *adj.* final; finite. **2.** *adv.* at last.

endlos, *adj.* endless.

Endstation, -en, *n.f.* terminus.

Energieʹ, -n, *n.f.* energy.

energieʹlos, *adj.* languid.

enerʹgisch, *adj.* energetic.

eng, *adj.* narrow, tight.

engagieʹren, *vb.* engage, hire.

Enge, -n, *n.f.* narrowness; narrow place; **(in die E. treiben*)** drive into a corner.

Engel, -, *n.m.* angel.

England, *n.nt.* England.

Engländer, -, *n.m.* English-man.

englisch, *adj.* English.

Enkel, -, *n.m.* grandson.

Enkelin, -nen, *n.f.* grand-daughter.

Enkelkind, -er, *n.nt.* grand-child.

enorm', *adj.* enormous.

Ensem'ble, -s, *n.nt.* ensem-ble.

entar'ten, *vb.* degenerate.

entbeh'ren, *vb.* go without.

entbehr'lich, *adj.* dispen-sable.

Entbeh'rung, -en, *n.f.* pri-vation.

entbin'den*, *vb.* set free; deliver.

Entbin'dung, -en, *n.f.* de-livery.

entblö'ßen, *vb.* denude, un-cover, bare.

entde'cken, *vb.* discover.

Entde'ckung, -en, *n.f.* dis-covery.

Ente, -n, *n.f.* duck.

enteh'ren, *vb.* dishonor.

enteig'nen, *vb.* dispossess.

entfa'chen, *vb.* kindle.

entfal'len*, *vb.* fall to; slip from (memory).

entfal'ten, *vb.* unfold.

entfer'nen, *vb.* remove.

entfernt', *adj.* removed; distant.

Entfer'nung, -en, *n.f.* re-moval; distance.

entfes'seln, *vb.* unchain, release.

entflam'men, *vb.* inflame.

entflie'hen*, *vb.* flee, escape.

entfrem'den, *vb.* estrange, alienate.

entfüh'ren*, *vb.* carry off, abduct, kidnap.

Entfüh'rung, -en, *n.f.* ab-duction.

entge'gen, *adv.&prep.* oppo-site, contrary to; towards.

entge'gengesetzt, *adj.* op-posite.

entge'gen-kommen*, *vb.* come towards; be obliging.

entge'gen-setzen, *vb.* oppose.

entgeg'nen, *vb.* reply, re-tort.

entge'hen*, *vb.* elude.

Entgelt', *n.nt.* remunera-tion.

entglei'sen*, *vb.* jump the track; make a slip.

Entglei'sung, -en, *n.f.* de-railment; blunder.

enthal'ten*, *vb.* hold, con-tain; **(sich e.)** refrain.

enthalt'sam, *adj.* abste-mious.

Enthalt'samkeit, -en, *n.f.* abstinence.

Enthal'tung, *n.f.* forbear-ance.

enthe'ben*, *vb.* oust.

Enthe'bung, -en, *n.f.* ouster.

enthül'len, *vb.* unveil, dis-close.

Enthül'lung, -en, *n.f.* dis-closure, exposé.

Enthusiast', -en, -en, *n.m.* enthusiast.

entklei'den, *vb.* undress, divest.

entkom'men*, *vb.* escape.

entkräf'ten, *vb.* debilitate.

entla'den*, *vb.* unload.

entlang', *adv.&prep.* along.

entlas'sen*, *vb.* dismiss, re-lease.

Entlas'sung, -en, *n.f.* dis-missal, release.

entlau'fen*, *vb.* run away.

entle'digen, *vb.* free from; exempt.

entle'gen, *adj.* remote.

entmilitarisie'ren, *vb.* de-militarize.

entmu'tigen, *vb.* discourage.

Entmu'tigung, -en, *n.f.* dis-couragement.

entneh'men*, *vb.* take from, infer from.

entner'ven, *vb.* enervate.

entrah'men, *vb.* skim.

enträt'seln, *vb.* decipher.

entrei'ßen*, *vb.* snatch from.

entrich'ten, *vb.* pay, settle.

entrin'nen*, *vb.* run away from.

entrüs'ten, *vb.* make indig-nant; **(sich e.)** become in-dignant.

entrüs'tet, *adj.* indignant.

Entrüs'tung, -en, *n.f.* in-dignation.

entsa'gen, *vb.* renounce, abjure.

entschä'digen, *vb.* compensate, indemnify.

Entschä'digung, -en, *n.f.* compensation, indemnification.

entschei'den*, *vb.* decide.

entschei'dend, *adj.* decisive.

Entschei'dung, -en, *n.f.* decision.

entschie'den, *adj.* decided, definite.

entschlie'ßen*, *vb.* (**sich e.**) decide.

entschlo'ssen, *adj.* determined.

Entschlos'senheit, *n.f.* determination.

entschlüp'fen, *vb.* slip away from.

Entschluß', ¨sse, *n.m.* decision.

entschul'digen, *vb.* excuse; (**sich e.**) apologize.

Entschul'digung, -en, *n.f.* excuse, apology.

entset'zen, *vb.* dismiss; horrify; (**sich e.**) be horrified.

Entset'zen, *n.nt.* horror.

entsetz'lich, *adj.* horrible.

entsin'nen*, *vb.* (**sich e.**) recollect.

entspan'nen, *vb.* relax.

entspre'chen*, *vb.* correspond.

entspre'chend, *adj.* corresponding (to), respective.

entste'hen*, *vb.* arise, originate.

entstel'len, *vb.* disfigure, deform, distort, mutilate, garble.

enttäu'schen, *vb.* disappoint.

Enttäu'schung, -en, *n.f.* disappointment.

entthro'nen, *vb.* dethrone.

entwaff'nen, *vb.* disarm.

entwäs'sern, *vb.* drain.

entweder, *conj.* (**e. . . . oder**) either . . . or.

entwei'chen*, *vb.* escape.

entwen'den*, *vb.* steal.

entwer'fen*, *vb.* sketch, draft, plan.

entwer'ten, *vb.* depreciate; cancel.

entwi'ckeln, *vb.* develop.

Entwick'ler, -, *n.m.* developer.

Entwicklung, -en, *n.f.* development.

entwir'ren, *vb.* disentangle.

entwi'schen, *vb.* slip away from.

entwür'digen, *vb.* dishonor.

Entwurf', ¨e, *n.m.* sketch, design, draft, plan.

entzie'hen*, *vb.* remove, extract.

entzü'cken, *vb.* delight.

Entzü'cken, -, *n.nt.* delight.

entzü'ckend, *adj.* delightful, charming.

Entzü'ckung, -en, *n.f.* rapture.

entzünd'bar, *adj.* inflammable.

entzün'den, *vb.* inflame.

entzün'det, *adj.* infected.

Entzün'dung, -en, *n.f.* inflammation, infection.

entzwei', *adv.* in two, apart.

Enzy'klika, -ken, *n.f.* encyclical.

Enzyklopädie', -i'en, *n.f.* encyclopaedia.

Epidemie', -i'en, *n.f.* epidemic.

epide'misch, *adj.* epidemic.

Epilepsie', *n.f.* epilepsy.

Epilog', -e, *n.m.* epilogue.

Episo'de, -n, *n.f.* episode.

Epo'che, -n, *n.f.* epoch.

Epos (*pl.* **Epopen**) *n.f.* epic poem.

er, *pron.* he, it.

erach'ten *vb.* consider.

erbar'men, *vb.* have pity. (**sich e.**) pity.

Erbar'men, *n.nt.* pity.

erbärm'lich, *adj.* pitiful.

erbar'mungslos, *adj.* pitiless.

erbau'en, *vb.* construct; edify.

erbau'lich, *adj.* edifying.

Erbau'ung, *n.f.* edification.

Erbe, -n, -n, *n.m.* heir.

Erbe, *n.nt.* inheritance, heritage.

erben, *vb.* inherit.

Erbfolge, *n.f.* succession.

erbie′ten*, *vb.* (sich e.) offer, volunteer.

erbit′ten, *vb.* ask for.

erbit′tern, *vb.* embitter.

erblas′sen, *vb.* turn pale.

erblei′chen*, *vb.* turn pale.

erblich, *adj.* hereditary.

Erblichkeit, *n.f.* heredity.

erblicken, *vb.* catch sight of.

erbo′sen, *vb.* make angry; (sich e.) get angry.

erbre′chen*, *vb.* break open; (sich e.) vomit.

Erbschaft, -en, *n.f.* inheritance.

Erbse, -n, *n.f.* pea.

Erbstück, -e, *n.nt.* heirloom.

Erdbeben, -, *n.nt.* earthquake.

Erdbeere, -n, *n.f.* strawberry.

Erdboden, *n.m.* ground, soil.

Erde, *n.f.* earth.

erden, *vb.* ground.

erden′ken*, *vb.* think up.

erdenk′lich, *adj.* imaginable.

Erdgeschoß, *n.nt.* ground floor.

Erdhügel, -, *n.m.* mound.

erdich′ten, *vb.* invent, imagine.

erdich′tet, *adj.* fictional.

Erdich′tung, *n.f.* fiction.

erdig, *adj.* earthy.

Erdkreis, -e, *n.m.* sphere.

Erdkugel, -n, *n.f.* globe.

Erdkunde, *n.f.* geography.

Erdnuß, ˝sse, *n.f.* peanut.

Erdöl, -e, *n.nt.* petroleum.

erdrei′sten, *vb.* (sich e.) be so bold.

erdros′seln, *vb.* strangle.

erdrü′cken, *vb.* crush (to death), stifle.

Erdteil, -e, *n.m.* continent.

erdul′den, *vb.* endure.

ereig′nen, *vb.* (sich e.) happen.

Ereig′nis, -se, *n.nt.* event.

ereig′nisreich, *adj.* eventful.

erfah′ren*, *vb.* come to know, learn, experience.

erfah′ren, *adj.* experienced, adept.

Erfah′rung, -en, *n.f.* experience.

erfas′sen, *vb.* grasp, realize; apprehend.

erfin′den*, *vb.* invent; contrive.

Erfin′der, -, *n.m.* inventor.

erfin′derisch, *adj.* inventive; ingenious.

Erfin′dung, -en, *n.f.* invention.

Erfolg′, -e, *n.m.* success.

erfolg′los, *adj.* unsuccessful.

erfolg′reich, *adj.* successful; (e. sein*) to succeed.

erfor′derlich, *adj.* required.

erfor′dern, *vb.* require.

Erfor′dernis, -se, *n.nt.* requirement, requisite.

erfor′schen, *vb.* explore.

Erfor′schung, -en, *n.f.* exploration.

erfreu′en, *vb.* delight, gratify; (sich e.) enjoy.

erfreu′lich, *adj.* enjoyable.

erfrie′ren*, *vb.* freeze.

erfri′schen, *vb.* refresh, invigorate.

Erfri′schung, -en, *n.f.* refreshment.

erfül′len, *vb.* fill; fulfill.

Erfül′lung, -en, *n.f.* fulfillment.

ergän′zen, *vb.* supplement; amend.

Ergän′zung, -en, *n.f.* supplement, complement.

erge′ben*, *vb.* yield; result in; (sich e.) result, follow; surrender.

erge′ben, *adj.* devoted.

Ergeb′nis, -se, *n.nt.* result, outcome.

ergie′big, *adj.* productive.

ergöt′zen, *vb.* delight.

ergötz′lich, *adj.* delectable.

ergrei′fen*, *vb.* grasp, seize.

Ergrif′fenheit, *n.f.* emotion.

Erguß′, ˝sse, *n.m.* effusion.

erha′ben, *adj.* elevated; lofty, sublime.

Erha′benheit, *n.f.* grandeur.

erhal′ten*, *vb.* maintain, preserve; get, obtain.

Erhal′tung, *n.f.* maintenance, preservation; acquisition.

erhär′ten, *vb.* harden.

erha′schen, *vb.* snatch.

erhe'ben*, *vb.* raise.

erheb'lich, *adj.* considerable.

erhei'tern, *vb.* brighten, cheer.

erhel'len, *vb.* illuminate.

erhit'zen, *vb.* heat.

erhö'hen, *vb.* raise, heighten; ennoble.

Erhö'hung, **-en**, *n.f.* elevation, rise; enhancement.

erho'len, *vb.* (sich e.) get better, recuperate.

Erho'lung, *n.f.* recuperation, recreation.

erhö'ren, *vb.* hear.

erin'nern, *vb.* remind; (sich e.) remember, recollect.

Erin'nerung, **-en**, *n.f.* remembrance, memory.

erkäl'ten, *vb.* (sich e.) catch cold.

Erkäl'tung, **-en**, *n.f.* cold.

erken'nen*, *vb.* recognize.

erkennt'lich, *adj.* recognizable; thankful.

Erkennt'nis, **-se**, *n.f.* realization, knowledge.

erklä'ren, *vb.* explain, declare.

erklä'rend, *adj.* explanatory.

Erklä'rung, **-en**, *n.f.* explanation; declaration.

erklet'tern, *vb.* climb up, scale.

erklin'gen*, *vb.* (re)sound.

erkran'ken, *vb.* be taken ill.

erkun'digen, *vb.* (sich e.) inquire.

Erkun'digung, **-en**, *n.f.* inquiry.

erlan'gen, *vb.* obtain, attain.

Erlaß', **-sse**, *n.m.* decree.

erlas'sen*, *vb.* decree; forgive.

erlau'ben, *vb.* allow, permit.

Erlaub'nis, *n.f.* permission, permit.

erläu'tern, *vb.* illustrate; elucidate.

Erläu'terung, **-en**, *n.f.* illustration; elucidation.

Erleb'nis, **-se**, *n.nt.* event, experience.

erle'digen, *vb.* take care of, settle.

erle'digt, *adj.* settled; exhausted.

erleich'tern, *vb.* lighten, facilitate; relieve.

Erleich'terung, **-en**, *n.f.* ease, relief.

erlei'den*, *vb.* suffer.

erle'sen, *adj.* chosen.

erleuch'ten, *vb.* illuminate.

erlie'gen*, *vb.* succumb.

Erlös', *n.m.* proceeds.

erlö'schen*, *vb.* go out, be extinguished; become extinct.

erlö'sen, *vb.* deliver, redeem.

Erlö'ser, *n.m.* redeemer.

Erlö'sung, **-en**, *n.f.* deliverance, redemption.

ermäch'tigen, *vb.* empower, enable.

Ermäch'tigung, **-en**, *n.f.* authorization.

ermah'nen, *vb.* admonish.

ermann'geln, *vb.* lack.

ermä'ßigen, *vb.* reduce.

Ermä'ßigung, **-en**, *n.f.* reduction.

ermat'ten, *vb.* tire.

ermes'sen*, *vb.* calculate; comprehend.

ermit'teln, *vb.* ascertain.

Ermitt'lung, **-en**, *n.f.* detection.

ermög'lichen, *vb.* make possible, enable.

ermor'den, *vb.* murder.

Ermor'dung, **-en**, *n.f.* murder, assassination.

ermü'den, *vb.* tire.

ermun'tern, *vb.* rouse; cheer up.

ermu'tigen, *vb.* encourage.

Ermu'tigung, **-en**, *n.f.* encouragement.

ernäh'ren, *vb.* nourish, nurture.

Ernäh'rung, *n.f.* nourishment, nutrition.

ernen'nen*, *vb.* appoint, nominate.

Ernen'nung, **-en**, *n.f.* appointment, nomination.

erneu'ern, *vb.* renew.

Erneu'erung, **-en**, *n.f.* renewal.

ernie'drigen, *vb.* debase, degrade.

Ernie'drigung, **-en**, *n.f.* degradation.

ernst, *adj.* earnest; severe, serious.

Ernst, *n.m.* earnestness; gravity, seriousness.

Ernte -n, *n.f.* harvest, crop.

ernten, *vb.* harvest, reap.

ero'bern, *vb.* conquer.

Ero'berer, -, *n.m.* conqueror.

Ero'berung, -en, *n.f.* conquest.

eröff'nen, *vb.* open.

Eröff'nung, -en, *n.f.* opening.

erör'tern, *vb.* discuss, debate.

Erör'terung, -en, *n.f.* discussion, debate.

Ero'tik, *n.f.* eroticism.

ero'tisch, *adj.* erotic.

erpicht', *adj.* intent.

erpres'sen, *vb.* blackmail.

Erpres'sung, -en, *n.f.* blackmail, extortion.

erqui'cken, *vb.* refresh.

erra'ten*, *vb.* guess.

erre'gen, *vb.* arouse, excite.

Erre'gung, -en, *n.f.* excitement; emotion.

errei'chen, *vb.* reach; achieve.

errich'ten, *vb.* erect, establish.

Errich'tung, -en, *n.f.* erection.

errin'gen*, *vb.* achieve; gain.

Errun'genschaft, -en, *n.f.* achievement, attainment.

Ersatz', *n.m.* compensation; substitute; *cpds.* spare.

erschaf'fen*, *vb.* create.

Erschaf'fung, -en, *n.f.* creation.

erschei'nen*, *vb.* appear.

Erschei'nung, -en, *n.f.* appearance; apparition; phenomenon.

erschie'ßen*, *vb.* shoot (dead).

erschla'gen*, *vb.* slay.

erschlie'ßen*, *vb.* open, unfold.

erschöp'fen, *vb.* exhaust.

erschöpft', *adj.* weary, exhausted.

Erschöp'fung, *n.f.* exhaustion.

erschre'cken, *vb.* scare, frighten, startle.

erschre'cken*, *vb.* become

scared, become frightened, be startled.

erschü'ttern, *vb.* shake, shock.

Erschüt'terung, -en, *n.f.* shock; vibration.

erschwe'ren, *vb.* make more difficult, aggravate.

erschwing'lich, *adj.* within one's means.

erse'hen*, *vb.* see, learn.

erset'zen, *vb.* make good, replace; supersede.

ersicht'lich, *adj.* evident.

ersin'nen*, *vb.* devise.

erspa'ren, *vb.* save.

erst, 1. *adj.* first. **2.** *adv.* not until, only.

erstens, *adv.* in the first place, firstly.

erstar'ren, *vb.* get numb, stiffen; congeal.

erstat'ten, *vb.* refund, recompense.

erstau'nen, *vb.* astonish, amaze.

Erstau'nen, *n.nt.* amazement, astonishment.

erstaun'lich, *adj.* amazing.

erste'hen*, *vb.* arise; get, obtain.

erstei'gen*, *vb.* climb.

erster-, *adj.* former.

ersti'cken, *vb.* stifle, suffocate, smother.

Ersti'ckung, -en, *n.f.* suffocation, asphyxiation, choking.

erstklassig, *adj.* first-class, first-rate.

erstre'ben, *vb.* aspire to.

erstreck'en, *vb.* (sich e.) extend, range.

ersu'chen, *vb.* request.

ertap'pen, *vb.* catch, surprise.

ertei'len, *vb.* give, administer.

Ertrag', ⸚e, *n.m.* yield, return.

ertrag'bar, *adj.* bearable.

ertra'gen*, *vb.* bear, endure.

erträg'lich, *adj.* passable.

erträn'ken, *vb.* (tr.) drown.

ertrin'ken*, *vb.* (intr.) drown.

erü'brigen, *vb.* (sich e.) not be necessary.

erwa'chen, vb. wake.

erwach'sen*, vb. arise, grow.

erwach'sen, adj. grown, grown-up, adult.

Erwach'sene-, n.m.&f. adult.

erwä'gen, vb. deliberate, ponder.

Erwä'gung, -en, n.f. consideration.

erwäh'nen, vb. mention.

Erwäh'nung, -en, n.f. mention.

erwar'ten, vb. expect, await.

Erwar'tung, -en, n.f. expectation, anticipation.

erwe'cken, vb. awaken.

erwei'chen, vb. soften, mollify; (sich e. lassen) relent.

erwei'sen*, vb. prove; render.

erwei'tern, vb. widen, extend.

erwer'ben*, vb. acquire.

Erwer'bung, -en, n.f. acquisition.

erwi'dern, vb. reply; return, reciprocate.

Erwi'derung, -en, n.f. reply; return.

erwir'ken, vb. bring about.

erwi'schen, vb. catch, get hold of.

erwünscht', adj. desired.

erwür'gen, vb. strangle.

erzäh'len, vb. tell, narrate, relate.

Erzäh'lung, -en, n.f. story, narrative, tale.

Erzbischof, -e, n.m. archbishop.

Erzdiözese, -n, n.f. archdiocese.

erzeu'gen, vb. create, produce; (elec.) generate.

Erzeug'nis, -se, n.nt. product.

Erzherzog, -e, n.m. archduke.

erzie'hen*, vb. educate.

Erzie'her, -, n.m. educator.

Erzie'herin, -nen, n.f. governess.

erzie'herisch, adj. educational.

Erzie'hung, n.f. education; breeding.

erzür'nen, vb. (sich e.) become angry.

erzwin'gen*, vb. force.

es, pron. it.

Esche, -n, n.f. ash (tree).

Esel, -, n.m. donkey, ass, jackass.

eßbar, adj. edible.

essen*, vb. eat.

Essen, n.nt. food.

Essenz', -en, n.f. essence; flavoring.

Essig, n.m. vinegar.

Eßlöffel, -, n.m. tablespoon.

Eta'ge, -n, n.f. floor, story.

Etat', -s, n.m. budget.

Etikett', -e, n.nt. tag, label, sticker.

Etiket'te, n.f. etiquette.

etliche, pron. several.

etwa, adv. about, approximately, more or less, maybe.

etwaig, adj. eventual.

etwas, 1. pron. something. 2. adv. somewhat.

Eule, -n, n.f. owl.

Euro'pa, n.nt. Europe.

Europä'er, -, n.m. European.

europä'isch, adj. European.

evakuie'ren, vb. evacuate.

evange'lisch, adj. evangelical, Protestant.

Evangelist', -en, -en, n.m. evangelist.

Evange'lium, n.nt. gospel.

Eventualität', -en, n.f. contingency.

eventuell', adj. possible, potential.

ewig, 1. adj. eternal, everlasting. 2. adv. forever.

Ewigkeit, -en, n.f. eternity.

Exa'men, -, n.nt. examination.

Exemplar', -e, n.nt. specimen, copy.

exerzie'ren, vb. drill.

Existenz', -en, n.f. existence.

existie'ren, vb. exist.

exo'tisch, adj. exotic.

Experiment', -e, n.nt. experiment.

experimentie'ren, vb. experiment.

explodie'ren, vb. explode, detonate.

Explosion', -en, n.f. explosion.

explosiv, adj. explosive.

Export', -e, *n.m.* export.
exportie'ren, *vb.* export.
Expreß', -sse, *n.m.* express train.
extra, *adj.* extra.
Extravaganz, -en, *n.f.* extravagance.
extrem', *adj.* extreme.
Exzellenz', -en, *n.f.* Excellency.
exzen'trisch, *adj.* eccentric.
Exzentrizität', -en, *n.f.* eccentricity.

F

Fabel, -n, *n.f.* fable.
fabelhaft, *adj.* fabulous, wonderful.
Fabrik', -en, *n.f.* factory, plant.
Fabrikant', -en, -en, *n.m.* manufacturer.
Fabrikat', -e, *n.nt.* manufactured article; **(deutsches F.)** made in Germany.
Fach, ⸚er, *n.nt.* compartment; profession; (academic) subject.
Fächer, -, *n.m.* fan.
fächern, *vb.* fan.
fachmännisch, *adj.* professional.
Fackel, -, *n.f.* torch.
fade, *adj.* flavorless, insipid.
Faden, ⸚, *n.m.* thread, filament.
fadenscheinig, *adj.* threadbare.
fähig, *adj.* able, capable, competent.
Fähigkeit, -en, *n.f.* ability, capability, competence.
fahnden, *vb.* search.
Fahne, -n, *n.f.* flag.
Fahnenflucht, *n.f.* desertion.
Fahnenflüchtig-, *n.m.* deserter.
Fähnrich, -e, *n.m.* ensign.
Fahrbahn, -en, *n.f.* lane.
Fähre, -n, *n.f.* ferry.

fahren*, *vb.* drive, ride, go.
Fahrer, -, *n.m.* driver.
Fahrgeld, -er, *n.nt.* fare.
Fahrkarte, -n, *n.f.* ticket.
fahrlässig, *adj.* negligent.
Fahrplan, ⸚e, *n.m.* timetable, schedule.
fahrplanmäßig, *adj.* scheduled.
Fahrpreis, -e, *n.m.* fare.
Fahrrad, ⸚er, *n.nt.* bicycle.
Fahrrinne, -n, *n.f.* lane.
Fahrstuhl, ⸚e, *n.m.* elevator.
Fahrt, -en, *n.f.* ride; trip.
Fährte, -n, *n.f.* track, trail.
Fahrzeug, -e, *n.nt.* vehicle, conveyance.
Faktor, -o'ren, *n.m.* factor.
Fakultät', -en, *n.f.* faculty.
fakultativ', *adj.* optional.
Fall, ⸚e, *n.m.* fall; case.
Falle, -n, *n.f.* trap; pitfall.
fallen*, *vb.* fall, drop; **(f. lassen)** drop.
fällen, *vb.* fell.
fällig, *adj.* due; **(f. werden)** become due, mature.
Fälligkeit, *n.f.* maturity.
falls, *conj.* in case, if.
falsch, *adj.* false, wrong; fake; deceitful.
fälschen, *vb.* forge, counterfeit.
Fälscher, -, *n.m.* forger.
Falschheit, -en, *n.f.* falseness, deceit.
Fälschung, -en, *n.f.* forgery.
Falte, -n, *n.f.* fold, crease, pleat; wrinkle.
falten, *vb.* fold, pleat, crease.
familiär', *adj.* familiar; intimate.
Fami'lie, -n, *n.f.* family.
Fami'lienname(n), -, *n.m.* surname.
famos', *adj.* splendid.
Fana'tiker, -n, *n.m.* fanatic.
fana'tisch, *adj.* fanatic, rabid.
Fanatis'mus, *n.m.* fanaticism.
Fanfa're, -n, *n.f.* fanfare.
Fang, ⸚e, *n.m.* catch.
fangen*, *vb.* catch, capture.
Fänger, -, *n.m.* catcher.
Farbe, -n, *n.f.* color; paint; dye; (cards) suit.

färben, vb. color, dye.
farbenreich, adj. colorful.
Färber, -, n.m. dyer.
farbig, adj. colored.
farblos, adj. colorless, drab.
Farbstoff, -e, n.m. dye(stuff).
Farbton, ¨e, n.m. shade.
Farbtönung, -en, n.f. tint.
Färbung, -en, n.f. coloring, hue.
Farce, -n, n.f. farce.
Farmer, -, n.m. farmer.
Fasching, n.m. carnival, Mardi gras.
Faschis′mus, n.m. fascism.
Faschist′, -en, -en, n.m. fascist.
faschis′tisch, adj. fascist.
faseln, vb. talk nonsense.
Faser, -n, n.f. fiber.
Faß, ¨sser, n.nt. barrel, keg, vat, cask.
Fassa′de, -n, n.f. façade.
fassen, vb. grasp; seize; **(sich f.)** compose oneself; **(fasse dich kurz!)** make it short.
Fasson′, -s, n.f. shape.
Fassung, -en, n.f. version; gem setting; (fig.) composure; **(aus der F. bringen)** rattle.
fassungslos, adj. bewildered, staggered.
Fassungsvermögen, -, n.nt. capacity; comprehension.
fast, adv. almost, nearly.
fasten, vb. fast.
Fastenzeit, n.f. Lent.
faszinie′ren, vb. fascinate.
fauchen, vb. puff; (of cats) spit.
faul, adj. lazy; rotten.
faulenzen, vb. loaf.
Faulenzer, -n, n.m. loafer.
Fäulnis, n.f. decay, putrefaction.
Faultier, -e, n.nt. sloth.
Faust, ¨e, n.f. fist.
Februar, -e, n.m. February.
fechten, vb. fence.
Feder, -n, n.f. feather, plume; pen.
federleicht, adj. feathery.
federn, vb. feather; have good springs.
Fee, Fe′en, n.f. fairy.

Fegefeuer, n.nt. purgatory.
Fehde, -n, n.f. feud.
fehlbar, adj. fallible.
fehlen, vb. lack; be absent or missing.
Fehler, -, n.m. mistake, error; flaw, imperfection, defect; blunder.
fehlerfrei, adj. flawless.
fehlerhaft, adj. faulty, imperfect, defective.
fehlerlos, adj. faultless.
fehl-gebären*, vb. abort, have a miscarriage.
Fehlgeburt, -en, n.f. miscarriage, abortion.
fehl-gehen*, vb. err, go astray.
Fehlschlag, ¨e, n.m. failure; setback.
Fehltritt, -e, n.m. slip.
Feier, -n, n.f. celebration.
feierlich, adj. ceremonious; solemn.
Feierlichkeit, -en, n.f. ceremony, solemnity.
feiern, vb. celebrate.
Feiertag, -e, n.m. holiday.
feige, adj. cowardly.
Feige, -n, n.f. fig.
Feigheit, -en, n.f. cowardice.
Feigling, -e, n.m. coward.
Feile, -n, n.f. file.
feilen, vb. file.
feilschen, vb. bargain, haggle.
fein, adj. fine, delicate; elegant; subtle.
Feind, -e, n.m. foe, enemy.
feindlich, adj. hostile.
Feindschaft, -en, n.f. enmity; feud.
Feindseligkeit, -en, n.f. hostility.
Feingefühl, n.nt. sensitivity.
Feinheit, -en, n.f. purity; delicacy; elegance; subtlety.
feinsinnig, adj. ingenious.
feist, adj. fat, plump.
Feld, -er, n.nt. field.
Feldbett, -en, n.nt. cot.
Feldherr, -n, -en, n.m. commander.
Feldstecher, -, n.m. binoculars.
Feldzug, ¨e, n.m. campaign.

Fell, -e, *n.nt.* skin, pelt, hide.

Fels(en), -, *n.m.* rock, boulder.

Felsblock, ⸚e, *n.m.* boulder.

felsig, *adj.* rocky, craggy

Fenster, -, *n.nt.* window.

Fensterladen, ⸚, *n.m.* shutter.

Fensterscheibe, -n, *n.f.* windowpane.

Ferien, *n.pl.* vacation.

Ferienort, -e, *n.m.* resort.

fern, *adj.* far, distant, remote.

Fernanruf, -e, *n.m.* long-distance call.

ferner, *adv.* moreover, furthermore.

Ferngespräch, -e, *n.nt.* long-distance call.

Fernglas, ⸚er, *n.nt.* binocular(s).

Fernrohr, -e, *n.nt.* telescope.

Fernsehapparat, -e, *n.m.* television set.

Fernsehen, *n.nt.* television.

Fernsprecher, -, *n.m.* telephone.

Ferse, -n, *n.f.* heel.

fertig, *adj.* finished, complete, ready, done; **(f. sein)** be through; **(f. bringen)** complete, accomplish.

Fertigkeit, -en, *n.f.* dexterity, knack.

fesch, *adj.* chic.

Fessel, -n, *n.f.* fetter, irons, handcuffs; ankle.

Fesselgelenk, -e, *n.nt.* ankle.

fesseln, *vb.* chain; (fig.) captivate, fascinate.

fest, *adj.* firm, solid; fixed, steady; tight.

Fest, -e, *n.nt.* feast, celebration.

Feste, -n, *n.f.* fort, stronghold.

Festessen, -, *n.nt.* banquet, feast.

fest-fahren*, *vb.* run aground; (fig.) come to an impasse.

fest-halten*, *vb.* hold fast to, adhere to; detain.

festigen, *vb.* solidify, consolidate.

Festigkeit, *n.f.* firmness, solidity.

fest-klammern, *vb.* clamp; **(sich f.)** hold fast.

Festland, *n.nt.* mainland.

fest-legen, *vb.* fix, lay down.

festlich, *adj.* festive.

Festlichkeit, -en, *n.f.* festivity.

fest-machen, *vb.* fasten, make fast.

Festmahl, -e, *n.nt.* feast.

fest-nehmen*, *vb.* arrest.

fest-setzen, *vb.* fix, establish; determine.

Festspiel, -e, *n.nt.* festival.

fest-stehen*, *vb.* be stable; be certain.

feststehend, *adj.* stationary.

fest-stellen, *vb.* determine, ascertain; state.

Festtag, -e, *n.m.* holiday.

fett, *adj.* fat, greasy.

Fett, -e, *n.nt.* fat, grease.

fetten, *vb.* grease.

fettig, *adj.* fatty, greasy, oily.

fettleibig, *adj.* obese.

Fetzen, -, *n.m.* rag; scrap.

feucht, *adj.* moist, damp, humid.

Feuchtigkeit, *n.f.* moisture, dampness, humidity.

feuchtkalt, *adj.* clammy.

Feuer, -, *n.nt.* fire, (fig.) verve.

feuergefährlich, *adj.* inflammable.

Feuerleiter, -n, *n.f.* fire escape.

feuern, *vb.* fire.

Feuersbrunst, *n.f.* conflagration.

Feuerspritze, -n, *n.f.* fire engine.

Feuerstein -e, *n.m.* flint.

Feuerwaffe, -n, *n.f.* firearm.

Feuerwechsel, -n, *n.m.* skirmish.

Feuerwehrmann, ⸚er, *n.m.* fireman.

Feuerwerk, -e, *n.nt.* fireworks.

Feuerzeug, -e, *n.nt.* cigarette lighter.

feurig, *adj.* fiery.

Fichte, -n, *n.f.* pine, fir.

fidel*, *adj.* jolly.

Fieber, *n.nt.* fever.

fieberhaft, *adj.* feverish.

fiebern, *vb.* be feverish.

Fieberwahnsinn, -e, *n.m.* delirium.

Fiedel, -n, *n.f.* fiddle.

Figur', -en, *n.f.* figure.

figür'lich, *adj.* figurative.

Fiktion', -en, *n.f.* figment.

Filet', -s, *n.nt.* fillet.

Film, -e, *n.m.* film, movie, motion-picture.

filmen, *vb.* film.

Filmschauspieler, -, *n.m.* movie actor.

Filter, -, *n.m.* filter.

filtrie'ren, *vb.* filter.

Filz, -e, *n.m.* felt.

Fina'le, -s, *n.nt.* finale.

Finan'zen, *n.pl.* finances.

finanziell', *adj.* financial.

finanzie'ren, *vb.* finance.

Finanz'mann, ̈**er,** *n.m.* financier.

Finanz'wirtschaft, -en, *n.f.* finance.

finden*, *vb.* find, locate.

Finderlohn, *n.m.* reward (for returning lost articles).

findig, *adj.* ingenious, resourceful.

Findigkeit, *n.f.* ingenuity.

Findling, -e, *n.m.* foundling.

Finger, -, *n.m.* finger.

Fingerabdruck, ̈**e,** *n.m.* fingerprint.

Fingernagel, ̈, *n.m.* fingernail.

fingie'ren, *vb.* feign, simulate.

fingiert', *adj.* fictitious.

finster, *adj.* dark; saturnine.

Finsternis, -se, *n.f.* darkness; eclipse.

Firma *(pl.* **Firmen),** *n.f.* firm, company.

Firnis, -se, *n.m.* varnish.

firnissen, *vb.* varnish.

Fisch, -e, *n.m.* fish.

fischen, *vb.* fish.

Fischer, -, *n.m.* fisherman.

Fischgeschäft, -e, *n.nt.* fish-store.

Fixie'rung, -en, *n.f.* fixation.

flach, *adj.* flat, shallow.

Fläche, -n, *n.f.* plane, area.

Flachheit, -en, *n.f.* flatness.

Flachs, *n.m.* flax.

flackern, *vb.* flare, flicker.

Flagge, -n, *n.f.* flag.

Flak, -(s), *n.f.* (=Fliegerabwehrkanone) antiaircraft (fire, troops).

Flak-, *cpds.* antiaircraft.

Flamme, -n, -n, *n.m.* Fleming.

Flamme, -n, *n.f.* flame, blaze.

flammend, *adj.* flaming; *(fig.)* enthusiastic.

Flanell', -e, *n.m.* flannel.

Flanke, -n, *n.f.* flank.

flankie'ren, *vb.* flank.

Flasche, -n, *n.f.* bottle, flask.

flattern, *vb.* flutter, flap.

flau, *adj.* slack, dull.

Flaum, *n.m.* down, fuzz.

flaumig, *adj.* downy, fuzzy, fluffy.

Flechte, -n, *n.f.* braid.

Fleck, -e, *n.m.* spot, stain, blotch.

Fledermaus, ̈**e,** *n.f.* bat.

Flegel, -, *n.m.* rowdy, boor.

flehen, *vb.* implore, beseech.

flehentlich, *adj.* beseeching.

Fleisch, *n.nt.* flesh, meat.

fleischig, *adj.* fleshy.

fleischlich, *adj.* carnal.

Fleiß, *n.m.* diligence, hard work.

fleißig, *adj.* industrious, hard working.

flicken, *vb.* patch.

Flicken, -, *n.m.* patch.

Flickwerk, *n.nt.* patchwork.

Flieder, *n.m.* lilac.

Fliege, -n, *n.f.* fly.

fliegen*, *vb.* fly.

Flieger, -, *n.m.* flier, aviator.

fliehen*, *vb.* flee.

Fliese, -n, *n.f.* tile, flagstone.

fließen*, *vb.* flow.

fließend, *adj.* fluent.

flimmern, *vb.* flicker.

flink, *adj.* nimble, spry.

Flirt, -s, *n.m.* flirt, flirtation.

flirten, *vb.* flirt.

Flitterwochen, *n.pl.* honeymoon.

Flocke, -n, *n.f.* flake.

Floh, ̈**e,** *n.m.* flea.

Floß, ̈**e,** *n.nt.* float, raft.

Flosse, -n, *n.f.* fin.

Flöte, -n, *n.f.* whistle; flute.

flott, *adj.* afloat; smart, dashing.

Flotte, -n, *n.f.* fleet, navy.

Fluch, -e, *n.m.* curse.

fluchen, *vb.* swear, curse.

Fluchen, *n.nt.* profanity.

Flucht, *n.f.* escape, flight, getaway; **(in die F. schlagen)** rout.

flüchten, *vb.* flee.

flüchtig, *adj.* fleeting, cursory; superficial.

Flüchtling, -e, *n.m.* refugee, fugitive.

Flug, -e, *n.m.* flight.

Flugblatt, -er, *n.nt.* leaflet.

Flügel, -, *n.m.* wing.

Flughafen, -, *n.m.* airport.

Flugzeug, -e, *n.nt.* airplane.

Flunder, -n, *n.nf.* flounder.

flunkern, *vb.* fib.

fluoreszie'rend, *adj.* fluorescent.

Fluß, -sse, *n.m.* river; flux.

flüssig, *adj.* liquid, fluid; **(f. machen)** liquefy.

Flüssigkeit, -en, *n.f.* fluid, liquid.

flüstern, *vb.* whisper.

Flut, -en, *n.f.* flood, high tide.

fluten, *vb.* flood.

Folge, -n, *n.f.* consequence, outgrowth; succession; **(zur F. haben)** result in.

folgen, *vb.* follow; succeed.

folgend, *adj.* subsequent.

folgenreich, *adj.* consequential.

folgenschwer, *adj.* momentous.

folgerichtig, *adj.* consistent.

folgern, *vb.* infer, deduce.

Folgerung, -en, *n.f.* inference, deduction.

folglich, *adv.* consequently.

Folter, -n, *n.f.* torture.

foltern, *vb.* torture.

Fond, -s, *n.m.* fund.

Fondant', -s, *n.m.* bonbon.

Förderer, -, *n.m.* sponsor.

förderlich, *adj.* helpful, conducive.

fordern, *vb.* demand.

fördern, *vb.* promote, further; (mining) mine, haul.

Forderung, -en, *n.f.* demand, claim.

Förderung, -en, *n.f.* furtherance, advancement.

Forel'le, -n, *n.f.* trout.

Form, -en, *n.f.* form, shape; mold; **(in F. sein*)** be fit, be in fine shape.

Formalität', -en, *n.f.* formality.

Format', -e, *n.nt.* format; *(fig.)* stature.

Formation', -en, *n.f.* formation.

Formel, -n, *n.f.* formula.

formell', *adj.* formal.

formen, *vb.* form, shape, mold.

Förmlichkeit, -en, *n.f.* formality.

formlos, *adj.* formless.

Formular', -e, *n.nt.* form, blank.

formulie'ren, *vb.* formulate.

forschen, *vb.* explore, search.

Forscher, -, *n.m.* explorer.

Forschung, -en, *n.f.* research.

fort, *adv.* away, gone; forward.

Fortdauer, *n.f.* continuity.

fortdauernd, *adj.* continuous.

fort-fahren*, *vb.* drive away; proceed, continue.

fort-gehen*, *vb.* leave; continue.

fortgeschritten, *adj.* advanced.

fort-pflanzen, *vb.* propagate.

fort-schreiten*, *vb.* progress.

Fortschritt, -e, *n.m.* progress, advance.

fortschrittlich, *adj.* progressive.

fort-setzen, *vb.* continue.

Fortsetzung, -en, *n.f.* continuation.

fortwährend, *adj.* continuous.

Foyer', -s, *n.nt.* foyer.

Fracht, -en, *n.f.* freight, cargo.

Frachtbrief, -e, *n.m.* bill of lading.

Frachter, -, *n.m.* freighter.

Frachtschiff, -e, *n.nt.* freighter.

Frachtspesen, *n.pl.* freight charges.

Frage, -n, *n.f.* question.

Fragebogen, ⍩, *n.m.* questionnaire.

fragen, *vb.* ask, inquire.

fragend, *adj.* interrogative.

Fragezeichen, -, *n.nt.* question mark.

fraglich, *adj.* questionable.

fragmenta'risch, *adj.* fragmentary.

fragwürdig, *adj.* questionable.

Fraktur', *n.f.* German type (print).

Frankreich, *n.nt.* France.

Franse, -n, *n.f.* fringe.

Franzo'se, -n, -n, *n.m.* Frenchman.

Franzö'sin, -nen, *n.f.* French woman.

franzö'sisch, *adj.* French.

frappant', *adj.* striking.

fraternisie'ren, *vb.* fraternize.

Fratze, -n, *n.f* grimace; face, mug.

Frau, -en, *n.f.* woman, wife; Mrs.

Frauenarzt, ⍩e, *n.m.* gynecologist.

Fräulein, -, *n.nt.* Miss.

fraulich, *adj.* womanly.

frech, *adj.* impudent; saucy.

Frechheit, -en, *n.f.* impertinence, effrontery.

frei, *adj.* free; frank; vacant.

Frei-, *n.nt.* outdoors.

Freier, -, *n.m.* suitor.

freigebig, *adj.* generous.

Freigebigkeit, *n.f.* liberality, generosity.

freigestellt, *adj.* optional.

frei·halten*, *vb.* keep free; treat.

Freiheit, -en, *n.f.* liberty, freedom.

Freiherr, -n, -en, *n.m.* baron.

frei·lassen*, *vb.* free; leave blank.

freilich, *adv.* to be sure.

Freimarke, -n, *n.f.* stamp.

Freimaurer, -, *n.m.* Mason.

freimütig, *adj.* candid, heart-to-heart.

freisinnig, *adj.* liberal.

frei·sprechen*, *vb.* acquit, absolve.

Freispruch, ⍩e, *n.m.* acquittal.

Freitag, -e, *n.m.* Friday.

freiwillig, *adj.* voluntary; **(sich f. melden)** volunteer; enlist.

Freiwillig-, *n.m.&f.* volunteer.

fremd, *adj.* strange; foreign, alien.

Fremd-, *n.m.&f.* stranger.

Fremdenführer, -, *n.m.* guide.

Fremdenzimmer, -, *n.nt.* guest room, room to let.

frequentie'ren, *vb.* habituate

Frequenz', -en, *n f.* frequency.

Fresko, -ken, *n.nt.* fresco.

fressen*, *vb.* (of animals) eat; stuff oneself.

Freude, -n, *n.f.* joy, pleasure.

Freudenfeuer, -, *n.nt.* bonfire.

freudig, *adj.* joyful, joyous.

freudlos, *adj.* cheerless.

freuen, *vb.* make glad; **(sich f.)** be glad, rejoice.

Freund, -e, *n.m.* friend.

Freundin, -nen, *n.f.* friend (female).

freundlich, *adj.* friendly, kind.

freundlicherweise, *adv.* kindly.

Freundlichkeit, *n.f.* kindness, friendliness.

freundlos, *adj.* friendless.

Freundschaft, -en, *n.f.* friendship.

freundschaftlich, *adj.* amicable.

Frevel, -, *n.m.* outrage.

frevelhaft, *adj.* sacrilegious; flagrant.

Friede(n), *n.m.* peace.

Friedensvertrag, ⍩e, *n.m.* peace treaty.

friedfertig, *adj.* peaceable.

Friedhof, ⍩e, *n.m.* cemetery, graveyard.

friedlich, *adj.* peaceable, peaceful.
frieren*, *vb.* freeze.
Frikassee', -s, *n.nt.* fricassee.
frisch, *adj.* fresh, crisp.
Frische, *n.f.* freshness.
Friseur', -e, *n.m.* barber, hairdresser.
Friseu'se, -n, *n.f.* hairdresser (female).
frisie'ren, *vb.* dress the hair; *(fig.)* tamper with.
Frist, -en, *n.f.* limited period; respite.
Frisur', -en, *n.f.* coiffure, hairdo.
frivol', *adj.* frivolous.
froh, *adj.* glad.
fröhlich, *adj.* gay, cheerful.
Fröhlichkeit, *n.f.* cheerfulness, merriment.
frohlo'cken, *vb.* rejoice.
frohlo'ckend, *adj.* jubilant.
fromm (ö, -) *adj.* pious, religious, devout.
Frömmelei', -en, *n.f.* bigotry.
Frömmigkeit, *n.f.* piety.
Frömmler, -, *n.m.* bigot.
frönen, *vb.* indulge.
Front, -en, *n.f.* front.
Frosch, ⸚e, *n.m.* frog.
Frost, *n.m.* frost, chill.
frösteln, *vb.* feel chilly.
frostig, *adj.* frosty.
Frucht, ⸚e, *n.f.* fruit.
fruchtbar, *adj.* fruitful, fertile; prolific.
Fruchtbarkeit, *n.f.* fertility.
fruchtlos, *adj.* fruitless.
früh, *adj.* early.
früher, *adj.* earlier; former.
Frühjahr, *n.nt.* spring.
Frühling, -e, *n.m.* spring.
frühreif, *adj.* precocious.
Frühstück, -e, *n.nt.* breakfast.
frühzeitig, *adj.* early.
Fuchs, ⸚e, *n.m.* fox.
fügen, *vb.* join; **(sich f.)** comply, submit.
fügsam, *adj.* docile.
fühlbar, *adj.* tangible.
fühlen, *vb.* feel, sense.
führen, *vb.* lead, guide, direct.
Führer, -, *n.m.* leader, guide.

Führerschein, -e, *n.m.* driver's license.
Führung, *n.f.* leadership, guidance.
Fülle, *n.f.* fullness, wealth; **(in Hülle und F.)** galore.
füllen, *vb.* fill.
Füllfederhalter, -, *n.m.* fountain pen.
Füllung, -en, *n.f.* filling.
Fund, -e, *n.m.* find, discovery.
Fundament', -e, *n.nt.* foundation.
fundie'ren, *vb.* base.
fünf, *num.* five.
fünft-, *adj.* fifth.
Fünftel, -, *n.nt.* fifth; **(ein f.)** one-fifth.
fünfzig, *num.* fifty.
fünfzigst-, *adj.* fiftieth.
Fünfzigstel, -, *n.nt.* fiftieth; **(ein f.)** one-fiftieth.
Funke(n), -, *n.m.* spark.
funkeln, *vb.* sparkle.
funkelnagelneu, *adj.* brandnew.
funken, *vb.* radio.
Funktion', -en, *n.f.* function.
Funktionär', -e, *n.m.* functionary.
funktionie'ren, *vb.* function.
für, *prep.* for.
Furche, -n, *n.f.* furrow.
Furcht, *n.f.* fright, fear, dread.
furchtbar, *adj.* terrible.
fürchten, *vb.* fear; **(sich f. vor)** be afraid of.
furchtlos, *adj.* fearless.
Furchtlosigkeit, *n.f.* fearlessness.
furchtsam, *adj.* fearful.
Fürst, -en, -en, *n.m.* prince, ruler.
fürstlich, *adj.* princely.
Furt, -en, *n.f.* ford.
Furun'kel, -n, *n.m.* boil.
Fürwort, ⸚er, *n.nt.* pronoun.
Fusion', -en, *n.f.* fusion, merger.
Fuß, ⸚e, *n.m.* foot.
Fußball, ⸚e, *n.m.* football.
Fußboden, ⸚, *n.m.* floor; flooring.

Fußgänger, -, *n.m.* pedestrian.

Fußnote, -n, *n.f.* footnote.

Fußpfleger, -, *n.m.* chiropodist.

Futter, -, *n.nt.* feed, fodder; lining.

füttern, *vb.* feed; (clothing) line.

G

Gabardine, *n.m.* gabardine.

Gabe, -n, *n.f.* gift, donation; faculty.

Gabel, -n, *n.f.* fork.

gaffen, *vb.* gape.

gähnen, *vb.* yawn.

galant', *adj.* gallant.

Galanterie', -en, *n.f.* gallantry.

Gala-Uniform, *n.f.* full dress.

Galerie', -i'en, *n.f.* gallery.

Galgen, -, *n.m.* gallows.

Galle, -n, *n.f.* gall, bile.

Gallenblase, -n, *n.f.* gall bladder.

gallertartig, *adj.* gelatinous.

gallig, *adj.* bilious.

Galopp', -s, *n.m.* gallop; **(leichter G.)** canter.

galoppie'ren, *vb.* gallop.

galvanisie'ren, *vb.* galvanize.

Gama'sche, -n, *n.f.* gaiters, leggings.

Gang, ²e, *n.m.* walk; corridor, aisle; course; (auto) gear.

Gangrän', -e, *n.nt.* gangrene.

Gangster, -, *n.m.* gangster.

Gans, ²e, *n.f.* goose.

Gänsemarsch, *n.m.* single file.

ganz, 1. *adj.* whole, entire. **2.** *adv.* quite, rather; **(g. gut)** pretty good. **(g. und gar)** completely.

Ganz-, *n.nt.* whole (thing).

Ganzheit, *n.f.* entirety.

gänzlich, *adj.* complete.

gar, 1. *adj.* cooked, done. **2.** *adv.* **(g. nicht)** not at all; **(g. nichts)** nothing at all.

Gara'ge, -n, *n.f.* garage.

Garantie', -i'en, *n.f.* guarantee.

garantie'ren, *vb.* guarantee, warrant.

Garbe, -n, *n.f.* sheaf.

Gardero'be, -n, *n.f.* clothes, cloakroom.

gären*, *vb.* ferment.

Garn, -e, *n.nt.* yarn; thread.

Garne'le, -n, *n.f.* shrimp.

garnie'ren, *vb.* garnish.

Garnison', -en, *n.f.* garrison.

Garnitur', -en, *n.f.* set.

garstig, *adj.* nasty.

**Garten, ², ** *n.m.* garden, yard.

Gartenbau, *n.m.* horticulture.

Gärtner, -, *n.m.* gardener.

Gas, -e, *n.nt.* gas.

Gashebel, -, *n.m.* accelerator.

gasig, *adj.* gassy.

Gasse, -n, *n.f.* narrow street, alley.

Gast, ²e, *n.m.* guest.

gastfrei, *adj.* hospitable.

Gastfreiheit, *n.f.* hospitality.

gastfreundlich, *adj.* hospitable.

Gastfreundschaft, *n.f.* hospitality.

Gastgeber, -, *n.m.* host.

Gastgeberin, -nen, *n.f.* hostess.

Gasthaus, ²er, *n.nt.* inn.

gastrono'misch, *adj.* gastronomical.

Gaststube, -n, *n.f.* taproom.

Gatte, -n, -n, *n.m.* husband.

Gattin, -nen, *n.f.* wife.

Gattung, -en, *n.f.* species, genus.

Gau, -e, *n.m.* district, province.

Gaul, ²e, *n.m.* nag.

Gaumen, -, *n.m.* palate.

Gaze, -n, *n.f.* gauze.

**Geäch'tet-, ** *n.m.* outlaw.

Gebäck', *n.nt.* pastry.

Gebär'de, -n, *n.f.* gesticulation; gesture.

geba'ren, *vb.* **(sich g.)** behave.

gebä'ren*, *vb.* bear.

Gebäu'de, -, *n.nt.* building.

geben*, *vb.* give; deal (cards); **(es gibt)** there is, there are.

Geber', -, *n.m.* giver.

Gebet', -e, *n.nt.* prayer.

Gebiet', -e, *n.nt.* territory, region, field.

gebie'ten*, *vb.* command.

Gebie'ter, -, *n.m.* master.

Gebil'de, -, *n.nt.* form, structure.

gebil'det, *adj.* educated, civilized, cultured.

Gebir'ge, -, *n.nt.* mountainous area, mountains; mountain range.

gebir'gig, *adj.* mountainous.

Gebiß', -sse, *n.nt.* teeth; denture; (horse) bit.

Geblüt', *n.nt.* descent, family.

gebo'ren, *adj.* born.

Gebor'genheit, *n.f.* safety.

Gebot', -e, *n.nt.* command(ment).

Gebräu', -e, *n.nt.* brew, concoction.

Gebrauch', ⸚e, *n.m.* use; usage, custom.

gebrau'chen, *vb.* use.

gebräuch'lich, *adj.* customary.

Gebrauchs'anweisung, -en, *n.f.* directions (for use).

Gebre'chen, -, *n.nt.* infirmity.

gebrech'lich, *adj.* decrepit.

Gebrü'der, *n.pl.* brothers.

Gebrüll', *n.nt.* roar, howl.

gebückt', *adj.* stooped.

Gebühr', -en, *n.f.* charge, fee; **(nach G.)** duly; **(über alle G.)** excessively.

gebüh'ren, *vb.* be due; **(sich g.)** be proper.

gebüh'rend, *adj.* duly.

gebühr'lich, *adj.* proper.

Geburt', -en, *n.f.* birth; childbirth; **(von G. an)** congenital.

gebür'tig, *adj.* native.

Geburts'datum, -ten, *n.nt.* date of birth.

Geburts'helfer, -, *n.m.* obstetrician.

Geburts'ort, -e, *n.nt.* birthplace.

Geburts'schein, -e, *n.m.* birth certificate.

Geburts'tag, -e, *n.m.* birthday.

Gebüsch', -e, *n.nt.* bushes, shrubbery.

Geck, -en, -en, *n.m.* dandy.

Gedächt'nis, -se, *n.nt.* memory.

Gedächt'nisfeier, -n, *n.f.* commemoration.

Gedan'ke(n), -, *n.m.* thought, idea.

gedan'kenlos, *adj.* thoughtless, unthinking.

gedan'kenvoll, *adj.* thoughtful.

Gedeck', -e, *n.nt.* cover, table setting.

gedei'hen*, *vb.* thrive.

geden'ken*, *vb.* remember; commemorate.

Gedicht', -e, *n.nt.* poem.

gedie'gen, *adj.* solid.

Gedrän'ge, *n.nt.* crush.

gedrängt', *adj.* concise.

Geduld', *n.f.* patience.

gedul'den, *vb.* **(sich g.)** have patience, forbear.

gedul'dig, *adj.* patient.

geeig'net, *adj.* qualified; suitable.

Gefahr', -en, *n.f.* danger, jeopardy.

gefähr'den, *vb.* endanger, jeopardize.

gefähr'lich, *adj.* dangerous.

gefahr'los, *adj.* without danger.

Gefähr'te, -n, -n, *n.m.* companion.

gefal'len*, *vb.* please; **(es gefällt mir)** I like it.

Gefal'len, -, *n.m.* favor.

gefäl'lig, *adj.* obliging, pleasing.

Gefan'gen-, *n.m.&f.* prisoner, captive.

Gefan'gennahme, -n, *n.f.* capture.

Gefan'genschaft, -en, *n.f.* captivity.

Gefäng'nis, -se, *n.nt.* prison, jail.

Gefäng'niswärter, -, *n.m.* jailer.

Gefäß', -e, *n.nt.* container.

gefaßt', *adj.* composed.

Gefecht', -e, *n.nt.* battle; engagement.

gefeit', *adj* fortified against.

Gefie'der, *n.nt.* plumage.

gefleckt', *adj.* dappled.

ge'flis'sentlich, *adj.* intentional; studied.

Geflü'gel, *n.nt.* poultry.

Geflüs'ter, *n.nt.* whispering.

Gefol'ge, *n.nt.* retinue.

gefrä'ßig, *adj.* gluttonous.

Gefrei'te-, *n.m.* corporal.

gefrie'ren*, *vb.* freeze.

Gefrier'fach, ⁻er, *n.nt.* freezer (in refrigerator).

Gefro'ren-, *n.nt.* ice (cream).

gefü'gig, *adj.* compliant.

Gefühl', -e, *n.nt.* feeling, sensation; emotion, sentiment.

gefühl'los, *adj.* insensible, callous.

gefühls'mäßig, *adj.* emotional.

gefühl'voll, *adj.* sentimental.

gegen, *prep.* against; toward; about.

Gegenangriff, -e, *n.m.* counterattack.

Gegend, -en, *n.f.* region.

Gegengewicht, -e, *n.nt.* counterbalance.

Gegengift, -e, *n.nt.* antidote, antitoxin.

Gegenmaßnahme, -n, *n.f.* countermeasure.

Gegensatz, ⁻e, *n.m.* contrast, opposite.

gegenseitig, *adj.* mutual.

Gegenstand, ⁻e, *n.m.* object.

Gegenteil, *n.nt.* reverse, opposite.

gegenü'ber, *prep.&adv.* opposite.

gegenü'ber-stellen, *vb.* confront.

Gegenwart, *n.f.* present, presence.

gegenwärtig, *adj.* present.

Gegenwirkung, -en, *n.f.* counteraction.

Gegner, -, *n.m.* adversary, opponent.

Gehalt', -e, *n.m.* content, substance.

Gehalt', ⁻er, *n.nt.* salary, pay.

gehar'nischt, *adj.* armed; *(fig.)* vehement.

gehäs'sig, *adj.* malicious.

Gehäu'se, -, *n.nt.* casing.

geheim', *adj.* secret, cryptic.

Geheim'dienst, -e, *n.m.* secret service.

geheim'halten*, *vb.* keep secret.

Geheim'nis, -se, *n.nt.* secret, mystery.

geheim'nisvoll, *adj.* secretive, mysterious.

Geheiß', *n.nt.* command, behest.

gehen*, *vb.* go, walk; **(wie geht es Ihnen?)** how are you?

gehen·lassen*, *vb.* **(sich g.)** let oneself go.

Gehil'fe, -n, -n, *n.m.* helper, assistant.

Gehirn', -e, *n.nt.* brain.

Gehöft', -e, *n.nt.* farmstead.

Gehölz', -e, *n.nt.* woods.

Gehör', *n.nt.* hearing.

gehor'chen, *vb.* obey.

gehö'ren, *vb.* belong to.

gehö'rig, *adj.* belonging to; thorough, sound; appropriate.

gehor'sam, *adj.* obedient.

Gehor'sam, *n.m.* obedience, allegiance.

Geige, -n, *n.f.* violin.

Geisel, -n, *n.m.* hostage.

Geiser, -, *n.m.* geyser.

Geißel, -n, *n.f.* whip, scourge.

geißeln, *vb.* flagellate, scourge.

Geist, -er, *n.m.* mind, spirit; ghost; **(Heiliger G.)** Holy Spirit, Ghost.

geistesabwesend, *adj.* absent-minded.

Geistesgegenwart, *n.f.* presence of mind.

geistesgestört, *adj.* deranged.

Geisteswissenschaften, *n.pl.* arts.

geistig, *adj.* mental, spiritual.

geistlich, *adj.* ecclesiastic(al).

Geistlich-, *n.m.* minister, clergyman.

Geistlichkeit, *n.f.* clergy.

geistlos, *adj.* inane, vacuous.

geistreich, *adj.* bright, witty.

geisttötend, *adj.* dull.

Geiz, -e, *n.m.* avarice.

Geizhals, ⸚e, *n.m.* miser.

geizig, *adj.* avaricious, miserly.

Geklap'per, *n.nt.* clatter.

Gekrit'zel, *n.nt.* scribbling.

gekün'stelt, *adj.* contrived.

Geläch'ter, *n.nt.* laughter.

Gela'ge, -, *n.nt.* banquet.

gelähmt', *adj.* crippled.

Gelän'de, -, *n.nt.* terrain.

Gelän'der, -, *n.nt.* railing, banister.

gelan'gen, *vb.* reach, get to.

gelas'sen, *adj.* placid, composed.

Gelati'ne, -n, *n.f.* gelatine.

geläu'fig, *adj.* familiar, fluent.

Geläu'figkeit, *n.f.* fluency.

gelaunt', *adj.* (gut g.) in good humor.

gelb, *adj.* yellow.

gelbbraun, *adj.* tan.

Geld, -er, *n.nt.* money.

Geldbeutel, -, *n.m.* purse.

geldlich, *adj.* monetary.

Geldschein, -, *n.m.* bill.

Gel'schrank, ⸚e, *n.m.* safe.

Geldstrafe, -n, *n.f.* fine; (zu einer G. verurteilen) fine.

Geldwechsler, -, *n.m.* money-changer.

Gelee', -s, *n.nt.* jelly.

gele'gen, *adj.* situated; opportune.

Gele'genheit, -en, *n.f.* occasion, chance.

gele'gentlich, *adj.* occasional.

Gelehr'samkeit, *n.f.* erudition, scholarship.

gelehrt', *adj.* learned, erudite.

Gelehr't-, *n.m.&f.* scholar.

Gelei'se, -, *n.nt.* track.

Geleit', *n.nt.* accompaniment; (freies G.) safe conduct.

Geleit'zug, ⸚e, *n.m.* convoy.

gelei'ten, *vb.* escort.

Gelenk', -e, *n.nt.* joint.

gelen'kig, *adj.* supple.

geliebt', *adj.* beloved.

Gelieb'te, -n, *n.f.* beloved; mistress.

gelind', *adj.* mild, light.

gellen, *vb.* shriek.

gellend, *adj.* shrill.

gelo'ben, *vb.* vow, pledge.

gelten*, *vb.* be valid, apply, hold; be intended for; be considered; (das gilt nicht) that's not fair.

Geltung, *n.f.* standing, value.

Gelüb'de, -, *n.nt.* vow.

Gelüst', -e, *n.nt.* lust.

Gemach', -er, *n.nt.* chamber.

gemach', *adv.* slowly, gently.

gemäch'lich, *adj.* leisurely, slow and easy.

Gemahl', -e, *n.m.* husband; consort.

gemäß', *prep.* according to.

gemä'ßigt, *adj.* moderate.

gemein', 1. *adj.* mean, vile, vicious. 2. *adv.* in common.

Gemein'de, -n, *n.f.* community; municipality; congregation.

gemein'gültig, *adj.* generally accepted.

Gemein'platz, ⸚e, *n.m.* platitude.

gemein'sam, *adj.* common, joint.

Gemein'schaft, *n.f.* community, fellowship.

Gemur'mel, -, *n.nt.* murmur.

Gemü'se, -, *n.nt.* vegetable.

Gemüt', -er, *n.nt.* mind, spirit, temper, heart.

gemüt'lich, *adj.* comfortable, homey, genial.

Gemüts'art, -en, *n.f.* temperament.

Gemüts'ruhe, *n.f.* placidity, fussy.

genau', *adj.* accurate, exact; fussy.

Genau'igkeit, -en, *n.f.* accuracy.

geneh'migen, *vb.* grant, approve.

Geneh'migung, -en, *n.f.* permission, license.

geneigt', *adj.* inclined.

General', -e, *n.m.* general.

Genera'tor, -o'ren, *n.m.* generator.

gene'sen*, *vb.* recover.

Gene'sung, *n.f.* convalescence, recovery.

genial', *adj.* ingenious, having genius.

Genialität', *n.f.* ingenuity; genius.

Genie', **-s**, *n.nt.* genius.

genie'ßen*, *vb.* enjoy, relish.

Genitiv, *n.m.* genitive.

Genos'se, **-n**, *n.m.* companion; (derogatory) character.

Genos'senschaft, **-en**, *n.f.* association, co-operative society.

genug', *adj.* enough.

genü'gen, *vb.* be enough, suffice.

genü'gend, *adj.* satisfactory, sufficient.

genüg'sam, *adj.* modest.

Genüg'samkeit, *n.f.* frugality.

Genugtuung, **-en**, *n.f.* satisfaction.

Genuß', **-sse**, *n.m.* enjoyment; relish.

Geograph', **-en**, *n.m.* geographer.

Geographie', *n.f.* geography.

geogra'phisch, *adj.* geographical.

Geometrie', *n.f.* geometry.

geome'trisch, *adj.* geometric.

geord'net, *adj.* orderly.

Gepäck', *n.nt.* luggage, baggage.

Gepäck'träger, **-**, *n.m.* porter.

Gepäck'schein, **-e**, *n.m.* baggage check.

Geplau'der, *n.nt.* chat, small talk.

Geprä'ge, *n.nt.* stamp; character.

Gerad'heit, *n.f.* erectness; directness.

gera'de, **1.** *adj.* straight, even. **2.** *adv.* just; (**g. aus**) straight ahead.

gera'de·stehen*, *vb.* stand straight; answer for.

geradezu', *adv.* downright.

Gerät', *n.nt.* tool, appliance, utensil.

Geratewohl', *n.* (**aufs G.**) at random, haphazardly.

geraum', *adj.* considerable.

geräu'mig, *adj.* spacious.

Geräusch', **-e**, *n.nt.* noise.

geräusch'los, *adj.* noiseless.

gerben, *vb.* tan.

gerecht', *adj.* just, fair.

Gerech'tigkeit, *n.f.* justice.

Gere'de, *n.nt.* chatter; (**ins G. bringen**) make someone the talk of the town.

gereift', *adj.* mellow.

gereizt', *adj.* irritated, edgy.

Gereizt'heit, *n.f.* irritability.

gereu'en, *vb.* repent, regret.

Gericht', **-e**, *n.nt.* court, bar, tribunal; (food) course; (**Jüngstes G.**) doomsday, judgment day.

gericht'lich, *adj.* legal, judicial, forensic.

Gerichts'barkeit, *n.f.* jurisdiction.

Gerichts'gebäude, **-**, *n.nt.* courthouse.

Gerichts'saal, **-säle**, *n.m.* courtroom.

Gerichts'verhandlung, **-en**, *n.f.* court proceedings, trial.

gerie'ben, *adj.* cunning, sly.

gering', *adj.* slight, slim.

gering'fügig, *adj.* negligible, petty.

gering'·achten, *vb.* look down upon.

gering'·schätzen, *vb.* hold in low esteem.

gering'schätzig, *adj.* disparaging, derogatory.

gerin'nen*, *vb.* curdle, clot, coagulate.

Gerip'pe, **-**, *n.nt.* skeleton.

geris'sen, *adj.* shrewd.

Germa'ne, **-n**, **-n**, *n.m.* Teuton.

germa'nisch, *adj.* Germanic.

gern, *adv.* gladly, readily; (**g. haben***) like, be fond of; (**g. tun***) like to do.

Gerste, **-n**, *n.f.* barley.

Gerstenkorn, **-er**, *n.nt.* sty.

Geruch', **-e**, *n.m.* smell, odor, scent.

Gerücht', **-e**, *n.nt.* rumor.

geru'hen, *vb.* deign.

Gerüst', **-e**, *n.nt.* scaffold, scaffolding.

gesamt', *adj.* total.

Gesamt'heit, *n.f.* entirety.

Gesandt'·, *n.m.* ambassador, envoy.

Gesandt'schaft, **-en**, *n.f.* legation.

Gesang', -̈e, *n.m.* song, chant.
Gesang'buch, -̈er, *n.nt.* hymnal.
Geschäft', -e, *n.nt.* business, deal; shop, store.
geschäf'tig, *adj.* busy.
Geschäf'tigkeit, -en, *n.f.* bustle.
Geschäfts'mann, -̈er *or* -leute, *n.m.* businessman.
geschäfts'mäßig, *adj.* businesslike.
Geschäfts'viertel, -, *n.nt.* downtown, business section.
gesche'hen*, *vb.* occur, happen.
Gescheh'nis, -se, *n.nt.* happening, occurrence.
gescheit', *adj.* bright, clever.
Geschenk', -e, *n.nt.* present.
Geschich'te, -n, *n.f.* story; history.
Geschick', *n.nt.* skill.
Geschick'lichkeit, -en, *n.f.* dexterity, facility.
geschickt', *adj.* skillful, clever, deft.
Geschirr', -e, *n.nt.* dishes; harness.
Geschlecht', -er, *n.nt.* genus, sex; gender; lineage, family.
geschlecht'lich, *adj.* sexual.
Geschmack', -̈e, *n.m.* taste, flavor.
geschmack'los, *adj.* tasteless; in bad taste.
geschmei'dig, *adj.* lithe.
Geschöpf', -e, *n.nt.* creature.
Geschoß', -sse, *n.nt.* missile, projectile.
Geschrei', *n.nt.* clamor.
Geschütz', -e, *n.nt.* gun.
Geschwa'der, -, *n.nt.* squadron.
Geschwätz', *n.nt.* idle talk, babble.
geschwät'zig, *adj.* talkative, gossipy.
geschwind', *adj.* swift.
Geschwin'digkeit, -en, *n.f.* speed, velocity.
Geschwin'digkeitsgrenze, -n, *n.f.* speed limit.
Geschwo'ren-, *n.m.&f.* juror; (*pl.*) jury.
Geschwulst', -̈e, *n.nt.* swelling, growth.

Geschwür', -e, *n.nt.* abscess, ulcer.
geseg'net, *adj.* blessed.
Gesel'le, -n, -n, *n.m.* journeyman; fellow.
gesel'len, *vb.* (si h g.) join.
gesel'lig, *adj.* sociable, gregarious.
Gesell'schaft, -en, *n.f.* society; company; party.
Gesell'schafter n, -nen, *n.f.* companion.
gesell'schaftlich, *adj.* social.
Gesell'schaftskleidung, -en, *n.f.* evening dress, dress clothes.
Gesell'schaftsreise, -n, *n.f.* group tour.
Gesetz', -e, *n.nt.* law, act.
Gesetz'antrag, -̈e, *n.m.* bill.
gesetz'gebend, *adj.* legislative.
Gesetz'geber, -, *n.m.* legislator.
Gesetz'gebung, *n.f.* legislation.
gesetz'lich, *adj.* lawful, legal.
gesetz'los, *adj.* lawless.
gesetz'mäßig, *adj.* legal.
Gesetz'mäßigkeit, *n.f.* legality.
gesetz'widrig, *adj.* illegal, unlawful.
Gesicht', -er, *n.nt.* face.
Geichts'ausdruck, -̈e, *n.m.* facial expression, mien.
Gesichts'farbe, -n, *n.f.* complexion.
Gesichts'kreis, *n.m.* horizon.
Gesichts'punkt, -e, *n.m.* point of view, aspect.
Gesichts'massage, -n, *n.f.* facial.
Gesichts'zug, -̈e, *n.m.* feature.
Gesin'del, *n.nt.* rabble.
gesinnt', *adj.* (g. sein) be of a mind, be disposed.
Gesin'nung, -en, *n.f.* attitude, way of thinking, views.
gesit'tet, *adj.* well-mannered, civilized.
gespannt', *adj.* tense; eager to know, curious.
Gespenst', -er, *n.nt.* ghost.

Gespie'le, -n, -n, *n.m.* playmate.

Gespräch', -e, *n.nt.* talk, conversation.

gesprä'chig, *adj.* talkative.

Gestalt', -en, *n.f.* figure, form, shape.

gestal'ten, *vb.* form, shape, fashion.

Gestal'tung, -en, *n.f.* formation, fashioning.

Gestam'mel, -, *n.nt.* stammering.

gestän'dig, *adj.* **(g. sein)** make a confession.

Geständ'nis, -se, *n.nt.* confession, avowal.

Gestank', *n.m.* stench.

gestat'ten, *vb.* permit.

Geste, -n, *n.f.* gesture.

geste'hen*, *vb.* confess, avow.

Gestein', *n.nt.* rock.

Gestell', -e, *n.nt.* stand, rack, frame.

gestern, *adv.* yesterday.

gestikulie'ren, *vb.* gesticulate.

Gestirn', -e, *n.nt.* star; constellation.

Gestirns'bahn, -en, *n.f.* orbit.

Gestrüpp', *n.nt.* scrub, brush.

Gesuch', -e, *n.nt.* application, petition, request.

gesucht', *adj.* far-fetched, contrived.

gesund', *adj.* healthy, sound, wholesome.

Gesund'heit, *n.f.* health, fitness; **(geistige G.)** sanity.

Gesund'heitsattest, -e, *n.nt.* certificate of health.

Gesund'heitswesen, *n.nt.* sanitation.

gesund'heitsschädlich, *adj.* **unhealthy.**

gesun'den, *vb.* recover.

Gesun'dung, *n.f.* recovery.

Getö'se, *n.nt.* uproar.

Getränk', -e, *n.nt.* drink, beverage; **(alkoholfreies G.)** soft drink.

getrau'en, *vb.* **(sich g.)** dare.

Getrei'de, *n.nt.* grain, cereal.

getrennt', *adj.* separate.

getreu', *adj.* faithful.

Getrie'be, -n, *n.nt.* gear.

getrost', *adv.* confidently.

Getu'e, *n.nt.* affectation, goings-on.

geübt', *adj.* experienced.

Gewächs', -e, *n.nt.* growth.

gewagt', *adj.* daring, hazardous.

Gewähr', *n.f.* guarantee.

gewäh'ren, *vb.* grant.

gewähr'leisten, *vb.* warrant, guarantee.

Gewahr'sam, *n.m.* custody.

Gewalt', -en, *n.f.* force, power.

Gewalt'herrschaft, *n.f.* despotism.

gewal'tig, *adj.* powerful, tremendous.

gewalt'sam, *adj.* forcible, violent.

gewalt'tätig, *adj.* violent.

Gewalt'tätigkeit, -en, *n.f.* violence.

Gewand', :er, *n.nt.* garb, garment.

gewandt', *adj.* facile, versatile.

Gewandt'heit, -en, *n.f.* deftness.

gewär'tig, *adv.* **(g. sein)** be prepared.

Gewäs'ser, *n.nt.* waters.

Gewe'be, -, *n.nt.* tissue, texture.

Gewehr', -e, *n.nt.* rifle, gun.

Gewer'be, -, *n.nt.* trade, business.

Gewerk'schaft, -en, *n.f.* labor union.

Gewicht', -e, *n.nt.* weight.

gewiegt', *adj.* crafty.

gewillt', *adj.* willing.

Gewinn', -e, *n.m.* gain, profit.

gewinn'bringend, *adj.* lucrative.

gewin'nen*, *vb.* win, gain.

Gewin'ner, -, *n.m.* winner.

gewinn'süchtig, *adj.* mercenary, greedy.

Gewirr', *n.nt.* tangle, confusion.

gewiß', *adj.* certain.

Gewis'sen, -, *n.nt.* conscience.

gewis'senhaft, *adj.* conscientious.

gewis'senlos, *adj.* unprincipled.

Gewis'sensbiß, -sse, *n.m.* remorse, qualms.

gewisserma'ßen, *adv.* so to speak, as it were.

Gewiß'heit, -en, *n.f.* certainty.

Gewit'ter, -, *n.nt.* thunderstorm.

gewit'zigt, *adj.* clever.

gewo'gen, *adj.* **(g. sein)** be disposed towards.

gewöh'nen, *vb.* accustom; **(sich g. an)** become accustomed to.

Gewohn'heit, -en, *n.f.* habit, custom, practice.

gewohn'heitsmäßig, *adj.* customary, habitual.

gewöhn'lich, *adj.* ordinary, usual, regular; common, vulgar.

gewohnt', *adj.* accustomed.

Gewöl'be, -, *n.nt.* vaulting, vault.

Gewühl', *n.nt.* shuffle, melee.

gewun'den, *adj.* coiled; sinuous.

Gewürz', -e, *n.nt.* spice, condiment, seasoning.

Gewürz'kraut, ⸚er, *n.nt.* herb.

Gezei'ten, *n.pl.* tide.

gezie'men, *vb.* be proper, befit.

Gicht, -en, *n.f.* gout, arthritis.

Giebel, -, *n.m.* gable.

Gier, *n.f.* greed(iness).

gierig, *adj.* greedy.

gießen*, *vb.* pour; cast (metal).

Gift, -e, *n.nt.* poison.

giftig, *adj.* poisonous.

Gilde, -n, *n.f.* guild.

Gin, -s, *n.m.* gin.

Gipfel, -, *n.m.* peak.

gipfeln, *vb.* culminate.

Gips, -e, *n.m.* gypsum, plaster.

Giraf'fe, -n, *n.f.* giraffe.

Girant', -en, -en, *n.m.* endorser.

Girat', -en, -en, *n.m.* endorsee.

girie'ren, *vb.* endorse (a check, note, etc.), put into circulation.

Giro, -s, *n.nt.* endorsement, circulation (of endorsed notes, etc.).

Gischt, -e, *n.m.* spray, foam.

Gitar're, -n, *n.f.* guitar.

Gitter, -, *n.nt.* grating; gate.

Gitterwerk, -e, *n.nt.* grating.

glaciert', *adj.* glacé.

Glanz, *n.m.* shine, sheen, gloss; brilliance, splendor.

glänzen, *vb.* shine.

glänzend, *adj.* shiny, brilliant.

Glas, ⸚er, *n.nt.* glass.

Glaser, -, *n.m.* glazier.

gläsern, *adj.* made of glass.

glasie'ren, *vb.* glaze.

glasig, *adj.* glassy.

Glasscheibe, -n, *n.f.* pane.

Glasur, -en, *n.f.* glaze.

Glasware, -n, *n.f.* glassware.

glatt, *adj.* smooth, slippery; outright.

glätten, *vb.* smooth.

Glatzkopf, ⸚e, *n.m.* bald head.

Glaube(n), -, *n.m.* belief, faith.

glauben, *vb.* believe.

Glaubensbekenntnis, -se, *n.nt.* confession of faith; creed.

glaubhaft, *adj.* believable.

gläubig, *adj.* believing, devout.

Gläubig-, *n.m.&f.* believer; creditor.

glaublich, *adj.* credible.

glaubwürdig, *adj.* credible.

Glaubwürdigkeit, *n.f.* credibility.

gleich, 1. *adj.* equal, same, even. **2.** *adv.* right away.

gleichaltig, *adj.* of the same age.

gleichartig, *adj.* similar, homogeneous.

gleichberechtigt, *adj.* having equal rights.

Gleichberechtigung, -en, *n.f.* equality of rights.

gleichen*, *vb.* be like, equal, resemble.

gleichfalls, *adv.* likewise.

gleichförmig, *adj.* uniform.

gleichgesinnt, adj. like-minded.

gleichgestellt, adj. coordinate.

Gleichgewicht, n.nt. equilibrium.

gleichgültig, adj. indifferent.

Gleichgültigkeit, n.f. indifference.

Gleichheit, n.f. equality.

gleich·machen, vb. equalize.

Gleichmaß, n.nt. proportion, symmetry.

gleichmäßig, adj. even, regular.

Gleichmut, n.m. equanimity.

gleichmütig, adj. even-tempered.

Gleichnis, -se, n.nt. simile, parable.

gleichsam, adv. as it were.

gleichseitig, adj. equilateral.

gleich·setzen, vb. equate.

Gleichstrom, -e, n.m. direct current.

gleich·tun*, vb. do like, match up to.

Gleichung, -en, n.f. equation.

gleichwertig, adj. equivalent.

gleichwie, adv.&conj. just as.

gleichwohl, adv. nevertheless.

gleichzeitig, adj. simultaneous.

Gleis, -e, n.nt. track.

gleiten*, vb. glide, slide, slip.

Gletscher, -, n.m. glacier.

Gletscherspalte, -n, n.f. crevasse.

Glied, -er, n.nt. limb; link.

gliedern, vb. segment, classify.

Gliederung, -en, n.f. arrangement, structure.

Gliedmaßen, n.pl. limbs, extremities.

glitzern, vb. glitter.

Globus, -ben (-busse), n.m. globe.

Glocke, -n, n.f. bell.

Glockenschlag, -e, n.m. stroke of the clock.

Glockenspiel, -e, n.nt. chimes, carillon.

Glockenturm, -e, n.m. belfry, bell-tower.

Glorie, -n, n.f. glory.

Glorienschein, -e, n.m. halo.

glorreich, adj. glorious.

glotzen, vb. stare.

Glück, n.nt. happiness, luck.

gluckern, vb. gurgle.

glücklich, adj. happy.

glücklicherweise, adj. fortunately.

glückselig, adj. blissful.

Glückseligkeit, -en, n.f. bliss.

glucksen, vb. gurgle.

Glücksfall, -e, n.m. stroke of luck.

Glücksspiel, -e, n.nt. gamble; gambling.

Glücksspieler, -, n.m. gambler.

Glückwunsch, -e, n.m. congratulation.

Glühbirne, -n, n.f. electric light bulb.

glühen, vb. glow.

glühend, adj. glowing, incandescent; ardent.

Glut, -en, n.f. heat, live coals; ardor, passion.

Glyzerin', n.nt. glycerine.

G.m.b.H., abbr. (= Gesell'-schaft mit beschränk'ter Haftung) incorporated, inc.

Gnade, n.f. grace, mercy.

gnadenreich, adj. merciful.

gnädig, adj. gracious, merciful; **(g.e Frau)** madam.

Gold, n.nt. gold.

Goldbarren, -, n.m. bullion.

golden, adj. golden.

Goldfisch, -e, n.m. goldfish.

goldig, adj. darling, cute.

Goldschmied, -e, n.m. goldsmith.

Golf, -e, n.m. gulf, bay.

Golf, n.nt. golf.

Golfplatz, -e, n.m. golf course.

Gondel, -n, n.f. gondola.

gönnen, vb. grant, not begrudge; **(sich g.)** allow oneself; **(das gönne ich ihm!)** that serves him right!

Gör, -en, n.nt. brat, girl.

Goril'la, -s, n.m. gorilla.

Gosse, -n, n.f. gutter, drain.

Gotik, *n.f.* Gothic architecture.

gotisch, *adj.* Gothic.

Gott, ⸚er, *n.m.* god, deity.

gottähnlich, *adj.* godlike.

Götterdämmerung, *n.f.* twilight of the gods.

Gottesacker, ⸚, *n.m.* cemetery.

Gottesdienst, -e, *n.m.* (church) service.

Gottesgabe, -, *n.f.* god send.

Gotteshaus, ⸚er, *n.nt.* church.

Gotteslästerung, -en, *n.f.* blasphemy.

Gottheit, -en, *n.f.* deity, divinity.

Göttin, -nen, *n.f.* goddess.

göttlich, *adj.* godly, divine.

gottlob', *interj.* praise God.

gottlos, *adj.* godless.

Götze, -n, -n, *n.m.* idol, false god.

Götzenbild, -er, *n.nt.* idol.

Götzendienst, -e, *n.m.* idolatry.

Gouvernan'te, -n, *n.f.* governess.

Gouverneur', -e, *n.m.* governor.

Gouverneurs'amt, ⸚er, *n.nt.* governorship.

Grab, ⸚er, *n.nt.* grave.

graben*, *vb.* dig.

Graben, ⸚, *n.m.* trench, ditch.

Grablegung, -en, *n.f.* burial.

Grabmal, ⸚er, *n.nt.* tomb(stone).

Grabschrift, -en, *n.f.* epitaph.

Grabstein, -e, *n.m.* gravestone.

Grad, -e, *n.m.* degree.

Graf, -en, -en, *n.m.* count.

Gräfin, -nen, *n.f.* countess.

Grafschaft, -en, *n.f.* county.

Gram, *n.m.* grief, care.

grämen, *vb.* (sich g.) grieve, fret.

Gramm, -, *n.nt.* gram.

Gramma'tik, -en, *n.f.* grammar.

Gramma'tiker, -, *n.m.* grammarian.

gramma'tisch, *adj.* grammatical.

Grammophon', -e, *n.nt.* phonograph.

Grammophon'platte, -n, *n.f.* phonograph record.

Granat', -e, *n.m.* garnet.

Grana'te, -n, *n.f.* grenade.

Granit', *n.m.* granite.

granulie'ren, *vb.* granulate.

Graphiker, -, *n.m.* illustrator, commercial artist.

graphisch, *adj.* graphic.

Gras, ⸚er, *n.nt.* grass.

grasartig, *adj.* grasslike, grassy.

grasen, *vb.* graze.

grasig, *adj.* grassy.

gräßlich, *adj.* hideous.

Grat, -e, *n.m.* ridge.

Gräte, -n, *n.f.* bone (of a fish).

gratis, *adj.* gratis.

gratulie'ren, *vb.* congratulate.

grau, *adj.* gray.

Grauen, *n.nt.* horror.

grauenhaft, *adj.* ghastly.

grausam, *adj.* cruel.

grausig, *adj.* lurid.

Graveur', -e, *n.m.* engraver.

gravie'ren, *vb.* engrave.

gravitie'ren, *vb.* gravitate.

Grazie, -n, *n.f.* grace, charm.

graziös', *adj.* graceful.

greifbar, *adj.* tangible.

greifen*, *vb.* seize, grasp.

Greis, -e, *n.m.* old man.

Greisenalter, -, *n.nt.* old age.

Greisin, -nen, *n.f.* old woman.

grell, *adj.* garish, gaudy, shrill.

Grenze, -n, *n.f.* limit, border, boundary.

grenzen, *vb.* (g. an) border on.

grenzenlos, *adj.* boundless.

Greuel, -, *n.m.* horror, outrage.

greulich, *adj.* horrible.

Grieche, -n, -n, *n.m.* Greek.

Griechenland, *n.nt.* Greece.

griechisch, *adj.* Greek.

Griesgram, -e, *n.m.* grouch.

griesgrämig, *adj.* sullen.

Grieß, -e, *n.m.* coarse meal; gravel.

Griff, -e, *n.m.* grasp, grip, handle.

Grill, -s, *n.m.* grill; grill-room.

Grille, -n, *n.f.* cricket; whim.

grillen, *vb.* broil.

grillenhaft, *adj.* whimsical.

Grimas'se, -n, *n.f.* grimace.

Grimm, *n.m.* anger.

grimmig, *adj.* angry.

grinsen, *vb.* grin.

Grinsen, -, *n.nt.* grin.

Grippe, -n, *n.f.* grippe, influenza.

grob(-), *adj.* coarse, rough, crude.

Grobian, -e, *n.m.* boor, ruffian.

Grog, -s, *n.m.* grog.

Groll, *n.m.* anger, grudge.

grollen, *vb.* be angry, bear a grudge.

Gros, -se, *n.nt.* gross.

Groschen, -, *n.m.* ten pfennig piece; 1/100 of an Austrian schilling.

groß(-), *adj.* big, tall, great.

großartig, *adj.* grand, magnificent.

Großbritan'ien, *n.nt.* Great Britain.

Größe, -n, *n.f.* size, height, greatness.

Großeltern, *n.pl.* grandparents.

großenteils, *adv.* in large part, largely.

Großhandel, *n.m.* wholesale trade.

großherzig, *adj.* magnanimous.

großjährig, *adj.* of age.

Großmacht, ⸚e, *n.f.* major power.

Großmut, *n.m.* magnanimity, generosity.

großmütig, *adj.* magnanimous, generous.

Großmutter, ⸚, *n.f.* grandmother.

großsprecherisch, *adj.* boastful.

Großstaat, -en, *n.m.* major power.

Großstadt, ⸚e, *n.f.* large city, metropolis.

Großstädter, -e, *n.m.* big city person.

größtenteils, *adv.* for the most part, mostly.

groß-tun*, *vb.* act big, boast.

Großvater, ⸚, *n.m.* grandfather.

groß-ziehen*, *vb.* bring up, raise.

großzügig, *adj.* on a grand scale, generous, broadminded.

grotesk', *adj.* grotesque.

Grotte, -n, *n.f.* grotto.

Grube, -n, *n.f.* pit; mine.

grübeln, *vb.* brood.

Grubenarbeiter, -, *n.m.* miner.

Gruft, ⸚e, *n.f.* crypt, vault.

grün, *adj.* green.

Grund, -e, *n.m.* ground, bottom, basis, reason; **(G. und Boden)** land, real estate.

Grundbegriff, -e, *n.m.* basic concept.

Grundbesitz, -e, *n.m.* landed property.

Grundbesitzer, -, *n.m.* landholder.

gründen, *vb.* found.

Grundgesetz, -e, *n.nt.* basic law; constitution.

Grundlage, -n, *n.f.* basis.

grundlegend, *adj.* fundamental.

gründlich, *adj.* thorough.

Grundlinie, -n, *n.f.* base.

grundlos, *adj.* bottomless; unfounded.

Grundriß, -sse, *n.m.* outline, sketch.

Grundsatz, ⸚e, *n.m.* principle.

grundsätzlich, *adj.* fundamental, on principle.

Grundschule, -n, *n.f.* elementary school.

Grundstoff, -e, *n.m.* basic material.

Grundstück, -e, *n.nt.* lot.

Gründung, -en, *n.f.* founding, establishment.

grunzen, *vb.* grunt.

Gruppe, -n, *n.f.* group.

gruppie'ren, *vb.* group.

gruselig, *adj.* uncanny, creepy.

Gruß, ⸚e, *n.m.* greeting; salute.

grüßen, *vb.* greet; salute.

gucken, *vb.* look.

gültig, *adj.* valid.

Gültigkeit, *n.f.* validity.

Gummi, -s, *n.m.* rubber; eraser.

Gummi, -s, *n.nt.* gum.

gummiartig, *adj.* gummy.

Gummiband, -er, *n.nt.* elastic (band).

Gummischuhe, *n.pl.* overshoes, galoshes, rubbers.

Gunst, -e, *n.f.* favor.

günstig, *adj.* favorable.

Günstling, -e, *n.m.* favorite.

Gurgel, -n, *n.f.* throat, gullet.

gurgeln, *vb.* gargle.

Gurke, -n, *n.f.* cucumber; (saure G.) pickle.

Gurt, -e, *n.m.* girth, harness.

Gürtel, -, *n.m.* belt, girdle.

gürten, *vb.* gird.

Guß, -sse, *n.m.* downpour; frosting; casting.

Gußstein, -e, *n.m.* sink, drain.

gut, 1. *adj.* good. **2.** *adv.* well.

Gut, -er, *n.nt.* property; landed estate; (*pl.*) goods.

Gutachten, -, *n.nt.* (expert) opinion, (legal) advice.

gutaussehend, *adj.* good-looking.

Gutdünken, *n.nt.* opinion, discretion.

Güte, *n.f.* kindness; quality, purity.

gutgläubig, *adj.* credulous.

Guthaben, -, *n.nt.* credit; assets.

gut-heißen*, *vb.* approve.

gutherzig, *adj.* good-hearted.

gütig, *adj.* kind, friendly, gracious.

gütlich, *adj.* kind, friendly.

gut-machen, *vb.* make good; (wieder g.) make amends for.

gutmütig, *adj.* good-natured.

gut-schreiben*, *vb.* credit.

Gutschrift, -en, *n.f.* credit.

Gymna'sium, -ien, *n.nt.* secondary school preparing for university.

Gymnas'tik, *n.f.* gymnastics.

gymnas'tisch, *adj.* gymnastic.

H

ha, *abbr.* (= Hektar') hectare.

Haar, -e, *n.nt.* hair.

haarig, *adj.* hairy.

Haarklammer, -n, *n.f.* bobby pin.

Haarnadel, -n, *n.f.* hairpin.

haarscharf, *adj.* very sharp.

Haarschneiden, *n.nt.* haircut.

Haarschnitt, -e, *n.m.* (style of) haircut.

Habe, -n *n.f.* property; (Hab und Gut) goods and chattels, all one's property.

haben*, *vb.* have.

Haben, *n.nt.* credit; (Soll und H.) debit and credit.

Habgier, *n.f.* greed.

habgierig, *adj.* greedy.

Habseligkeiten, *n.pl.* belongings.

Habsucht, *n.f.* greed.

habsüchtig, *adj.* greedy.

Hacke, -n, *n.f.* hoe, pick; heel.

hacken, *vb.* chop.

Hader, *n.m.* quarrel, strife.

hadern, *vb.* quarrel.

Hafen, -, *n.m.* harbor, port.

Hafenstadt, -e, *n.f.* seaport.

Hafer, *n.m.* oats.

Hafergrütze, *n.f.* oatmeal.

Haft, *n.f.* arrest, detention.

haftbar, *adj.* liable.

Haftbefehl, -e, *n.m.* warrant.

haften, *vb.* stick, adhere; be responsible.

Haftpflicht, -en, *n.f.* liability.

Hagel, *n.m.* hail.

Hagelwetter, -, *n.nt.* hailstorm.

hager, *adj.* gaunt.

Hahn, ꞏe, *n.m.* rooster; faucet.

Haifisch, -e, *n.m.* shark.

Hain, -e, *n.m.* grove.

Haken, -, *n.m.* hook.

halb, *adj.* half.

halber, *prep.* because of, for the sake of.

halbieren, *vb.* halve.

Halbinsel, -n, *n.f.* peninsula.

halbjährlich, *adj.* semiannual.

Halbkreis, -e, *n.m.* semicircle.

Halbkugel, -n, *n.f.* hemisphere.

Halbmesser, -, *n.m.* radius.

Halbschuhe, *n.pl.* low shoes, oxfords.

halbwegs, *adv.* halfway.

Hälfte, -n, *n.f.* half.

Halfter, -, *n.nt.* halter.

Halle, -n, *n.f.* hall.

hallen, *vb.* sound, echo.

Halm, -e, *n.m.* blade, stalk.

hallo, *interj.* hello.

Hals, ꞏe, *n.m.* neck.

Halsband, ꞏer, *n.nt.* necklace.

halsbrecherisch, *adj.* breakneck.

Halskette, -n, *n.f.* necklace.

Halsschmerzen, *n.pl.* sore throat.

halsstarrig, *adj.* obstinate.

Halstuch, ꞏer, *n.nt.* kerchief.

Halsweh, *n.nt.* sore throat.

halt, *interj.* halt.

halt, *adv.* after all, I think.

Halt, -e, *n.m.* halt; hold, support.

haltbar, *adj.* tenable.

halten*, *vb.* hold, keep, stop; (**h. für**) consider as.

Halter, -, *n.m.* holder.

Haltestelle, -n, *n.f.* stop.

halt-machen, *vb.* halt, stop.

Haltung, -en, *n.f.* attitude, posture.

Hammelbraten, -, *n.m.* roast mutton.

Hammelfleisch, *n.nt.* mutton.

Hammelkeule, -n, *n.f.* leg of mutton.

Hammer, ꞏ, *n.m.* hammer.

hämmern, *vb.* hammer.

Hämorrhoi'de, -n, *n.f.* hemorrhoid.

hamstern, *vb.* hoard.

Hand, ꞏe, *n.f.* hand.

Handarbeit, -en, *n.f.* manual labor; needlework.

Handbremse, -n, *n.f.* hand brake, emergency brake.

Handbuch, ꞏer, *n.nt.* handbook, manual.

Händedruck, *n.m.* clasp (of hands).

Handel, *n.m.* trade, commerce.

handeln, *vb.* act, trade, deal; (**es handelt sich um . . .**) it is a question of . . .

Handelsgeist, *n.m.* commercialism.

Handelsmarine, *n.f.* merchant marine.

Handelsreisend-, *n.m.* traveling salesman.

handfest, *adj.* sturdy.

Handfläche, -n, *n.f.* palm.

Handgelenk, -e, *n.nt.* wrist.

handhaben, *vb.* handle, manage.

Handikap, -s, *n.nt.* handicap.

Handlanger, -, *n.m.* handy man, general worker.

Händler, -, *n.m.* dealer, trader.

handlich, *adj.* handy.

Handlung, -en, *n.f.* action; plot.

Handschelle, -n, *n.f.* handcuff.

Handschrift, -en, *n.f.* handwriting.

Handschuh, -e, *n.m.* glove.

Handtasche, -n, *n.f.* pocketbook.

Handtuch, ꞏer, *n.nt.* towel.

Handvoll, -, *n.f.* handful.

Handwerk, *n.nt.* handicraft, handiwork.

Handwerker, -, *n.m.* craftsman, artisan.

Hang, ꞏe, *n.m.* slope; inclination.

Hängebrücke, -n, *n.f.* suspension bridge.

Hängematte, -n, *n.f.* hammock.

hängen*, *vb.* (*intr.*) hang, be

suspended; **(an jemandem h.)** be attached to someone.

hängen(*), *vb.* *(tr.)* hang, suspend.

Hans, *n.m.* Hans; **(H. Dampf in allen Gassen)** jack-of-all-trades.

hänseln, *vb.* tease.

hantie'ren, *vb.* handle, manipulate.

hapern, *vb.* get stuck, be wrong.

Happen, -, *n.m.* morsel.

Harfe, -n, *n.f.* harp.

Harke, -n, *n.f.* rake.

harken, *vb.* rake.

Harm, *n.m.* grief.

harmlos, *adj.* harmless.

Harmonie', -i'en, *n.f.* harmony.

Harmo'nika, -s, *n.f.* harmonica.

harmo'nisch, *adj.* harmonious.

harmonisie'ren, *vb.* harmonize.

Harn, *n.m.* urine.

Harnblase, -n, *n.f.* (urinary) bladder.

harnen, *vb.* urinate.

Harnisch, -e, *n.m.* harness, armor.

Harpu'ne, -n, *n.f.* harpoon.

hart (˙), *adj.* hard, severe.

Härte, -n, *n.f.* hardness, severity.

härten, *vb.* harden, temper.

hartgekocht, *adj.* hard-boiled.

hartherzig, *adj.* hard-hearted.

hartnäckig, *adj.* stubborn.

Harz, -e, *n.nt.* resin, rosin.

haschen, *vb.* catch, snatch.

Hase, -n, -n, *n.m.* hare.

Haselnuß, -sse, *n.f.* hazelnut.

Hasenbraten, -, *n.m.* roast hare.

Haspe, -n, *n.f.* hasp, hinge.

Haß, *n.m.* hatred.

hassen, *vb.* hate.

häßlich, *adj.* ugly.

Häßlichkeit, *n.f.* ugliness.

Hast, *n.f.* haste, hurry.

hasten, *vb.* hasten, hurry.

hastig, *adj.* hasty.

Haube, -n, *n.f.* hood.

Hauch, -e, *n.m.* breath.

hauchdünn, *adj.* extremely thin.

hauen*, *vb.* hew, chop, strike, spank; **(sich h.)** fight.

Haufen, -, *n.m.* pile, heap; crowd; large amount.

häufen, *vb.* heap.

häufig, *adj.* frequent.

Häufigkeit, -en, *n.f.* frequency.

Häufung, -en, *n.f.* accumulation.

Haupt, ˙er, *n.nt.* head.

Hauptamt, ˙er, *n.nt.* main office.

Hauptbahnhof, ˙e, *n.m.* main railroad station.

Häuptling, -e, *n.m.* chieftain.

Hauptmann, -leute, *n.m.* captain.

Hauptquartier, -e, *n.nt.* headquarters.

Hauptsache, -n, *n.f.* main, essential thing; principal matter.

hauptsächlich, *adj.* main, principal.

Hauptstadt, ˙e, *n.f.* capital.

Hauptwort, ˙er, *n.nt.* noun, substantive.

Haus, *n.nt.* house.

Hausangestellt-, *n.m.&f.* servant.

Hausarbeit, -en, *n.f.* housework.

Hausaufgabe, -n, *n.f.* homework.

hausbacken, *adj.* homemade; plain.

hausen, *vb.* dwell, reside.

Häuserblock, -s, *n.m.* block.

Hausfrau, -en, *n.f.* housewife.

Haushalt, -e, *n.m.* household.

haus-halten*, *vb.* economize.

Haushälterin, -nen, *n.f.* housekeeper.

Haushaltung, *n.f.* housekeeping.

hausie'ren, *vb.* peddle.

Hausie'rer, -, *n.m.* peddler.

häuslich, *adj.* domestic.

Hausmeister, -, *n.m.* janitor.

Hausrat, _m._ household goods.

Hausschuh, -e, _n.m._ slipper.

Haut, -e, _n.f._ skin, hide.

hautstraffend, _adj._ astringent.

Hebamme, -n, _n.f._ midwife.

Hebel, -, _n.m._ lever.

heben*, _vb._ raise, lift.

Hebräer, -, _n.m._ Hebrew.

hebräisch, _adj._ Hebrew.

hecheln, _vb._ heckle.

Hecht, -e, _n.m._ pike (fish).

Heck, -e, _n.nt._ stern, rear, tail.

Hecke, -n, _n.f._ hedge.

Heer, -e, _n.nt._ army.

Heft, -e, _n.nt._ notebook; handle, hilt.

heften, _vb._ fasten, pin, stitch, tack.

Hefter, -, _n.m._ folder.

heftig, _adj._ vehement.

Heftigkeit, _n.f._ vehemence.

hegen, _vb._ nurture.

Heide, -n, -n, _n.m._ heathen.

Heide, -n, _n.f._ heath.

Heidelbeere, -n, _n.f._ huckleberry.

heidnisch, _adj._ heathen.

heikel, _adj._ ticklish, tricky, delicate.

Heil, _n.nt._ welfare, safety, salvation.

heil, _adj._ whole; well, healed, unhurt.

Heiland, _n.m._ Savior.

Heilbad, -er, _n.nt._ spa.

heilbar, _adj._ curable.

Heilbutt, -e, _n.m._ halibut.

heilen, _vb._ heal, cure.

heilig, _adj._ holy, sacred.

Heilig-, _n.m.&f._ saint.

heiligen, _vb._ hallow, sanctify.

Heiligenschein, -e, _n.m._ halo.

Heiligkeit, _n.f._ holiness, sanctity.

Heiligtum, -er, _n.nt._ sanctuary.

Heiligung, -en, _n.f._ sanctification, consecration.

Heilmittel, -, _n.nt._ remedy, cure.

Heilung, -en, _n.f._ healing, cure.

Heim, -e, _n.nt._ home.

heim, _adv._ home.

Heimat, _n.f._ home (town, country).

Heimatland, -er, _n.nt._ homeland.

heimatlos, _adj._ homeless.

heimatlich, _adj._ native.

Heimchen, -, _n.nt._ cricket.

heimisch, _adj._ domestic, home-like.

heimlich, _adj._ secret.

heim-suchen, _vb._ scourge.

Heimsuchung, -en, _n.f._ scourge.

heimtückisch, _adj._ malicious, treacherous.

heimwärts, _adv._ homeward.

Heimweh, _n.nt._ homesickness.

Heirat, -en, _n.f._ marriage.

heiraten, _vb._ marry.

Heiratsantrag, -e, _n.m._ proposal.

heiser, _adj._ hoarse.

heiß, _adj._ hot.

heissen*, _vb._ be called, be named; mean; call, order.

heiter, _adj._ cheerful; clear.

heizen, _vb._ heat, have the heat on.

Heizkörper, -, _n.m._ radiator.

Heizvorrichtung, -en, _n.f._ heater.

Heizung, -en, _n.f._ heating, heat.

Hektar', -e, _n.m._ hectare.

hektisch, _adj._ hectic.

Hektogramm', -e, _n.nt._ hectogram.

Held, -en, -en, _n.m._ hero.

heldenhaft, _adj._ heroic.

Heldenmut, _n.m._ heroism.

Heldin, -nen, _n.f._ heroine.

helfen*, _vb._ help, aid, assist.

Helfer, -, _n.m._ helper.

Helfershelfer, -, _n.m._ confederate, accomplice.

hell, _adj._ bright, light.

Helligkeit, _n.f._ brightness.

Helm, -e, _n.m._ helmet.

Hemd, -en, _n.nt._ shirt.

hemmen, _vb._ stop, hinder.

Hemmnis, -se, _n.nt._ hindrance, obstacle.

Hemmschuh, -e, _n.m._ brake, drag, skid.

Hemmung, -en, *n.f.* restraint, inhibition.

Henkel, -, *n.m.* handle.

Henna, *n.f.* henna.

Henne, -n, *n.f.* hen.

her, *adv.* towards here; ago.

herab', *adv.* downwards.

herab'-hängen, *vb.* droop.

herab'-lassen, *vb.* let down; **(sich h.)** condescend.

herab'lassend, *adj.* condescending.

Herab'lassung, -en, *n.f.* condescension.

herab'setzen, *vb.* set down, lower, reduce, disparage.

Herab'setzung, -en, *n.f.* reduction, disparagement.

heran', *adv.* up to, toward.

heran'-gehen*, *vb.* walk up to, approach.

heran'-nahen, *vb.* approach, draw near.

heran'wachsen*, *vb.* grow up.

herauf', *adv.* upwards.

heraus', *adv.* out.

heraus'-bringen*, *vb.* bring out, publish.

heraus'-fordern, *vb.* challenge.

heraus'fordernd, *adj.* defiant.

Heraus'forderer, -, *n.m.* challenger.

Heraus'forderung, -en, *n.f.* challenge, defiance.

heraus'-geben*, *vb.* edit, publish.

Heraus'geber, -, *n.m.* editor, publisher.

heraus'-kommen*, *vb.* come out, be published.

heraus'-lassen*, *vb.* let out.

heraus'-putzen, *vb.* dress up

heraus'-stellen, *vb.* put out; **(sich h.)** turn out to be.

heraus'-ziehen*, *vb.* extract.

herb, *adj.* tart, bitter.

herbei', *adv.* toward here.

herbei'-schaffen, *vb.* procure.

Herberge, -n, *n.f.* hostel.

herbergen, *vb.* shelter, lodge.

Herbheit, -en, *n.f.* tartness.

Herbst, -e, *n.m.* fall, autumn.

herbstlich, *adj.* autumnal.

Herd, -e, *n.m.* kitchen stove; hearth.

Herde, -n, *n.f.* herd.

herein', *adv.* in; **(h. !)** come in!

Hergang, "e, *n.m.* course of events.

hergebracht, *adj.* customary.

hergelaufen, *adj.* of uncertain origin.

Hering, -e, *n.m.* herring.

Herkommen, -, *n.nt.* tradition; origin.

Herkömmlich, *adj.* traditional.

Herkunft, "e, *n.f.* origin, extraction.

her-leiten, *vb.* derive.

herme'tisch, *adj.* hermetic.

hernach', *adv.* afterwards.

hernie'der, *adv.* downwards, from above.

Herr, -n, -en, *n.m.* Mr. gentleman, lord, master.

Herrenfriseur, -e, *n.m.* men's barber

Herrenvolk, "er, *nt.* master race.

Herrin, -nen, *n.f.* mistress.

herrisch, *adj.* imperious.

herrlich, *adj.* wonderful, splendid.

Herrlichkeit, *n.f.* glory, magnificence.

Herrschaft, *n.f.* rule, reign; estate.

Herrschaften, *n.pl.* master and mistress of the house; people of high rank; **(meine H.)** ladies and gentlemen.

herrschen, *vb.* rule, reign.

herrschend, *adj.* ruling, prevailing.

Herrscher, -, *n.m.* ruler.

herrschsüchtig, *adj.* imperious, tyrannical.

her-richten, *vb.* set up, arrange.

her-sagen, *b.* recite.

her-stellen, *vb.* make, manufacture.

Herstellung, - n, *n.f.* manufacture.

herü'ber, *adv.* over (towards here).

herum', *adv.* around, about.

herum'·kriegen, *vb.* talk over, win over.

herum'·lungern, *vb.* loaf around.

herum'·nörgeln, *vb.* nag.

herum'·pfuschen, *vb.* tamper.

herum'·schnüffeln, *vb.* pry, snoop.

herum'·stehen*, *vb.* stand around, loiter.

herun'ter, *adv.* down.

herun'tergekommen, *adj.* run-down, down at the heels.

herun'ter·lassen*, *vb.* lower.

herun'ter·machen, *vb.* dress down, tear apart, pan.

hervor', *adv.* forth, forward.

hervor'·brechen*, *vb.* erupt.

hervor'·bringen*, *vb.* bring forth, produce.

hervor'·heben*, *vb.* emphasize.

hervor'·quellen*, *vb.* gush; ooze.

hervor'ragend, *adj.* prominent, outstanding, superb.

hervor'·rufen*, *vb.* evoke; provoke.

hervor'·schießen*, *vb.* spurt.

hervor'·stehen*, *vb.* protrude.

Herz(en), -, *n.nt.* heart.

her·zeigen, *vb.* show.

herzen, *vb.* hug, cuddle.

herzhaft, *adj.* hearty.

herzig, *adj.* lovable, darling.

Herzinfarkt, -e, *n.m.* heart attack.

herzlich, *adj.* cordial, affectionate.

Herzlichkeit, *n.f.* cordiality.

herzlos, *adj.* heartless.

Herzog, ⸚e, *n.m.* duke.

Herzogin, -nen, *n.f.* duchess.

Herzogtum, ⸚er, *n.nt.* dukedom, duchy.

Hetze, -n, *n.f.* rush; agitation, inflammatory talk.

hetzen, *vb.* rush; hound, agitate, rabble-rouse.

Hetzerei', -en, *n.f.* rush; demagoguery.

hetzerisch, *adj.* inflammatory, demagogic.

Hetzredner, -, *n.m.* rabble rouser, demagogue.

Heu, *n.nt.* hay.

Heuchelei', -en, *n.f.* hypocrisy.

heucheln, *vb.* fake, feign; play the hypocrite.

Heuchler, -, *n.m.* hypocrite.

heuchlerisch, *adj.* hypocritical.

heuer, *adv.* this year.

Heugabel, -n, *n.f.* pitchfork.

Heuhaufen, -, *n.m.* haystack.

heulen, *vb.* howl; cry.

heurig, *adj.* of this year.

Heuschnupfen, -, *n.m.* hay fever.

heute, *adv.* today; (**h. abend**) tonight.

heutig, *adj.* today's.

Heuwiese, -n, *n.f.* hayfield.

Hexe, -n, *n.f.* witch.

hexen, *vb.* perform witchcraft; be a magician.

Hexenschuß, *n.m.* lumbago.

Hieb, -e, *n.m.* blow, stroke.

hinie'den, *adv.* here below.

hier, *adv.* here.

hierar'chisch, *adj.* hierarchical.

hierbei, *adv.* hereby.

hierher, *adv.* hither.

hiermit, *adv.* hereby, herewith.

Hilfe, -n, *n.f.* help, aid.

hilfeflehend, *adj.* imploring.

Hilfeleistung, -en, *n.f.* assistance, aid.

hilflos, *adj.* helpless, defenseless.

Hilflosigkeit, *n.f.* helplessness.

hilfreich, *adj.* helpful.

hilfsbedürftig, *adj.* needy.

hilfsbereit, *adj.* cooperative.

Hilfsquelle, -n, *n.f.* resource.

Himbeere, -n, *n.f.* raspberry.

Himmel, -, *n.m.* heaven, sky.

Himmelfahrt, -en, *n.f.* ascension to heaven; (**H. Christi**) Ascension (Day) (40 days after Easter); (**Mariä H.**) Assumption (of the Blessed Virgin) (August 15).

himmelhochjauchzend, *adj.* jubilant.

himmelschreiend, *adj.* scandalous.

Himmelsrichtung, -en, *n.f.* point of the compass, direction.

himmlisch, *adj.* heavenly.

hin, *adv.* to there; gone; (**h. und her**) back and forth; (**h. und wieder**) now and then.

hinab', *prep.* down.

hinaus', *adv.* out.

hinaus'·zögern, *vb.* procrastinate.

Hinblick, *n.m.* aspect. (**in H. auf . . .**) with regard to . . .

hinderlich, *adj.* hindering, inconvenient.

hindern, *vb.* hinder, deter.

Hindernis, -se, *n.nt.* hindrance, obstacle.

hin·deuten, *vb.* point to.

hinein', *adv.* in.

Hingabe, *n.f.* fervency.

hin·geben*, *vb.* give away, up; (**sich h.**) devote oneself; surrender.

Hingebung, *n.f.* devotion.

hingestreckt, *adj.* prostrate.

hin·halten*, *vb.* (*fig.*) delay.

hinken, *vb.* limp.

hin·legen, *vb.* lay down; (**sich h.**) lie down.

hin·purzeln, *vb.* tumble.

hin·reißen*, *vb.* (**sich h. lassen**) let oneself be carried away.

hinreißend, *adj.* captivating, ravishing.

hin·richten, *vb.* execute.

Hinrichtung, -en, *n.f.* execution.

Hinsicht, -en, *n.f.* respect, regard.

hinsichtlich, *prep.* in regard to, regarding, concerning.

hinten, *adv.* behind.

hintenherum', *adv.* from behind; (*fig.*) roundabout, through the back door.

hinter, *prep.* behind, beyond.

hinter-, *adj.* hind, back.

Hintergedanke(n), -, *n.m.* ulterior motive.

hinterge'hen*, *vb.* doublecross.

Hintergrund, ·̈e, *n.m.* background.

Hinterhalt, *n.m.* ambush.

hinterher', *adv.* afterward(s).

Hinterland, *n.nt.* hinterland.

hinterle'gen, *vb.* deposit.

Hinterlist, *n.f.* insidiousness, underhanded act.

hinterlistig, *adj.* insidious, designing, underhanded.

Hintertreffen, *n.nt.* (**ins H. geraten**) fall behind.

Hintertür, -en, *n.f.* back door; (*fig.*) loophole.

hinterzie'hen*, *vb.* (*fig.*) defraud.

hinü'ber, *adv.* over, across.

hinun'ter, *adv.* down.

Hinweis, -e, *n.m.* reference; indication.

hin·weisen*, *vb.* point, refer, allude.

hinzu'·fügen, *vb.* add.

Hirn, -e, *n.nt.* brain.

Hirsch, -e, *n.m.* stag.

Hirschleder, -, *n.nt.* deerskin.

Hirt, -en, -en (*Biblical* **Hirte, -n, -n**) *n.m.* shepherd.

hissen, *vb.* hoist.

Histo'riker, -, *n.m.* historian.

histo'risch, *adj.* historic(al).

Hitze, *n.m.* heat.

hitzig, *adj.* heated, fiery, heady.

hitzköpfig, *adj.* hot-headed.

Hitzschlag, ·̈e, *n.m.* heatstroke.

Hobel, -, *n.m.* plane.

hobeln, *vb.* plane.

hoch (hoh-, höher, höchst), 1. *adj.* high, tall. 2. *adv.* up.

Hochebene, -n, *n.f.* plateau.

hocherfreut, *adj.* elated.

hochgradig, *adj.* intense, extreme.

Hochmut, *n.m.* haughtiness, pride.

hochmütig, *adj.* haughty, arrogant.

hoch·schätzen, *vb.* treasure.

Hochschule, -n, *n.f.* university.

Hochsommer, -, *n.m.* midsummer.

höchst, *adv.* highly, extremely.

Hochstapler, -, *n.m.* swindler, impersonator.

höchstens, *adv.* at best, at the outside.

höchstenfalls, *adv.* at best, at the outside.

Höchstgrenze, -n, *n.f.* top limit.

hochtrabend, *adj.* pompous, grandiloquent.

Hochverrat, *n.m.* high treason.

Hochzeit, -en, *n.f.* wedding.

Hochzeitsreise, -n, *n.f.* honeymoon.

hoch-ziehen*, *vb.* hoist.

hocken, *vb.* squat.

Hocker, -, *n.m.* stool.

Höcker, -, *n.m.* bump, hump.

Hockey, *n.nt.* hockey.

Hof, -ºe, *n.m.* court, courtyard; **(den H. machen)** court.

hoffen, *vb.* hope.

hoffentlich, *adv.* I hope.

Hoffnung, -en, *n.f.* hope.

hoffnungslos, *adj.* hopeless.

hoffnungsvoll, *adj.* hopeful.

höfisch, *adj.* courtly.

höflich, *adj.* polite, courteous, respectful, civil.

Höflichkeit, -en, *n.f.* courtesy.

höher, *adj.* higher.

hohl, *adj.* hollow.

Höhle, -n, *n.f.* cave, den.

Hohlraum, -ºe, *n.m.* hollow space, vacuum.

Hohn, *n.m.* mockery, derision.

höhnisch, *adj.* derisive, mocking.

hohnlächeln, *vb.* sneer, deride.

hold, *adj.* gracious, lovely.

holdselig, *adj.* gracious.

holen, *vb.* (go and) get, fetch.

Holland, *n.nt.* Holland.

Holländer, -, *n.m.* Dutchman.

holländisch, *adj.* Dutch.

Hölle, *n.f.* inferno, hell.

höllisch, *adj.* infernal, hellish.

holprig, *adj.* bumpy.

Holz, -ºer, *n.nt.* wood, lumber, timber.

hölzern, *adj.* wooden.

Holzklotz, -ºe, *n.m.* block (of wood); log.

Holzkohle, -n, *n.f.* charcoal.

Holzschnitt, -e, *n.m.* woodcut.

Honig, *n.m.* honey.

Honorar', -e, *n.nt.* honorarium.

honorie'ren, *vb.* honor; remunerate.

Hopfen, -, *n.m.* hop(s).

hopsen, *vb.* hop, skip.

hops-gehen*, *vb.* go down the drain, go west.

hörbar, *adj.* audible.

horchen, *vb.* listen to; eavesdrop.

Horde, -n, *n.f.* horde.

hören, *vb.* hear.

Hörensagen, *n.nt.* hearsay.

Hörer, -, *n.m.* (telephone) receiver; (student) auditor.

hörig, *adj.* submissive; subservient.

Horiz = t', -e, *n.m.* horizon.

horizoutal', *adj.* horizontal.

Hormon', -e, *n.nt.* hormone.

Horn, ºer, *n.nt.* horn.

hörnern, *adj.* horny.

Hornhaut, -ºe, *n.f.* callous skin; cornea.

hornig, *adj.* horny.

Hornis'se, -en, *n.f.* hornet.

Horoskop', -e, *n.nt.* horoscope.

Hort, -e, *n.m.* hoard; refuge, retreat.

Hörweite, *n.f.* earshot.

Hose, -n, *n.f.* trousers, pants.

Hosenband, -ºer, *n.nt.* garter.

Hostie, *n.f.* host.

Hotel', -s, *n.nt.* hotel.

Hotel'boy, -s, *n.m.* bellboy.

hübsch, *adj.* pretty, handsome.

Hubschrauber, -, *n.m.* helicopter.

Huf, -e, *n.nt.* hoof.

Hüfte, -n, *n.f.* hip.

Hügel, -, *n.m.* hill.

Huhn, ⁻er, *n.nt.* chicken, fowl.

Hühnerauge, -n, *n.nt.* corn.

huldigen, *vb.* do homage to.

Hülle, -n, *n.f.* covering, casing; **(in H. und Fülle)** abundantly, in profusion.

hüllen, *vb.* clothe, wrap, envelope.

Hülse, -n, *n.f.* hull, husk; case.

human', *adj.* humane.

Humanis'mus, *n.m.* humanism.

Humanist', -en, -en, *n.m.* humanist.

humanitär', *adj.* humanitarian.

Humanität', *n.f.* humanity.

Hummel, -n, *n.f.* bumblebee.

Hummer, -, *n.m.* lobster.

Humor', *n.m.* humor, wit.

Humorist', -en, -en, *n.m.* humorist.

humor'voll, *adj.* humorous.

humpeln, *vb.* hobble.

Hund, -e, *n.m.* dog, hound.

hundert, *num.* a hundred.

Hundert, -e, *n.nt.* hundred.

Hundertjahr'feier, -n, *n.f.* centenary, centennial.

hundertjährig, *adj.* centennial.

hundertst-, *adj.* hundredth.

Hundertstel, -, *n.nt.* hundredth; **(ein h.)** one one-hundredth.

Hundezwinger, -, *n.m.* kennel.

Hündin, -nen, *n.f.* bitch.

hünenhaft, *adj.* gigantic.

Hunger, *n.m.* hunger.

hungern, *vb.* starve.

Hungersnot, ⁻e, *n.f.* famine.

Hungertod, *n.m.* starvation.

hungrig, *adj.* hungry.

Hupe, -n, *n.f.* auto horn.

hupen, *vb.* blow the horn.

hüpfen, *vb.* hop.

Hürde, -n, *n.f.* hurdle.

Hure, -n, *n.f.* whore.

husten, *vb.* cough.

Husten, *n.m.* cough.

Hut, ⁻e, *n.m.* hat.

Hut, *n.f.* care, protection; **(auf der H. sein*)** be on the alert.

hüten, *vb.* tend; **(sich h.)** beware, be careful not to do.

Hütte, -n, *n.f.* hut; shed, hovel; *(tech.)* foundry.

Hyazin'the, -n, *n.f.* hyacinth.

Hydrant', -en, -en, *n.m.* hydrant.

Hygie'ne, *n.f.* hygiene.

hygie'nisch, *adj.* hygienic, sanitary.

Hymne, -n, *n.f.* hymn, anthem.

Hypno'se, -n, *n.f.* hypnosis.

hypno'tisch, *adj.* hypnotic.

hypnotisie'ren, *vb.* hypnotize.

Hypothek', -en, *n.f.* mortgage.

Hypothe'se, -n, *n.f.* hypothesis.

hypothe'tisch, *adj.* hypothetical.

Hysterie', *n.f.* hysteria, hysterics.

hyste'risch, *adj.* hysterical.

I

ich, *pron.* I.

Ich, *n.nt.* ego.

ideal', *adj.* ideal.

Ideal', -e, *n.nt.* ideal.

idealisie'ren, *vb.* idealize.

Idealis'mus, *n.m.* idealism.

Ideé, -e'en, *n.f.* idea, notion; **(fixe I.)** obsession.

identifizier'bar, *adj.* identifiable.

identifizie'ren, *vb.* identify.

iden'tisch, *adj.* identical.

Identität', -en, *n.f.* identity.

Idiot', -en, -en, *n.m.* idiot.

idio'tisch, *adj.* idiotic.

Idyll', -e, *n.nt.* idyl.

idyl'lisch, *adj.* idyllic.

ignorie'ren, *vb.* ignore.

illuminie′ren, *vb.* illuminate.

illuso′risch, *adj.* illusive, illusory.

Illustration′, -en, *n.f.* illustration.

illustrie′ren, *vb.* illustrate.

imaginär′, *adj.* imaginary.

Imbiß, -sse, *n.m.* snack.

Imita′tor, -o′ren, *n.m.* impersonator.

imitie′ren, *vb.* imitate.

immatrikulie′ren, *vb.* (sich i.) register in a university.

immer, *adv.* always.

immergrün, *adj.* evergreen.

immerhin′, *adv.* after all, anyway.

Immobi′lien, *n.pl.* real estate.

immun′, *adj.* immune.

Immunität′, -en, *n.f.* immunity.

Imperfekt, -e, *n.nt.* imperfect tense.

Imperialis′mus, *n.m.* imperialism.

imperialis′tisch, *adj.* imperialist.

impfen, *vb.* vaccinate.

Impfstoff, -e, *n.m.* vaccine.

Impfung, -en, *n.f.* vaccination.

impli′cite, *adv.* by implication.

implizie′ren, *vb.* imply, implicate.

Import′, -e, *n.m.* import.

importie′ren, *vb.* import.

imposant′, *adj.* imposing.

impotent′, *adj.* impotent.

Impotenz′, *n.f.* impotence.

imprägnie′ren, *vb.* waterproof.

Impresa′rio, -s, *n.m.* impresario.

improvisie′ren, *vb.* improvise.

Impuls′, -e, *n.m.* impulse.

impulsiv′, *adj.* impulsive.

Impulsivität′, *n.f.* spontaneity.

imstan′de, *adj.* able, capable.

in, *prep.* in, into.

Inbegriff, -e, *n.m.* essence, embodiment.

inbegriffen, *adj.* included; implicit.

Inbrunst, *n.f.* ardor, fervor.

inbrünstig, *adj.* zealous, ardent.

Inder, -, *n.m.* Indian.

Index, -e *or* **-dizes**, *n.m.* index.

India′ner, -, *n.m.* (American) Indian.

india′nisch, *adj.* (American) Indian.

Indien, *n.nt.* India.

Indikativ, -e, *n.m.* indicative.

Indika′tor, -o′ren, *n.m.* indicator.

indirekt′, *adj.* indirect.

indisch, *adj.* Indian.

indiskret, *adj.* indiscreet

Individualität′, -en, *n.f.* individuality

individuell′, *adj.* individual.

Indivi′duum, -duen, *n.nt.* individual.

Indone′sien, *n.nt.* Indonesia.

Induktion′, -en, *n.f.* induction.

induktiv′, *adj.* inductive.

Industrie, -i′en, *n.f.* industry.

industriell′, *adj.* industrial.

Industriell′-, *n.m.* industrialist.

induzie′ren, *vb.* induce.

infam′, *adj.* infamous; beastly.

Infanterie, -n, *n.f.* infantry.

Infanterist, -en, -en, *n.m.* infantryman.

infiltrie′ren, *vb.* infiltrate.

Infinitiv, -e, *n.m.* infinitive.

infizie′ren, *vb.* infect.

Inflation′, -en, *n.f.* inflation.

infolgedes′sen, *adv.* consequently.

informie′ren, *vb.* inform.

Ingenieur′, -e, *n.m.* engineer.

Ingwer, *n.m.* ginger.

Inhaber, -, *n.m.* proprietor; (of an apartment) occupant.

Inhalt, *n.m.* content, volume, capacity.

Inhaltsangabe, -n, table of contents.

inhaltschwer, *adj.* momentous, weighty.

Inhaltsverzeichnis, -se, *n.nt.* table of contents, index.

Initiati've, -n, *n.f.* initiative.

inkog'nito, *adv.* incognito.

Inland, -e, *n.nt.* homeland: **(im In- und Ausland)** at home and abroad.

inländisch, *adj.* domestic.

inmit'ten, *prep.* amid, in the midst of.

innen, *adv.* inside.

Innen-, *cpds.* interior, inner; domestic.

Innenpolitik, *n.f.* domestic policy.

Innenseite, -n, *n.f.* inside.

inner-, *adj.* inner, interior, internal.

Inner-, *n.nt.* interior, inside; soul.

innerhalb, *prep.* within.

innerlich, *adj.* inward, intrinsic.

innerst-, *adj.* innermost.

innig, *adj.* intimate; fervent.

Innigkeit, *n.f* fervor.

Innung, -en, *n.f.* guild.

Insasse, -n, -n, *n.m.* occupant; inmate.

insbeson'dere, *adv.* especially.

Inschrift, -en, *n.f.* inscription.

Insekt', -en, *n.nt.* insect.

Insek'tenpulver, -, *n.nt.* insecticide.

Insel, -n, *n.f.* island.

Inserat', -e, *n.nt.* advertisement.

Inserent', -en, -en, *n.m.* advertiser.

insgeheim', *adv.* secretly.

insgesamt', *adv.* altogether.

Insig'nien, *n.pl.* insignia.

inso'fern, inso'weit, *adv.* to that extent, to this extent.

insofern', insoweit', *conj.* insofar as, to the extent that.

Inspek'tor, -o'ren, *n.m.* inspector.

inspizie'ren, *vb.* inspect.

Installation', -en, *n.f.* installation.

instand/halten*, *vb.* keep up, keep in good repair.

Instand/haltung, *n.f.* maintenance.

instän'dig, *adj.* earnest.

instand'/setzen, *vb.* repair, recondition; enable.

Instanz', -en, *n.f.* instance.

Instan'zenweg, -e, *n.m.* stages of appeal, channels.

Instinkt', -e, *n.m.* instinct.

instinktiv', *adj.* instinctive.

Institut', -e, *n.nt.* institute, institution.

Instrument', -e, *n.nt.* instrument.

Insulin', *n.nt.* insulin.

inszenie'ren, *vb.* stage.

intakt', *adj.* intact.

integrie'ren, *vb.* integrate.

Intellekt', *n.m.* intellect.

intellektuell', *adj.* intellectual.

Intellektuell'-, *n.m.&f.* intellectual, highbrow, egghead.

intelligent', *adj.* intelligent.

ntelligenz', *n.f.* intelligence.

intensiv', *adj.* intense, intensive.

interessant', *adj.* interesting.

Interes'se, -n, *n.nt.* interest, concern.

interessie'ren, *vb.* interest.

Interjektion', -en, *n.f.* interjection.

international', *adj.* international.

internie'ren, *vb.* intern.

Internist', -en, -en, *n.m.* specialist for internal medicine.

interpretie'ren, *vb.* interpret.

interpunktie'ren, *vb.* punctuate.

Interpunktion', *n.f.* punctuation.

Interview', -s, *n.nt.* interview.

interview'en, *vb.* interview.

intim', *adj.* intimate.

Intoleranz, *n.f.* intolerance.

intransitiv, *adj.* intransitive.

intravenös', *adj.* intravenous.

Intri'ge, -n, *n.f.* intrigue.

intrigie'ren, *vb.* plot, scheme.

Intuition', -en, n.f. intuition.

intuitiv', adj. intuitive.

Invali'de, -n, -n, n.m. invalid.

Invasion', -en, n.f. invasion.

Inventar', -e, n.nt. inventory.

Inventur', -en, n.f. inventory.

investie'ren, vb. invest.

inwendig, adj. inward, inner.

inzwi'schen, adv. in the meantime.

Irak', n.nt. Iraq.

Iran', n.nt. Iran.

irdisch, adj. earthly.

Ire, -n, -n, n.m. Irishman.

irgendein, -, -e, adj. any (at all), any old.

irgendeiner, -e, pron. anyone, anybody.

irgendetwas, pron. something or other, anything at all.

irgendjemand, pron. somebody or other.

irgendwann', adv. sometime.

irgendwelcher, -es, -e, adj. any.

irgendwie', adv. somehow.

irgendwo', adv. somewhere, anywhere.

irgendwohin', adv. (to) somewhere, anywhere.

irisch, adj. Irish.

Irland, n.nt. Ireland.

Ironie', n.f. irony.

tro'nisch, adj. ironical.

irre, adj. astray, wrong; wandering, lost; insane.

irre·führen, vb. mislead.

irreführend, adj. misleading.

irren, vb. err, go astray; (sich i.) err, be mistaken.

irrig, adj. mistaken.

irritie'ren, vb. irritate, annoy.

Irrsinn, n.m. nonsense, lunacy.

irrsinnig, adj. lunatic.

Irrtum, ⁻er, n.m. error.

irrtümlich, adj. erroneous.

Isolationist', -en, -en, n.m. isolationist.

Isola'tor, -o'ren, n.m. - insulator.

isolie'ren, vb. isolate; insulate.

Isolie'rung, -en, n.f. isolation; insulation.

Israel, n.nt. Israel.

Israe'li, -s, n.m. Israeli.

israe'lisch, adj. Israeli.

Israelit', -en, -en, n.m. Israelite.

Ita'lien, n.nt. Italy.

Italie'ner, -, n.m. Italian.

italie'nisch, adj. Italian.

J

ja, 1. interj. yes. 2. adv. as is well known, to be sure; (j. nicht) not at all.

Jacht, -en, n.f. yacht.

Jacke, -n, n.f. jacket.

Jade, n.m. jade.

Jagd, -en, n.f. hunt; chase, pursuit.

jagen, vb. hunt; chase.

Jäger, -, n.m. hunter.

jäh, adj. sudden.

Jahr, -e, n.nt. year.

jahraus', **jahrein'**, adv. year in, year out.

Jahrbuch, ⁻er, n.nt. yearbook, almanac, annual; (pl.) annals.

Jahrestag, -e, n.m. anniversary.

Jahreszeit, -en, n.f. season.

Jahrgang, ⁻e, n.m. (school) class; (wine) vintage.

Jahrhun'dert, -e, n.nt. century.

jährlich, adj. yearly, annual.

Jahrmarkt, -e, n.m. fair.

Jahrzehnt', -e, n.nt. decade.

Jähzorn, n.m. quick temper.

jähzornig, adj. quick-tempered.

Jammer, n.m. misery.

jämmerlich, adj. miserable; dismal.

Januar, -e, n.m. January.

Japan, n.nt. Japan.

Japa'ner, -, n.m. Japanese.

japa'nisch, adj. Japanese.

Jargon', -s, *n.m.* jargon, slang.

jäten, *vb.* weed.

jauchzen, *vb.* jubilate, cheer.

jawohl', *interj.* yes, sir.

Jazz, *n.m.* jazz.

je, *adv.* ever; apiece, each; **(j. nach)** in each case according to; **(j. nachdem')** according to whether, as the case may be; **(je mehr, je [desto, umso] besser)** the more the better.

jeder, -es, -e, *pron.&adj.* each, every.

jedoch', *conj.* yet; nevertheless.

jemals, *adv.* ever.

jemand, *pron.* someone, somebody; anyone, anybody.

jener, -es, -e, *pron.&adj.* that, yonder; the former.

jenseits, *adv. and prep.* beyond, on the other side.

Jenseits, *n.nt.* beyond, life after death.

Jeru'salem, *n.nt.* Jerusalem.

Jesuit', *-en, -en, n.m.* Jesuit.

jetzt, *adv.* now.

jetzig, *adj.* present.

jeweilig, *adj.* in question, under consideration.

Joch, -e, *n.nt.* yoke.

Jockei, -s, *n.m.* jockey.

Jod, *n.nt.* iodine.

jodeln, *vb.* yodel.

Joghurt', *n.m. or nt.* yogurt.

johlen, *vb.* howl.

Joker, -, *n.m.* joker.

jonglie'ren, *vb.* juggle.

Jota, -s, *n.nt.* iota.

Journalist', -en, -en, *n.m.* journalist.

Jubel, *n.m.* jubilation, rejoicing.

jubeln, *vb.* shout with joy, rejoice.

Jubilä'um, -en, *n.nt.* jubilee.

jucken, *vb.* itch.

Jude, -n, -n, *n.m.* Jew.

Judentum, *n.nt.* Judaism, Jewry.

Judenverfolgung, -en, *n.f.* pogrom.

jüdisch, *adj.* Jewish.

Jugend, *n.f.* youth.

jugendlich, *adj.* youthful; adolescent, juvenile.

Jugendverbrecher, -, *n.m.* juvenile delinquent.

Jugendzeit, -en, *n.f.* youth, adolescence.

Jugosla'we, -n, -n, *n.m.* Yugoslav.

Jugosla'wien, *n.nt.* Yugoslavia.

jugosla'wisch, *adj.* Yugoslavian.

Juli, *n.m.* July.

jung(⁼), *adj.* young.

Junge, -n, -n, *n.m.* boy.

Jung-, *n.nt.* young (of an animal).

jungenhaft, *adj.* boyish.

Jünger, -, *n.m.* disciple.

Jungfer, -n, *n.f.* (**alte J.**) old maid, spinster.

Jungfrau, -en, *n.f.* virgin.

Junggeselle, -n, -n, *n.m.* bachelor.

Jüngling, -e, *n.m.* young man.

Juni, *n.m.* June.

Junker, -, *n.m.* aristocratic landowner (especially in Prussia).

Jurist', -en, -en, *n.m.* jurist; law student.

juris'tisch, *adj.* juridical, legal.

Justiz', *n.f.* justice.

Juwel', -en, *n.nt.* jewel.

Juwelier', -e, *n.m.* jeweler.

Jux, *n.m.* fun.

K

Kabarett', -e, *n.nt.* cabaret.

Kabel, -, *n.nt.* cable; cablegram.

Kabeljau, -e, *n.m.* cod.

kabeln, *vb.* cable.

Kabi'ne, -n, *n.f.* cabin, stateroom.

Kabinett', -e, *n.nt.* cabinet.

Kabriolett', -s, *n.nt.* convertible.

Kachel, -n, *n.f.* tile.

Kada'ver, -, *n.m.* carcass.

Kadett', -en, -en, *n.m.* cadet.

Käfer, -, *n.m.* beetle, bug.

Kaffee, *n.m.* coffee.

Kaffein', *n.nt.* caffeine.

Käfig, -e, *n.m.* cage.

kahl, *adj.* bald; bare.

Kahn, ⸚e, *n.m.* boat, barge.

Kaiser, -, *n.m.* emperor.

Kaju'te, -n, *n.f.* cabin (on a boat).

Kaka'o, -s, *n.m.* cocoa.

Kalb, ⸚er, *n.nt.* calf.

Kalbfleisch, *n.nt.* veal.

Kalbleder, -, *n.nt.* calfskin.

Kalen'der, -, *n.m.* calendar.

Kali, *n.nt.* potash, potassium.

Kali'ber, -, *n.nt.* caliber.

Kalium, *n.nt.* potassium.

Kalk, *n.m.* lime, chalk, calcium.

Kalkstein, *n.m.* limestone.

Kalorie', -i'en, *n.f.* calorie.

kalt(⸚), *adj.* cold.

kaltblütig, *adj.* cold-blooded.

Kälte, -n, *n.f.* cold(ness).

Kalva'rienberg, *n.m.* Calvary.

Kalzium, *n.nt.* calcium.

Kame'e, -n, *n.f.* cameo.

Kamel', -e, *n.nt.* camel.

Kamera, -s, *n.f.* camera.

Kamerad', -en, -en, *n.m.* comrade.

Kamerad'schaft, -en, *n.f.* comradeship, camaraderie.

Kamil'le, -n, *n.f.* camomile.

Kamin', -e, *n.m.* fireplace, hearth; fireside.

Kamm, ⸚e, *n.m.* comb; (mountain) crest.

kämmen, *vb.* comb.

Kammer, -n, *n.f.* room; chamber.

Kammermusik, *n.f.* chamber music.

Kampag'ne, -n, *n.f.* campaign.

Kampf, ⸚e, *n.m.* fight, fighting, combat.

kämpfen, *vb.* fight.

Kampfer, *n.m.* camphor.

Kämpfer, -, *n.m.* fighter, combatant; champion.

kampfunfähig, *adj.* disabled.

Kanada, *n.nt.* Canada.

Kana'dier, -, *n.m.* Canadian.

kana'disch, *adj.* Canadian.

Kanal', ⸚e, *n.m.* canal, channel; duct.

Kanalisation', *n.f.* canalization; sewer.

kanalisie'ren, *vb.* canalize; drain by sewer.

Kana'rienvogel, ⸚, *n.m.* canary.

Kanda're, -n, *n.f.* curb (of a horse); **(an die K. nehmen)** take a person in hand.

Kandidat', -en, -en, *n.m.* candidate, nominee.

Kandidatur', -en, *n.f.* candidacy, nomination.

kandiert', *adj.* candied.

Känguruh', -s, *n.nt.* kangaroo.

Kanin'chen, -, *n.nt.* rabbit, bunny.

Kanne, -n, *n.f.* can, jug, pitcher.

Kanniba'le, -n, -n, *n.m.* cannibal.

Kanon, -s, *n.m.* canon.

Kanona'de, -n, *n.f.* cannonade.

Kano'ne, -n, *n.f.* cannon.

Kano'nenboot, -e, *n.nt.* gunboat.

Kanonier', -e, *n.m.* cannoneer.

kano'nisch, *adj.* canonical.

kanonisie'ren, *vb.* canonize.

Kanta'te, -n, *n.f.* cantata.

Kante, -n, *n.f.* edge, border.

Kanti'ne, -n, *n.f.* canteen.

Kanu', -s, *n.nt.* canoe.

Kanzel, -n, *n.f.* pulpit.

Kanzlei', -en, *n.f.* chancellery.

Kanzler, -, *n.m.* chancellor.

Kap, -s, *n.nt.* cape.

Kapaun', -e, *n.m.* capon.

Kapel'le, -n, *n.f.* chapel; orchestra, band.

Kapell'meister, -, *n.m.* conductor, bandmaster.

kapern, *vb.* capture.

kapie'ren, *vb.* understand.

kapital', *adj.* capital.

Kapital', -ien, *n.nt.* capital.

kapitalisie'ren, *vb.* capitalize.

Kapitalis'mus, *n.m.* capitalism.

kapitalis'tisch, *adj.* capitalistic.

Kapitän', -e, *n.m.* captain.

Kapi'tel, -, *n.nt.* chapter.

kapitulie'ren, *vb.* capitulate.

Kappe, -n, *n.f.* cap, hood.

Kapsel, -n, *n.f.* capsule.

kaputt', *adj.* broken, busted; **(k. machen)** bust, wreck.

Kapu'ze, -n, *n.f.* hood.

Karabi'ner, -, *n.m.* carbine.

Karaf'fe, -n, *n.f.* decanter, carafe.

Karamel', *n.nt.* caramel.

Karawa'ne, -n, *n.f.* caravan.

Karbid', *n.nt.* carbide.

Karbun'kel, -, *n.m.* carbuncle.

Kardinal', ̈e, *n.m.* cardinal.

Karfrei'tag, *n.m.* Good Friday.

Karies, *n.f.* caries.

Karikatur', -en, *n.f.* caricature; cartoon.

karikie'ren, *vb.* caricature.

karmin'rot(̈), *adj.* crimson.

Karneval', -s, *n.m.* carnival.

Karo, *n.nt.* (cards) diamond(s).

Karpfen, -, *n.m.* carp.

Karre, -n, *n.f.* cart.

Karree', -s, *n.nt.* square.

Karren, -, *n.m.* cart.

Karrie're, -n, *n.f.* career; **(K. machen)** be successful, get far in one's profession.

Karte, -n, *n.f.* card; chart, map.

Kartei', -en, *n.f.* card index, file.

Kartell', -e, *n.nt.* cartel.

Kartenspiel, -e, *n.nt.* card game; deck of cards.

Kartof'fel, -n, *n.f.* potato.

Karton', -s, *n.m.* carton.

Karussell', -s, *n.nt.* merrygo-round.

Karwoche, *n.f.* Holy Week.

Kaschmir, -e, *n.m.* cashmere.

Käse, *n.m.* cheese.

Kaser'ne, -n, *n.f.* barracks.

Kasi'no, -s, *n.nt.* casino.

Kasse, -n, *n.f.* cash box; cash register; box-office; **(bei K. sein*)** be flush; **(an der K. bezahlen)** pay the cashier.

Kassenzettel, -, *n.m.* salesslip.

kassie'ren, *vb.* collect (money due); dismiss.

Kassie'rer, -, *n.m.* teller, cashier.

Kaste, -n, *n.f.* caste.

kastei'en, *vb.* chastise, mortify.

Kasten, ̈, *n.m.* box, case.

Katalog', -e, *n.m.* catalogue.

Katapult', -e, *n.m.* catapult.

Katarrh', -e, *n.m.* catarrh.

Bats'ter, -, *n.nt.* register.

katastrophal', *adj.* disastrous, ruinous.

Katechis'mus, -men, *n.m.* catechism.

Kategorie', -i'en, *n.f.* category.

katego'risch, *adj.* categorical.

Kater, -, *n.m.* tomcat; hangover.

Kathedra'le, -n, *n.f.* cathedral.

Katho'de, -n, *n.f.* cathode.

Katholik', -en, -en, *n.m.* Catholic.

katho'lisch, *adj.* Catholic.

Katholizis'mus, -men, *n.m.* Catholicism.

Kattun', -e, *n.m.* gingham, calico.

Kätzchen, -, *n.nt.* kitten.

Katze, -n, *n.f.* cat.

katzenartig, *adj.* feline.

Katzenjammer, *n.m.* hangover.

kauen, *vb.* chew.

kauern, *vb.* crouch, cower.

Kauf, -e, *n.m.* purchase.

kaufen, *vb.* purchase, buy.

Käufer, -, *n.m.* buyer.

Kaufkontrakt, -e, *n.m.* bill of sale.

Kaufmann, -leute, *n.m.* businessman, merchant.

kaufmännisch, *adj.* commercial.

Kaugummi, -s, *n.nt.* chewing gum.

kaum, *adv.* scarcely, hardly, barely.

Kausalität', -en, *n.f.* causation.

Kaution', -en, *n.f.* surety; security; bail.

Kavalier', -e, *n.m.* cavalier.

Kavallerie', -n, *n.f.* cavalry.

Kaviar, *n.m.* caviar.

keck, *adj.* saucy.

Kegel, -, *n.m.* cone.

kegelförmig, *adj.* conic.

kegeln, *vb.* bowl.

Kehle, -n, *n.f.* throat.

Kehlkopfentzündung, -en, *n.f.* laryngitis.

kehren, *vb.* turn; brush, sweep.

Kehricht, *n.m.* sweepings; garbage.

Kehrseite, -n, *n.f.* reverse side; other side of the picture.

kehrt-machen, *vb.* turn around, about-face.

Kehrtwendung, *n.f.* about-face.

keifen, *vb.* nag, scold.

Keil, -e, *n.m.* wedge.

Keilerei', -en, *n.f.* fracas, brawl.

Keim, -e, *n.m.* germ, bud.

keimen, *vb.* germinate.

keimfrei, *adj.* germ free, sterile.

keimtötend, *adj.* germicidal.

kein, -, -e, *adj.* not a, not any, no.

keiner, -es, -e, *pron.* no one, not any, none.

keinerlei, *adj.* not of any sort.

keineswegs, *adv.* by no means.

Keks, -e, *n.m.* biscuit, cookie.

Kelch, -e, *n.m.* cup, goblet, chalice; calyx.

Kelchglas, -er, *n.nt.* goblet.

Kelle, -n, *n.f.* ladle, scoop.

Keller, -, *n.m.* cellar.

Kellner, -, *n.m.* waiter.

Kellnerin, -nen, *n.f.* waitress.

kennen*, *vb.* know, be acquainted with.

kennen-lernen, *vb.* meet, become acquainted with.

Kenner, -, *n.m.* connoisseur.

Kennkarte, -n, *n.f.* identity card.

kenntlich, *adj.* recognizable.

Kenntnis, -se, *n.f.* knowledge, notice.

Kennzeichen, -, *n.nt.* sign, distinguishing mark, feature.

kennzeichnen, *vb.* mark, stamp, distinguish, characterize.

kentern, *vb.* capsize.

Kera'mik, -en, *n.f.* ceramics.

kera'misch, *adj.* ceramic.

Kerbe, -n, *n.f.* notch.

kerben, *vb.* notch.

Kerker, -, *n.m.* jail, prison.

Kerl, -e, *n.m.* fellow, guy.

Kern, -e, *n.m.* kernel, pit, core; nucleus; gist.

Kernenergie, *n.f.* nuclear energy.

Kerngehäuse, -, *n.nt.* core.

Kernhaus, -er, *n.nt.* core.

Kernphysik, *n.f.* nuclear physics.

Kernspaltung, -en, *n.f.* nuclear fission.

Kerosin', *n.nt.* kerosene.

Kerze, -n, *n.f.* candle.

Kessel, -, *n.m.* kettle, boiler.

Kette, -n, *n.f.* chain.

ketten, *vb.* chain, link.

Kettenreaktion, -en, *n.f.* chain reaction.

Ketzer, -, *n.m.* heretic.

Ketzerei', *n.f.* heresy.

keuchen, *vb.* gasp.

Keuchhusten, *n.m.* whooping-cough.

Keule, -n, *n.f.* club, cudgel; (meat) leg, joint.

keusch, *adj.* chaste.

Keuschheit, *n.f.* chastity.

kichern, *vb.* giggle.

Kiefer, -, *n.m.* jaw.

Kiefer, -n, *n.f.* pine.

Kiel, -e, *n.m.* keel.

Kielwasser, *n.nt.* wake.

Kieme, -n, *n.f.* gill.

Kiepe, -n, *n.f.* basket (carried on the back).

Kies, -e, *n.m.* gravel.

Kilo, -, *n.nt.* kilogram.

Kilome'ter, *n.m. or nt.* kilometer.

Kilowatt', -, *n.nt.* kilowatt.

Kind, -er, *n.nt.* child.

Kinderarzt, ⸚e, *n.m.* pediatrician.

Kinderbett, -en, *n.nt.* crib.

Kindergarten, ⸚, *n.m.* kindergarten.

Kinderlähmung, -en, *n.f.* infantile paralysis, polio.

kinderlos, *adj.* childless.

Kinderraub, *n.m.* kidnapping.

Kinderräuber, -, *n.m.* kidnapper.

Kindersportwagen, -, *n.m.* stroller.

Kinderwagen, -, *n.m.* baby carriage.

Kinderzimmer, -, *n.nt.* nursery.

Kindheit, -en, *n.f.* childhood.

kindisch, *adj.* childish.

kindlich, *adj.* childlike.

Kinn, -e, *n.nt.* chin.

Kino, -s, *n.nt.* movie theater.

Kiosk', -e, *n.m.* kiosk, newsstand.

kippen, *vb.* tip, tilt.

Kirche, -n, *n.f.* church.

Kirchenlied, -er, *n.nt.* hymn.

Kirchenschiff, -e, *n.nt.* nave.

Kirchenstuhl, ⸚e, *n.m.* pew.

Kirchhof, ⸚e, *n.m.* churchyard.

kirchlich, *adj.* ecclesiastical.

Kirchspiel, -e, *n.nt.* parish.

Kirchturm, ⸚e, *n.m.* steeple.

Kirsche, -n, *n.f.* cherry.

Kissen, -, *n.nt.* cushion, pillow.

Kissenbezug, ⸚e, *n.m.* pillowcase.

Kiste, -n, *n.f.* crate, chest.

Kitsch, *n.m.* trash.

Kittel, -, *n.m.* smock.

kitzeln, *vb.* tickle.

kitzlig, *adj.* ticklish.

klaffen, *vb.* gape, yawn.

Klage, -n, *n.f.* complaint; suit.

Kläger, -, *n.m.* plaintiff.

kläglich, *adj.* miserable.

Klammer, -n, *n.f.* clamp, clasp; parenthesis.

Klamot'ten, *n.pl.* duds, rags, stuff.

Klampe, -n, *n.f.* cleat.

Klang, ⸚e, *n.m.* sound, ring (ing).

Klappbett, -en, *n.nt.* folding bed.

Klappe, -n, *n.f.* flap, lid, valve.

klappen, *vb.* flap, fold; come out right.

klappern, *vb.* clatter, chatter, rattle.

Klaps, -e, *n.m.* slap.

klar, *adj.* clear.

klären, *vb.* clear.

Klarheit, -en, *n.f.* clarity.

Klarinet'te, -n, *n.f.* clarinet.

klar-legen, *vb.* clarify.

klar-stellen, *vb.* clarify.

Klasse, -n, *n.f.* class.

Klassenkamerad, -en, -en, *n.m.* classmate.

Klassenzimmer, -, *n.nt.* classroom.

klassifizie'ren, *vb.* classify.

Klassifizie'rung, -en, *n.f.* classification.

klassisch, *adj.* classic(al).

Klatsch, *n.m.* gossip.

klatschen, *vb.* clap; gossip.

Klaue, -n, *n.f.* claw.

klauen, *vb.* snitch.

Klausel, -n, *n.f.* clause, proviso.

Klavier', -e, *n.nt.* piano.

Klebemittel, -, *n.nt.* glue, adhesive.

kleben, *vb.* paste; stick.

Klebgummi, *n.m.* mucilage.

klebrig, *adj.* sticky.

Klebstoff, -e, *n.m.* paste.

kleckern, *vb.* spill, make a spot.

Klecks, -e, *n.m.* spot, stain.

Klee, *n.m.* clover.

Kleid, -er, *n.nt.* dress; *(pl.)* clothes.

kleiden, *vb.* clothe, dress.

Kleiderbügel, -, *n.m.* hanger.

Kleiderhändler, -, *n.m.* clothier.

Kleiderschrank, ⸚e, *n.m.* clothes closet, wardrobe.

kleidsam, *adj.* becoming.

Kleidung, -en *n.f.* clothing.

Kleidungsstück, -e, *n.nt.* garment.

klein, *adj.* little, small.

Kleingeld, -er, *n.nt.* change.

Kleinheit, -en, *n.f.* small-
ness.

Kleinigkeit, -en *n,.f.* trifle.

kleinlaut, *adj.* meek, sub-
dued.

kleinlich, *adj.* petty.

Kleinod, -ien, *n.nt.* jewel,
gem.

Kleister, -, *n.m.* paste.

Klemme, -n, *n.f.* clamp;
dilemma, jam, tight spot.

klemmen, *vb.* pinch, jam.

Klempner, -, *n.m.* plumber.

Klepper, -, *n.m.* hack.

klerikal', *adj.* clerical.

Kleriker, -, *n.m.* clergyman.

Klerus, *n.m.* clergy.

klettern, *vb.* climb.

Klient', -en, -en, *n.m.* client.

Klima, -a'te, *n.nt.* climate.

Klimaanlage, -n, *n.f.* air-
conditioning (system).

klima'tisch, *adj.* climatic.

klimatisie'ren, *vb.* air-condition.

klimmen*, *vb.* climb.

Klinge, -n, *n.f.* blade.

Klingel, -n, *n.f.* (small) bell;
buzzer.

klingeln, *vb.* ring.

klingen*, *vb.* ring, sound.

Klinik, -en, *n.f.* clinic, hospital.

klinisch, *adj.* clinical.

Klippe, -n, *n.f.* cliff, crag.

Klistier', -e, *n.nt.* enema.

Klo, -s, *n.nt.* (short for
Klosett') bathroom, toilet.

Kloa'ke, -n, *n.f.* sewer, drain.

klobig, *adj.* clumsy.

klopfen, *vb.* knock, beat.

Klops, -e, *n.m.* meatball.

Klosett', -e, *n.nt.* water
closet.

Kloß, ⸚e, *n.m.* clump; dumpling.

Kloster, ⸚, *n.nt.* monastery,
nunnery.

Klosterbruder, ⸚, *n.m.* friar.

Klostergang, ⸚e, *n.m.* cloi-
ster(s).

Klotz, ⸚e, *n.m.* block.

Klub, -s, *n.m.* club (social).

Kluft, ⸚e, *n.f.* gap, cleft,
fissure.

klug(⸚), *adj.* clever.

Klugheit, -en, *n.f.* cleverness.

Klumpen, -, *n.m.* lump.

klumpig, *adj.* lumpy.

knabbern, *vb.* nibble.

Knabe, -n, -n, *n.m.* lad,
youth.

knacken, *vb.* click.

Knall, -e, *n.m.* bang, crack,
pop.

knallen, *vb.* bang, pop.

knapp, *adj.* scarce, scant,
tight, terse.

Knappheit, -en, *n.f.* scarcity, shortage, terseness.

knarren, *vb.* creak, rattle.

knauserig, *adj.* niggardly.

Knebel, -, *n.m.* cudgel; gag.

knebeln, *vb.* bind, gag.

Knecht, -e, *n.m.* servant,
farm hand.

Knechtschaft, -en, *n.f.*
bondage, servitude.

kneifen*, *vb.* pinch.

Kneifzange, -n, *n.f.* pliers.

Kneipe, -n, *n.f.* tavern, pub,
joint.

kneten, *vb.* knead.

Knick, -e, *n.m.* bend, crack.

knicken, *vb.* bend, fold,
crack.

Knicks, -e, *n.m.* curtsy.

Knie, -i'e, *n.nt.* knee.

kni'en, *vb.* kneel.

Kniff, -e, *n.m.* pinch; trick.

knifflig, *adj.* tricky.

knipsen, *vb.* snap, punch
(ticket), take a snapshot,
snap one's fingers.

knirschen, *vb.* grate, crunch;
gnash (teeth).

knistern, *vb.* crackle.

knittern, *vb.* wrinkle.

Knöchel, -, *n.m.* knuckle.

Knochen, -, *n.m.* bone

knochig, *adj.* bony.

knochenlos, *adj.* boneless.

Knödel, -, *n.m.* dumpling.

Knopf, ⸚e, *n.m.* button.

Knopfloch, ⸚er, *n.nt.* buttonhole.

Knorpel, -, *n.m.* cartilage.

Knorren, -, *n.m.* knot, gnarl.

knorrig, *adj.* knotty, gnarled.

Knospe, -n, *n.f.* bud.

knospen, *vb.* bud.

Knoten, -, *n.m.* knot.

knoten, vb. knot.

Knotenpunkt, -e, n.m. junction.

knüpfen, vb. tie, knot.

Knüppel, -, n.m. cudgel, club.

knurren, vb. growl.

knusp(e)rig, adj. crisp, crusty.

Kobalt, n.m. cobalt.

Koch, -̈e, n.m. cook.

Kochbuch, -̈er, n.nt. cookbook.

kochen, vb. cook, boil.

Köchin, -nen, n.f. cook.

Kode, -s, n.m. code.

Kodein', n.nt. codein.

ködern, vb. decoy.

Kodex, -dizes, n.m. code.

kodifizie'ren, vb. codify.

Koffein', -e, n.nt. caffeine.

Koffer, -, n.m. suitcase, trunk.

Kognak, -s, n.m. brandy, cognac.

Kohl, -e, n.m. cabbage.

Kohle, -n, n.f. coal.

kohlen, vb. char.

Kohlenoxyd', n.nt. carbon monoxide.

Kohlenstoff, -e, n.m. carbon.

Koje, -n, n.f. bunk.

Kokain', n.nt. cocaine.

kokett', adj. coquettish.

Koket'te, -n, n.f. coquette.

kokettie'ren, vb. flirt.

Kokon', -s, n.m. cocoon.

Koks, -e, n.m. coke.

Kolben, -, n.m. butt, piston.

Kolle'ge, -n, -n, n.m. colleague.

kollektiv', adj. collective.

Koller, n.m. rage, frenzy.

kölnisch Wasser, n.nt. eau-de-cologne.

kolonial', adj. colonial.

Kolonial'waren, n.pl. groceries.

Kolonial'warenhändler, -, n.m. grocer.

Kolonie', -i'en, n.f. colony.

Kolonisation', n.f. colonization.

kolonisie'ren, vb. colonize.

Kolon'ne, -n, n.f. column.

Kolorit', -e, n.nt. color(ing).

kolossal', adj. colossal.

Knäuel, -, n.m. or nt. clew, ball; throng, crowd.

Koma, n.nt. coma.

kombinie'ren, vb. combine.

Komet', -en, -en, n.m. comet.

Komiker, -, n.m. comedian.

Komikerin, -nen, n.f. comedienne.

komisch, adj. funny.

Komitee', -s, n.nt. committee.

Komma, -s (or -ta), n.nt. comma.

Kommandant', -en, -en, n.m. commander, commanding officer.

Kommandantur', -en, n.f. commander's office.

kommen*, vb. come.

Kommentar', -e, n.m. commentary.

Kommenta'tor, -o'ren, n.m. commentator.

kommentie'ren, vb. comment on.

Kommissar', -e, n.m. commissary, commissioner.

Kommission', -en, n.f. commission.

Kommo'de, -n, n.f. bureau.

kommunal', adj. communal, municipal.

Kommunikant', -en, -en, n.m. communicant.

Kommunion', -en, n.f. communion.

Kommuniqué, -s, n.nt. communiqué.

Kommunis'mus, n.m. communism.

Kommunist', -en, -en, n.m. communist.

kommunis'tisch, adj. communistic.

kommunizie'ren, vb. commune; communicate.

Komödiant', -en, -en, n.m. comedian.

Komö'die, -n, n.f. comedy.

Kompagnon, -s, n.m. (business) partner.

kompakt', adj. compact.

Komparative, -e, n.m. comparative (degree).

Kompaß, -sse, n.m. compass.

kompensie'rend, adj. compensatory.

kompetent', *adj.* competent, authoritative.

Kompetenz', **-en**, *n.f.* competence, authority, jurisdiction.

Komplex', **-e**, *n.m.* complex.

komplex', *adj.* complex.

Komplikation', **-en**, *n.f.* complication.

Kompliment', **-e**, *n.nt.* compliment.

Kompli'ze, **-n**, **-n**, *n.m.* accomplice.

komplizie'ren, *vb.* complicate.

kompliziert', *adj.* complicated.

Komplott', **-e**, *n.nt.* plot.

komponie'ren, *vb.* compose.

Komponist', **-en**, **-en**, *n.m.* composer.

Komposition', **-en**, *n.f.* composition.

Kompott', **-e**, *n.nt.* compote.

Kompres'se, **-n**, *n.f.* compress.

Kompression', **-en**, *n.f.* compression.

Kompres'sor, **-o'ren**, *n.m.* compressor.

Kompromiß', **-sse**, *n.m.* compromise.

kompromittie'ren, *vb.* compromise.

Kondensation', **-en**, *n.f.* condensation.

Kondensa'tor, **-o'ren**, *n.m.* condenser.

kondensie'ren, *vb.* condense.

Kondi'tor, **-o'ren**, *n.m.* confectioner, pastry baker.

Konditorei', **-ei'en**, *n.f.* café and pastry shop.

Konfekt', **-e**, *n.nt.* candy.

Konfektion', *n.f.* ready-made clothing.

Konferenz', **-en**, *n.f.* conference.

Konfirmation', **-en**, *n.f.* confirmation.

konfiszie'ren, *vb.* confiscate.

Konfitü're, **-n**, *n.f.* jam.

Konflikt', **-e**, *n.m.* conflict.

konform', *adj.* in conformity.

konfrontie'ren, *vb.* confront.

konfus', *adj.* confused.

Kongreß', **-sse**, *n.m.* congress.

König, **-e**, *n.m.* king.

Königin, **-nen**, *n.f.* queen.

königlich, *adj.* royal.

Königreich, **-e**, *n.nt.* kingdom.

Königtum, *n.nt.* kingship, royalty.

Konjugation', **-en**, *n.f.* conjugation.

konjugie'ren, *vb.* conjugate.

Konjunktiv', **-e**, *n.m.* subjunctive.

Konjunktion', **-en**, *n.f.* conjunction.

konkav', *adj.* concave.

konkret', *adj.* concrete.

Konkurrent', **-en**, **-en**, *n.m.* competitor.

Konkurrenz', **-en**, *n.f.* competition.

konkurrie'ren, *vb.* compete.

Konkurs', **-e**, *n.m.* bankruptcy.

können*, *vb.* can, be able to.

konsequent', *adj.* consistent.

Konservatis'mus, *n.m.* conservatism.

konservativ', *adj.* conservative.

Konservato'rium, **-en**, *n.nt.* conservatory.

Konser'venfabrik, **-en**, *n.f.* cannery.

konservie'ren, *vb.* preserve.

Konservie'rung, **-en**, *n.f.* conservation.

Konsistenz', *n.f.* consistency.

konsolidie'ren, *vb.* consolidate.

Konsonant', **-en**, **-en**, *n.m.* consonant.

konstant', *adj.* constant.

Konstellation', **-en**, *n.f.* constellation.

konstituie'ren, *vb.* constitute.

Konstitution', **-en**, *f.* constitution.

konstitutionell', *adj.* constitutional.

konstruie'ren, *vb.* construct.

Konstrukteur', **-e**, *n.m.* constructor, designer.

Konstruktion', -en, n.f. construction.

Konsul, -n, n.m. consul.

konsula'risch, adj. consular.

Konsulat', -e, n.nt. consulate.

Konsum', -s, n.m. consumption; (short for **Konsum'laden**, ∵, n.m.) cooperative store, co-op.

Konsument', -en, -en, n.m. consumer.

Konsum'verein, -e, n.m. cooperative (society).

Kontakt', -e, n.m. contact.

Kontinent, -e, n.m. continent.

kontinental', adj. continental.

Konto, -s or -ten or -ti, n.nt. account.

Kontobuch, ∵er, n.nt. bankbook, account book.

Kontor', -e, n.nt. office.

Kontorist', -en, -en, n.m. clerk.

Kontroll'abschnitt, -e, n.m. stub.

Kontrol'le, -n, n.f. control. check.

kontrollier'bar, adj. controllable.

kontrollie'ren, vb. control, check.

Kontroll'marke, -n, n.f. check.

Kontur', -en, n.f. contour. outline.

Konvaleszenz', n.f. convalescence.

Konvention', -en, n.f. convention.

konventionell', adj. conventional.

konvergie'ren, vb. converge.

konvertie'ren, vb. convert.

konvex', adj. convex.

Konvulsion', -en, n.f. convulsion.

konvulsiv', adj. convulsive.

Konzentration', -en, n.f. concentration.

Konzentrations'lager, ∵, n.nt. concentration camp.

konzentrie'ren, vb. concentrate.

konzen'trisch, adj. concentric.

Konzept', -e, n.nt. plan, draft; (**aus dem K. bringen*****) confuse.

Konzern', -e, n.m. (business) trust, pool.

Konzert', -e, n.nt. concert.

Konzession', -en, n.f. concession.

koordinie'ren, vb. coordinate.

Kopf, ∵e, n.m. head.

Kopfhaut, ∵e, n.f. scalp.

Kopfhörer, -, n.m. earphone.

Kopfkissen, -, n.nt. pillow.

Kopfsalat, -e, n.m. lettuce.

Kopfschmerzen, n.pl. headache.

Kopfsprung, ∵e, n.m. dive.

Kopftuch, ∵er, n.nt. kerchief.

Kopie', -i'en, n.f. copy.

kopie'ren, vb. copy, duplicate.

koppeln, vb. couple.

Koral'le, -n, n.f. coral.

Korb, ∵e, n.m. basket.

Korbball, ∵e, n.m. basketball.

Korbwiege, -n, n.f. bassinet.

Korduanleder, -, n.nt. cordovan.

Kore'a, n.nt. Korea.

Korin'the, -n, n.f. currant.

Kork, -e, n.m. cork (material).

Korken, -, n.m. cork (stopper).

Korkenzieher, -, n.m. corkscrew.

Korn, -, n.m. grain whiskey.

Korn, -e, n.nt. (type of) grain.

Korn, ∵er, n.nt. (individual) grain.

Körnchen, -, n.nt. granule.

Kornett', -e, n.nt. cornet.

körnig, adj. granular.

Kornkammer, -n, n.f. granary.

Kornspeicher, -, n.m. granary.

Körper, -, n.m. body.

Körperbau, n.m. physique.

Körperchen, -, n.nt. corpuscle.

Körperbehinderung, **-en**, *n.f.* physical disability.

Körperkraft, *n.f.* physical strength.

körperlich, *adj.* physical, corporeal.

Körperschaft, **-en**, *n.f.* corporation.

Korps, **-**, *n.nt.* corps.

korpulent′, *adj.* corpulent.

korrekt′, *adj.* correct.

Korrekt′heit, **-en**, *n.f.* correctness.

korrektiv′, *adj.* corrective.

Korrespondent′, **-en**, **-en**, *n.m.* correspondent.

Korrespondenz′, **-en**, *n.f.* correspondence.

korrespondie′ren, *vb.* correspond.

Korridor, **-e**, *n.m.* corridor.

korrigie′ren, *vb.* correct.

korrumpie′ren, *vb.* corrupt.

korrupt′, *adj.* corrupt.

Korruption′, **-en**, *n.f.* corruption.

Korsett′, **-s**, *n.nt.* corset.

kosen, *vb.* fondle, caress.

Kosename(n), **-**, *n.m.* pet name.

kosme′tisch, *adj.* cosmetic.

kosmisch, *adj.* cosmic.

kosmopoli′tisch, *adj.* cosmopolitan.

Kosmos, *n.m.* cosmos.

Kost, *n.f.* food, fare, board.

kostbar, *adj.* costly, precious.

Kosten, *n.pl.* cost, charges, expenses.

kosten, *vb.* cost; taste.

Kostenanschlag, **ᵘe**, *n.m.* estimate.

kostenfrei, *adj.* free of charge.

kostenlos, *adj.* free, without cost.

Kostgänger, **-**, *n.m.* boarder.

köstlich, *adj.* delicious.

kostspielig, *adj.* expensive.

Kostspieligkeit, **-en**, *n.f.* costliness.

Kostüm′, **-e**, *n.nt.* costume; matching coat and skirt.

Kot, *n.m.* dirt, mud, filth.

Kotelett′, **-s**, *n.nt.* cutlet, chop.

Köter, **-**, *n.m.* cur.

kotzen, *vb.* vomit.

Krabbe, **-n**, *n.f.* shrimp, crab.

Krach, **-e** or **-s**, *n.m.* bang, crash, racket; row, fight.

krachen, *vb.* crash.

Kraft, **ᵘe**, *n.f.* strength, force, power.

kraft, *prep.* by virtue of.

Kraftbrühe, **-**, *n.f.* bouillon.

Kraftfahrer, **-**, *n.m.* motorist.

Kraftfahrzeug, **-e**, *n.nt.* motor vehicle.

kräftig, *adj.* strong.

kraftlos, *adj.* powerless.

kraftstrotzend, *adj.* vigorous.

kraftvoll, *adj.* powerful.

Kraftwagen, **-**, *n.m.* automobile.

Kragen, **-**, *n.m.* collar.

Krähe, **-n**, *n.f.* crow.

Kralle, **-n**, *n.f.* claw.

Kram, **ᵘe**, *n.m.* stuff, junk; business, affairs; retail trade, goods.

kramen, *vb.* rummage.

Krämer, **-**, *n.m.* small tradesman.

Krampf, **ᵘe**, *n.m.* cramp, spasm.

krampfhaft, *adj.* spasmodic.

Kran, **ᵘe**, *n.m.* crane, derrick.

Kranich, **-e**, *n.m.* crane.

krank(ᵘ), *adj.* sick.

kranken, *vb.* suffer from, ail.

kränken, *vb.* offend.

Krankenauto, **-s**, *n.nt.* ambulance.

Krankenhaus, **ᵘer**, *n.nt.* hospital.

Krankenschwester, **-n**, *n.f.* nurse.

Krankenwagen, **-**, *n.m.* ambulance.

krankhaft, *adj.* morbid.

Krankheit, **-en**, *n.f.* sickness, disease.

kränklich, *adj.* sickly.

Kränkung, **-en**, *n.f.* offense.

Kranz, **ᵘe**, *n.m.* wreath.

kraß, *adj.* crass, gross.

Kraßheit, **-en**, *n.f.* grossness.

kratzen, *vb.* scrape, scratch.

kraulen, *vb.* crawl.

kraus, *adj.* curly, crisp.

Krause, -n, *n.f.* frill.

kräuseln, *vb.* curl, ruffle.

Kraut, ⁻er, *n.nt.* herb, plant.

Krawat'te, -n, *n.f.* necktie.

Krebs, -e, *n.m.* crayfish; *(med.)* cancer.

kreden'zen, *vb.* serve, offer.

Kredit', -e, *n.m.* credit.

Kreide, -n, *n.f.* chalk.

kreidig, *adj.* chalky.

Kreis, -e, *n.m.* circle; district.

Kreisbahn, -en, *n.f.* orbit.

kreischen, *vb.* shriek.

Kreisel, -, *n.m.* top.

kreiseln, *vb.* spin like a top, gyrate.

kreisen, *vb.* circle, revolve.

kreisförmig, *adj.* circular.

Kreislauf, ⁻e, *n.m.* circulation, circuit.

Kremato'rium, -ien, *n.nt.* crematorium.

Krempe, -n, *n.f.* brim.

Krepp, *n.m.* crepe.

Kretonn'e, -s, *n.m.* cretonne.

Kreuz, -e, *n.nt.* cross; back; *(music)* sharp.

kreuzen, *vb.* cross; cruise, tack.

Kreuzer, -, *n.m.* cruiser.

Kreuzgang, ⁻e, *n.m.* cloister.

kreuzigen, *vb.* crucify.

Kreuzigung, -en, *n.f.* crucifixion.

kreuz und quer, *adv.* crisscross.

Kreuzung, -en, *n.f.* cross- (breed); crossing, intersection.

Kreuzverhör, -e, *n.nt.* cross-examination.

Kreuzzug, ⁻e, *n.m.* crusade.

Kreuzzügler, -, *n.m.* crusader.

kribbelig, *adj.* jittery.

kriechen*, *vb.* crawl, creep; grovel.

Krieg, -e, *n.m.* war.

kriegen, *vb.* get.

Krieger, -, *n.m.* warrior.

kriegerisch, *adj.* warlike.

Kriegsdienst, -e, *n.m.* military service.

Kriegsdienstverweigerer, -, *n.m.* conscientious objector.

Kriegsgefangen-, *n.m.* prisoner of war.

Kriegsgericht, -e, *n.nt.* court-martial.

Kriegslist, -en, *n.f.* stratagem.

Kriegslust, ⁻e, *n.f.* belligerence.

kriegslustig, *adj.* bellicose.

Kriegsmacht, ⁻e, *n.f.* military forces.

Kriegsschiff, -e, *n.nt.* warship.

kriegsversehrt, *adj.* disabled (by war).

Kriegszug, ⁻e, *n.m.* military expedition.

Kriegszustand, ⁻e, *n.m.* state of war.

kriminal', *adj.* criminal.

Krippe, -n, *n.f.* crib.

Krise, -n, *n.f.* crisis.

Kristall', -e, *n.nt.* crystal.

kristal'len, *adj.* crystal, crystalline.

kristallisie'ren, *vb.* crystallize.

Kritik', -en, *n.f.* criticism, critique, review.

Kritiker, -, *n.m.* critic.

kritisch, *adj.* critical.

kritisie'ren, *vb.* criticize.

kritzeln, *vb.* scribble.

Krocket'spiel, -e, *n.nt.* croquet.

Krokodil', -e, *n.nt.* crocodile.

Krone, -n, *n.f.* crown.

krönen, *vb.* crown.

Kronleuchter, -, *n.m.* chandelier.

Kronprinz, -en, -en, *n.m.* crown prince.

Krönung, -en, *n.f.* coronation.

Kropf, ⁻e, *n.m.* crop; goiter.

Krücke, -n, *n.f.* crutch.

Krug, ⁻e, *n.m.* pitcher.

Krümel, -, *n.m.* crumb.

krümeln, *vb.* crumble.

krumm (⁻, -), *adj.* crooked.

krümmen, *vb.* bend; **(sich k.)** warp, buckle, double up (with pain or laughter).

Krümmung, -en, *n.f.* bend; curve; curvature.

Krüppel, -, *n.m.* cripple.
Kruste, -n, *n.f.* crust.
Kruzifix, -e, *n.nt.* crucifix.
Kübel, -, *n.m.* bucket.
Kubik'-, *cpds.* cubic.
kubisch, *adj.* cubic.
Küche, -n, *n.f.* kitchen.
Kuchen, -, *n.m.* cake.
Küchenchef, -s, *n.m.* chef.
Küchenzettel, -, *n.m.* menu, bill of fare.
Kugel, -n, *n.f.* sphere, ball, bullet.
kugelförmig, *adj.* spherical; globular.
Kuh, -e, *n.f.* cow.
kühl, *adj.* cool.
Kühle, *n.f.* coolness.
kühlen, *vb.* cool.
Kühler, -, *n.m.* auto radiator.
Kühlschrank, -e, *n.m.* refrigerator.
kühn, *adj.* bold.
Kühnheit, -en, *n.f.* boldness.
Küken, -, *n.nt.* chick.
kulina'risch, *adj.* culinary.
Kult, -e, *n.m.* cult.
kultivie'ren, *vb.* cultivate.
kultiviert', *adj.* cultured.
Kultivie'rung, *n.f.* cultivation.
Kultur', -en, *n.f.* culture.
kulturell', *adj.* cultural.
Kummer, -, *n.f.* sorrow, grief.
kümmerlich, *adj.* miserable.
kümmern, *vb.* grieve, trouble, concern; (**sich k. um**) care about, look out for.
kummervoll, *adj.* sorrowful.
kund, *adj.* known.
Kunde, -n, -n, *n.m.* customer, client.
Kunde, -n, *n.f.* knowledge, information.
kund-geben*, *vb.* make known.
Kundgebung, -en, *n.f.* demonstration.
kundig, *adj.* well informed, knowing.
kündigen, *vb.* give notice; cancel.
Kündigung, -en, *n.f.* cancellation.

Kundschaft, -en, *n.f.* clientele.
künftig, *adj.* future.
Kunst, -e, *n.f.* art.
künsteln, *vb.* contrive.
kunstfertig, *adj.* skillful.
Künstler, -, *n.m.* artist.
künstlerisch, *adj.* artistic.
Künstlertum, *n.nt.* artistry.
künstlich, *adj.* artificial.
kunstlos, *adj.* artless.
Kunstseide, -n, *n.f.* rayon.
Kunststoff, -e, *n.m.* plastic.
Kunststück, -e, *n.nt.* feat, stunt.
kunstvoll, *adj.* artistic.
Kunstwerk, -e, *n.nt.* work of art.
Kunstwissenschaft, *n.f.* fine arts.
Kupfer, *n.nt.* copper.
kuppeln, *vb.* couple, join; pander.
Kuppelung, -en, *n.f.* clutch.
Kur, -en, *n.f.* cure.
Kurbel, -n, *n.f.* crank.
Kürbis, -se, *n.m.* pumpkin, gourd.
Kurier', -e, *n.m.* courier.
kurie'ren, *vb.* cure.
kurios', *adj.* odd, strange.
Kuriosität', -en, *n.f.* curio.
Kurio'sum, -sa, *n.nt.* freak.
Kurort, -e, *n.m.* resort.
Kurs, -e, *n.m.* course; rate of exchange.
Kursbuch, -er, *n.nt.* timetable.
kursie'ren, *vb.* circulate.
kursiv', *adj.* italic.
Kursus, Kurse, *n.m.* course.
Kurve, -n, *n.f.* curve.
kurz(÷), *adj.* short; (**k. und bündig**) short and to the point.
Kürze, -n, *n.f.* shortness, brevity.
kürzen, *vb.* shorten.
kürzlich, *adj.* recently.
kurzsichtig, *adj.* nearsighted.
kurzum', *adv.* in short.
Kürzung, -en, *n.f.* shortening, cut.
Kurzwaren, *n.pl.* notions.
Kuß, -sse, *n.m.* kiss.
küssen, *vb.* kiss.

L

Küste, -n, *n.f.* coast, shore.
Küster, -, *n.m.* sexton.
Kutsche, -n, *n.f.* coach.
Kuvert', -s, *n.nt.* envelope.

Labe, -n, *n.f.* refreshment, comfort.
laben, *vb.* refresh, comfort.
Laborato'rium, -rien, *n.nt.* laboratory.
Labsal, -e, *n.nt.* refreshment, comfort.
Labyrinth', -e, *n.nt.* labyrinth.
Lache, -n, *n.f.* puddle.
lächeln, *vb.* smile.
Lächeln, -, *n.nt.* smile.
lachen, *vb.* laugh.
Lachen, -, *n.nt.* laugh(ing).
lächerlich, *adj.* ridiculous.
Lachs, *n.m.* salmon.
Lack, -e, *n.m.* lacquer.
Lackleder, *n.nt.* patent leather.
Lade, -n, *n.f.* box, chest, drawer.
laden*, *vb.* load, charge; summon.
Laden, -, *n.m.* shop; shutter.
Ladenkasse, -n, *n.f.* till.
Ladentisch, -e, *n.m.* counter.
Ladung, -en, *n.f.* load, cargo, shipment; charge.
Kümmel, *n.m.* caraway.
Lage, -n, *n.f.* location, situation, condition.
Lager, -, *n.nt.* camp, lair, bed; deposit, depot, supply; bearing.
Lagerhaus, ᵉer, *n.nt.* storehouse.
lagern, *vb.* lay down, store, deposit; **(sich l.)** camp; be deposited.
Lagerung, -en, *n.f.* storage, bearing; stratification, grain.
Lagu'ne, -n, *n.f.* lagoon.
lahm, *adj.* lame.
lähmen, *vb.* lame, cripple, paralyze.

Lähmung, -en, *n.f.* paralysis.
Laib, -e, *n.m.* loaf.
Laie, -n, -n, *n.m.* layman.
Laienstand, *n.m.* laity.
Laken, -, *n.nt.* sheet.
Lamm, ᵉer, n.nt. lamb.
Lampe, -n, *n.f.* lamp.
lancie'ren, *vb.* launch.
Land, ᵉer, *n.nt.* land, country.
Landbau, *n.m.* agriculture.
Landebahn, -en, *n.f.* flight strip, runway.
landen, *vb.* land.
Landesverrat, *n.m.* high treason.
Landkarte, -n, *n.f.* map.
landläufig, *adj.* usual, ordinary.
ländlich, *adj.* rural.
Landschaft, -en, *n.f.* landscape, countryside.
Landser, -, *n.m.* common soldier, GI.
Landsmann, -leute, *n.m.* compatriot.
Landstraße, -n, *n.f.* highway.
Landstrich, -e, *n.m.* region.
Landung, -en, *n.f.* landing.
Landwirt, -e, *n.m.* farmer.
Landwirtschaft, *n.f.* agriculture.
landwirtschaftlich, *adj.* agricultural.
lang(ᵉ), *adj.* long, tall.
lange, *adv.* for a long time.
Länge, -n, *n.f.* length; longitude.
langen, *vb.* hand; suffice.
Langeweile, *n.f.* boredom.
langlebig, *adj.* long-lived.
länglich, *adj.* oblong.
Langmut, *n.m.* patience.
langmütig, *adj.* long-suffering.
längs, *adv.&prep.* along.
langsam, *adj.* slow.
Langsamkeit, *n.f.* slowness.
längst, *adv.* long since.
langweilen, *vb.* bore.
langweilig, *adj.* boring.
langwierig, *adj.* lengthy.
Lanze, -n, *n.f.* lance.
Lappa'lie, -n, *n.f.* trifle.
Lappen, -, *n.m.* rag; lobe.
Lärm, *n.m.* noise.

Larve, -n, *n.f.* mask; larva.

lassen*, *vb.* let, permit; cause to, have (someone do something, something done); leave; leave off, stop.

lässig, *adj.* indolent, careless.

Last, -en, *n.f.* burden, encumbrance; load, weight, cargo.

Lastauto, -s, *n.nt.* truck.

lasten, *vb.* weigh heavily, be a burden.

Laster, -, *n.nt.* vice.

lasterhaft, *adj.* vicious, wicked.

lästern, *vb.* slander, blaspheme.

lästig, *adj.* troublesome, disagreeable.

Lastkraftwagen, -, *n.m.* (motor) truck.

Lastwagen, -, *n.m.* (motor) truck.

Latein', *n.nt.* Latin.

latei'nisch, *adj.* Latin.

Later'ne, -n, *n.f.* lantern.

Latri'ne, -n, *n.f.* latrine.

latschen, *vb.* shuffle, slouch.

Latz, ⸗e, *n.m.* bib, flap.

lau, *adj.* tepid, lukewarm.

Laub, *n.nt.* foliage.

Lauer, *n.f.* ambush.

lauern, *vb.* lurk, lie in wait for.

Lauf, ⸗e, *n.m.* course, race, run; (gun) barrel.

Laufbahn, -en, *n.f.* career; runway, race track.

laufen*, *vb.* run, walk.

laufend, *adj.* running, current.

Läufer, -, *n.m.* runner; stair carpet; (chess) bishop.

Lauge, -n, *n.f.* lye.

Laune, -n, *n.f.* whim, caprice, fancy; mood, humor.

launenhaft, *adj.* capricious.

launig, *adj.* humorous.

launisch, *adj.* moody.

Laus, ⸗e, *n.f.* louse.

lausig, *adj.* lousy.

lauschen, *vb.* listen.

laut, *adj.* loud, aloud.

laut, *prep.* according to.

Laut, -e, *n.m.* sound.

Laute, -n, *n.f.* lute.

lauten, *vb.* read, say.

läuten, *vb.* ring, peal, sound.

lauter, *adj.* pure, sheer, nothing but.

Lauterkeit, -en, *n.f.* purity.

läutern, *vb.* purify.

lautlos, *adj.* soundless, silent.

Lautsprecher, -, *n.m.* loudspeaker.

lauwarm, *adj.* lukewarm; half-hearted.

Lava', *n.f.* lava.

Laven'del, *n.m.* lavender.

lax, *adj.* lax.

Laxheit, *n.f.* laxity.

leben, *vb.* live, be alive.

Leben, -, *n.nt.* life.

lebend, *adj.* living.

leben'dig, *adj.* living, alive; lively.

Leben'digkeit, *n.f.* liveliness, vivacity.

lebenserfahren, *adj.* experienced, sophisticated.

Lebensgefahr, -en, *n.f.* danger (to life).

lebensgefährlich, *adj.* highly dangerous.

Lebenskraft, *n.f.* vitality.

lebenslänglich, *adj.* lifelong, for life.

Lebensmittel, *n.pl.* provisions, groceries.

Lebensmittelgeschäft, -e, *n.nt.* grocery store.

Lebensunterhalt, *n.m.* livelihood.

Leber, -n, *n.f.* liver.

Lebewesen, -, *n.nt.* living being, organism.

lebewohl, *interj.* farewell, adieu.

lebhaft, *adj.* lively.

leblos, *adj.* lifeless.

Lebzeiten, *n.pl.* lifetime.

lechzen, *vb.* thirst, languish.

leck, *adj.* leaky, having a leak.

Leck, -e, *n.nt.* leak.

lecken, *vb.* leak; lick.

lecker, *adj.* tasty, appetizing.

Leder, -, *n.nt.* leather.

ledern, *adj.* leather(y).

ledig, *adj.* unmarried, single; vacant; exempt.

lediglich, *adv.* merely.

leer, *adj.* empty, vacant, blank.

Leere, -, *n.f.* emptiness.
leeren, *vb.* empty.
Leerlauf, *n.m.* neutral (gear).
legal', *adj.* legal.
legalisie'ren, *vb.* legalize.
Legat', -e, *n.nt.* bequest.
legen, *vb.* lay, place, put; **(sich l.)** lie down, subside.
legendär', *adj.* legendary.
Legen'de, -n, *n.f.* legend.
Legie'rung, -en, *n.f.* ´alloy.
Legion', -en, *n.f.* legion.
legitim', *adj.* legitimate.
legitimie'ren, *vb.* legitimize; **(sich l.)** prove one's identity.
Lehm, *n.m.* loam, clay.
Lehne, -n, *n.f.* back, arm (of a chair), support.
lehnen, *vb.* lean.
Lehnstuhl, ¨e, *n.m.* armchair.
Lehrbuch, ¨er, *n.nt.* textbook.
Lehre, -n, *n.f.* doctrine, teaching, lesson; apprenticeship.
lehren, *vb.* teach.
Lehrer, -, *n.m.* teacher.
Lehrgang, ¨e, *n.m.* course of instruction.
Lehrplan, ¨e, *n.m.* curriculum.
lehrreich, *adj.* instructive.
Lehrsatz, ¨e, *n.m.* proposition.
Lehrstunde, -n, *n.f.* lesson.
Leib, -er, *n.m.* body; abdomen; womb.
leibhaft(ig), *adj.* incarnate, personified.
leiblich, *adj.* bodily.
Leiche, -n, *n.f.* corpse.
leicht, *adj.* light; easy.
Leichter, -, *n.m.* barge.
leichtfertig, *adj.* frivolous.
Leichtfertigkeit, *n.f.* frivolity.
leichtgläubig, *adj.* gullible, credulous.
Leichtigkeit, -en, *n.f.* ease.
Leichtsinn, *n.m.* frivolity.
leichtsinnig, *adj.* frivolous, reckless.
leid, *adj.* **(es tut* mir l.)** I'm sorry.

Leid, *n.nt.* suffering, sorrow, harm.
leiden*, *vb.* suffer; stand, endure; **(gern l. mögen*)** like.
Leiden, -, *n.nt.* suffering; illness.
Leidenschaft, -en, *n.f.* passion.
leidenschaftlich, *adj.* passionate.
leidenschaftslos, *adj.* dispassionate.
leider, *adv.* unfortunately.
leidig, *adj.* unpleasant.
leidlich, *adj.* tolerable.
Leier, -n, *n.f.* lyre.
leihen*, *vb.* lend; borrow.
leihweise, *adv.* on loan.
Leim, *n.m.* glue.
leimen, *vb.* glue.
Leine, -n, *n.f.* line, leash.
Leinen, -, *n.nt.* linen.
leinen, *adj.* linen.
Leinsamen, *n.m.* linseed.
Leinwand, *n.f.* canvas; (movie) screen.
leise, *adj.* soft, quiet, gentle.
leisten, *vb.* perform, accomplish; **(sich l.)** afford.
Leisten, -, *n.m.* last.
Leistung, -en, *n.f.* performance, accomplishment, achievement, output.
leistungsfähig, *adj.* efficient.
Leitartikel, -, *n.m.* editorial.
leiten, *vb.* lead, direct, conduct, manage.
Leiter, -, *n.m.* leader, director, manager.
Leiter, -n, *n.f.* ladder.
Leitfaden, ¨, *n.m.* key, guide.
Leitsatz, ¨e, *n.m.* guiding principle.
Leitung, -en, *n.f.* guidance, direction, management; wire, line, duct, tube; conduction.
Leitungsrohr, -e, *n.nt.* conduit.
Lektion', -en, *n.f.* lesson.
Lektor, -o'ren, *n.m.* university instructor.
Lektü're, -n, *n.f.* reading.
Lende, -n, *n.f.* loin.
Lendenstück, -e, *n.nt.* sirloin.

lenkbar, *adj.* steerable, dirigible, manageable.

lenken, *vb.* direct, steer, guide.

Lenkung, -en, *n.f.* guidance, steering, control.

Lenz, -e, *n.m.* spring.

Leopard', -en, -en, *n.m.* leopard.

Lerche, -n, *n.f.* lark.

lernen, *vb.* learn.

Lesart, -en, *n.f.* reading, version.

lesbar, *adj.* legible; worth reading.

Lese, -n, *n.f.* vintage.

Lesebuch, -er, *n.nt.* reader.

lesen*, *vb.* read; lecture; gather.

Leser, -, *n.m.* reader.

leserlich, *adj.* legible.

Lethargie', -, *n.f.* lethargy.

lethar'gisch, *adj.* lethargic.

Lettland, *n.nt.* Latvia.

letzt-, *adj.* last.

letzter-, *adj.* latter.

leuchten, *vb.* give forth light, shine.

Leuchter, -, *n.m.* candlestick.

Leuchtschirm, -e, *n.m.* fluorescent screen, television screen.

Leuchtsignal, -e, *n.nt.* flare.

Leuchtturm, -e, *n.m.* lighthouse.

leugnen, *vb.* deny.

Leukoplast', *n.nt.* adhesive tape, band-aid.

Leumund, -e, *n.m.* reputation.

Leute, *n.pl.* people.

Leutnant, -s, *or* **-e,** *n.m.* lieutenant.

leutselig, *adj.* affable.

Lexikon, -ka, *n.nt.* dictionary.

Liaison', -s, *n.f.* liaison.

liberal', *adj.* liberal.

Liberalis'mus, *n.m.* liberalism.

Libret'to, -s, *n.nt.* libretto.

Licht, -er, *n.nt.* light.

Lichtbild, -er, *n.nt.* photograph.

Lichtschimmer, -, *n.m.* glint.

Lichtspiel, -e, *n.nt.* moving picture.

Lid, -er, *n.nt.* eyelid.

lieb, *adj.* dear.

liebäugeln, *vb.* make eyes at.

Liebchen, -, *n.nt.* dearest, darling.

Liebe, -n, *n.f.* love.

Liebelei', -en, *n.f.* flirtation.

liebeln, *vb.* flirt, make love.

liebenswert, *adj.* lovable.

liebenswürdig, *adj.* amiable, kind.

lieber, *adv.* rather.

Liebesaffäre, -n, *n.f.* love affair.

liebevoll, *adj.* loving, affectionate.

lieb-haben*, *vb.* love.

Liebhaber, -, *n.m.* lover.

Liebhaberei', -en, *n.f.* hobby.

liebkosen, *vb.* fondle, caress.

Liebkosung, -en, *n.f.* caress.

lieblich, *adj.* lovely.

Liebling, -e, *n.m.* darling.

Lieblings-, *cpds.* favorite.

lieblos, *adj.* loveless.

Liebreiz, -e, *n.m.* charm.

Liebschaft, -en, *n.f.* love affair.

Liebst-, *n.m.&f.* dearest, sweetheart.

Lied, -er, *n.nt.* song.

liederlich, *adj.* slovenly; dissolute.

Lieferant', -en, -en, *n.m.* supplier.

liefern, *vb.* supply, deliver.

Lieferung, -en, *n.f.* delivery.

Lieferwagen, -, *n.m.* delivery van.

liegen*, *vb.* lie, be located.

Lift, -e, *n.m.* elevator.

Likör', -e, *n.m.* liqueur.

lila, *adj.* lilac, purple.

Lilie, -n, *n.f.* lily.

Limona'de, -n, *n.f.* lemonade.

Limo'ne, -n, *n.f.* lime.

Limousi'ne, -n, *n.f.* limousine, sedan.

lind, *adj.* mild, gentle.

lindern, *vb.* alleviate, ease, soothe.

Lineal', -e, *n.nt.* ruler.

linear', *adj.* linear.

Linguist', -en, -en, *n.m.* linguist.

linguis'tisch, *adj.* linguistic.

Linie, -n, *n.f.* line.

link-, *adj.* left.

Link-, *n.f.* left.

linkisch, *adj.* awkward, clumsy.

links, *adv.* to the left.

Linse, -n, *n.f.* lens; lentil.

Lippe, -n, *n.f.* lip.

Lippenstift, -e, *n.m.* lipstick.

liquidie'ren, *vb.* liquidate.

lispeln, *vb.* lisp, whisper.

List, -en, *n.f.* cunning, trick, ruse.

Liste, -n, *n.f.* list.

listig, *adj.* cunning, crafty.

Litanei', *n.f.* litany.

Litauen, *n.nt.* Lithuania.

Liter, -, *n.m. or nt.* liter.

litera'risch, *adj.* literary.

Literatur', -en, *n.f.* literature.

Lithographie', -i'en, *n.f.* lithograph(y).

Liturgie', -i'en, *n.f.* liturgy.

litur'gisch, *adj.* liturgical.

Livree', -e'en, *n.f.* livery.

Lizenz', -en, *n.f.* license.

Lob, *n.nt.* praise.

loben, *vb.* praise.

lobenswert, *adj.* praiseworthy.

löblich, *adj.* praiseworthy.

lobpreisen, *vb.* praise, extol.

Lobrede, -n, *n.f.* eulogy.

Loch, ⁝er, *n.nt.* hole.

lochen, *vb.* put a hole in, punch.

Locke, -n, *n.f.* lock, curl.

locken, *vb.* curl; lure.

locker, *adj.* loose.

lockern, *vb.* loosen.

lockig, *adj.* curly.

lodern, *vb.* blaze.

Löffel, -, *n.m.* spoon.

Logbuch, ⁝er, *n.nt.* log.

Loge, -n, *n.f.* loge, box; (fraternal) lodge.

Logik, *n.f.* logic.

logisch, *adj.* logic.

Lohn, ⁝e, *n.m.* reward; wages.

lohnen, *vb.* reward, pay, be

of value; **(sich l.)** be worth the trouble.

lokal', *adj.* local.

Lokal', -e, *n.nt.* night club, bar, place of amusement; premises.

Lokomoti've, -n, *n.f.* locomotive.

Lokus, -se, *n.m.* toilet.

los, *adj.* loose; wrong; **(was ist l.?)** what's the matter?

Los, -e, *n.nt.* lot.

lösbar, *adj.* soluble.

los-binden*, *vb.* untie.

Löschblatt, ⁝er, *n.nt.* blotter.

löschen, *vb.* extinguish, quench; unload.

lose, *adj.* loose, slack, lax, dissolute.

Lösegeld, -er, *n.nt.* ransom.

lösen, *vb.* undo, solve, dissolve; buy (a ticket).

los-fahren*, *vb.* start out.

los-gehen*, *vb.* start out, go off, begin.

los-kommen*, *vb.* get loose.

los-lassen*, *vb.* get loose, let go.

los-lösen, *vb.* disconnect.

los-machen, *vb.* unfasten, free.

Lösung, -en, *n.f.* solution.

Lösungsmittel, -, *n.nt.* solvent.

los-werden*, *vb.* get rid of.

Lot, -e, *n.nt.* lead, plumbline.

löten, *vb.* solder.

lotrecht, *adj.* perpendicular.

Lotse, -n, -n, *n.m.* pilot.

lotsen, *vb.* pilot.

Lotterie', -i'en, *n.f.* lottery.

Löwe, -n, -n, *n.m.* lion.

Lücke, -n, *n.f.* gap.

lückenhaft, *adj.* with gaps, incomplete.

lückenlos, *adj.* without gaps, complete.

Luder, -, *n.nt.* scoundrel, slut; carrion.

Luft, ⁝e, *n.f.* air.

Luftabwehr, *n.f.* anti-aircraft, air defense.

Luftangriff, -e, *n.m.* air raid.

Luftballon, -s, *n.m.* balloon.

Luftblase, -n, *n.f.* bubble.

Luftbrücke, -n, *n.f.* air lift.
luftdicht, *adj.* airtight.
Luftdruck, -e, *n.m.* air pressure.
lüften, *vb.* air, ventilate.
Luftfahrt, *n.nt.* aviation.
Luftflotte, -n, *n.f.* air fleet.
luftig, *adj.* airy.
luftkrank, *adj.* air-sick.
Luftlinie, -n, *n.f.* air line.
Luftpost, *n.f.* air mail.
Luftschiff, -e, *n.nt.* airship, dirigible.
Luftsprung, -e, *n.m.* caper.
Luftstützpunkt, -e, *n.m.* air base.
Lüftung, *n.f.* ventilation.
Luftwaffe, -n, *n.f.* air force.
Luftzug, -e, *n.m.* draft.
Lüge, -n, *n.f.* lie.
lugen, *vb.* peep.
lügen*, *vb.* lie.
Lügner, -, *n.m.* liar.
Lümmel, -, *n.m.* lout.
Lump, -en, -en, *n.m.* bum.
Lumpen, -, *n.m.* rag.
Lunge, -n, *n.f.* lung.
Lungenentzündung, -en, *n.f.* pneumonia.
Lust, -e, *n.f.* pleasure, desire; **(L. haben*)** feel like (doing something).
lüstern, *adj.* lecherous.
lustig, *adj.* merry, gay.
Lüstling, -e, *n.m.* libertine.
lustlos, *adj.* listless.
Lustspiel, -e, *n.nt.* comedy.
Luthera'ner, -, *n.m.* Lutheran.
lutherisch, *adj.* Lutheran.
lutschen, *vb.* suck.
Luxus, *n.m.* luxury.
Luxus-, *cpds.* de luxe.
Lymphe, -n, *n.f.* lymph.
lynchen, *vb.* lynch.
Lyrik, *n.f.* lyric poetry.
lyrisch, *adj.* lyric.
Lyze'um, -e'en, *n.nt.* girl's high school.

M

Maat, -e, *n.m.* mate.
machen, *vb.* make, do.

Macht, -e, *n.f.* power.
Machterweiterung, -en, *n.f.* aggrandizement.
mächtig, *adj.* powerful.
machtlos, *adj.* powerless.
mädchen, -, *n.nt.* girl.
mädchenhaft, *adj.* girlish.
Mädel, -, *n.nt.* girl.
Magazin', -e, *n.nt.* magazine, storeroom, store.
Magd, -e, *n.f.* hired girl.
Magen, - or -, *n.m.* stomach.
Magenbeschwerden, *n.pl.* indigestion.
Magengeschwür, -e, *n.nt.* stomach ulcer.
Magenschmerzen, *n.pl.* stomach ache.
Magenverstimmung, -en, *n.f.* stomach upset.
mager, *adj.* lean.
Magermilch, *n.f.* skim milk.
Magie', *n.f.* magic.
magisch, *adj.* magic.
Magnat', -en, -en, *n.m.* magnate, tycoon.
Magne'sium, *n.nt.* magnesium.
Magnet', -e, *or* **-en, -en,** *n.m.* magnet.
magne'tisch, *adj.* magnetic.
Magnetophon', -e, *n.nt.* tape recorder.
Mahago'ni, *n.nt.* mahogany.
mähen, *vb.* mow.
Mahl, -e, *or* **-er,** *n.nt.* meal, repast.
mahlen, *vb.* grind.
Mahlzeit, -en, *n.f.* meal.
mahnen, *vb.* remind, urge, warn, dun.
Mahnung, -en, *n.f.* admonition, warning.
Mähre, -n, *n.f.* mare.
Mai, *n.m.* May.
Mais, -e, *n.m.* corn, maize.
Maiskolben, -, *n.m.* corncob.
Majestät', -en, *n.f.* majesty.
majestä'tisch, *adj.* majestic.
Major', -e, *n.m.* major.
Majorität', -en, *n.f.* majority.
Majus'kel, -n, *n.f.* capital letter.
Makel, -, *n.m.* stain, blemish, flaw.

makellos, *adj.* spotless, flawless, immaculate.

Makkaro'ni, *n.pl.* macaroni.

Makler, -, *n.m.* broker.

Makre'le, -n, *n.f.* mackerel.

Makro'ne, -n, *n.f.* macaroon.

¹Mal, -e, *n.nt.* mark, sign, spot, mole.

²Mal, -e, *n.nt.* time; **(das erste M.)** the first time; **(2 mal** 2**)** 2 times 2.

mal, *adv.* (= einmal) once, just; **(nicht m.)** not even.

Mala'ria, *n.f.* malaria.

malen, *vb.* paint.

Maler, -, *n.m.* painter.

Malerei', -en, *n.f.* painting.

malerisch, *adj.* picturesque.

Malz, *n.nt.* malt.

man, *pron.* one, a person.

Manager, -, *n.m.* manager.

mancher, -es, -e, *pron.&adj.* many, many a.

mancherlei, *adj.* various.

manchmal, *adv.* sometimes.

Mandat', -e, *n.nt.* mandate.

Mandel, -n, *n.f.* almond, tonsil.

Mandoli'ne, -n, *n.f.* mandolin.

Mangel, ¨, *n.m.* lack, dearth, defect.

Mangel, -n, *n.f.* mangle.

mangelhaft, *adj.* faulty.

mangeln, *vb.* be lacking, deficient; **(es mangelt mir an . . .)** I lack . . .

mangels, *prep.* for lack of.

Manie', -i'en, *n.f.* mania.

Manier', -en, *n.f.* manner.

manier'lich, *adj.* mannerly, polite.

manikü'ren, *vb.* manicure.

manipulie'ren, *vb.* manipulate.

Manko, -s, *n.nt.* defect, deficiency.

Mann, ¨er, *n.m.* man, husband.

Männchen, -, *n.nt.* male (animal).

Mannesalter, *n.nt.* manhood.

mannhaft, *adj.* manly.

mannigfach, *adj.* manifold.

mannigfaltig, *adj.* manifold.

Mannigfaltigkeit, -en, *n.f.* diversity.

männlich, *adj.* male, masculine.

Männlichkeit, *n.f.* manliness.

Mannschaft, -en, *n.f.* crew, team, squad; **(pl.)** enlisted men.

Manö'ver, -, *n.nt.* maneuver.

manöv'rie'ren, *vb.* maneuver.

Manschet'te, -n, *n.f.* cuff.

Mantel, ¨, *n.m.* overcoat.

Manufaktur', -en, *n.f.* manufacture, factory.

Manuskript', -e, *n.nt.* manuscript.

Mappe, -n, *n.f.* portfolio, briefcase, folder.

Märchen, -, *n.nt.* fairy tale.

märchenhaft, *adj.* fabulous.

Märchenland, ¨er, *n.nt.* fairyland.

Margari'ne, *n.f.* margarine.

Mari'ne, -n, *n.f.* navy.

marinie'ren, *vb.* marinate.

Marionet'te, -n, *n.f.* marionette, puppet.

Mark, -, *n.f.* mark (unit of money); **(deutsche M.)** West German mark.

Mark, -en, *n.f.* border(land).

Marke, -n, *n.f.* mark; brand, sort; postage stamp, check, ticket.

markie'ren, *vb.* mark.

Marki'se, -n, *n.f.* awning.

Markstein, -e, *n.m.* boundary stone, landmark.

Markt, ¨e, *n.m.* market.

Marktplatz, ¨e, *n.m.* market place.

Marmela'de, -n, *n.f.* jam.

Marmor, -e, *n.m.* marble.

Maro'ne, -n, *n.f.* chestnut.

Marot'te, -n, *n.f.* whim, fad.

Marsch, ¨e, *n.m.* march.

Marsch, -en, *n.f.* marsh.

Marschall, ¨e, *n.m.* marshal.

marschie'ren, *vb.* march.

Marter, -n, *n.f.* torture.

martern, *vb.* torture.

Märtyrer, -, *n.m.* martyr.

Märtyrertum, *n.nt.* martyrdom.

März, *n.m.* March.

Marzipan', -e, *n.m.* or *nt.* marzipan, almond paste.

Masche, -n, *n.f.* stitch, mesh.

Maschi'ne, -n, *n.f.* machine.

Maschi'nenbau, *n.m.* engineering.

Maschi'nengewehr, -e, *n. nt.* machine gun.

Maschinist', -en, -en, *n.m.* machinist.

Masern, *n.pl.* measles.

Maske, -n, *n.f.* mask.

Maskera'de, -n, *n.f.* masquerade.

maskie'ren, *vb.* mask.

Maskot'te, -n, *n.f.* mascot.

mackulin', *adj.* masculine.

Maß, -e, *n.nt.* measure(ment), dimension, extent, rate, proportion.

Massa'ge, -n, *n.f.* massage.

Masse, -n, *n.f.* mass.

massenhaft, *adj.* in large quantity.

Massenversammlung, -en, *n.f.* mass meeting.

massenweise, *adv.* in large numbers.

Masseur', -e, *n.m.* masseur.

maßgebend, *adj.* authoritative, standard.

maßgeblich, *adj.* authoritative, standard.

massie'ren, *vb.* massage.

massig, *adj.* bulky, solid.

mäßig, *adj.* moderate.

mäßigen, *vb.* moderate.

Mäßigkeit, *n.f.* temperance.

Mäßigung, *n.f.* moderation.

massiv', *adj.* massive.

maßlos, *adj.* immoderate, excessive.

Maßnahme, -n, *n.f.* measure, step.

Maßregel, -n, *n.f.* measure, step.

maßregelnd, *adj.* disciplinary.

Maßstab, "e, *n.m.* scale, rate, gauge, standard.

maßvoll, *adj.* moderate.

Mast, -e or **-en,** *n.m.* mast.

mästen, *vb.* fatten.

Material', -ien, *n.nt.* material.

Materialis'mus, *n.m.* materialism.

Mate'rie, -n, *n.f.* matter, stuff.

materiell', *adj.* material.

Mathematik', *n.f.* mathematics.

Mathema'tiker, -, *n.m.* mathematician.

mathema'tisch, *adj.* mathematical.

Matrat'ze, -n, *n.f.* mattress.

Mätres'se, -n, *n.f.* mistress.

Matro'se, -n, -n, *n.m.* sailor.

matschig, *adj.* slushy.

matt, *adj.* dull, tired.

Matte, -n, *n.f.* mat.

Mattigkeit, *n.f.* lassitude.

Mätzchen, -, *n.nt.* antic, foolish trick.

Mauer, -n, *n.f.* (outside) wall.

Maul, "er, *n.nt.* mouth, snout.

Maulkorb, "e, *n.m.* muzzle.

Maultier, -e, *n.nt.* mule.

Maulwurf, "e, *n.m.* mole.

Maure, -n, -n, *n.m.* Moor.

Maurer, -, *n.m.* mason, bricklayer.

Maus, "e, *n.f.* mouse.

Mausole'um, -le'en, *n.nt.* mausoleum.

maximal', *adj.* maximum.

Maximum, -ma, *n.nt.* maximum.

Mayonnai'se, -n, *n.f.* mayonnaise.

m. E., *abbr.* (= meines Erach'tens) in my opinion.

Mecha'nik, *n.f.* mechanics, mechanism.

Mecha'niker, -, *n.m.* mechanic.

mecha'nisch, *adj.* mechanical.

mechanisie'ren, *vb.* mechanize.

Mechanis'mus, -men, *n.m.* mechanism.

Medai'lle, -n, *n.f.* medal.

Medikament', -e, *n.nt.* drug, medicine.

Medium, -ien, *n.nt.* medium.

Medizin', -en, *n.f.* medicine.

Medizi'ner, -, *n.m.* medical man, medical student.

medizi'nisch, *adj.* medical.

Meer, -e, *n.nt.* sea.

Meerbusen, -, *n.m.* bay.

Meerenge, -n, *n.f.* strait.

Meeresbucht, -en, *n.f.* bay.

Meerrettich, -e, *n.m.* horse-radish.

Mehl, *n.nt.* flour, meal.

mehr, *adj.* more.

mehren, *vb.* increase.

mehrere, *adj.* several.

mehrfach, *adj.* multiple.

Mehrheit, -en, *n.f.* majority.

mehrmalig, *adj.* repeated.

mehrmals, *adv.* repeatedly.

Mehrzahl, -en, *n.f.* majority; plural.

meiden*, *vb.* avoid.

Meile, -n, *n.f.* mile.

Meilenstein, -e, *n.m.* milestone.

mein, -, -e, *adj.* my.

meinen, *vb.* mean, think.

meiner, -es, -e, *pron.* mine.

meinetwegen, *adv.* for my sake; for all I care.

Meinung, -en, *n.f.* opinion.

Meißel, -, -en, *n.m.* chisel.

meist, 1. *adj.* most (of). **2.** *adv.* mostly, usually.

meistens, *adv.* mostly, usually.

Meister, -, *n.m.* master; champion.

meisterhaft, *adj.* masterly.

Meisterschaft, -en, *n.f.* championship.

Meisterstück, -e, *n.nt.* masterpiece.

Melancholie', *n.f.* melancholy.

melancho'lisch, *adj.* melancholy.

Melas'se, *n.f.* molasses.

melden, *vb.* announce, notify, report.

Meldung, -en, *n.f.* announcement, notification, report.

melken*, *vb.* milk.

Melodie', -i'en, *n.f.* melody, tune.

melo'disch, *adj.* melodious.

Melo'ne, -n, *n.f.* melon; derby.

Membra'ne, -n, *n.f.* membrane.

Memoi'ren, *n.pl.* memoirs.

Memoran'dum, -den, *n.nt.* memorandum.

Menagerie', -i'en, *n.f.* menagerie.

Menge, -n, *n.f.* quantity; crowd, multitude; **(eine M.)** a lot.

Mensch, -en, -en, *n.m.* human being, person; man.

Menschenfeind, -e, *n.m.* misanthrope.

Menschenfreund, -e, *n.m.* humanitarian.

Menschenliebe, *n.f.* philanthropy.

Menschenmenge, -n, *n.f.* mob.

Menschenrechte, *n.pl.* human rights.

Menschenverstand, *n.m.* **(gesunder M.)** common sense.

Menschheit, *n.f.* mankind, humanity.

menschlich, *adj.* human; humane.

Menschlichkeit, *n.f.* humanity.

Menstruation', *n.f.* menstruation.

Mentalität', *n.f.* mentality.

Menthol', *n.nt.* menthol.

Menü, -s, *n.nt.* menu.

merken, *vb.* realize, notice; **(sich m.)** keep in mind; **(sich nichts m. lassen*)** not give oneself away.

Merkmal, -e, *n.nt.* mark, characteristic.

merkwürdig, *adj.* peculiar, odd, queer.

Messe, -n, *n.f.* fair; *(eccles.)* mass.

messen*, *vb.* measure; gauge; **(sich m.)** match.

Messer, -, *n.nt.* knife.

Messi'as, *n.m.* Messiah.

Messing, *n.nt.* brass.

Metall', -e, *n.nt.* metal.

metal'len, *adj.* metallic.

Metall'waren, *n.pl.* hardware.

Meteor', -e, *n.m.* or *nt.* meteor.

Meteorologie', *n.f.* meteorology.

Meter, -, *n.m.* or *nt.* meter.

Metho'de, -n, *n.f.* method.

metrisch, *adj.* metric.

Metzger, -, *n.m.* butcher.

Metzgerei', -en, *n.f.* butcher shop.

Meuterei', -en, *n.f.* mutiny.

meutern, *vb.* mutiny.

Mexika'ner, -, *n.m.* Mexican.

mexika'nisch, *adj.* Mexican.

Mexiko, *n.nt.* Mexico.

Mieder, -, *n.nt.* bodice.

Miene, -n, *n.f.* mien.

Mienenspiel, -e, *n.nt.* pantomine.

Miete, -n, *n.f.* rent, rental.

mieten, *vb.* rent, lease, hire.

Mieter, -, *n.m.* tenant.

Mietvertrag, -e, *n.m.* lease.

Mietwohnung, -en, *n.f.* flat, apartment.

Migrä'ne, *n.f.* migraine.

Mikro'be, -n, *n.f.* microbe.

Mikrofilm, -e, *n.m.* microfilm.

Mikrophon', -e, *n.nt.* microphone.

Mikroskop', -e, *n.nt.* microscope.

Milbe, -n, *n.f.* mite.

Milch, *n.f.* milk.

Milchhändler, -, *n.m.* dairyman.

milchig, *adj.* milky.

Milchmann, ⁻er, *n.m.* milkman.

Milchwirtschaft, -en, *n.f.* dairy.

mild, *adj.* mild, gentle, lenient.

Milde, *n.f.* mildness, leniency, clemency.

mildern, *vb.* mitigate, alleviate, soften; **(mildernde Umstände)** extenuating circumstances.

Milderung, -en, *n.f.* alleviation.

Militär', -s, *n.nt.* military.

Militär'dienstpflicht, -en, *n.f.* conscription.

militä'risch, *adj.* military.

Militaris'mus, *n.m.* militarism.

militaris'tisch, *adj* militaristic.

Miliz', -en, *n.f.* militia.

Millime'ter, -, *n.nt.* millimeter.

Million', -en, *n.f.* million.

Millionär', -e, *n.m.* millionaire.

Milz, -en, *n.f.* spleen.

Minderheit, -en, *n.f.* minority.

minderjährig, *adj.* minor, not of age.

Minderjährigkeit, *n.f.* minority.

mindern, *vb.* reduce.

minderwertig, *adj.* inferior.

mindestens, *adv.* at least.

Mine, -n, *n.f.* mine.

Mineral', -e or -ien, *n.nt.* mineral.

minera'lisch, *adj.* mineral.

Miniatur', -en, *n.f.* miniature.

minimal', *adj.* minimum, minute.

Minimum, -ma, *n.nt.* minimum.

Mini'ster, -, *n.m.* (cabinet) minister.

Ministe'rium, -rien, *n.nt.* ministry, department.

Mini'sterpräsident, -en, *n.m.* prime minister.

minus, *adv.* minus.

Minu'te, -n, *n.f.* minute.

Minz'e, -n, *n.f.* mint.

mischen, *vb.* mix, mingle, blend.

Mischmasch, -e, *n.m.* hodgepodge.

Mischung, -en, *n.f.* mixture, blend.

mißachten, *vb.* disregard; slight.

Mißachtung, -en, *n.f.* disdain.

Mißbildung, -en, *n.f.* abnormality, deformity.

mißbilligen, *vb.* disapprove.

Mißbrauch, -e, *n.m.* abuse, misuse.

mißbrau'chen, *vb.* abuse.

missen, *vb.* do without.

mißdeu'ten, *vb.* misconstrue.

Mißerfolg, **-e**, *n.m.* failure.

Missetat, **-en**, *n.f.* misdeed, crime.

Missetäter, **-**, *n.m.* offender.

mißfal'len*, *vb.* displease.

Mißfallen, *n.nt.* displeasure.

Mißgeburt, **-en**, *n.f.* freak.

Mißgeschick, **-e**, *n.nt.* adversity, misfortune.

mißglü'cken, *vb.* fail.

mißglückt', *adj.* unsuccessful, abortive.

mißgön'nen, *vb.* begrudge.

mißhan'deln, *vb.* mistreat, maltreat.

Mission', **-en**, *n.f.* mission.

Missionar', **-e**, *n.m.* missionary.

Mißklang, **-e**, *n.m.* discord.

mißlin'gen*, *vb.* miscarry, fail.

mißra'ten, *adj.* ill-bred, low.

mißtrau'en, *vb.* distrust.

Mißtrauen, *n.nt.* distrust.

mißtrauisch, *adj.* suspicious, distrustful.

mißvergnügt, *adj.* cranky.

Mißverhältnis, **-se**, *n.nt.* disproportion.

Mißverständnis, **-se**, *n.nt.* misunderstanding.

mißverstehen*, *vb.* misunderstand.

Mist, *n.m.* manure, muck.

mistig, *adj.* misty.

mit, *prep.* with.

Mitarbeit, *n.f.* cooperation, collaboration.

mit-arbeiten, *vb.* collaborate.

Mitarbeiter, **-**, *n.m.* collaborator; (**anonymer M.**) ghost writer.

Mitbewerber, **-**, *n.m.* competitor.

mit-bringen*, *vb.* bring along; bring a present.

Mitbürger, **-**, *n.m.* fellow-citizen.

miteinan'der, *adv.* together, jointly.

mitein'begriffen, *adj.* included; implied.

mitempfunden, *adj.* sympathizing; vicarious.

mit-fühlen, *vb.* sympathize.

mitfühlend, *adj.* sympathetic.

Mitgefühl, *n.nt.* sympathy.

mitgenommen, *adj.* the worse for wear.

Mitgift, **-en**, *n.f.* dowry.

Mitglied, **-er**, *n.nt.* member, fellow.

Mitgliedschaft, *n.f.* membership.

Mithelfer, **-**, *n.m.* accessory.

Mitleid, *n.nt.* pity, compassion; mercy.

mitleidig, *adj.* compassionate.

mit-machen, *vb.* string along, join, conform.

Mitmacher, **-**, *n.m.* conformer.

Mitmensch, **-en**, **-en**, *n.m.* fellow-man.

Mitschuld, *n.f.* complicity.

mitschuldig, *adj.* being an accessory.

Mitschüler, **-**, *n.m.* classmate.

Mitspieler, **-**, *n.m.* player.

Mittag, *n.m.* midday, noon.

Mittagessen, **-**, *n.nt.* noon meal, lunch, dinner.

Mittäter, **-**, *n.m.* accomplice.

Mitte, **-**, *n.f.* middle, midst, center.

mittel, *adj.* mean.

mitteilbar, *adj.* communicable.

mit-teilen, *vb.* inform, communicate.

Mitteilung, **-en**, *n.f.* information, communication.

Mittel, **-**, *n.nt.* means, measure, expedient; medium.

Mittelalter, *n.nt.* Middle Ages.

mittelalterlich, *adj.* medieval.

mittellos, *adj.* penniless, destitute.

mittelmäßig, *adj.* mediocre.

Mittelmeer, *n.nt.* Mediterranean Sea.

Mittelpunkt, -e, *n.m.* center, focus.

mittels, *prep.* by means of.

Mittelstand, *n.m.* middle class.

Mitternacht, *n.f.* midnight.

mittler-, *adj.* medium, middle.

mittschiffs, *adv.* amidships.

mit-wirken, *vb.* cooperate, assist, contribute.

mitwirkend, *adj.* contributory.

Mittwoch, -e, *n.m.* Wednesday.

Möbel, -, *n.nt.* piece of furniture; (*pl.*) furniture.

Möbelwagen, -, *n.m.* moving van.

mobil', *adj.* mobile; (*fig.*) hale and hearty.

mobilisie'ren, *vb.* mobilize.

mobilisiert', *adj.* mobile.

möblie'ren, *vb.* furnish.

Mode, -n, *n.f.* mode, fashion.

Modell', -e, *n.nt.* model.

modellie'ren, *vb.* model.

Modenschau, *n.f.* fashion show.

modern, *vb.* rot.

modern', *adj.* modern, fashionable.

modernisie'ren, *vb.* modernize.

Modeschöpfer, -, *n.m.* designer.

modifizie'ren, *vb.* modify.

modisch, *adj.* modish, fashionable.

mögen*, *vb.* like; may.

möglich, *adj.* possible; potential.

möglicherweise, *adv.* possibly.

Möglichkeit, -en, *n.f.* possibility; potential; facility.

Mohr, -en, -en, *n.m.* Moor.

Mohrrübe, -n, *n.f.* carrot.

Mole, -n, *n.f.* mole, jetty, breakwater.

Molkerei', -en, *n.f.* dairy.

Moll, *n.nt.* minor.

mollig, *adj.* plump; snug.

Moment', -e, *n.m.* moment, instant.

Moment', -e, *n.nt.* factor, impulse, motive.

momentan', *adj.* momentary.

Monarch', -en, -en, *n.m.* monarch.

Monarchie', -i'en, *n.f.* monarchy.

Monat, -e, *n.m.* month.

monatlich, *adj.* monthly.

Monatschrift, -en, *n.f.* monthly

Mönch, -e, *n.m.* monk.

Mond, -e, *n.m.* moon.

Mondschein, *n.m.* moonlight.

Mondsichel, -n, *n.f.* crescent moon.

Monolog', -e, *n.m.* monologue.

Monopol', -e, *n.nt.* monopoly.

monopolisie'ren, *vb.* monopolize.

monoton', *adj.* monotonous.

Monotonie', *n.f.* monotony.

monströs', *adj.* monstrous, freak.

Montag, -e, *n.m.* Monday.

Montan'union, *n.f.* European Coal and Steel Community.

montie'ren, *vb.* assemble, mount.

monumental', *adj.* monumental.

Moor, -e, *n.nt.* moor.

Moos, -e, *n.nt.* moss.

Mop, -s, *n.m.* mop.

Moral, *n.f.* morals; morality; morale.

mora'lisch, *adj.* moral, ethical.

Moralist', -en, -en, *n.m.* moralist.

Morast', -e, *n.m.* morass, bog.

Mord, -e, *n.m.* murder, assasination.

morden, *vb.* murder.

Mörder, -, *n.m.* murderer.

Mords-, *cpds.* mortal; heck of a . . . .

Morgen, -, *n.m.* morning; acre.

morgen, *adv.* tomorrow.

Morgendämmerung, -en, *n.f.* dawn.

Morgenrock, ˙e, *n.m.* dressing gown.

morgens, *adv.* in the morning.

Morphium, *n.nt.* morphine.

morsch, *adj.* rotten.

Mörser, -, *n.m.* mortar.

Mörtel, -, *n.m.* mortar.

Mosaik', -e, *n.nt.* mosaic.

Most, -e, *n.m.* grape juice; new wine; **(Apfelmost)** cider.

Mostrich, *n.m.* mustard.

Motiv', -e, *n.nt.* motif.

motivie'ren, *vb.* motivate.

Motivie'rung, -en, *n.f.* motivation.

Motor('), -o'ren, *n.m.* motor, engine.

motorisie'ren, *vb.* motorize, mechanize.

Motor(')rad, ˙er, *n.nt.* motorcycle.

Motte, -n, *n.f.* moth.

Motto, -s, *n.nt.* motto.

Mücke, -n, *n.f.* mosquito.

mucksen, *vb.* stir.

müde, *adj.* tired, sleepy; weary.

Müdigkeit, *n.f.* fatigue.

Muff, -e, *n.m.* muff.

muffig, *adj.* musty.

Mühe, -n, *n.f.* trouble, inconvenience; effort; **(machen Sie sich keine M.)** don't bother.

mühelos, *adj.* effortless.

mühen, *vb.* **(sich m.)** try, take the trouble.

Mühle, -n, *n.f.* mill.

Muhme, -n, *n.f.* aunt.

Mühsal, -e, *n.f.* trouble, hardship.

mühsam, *adj.* difficult, tedious, inconvenient.

mühselig, *adj.* laborious.

Mull, *n.m.* gauze.

Müll, *n.m.* garbage.

Müller, -, *n.m.* miller.

Multiplikation', -en, *n.f.* multiplication.

multiplizie'ren, *vb.* multiply.

Mumie, -n, *n.f.* mummy.

Mund, ˙er, *n.m.* mouth.

Mundart, -en, *n.f.* dialect.

Mündel, -, *n.nt.* ward.

münden, *vb.* run, flow into, end.

mündlich, *adj.* oral, verbal.

Mündung, -en *n.f.* (river) mouth; (gun) muzzle.

Munition', -en, *n.f.* ammunition, munition.

munkeln, *vb.* rumor.

munter, *adj.* awake; sprightly, lusty.

Münze, -n, *n.f.* coin; mint.

mürbe, *adj.* mellow; (meat) tender; (cake) crisp; (*fig.*) weary.

murmeln, *vb.* murmur, mutter.

murren, *vb.* grumble.

mürrisch, *adj.* disgruntled, petulant, glum.

Mürrischkeit, *n.f.* glumness.

Muschel, -n, *n.f.* shell; mussel, clam.

Muse, -1 , *n.f.* muse.

Muse'um, -e'en, *n.nt.* museum.

Musik', *n.f.* music.

musika'lisch, *adj.* musical.

Musikant', -en, -en, *n.m.* musician.

Musiker, -, *n.m.* musician.

Musik'kapelle, -n, *n.f.* band, orchestra.

Musik'pavillon, -s, *n.m.* bandstand.

Muskat', *n.m.* nutmeg.

Muskel, -n, *n.m.* muscle.

Muskelkraft, ˙e, *n.f.* muscular strength, brawn.

muskulös', *adj.* muscular.

Muße, *n.f.* leisure.

Musselin', -e, *n.m.* muslin.

müßig, *adj.* idle.

Müßigkeit, *n.f.* idleness.

Muster, -, *n.nt.* model, sample; pattern, gauge.

Musterbeispiel, -e, *n.nt.* paragon, perfect example.

mustergültig, *adj.* exemplary, model.

musterhaft, *adj.* exemplary.

mustern, *vb.* examine; (*mil.*) muster.

Musterung, -en, *n.f.* exami

nation; (*mil.*) muster; (pattern) figuring.

Mut, *n.m.* courage, fortitude.

Mutation', **-en,** *n.f.* mutation.

mutig, *adj.* courageous.

Mutigkeit, *n.f.* pluck.

mutmaßen, *vb.* conjecture.

mutmaßlich, *adj.* presumable.

Mutmaßung, -en, *n.f.* conjecture.

Mutter, ", *n.f.* mother.

Mutterleib, *n.m.* womb.

mütterlich, *adj.* maternal.

Mutterschaft, *n.f.* maternity.

mutterseelenallein', *adj.* all alone.

Muttersprache, -n, *n.f.* native language.

mutwillig, *adj.* deliberate, wilful.

Mütze, -n, *n.f.* cap, bonnet.

Myrte, -n, *n.f.* myrtle.

mysteriös', *adj.* mysterious.

Mystik, *n.f.* mysticism.

mystisch, *adj.* mystic.

Mythe, -n, *n.f.* myth.

N

na, *interj.* well; **(n. also)** there you are; **(n. und ob)** I should say so.

Nabe, -n, *n.f.* hub.

nach, *prep.* towards, to; after; according to. **(n. und n.)** by and by, gradually.

nach·affen, *vb.* ape, imitate.

nach·ahmen, *vb.* imitate, simulate.

Nachahmung, -en, *n.f.* imitation.

Nachbar, (-n,)-n, *n.m.* neighbor.

Nachbarschaft, -en, *n.f.* neighborhood.

nachdem', *conj.* after.

nach·denken*, *vb.* think, meditate, reflect.

nachdenklich, *adj.* contemplative, pensive.

Nachdruck, *n.m.* emphasis.

nachdrücklich, *adj.* emphatic.

nach·eifern, *vb.* emulate.

Nachfolger, -, *n.m.* successor.

Nachforschung, -en, *n.f.* investigation; research.

Nachfrage, -n, *n.f.* inquiry; **(Angebot und N.)** supply and demand.

nach·fühlen, *vb.* understand, appreciate.

nach·füllen, *vb.* refill.

nach·geben*, *vb.* give in, yield.

nach·gehen*, *vb.* follow; seek; (clock) be slow.

nachgiebig, *adj.* compliant.

nachhaltig, *adj.* lasting.

nach·helfen*, *vb.* assist, boost.

nachher, *adv.* afterward(s)

Nachhilfe, *n.f.* assistance.

Nachhilfelehrer, -, *n.m.* tutor.

nach·holen, *vb.* make up for.

Nachkomme, -n, -n, *n.m.* descendant.

Nachlaß, ̈sse, *n.m.* estate.

nach·lassen*, *vb.* abate, subside.

nachlässig, *adj.* negligent, careless, derelict.

Nachlässigkeit, -en, *n.f.* negligence, carelessness.

nach·machen, *vb.* imitate.

Nachmittage, -e, *n.m.* afternoon.

Nachmittagsvorstellung, -en, *n.f.* matinee.

Nachnahme, -n, *n.f.* (**per N.**) C.O.D.

nach·prüfen, *vb.* check up, verify.

Nachricht, -en, *n.f.* information, message, notice; (*pl.*) news.

Nachrichtensendung, *n.f.* newscast.

nach·schlagen*, *vb.* look up, refer to.

Nachschrift, -en, *n.f.* postscript.

nach·sehen*, *vb.* look after; look up; examine, check; (*fig.*) excuse, indulge.

Nachsehen, *n.nt.* **(das N. haben)** be the loser.

Nachsicht, -en, *n.f.* indulgence, forbearance.

nachsichtig, *adj.* lenient, indulgent.

Nachspiel, -e, *n.nt.* postlude.

nach·spüren, *vb.* track down.

nach·stehen*, *vb.* be inferior.

nächst-, *adj.* next nearest.

nach·stellen, *vb.* pursue; (clock) put back.

Nächstenliebe, *n.f.* charity.

nächstens, *adv.* soon.

Nacht, ¨e, *n.f.* night.

Nachteil, -e, *n.m.* disadvantage, drawback.

nachteilig, *adj.* disadvantageous, adverse.

Nachthemd, -en, *n.nt.* nightgown.

Nachtigall, -en, *n.f.* nightingale.

Nachtisch, -e, *n.m.* dessert.

nächtlich, *adj.* nocturnal.

Nachtlokal, -e, *n.nt.* night club.

Nachtrag, ¨e, *n.m.* supplement.

nach·tragen*, *vb.* carry behind; *(fig.)* resent, bear a grudge.

Nachtwache, -n, *n.f.* vigil.

Nachweis, -e, *n.m.* proof, certificate.

nachweisbar, *adj.* demonstrable.

nach·weisen*, *vb.* demonstrate, prove.

Nachwelt, *n.f.* posterity.

Nachwirkung, -en, *n.f.* aftereffect.

nach·zählen, *vb.* count over again. count up.

nach·zeichnen, *vb.* trace.

nackt, *adj.* naked, nude; bare.

Nacktheit, *n.f.* nakedness, bareness.

Nadel, -n, *n.f.* needle, pin.

Nagel, ¨, *n.m.* nail.

nagen, *vb.* gnaw.

Nagetier, -e, *n.nt.* rodent.

nah(e) (näher, nächst-), *adj.* near.

Nähe, *n.f.* vicinity, proximity.

nähen, *vb.* sew.

Näherin, -nen, *n.f.* seamstress.

nähern, *vb.* **(sich n.)** approach.

nähren, *vb.* nourish; nurture.

nahrhaft, *adj.* nutritious, nourishing.

Nahrung, -en, *n.f.* nourishment, food.

Nahrungsmittel, *n.pl.* foodstuffs.

Naht, ¨e, *n.f.* seam.

naiv', *adj.* naïve.

Name(n), -, *n.m.* name.

namentlich, *adv.* by name, namely; considerable.

namhaft, *adj.* renowned.

nämlich, *adv.* that is to say, namely.

nanu', *interj.* well, what do you know?

Naphtha, *n.nt.* naphtha.

Narbe, -n, *n.f.* scar.

Narko'se, -n, *n.f.* anesthetic.

narko'tisch, *adj.* narcotic, anasthetic.

Narr, -en, -en, *n.m.* fool; **(zum N. halten*)** make a fool of.

narrensicher, *adj.* foolproof.

närrisch, *adj.* foolish, daffy.

Narzis'se, -n, *n.f.* narcissus; **(gelbe N.)** daffodil.

nasal', *adj.* nasal.

naschen, *vb.* nibble (secretly) on sweets.

Nase, -n, *n.f.* nose.

Nasenbluten, *n.nt.* nosebleed.

Nasenloch, ¨er, *n.nt.* nostril.

Nasenschleim, *n.m.* mucus.

naseweis, *adj.* fresh, know-it-all.

naß (-), *adj.* wet.

Nässe, *n.f.* wetness, moisture.

nässen, *vb.* wet.

Nation', -en, *n.f.* nation.

national', *adj.* national.

Nationalis'mus, *n.m.* nationalism.

Nationalität', -en, *n.f.* nationality.

National'ökonomie, *n.f.* economics.

Natrium, *n.nt.* sodium.

Natron, *n.nt.* sodium.

Natur', **-en,** *n.f.* nature.

Natura'lien, *n.pl.* food produce.

naturalisie'ren, *vb.* naturalize.

Naturalist', **-en,** **-en,** *n.m.* naturalist.

Natur'forscher, **-,** *n.m.* naturalist.

Natur'kunde, *n.f.* nature study.

natür'lich, 1. *adj.* natural. **2,** *adv.* of course.

Natür'lichkeit, *n.f.* naturalness.

Natur'wissenschaftler, *n.m.* scientist.

nautisch, *adj.* nautical.

Navigation', *n.f.* navigation.

Nebel, **-,** *n.m.* fog. mist.

Nebelfleck, **-e,** *n.m.* nebula.

nebelhaft, *adj.* nebulous.

neb(e)lig, *adj.* foggy.

neben, *prep.* beside.

nebeneinan'der, *adv.* beside one another, abreast.

Nebenanschluß, -sse, *n.m.* (telephone) extension.

nebenbei', *adv.* besides; by the way, incidentally.

Nebenbuhler, **-,** *n.m.* rival.

Nebengebäude, **-,** *n.nt.* annex.

Nebenprodukt, **-e,** *n.nt.* by-product.

Nebensache, -n, *n.f.* incidental matter.

nebensächlich, *adj.* incidental, irrelevant.

Nebenweg, **-e,** *n.m.* byway.

nebst, *prep.* with, including.

necken, *vb.* tease, kid.

neckisch, *adj.* playful, cute.

Neffe, -n, -n, *n.m.* nephew.

negativ, *adj.* negative.

Negativ', **-e,** *n.nt.* negative.

Neger, **-,** *n.m.* Negro.

Negligé, -s, *n.nt.* negligée.

nehmen*, *vb.* take.

Neid, *n.m.* envy.

neidisch, *adj.* envious.

neigen, *vb.* (*tr.*) incline, bow, bend; (*intr.*) lean, slant; (*fig.*) tend.

Neigung, **-en,** *n.f.* inclination; slant; tendency, trend; affection.

nein, *interj.* no.

Nelke, -n, *n.f.* carnation.

nennen*, *vb.* name, call.

nennenswert, *adj.* considerable, worth mentioning.

Nenner, **-,** *n.m.* denominator.

Nennwert, **-e,** *n.m.* denomination; face value.

Neon, *n.nt.* neon.

Nerv, **-en,** *n.m.* nerve.

Nervenkitzel, **-,** *n.m.* thrill.

nervös', *adj.* nervous, jittery; high-strung.

Nervosität', *n.f.* nervousness.

Nerz, **-e,** *n.m.* mink.

Nessel, -n, *n.f.* nettle.

Nest, -er, *n.nt.* nest.

nett, *adj.* nice, enjoyable.

netto, *adj.* net.

Netz, -e, *n.nt.* net, web; network.

Notzhaut, -e, *n.f.* retina.

neu, *adj.* new; (**aufs neue, von neuem**) anew.

Neubelebung, -en, *n.f.* revival.

Neuerung, -en, *n.f.* innovation.

Neugierde, *n.f.* curiosity.

neugierig, *adj.* curious, inquisitive.

Neuheit, -en, *n.f.* novelty.

Neuigkeit, -en, *n.f.* news; novelty.

Neujahr, *n.nt.* New Year; (**Fröhliches N.**) Happy New Year.

neulich, *adv.* the other day, recently.

Neuling, -e, *n.m.* novice.

neun, *num.* nine.

neunt-, *adj.* ninth.

Neuntel, **-,** *n.nt.* ninth; (**ein n.**) one-ninth.

neunzig, *num.* ninety.

neunzigst-, *adj.* ninetieth.

Neunzigstel, **-,** *n.nt.* ninetieth; (**ein n.**) one-ninetieth.

Neuralgie', *n.f.* neuralgia.

neuro'tisch, *adj.* neurotic.

neutral', *adj.* neutral.

Neutralität', *n.f.* neutrality.

nicht, *adv.* not; (**n. wahr**)

isn't that so, don't you, aren't we, won't they, etc.

Nichtachtung, *n.f.* disregard, disrespect.

Nichtanerkennung, -en, *n.f.* nonrecognition; repudiation.

Nichtbeachtung, *n.f.* disregard.

Nichte, -n, *n.f.* niece.

nichtig, *adj.* null, void.

Nichtjude, -n, -n, *n.m.* gentile.

nichtjüdisch, *adj.* gentile.

nichts, *pron.* nothing.

Nichts, *n.nt.* nothingness, nonentity.

nichtsdestoweniger, *adv.* notwithstanding, nevertheless.

Nichtswisser, -, *n.m.* ignoramus.

nichtswürdig, *adj.* worthless, condemnable.

Nickel, *n.nt.* nickel.

nicken, *vb.* nod.

nie, *adv.* never.

nieder, *adv.* down.

Niedergang, *n.m.* decline.

niedergedrückt, *adj.* depressed.

niedergeschlagen, *adj.* dejected.

Niederkunft, *n.f.* childbirth.

Niederlage, -n, *n.f.* defeat; branch office.

Niederlande, *n.pl.* Netherlands.

Niederländer, -, *n.m.* Netherlander, Dutchman.

niederländisch, *adj.* Netherlandic, Dutch.

nieder·lassen*, *vb.* (**sich** n.) settle.

Niederlassung, -en, *n.f.* settlement.

nieder·metzeln, *vb.* massacre.

Niederschlag, ⸗e, *n.m.* precipitation; sediment.

Niedertracht, *n.f.* meanness, infamy.

niederträchtig, *adj.* mean, vile, infamous.

niedlich, *adj.* pretty, cute.

niedrig, *adj.* low; base, menial.

niemals, *adv.* never.

niemand, *pron.* no one, nobody.

Niere, -n, *n.f.* kidney.

nieseln, *vb.* drizzle.

niesen, *vb.* sneeze.

Niete, -n, *n.f.* rivet; (lottery) blank; failure, washout.

Nihilis'mus, *n.m.* nihilism.

Nikotin', *n.nt.* nicotine.

nimmer, *adv.* never.

nimmermehr, *adv.* never again.

nirgends, nirgendwo, *adv.* nowhere.

Nische, -n, *n.f.* recess; niche.

nisten, *vb.* nestle.

Niveau', -s, *n.nt.* level.

nobel, *adj.* noble; liberal.

noch, *adv.* still, yet; (**n. einmal**) once more; (**n. ein**) another, an additional; (**weder . . . n.**) neither . . . nor.

nochmalig, *adj.* additional, repeated.

nochmal(s), *adv.* once more.

Noma'de, -n, -n, *n.m.* nomad.

nominal, *adj.* nominal.

Nonne, -n, *n.f.* nun.

Nonnenkloster, ⸗, *n.nt.* convent.

Nord, Norden, *n.m.* north.

nördlich, *adj.* northern; to the north.

Nordos'ten, *n.m.* northeast.

nordöst'lich, *adj.* northeastern; to the northeast.

Nordpol, *n.m.* North Pole.

Nordwes'ten, *n.m.* northwest.

nordwest'lich, *adj.* northwestern; to the northwest.

nörgeln, *vb.* gripe.

Norm, -en, *n.f.* norm, standard.

normal', *adj.* normal.

Norwegen, *n.nt.* Norway.

Norweger, -, *n.m.* Norwegian.

norwegisch, *adj.* Norwegian.

Not, ⸗e, *n.f.* need, necessity; hardship; distress.

Notar', -e, *n.m.* notary.

Notbehelf, *n.m.* makeshift, stop-gap.

Notdurft, *n.f.* want; need.

notdürftig, *adj.* scanty, bare.

Note, -n, *n.f.* note.

Notfall, ⁔e, *n.m.* emergency.

notgedrungen, *adv.* perforce.

notie'ren, *vb.* note, make a note.

Notie'rung, -en, *n.f.* quotation.

nötig, *adj.* necessary.

nötigen, *vb.* urge.

Notiz', -en, *n.f.* note.

Notiz'buch, ⁔er, *n.nt.* notebook.

notleidend, *adj.* needy.

notwendig, *adj.* necessary.

Notwendigkeit, -en, *n.f.* necessity.

Novel'le, -n, *n.f.* short story

Novem'ber, *n.m.* November.

Nu, *n.m.* jiffy.

nüchtern, *adj.* sober; **(auf nüchternen Magen)** on an empty stomach.

Nüchternheit, *n.f.* sobriety; unimaginativeness.

Nudeln, *n.pl.* noodles.

Null, -en, *n.f.* cipher; zero.

numerie'ren, *vb.* number.

nun, *adv.* now; **(von n. an)** henceforth.

nur, *adv.* only.

Nuß, ⁔sse, *n.f.* nut.

Nußschale, -n, *n.f.* nutshell.

Nüster, -n, *n.f.* nostril.

Nutzbarkeit, *n.f.* utility.

Nutzen, -, *n.m.* benefit.

nützen, *vb.* use, utilize; (*intr.*) be of use, help, benefit.

nützlich, *adj.* useful, beneficial.

nutzlos, *adj.* useless, futile.

Nutzlosigkeit, *n.f.* futility.

Nylon, *n.nt.* nylon.

Nymphe, -n, *n.f.* nymph.

O

Oa'se, -n, *n.f.* oasis.

ob, *conj.* whether; **(als o.)** as if.

Obdach, *n.nt.* shelter.

obdachlos, *adj.* homeless.

oben, *adv.* above; upstairs.

Ober, -, *n.m.* (= Oberkellner) headwaiter; waiter; **(Herr O.!)** waiter!

ober-, *adj.* upper.

Oberbefehlshaber, -, *n.m.* commander-in-chief.

Oberfläche, -n, *n.f.* surface.

oberflächlich, *adj.* superficial.

Oberhaupt, ⁔er, *n.nt.* chief.

Oberherrschaft, *n.f.* sovereignty.

Oberschicht, *n.f* upper stratum; upper classes; **(geistige O.)** intelligentsia.

oberst-, *adj.* supreme, paramount.

Oberst, -en, -en, *n.m.* colonel.

Oberstleut'nant, -s, *n.m.* lieutenant colonel.

obgleich', *conj.* although.

Obhut, *n.f.* keeping, charge.

obig, *adj.* above, aforesaid.

Objekt', -e, *n.nt.* object.

objektiv', *adj.* objective.

Objektiv', -e, *n.nt.* objective; lens.

Objektivität', *n.f.* objectivity, detachment.

Obliegenheit, -en, *n.f.* duty, obligation.

Obligation', -en, *n.f.* bond; obligation.

obligato'risch, *adj.* obligatory.

Obrigkeit, -en, *n.f.* authorities, government.

obschon', *conj.* although.

ob·siegen, *vb.* be victorious over.

Obst, *n.nt.* fruit.

Obstgarten, ⁔, *n.m.* orchard.

obszön', *adj.* obscene.

Obus, -se, *n.m.* (= Oberleitungsomnibus) trolley bus.

ob·walten, *vb.* prevail, exist.

obwohl', *conj.* although.

Ochse, -n, -n or **Ochs, -en, -en,** *n.m.* ox.

öde, *adj.* bleak, desolate.

Öde, -n, *n.f.* bleakness, waste place.

oder, *conj.* or.

Ofen, ⁓, *n.m.* stove, oven, furnace.

offen, *adj.* open, frank.

offenbar, *adj.* evident.

offenba'ren, *vb.* reveal.

Offenba'rung, -en, *n.f.* revelation.

Offenba'rungsschrift, -en, *n.f.* scripture.

Offenheit, *n.f.* frankness.

offenkundig, *adj.* manifest.

offensichtlich, *adj.* obvious.

Offensi've, -n, *n.f.* offense, offensive.

öffentlich, *adj.* public.

Öffentlichkeit, *n.f.* public.

offiziell', *adj.* official.

Offizier', -e, *n.m.* officer.

öffnen, *vb.* open.

Öffnung, -en, *n.f.* opening, aperture.

oft (⁓), *adv.* often.

oftmals, *adv.* often (times).

öfters, *adv.* quite often.

Oheim, -e, *n.m.* uncle.

ohne, *prep.* without.

ohnehin, *adv.* in any case.

ohneglei'chen, *adv.* unequalled.

Ohnmacht, *n.f.* faint, unconsciousness; **(in O. fallen*)** faint.

ohnmächtig, *adj.* in a faint, powerless.

Ohr, -en, *n.nt.* ear.

Öhr, -e, *n.nt.* eye (of a needle, etc.)

Ohrenschmerzen, *n.pl.* earache.

Ohrring, -e, *n.m.* earring.

okkult', *adj.* occult.

Ökonom', -en, -en, *n.m.* farmer, manager.

Ökonomie', -i'en, *n.f.* economy; agriculture.

ökono'misch, *adj.* economical.

Okta've, -n, *n.f.* octave.

Okto'ber, *n.m.* October.

Okzident, *n.m.* occident.

Öl, -e, *n.nt.* oil.

ölen, *vb.* oil.

ölig, *adj.* oily.

Oli've, -n, *n.f.* olive.

Ölung, -en, *n.f.* oiling; anointment; **(letzte Ö.)** extreme unction.

Oma, -s, *n.f.* granny, grandma.

Omelett', -e, *n.nt.* omelet.

Omnibus, -se, *n.m.* (omni)bus.

ondulie'ren, *vb.* wave (hair).

Onkel, -, *n.m.* uncle.

Opa, -s, *n.m.* grandpa.

Opal', -e, *n.m.* opal.

Oper, -n, *n.f.* opera.

Operation', -en, *n.f.* operation.

operativ', *adj.* operative.

Operet'te, -n, *n.f.* operetta.

operie'ren, *vb.* operate.

Opernglas, ⁓er, *n.nt.* opera glasses.

Opfer, -, *n.nt.* offering, sacrifice; victim, casualty.

opfern, *vb.* sacrifice.

Opium, *n.nt.* opium.

opponie'ren, *vb.* oppose.

Opposition', -en, *n.f.* opposition.

Optik, *n.f.* optics.

Optiker, -, *n.m.* optician.

Optimis'mus, *n.m.* optimism.

optimis'tisch, *adj.* optimistic.

optisch, *adj.* optic.

Oran'ge, -n, *n.f.* orange.

Orches'ter, -, *n.nt.* orchestra.

Orchide'e, -n, *n.f.* orchid.

Orden, -, *n.m.* order, medal, decoration.

ordentlich, *adj.* orderly, decent, regular.

ordinär, *adj.* vulgar.

ordnen, *vb.* put in order, sort, arrange.

Ordnung, -en, *n.f.* order.

Organ', -e, *n.nt.* organ.

orga'nisch, *adj.* organic.

Organisation', -en, *n.f.* organization.

Organis'mus, -men, *n.m.* organism.

organisie'ren, *vb.* organize; scrounge.

Organist', -en, -en, *n.m.* organist.

Orgel, -n, *n.f.* organ.

Orgie, -n, *n.f.* orgy.

Orient, *n.m.* Orient.

orienta'lisch, *adj.* oriental.

orientie'ren, *vb.* orient(ate).

Orientie'rung, -en, *n.f.* orientation.

Original', -e, *n.nt.* original.

Originalität', -en, *n.f.* originality.

originell', *adj.* original.

Ort, -e, *n.m.* place, locality, town.

Orter, -, *n.m.* navigator.

örtlich, *adj.* local.

orthodox', *adj.* orthodox.

ortsansässig, *adj.* resident, indigenous.

Ortschaft, -en, *n.f.* town, village.

Ost, Osten, *n.m.* east.

Ostern. *n.nt.* Easter.

Österreich, *n.nt.* Austria.

Österreicher, -, *n.m.* Austrian.

österreichisch, *adj.* Austrian.

östlich, *adj.* eastern, easterly.

Ostsee, *n.f.* Baltic Sea.

ostwärts, *adv.* eastward.

Otter, -, *n.m.* otter.

Otter, -n, *n.f.* adder.

Ouvertü're, -n, *n.f.* overture.

oval', *adj.* oval.

Ozean, -e, *n.m.* ocean.

Ozeandampfer, -, *n.m.* ocean liner.

Ozon', -e, *n.nt.* ozone.

P

Paar, -e, *n.nt.* pair, couple; **(ein paar)** a few.

paaren, *vb.* mate.

Pacht, -en, *n.f.* lease, tenure.

Pachtbrief, -e, *n.m.* lease (document).

pachten, *vb.* lease (from).

Pachtzins, *n.m.* rent (money).

Pächter, -, *n.m.* tenant.

Pack, -e, *n.nt.* pack; rabble.

Päckchen, -, *n.nt.* parcel.

packen, *vb.* pack, seize, thrill.

Packen, -, *n.m.* pack.

Packung, -en, *n.f.* packing, wrapper, pack(age).

Pädago'ge, -n, -n, *n.m.* pedagogue.

Pädago'gik, *n.f.* pedagogy.

Paddel, -, *n.nt.* paddle.

paff, *interj.* bang.

Page, -n, -n, *n.m.* page.

Paket', -e, *n.nt.* package.

Pakt, -e, *n.m.* pact.

Palast', -e, *n.m.* palace.

Palet'te, -n, *n.f.* palette.

Palme, -n, *n.f.* palm.

Pampelmu'se, -n, *n.f.* grapefruit.

Panik, *n.f.* panic.

Panne, -n, *n.f.* breakdown; flat tire.

Panora'ma, -men, *n.nt.* panorama.

Panther, -, *n.m.* panther.

Pantof'fel, -n, *n.f.* slipper.

Pantomi'me, -n, *n.f.* pantomime.

Panzer, -, *n.m.* armor; tank.

Panzer-, *cpds.* armored.

Papagei', -en, -en, *n.m.* parrot.

Papier', -e, *n.nt.* paper.

Papier'bogen, -, *n.m.* sheet of paper.

Papier'korb, -e, *n.m.* wastebasket.

Papier'krieg, -e, *n.m.* red tape, paper work.

Papier'waren, *n.pl.* stationery.

Papp, -e, *n.m.* pap, paste.

Pappe, -n, *n.f.* cardboard.

Papst, -e, *n.m.* pope.

päpstlich, *adj.* papal.

Papsttum, *n.nt.* papacy.

Para'de, -n, *n.f.* parade.

Paradies', *n.nt.* paradise.

paradox', *adj.* paradoxical.

Paradox', -e, *n.nt.* paradox.

Paraffin', -e, *n.nt.* paraffin.

Paragraph', -en, -en, *n.m.* paragraph.

parallel', *adj.* parallel.

Paralle'le, -n, *n.f.* parallel.

Paraly'se, -n, *n.f.* paralysis.

Parenthe'se, -n, *n.f.* parenthesis.

Parfüm', -e, *n.nt.* perfume.

pari, *adv.* at par.

Pari, *n.nt.* par.

Paris', *n.nt.* Paris.

Pari'ser, -, *n.m.* Parisian.

Park, -e *or* **-s,** *n.m.* park.

parken, *vb.* park.

Parkverbot, -e, *n.nt.* no parking.

Parlament', -e, *n.nt.* parliament.

parlamenta'risch, *adj.* parliamentary.

Parodie', -i'en, *n.f.* parody.

Paro'le, -n, *n.f.* password.

Partei', -en, *n.f.* party.

Partei'genosse, -n, -n, *n.m.* party comrade.

partei'isch, *adj.* partisan, biased.

partei'lich, *adj.* partisan, biased.

partei'los, *adj.* impartial.

Parte'rre, -s, *n.nt.* ground floor; orchestra (seats in theater).

Partie', -i'en, *n.f.* match.

Partisan', (-en,) -en, *n.m.* partisan; guerilla.

Partitur', -en, *n.f.* score.

Partizip', -ien, *n.nt.* participle.

Partner, -, *n.m.* partner, associate.

Parzel'le, -n, *n.f.* lot, plot.

Paß, ¨sse, *n.m.* pass; passport.

passa'bel, *adj.* passable.

Passagier', -e, *n.m.* passenger.

Passant', -en, -en, *n.m.* passer-by.

passen, *vb.* suit, fit; **(p. zu)** match.

passend, *adj.* fitting, suitable, proper.

passie'ren, *vb.* happen; pass.

Passion', *n.f.* passion.

passiv, *adj.* passive.

Passiv, -e, *n.nt.* passive.

Pasta, -sten, *n.f.* paste.

Paste, -n, *n.f.* paste.

Paste'te, -n, *n.f.* meat pie.

pasteurisie'ren, *vb.* pasteurize.

Pastil'le, -n, *n.f.* lozenge.

Pastor, -o'ren, *n.m.* minister.

Pate, -n, -n, *n.m.* godfather.

Pate, -n, *n.f.* godmother.

Patenkind, -er, *n.nt.* godchild.

Patenonkel, -, *n.m.* godfather.

Patentante, -n, *n.f.* godmother.

Patent', -e, *n.nt.* patent.

Pathos, *n.nt.* pathos.

Patient', -en, -en, *n.m.* patient.

Patin, -nen, *n.f.* godmother.

Patriot', -en, -en, *n.m.* patriot.

patrio'tisch, *adj.* patriotic.

Patriotis'mus, *n.m.* patriotism.

Patro'ne, -n, *n.f.* cartridge; pattern.

Patrouil'le, -n, *n.f.* patrol.

Pauschal'preis, -e, *n.m.* total price.

Pause, -n, *n.f.* pause, intermission, recess.

Pavillon, -s, *n.m.* pavillion.

Pazifis'mus, *n.m.* pacifism.

Pazifist', -en, -en, *n.m.* pacifist.

Pech, *n.nt.* pitch, bad luck.

Pedal', -e, *n.nt.* pedal.

Pedant', -en, -en, *n.m.* pedant.

Pein, *n.f.* pain, agony.

peinigen, *vb.* torment.

peinlich, *adj.* embarrassing; meticulous.

Peitsche, -n, *n.f* whip.

peitschen, *vb.* whip.

Pelz, -e, *n.m.* fur.

Pelzhändler, -, *n.m* furrier.

Pendel, -, *n.m. or nt.* pendulum.

pendeln, *vb.* swing, oscillate.

Penicillin', *n.nt.* penicillin.

Pension', -en, *n.f.* pension; board, boarding house.

pensionie'ren, *vb.* pension; **(sich p. lassen*)** retire.

per, *prep.* per, by, with.

perfekt', *adj.* perfect.

Perfekt', -e, *n.nt.* perfect (tense).

Pergament', -e, *n.nt.* parchment.

Perio'de, -n, *n.f.* period, term.

perio'disch, *adj.* periodic.

Peripherie', -i'en, *n.f.* periphery.

Perle, -n, *n.f.* pearl.

Perlmutter, *n.f.* mother-of-pearl.

Persia'ner, *n.m.* Persian lamb.

Persien, *n.nt.* Persia.

Person', -en, *n.f.* person.

Personal', *n.nt.* personnel, staff.

Persona'lien, *n.pl.* personal data.

persön'lich, *adj.* personal.

Persön'lichkeit, -en, *n.f.* personage; personality.

Perspekti've, -n, *n.f.* perspective.

pervers', *adj.* perverse.

Pessimis'mus, *n.m.* pessimism.

pessimis'tisch, *adj.* pessimistic.

Pest, *n.f.* plague, pestilence.

Petersi'lie, *n.f.* parsley.

Petro'leum, *n.nt.* petroleum.

Petschaft, -en, *n.f.* seal.

Pfad, -e, *n.m.* path.

Pfadfinder, -, *n.m.* boy scout.

Pfahl, -e, *n.m.* pole, pile, post, stake.

Pfand, -er, *n.m.* pawn, pledge, security.

Pfandbrief, -e, *n.m.* bond, mortgage bond.

pfänden, *vb.* seize, attach, impound.

Pfandhaus, -er, *n.nt.* pawn-shop.

Pfanne, -n, *n.f.* pan.

Pfannkuchen, -, *n.m.* pancake.

Pfarrer, -, *n.m.* minister, priest.

Pfau, -e, *n.m.* peacock.

Pfeffer, *n.m.* pepper.

Pfefferkuchen, -, *n.m.* gingerbread.

Pfeffermin'ze, *n.f.* peppermint.

Pfeife, -n, *n.f.* pipe, whistle.

pfeifen*, *vb.* whistle.

Pfeil, -e, *n.m.* arrow.

Pfeiler, -, *n.m.* pillar, pier.

Pfennig, -e, *n.m.* penny.

Pferd, -e, *n.nt.* horse.

Pferdestärke, -n, *n.f.* horsepower.

Pfiff, -e, *n.m.* whistle; trick.

pfiffig, *adj.* tricky, sly.

Pfingsten, *n.nt.* Pentecost, Whitsuntide.

Pfirsich, -e, *n.m.* peach.

Pflanze, -n, *n.f.* plant.

pflanzen, *vb.* plant.

Pflaster, -, *n.nt.* plaster; pavement.

pflastern, *vb.* plaster, pave.

Pflaume, -n, *n.f.* plum.

Pflege, -n, *n.f.* care, nursing, cultivation.

pflegen, *vb.* take care of, nurse, cultivate; be accustomed.

Pflegeeltern, *n.pl.* foster parents.

Pflicht, -en, *n.f.* duty.

pflichtgemäß, *adj.* dutiful.

Pflock, -e, *n.m.* peg.

pflücken, *vb.* pick, gather.

Pflug, -e, *n.m.* plow.

pflügen, *vb.* plow.

Pforte, -n, *n.f.* gate, door, entrance.

Pförtner, -, *n.m.* janitor, doorman.

Pfosten, -, *n.m.* post, jamb.

Pfote, -n, *n.f.* paw.

Pfropf, -e, = Pfropfen, -, *n.m.* stopper, plug.

pfropfen, *vb.* graft.

Pfund, -e, *n.nt.* pound.

pfuschen, *vb.* botch, bungle.

Pfütze, -n, *n.f.* puddle.

Phänomen', -e, *n.nt.* phenomenon.

Phantasie', -i'en, *n.f.* fantasy.

phantas'tisch, *adj.* fantastic.

Phase, -n, *n.f.* phase.

Philosoph', -en, -en, *n.m.* philosopher.

Philosophie', -i'en, *n.f.* philosophy.

philoso'phisch, *adj.* philosophical.

phlegma'tisch, *adj.* phlegmatic.

phone'tisch, *adj.* phonetic.

Phosphor, *n.m.* phosphorus.

Photoapparat, **-e**, *n.m.* camera.

photoelek'trisch, *adj.* photoelectric.

Photograph', **-en**, **-en**, *n.m.* photographer.

Photographie', **-i'en**, *n.f.* photograph(y).

Photokopie', **-i'en**, *n.f.* photostat.

Physik', *n.f.* physics.

Physiker, **-**, *n.m.* physicist.

Physiologie', *n.f.* physiology.

physisch, *adj.* physical.

Pianist', **-en**, **-en**, *n. m.* pianist.

Pickel, **-**, *n.m.* pimple; ice axe.

picken, *vb.* peck.

Picknick, **-s**, *n.nt.* picnic.

piepsen, *vb.* peep.

Pier, **-s**, *n.m.* pier.

Pietät', *n.f.* piety.

Pigment', **-e**, *n.nt.* pigment.

pikant', *adj.* piquant.

Pilger, **-**, *n.m.* pilgrim.

Pille, **-n**, *n.f.* pill.

Pilot', **-en**, **-en**, *n.m.* pilot.

Pilz, **-e**, *n.m.* mushroom.

Pinsel, **-**, *n.m.* brush.

Pionier', **-e**, *n.m.* pioneer; (*mil.*) engineer.

Pisto'le, **-n**, *n.f.* pistol.

Pisto'lenhalter, **-**, *n.m.* holster.

Plackerei', **-en**, *n.f.* drudgery.

plädie'ren, *vb.* plead.

Plädoyer', **-s** *n.nt.* plea.

Plage, **-n**, *n.f.* trouble, affliction.

plagen, *vb.* plague, annoy, afflict.

Plagiat', *n.nt.* plagiarism.

Plakat', **-e**, *n.nt.* placard, poster.

Plan, **-e**, *n.m.* plan.

planen, *vb.* plan.

Planet', **-en**, **-en**, *n.m.* planet.

Planke, **-n**, *n.f.* plank.

planlos, *adj.* aimless.

planmäßig, *adj.* according to plan.

planschen, *vb.* splash.

Planta'ge, **-n**, *n.f.* plantation.

Plappermaul, **-er**, *n.nt.* chatterbox.

plappern, *vb.* babble.

Plasma, **-men**, *n.nt.* plasma.

Plastik, **-en**, *n.f.* sculpture.

plastisch, *adj.* plastic.

Plateau', **-s**, *n.nt.* plateau.

Platin, *n.nt.* platinum.

platt, *adj.* flat.

Plättbrett, **-er**, *n.nt.* ironing board.

Platte, **-n**, *n.f.* plate, slab, sheet, tray; (photographic) slide; (phonograph) record.

Plätteisen, **-**, *n.nt.* (flat) iron.

plätten, *vb.* iron.

Plattenspieler, **-**, *n.m.* record player.

Plattform, **-en**, *n.f.* platform.

Plattfuß, **-e**, *n.m.* flat foot.

plattie'ren, *vb.* plate.

Platz, **-e**, *n.m.* place, seat, square.

platzen, *vb.* burst.

Plauderei', **-en**, *n.f.* chat.

plaudern, *vb.* chat.

pleite, *adj.* broke.

Plombe, **-n**, *n.f.* (tooth) filling.

plötzlich, *adj.* sudden.

plump, *adj.* clumsy, tactless.

Plunder, *n.m.* old clothes, rubbish.

plündern, *vb.* plunder, pillage.

Plünderung, **-en**, *n.f.* pillage.

Plural, **-e**, *n.m.* plural.

plus, *adv.* plus.

Plüsch, **-e**, *n.m.* plush.

Plutokrat', **-en**, **-en**, *n.m.* plutocrat.

pneuma'tisch, *adj.* pneumatic.

Pöbel, *n.m.* mob, rabble.

pöbelhaft, *adj.* vulgar.

pochen, *vb.* knock, throb.

Pocke, **-n**, *n.f.* pock; (*pl.*) smallpox.

Podium, **-ien**, *n.nt.* rostrum.

Poesie', -i'en, *n.f.* poetry.

Poet', -en, -en, *n.m.* poet.

poe'tisch, *adj.* poetic.

Poin'te, -n, *n.f.* point (of a joke), punch line.

Pokal', -e, *n.m.* goblet, cup.

Pol, -e, *n.m.* pole.

polar', *adj.* polar.

Polar'stern, *n.m.* North Star.

Pole, -n, -n, *n.m.* Pole.

Polen, *n.nt.* Poland.

Poli'ce, -n, *n.f.* (insurance) policy.

polie'ren, *vb.* polish.

Politik', *n.f.* politics, policy.

Poli'tiker, -, *n.m.* politician.

poli'tisch, *adj.* politic(al).

Politur', -en, *n.f.* polish.

Polizei', -en, *n.f.* police.

polizei'lich, *adj.* by the police.

Polizei'präsident, -en, -en, *n.m.* chief of police.

Polizei'präsidium, -ien, *n.nt.* police headquarters.

Polizei'revier, -e, *n.nt.* police station.

Polizei'richter, -, *n.m.* magistrate.

Polizei'staat, -en, -en, *n.m.* police state.

Polizei'stunde, -n, *n.f.* curfew.

Polizei'wache, -n, *n.f.* police station.

Polizist', -en, -en, *n.m.* policeman.

polnisch, *adj.* Polish.

Polonä'se, -n, *n.f.* polonaise.

Polster, -, *n.nt.* pad, cushion.

polstern, *vb.* pad, upholster.

Polsterung, -en, *n.f.* padding, upholstery.

poltern, *vb.* rattle, bluster.

Polygamie', *n.f.* polygamy.

Poly'pen, *n.pl.* adenoids.

Polytech'nikum, -ken, *n.nt.* technical college.

Pomeran'ze, -n, *n.f.* orange.

Pony, -s, *n.nt.* pony; (*pl.*) bangs.

populär', *adj.* popular.

popularisie'ren, *vb.* popularize.

Popularität', *n.f.* popularity.

Pore, -n, *n.f.* pore.

porös', *adj.* porous.

Portal', -e, *n.nt.* portal.

Portefeuille', -s, *n.nt.* portfolio.

Portemonnaie', -s, *n.nt.* purse.

Portier', -s. *n.m.* doorman, concierge.

Portion', -en, *n.f.* portion, helping.

Porto, *n.nt.* postage.

Porträt', -s, *n.nt.* portrait.

Portugal, *n.nt.* Portugal.

Portugie'se, -n, -n, *n.m.* Portuguese.

portugie'sisch, *adj.* Portuguese.

Porzellan', -en, *n.nt.* porcelain, china.

Posau'ne, -n, *n.f.* trumpet.

Pose, -n, *n.f.* pose.

posie'ren, *vb.* strike a pose.

Position', -en, *n.f.* position.

positiv, *adj.* positive.

Posse, -n, *n.f.* prank, antic; farce.

Post, *n.f.* mail; post office.

Postamt, "er, *n.nt.* post office.

Postanweisung, -en, *n.f.* money order.

Postbote, -n, -n, *n.m.* postman.

Posten, -, *n.m.* post, station; item.

Postfach, "er, *n.nt.* post office box.

Postkarte, -n, *n.f.* post card.

postlagernd, *adv.* general delivery.

Poststempel, -, *n.m.* post mark.

Pracht, *n.f.* splendor.

prächtig, *adj.* splendid.

prachtvoll, *adj.* gorgeous.

Prädikat', -e, *n.nt.* predicate.

Präfix, -e, *n.nt.* prefix.

prägen, *vb.* stamp, coin, impress.

Prägung, -en, *n.f.* coinage.

prähistorisch, *adj.* prehistoric.

prahlen, *vb.* boast.

praktisch, *adj.* practical.

Prali'ne, -n, *n.f.* chocolate candy.

prallen, *vb.* bounce, be reflected.

Prämie, -n, *n.f.* premium, prize.

präparie'ren, *vb.* prepare.

Präposition', -en, *n.f.* preposition.

Präsens, *n.nt.* present.

präsentie'ren, *vb.* present.

Präsident', -en, -en, *n.m.* president.

prasseln, *vb.* patter, crackle.

Praxis, *n.f.* practice; doctor's office.

Präzedenz'fall, -e, *n.m.* precedent.

Präzision', *n.f.* precision.

predigen, *vb.* preach.

Prediger, -, *n.m.* preacher.

Predigt, -en, *n.f.* sermon.

Preis, -e, *n.m.* price; cost; prize, praise.

Preiselbeere, -n, *n.f.* cranberry.

preisen*, *vb.* praise.

Preisgabe, -n, *n.f.* surrender, abandonment.

preis-geben*, *vb.* surrender, abandon.

prellen, *vb.* toss; cheat.

Premie're, -n, *n.f.* première.

Premier'minister, -, *n.m.* prime minister.

Presse, *n.f.* press.

pressen, *vb.* press.

Prestige', *n.nt.* prestige.

Preußen, *n.nt.* Prussia.

Preuße, -n, -n, *n.m.* Prussian.

preußisch, *adj.* Prussian.

Priester, -, *n.m.* priest.

prima, *adj.* first class, swell.

primär', *adj.* primary.

Primel, -n, *n.f.* primrose.

primitiv', *adj.* primitive.

Prinz, -en, -en, *n.m.* prince.

Prinzes'sin, -nen, *n.f.* princess.

Prinzip', -ien, *n.nt.* principle.

Priorität', -en, *n.f.* priority.

Prise, -n, *n.f.* pinch.

Prisma, -men, *n.nt.* prism.

privat', *adj.* private.

Privileg', -ien, *n.nt.* privilege.

pro, *prep.* per.

Probe, -n, *n.f.* experiment, test; rehearsal; sample.

proben, *vb.* rehearse.

probeweise, *adj.* tentative.

Probezeit, -en, *n.f.* probation.

probie'ren, *vb.* try (out).

Problem', -e, *n.nt.* problem.

Produkt', -e, *n.t.* product.

Produktion', *n.f.* production.

produktiv', *adj.* productive.

Produzent', -en, -en, *n.m.* producer.

produzie'ren, *vb.* produce.

profan', *adj.* profane.

Profes'sor, -o'ren, *n.m.* professor.

Profil', -e, *n.nt.* profile.

Profit', -e, *n.m.* profit.

profitie'ren, *vb.* profit.

Progno'se, -n, *n.f.* prognosis.

Programm', -e, *n.nt.* program.

Projekt', -e, *n.nt.* project.

Projektion', -en, *n.f.* projection.

Projek'tor, -o'ren, *n.m.* projector.

projizie'ren, *vb.* project.

Proklamation', -en, *n.f.* proclamation.

Prokurist', -en, -en, *n.m.* manager.

Proletariat', *n.nt.* proletariat.

Proleta'rier, -, *n.m.* proletarian.

proleta'risch, *adj.* proletarian.

Prolog', -e, *n.m.* prologue.

prominent', *adj.* prominent.

Prono'men, -mina, *n.nt.* pronoun.

Propagan'da, *n.f.* propaganda, publicity.

Propel'ler, -, *n.m.* propeller.

Prophet', -en, -en, *n.m.* prophet.

prophe'tisch, *adj.* prophetic.

prophezei'en, *vb.* prophesy.

Prophezei'ung, -en, *n.f.* prophecy.

Proportion', -en, *n.f.* proportion.

proppenvoll, *adj.* chock full.

Prosa, *n.f.* prose.

prosa'isch, *adj.* prosaic.

Prospekt', **-e,** *n.m.* prospectus.

Prostituiert'-, *n.f.* prostitute.

Protein', *n.nt.* protein.

Protest', **-e,** *n.m.* protest.

Protestant', **-en, -en,** *n.m.* Protestant.

protestie'ren, *vb.* protest.

Protokoll', **-e,** *n.nt.* minutes, record.

protzen, *vb.* show off.

protzig, *adj.* gaudy.

Proviant', *n.m.* food, supplies.

Provinz', **-en,** *n.f.* province.

provinziell', *adj.* provincial.

Provision', **-en,** *n.f.* commission.

proviso'risch, *adj.* temporary.

Provokation', **-en,** *n.f.* provocation.

provozie'ren, *vb.* provoke.

Prozent', **-e,** *n.nt.* per cent.

Prozent'satz, **-e,** *n.m.* percentage.

Prozeß', **-sse,** *n.m.* process, trial, lawsuit.

Prozession', **-en,** *n.f.* procession.

prüde, *adj.* prudish.

prüfen, *vb.* test, examine, verify.

Prüfung, **-en,** *n.f.* test, examination, scrutiny.

Prügel, **-,** *n.m.* cudgel; (*pl.*) beating.

Prügelei', **-en,** *n.f.* brawl.

prügeln, *vb.* beat, thrash.

Prunk, *n.m.* pomp, show.

prunkvoll, *adj.* pompous, showy.

PS, *abbr.* (= Pferdestärke) horsepower.

Psalm, **-en,** *n.m.* psalm.

Pseudonym', **-e,** *n.nt.* pseudonym.

Psychia'ter, **-,** *n.m.* psychiatrist.

Psychiatrie', *n.f.* psychiatry.

Psychoanaly'se, **-n,** *n.f.* psychoanalysis.

Psycholo'ge, **-n, -n,** *n.m.* psychologist.

Psychologie', *n.f.* psychology.

psycholo'gisch, *adj.* psychological.

Psycho'se, **-n,** *n.f.* psychosis.

Publikation', **-en,** *n.f.* publication.

Publikum, *n.nt.* public, audience.

publizie'ren, *vb.* publish.

Pudding, **-e,** *n.m.* pudding.

Pudel, **-,** *n.m.* poodle.

Puder, **-,** *n.nt.* powder.

Puderdose, **-n,** *n.f.* compact.

pudern, *vb.* powder.

Puderquaste, **-n,** *n.f.* powder puff.

Puffer, **-,** *n.m.* buffer; potato pancake.

Pullo'ver, **-,** *n.m.* sweater.

Puls, **-e,** *n.m.* pulse.

Pulsader, **-n,** *n.f.* artery.

pulsie'ren, *vb.* pulsate, throb.

Pult, **-e,** *n.nt.* desk, lectern.

Pulver, **-,** *n.nt.* powder.

Pumpe, **-n,** *n.f.* pump.

pumpen, *vb.* pump; borrow, lend.

Pumps, *n.pl.* pumps.

Punkt, **-e,** *n.m.* point, dot, period.

Punktgleichheit, *n.f.* tie.

Punktion', **-en,** *n.f.* puncture.

pünktlich, *adj.* punctual.

Punktzahl, **-en,** *n.f.* score.

Punsch, *n.m.* punch.

Pupil'le, **-n,** *n.f.* pupil.

Puppe, **-n,** *n.f.* doll; chrysalis.

pur, *adj.* pure; (alcohol) straight.

Püree', **-s,** *n.nt.* purée.

Purpur, *n.m.* purple.

purpurn, *adj.* purple.

Puter, **-,** *n.m.* turkey.

Putsch, **-e,** *n.m.* attempt to overthrow the government.

Putz, *n.m.* finery.

putzen, *vb.* clean, polish.

Putzfrau, **-en,** *n.f.* cleaning woman.

putzig, *adj.* funny, droll, quaint.

Putzwaren, *n.pl.* millinery.

Puzzle, **-s,** *n.nt.* puzzle.

Pyja'ma, -s, *n.m.* pajamas.
Pyrami'de, -n, *n.f.* pyramid.

Q

Quadrat', -e, *n.nt.* square.
Quadrat'-, *cpds.* square.
quadra'tisch, *adj.* square.
quaken, *vb.* quack, croak.
Qual, -en, *n.f.* torment, agony, ordeal.
quälen, *vb.* torment, torture.
Qualifikation', -en, *n.f.* qualification.
qualifizie'ren, *vb.* qualify.
Qualität', -en, *n.f.* quality.
qualmen, *vb.* smoke.
qualvoll, *adj.* agonizing.
Quantität', -en, *n.f.* quantity.
Quarantä'ne, -n, *n.f.* quarantine.
Quark, *n.m.* curds.
Quarkkäse, *n.m.* cottage cheese.
Quartal', -e, *n.nt.* quarter of a year.
Quartett', -e, *n.nt.* quartet.
Quartier', -e, *n.nt.* lodging, billet.
Quarz, -e, *n.m.* quartz.
Quaste, -n, *n.f.* tuft.
Quatsch, *n.m.* nonsense, bunk, baloney.
Quecksilber, *n.nt.* mercury.
Quelle, -n, *n.f.* spring, source, well, fountain.
quellen*, *vb.* well, gush, flow.
quer, *adj.* cross(wise), diagonal.
Querschnitt, -, *n.m.* cross section.
Querstraße, -n, *n.f.* cross street.
Querverweis, -e, *n.m.* cross reference.
quetschen, *vb.* squeeze, bruise.
Quetschung, -en, *n.f.* contusion.
quietschen, *vb.* squeak.
Quintett', -e, *n.nt.* quintet.

quitt, *adj.* quits, even, square.
quittie'ren, *vb.* receipt.
Quittung, -en, *n.f.* receipt.
Quote, -n, *n.f.* quota.

R

Rabatt', -e, *n.m.* discount.
Rabau'ke, -n, -n, *n.m.* tough.
Rabbi'ner, -, *n.m.* rabbi.
Rabe, -n, -n, *n.m.* raven.
Rache, *n.f.* revenge.
rächen, *vb.* revenge, avenge.
Rachen, -, *n.m.* throat, jaws.
Rad, ˃er, *n.nt.* wheel.
Radar, *n.nt.* radar.
Radau', *n.m.* noise, racket.
radeln, *vb.* (bi)cycle.
rad-fahren*, *vb.* (bi)cycle.
Radfahrer, -, *n.m.* (bi)cyclist.
radie'ren, *vb.* erase; etch.
Radier'gummi, -s, *n.m.* (rubber) eraser.
Radie'rung, -en, *n.f.* etching.
Radies'chen, -, *n.nt.* radish.
radikal', *adj.* radical.
Radio, -s, *n.nt.* radio.
radioaktiv', *adj.* radioactive.
Radioapparat, -e, *n.m.* radio set.
Radioempfänger, -, *n.m.* radio receiver.
Radiosender, -, *n.m.* radio transmitter, broadcasting station.
Radiosendung, -en, *n.f.* radio broadcast.
Radium, *n.nt.* radium.
Radius, -ien, *n.m.* radius.
Radspur, -en, *n.f.* rut.
raffinie'ren, *vb.* refine.
raffiniert', *adj.* tricky, shrewd; sophisticated.
ragen, *vb.* extend, loom.
Rahm, *n.m.* cream.
Rahmen, -, *n.m.* frame.
rahmen, *vb.* frame.
Rake'te, -n, *n.f.* rocket.
Rake'tenwaffe, -n, *n.f.* missile.

rammen, *vb.* ram.

Rampe, -n, *n.f.* ramp.

Rand, -er, *n.m.* edge, rim, margin.

Rang, -e, *n.m.* rank.

rangie'ren, *vb.* switch, shunt.

Rangordnung, -en, *n.f.* hierarchy.

ranzig, *adj.* rancid.

Rapier', -e, *n.nt.* foil.

rasch, *adj.* quick.

rascheln, *vb.* rustle.

rasen, *vb.* rage.

Rasen, *n.m.* lawn. turf.

rasend, *adj.* frenzied.

Raserei', -en, *n.f.* frenzy.

Rasierapparat, -e, *n.m.* safety razor.

rasie'ren, *vb.* shave.

Rasier'klinge, -n, *n.f.* razor blade.

Rasier'messer, -, *n.nt.* (straight) razor.

Rasse, -n, *n.f.* race.

rasseln, *vb.* rattle.

Rast, -en, *n.f.* rest.

rasten, *vb.* rest.

rastlos, *adj.* restless.

Rasur', -en, *n.f.* erasure. shave.

Rat, -e, *n.m.* advice; councilor.

Rate, -n, *n.f.* payment, installment.

raten*, *vb.* guess, advise.

Ratenzahlung, *n.f.* payment by installments.

ratifizie'ren, *vb.* ratify.

Ration', -en, *n.f.* ration.

rationell', *adj.* rational, reasonable.

rationie'ren, *vb.* ration.

ratlos, *adj.* helpless, perplexed, at one's wit's end.

Ratlosigkeit, *n.f.* perplexity.

ratsam, *adj.* advisable.

Ratsamkeit, *n.f.* advisability.

Rätsel, -, *n.nt.* riddle, puzzle; enigma, mystery.

rätselhaft, *adj.* puzzling, mysterious.

Ratte, -n, *n.f.* rat.

rattern, *vb.* rattle.

Raub, *n.m.* robbery, plunder.

rauben, *vb.* rob.

Räuber, -, *n.m.* robber.

Rauch, *n.m.* smoke.

rauchen, *vb.* smoke.

Raucher, -, *n.m.* smoker.

räuchern, *vb.* smoke (fish, meat).

raufen, *vb.* pull, tear; (**sich r.**) fight, brawl.

Rauferei', -en, *n.f.* brawl.

rauh, *adj.* rough; hairy, rugged.

Rauheit, -en, *n.f.* roughness.

Raum, -e, *n.m.* room, space.

Rauminhalt, *n.m.* volume, capacity, contents.

räumen, *vb.* vacate.

räumlich, *adj.* spatial.

Räumung, *n.f.* (*comm.*) clearance; (*mil.*) evacuation.

raunen, *vb.* whisper.

Rausch, -e, *n.m.* intoxication.

Rauschgift, -e, *n.nt.* narcotic, dope.

rauschen, *vb.* roar, rustle.

Razzia, -ien, *n.f.* raid.

reagie'ren, *vb.* react, respond.

Reaktion', -en, *n.f.* reaction, response.

Reaktionär', -e, *n.m.* reactionary.

reaktionär', *adj.* reactionary.

reaktivie'ren, *vb.* recommission.

Reak'tor, -o'ren, *n.m.* reactor.

realisie'ren, *vb.* realize, put into effect.

Realisie'rung, -en, *n.f.* realization.

Realis'mus, *n.m.* realism.

Realist', -en, -en, *n.m.* realist.

Realität', -en, *n f.* reality.

Rebe, -n, *n.f.* vine; grape.

Rebstock, -e, *n.m.* vine.

Rechen, -, *n.m.* rake.

Rechenaufgabe, -n, *n.f.* arithmetic problem.

Rechenmaschine, -n, *n.f.* calculating machine.

Rechenschaft, *n.f.* account, responsibility; (**R. ablegen**) account for.

Rechenschieber, -, _n.m._ slide rule.

rechnen, _vb._ count, do sums, figure.

Rechnen, _n.nt._ arithmetic.

Rechnung, -en, _n.f._ figuring, computation; bill; (**R. tragen**) take into account.

Rechnungsbuch, ̈er, _n.nt._ account book.

recht, _adj._ right; (**r. haben**) be right.

Recht, -e, _n.nt._ right; (system of) law.

Rechteck, -e, _n.nt._ rectangle.

rechteckig, _adj._ rectangular, oblong.

rechtfertigen, _vb._ justify; vindicate.

Rechtfertigung, -en, _n.f._ justification.

rechtlich, _adj._ legal, judicial.

rechtmäßig, _adj._ lawful.

rechts, _adv._ (to the) right.

Rechtsanwalt, ̈e, _n.m._ lawyer.

rechtschaffen, _adj._ honest, righteous.

Rechtschaffenheit, _n.f._ honesty, righteousness.

Rechtschreibung, _n.f._ orthography, spelling.

Rechtsgelehrt-, _n.m._ jurist.

Rechtsprechung, _n.f._ jurisdiction.

Rechtsspruch, ̈e, _n.m._ judgment, sentence.

Rechtsstreit, -e, _n.m._ litigation.

Rechtswissenschaft, _n.f._ jurisprudence.

recken, _vb._ stretch.

Redakteur', -e, _n.m._ editor.

Redaktion', -en, _n.f._ editorial office; editor.

Rede, -n, _n.f._ speech, talk; (**eine R. halten***) give a speech; (**keine R. sein* von**) be no question of; (**jemanden zur R. stellen**) confront a person with, take to task.

redegewandt, _adj._ eloquent.

Redekunst, _n.f._ rhetoric, oratory.

reden, _vb._ talk, speak;

(**vernünftig r. mit**) reason with.

Redensart, -en, _n.f._ way of speaking; saying, idiom.

Redeteil, -e, _n.m._ part of speech.

Redewendung, -en, _n.f._ phrase, figure of speech.

redlich, _adj._ honest, upright.

Redner, -, _n.m._ speaker, orator.

redselig, _adj._ loquacious.

Reduktion', -en, _n.f._ reduction.

reduzie'ren, _vb._ reduce.

reell', _adj._ honest, sound.

Reflex', -e, _n.m._ reflex.

reflektie'ren, _vb._ reflect.

Reflexion', -en, _n.f._ reflection.

Reform', -en, _n.f._ reform.

reformie'ren, _vb._ reform.

Refrain', -s, _n.m._ refrain.

Regal', -e, _n.nt._ shelf.

rege, _adj._ alert; active.

Regel, -n, _n.f._ rule.

regelmäßig, _adj._ regular.

Regelmäßigkeit, _n.f._ regularity.

regeln, _vb._ regulate.

regelrecht, _adj._ regular, downright.

Regelung, -en, _n.f._ regulation.

regen, _vb._ stir, move.

Regen, _n.m._ rain.

Regenbogen, ̈, _n.m._ rainbow.

Regenguß, ̈sse, _n.m._ downpour.

Regenmantel, ̈, _n.m._ raincoat.

Regenschirm, -e, _n.m._ umbrella.

Regie', _n.f._ direction.

regie'ren, _vb._ govern.

Regie'rung, -en, _n.f._ government.

Regi'me, -s, _n.nt._ regime.

Regiment', -er, _n.nt._ regiment.

Region', -en, _n.f._ region.

Regisseur', -e, _n.m._ director.

Regis'ter, -, _n.nt._ register, index.

Registrie'rung, -en, _n.f._ registration.

regnen, vb. rain.

regnerisch, adj. rainy.

regsam, adj. alert, quick.

regulie'ren, vb. regulate.

Reh, -e, n.nt. deer, roe.

rehabilitie'ren, vb. rehabilitate.

Rehleder, -, n.nt. deerskin.

Reibe, -n, n.f. grater.

reiben*, vb. rub; grate; chafe.

Reibung, -en, n.f. friction.

reich, adj. rich.

Reich, -e, n.nt. kingdom, empire, realm.

reichen, vb. (tr.) pass, hand, reach; (intr.) extend.

reichlich, adj. plentiful, ample, abundant.

Reichtum, -er, n.m. wealth, affluence.

Reichweite, n.f. reach, range.

reif, adj. ripe, mature.

Reife, n.f. maturity.

reifen, vb. ripen, mature.

Reifen, -, n.m. hoop; (auto, etc.) tire.

Reifenpanne, -n, n.f. puncture, blowout.

reiflich, adj. carefully considerate.

Reigen, -, n.m. (dance) round; (music) song.

Reihe, -n, n.f. row; series; succession.

reihen, vb. (sich r.) rank.

Reihenfolge, -n, n.f. sequence, succession.

Reim, -, n.m. rhyme.

rein, adj. clean, pure.

Reinfall, -e, n.m. flop.

rein-fallen*, vb. be taken in.

Reinheit, n.f. purity.

reinigen, vb. clean, cleanse.

Reinigung, -en, n.f. cleaning, cleansing; **(chemische R.)** dry-cleaner, dry-cleaning.

rein-legen, vb. trick, take in.

Reis, -, n.m. rice.

Reise, -n, n.f. trip, journey.

Reiseandenken, -, n.nt. souvenir.

Reisebüro, -s, n.nt. travel agency.

Reiseführer, -, n.m. guidebook.

reisen, vb. travel.

Reisend-, n.m.&f. traveler.

Reiseroute, -n, n.f. itinerary.

reißen*, vb. rip, tear; **(sich r. um)** scramble for.

reißend, adj. rapid, racing.

Reißer, -, n.m. thriller, bestseller.

reiten*, vb. ride, horseback.

Reiter, -, n.m. rider.

Reiz, -e, n.m. charm, appeal; irritation.

reizbar, adj. sensitive, irritable.

reizen, vb. excite, tempt; irritate.

reizend, adj. adorable, lovely.

Reizfaktor, -en, n.m. irritant.

Reizmittel, -, n.nt. stimulant.

Reizung, -en, n.f. irritation.

rekeln, vb. (sich r.) stretch, sprawl.

Rekla'me, n.f. advertisement, advertising, publicity.

reklamie'ren, vb. reclaim; complain.

Rekord', -e, n.m. record.

Rekrut', -en, -en, n.m. draftee, recruit.

Rektor, -o'ren, n.m. headmaster; (university) president, chancellor.

relativ', adj. relative.

Religion', -en, n.f. religion.

religiös', adj. religious.

Rendezvous', -, n.nt. rendezvous, tryst.

Rennen, -, n.nt. race.

rennen*, vb. run, dash; race.

Renntier, -e, n.nt. reindeer.

renta'bel, adj. profitable.

Rente, -n, n.f. pension, income.

rentie'ren, vb. (sich r.) be profitable.

Reparation', -en, n.f. reparation.

Reparatur', -en n.f. repair.

reparie'ren, vb. repair.

repatriie'ren, vb. repatriate.

Repertoire', -s, n.nt. repertoire.

Repor'ter, -, n.m. reporter.

Repräsentant', -en, -en, n.m. representative.

Repräsentation', **-en**, *n.f.* representation.

reproduzie'ren, *vb.* reproduce.

Reptil', **-e**, *or* **-ien**, *n.nt.* reptile.

Republik', **-en**, *n.f.* republic.

republika'nisch, *adj.* republican.

requirie'ren, *vb.* requisition.

Requisition', **-en**, *n.f.* requisition.

Reservation', **-en**, *n.f.* reservation.

Reser've, **-n**, *n.f.* reserve.

reservie'ren, *vb.* reserve.

Reservoir', **-s**, *n.nt.* reservoir.

Residenz', **-en**, *n.f.* residence.

Resignation', **-en**, *n.f.* resignation.

resignie'ren, *vb.* resign.

resolut', *adj.* determined.

resonant', *adj.* resonant.

Resonanz', **-en**, *n.f.* resonance.

Respekt', *n.m.* respect, regard.

Rest, **-e**, *n.m.* rest, remnant.

Restaurant', **-s**, *n.nt.* restaurant.

restaurie'ren, *vb.* restore.

restlos, *adj.* without remainder, entire.

Restbestand, **˗e**, *n.m.* residue.

Resultat', **-e**, *n.nt.* result.

Resümee', **-s**, *n.nt.* resumé.

retten, *vb.* rescue, save, salvage.

Retter, **-**, *n.m.* savior.

Rettung, **-en**, *n.f.* rescue; salvation.

Rettungsboot, **-e**, *n.nt.* lifeboat.

rettungslos, *adj.* irretrievable, hopeless.

Rettungsring, **-e**, *n.m.* life preserver.

Reue, *n.f.* repentance.

reuevoll, *adj.* repentant.

reuig, *adj.* penitent.

Revan'che, **-n**, *n.f.* revenge; return match.

Revers', **-**, *n.m.* lapel.

revidie'ren, *vb.* revise.

Revier', **-e**, *n.nt.* district.

Revision', **-en**, *n.f.* revision.

Revol'te, **-n**, *n.f.* revolt.

revoltie'ren, *vb.* revolt.

Revolution', **-en**, *n.f.* revolution.

revolutionär', *adj.* revolutionary.

Revol'ver, **-**, *n.m.* revolver, gun.

Rezept', **-e**, *n.nt.* receipt, recipe; prescription.

Rhabar'ber, *n.m.* rhubarb.

Rhapsodie', **-i'en**, *n.f.* rhapsody.

Rhein, *n.m.* Rhine.

rheto'risch, *adj.* rhetorical.

Rheuma, *n.nt.* rheumatism.

Rheumatis'mus, *n.m.* rheumatism.

rhythmisch, *adj.* rhythmical.

Rhythmus, **-men**, *n.m.* rhythm.

richten, *vb.* set right; (**r. auf**) turn to; (**sich r. an**) turn to; (**sich r. nach**) go by, be guided by, depend on; (*jur.*) judge.

Richter, **-**, *n.m.* judge.

richterlich, *adj.* judicial, judiciary.

Richterstand, *n.m.* judiciary.

richtig, *adj.* true, correct.

Richtigkeit, *n.f.* correctness.

Richtung, **-en**, *n.f.* direction; tendency.

riechen*, *vb.* smell.

Riecher, **-**, *n.m.* (*fig.*) hunch.

Riegel, **-**, *n.m.* bolt.

Riemen, **-**, *n.m.* strap; oar.

Riese, **-n**, **-n**, *n.m.* giant.

riesenhaft, *adj.* gigantic.

riesig, *adj.* tremendous, vast.

rigoros', *adj.* rigorous.

Rind, **-er**, *n.nt.* ox, cow, cattle.

Rinde, **-n**, *n.f.* bark.

Rindfleisch, *n.nt.* beef.

Rindsleder, **-**, *n.nt.* cowhide.

Ring, **-e**, *n.m.* ring.

ringeln, *vb.* curl.

ringen*, *vb.* struggle, wrestle,

Ringkampf, ≃e, *n.m.* wrestling match.

Rinne, -n, *n.f.* rut, groove.

Rinnstein, -e, *n.m.* curb, gutter.

Rippe, -n, *n.f.* rib.

Rippenfellentzündung, -en, *n.f.* pleurisy.

Risiko, -s, *n.t.* risk, hazard, gamble.

riskie'ren, *vb.* risk, gamble.

Riß, -sse, *n.m.* tear, crack.

Ritt, -e, *n.m.* ride.

Ritter, -, *n.m.* knight.

ritterlich, *adj.* chivalrous.

rittlings, *adv.* astride.

Rituele', *-e,* *n.nt.* ritual.

rituell', *adj.* ritual.

Ritus, -en, *n.m.* rite.

Ritze, -n, *n.f.* crack.

Riva'le, -n, -n, *n.m.* rival.

rivalisie'ren, *vb.* rival.

Rivalität', -en, *n.f.* rivalry.

Rizinusöl, *n.nt.* castor oil.

Robbe, -n, *n.f.* seal.

Roboter, -, *n.m.* robot.

robust', *adj.* robust.

röcheln, *vb.* breathe heavily.

Rock, ≃e, *n.m.* (men) jacket; (women) skirt.

rodeln, *vb.* go sledding.

Rodelschlitten, -, *n.m.* sled.

Rogen, -, *n.m.* roe.

Roggen, *n.m.* rye.

roh, *adj.* raw, crude; (*fig.*) brutal.

Roheit, -en, *n.f.* crudeness, brutality.

Rohling, -e, *n.m.* rowdy.

Rohr, -e, *n.nt.* pipe; (gun) barrel; (bamboo, sugar) cane.

Röhre, -n, *n.f.* pipe, tube.

Rohrflöte, -n, *n.f.* reed pipe.

Rolle, -n, *n.f.* roll, coil; spool; role, part.

rollen, *vb.* roll.

Roller, -, *n.m.* scooter.

Rolltreppe, -n, *n.f.* escalator.

Rom, *n.nt.* Rome.

Roman', *-e,* *n.m.* novel.

roma'nisch, *adj.* Romance.

Roman'schriftsteller, -, *n.m.* novelist.

Roman'tik, *n.f.* romanticism, Romantic Movement.

roman'tisch, *adj.* romantic.

Roman'ze, -n, *n.f.* romance.

Römer, -, *n.m.* Roman.

römisch, *adj.* Roman.

röntgen, *vb.* x-ray.

Röntgenaufnahme, -n, *n.f.* x-ray.

Röntgenstrahlen, *n.pl.* x-rays.

rosa, *adj.* pink.

Rose, -n, *n.f.* rose.

Rosenkranz, ≃e, *n.m.* rosary.

rosig, *adj.* rosy.

Rosi'ne, -n, *n.f.* raisin.

Roß, -sse, *n.nt.* horse, steed.

Rost, -e, *n.m.* rust; (oven) grate.

rosten, *vb.* rust.

rösten, *vb.* roast; toast.

rostig, *adj.* rusty.

rot(≃), *adj.* red.

rotbraun, *adj.* red-brown, maroon.

Röteln, *n.pl.* German measles.

rotie'ren, *vb.* rotate.

Rotwein, -e, *n.m.* red wine, claret.

Roué', -s, *n.m.* roué, rake.

Rouge, *n.nt.* rouge.

Roula'de, -n, *n.f.* meat roll.

Route, -n, *n.f.* route.

Routi'ne, -n, *n.f.* routine.

routiniert', *adj.* experienced.

Rowdy, -s, *n.m.* hoodlum.

Rübe, -n, *n.f.* (**gelbe R.**) carrot; (**rote R.**) beet; (**weisse R.**) turnip.

Rubin', -e, *n.m.* ruby.

Rubrik', -en, *n.f.* category, heading.

ruchbar, *adj.* notorious.

ruchlos, *adj.* infamous, profligate.

Ruck, -e, *n.m.* jerk, wrench.

ruckartig, *adj.* jerky.

rückbezüglich, *adj.* reflexive.

Rückblick, *n.m.* retrospect.

Rücken, -, *n.m.* back.

rücken, *vb.* move, move over.

rückerstatten, *vb.* refund.

Rückfahrkarte, -n, *n.f.* return ticket.

Rückfahrt, -en, *n.f.* return trip.

Rückfall, ⸚e, *n.m.* relapse.

Rückgabe, *n.f.* return, restitution.

Rückgang, ⸚e, *n.m.* retrogression, decline.

rückgängig, *adj.* declining; (**r. machen**) cancel, revoke.

Rückgrat, -e, *n.nt.* spine. backbone.

Rückhalt, *n.m.* support, reserve.

rückhaltlos, *adj.* unreserved, frank.

Rückhand, ⸚e, *n.f.* backhand.

Rückkaufswert, -e, *n.m.* equity (mortgage, etc.).

Rückkehr, *n.f.* return; reversion.

Rückmarsch, ⸚e, *n.m.* retreat.

Rucksack, ⸚e, *n.m.* knapsack.

Rückschlag, ⸚e, *n.m.* reverse, upset.

Rückschluß, ⸚sse, *n.m.* conclusion.

Rückseite, -n, *n.f.* reverse, rear.

Rücksicht, -en, *n.f* consideration.

Rücksichtnahme, *n.f.* consideration.

rücksichtslos, *adj.* inconsiderate; reckless, ruthless.

Rücksichtslosigkeit, -en, *n.f.* lack of consideration, ill-mannered behavior; ruthlessness.

rücksichtsvoll, *adj.* thoughtful. considerate.

Rückstand, ⸚e, *n.m.* arrears; (**in R. geraten***) fall behind, lag.

rückständig, *adj.* in arrears; backward, antiquated.

Rücktritt, -e, *n.m.* resignation.

rückwärts, *adv.* backward(s).

Rückwärtsgang, ⸚e, *n.m..* reverse (gear).

ruckweise, *adv.* by fits and starts.

Rückzug, -e, *n.m.* retreat.

Rudel, -, *n.nt.* pack.

Ruder, -, *n.nt.* oar.

Ruderboot, -e, *n.nt.* rowboat.

rudern, *vb.* row.

Ruf, -e, *n.m.* call; reputation, standing.

rufen*, *vb.* call, shout.

Rufnummer, -n, *n.f.* (telephone) number.

Rüge, -n, *n.f.* reprimand.

rügen, *vb.* reprimand.

Ruhe, *n.f.* rest; calmness, tranquility; silence.

ruhelos, *adj.* restless.

ruhen, *vb.* rest, repose.

Ruhestand, *n.m.* retirement.

Ruhestätte, -n, *n.f.* resting place.

ruhig, *adj.* calm, composed; quiet; (**das kannst du r. machen**) go ahead and do it.

Ruhm, *n.m.* fame, glory.

rühmen, *vb.* praise, extol.

rühmenswert, *adj.* praiseworthy.

rühmlich, *adj.* laudable.

ruhmlos, *adj.* inglorious.

ruhmreich, *adj.* glorious.

Ruhr, *n.f.* dysentery.

Rührei, -er, *n.nt.* scrambled eggs.

rühren, *vb.* move, stir; (**sich r.**) stir.

rührend, *adj.* touching, pathetic.

rührig, *adj.* lively, hustling.

Rührung, *n.f.* emotion, compassion.

Rui'ne, -n, *n.f.* ruin.

ruinie'ren, *vb.* ruin.

Rum, *n.m.* rum.

Rummel, *n.m.* hubbub, racket.

rumpeln, *vb.* rumble.

Rumpf, ⸚e, *n.m.* torso, fuselage, hull.

rund, *adj.* round, circular.

Runde, -n, *n.f.* round; (sports) lap.

Rundfunk, *n.m.* radio.

Rundfunksendung, -en, *n.f.* broadcast.

Rundfunksprecher, -, *n.m.* broadcaster.

Rundfunkübertragung, -en, *n.f.* broadcast.

rundlich, *adj.* plump.

Rundschreiben, -, *n.nt.* circular.

Runzel, -n, *n.f.* wrinkle.

runzeln, *vb.* wrinkle; **(die Stirn r.)** frown.

rupfen, *vb.* pluck.

Rüsche, -n, *n.f.* ruffle.

Ruß, *n.m.* soot, grime.

Russe, -n, *n.m.* Russian.

Rüssel, -, *n.m.* trunk.

russisch, *adj.* Russian.

Rußland, *n.nt.* Russia.

rüsten, *vb.* prepare; *(mil.)* arm.

rüstig, *adj.* vigorous, spry.

Rüstung, -en, *n.f.* armament; armor.

rutschen, *vb.* slide, skid.

rütteln, *vb.* shake, jolt.

S

Saal, Säle, *n.m.* large room, hall.

Saat, -en, *n.f.* seed, sowing.

Sabbat, -en, *n.m.* Sabbath.

Säbel, -, *n.m* saber.

Sabota′ge, *n.f.* sabotage.

Saboteur′, -e, *n.m.* saboteur.

sabotie′ren, *vb.* sabotage.

Sache, -n, *n.f.* thing, matter; cause.

Sacharin′, *n.nt.* saccharine.

Sachkundig-, *n.m.* expert.

sachlich, *adj.* objective, relevant, matter-of-fact; (art) functional.

Sachlichkeit, *n.f.* objectivity, detachment.

sacht, *adj.* soft.

sachte, *adv.* cautiously, gingerly.

Sachverständig-, *n.m.* expert.

Sack, -e, *n.m.* sack, bag.

Sadis′mus, *n.m.* sadism.

Sadist′, -en, -en, *n.m.* sadist.

sadis′tisch, *adj.* sadistic.

säen, *vb.* sow.

Saft, -e, *n.m.* juice, sap.

saftig, *adj.* juicy, succulent.

Sage, -n, *n.f.* myth.

Säge, -n, *n.f.* saw.

sagen, *vb.* say, tell.

sägen, *vb.* saw.

sagenhaft, *adj.* mythical, fabulous.

Sago, *n.nt.* tapioca.

Sahne, *n.f.* cream.

Sahneeis, *n.nt.* ice cream.

Saison′, -s, *n.f.* season.

Saite, -n, *n.f.* string, chord.

Sakrament′, -e, *n.nt.* sacrament.

Sakrileg′, -e, *n.nt.* sacrilege.

Sakristei′, -en, *n.f.* sacristy, vestry.

Salat′, -e, *n.m.* salad.

Salat′soße, -n, *n.f.* salad dressing.

Salbe, -n, *n.f.* salve, ointment.

salben, *vb.* anoint.

Saldo, -den, *n.m.* balance, remainder.

Salm, -e, *n.m.* salmon.

Salon′, -s, *n.m.* salon.

salopp′, *adj.* nonchalant.

salutie′ren, *vb.* salute.

Salve, -n, *n.f.* salvo.

Salz, -e, *n.nt.* salt.

salzen, *vb.* salt.

salzig, *adj.* salty.

Salzwasser, -, *n.nt.* brine.

Samen, -, *n.m.* seed.

sammeln, *vb.* collect, gather; **(sich s.)** *(mil.)* rally.

Sammler, -, *n.m.* collector.

Sammlung, -en, *n.f.* collection.

Samstag, -e, *n.m.* Saturday.

Samt, *n.m.* velvet.

samt, *adv. & prep.* together with.

sämtlich, *adj.* entire.

Sanato′rium, -rien, *n.nt.* sanatorium.

Sand, -e, *n.m.* sand.

Sanda′le, -n, *n.f.* sandal.

sandig, *adj.* sandy.

Sandtorte, -n, *n.f.* pound cake.

sanft, *adj.* gentle, meek.

Sanftmut, *n.m.* gentleness.

sanftmütig, *adj.* gentle, meek.

Sänger, -, *n.m.* singer.

sang- und klanglos, *adv.* quietly.

Sankt, *adj.* Saint.

Saphir', **-e**, *n.m.* sapphire.

Sardel'le, **-n**, *n.f.* anchovy.

Sardi'ne, **-n**, *n.f.* sardine.

Sarg, **ᵉe**, *n.m.* coffin.

Sarkas'mus, *n.m.* sarcasm.

sarkas'tisch, *adj.* sarcastic.

Satan, *n.m.* Satan.

sata'nisch, *adj.* diabolical.

Satellit', **-en**, **-en**, *n.m.* satellite.

Satin', **-s**, *n.m.* satin.

Sati're, **-n**, *n.f.* satire.

sati'risch, *adj.* satirical.

satt, *adj.* satiated; **(ich bin s.)** I have had enough to eat; **(ich habe es s.)** I am sick of it; **(sich s. essen*, sehen*)** have one's fill.

Sattel, **-**, *n.m.* saddle.

satteln, *vb.* saddle.

sättigen, *vb.* satiate, saturate.

Sättigung, *n.f.* satiation, saturation.

sattsam, *adv.* sufficiently.

Satz, **ᵉe**, *n.m.* (*gram.*) sentence, clause; (*music*) movement; (*dishes, tennis*) set.

Satzlehre, *n.f.* syntax.

Satzung, **-en**, *n.f.* statute, by-law.

Satzzeichen, **-**, *n.nt.* punctuation mark.

Sau, **ᵉe**, *n.f.* sow.

sauber, *adj.* clean, neat.

Sauberkeit, *n.f.* cleanliness, neatness.

säuberlich, *adj.* clean, careful.

säubern, *vb.* cleanse, purge.

Säuberungsaktion, **-en**, *n.f.* purge.

sauer, *adj.* sour, acid.

Säuerlichkeit, **-en**, *n.f.* acidity.

Sauerstoff, *n.m.* oxygen.

saufen*, *vb.* drink heavily, guzzle.

Säufer, **-**, *n.m.* drunkard.

saugen*, *vb.* suck.

Saugen, *n.nt.* suction.

Sauger, **-**, *n.m.* nipple (baby's bottle).

Säugling, **-e**, *n.m.* infant, baby.

Säule, **-n**, *n.f.* pillar, column.

Saum, **ᵉe**, *n.m.* seam, hem.

säumen, *vb.* hem; delay.

säumig, *adj.* tardy, delinquent.

Säure, **-n**, *n.f.* acid.

säuseln, *vb.* rustle.

sausen, *vb.* (wind) whistle; run, dash.

schaben, *vb.* scrape.

Schabernack, **-e**, *n.m.* hoax.

schäbig, *adj.* shabby.

Schach, *n.nt.* chess; **(in S. halten)** keep at bay.

Schachbrett, **-er**, *n.nt.* chessboard.

Schachfigur, **-en**, *n.f.* chessman.

Schachspiel, **-e**, *n.nt.* chess.

Schacht, **ᵉe**, *n.m.* shaft.

Schachtel, **-n**, *n.f.* box.

schade, *adv.* too bad.

Schädel, **-**, *n.m.* skull.

schaden, *vb.* harm; be harmful.

Schaden, **ᵉ**, *n.m.* harm, damage.

Schadenersatz, *n.m.* indemnity, compensation, damages.

schadenfroh, *adj.* gloating; **(s. sein*)** gloat.

schadhaft, *adj.* defective.

schädigen, *vb.* wrong, damage.

schädlich, *adj.* harmful, injurious.

Schädling, **-e**, *n.m.* pest, destructive insect.

Schaf, **-e**, *n.nt.* sheep.

Schäfer, **-**, *n.m.* shepherd.

schaffen*, *vb.* make, create.

schaffen, *vb.* get done, achieve; **(sich zu s. machen mit)** to busy oneself with, tangle.

Schaffner, **-**, *n.m.* conductor.

Schafott', **-e**, *n.nt.* scaffold.

Schafskopf, **ᵉe**, *n.m.* idiot.

Schaft, **ᵉe**, *n.m.* shaft.

Schakal', **-e**, *n.m.* jackal.

Schal, **-s**, *n.m.* shawl, scarf.

schal, *adj.* stale.

Schale, -n, *n.f.* skin, rind; shell; dish, bowl.

schälen, *vb.* pare, peel.

Schalk, -e, *n.m.* rogue.

schalkhaft, *adj.* roguish.

Schall, ⁻e, *n.m.* sound, ring.

Schalldämpfer, -, *n.m.* (auto) muffler; (gun) silencer.

Schallgrenze, -n, *n.f.* sound barrier.

Schallplatte, -n, *n.f.* phonograph record.

Schalot'te, -n, *n.f.* scallion.

Schaltanlage, -n, *n.f.* switchboard.

Schaltbrett, -er, *n.nt.* switchboard; control panel.

schalten, *vb.* shift; command; **(s. und walten)** do as one pleases.

Schalter, -, *n.m.* (*elec.*) switch; (ticket, etc.) window.

Schaltjahr, -e, *n.nt.* leap year.

Schaltung, -en, *n.f.* (*elec.*) connection; (auto) shift.

Scham, *n.f.* shame; chastity.

schämen, *vb.* shame; (**sich s.**) be ashamed.

Schamgefühl, -e, *n.nt.* sense of modesty.

schamhaft, *adj.* modest, chaste.

schamlos, *adj.* shameless, infamous.

Schamlosigkeit, *n.f.* shamelessness.

Schampun', -s, *n.nt.* shampoo.

schandbar, *adj.* shameful, disgraceful.

Schande, *n.f.* shame, dishonor.

schänden, *vb.* dishonor, ravish.

Schandfleck, -e, *n.m.* blemish, stigma.

schändlich, *adj.* infamous.

Schandtat, -en, *n.f.* crime.

Schändung, -en, *n.f.* desecration; rape.

Schankstube, -n, *n.f.* barroom.

Schanze, -n, *n.f.* entrenchment; **(sein Leben in die**

S. schlagen*) risk one's life.

Schar, -en, *n.f.* flock, group, host.

scharf(⁴), *adj.* sharp, acute, keen.

Scharfblick, *n.m.* quick eye; acuteness.

Schärfe, -n, *n.f.* sharpness, acuteness.

schärfen, *vb.* sharpen.

Scharfrichter, -, *n.m.* executioner.

Scharfsinn, *n.m.* acumen, discernment.

scharfsinnig, *adj.* acute, shrewd.

Scharlach, *n.m.* scarlet fever.

scharlachrot, *adj.* scarlet.

Scharnier', -e, *n.nt.* hinge.

Schärpe, -n, *n.f.* sash.

Scharte, -n, *n.f.* crack.

Schatten, -, *n.m.* shade; shadow.

Schattenbild, -er, *n.nt.* silhouette.

Schattengestalt, -en, *n.f.* phantom, phantasm.

Schattenseite, -n, *n.f.* shady side; (*fig.*) disadvantage, drawback.

schattie'ren, *vb.* shade.

schattig, *adj.* shady.

Schatz, ⁻e, *n.m.* treasure.

schätzen, *vb.* treasure, prize; estimate, gauge; esteem.

schätzenswert, *adj.* estimable.

Schatzmeister, -, *n.m.* treasurer.

Schätzung, -en, *n.f.* estimate.

schätzungsweise, *adv.* approximately.

Schau, *n.f.* show, exhibition; **(zur S. tragen*)** display.

Schauder, -, *n.m.* shudder, shiver.

schauderhaft, *adj.* horrible, ghastly.

schaudern, *vb.* shudder.

schauen, *vb.* see, look.

Schauer, -, *n.m.* shower; (fever) chill.

schauerlich, *adj.* gruesome.

Schaufel, -n, *n.f.* shovel; dustpan.

Schaufenster, -, *n.nt.* store window, display window.

schachmatt', *adj.* checkmate; *(fig.)* exhausted.

Schaukel, -n, *n.f.* swing.

schaukeln, *vb.* swing, rock.

Schaukelstuhl, ⸗e, *n.m.* rocking chair.

Schaum, *n.m.* froth, foam; lather.

schäumen, *vb.* froth, foam; lather.

Schaumgummi, *n.m.* foam rubber.

Schaumwein, -e, *n.m.* champagne.

Schauplatz, ⸗e, *n.m.* scene, theater, locale.

schaurig, *adj.* horrible.

Schauspiel, -e, *n.nt.* drama; spectacle.

Schauspieler, -, *n.m.* actor.

Schauspielerin, -nen, *n.f.* actress.

Schaustellung, *n.f.* exhibition; ostentation.

Scheck, -s, *n.m.* check.

scheel, *adj.* **(s. an·sehen)** look askance at.

Scheffel, -, *n.m.* bushel.

Scheibe, -n, *n.f.* disk; slice.

Scheide, -n, *n.f.* sheath; (water) divide; vagina.

scheiden*, *vb.* leave, part; **(sich s. lassen*)** get divorced.

Scheidewand, ⸗e, *n.f.* partition.

Scheideweg, -e, *n.m.* crossroads.

Scheidung, -en, *n.f.* divorce.

Schein, *n.m.* shine, light, shimmer; brilliance.

scheinbar, *adj.* apparent; imaginary.

scheinen*, *vb.* shine; seem.

scheinheilig, *adj.* hypocritical.

Scheinwerfer, -, *n.m.* spotlight; headlight.

Scheinwerferlicht, *n.nt.* floodlight.

Scheitel, -, *n.m.* part (in the hair).

scheitern, *vb.* fail.

Schelle, -n, *n.f.* bell.

schellen, *vb.* ring.

Schelm, -e, *n.m.* rogue.

schelmisch, *adj.* roguish, mischievous.

Schelte, -n, *n.f.* scolding.

schelten*, *vb.* scold.

Schema, -s, *n.nt.* scheme.

Schenke, -n, *n.f.* tavern, bar.

Schenkel, -, *n.m.* thigh.

schenken, *vb.* give (as a present).

Schenkstube, -n, *n.f.* taproom, bar.

Schenkung, -en, *n.f.* donation.

Schere, -n, *n.f.* scissors, shears.

Schererei', -en, *n.f.* bother.

scheren*, *vb.* shear.

Scherz, -e, *n.m.* joke, jest.

scherzen, *vb.* joke, jest, kid.

scherzhaft, *adj.* jocular.

scheu, *adj.* shy.

Scheu, *n.f.* timidity.

scheuchen, *vb.* scare, shoo.

scheuen, *vb.* shy, shun.

Scheuer, -n, *n.f.* barn, shed.

scheuern, *vb.* scour.

Scheuklappe, -n, *n.f.* blinder.

Scheune, -n, *n.f.* barn, shed.

Scheusal, -e, *n.nt.* monster; fright.

scheußlich, *adj.* horrible.

Schi, -er, *n.m.* ski.

Schicht, -en, *n.f.* layer, stratum, class.

Schick, *n.m.* skill; stylishness.

schick, *adj.* chic, stylish.

schicken, *vb.* send; **(sich s.)** be proper.

schicklich, *adj.* proper.

Schicksal, -e, *n.nt.* fate.

schicksalsschwer, *adj.* fateful.

Schickung, *n.f.* providence.

schieben*, *vb.* push, shove; engage in illegal transactions.

Schieber, -, *n.m.* profiteer.

Schiebung, -en, *n.f.* racketeering.

Schiedsrichter, -, *n.m.* umpire, referee.

schief, *adj.* crooked, askew.

Schiefer, *n.m.* slate.

schielen, *vb.* be cross-eyed, look cross-eyed.

Schienbein, **-e**, *n.nt.* shin.

Schiene, **-n**, *n.f.* rail; (*med.*) splint.

schier, 1. *adj.* sheer, pure. 2. *adv.* almost.

Schierling, *n.m.* hemlock.

schießen*, *vb.* shoot.

Schießgewehr, **-e**, *n.nt.* gun.

Schiff, **-e**, *n.nt.* ship; nave (of a church).

Schiffahrt, *n.f.* navigation.

schiffbar, *adj.* navigable.

Schiffbau, *n.m.* ship building.

Schiffbruch, **ᵉe**, *n.m.* shipwreck.

schiffen, *vb.* ship, navigate.

Schiffer, **-**, *n.m.* mariner.

Schiffsrumpf, **ᵉe**, *n.m.* hull.

schi·laufen*, *vb.* ski.

schikanie'ren, *vb.* annoy.

Schild, **-e**, *n.m.* shield.

Schild, **-er**, *n.nt.* sign.

Schilddrüse, **-n**, *n.f.* thyroid gland.

schildern, *vb.* portray.

Schilderung, **-en**, *n.f.* portrayal.

Schildkröte, **-n**, *n.f.* turtle, tortoise.

Schilf, *n.nt.* reed.

Schilift, **-s**, *n.m.* ski lift.

schillern, *vb.* be iridescent.

Schilling, **-e**, *n.m.* shilling.

Schimmel, **-**, *n.m.* mold, mildew; white horse.

schimmelig, *adj.* moldy.

Schimmer, **-**, *n.m.* glimmer, gleam.

Schimpan'se, **-n**, **-n**, *n.m.* chimpanzee.

Schimpf, **-e**, *n.m.* insult, abuse, disgrace.

schimpfen, *vb.* insult, abuse, complain, gripe.

Schimpfwort, **-e**, *n.nt.* term of abuse.

schinden*, *vb.* flay; (*fig.*) torment; (**sich s.**) work hard, slave.

Schinken, **-**, *n.m.* ham.

Schirm, **-e**, *n.m.* screen; umbrella, parasol; shelter.

schirmen, *vb.* protect.

Schirmherr, **-n**, **-en**, *n.m.* patron.

Schlacht, **-en**, *n.f.* battle.

schlachten, *vb.* slaughter.

Schlächter, **-**, *n.m.* butcher.

Schlachtfeld, **-er**, *n.nt.* battlefield.

Schlachtschiff, **-e**, *n.nt.* battleship.

Schlacke, **-n**, *n.f.* slag, clinker, cinder.

Schlaf, *n.m.* sleep.

Schlafanzug, **ᵉe**, *n.m.* pajamas.

Schläfe, **-n**, *n.f.* temple.

schlafen*, *vb.* sleep, be asleep.

Schlafenszeit, **-en**, *n.f.* bedtime.

schlaff, *adj.* limp.

Schlaffheit, *n.f.* limpness, laxity.

Schlaflosigkeit, *n.f.* insomnia.

Schlafmittel, **-**, *n.nt.* sleeping pill.

schläfrig, *adj.* sleepy.

Schlafrock, **ᵉe**, *n.m.* dressing gown.

Schlafwagen, **-**, *n.m.* sleeping car.

Schlafzimmer, **-**, *n.nt.* bedroom.

Schlag, **ᵉe**, *n.m.* blow, stroke, shock.

Schlagader, **-n**, *n.f.* artery.

Schlaganfall, **ᵉe**, *n.m.* stroke; apoplexy.

Schlagbaum, **ᵉe**, *n.m.* wooden bar, (railroad customs) barrier.

schlagen*, *vb.* hit, strike, beat; fell, (trees); coin (money).

schlagen*, *vb.* hit, strike, beat.

Schlager, **-**, *n.m.* hit (song, play, book).

Schläger, **-**, *n.m.* hitter; bat, club.

Schlägerei', **-en**, *n.f.* brawl.

Schlagholz, **ᵉer**, *n.nt.* bat, club.

Schlagobers, *n.nt.* whipped cream.

Schlagsahne, *n.f.* whipped cream.

Schlagseite, *n.f.* list.

Schlagwort, -e, *n.nt.* slogan.

Schlagzeile, -n, *n.f.* headline.

Schlamm, *n.m.* muck, mud.

schlampig, *adj.* frowsy.

Schlange, -n, *n.f.* snake, serpent.

schlängeln, *vb.* **(sich s.)** wind, wriggle.

schlank, *adj.* slender, slim.

schlapp, *adj.* slack, flabby.

Schlappe, -n, *n.f.* rebuff, setback, defeat.

schlau, *adj.* sly, clever, astute.

Schlauch, ⸗e, *n.m.* hose, tube.

Schlaufe, -n, *n.f.* loop.

schlecht, *adj.* bad.

schlechterdings, *adv.* absolutely.

schlechthin, *adv.* quite, simply.

Schlegel, -, *n.m.* mallet, sledge hammer, drumstick.

schleichen*, *vb.* sneak, slink, crawl.

Schleier, -, *n.m.* veil.

schleierhaft, *adj.* veil-like; inexplicable, mysterious.

Schleife, -n, *n.f.* bow.

schleifen, *vb.* drag.

schleifen*, *vb.* grind, polish, sharpen.

Schleifmittel, -, *n.nt.* abrasive.

Schleifstein, -e, *n.m.* grindstone.

Schleim, *n.m.* slime; mucus.

Schleimhaut, ⸗e, *n.f.* mucous membrane.

schleimig, *adj.* slimy; mucous.

schlendern, *vb.* saunter, stroll.

schlenkern, *vb.* shamble, dangle, swing.

Schleppe, -n, *n.f.* train.

schleppen, *vb.* drag, lug, haul, tow.

Schlepper, -, *n.m.* tugboat, tractor.

Schleuder, -n, *n.f.* slingshot, catapult, centrifuge.

schleudern, *vb.* hurl, fling, skid.

schleunig, *adj.* speedy.

Schleuse, -n, *n.f.* sluice, lock.

Schlich, -e, *n.m.* trick.

schlicht, *adj.* plain, simple.

schlichten, *vb.* smooth; arbitrate.

Schlichter, -, *n.m.* arbitrator.

Schlichtung, -en, *n.f.* arbitration.

schließen*, *vb.* shut; close; conclude.

schließlich, **1.** *adj.* final. **2.** *adv.* at last.

Schliff, -e, *n.m.* cut, polish(ing), grind(ing); good manners, style; **(letzter S.)** final touch.

schlimm, *adj.* bad, serious.

Schlinge, -n, *n.f.* sling, noose.

schlingen*, *vb.* twist, wind; gulp.

schlingern, *vb.* roll.

Schlips, -e, *n.m.* necktie.

Schlitten, -, *n.m.* sled, sleigh.

Schlittschuh, -e, *n.m.* skate.

Schlittschuh-laufen*, *vb.* skate.

Schlitz, -e, *n.m.* slit, slot, slash.

schlitzen, *vb.* slit, slash.

Schloß, ⸗sser, *n.nt.* lock; castle.

Schlot, -e, *n.m.* chimney, flue.

schlottern, *vb.* hang loosely, flop, shake.

Schlucht, -en, *n.f.* gorge, gulch.

schluchzen, *vb.* sob.

Schluck, -e, *n.m.* swallow.

Schluckauf, *n.m.* hiccup(s).

Schlückchen, -, *n.nt.* nip.

schlucken, *vb.* swallow.

Schlummer, *n.m.* slumber.

schlummern, *vb.* slumber.

Schlund, ⸗e, *n.m.* throat, gullet; chasm.

schlüpfen, *vb.* slip.

Schlüpfer, -, *n.m.* panties.

schlüpfrig, *adj.* slippery.

schlürfen, *vb.* sip.

Schluß, ⸗sse, *n.m.* end, close, conclusion.

Schlüssel, -, *n.m.* key.

Schlußfolgerung, -en, *n.f.* deduction, conclusion.

Schmach, *n.f.* disgrace, insult.

schmachten, *vb.* languish.

schmächtig, *adj.* slim, slight.

schmachvoll, *adj.* ignominious.

schmackhaft, *adj.* tasty.

schmähen, *vb.* abuse, revile.

schmal (-, ˵), *adj.* narrow.

schmälern, *vb.* curtail, detract from.

Schmalz, *n.nt.* lard.

schmarotzen, *vb.* sponge (on).

Schmarot'zer, -, *n.m.* hanger-on; parasite.

schmatzen, *vb.* smack one's lips.

Schmaus, ˵e, *n.m.* feast.

schmausen, *vb.* feast.

schmecken, *vb.* taste.

Schmeichelei', -en, *n.f.* flattery.

schmeichelhaft, *adj.* flattering.

schmeicheln, *vb.* flatter.

schmeißen*, *vb.* throw, hurl, chuck, hit.

schmelzen*, *vb.* melt.

Schmerz, -en, *n.m.* ache, pain.

schmerzen, *vb.* ache, pain, hurt.

schmerzhaft, *adj.* painful.

Schmetterling, -e, *n.m.* butterfly.

schmettern, *vb.* dash, smash; bray, blare.

Schmied, -e, *n.m.* blacksmith.

Schmiede, -n, *n.f.* forge.

schmieden, *vb.* forge.

schmiegen, *vb.* bend, press close, nestle, cling.

schmiegsam, *adj.* pliant, flexible.

Schmiere, -n, *n.f.* grease.

schmieren, *vb.* grease, smear, scribble; **(wie geschmiert')** like clockwork.

schmierig, *adj.* greasy, dirty, sordid.

Schmiermittel, -, *n.nt.* lubricant.

Schminke, -n, *n.f.* rouge, make-up, grease paint.

schminken, *vb.* put on make-up.

Schmiß, -sse, *n.m.* stroke, cut; dueling scar; verve.

schmökern, *vb.* browse.

schmollen, *vb.* pout, sulk.

schmoren, *vb.* stew.

Schmuck, *n.m.* ornament, jewelry.

schmuck, *adj.* smart, trim.

schmücken, *vb.* decorate.

Schmucknadel, -n, *n.f.* clip.

Schmuggel, -, *n.m.* smuggling.

schmuggeln, *vb.* smuggle.

Schmuggelware, -n, *n.f.* contraband.

Schmuggler, -, *n.m.* smuggler.

schmunzeln, *vb.* smirk, grin.

schmusen, *vb.* spoon, neck.

Schmutz, *n.m.* dirt, filth.

schmutzig, *adj.* dirty.

Schnabel, ˵, *n.m.* beak.

Schnake, -n, *n.f.* gnat.

Schnalle, -n, *n.f.* buckle, clasp.

schnallen, *vb.* buckle.

schnalzen, *vb.* click (one's tongue), snap (one's fingers), crack (a whip).

schnappen, *vb.* snap, snatch, grab, catch, gasp (for breath).

Schnappschuß, -sse, *n.m.* snapshot.

Schnaps, ˵e, *n.m.* hard liquor, whisky, brandy.

schnarchen, *vb.* snore.

schnarren, *vb.* buzz, whir, rattle, burr.

schnattern, *vb.* cackle.

schnauben, *vb.* pant, snort.

schnaufen, *vb.* breathe hard.

Schnauze, -, *n.f.* snout.

Schnecke, -n, *n.f.* snail.

Schnee, *n.m.* snow.

Schneesturm, ˵e, *n.m.* blizzard.

Schneid, *n.m.* bravado.

Schneide, -n, *n.f.* edge.

schneiden, *vb.* cut.

schneidend, *adj.* cutting. scathing.

Schneider, -, *n.m.* tailor.

Schneiderin, -nen, *n.f.* dressmaker.

schneidig, *adj.* dashing.

schneien, *vb.* snow.

schnell, *adj.* quick.

schnellen, *vb.* flip, jerk.

Schnelligkeit, -en, *n.f.* swiftness.

Schnellzug, ⁀e, *n.m.* express train.

schneuzen, *vb.* (**sich s.**) blow one's nose.

schnippisch, *adj.* saucy.

Schnitt, -e, *n.m.* cut, slice, incision.

Schnittbohne, -n, *n.f.* string bean.

Schnitte, -n, *n.f.* slice, sandwich.

Schnittlauch, *n.m.* chive(s).

Schnittmuster, -, *n.nt.* pattern.

Schnittpunkt, -e, *n.m.* intersection.

Schnittwaren, *n.pl.* dry goods.

Schnittwunde, -n, *n.f.* cut.

Schnitzel, -, *n.nt.* chip; cutlet.

schnitzen, *vb.* carve, whittle.

Schnitzwerk, -e, *n.nt.* carving.

schnodd(e)rig, *adj.* insolent.

schnöde, *adj.* scornful, base.

Schnorchel, -, *n.m.* snorkel.

schnüffeln, *vb.* sniffle, snoop.

Schnuller, -, *n.m.* pacifier.

Schnupfen, -, *n.m.* cold (in the head).

Schnupftuch, ⁀er, *n.nt.* handkerchief.

Schnuppe, -n, *n.f.* shooting star; (**das ist mir S.**) I don't care a hoot.

Schnur, ⁀e, *n.f.* cord, string.

schnüren, *vb.* lace.

Schnurrbart, ⁀e, *n.m.* mustache.

Schnürsenkel, -, *n.m.* shoelace.

Shock, -s, *n.m.* shock.

schockie'ren, *vb.* shock.

schofel(ig), *adj.* shabby, mean.

Schokola'de, -n, *n.f.* chocolate.

Scholle, -n, *n.f.* clod, soil.

schon, *adv.* already; even.

schön, *adj.* beautiful, nice.

schonen, *vb.* treat carefully, spare.

Schönheit, -en, *n.f.* beauty.

Schönheitssalon, -s, *n.m.* beauty parlor.

Schonung, -en, *n.f.* careful treatment, consideration.

schonungslos, *adj.* merciless.

Schopf, ⁀e, *n.m.* forelock, crown.

schöpfen, *vb.* draw (water, breath); take from.

Schöpfer, -, *n.m.* creator.

schöpferisch, *adj.* creative.

Schöpfkelle, -n, *n.f.* scoop.

Schöpflöffel, -, *n.m.* ladle, dipper.

Schöpfung, -, *n.f.* creation.

Schoppen, -, *n.m.* glass of beer or wine; pint.

Schorf, -e, *n.m.* scab.

Schornstein, -e, *n.m.* chimney, smokestack.

Schoß, ⁀e, *n.m.* lap.

Schößling, -e, *n.m.* shoot.

Schote, -n, *n.f.* pod.

Schotte, -n, -n, *n.m.* Scotsman.

schottisch, *adj.* Scotch.

Schottland, *n.nt.* Scotland.

schräg, *adj.* oblique.

Schrägschrift, *n.f.* italics.

Schramme, -n, *n.f.* scratch.

Schrank, ⁀e, *n.m.* wardrobe, locker, cupboard, cabinet.

Schranke, -n, *n.f.* barrier.

Schrapnell', -s, *n.nt.* shrapnel.

Schraube, -n, *n.f.* screw.

schrauben, *vb.* screw.

Schraubenschlüssel, -, *n.m.* wrench.

Schraubenzieher, -, *n.m.* screwdriver.

Schreck, -e, *n.m.* fright, scare.

Schrecken, -, *n.m.* terror, fear.

schreckhaft, *adj.* easily frightened.

schrecklich, adj. awful, terrible.

Schrei, -e, n.m. cry, scream, shout.

Schreibdame, -n, n.f. typist.

schreiben*, vb. write.

Schreiben, -, n.nt. letter.

Schreibheft, -e, n.nt. notebook.

Schreiber, -, n.m. clerk, scribe.

Schreibmaschine, -n, n.f. typewriter.

Schreibtisch, -e, n.m. desk.

Schreibung, -en, n.f. spelling.

Schreibwaren, n.pl. stationery.

schreien*, vb. cry, scream, shout.

schreiend, adj. flagrant.

Schrein, -e, n.m. shrine, casket, cabinet.

schreiten*, vb. stride, step.

Schrift, -en, n.f. writing, script; **(Heilige S.)** scripture(s).

Schriftführer, -, n.m. secretary (of an organization).

schriftlich, adj. written, in writing.

Schriftsatz, -e, n.m. type.

Schriftsteller, -, n.m. writer, author.

schrill, adj. shrill.

Schritt, -e, n.m. step, pace; crotch (of trousers).

schroff, adj. steep, abrupt, curt.

Schrotmehl, n.m. coarse meal, grits.

schrubben, vb. scrub.

Schrulle, -n, n.f. whim.

schrumpfen, vb. shrink.

Schub, -e, n.m. shove, thrust; batch.

Schublade, -n, n.f. drawer.

schüchtern, adj. shy, bashful.

Schüchternheit, -en, n.f. bashfulness, shyness.

Schuft, -e, n.m. cad, scoundrel.

schuften, vb. work hard, drudge.

Schuh, -e, n.m. shoe.

Schuhmacher, -, n.m. shoemaker.

Schuhputzer, -, n.m. bootblack.

Schuhwerk, -e, n.nt. footwear.

Schularbeiten, n.pl. homework.

Schulbeispiel, -e, n.nt. typical example.

Schuld, -en, n.f. fault, guilt, blame, debt.

schulden, vb. owe.

schuldhaft, adj. culpable.

schuldig, adj. guilty; due, owing.

Schuldigsprechung, -en, n.f. conviction.

Schuldirektor, -en, n.m. headmaster, principal.

schuldlos, adj. guiltless.

Schuldner, -, n.m. debtor.

Schule, -n, n.f. school.

schulen, vb. train, indoctrinate.

Schüler, -, n.m. (boy) pupil.

Schülerin, -nen, n.f. (girl) pupil.

Schulgeld, -er, n.nt. tuition.

Schulter, -n, n.f. shoulder.

schultern, vb. shoulder.

Schund, n.m. trash.

Schupo, -s, n.m. (=Schutzpolizist) cop.

Schuppe, -n, n.f. scale; (pl.) dandruff.

Schuppen, -, n.m. shed, hangar.

schüren, vb. poke, stir up, foment.

Schurke, -n, -n, n.m. villain, scoundrel.

Schürze, -n, n.f. apron.

Schuß, -sse, n.m. shot.

Schüssel, -n, n.f. dish, bowl.

Schuster, -, n.m. shoemaker.

Schutt, n.m. rubbish.

schütteln, vb. shake.

schütten, vb. shed, pour.

Schutz, n.m. protection.

Schütze, -n, -n, n.m. rifleman, marksman, shot.

schützen, vb. protect.

Schützengraben, -, n.m. trench, dugout.

Schutzhaft, n.f. protective custody.

Schutzheilig-, *n.m.&f.* patron saint.

Schutzherr, -n, -en, *n.m.* patron.

schutzlos, *adj.* unprotected, defenseless.

Schutzmann, ⁼er, *n.m.* patrolman.

Schutzmarke, -n, *n.f.* trade mark.

schwach(⁼), *adj.* weak.

Schwäche, -n, *n.f.* weakness.

schwächen, *vb.* weaken.

Schwachheit, -en, *n.f.* frailty.

schwächlich, *adj.* feeble.

Schwächling, -e, *n.m.* weakling.

Schwachsinn, *n.m.* feeblemindedness.

schwachsinnig, *adj.* feebleminded.

Schwachsinnig-, *n.m.&f.* moron.

Schwager, ⁼r, *n.m.* brother-in-law.

Schwägerin, -nen, *n.f.* sister-in-law.

Schwalbe, -n, *n.f.* swallow.

Schwall, -e, *n.m.* flood.

Schwamm, ⁼e, *n.m.* sponge.

Schwan, ⁼e, *n.m.* swan.

schwanger, *adj.* pregnant.

Schwangerschaft, -en, *n.f.* pregnancy.

schwanken, *vb.* totter, sway, vacillate, waver.

Schwankung, -en, *n.f.* fluctuation.

Schwanz, ⁼e, *n.m.* tail.

schwänzen, *vb.* cut (a class).

Schwarm, ⁼e, *n.m.* swarm.

schwärmen, *vb.* swarm; (s. **für**) be crazy about.

Schwärmer, -, *n.m.* enthusiast.

schwarz(⁼), *adj.* black; illegal.

Schwarzbrot, -e, *n.nt.* black bread.

schwärzen, *vb.* blacken.

Schwarzmarkt, ⁼e, *n.m.* black market.

Schwarzseher, -, *n.m.* alarmist, pessimist.

schwatzen, schwätzen, *vb.* chatter, gab.

Schwebe, *n.f.* suspense, suspension; **(in der S.)** undecided.

schweben, *vb.* hover, be suspended, be pending.

Schwebezustand, ⁼e, *n.m.* abeyance.

Schwede, -n, -n, *n.m.* Swede.

Schweden, *n.nt.* Sweden.

schwedisch, *adj.* Swedish.

Schwefel, *n.m.* sulphur.

Schweif, -e, *n.m.* tail, train.

schweifen, *vb.* roam, range.

schweigen*, *vb.* keep quiet, be silent.

Schweigen, *n.nt.* silence.

schweigsam, *adj.* silent.

Schwein, -e, *n.nt.* swine, hog, pig; good luck.

Schweinebraten, -, *n.m.* roast of pork.

Schweinefleisch, *n.nt.* pork.

Schweinerei', -en, *n.f.* awful mess, dirty business.

Schweinestall, ⁼e, *n.m.* pigsty.

Schweinsleder, *n.nt.* pigskin.

Schweiß, *n.m.* sweat.

Schweiz, *n.f.* Switzerland.

Schweizer, -, *n.m.* Swiss.

schweizerisch, *adj.* Swiss.

schwelen, *vb.* smolder.

schwelgen, *vb.* revel.

Schwelgerei', -en, *n.f.* revelry.

Schwelle, -n, *n.f.* sill, threshold; (railroad) tie.

schwellen*, *vb.* swell.

schwenken, *vb.* wave, flourish, brandish.

schwer, *adj.* heavy; difficult.

Schwere, *n.f.* heaviness.

schwerfällig, *adj.* clumsy, ponderous, stolid.

Schwergewicht, *n.nt.* heavyweight.

schwerhörig, *adj.* hard of hearing.

Schwerkraft, *n.f.* gravity.

schwerlich, *adj.* with difficulty, hardly.

Schwermut, *n.f.* melancholy.

schwermütig, *adj.* moody, melancholy.

Schwert, -er, *n.f.* sword; centerboard.

schwerwiegend, *adj.* grave.

Schwester, -n, *n.f.* sister; nurse.

Schwiegereltern, *n.pl.* parents-in-law.

Schwiegermutter, ", *n.f.* mother-in-law.

Schwiegersohn, "e, *n.m.* son-in-law.

Schwiegertochter, ", *n.f.* daughter-in-law.

Schwiegervater, ", *n.m.* father-in-law.

Schwiele, -n, *n.f.* callus.

schwielig, *adj.* callous.

schwierig, *adj.* difficult.

Schwierigkeit, -en, *n.f.* difficulty, trouble.

Schwimmbad, "er, *n.nt.* swimming pool.

schwimmen*, *vb.* swim.

Schwimmweste, -n, *n.f.* life-preserver.

Schwindel, -, *n.m.* dizziness; swindle, hoax; bunk.

Schwindelgefühl, *n.nt.* vertigo.

schwindeln, *vb.* swindle, cheat, fraud.

schwinden*, *vb.* disappear.

Schwindler, -, *n.m.* swindler, cheat, fraud.

schwindlig, *adj.* dizzy.

Schwindsucht, *n.f.* consumption.

schwindsüchtig, *adj.* consumptive.

schwingen*, *vb.* swing, brandish, oscillate.

Schwingung, -en, *n.f.* oscillation.

Schwips, *n.m.* **(einen S. haben*)** be tipsy.

schwirren, *vb.* whir.

schwitzen, *vb.* sweat.

schwören, *vb.* swear.

schwül, *adj.* sultry, muggy.

Schwulst, "e, *n.m.* bombast.

Schwund, *n.m.* disappearance, loss.

Schwung, "e, *n.m.* swing, verve, animation, motion.

Schwungkraft, *n.f.* drive.

schwunglos, *adj.* lackadaisical.

schwungvoll, *adj.* spirited.

Schwur, "e, *n.m.* oath.

sechs, *num.* six.

sechst-, *adj.* sixth.

Sechstel, -, *n.nt.* sixth; **(ein s.)** one-sixth.

sechzig, *num.* sixty.

sechzigst-, *adj.* sixtieth.

Sechzigstel, -, *n.nt.* sixtieth; **(ein s.)** one-sixtieth.

See, Se'en, *n.m.* lake.

See, Se'en, *n.f.* sea.

See-, *cpds.* naval, marine.

Seegang, *n.m.* (rough, calm) sea.

Seehund, -e, *n.m.* seal.

seekrank, *adj.* seasick.

Seekrankheit, *n.f.* seasickness.

Seele, -n, *n.f.* soul, spirit, mind.

Seeleute, *n.pl.* seamen.

seelisch, *adj.* spiritual.

Seelsorge, *n.f.* ministry.

Seemann, -leute, *n.m.* mariner.

Seemeile, -n, *n.f.* nautical mile.

Seeräuber, -, *n.m.* pirate.

Seereise, -n, *n.f.* cruise.

Seetang, *n.m.* seaweed.

seetüchtig, *adj.* seaworthy.

Seezunge, -n, *n.f.* sole.

Segel, -, *n.nt.* sail.

Segelboot, -e, *n.nt.* sailboat.

Segelflug, *n.m.* gliding.

Segelflugzeug, -e, *n.nt.* glider, sailplane.

segeln, *vb.* sail.

Segeltuch, *n.nt.* canvas, duck.

Segen, -, *n.m.* blessing.

Segment', -e, *n.nt.* segment.

segnen, *vb.* bless.

Segnung, -en, *n.f.* blessing, benediction.

sehen*, *vb.* see.

sehenswert, *adj.* worth seeing.

Sehenswürdigkeit, -en, *n.f.* sight(s).

Seher, -, *n.m.* seer, prophet.

Sehkraft, "e, *n.f.* (power of) sight, vision.

Sehne, -n, *n.f.* tendon, ligament, sinew.

sehnen, *vb.* **(sich s.)** long, yearn.

Sehnsucht, *n.f.* longing.

sehnsüchtig, *adj.* longing.

sehnsuchtsvoll, *adj.* longing.

sehr, *adv.* very, much, a lot.

Sehweite, -n, *n.f.* range of sight.

seicht, *adj.* shallow, insipid.

Seide, -n, *n.f.* silk.

seiden, *adj.* silk.

Seidenpapier, *n.nt.* tissue paper.

seidig, *adj.* silky.

Seidel, -, *n.nt.* beer mug.

Seife, -n, *n.f.* soap.

Seifenschaum, *n.m.* suds.

seihen, *vb.* strain.

Seil, -e, *n.nt.* rope, cable.

Seilbahn, -en, *n.f.* cableway.

sein*, *vb.* be.

Sein, *n.nt.* being.

sein, -, -e, *adj.* his, its.

seiner, -es, -e, *pron.* his, its.

seinerseits, *adv.* for his part.

seinerzeit, *adv.* at the time.

seinesgleichen, *pron.* equal to him, such as he.

seinetwegen, *adv.* for his sake; for all he cares.

seinetwillen, *adv.* **(um s.)** for his sake, because of him.

seit, 1. *prep.* since, for. **2.** *conj.* since.

seitab', *adv.* aside.

seitdem, 1. *conj.* since. **2.** *adv.* since then.

seither, *adv.* since then.

Seite, -n, *n.f.* side; page.

seitenlang, *adj.* going on for pages.

seitens, *prep.* on behalf of.

Seitensprung, -e, *n.m.* escapade.

Seitenstraße, -n, *n.f.* side street.

Seitenzahl, -en, *n.f.* number of pages.

seitlich, *adj.* lateral.

seitwärts, *adv.* sideways.

Sekretär', -e, *n.m.* secretary.

Sekretä'rin, -nen, *n.f.* secretary.

Sekt, -e, *n.m.* champagne.

Sekte, -n, *n.f.* sect, denomination.

Sekundant', -en, -en, *n.m.* second (at a duel).

sekundär', *adj.* secondary.

Sekun'de, -n, *n.f.* second.

selb-, *adj.* same.

selber, *adv.* (my-, your-, him-, etc.)self; (our-, your-, them-)selves.

selbst, *adv.* even; (my-, your-, him-, etc.)self; (our-, your-, them-)selves.

Selbstachtung, *n.f.* self-respect.

selbständig, *adj.* independent.

Selbständigkeit, *n.f.* independence.

Selbstbestimmung, *n.f.* self-determination.

selbstbewußt, *adj.* self-conscious.

Selbstbiographie, -n, auto-biography.

selbstgefällig, *adj.* self-satisfied, smug.

selbstgefertigt, *adj.* home-made.

selbstgerecht, *adj.* self-righteous.

Selbstgespräch, -e, *n.nt.* monologue.

selbstlos, *adj.* unselfish.

Selbstmord, -e, *n.m.* suicide.

selbstredend, *adj.* self-evident.

selbstsicher, *adj.* self-confident.

Selbstsucht, *n.f.* selfishness.

selbstsüchtig, *adj.* selfish.

selbsttätig, *adj.* automatic.

selbstverständlich, *adj.* obvious.

Selbstverwaltung, *n.f.* home rule.

selbstzufrieden, *adj.* complacent.

Selbstzufriedenheit, *n.f.* complacency.

selig, *adj.* blessed; blissfully happy; deceased, late.

Seligkeit, -en, *n.f.* salvation, bliss.

selig-sprechen*, *vb.* beatify.

Sellerie, *n.m.* celery.

selten, 1. *adj.* rare, scarce. **2.** *adv.* seldom.

Seltenheit, -en, *n.f.* rarity.

eltsam, *adj.* strange, queer, curious.

elters, Selter(s)wasser, *n.nt.* soda water.

eman'tik, *n.f.* semantics.

eman'tisch, *adj.* semantic.

emes'ter, -, *n.nt.* semester, term.

emiko'lon, -s, *n.nt.* semicolon.

eminar', -e, *n.nt.* seminar(y).

emit', -en, -en, *n.m.* Semite.

emi'tisch, *adj.* Semitic.

emmel, -n, *n.f.* roll.

enat', -e, *n.m.* senate.

ena'tor, -o'ren, *n.m.* senator.

enden*, *vb.* send, ship.

enden, *vb.* broadcast.

ender, -, *n.m.* sender, transmitter, broadcasting station.

endung, -en, *n.f.* shipment, broadcast, transmission.

enf, *n.m.* mustard.

engen, *vb.* scorch, singe.

enken, *vb.* sink, lower, reduce.

enkrecht, *adj.* perpendicular.

enkung, -en, *n.f.* depression, reduction.

ensationell', *adj.* sensational.

ensation', -en, *n.f.* sensation, thrill.

ense, -n, *n.f.* scythe.

entimental', *adj.* sentimental.

eptem'ber, -, *n.m.* September.

erbe, -n, -n, *n.m.* Serbian.

erbien, *n.nt.* Serbia.

erbisch, *adj.* Serbian.

erie, -n, *n.f.* series.

erum, -ra, *n.nt.* serum.

ervi'ce, *n.nt.* service, set.

ervie'ren, *vb.* serve.

ervier'platte, -n, *n.f.* platter.

erviet'te, -n, *n.f.* napkin.

essel, -, *n.m.* easy-chair.

eßhaft, *adj.* settled, established.

etzen, *vb.* set, put, place; **(sich s.)** sit down.

Seuche, -n, *n.f.* plague, epidemic.

seufzen, *vb.* sigh.

Seufzer, -, *n.m.* sigh.

sexuell', *adj.* sexual.

Siam, *n.nt.* Siam.

Siame'se, -n, -n, *n.m.* Siamese.

siame'sisch, *adj.* Siamese.

Sibi'rien, *n.nt.* Siberia.

sich, *pron.* (him-, her-, it-, your-)self, (them-, your-)selves; each other, one another.

Sichel, -n, *n.f.* sickle; crescent.

sicher, *adj.* sure, certain, safe, secure.

Sicherheit, -en, *n.f.* safety, security, certainty.

Sicherheitsnadel, -n, *n.f.* safety-pin.

sicherlich, *adv.* surely.

sichern, *vb.* secure, safeguard.

Sicht, *n.f.* sight.

sichtbar, *adj.* visible.

sichten, *vb.* sift; sight.

sickern, *vb.* seep.

sie, *pron.* she; they.

Sie, *pron.* you (normal polite).

Sieb, -e, *n.nt.* sieve, strainer.

sieben, *vb.* sift, strain.

sieben, *num.* seven.

sieb(en)t-, *adj.* seventh.

Sieb(en)tel, -, *n.nt.* seventh: **(ein s.)** one-seventh.

siebzig, *num.* seventy.

siebzigst-, *adj.* seventieth.

Siebzigstel, -, *n.nt.* seventieth; **(ein s.)** one-seventieth.

siedeln, *vb.* settle.

sieden*, *vb.* boil.

Siedler, -, *n.m.* settler.

Siedlung, -en, *n.f.* settlement.

Sieg, -e, *n.m.* victory.

Siegel, -, *n.nt.* seal.

siegeln, *vb.* seal.

siegen, *vb.* win, be victorious.

Sieger, -, *n.m.* winner, victor.

sieghaft, *adj.* triumphant.

siegreich, *adj.* victorious.

Signal, -e, *n.nt.* signal.

Signal'horn, ˸er, *n.nt.* bugle.

Silbe, -n, *n.f.* syllable.

Silber, *n.nt.* silver.

silbern, *adj.* silver.

Silberwaren, *n.f.* silverware.

silbisch, *adj.* syllabic.

silbrig, *adj.* silvery.

Silves'ter, *n.nt.* New Year's Eve.

Sims, -e, *n.m.* cornice; ledge, sill; mantelpiece.

singen*, *vb.* sing.

Singular, -e, *n.m.* singular.

sinken*, *vb.* sink, decline, fall.

Sinn, -e, *n.m.* sense, mind, meaning, taste.

Sinnbild, -er, *n.nt.* symbol.

sinnen*, *vb.* think, meditate, plot.

sinnig, *adj.* thoughtful, appropriate.

sinnlich, *adj.* sensual.

sinnlos, *adj.* senseless.

Sintflut, *n.f.* flood, deluge.

Sippe, -n, *n.f.* kin; clan, tribe.

Sire'ne, -n, *n.f.* siren.

Sirup, *n.m.* molasses; syrup.

Sitte, -n, *n.f.* custom; (*pl.*) mores, manners, morals.

Sittenlehre, -n, *n.f.* ethics.

sittenlos, *adj.* immoral.

sittig, *adj.* chaste, well-bred.

sittlich, *adj.* moral.

Situation', -en, *n.f.* situation.

Sitz, -e, *n.m.* seat, residence.

sitzen*, *vb.* sit, be seated; fit; be in jail.

sitzen-bleiben*, *vb.* remain seated; get stuck (with); not be promoted.

sitzen-lassen*, *vb.* jilt.

Sitzplatz, -e, *n.m.* seat.

Sitzung, -en, *n.f.* session.

Sizilia'ner, -, *n.m.* Sicilian.

sizilia'nisch, *adj.* Sicilian.

Sizi'lien, *n.nt.* Sicily.

Skala, -len, *n.f.* scale.

Skandal', -e, *n.m.* scandal.

Skandina'vien, *n.nt.* Scandinavia.

Skandina'vier, -, *n.m.* Scandinavian.

skandina'visch, *adj.* Scandinavian.

Skelett', -e, *n.nt.* skeleton.

Skepsis, *n.f.* skepticism.

Skeptiker, -, *n.m.* skeptic.

skeptisch, *adj.* skeptic(al).

Skizze, -n, *n.f.* sketch.

skizzie'ren, *vb.* sketch.

Sklave, -n, -n, *n.m.* slave.

Sklaverei', *n.f.* slavery.

Skrupel, -, *n.m.* scruple.

Slang, *n.m.* slang.

Slawe, -n, -n, *n.m.* Slav.

slawisch, *adj.* Slavic.

Sicherung, -en, *n.f.* fuse.

Slowa'ke, -n, -n, *n.m.* Slovak.

Slowakei', *n.f.* Slovakia.

slowa'kisch, *adj.* Slovakian

Smaragd', -e, *n.m.* emerald

Smoking, -s, *n.m.* dinner jacket, tuxedo.

Snob, -s, *n.m.* snob.

so, *adv.* so, thus; (**s. groß wie**) as big as.

Socke, -n, *n.f.* sock.

Sockenhalter, -, *n.m.* garter.

Soda, *n.nt.* soda.

Sodbrennen, *n.nt.* heart burn.

soe'ben, *adv.* just now.

Sofa, -s, *n.nt.* sofa.

sofort', *adv.* immediately.

sofor'tig, *adj.* instantaneous

Sog, *n.m.* suction; undertow

sogar', *adv.* yet, even.

sogenannt, *adj.* so-called.

Sohle, -n, *n.f.* sole.

Sohn, -e, *n.m.* son.

solch(er, -es, -e), *adj.* such.

solcherlei, *adj.* of such a kind.

solchermaßen, *adv.* in such a way.

Sold, -e, *n.m.* pay.

Soldat', -en, -en, *n.m.* soldier.

solid', *adj.* solid.

Solidarität', *n.f.* solidarity

Solist', -en, -en, *n.m.* soloist.

Soll, *n.nt.* debit; quota.

sollen, *vb.* be supposed to, be said to; shall; (**er sollte gehen***) he should, ought to go; (**er hätte gehen sollen**) he should, ought to have gone.

Solo, -s, *n.nt.* solo.

Sommer, -, *n.m.* summer.

Sommersprosse, -n, *n.f.* freckle.

Sommerzeit, -en, *n.f.* summer time; daylight-saving time.

Sona'te, -n, *n.f.* sonata.

Sonde, -n, *n.f.* probe.

sonder, *prep.* without.

Sonder-, *cpds.* special.

Sonderangebot, -e, *n.nt.* bargain, special sale.

sonderbar, *adj.* strange, queer.

sonderbarerwei'se, *adv.* strange to say.

sonderglei'chen, *adv.* without equal, unparalleled.

sonderlich, *adj.* peculiar.

sondern, *vb.* separate.

sondern, *conj.* but (on the contrary).

sondie'ren, *vb.* sound, probe.

Sonett', -e, *n.nt.* sonnet.

Sonnabend, -e, *n.m.* Saturday.

Sonne, -n, *n.f.* sun.

sonnen, *vb.* (**sich s.**) sun oneself, bask.

Sonnenbrand, ̈e, *n.m.* sunburn.

Sonnenbräune, *n.f.* sun tan.

sonnenklar, *adj.* clear as daylight.

Sonnenschein, *n.m.* sunshine.

Sonnenstich, -e, *n.m.* sun stroke.

sonnenverbrannt, *adj.* sunburned.

sonnig, *adj.* sunny.

Sonntag, -e, *n.m.* Sunday.

sonst, *adv.* otherwise, else; formerly.

sonstig, *adj.* other; former.

sonstwie, *adv.* in some other way.

sonstwo, *adv.* somewhere else.

sonstwoher, *adv.* from some other place.

sonstwohin, *adv.* to some other place.

Sopran', -e, *n.m.* soprano.

Sorbett, -e, *n.nt.* sherbet.

Sorge, -n, *n.f.* sorrow; worry, anxiety, apprehension; care.

sorgen, *vb.* (**s. für**) care for,

provide; (**sich s.**) worry, concern oneself.

sorgenfrei, *adj.* carefree.

sorgenvoll, *adj.* worried, care-worn.

Sorgfalt, *n.f.* care.

sorgfältig, *adj.* careful, meticulous.

sorglos, *adj.* carefree.

sorgsam, *adj.* careful, painstaking.

Sorte, -n, *n.f.* sort, kind.

sortie'ren, *vb.* sort, assort, classify.

Soße, -n, *n.f.* sauce, gravy.

souverän, *adj.* sovereign.

Souveränität', *n.f.* sovereignty.

soviel, *adv.* so much, as much.

sowie, *conj.* as well as; as soon as.

sowieso, *adv.* in any case.

Sowjet, -s, *n.m.* Soviet.

sowje'tisch, *adj.* Soviet.

Sowjetunion, *n.f.* Soviet Union.

sowohl, *adv.* as well; (**s. A als B, s. A wie B**) both A and B.

sozial', *adj.* social.

sozialisie'ren, *vb.* socialize, nationalize.

Sozialis'mus, *n.m.* socialism.

Sozialist', -en, -en, *n.m.* socialist.

sozialis'tisch, *adj.* socialistic.

Soziologie', *n.f.* sociology.

sozusagen, *adv.* as it were, so to speak.

Spaghet'ti, *n.pl.* spaghetti.

Spalt, -e, *n.m.* crack, chink.

spaltbar, *adj.* fissionable.

Spalte, -n, *n.f.* crevice, gap; (newspaper) column.

spalten, *vb.* split.

Spaltung, -en, *n.f.* cleavage; fission.

Spange, -n, *n.m.* clasp, buckle.

Spanien, *n.nt.* Spain.

Spanier, -, *n.m.* Spaniard.

spanisch, *adj.* Spanish.

Spann, -e, *n.m.* arch, instep.

Spanne, -n, *n.f.* span.

spannen, vb. stretch; tighten.

spannend, adj. exciting, gripping.

Spannkraft, n.f. elasticity; (fig.) energy.

Spannung, -en, n.f. tension; (fig.) close attention, suspense.

sparen, vb. save.

Spargel, -, n.m. asparagus.

Sparkasse, -n, n.f. savings bank.

spärlich, adj. sparse, meager.

Sparren, -, n.m. spar, rafter.

sparsam, adj. thrifty, economical.

Sparsamkeit, n.f. thrift.

Spaß, ⸚e, n.m. joke, fun.

spaßeshalber, adv. for the fun of it.

spaßig, adj. funny.

Spaßmacher, -, n.m. jester.

spät, adj. late.

Spaten, -, n.m. spade.

spätestens, adv. at the latest.

Spatz, -en, -en, n.m. sparrow.

spazie'ren-gehen*, vb. go for a walk, stroll.

Spazier'fahrt, -en, n.f. drive.

Spazier'gang, ⸚e, n.m. walk.

Specht, -e, n.m. woodpecker.

Speck, n.m. fat; bacon.

spedie'ren, vb. dispatch.

Spediteur', -e, n.m. shipping agent.

Speer, -e, n.m. spear; javelin.

Speiche, -n, n.f. spoke.

Speichel, n.m. saliva.

Speicher, -, n.m. loft, storage place.

speien*, vb. spit.

Speise, -n, n.f. food, nourishment.

Speisekammer, -n, n.f. pantry.

Speisekarte, -n, n.f. bill of fare, menu.

speisen, vb. (tr.) feed; (intr.) eat.

Speiseröhre, -n, n.f. esophagus.

Speisewagen, -, n.m. diner, dining-car.

Speisezettel, -, n.m. menu.

Speisung, -en, n.f. feeding.

Spekta'kel, n.m. noise, racket.

spekulie'ren, vb. speculate.

spenda'bel, adj. free and easy with money; **(s. sein)** splurge.

Spende, -n, n.f. donation.

spenden, vb. give; donate.

Sperling, -e, n.m. sparrow.

Sperre, -n, n.f. barrier, blockade; gate.

sperren, vb. block, obstruct, blockade; (money) freeze.

Sperrfeuer, -, n.nt. barrage.

Sperrstunde, -n, n.f. curfew.

Spesen, n.pl. charges, expenses; **(auf S.)** on an expense account.

Spezialist', -en, n.m. specialist.

spezialisie'ren, vb. specialize.

Spezialität', -en, n.f. specialty.

speziell', adj. special, specific.

spezi'fisch, adj. specific.

spezifizie'ren, vb. specify.

Sphäre, -n, n.f. sphere.

Sphinx, -en, n.f. sphinx.

spicken, vb. lard, interlard.

Spiegel, -, n.m. mirror.

spiegeln, vb. mirror, reflect.

Spiegelung, -en, n.f. reflection.

Spiel, -e, n.nt. play, game; gambling; pack (of cards).

Spielbank, -en, n.f. gambling casino.

spielen, vb. play, act; **(um Geld s.)** gamble.

spielerisch, adj. playful.

Spielgefährte, -n, -n, n.m. playmate.

Spielplatz, ⸚e, n.m. playground.

Spielraum, ⸚e, n.m. room for action, range; elbow room; margin.

Spielwaren, n.pl. toys.

Spielzeug, -e, n.nt. toy.

Spieß, -e, n.m. spear; top sergeant.

Spinat', n.m. spinach.

Spindel, -n, n.f. spindle.

Spinett', **-e**, *n.nt.* spinet, harpsichord.

Spinne, **-n**, *n.f.* spider.

spinnen*, *vb.* spin; be crazy.

Spinngewebe, **-**, *n.nt.* cobweb.

Spion', **-e**, *n.m.* spy.

Spionag'e, *n.f.* espionage.

spionie'ren, *vb.* spy.

Spira'le, **-n**, *n.f.* spiral.

spiral'förmig, *adj.* spiral.

Spiritis'mus, *n.m.* spiritism.

Spiritualis'mus, *n.m.* spiritualism.

Spirituo'sen, *n.pl.* liquor, spirits.

spitz, *adj.* pointed, acute.

Spitzbart, **⸚e**, *n.m.* goatee.

Spitze, **-n**, *n.f.* point, tip, top; lace.

spitzenartig, *adj.* lacy.

spitzfindig, *adj.* shrewd; subtle.

Spitzhacke, **-n**, *n.f.* pick.

Spitzname(n), **-**, *n.m.* nickname.

Splitter, **-**, *n.m.* splinter, chip.

splittern, *vb.* splinter, shatter.

spontan', *adj.* spontaneous.

spora'disch, *adj.* sporadic.

Sporn, **Sporen**, *n.m.* spur.

Sport, **-e**, *n.m.* sport.

Sportler, **-**, *n.m.* sportsman; athlete.

sportlich, *adj.* athletic; sportsmanlike.

Sportplatz, **⸚e**, *n.m.* athletic field, stadium.

Spott, *n.m.* mockery, ridicule.

spottbillig, *adj.* dirt cheap.

spotten, *vb.* mock, scoff.

Spötter, **-**, *n.m.* scoffer.

spöttisch, *adj.* derisive.

Sprache, **-n**, *n.f.* speech; language.

spracheigen, *adj.* idiomatic.

Sprachfehler, **-**, *n.m.* speech impediment.

Sprachführer, **-**, *n.m.* phrase book.

sprachgewandt, *adj.* fluent.

sprachlos, *adj.* speechless.

Sprachschatz, *n.m.* vocabulary.

Sprachwissenschaft, **-en**, *n.f.* linguistics, philology.

sprechen*, *vb.* speak, talk.

Sprecher, **-**, *n.m.* speaker, spokesman.

Sprechstunde, **-n**, *n.f.* office hour.

spreizen, *vb.* spread apart.

sprengen, *vb.* explode, break; sprinkle.

Sprengstoff, **-e**, *n.m.* explosive.

Sprichwort, **⸚er**, *n.nt.* proverb, adage.

sprichwörtlich, *adj.* proverbial.

sprießen*, *vb.* sprout.

springen*, *vb.* jump; crack.

Springer, **-**, *n.m.* (chess) knight.

Springquell, **-e**, *n.m.* fountain.

sprinten, *vb.* sprint.

Spritze, **-n**, *n.f.* spray; injection; hypodermic.

spritzen, *vb.* spray, squirt, splash; inject.

spröde, *adj.* brittle; chapped; reserved, prim.

Sproß, **-sse**, *n.m.* sprout.

Sprößling, **-e**, *n.m.* shoot; offspring.

Sprotte, **-n**, *n.f.* sprat.

Spruch, **⸚e**, *n.m.* saying.

Sprudel, **-**, *n.m.* bubbling water; soda water.

sprudeln, *vb.* bubble.

Sprudeln, *n.nt.* effervescence.

sprühen, *vb.* spark, sparkle.

Sprühregen, *n.m.* drizzle.

Sprung, **⸚e**, *n.m.* jump; fissure, crack.

Sprungbrett, **-er**, *n.nt.* diving board; (*fig.*) stepping stone.

sprunghaft, *adj.* jumpy; erratic.

Sprungschanze, **-n**, *n.f.* ski-jump.

Spucke, *n.f.* spit, saliva.

spucken, *vb.* spit.

Spuk, **-e**, *n.m.* spook, ghost.

Spule, **-n**, *n.f.* spool, reel; (*elec.*) coil; bobbin.

spulen, *vb.* reel, wind.

spülen, *vb.* rinse, wash; (W.C.) flush.

Spülstein, -e, *n.m.* sink.

Spund, -e, *n.m.* spigot, tap.

Spur, -en, *n.f.* trace, track.

spuren, *vb.* follow the prescribed pattern.

spüren, *vb.* feel; trace.

spurlos, *adj.* without a trace.

Spurweite, -n, *n.f.* width of track, gauge.

sputen, *vb.* (sich s.) hurry up.

Staat, -en, *n.m.* state, government.

Staatenbund, ⸚e, *n.m.* federation.

staatlich, *adj.* national, governmental.

Staatsangehörig-, *n.m.&f.* national citizen.

Staatsangehörigkeit, -en, *n.f.* citizenship, nationality.

staatsfeindlich, *adj.* subversive.

Staatskunst, *n.f.* statesmanship.

Staatsmann, ⸚er, *n.m.* statesman.

Staatssekretär, -e, *n.m.* undersecretary of a ministry.

Staatsstreich, -e, *n.m.* coup d'état.

Stab, ⸚e, *n.m.* staff, rod.

stabil', *adj.* stable.

stabilisie'ren, *vb.* stabilize.

Stabilität', *n.f.* stability.

Stachel, -n, *n.m.* sting, thorn, spike.

Stachelbeere, -n, *n.f.* gooseberry.

Stachelschwein, -e, *n.nt.* porcupine.

Stadion, -dien, *n.nt.* stadium.

Stadium, -dien, *n.nt.* stage.

Stadt, ⸚e, *n.f.* town, city.

stadtbekannt, *adj.* known all over town, notorious.

städtisch, *adj.* municipal; urban.

Stadtteil, -e, *n.m.* borough.

Staffel, -n, *n.f.* rung, step; (*mil.*) echelon, squadron.

staffeln, *vb.* graduate, stagger.

stagnie'ren, *vb.* stagnate.

stagnie'rend, *adj.* stagnant.

Stahl, -e, *n.m.* steel.

Stahlhelm, -e, *n.m.* steel helmet.

Stahlwaren, *n.pl.* cutlery; hardware.

Stall, ⸚e, *n.m.* stall, stable, barn.

Stamm, ⸚e, *n.m.* (tree) trunk; (word) stem; tribe, clan.

Stammbaum, ⸚e, *n.m.* family tree; pedigree.

stammen, *vb.* stem, originate, be descended.

stammeln, *vb.* stammer.

Stammgast, ⸚e, *n.m.* habitué.

stämmig, *adj.* sturdy, burly.

stampfen, *vb.* stamp, trample.

Stand, ⸚e, *n.m.* stand(ing); position; level; status; class, estate.

Standard, -s, *n.m.* standard.

standardisie'ren, *vb.* standardize.

Ständchen, -, *n.nt.* serenade.

Ständer, -, *n.m.* rack, stand.

Standesamt, ⸚er, *n.nt.* marriage bureau, registrar.

standesbewußt, *adj.* classconscious.

standesgemäß, *adj.* according to one's rank.

standhaft, *adj.* steadfast.

Standhaftigkeit, *n.f.* constancy.

stand·halten*, *vb.* hold one's ground, withstand.

Standpunkt, -e, *n.m.* standpoint, point of view.

Stange, -n, *n.f.* rod, bar, pole; carton (of cigarettes).

Stapel, -, *n.m.* pile; stock; (ship) slip; (**vom S. lassen***) launch.

stapeln, *vb.* pile up.

stapfen, *vb.* stamp, plod.

Star, -e, *n.m.* (eye) cataract; (bird) starling; (film) star.

stark(⸚), *adj.* strong.

Stärke, -n, *n.f.* strength; starch.

stärken, *vb.* strengthen; starch.

Stärkungsmittel, -, *n.nt.* tonic.

starr, *adj.* rigid.

starren, *vb.* stare.

Starrheit, *n.f.* rigidity.

starrköpfig, *adj.* stubborn, headstrong.

Starrsinn, *n.m.* obstinacy.

Start, -s, *n.m.* start.

Startbahn, -en, *n.f.* runway.

starten, *vb.* start.

Startklappe, -n, *n.f.* choke (auto).

Station', -en, *n.f.* station.

stationär', *adj.* stationary.

Stations'vorsteher, -, *n.m* station master.

statisch, *adj.* static.

Statist', -en, -en, *n.m.* (theater) extra; (*fig.*) dummy.

Statis'tik, *n.f.* statistics.

Stativ', -e, *n.nt.* (photo) tripod.

statt, *prep.* instead of.

Stätte, -n, *n.f.* place.

statt-finden*, *vb.* take place.

stattlich, *adj.* imposing.

Statue, -n, *n.f.* statue.

Staub, *n.m.* dust.

staubig, *adj.* dusty.

Staudamm, ⁼e, *n.m.* dam.

stauen, *vb.* dam up; (**sich s.**) be dammed up, get jammed up.

staunen, *vb.* be astonished, wonder.

Stauung, -en, *n.f.* congestion.

stechen*, *vb.* prick, sting; pierce, stab.

Stechschritt, *n.m.* goose step.

Steckdose, -n, *n.f.* (*elec.*) outlet, socket.

stecken(*), *vb. intr.* be located, be hidden; (**wo steckt er denn?**) where *is* he, anyhow?; (**s. bleiben***) get stuck.

stecken, *vb. tr.* put, stick, pin, hide.

Steckenpferd, -e, *n.nt.* hobby-horse; hobby.

Stecknadel, -n, *n.f.* pin.

Steckrübe, -n, *n.f.* turnip.

Steg, ⁼e, *n.m.* path; foot-bridge.

stehen*, *vb.* stand, be located; be becoming; (**sich gut s.**) be on good terms;

(**es steht dahin'**) it has yet to be shown.

stehen·bleiben*, *vb.* stop.

stehen·lassen*, *vb.* leave standing; leave behind, forget.

Stehplatz, ⁼e, *n.m.* standing room.

stehlen*, *vb.* steal.

steif, *adj.* stiff, rigid.

Steifheit, -en, *n.f.* stiffness, rigidity.

Steig, -e, *n.m.* path.

steigen*, *vb.* climb, rise.

steigern, *vb.* increase, boost; (**sich s.**) increase, (*fig.*) work oneself up.

Steigung, -en, *n.f.* rise, slope, ascent.

steil, *adj.* steep.

Stein, -e, *n.m.* stone, rock.

Steingut, *n.nt.* earthenware, crockery.

steinigen, *vb.* stone.

Stelldichein, *n.nt.* rendezvous.

Stelle, -n, *n.f.* place, spot, point.

stellen, *vb.* place, put, set.

Stellenangebot, -e, *n.nt.* position offered.

Stellenvermittlung, -en, *n.f.* employment agency.

stellenweise, *adv.* in parts; in places.

Stellung, -en, *n.f.* position, place, stand; job; (**S. nehmen**) comment.

Stellungnahme, -n, *n.f.* comment, attitude.

stellvertretend, *adj.* assistant, deputy.

Stellvertreter, -, *n.m.* representative, deputy, alternate.

stemmen, *vb.* stem; (**sich s. gegen**) oppose, resist.

Stempel, -, *n.m.* stamp.

stempeln, *vb.* stamp; (**s. gehen**) be on the dole.

Stenographie', -i'en, *n.f.* shorthand.

stenographie'ren, *vb.* take shorthand, write shorthand.

Stenotypis'tin, -nen, *n.f.* stenographer.

Steppdecke, -n, *n.f.* quilt comforter.

Steppe, -n, *n.f.* steppe.

steppen, *vb.* stitch.

sterben*, *vb.* die.

sterblich, *adj.* mortal.

steril', *adj.* sterile.

sterilisie'ren, *vb.* sterilize.

Sterilität', *n.f.* sterility.

Sterling, -, *n.nt.* pound sterling.

Stern, -e, *n.m.* star.

Sternbild, -er, *n.nt.* constellation.

Sternchen, -, *n.nt.* asterisk.

Sternkunde, *n.f.* astronomy.

Sternwarte, -n, *n.f.* observatory.

stet(ig), *adj.* steady.

stets, *adv.* always.

Steuer, -, *n.nt.* rudder, helm.

Steuer, -n, *n.f.* tax.

steuern, *vb.* steer, pilot, navigate.

Steuerruder, -, *n.nt.* rudder.

Steuerzahler, -, *n.m.* taxpayer.

Steward, -s, *n.m.* steward.

Stewardeß, -ssen, *n.f.* stewardess.

Stich, -e, *n.m.* stab; bite, sting; stitch.

stichhaltig, *adj.* valid, sound.

Stichwort, ×er, *n.nt.* cue.

sticken, *vb.* embroider.

Stickerei', -en, *n.f.* embroidery.

Stickstoff, *n.m.* nitrogen.

Stiefel, -, *n.m.* boot.

Stief-, *cpds.* step-; (**Stiefvater**) stepfather; etc.

Stiel, -e, *n.m.* handle; stalk, stem.

stier, *adj.* glassy (look).

Stier, -e, *n.m.* steer.

stieren, *vb.* stare.

Stift, -e, *n.m.* peg, pin, tack; crayon, pencil.

Stift, -e(r), *n.nt.* charitable institution.

stiften, *vb.* donate; found; endow.

Stiftung, -en, *n.f.* foundation; donation.

Stil, -e, *n.m.* style.

stilgerecht, *adj.* in good style, in good taste.

still, *adj.* still, quiet.

Stille, *n.f.* stillness, silenc

stillen, *vb.* still, quenc nurse (a baby).

Stilleben, -, *n.nt.* still-life.

stillos, *adj.* in bad taste.

stillschweigend, *adj.* silen tacit, implicit.

Stillstand, *n.m.* halt.

Stimmabgabe, -n, *n.f.* vote voting.

Stimmband, ×er, *n.nt.* voca cord.

Stimme, -n, *n.f.* voice; vote

stimmen, *vb.* tune; vote; b correct.

Stimmengleichheit, *n.f.* ti vote.

Stimmenprüfung, -en, *n.y* canvass.

Stimmrecht, -e, *n.nt.* suf frage, franchise.

Stimmung, -en, *n.f.* mood morale.

stimmungsvoll, *adj.* festive moving; intimate.

Stimmzettel, -, *n.m.* ballot

stinken*, *vb.* stink.

Stinktier, -e, *n.nt.* skunk.

Stint, -e, *n.m.* smelt.

Stipen'dium, -dien, *n.nt* scholarship, grant.

Stirn, -en, *n.f.* forehead brow.

Stirnhöhle, -n, *n.f.* sinus.

Stock, ×e, *n.m.* stick, cane.

stockdunkel, *adj.* pitchdark.

stocken, *vb.* stop, come to a halt; falter.

Stockung, -en, *n.f.* stop standstill; deadlock.

Stockwerk, -e, *n.nt.* floor story.

Stoff, -e, *n.m.* matter, substance; material; cloth.

stofflich, *adj.* material.

stöhnen, *vb.* groan.

Stoiker, -, *n.m.* stoic.

stoisch, *adj.* stoical.

Stola, -len, *n.f.* stole.

stolpern, *vb.* stumble, trip

stolz, *adj.* proud.

Stolz, *n.m.* pride.

stolzie'ren, *vb.* strut.

stopfen, *vb.* stuff; (socks, etc.) darn.

stoppen, *vb.* stop.

Stöpsel, -, *n.m.* stopper; (*elec.*) plug.

Stör, -e, *n.m.* sturgeon.

stören, *vb.* disturb, bother.

Störenfried, -e, *n.m.* intruder, troublemaker.

Störung, -en, *n.f.* disturbance; (radio) interference, static.

Storch, ⁓e, *n.m.* stork.

Stoß, ⁓e, *n.m.* blow, hit, thrust.

stoßen*, *vb.* push, kick, hit, thrust.

Stoßstange, -n, *n.f.* bumper.

stottern, *vb.* stutter.

Strafanstalt, -en, *n.f.* penal institution.

strafbar, *adj.* liable to punishment.

Strafe, -n, *n.f.* punishment; fine; sentence.

strafen, *vb.* punish.

straff, *adj.* taut, tight.

straffen, *vb.* tighten.

Strafgebühr, -en, *n.f.* fine.

Strafgericht, -e, *n.nt.* criminal court.

Strafkammer, -n, *n.f.* criminal court.

Sträfling, -e, *n.m.* convict.

Strafmandat, -e, *n.nt.* traffic ticket.

Strafporto, *n.nt.* postage due.

Strahl, -en, *n.m.* ray, beam; (water) spout.

strahlen, *vb.* beam, gleam, radiate.

Strahlen, *n.nt.* radiance.

strahlend, *adj.* radiant.

Strahlflugzeug, -e, *n.nt.* jet plane.

Strahlung, -en, *n.f.* radiation.

Strähne, -n, *n.f.* strand, streak.

stramm, *adj.* tight; (*fig.*) strapping.

strampeln, *vb.* kick.

Strand, -e, *n.m.* beach, shore.

stranden, *vb.* strand.

Strandgut, *n.nt.* jetsam.

Strang, ⁓e, *n.m.* rope; (**über die Stränge schlagen***) run riot.

Strapaze, -n, *n.f.* exertion, drudgery.

Straße, -n, *n.f.* street, road.

Straßenbahn, -en, *n.f.* streetcar, trolley.

**Strategie', *n.f.* strategy.

strate'gisch, *adj.* strategic.

Stratosphä're, *n.f.* stratosphere.

sträuben, *vb.* (**sich s.**) bristle; (*fig.*) struggle against resist.

Strauch, ⁓er, *n.m.* shrub.

straucheln, *vb.* falter, stumble.

Strauß, ⁓e, *n.m.* bouquet; ostrich.

streben, *vb.* strive, endeavor, aspire.

Streben, *n.nt.* pursuit.

Strebepfeiler, -, *n.m.* flying buttress.

Streber, -, *n.m.* (school) grind; (society) social climber.

strebsam, *adj.* zealous.

Strecke, -n, *n.f.* stretch, distance.

strecken, *vb.* stretch; (**die Waffen s.**) lay down one's arms.

Streich, -e, *n.m.* stroke, blow; prank.

streichen*, *vb.* scratch; paint.

streicheln, *vb.* stroke, caress.

Streichholz, ⁓er, *n.nt.* match.

Streife, -n, *n.f.* patrol.

Streifen, -, *n.m.* strip.

streifen, *vb.* touch lightly.

Streik, -s, *n.m.* strike.

streiken, *vb.* strike.

Streikposten, -, *n.m.* picket.

Streit, *n.m.* quarrel, dispute.

streiten*, *vb.* fight; (**sich s.**) quarrel.

Streitfrage, -n, *n.f.* controversy.

Streitpunkt, -e, *n.m.* point at issue.

streitsüchtig, *adj.* pugnacious.

streng, *adj.* strict, stern, severe.

strenggläubig, *adj.* orthodox.

streuen, vb. strew, scatter; sprinkle.

Strich, -e, n.m. stroke; line; **(nach S. und Faden)** thoroughly; **(gegen den S.)** against the grain.

Strick, -e, n.m. rope.

stricken, vb. knit.

strittig, adj. controversial.

Stroh, n.nt. straw.

Strolch, -e, -e, n.m. vagabond.

Strom, ¨e, n.m. stream; (elec.) current.

strömen, vb. stream, flow.

Stromkreis, -e, n.m. circuit.

stromlinienförmig, adj. streamlined.

Stromspannung, -en, n.f. voltage.

Strömung, -en, n.f. current; trend, drift.

Strudel, -, n.m. whirlpool.

Struktur', -en, n.f. structure.

Strumpf, ¨e, n.m. stocking.

Strumpfband, ¨er, n.nt. garter.

Strumpfbandgürtel, n.m. girdle.

Strumpfwaren, n.pl. hosiery.

struppig, adj. shaggy.

Stube, -n, n.f. room.

Stuck, n.m. stucco.

Stück, -e, n.nt. piece; (theater) play.

stückeln, vb. patch, piece together.

stücken, vb. piece.

Student', -en, -en, n.m. student.

Studie, -n, n.f. study.

Studiengeld, -er, n.nt. tuition.

studie'ren, vb. study (at a university), be a student.

Studium, -dien, n.nt. study.

Stufe, -n, n.f. step.

stufenweise, adj. gradual, step by step.

Stuhl, ¨e, n.m. chair.

stumm, adj. mute, silent.

Stummel, -, n.m. stub, butt.

Stümper, -, n.m. beginner, amateur.

stumpf, adj. blunt; stupid; (angle) obtuse.

Stumpf, ¨e, n.m. stump.

Stunde, -n, n.f. hour; (school) class.

stündlich, adj. hourly.

stupsen, vb. joggle.

stur, adj. stubborn; obtuse.

Sturm, ¨e, n.m. storm.

stürmen, vb. storm.

stürmisch, adj. stormy.

Sturz, ¨e, n.m. fall; overthrow.

stürzen, vb. plunge, hurl, overthrow; rush, crash.

Stute, -n, n.f. mare.

Stütze, -n, n.f. support, prop, help.

stutzen, vb. trim.

stützen, vb. support.

Stützpunkt, -e, n.m. base.

Subjekt', -e, n.nt. subject.

sublime'ren, vb. sublimate.

Sündflut, n.f. the Flood; cataclysm.

Substantiv, -e, n.nt. noun.

Substanz', -en, n.f. substance.

subtrahie'ren, vb. subtract.

subtil', adj. subtle.

Subvention', -en, n.f. subvention, subsidy.

Suche, n.f. search.

suchen, vb. search, seek, look for.

Sucht, n.f. addiction.

Süd, Süden, n.m. south.

südlich, adj. southern; to the south.

Südos'ten, n.m. southeast.

südöst'lich, adj. southeast.

Südpol, n.m. South Pole.

Südwe'sten, n.m. southwest.

südwest'lich, adj. southwest.

suggerie'ren, vb. suggest.

Sühne, -n, n.f. atonement, expiation.

sühnen, vb. atone for, expiate.

Sülze, n.f. jellied meat.

summa'risch, adj. summary.

Summe, -n, n.f. sum.

summen, vb. hum, buzz.

Sumpf, ¨e, n.m. swamp, mire.

Sünde, -n, *n.f.* sin.

Sünder, -, *n.m.* sinner.

Sündenvergebung, *n.f.* absolution.

sündhaft, *adj.* sinful.

sündigen, *vb.* sin.

super, *adj.* super.

Suppe, -n, *n.f.* soup.

surren, *vb.* buzz.

suspendie'ren, *vb.* suspend.

süß, *adj.* sweet.

Süße, *n.f.* sweetness.

Sylve'ster, *n.nt.* New Year's Eve.

symbo'lisch, *adj.* symbolic.

Sympathie', -i'en, *n.f.* sympathy.

sympa'thisch, *adj.* likable, congenial; (*med.*) sympathetic.

Symphonie', -i'en, *n.f.* symphony.

sympho'nisch, *adj.* symphonic.

Symptom', -e, *n.nt.* symptom.

symptoma'tisch, *adj.* symptomatic.

synchronisie'ren, *vb.* synchronize.

Synago'ge, -n, *n.f.* synagogue.

Synonym', -e, *n.nt.* synonym.

Synthe'se, -n, *n.f.* synthesis.

synthe'tisch, *adj.* synthetic.

Syphilis, *n.f.* syphilis.

System', -e, *n.nt.* system.

systema'tisch, *adj.* systematic.

Szene, -n, *n.f.* scene.

T

Tabak, *n.m.* tobacco.

Tabel'le, -n, *n.f.* chart.

Tablett', -e, *n.nt.* tray.

Tablet'te, -n, *n.f.* tablet.

Tadel, -, *n.m.* reproof, reprimand; (school) demerit.

tadeln, *vb.* reprove, find fault with.

tadelnswert, *adj.* reprehensible.

Tafel, -n, *n.f.* tablet; table; chart; blackboard; bar (of chocolate).

täfeln, *vb.* panel.

Tag, -e, *n.m.* day; (**guten T.**) how do you do.

Tagebuch, ¨er, *n.nt.* diary.

Tagesanbruch, *n.m.* daybreak.

Tageslicht, *n.nt.* daylight.

Tageszeitung, -en, *n.f.* daily newspaper.

täglich, *adj.* daily.

Tagung, -en, *n.f.* convention, meeting.

Taille, -n, *n.f.* waist.

Takt, -e, *n.m.* tact; rhythm.

taktisch, *adj.* tactical.

Tal, ¨er, *n.nt.* valley.

Talent', -e, *n.nt.* talent.

talentiert', *adj.* talented.

tändeln, *vb.* dally.

Tango, -s, *n.m.* tango.

Tank, -s, *n.m.* tank.

Tankstelle, -n, *n.f.* filling station.

Tanne, -n, *n.f.* fir, spruce.

Tante, -n, *n.f.* aunt.

Tantie'me, -n, *n.f.* bonus.

Tanz, ¨e, *n.m.* dance.

tänzeln, *vb.* flounce, caper.

tanzen, *vb.* dance.

Tänzer, -, *n.m.* dancer.

Tanzsaal, -säle, *n.m.* dance hall, ballroom.

Tapezie'rer, -, *n.m.* upholsterer.

tapfer, *adj.* brave, valiant.

Tapisserie, -i'en, *n.f.* tapestry.

tappen, *vb.* grope.

tapsig, *adj.* gawky.

tarnen, *vb.* screen, camouflage.

Tarnung, -en, *n.f.* screen, camouflage.

Tasche, -n, *n.f.* pocket; handbag.

Taschendieb, -e, *n.m.* pickpocket.

Taschengeld, -er, *n.nt.* allowance, pocket money.

Taschenformat, *n.nt.* pocket-size.

Taschenlampe, -n, *n.f.* flashlight.

Taschentuch, ˙er, *n.nt.* handkerchief.

Tasse, -n, *n.f.* cup.

Tastatur', -en, *n.f.* keyboard.

Taste, -n, *n.f.* key.

tasten, *vb.* feel; grope.

Tastsinn, *n.m.* sense of touch.

Tat, -en, *n.f.* act, deed; (**in der T.**) indeed.

Tatbestand, *n.m.* facts, findings.

Täter, -, *n.m.* culprit.

tätig, *adj.* active.

Tätigkeit, -en, *n.f.* activity.

Tatkraft, ˙e, *n.f.* energy.

tatkräftig, *adj.* energetic.

tätlich, *adj.* violent.

Tätlichkeit, -en, *n.f.* violence.

Tatsache, -n, *n.f.* fact.

tatsächlich, *adj.* actual, real.

Tatze, -n, *n.f.* paw, claw.

Tau, *n.m.* dew.

Tau, -e, *n.nt.* rope.

taub, *adj.* deaf.

Taube, -n, *n.f.* pigeon, dove.

tauchen, *vb.* dive, plunge, dip.

Taucher, -, *n.m.* diver.

Taufe, -n, *n.f.* baptism, christening.

taufen, *vb.* baptize, christen.

Taufkapelle, -n, *n.f.* baptistry.

taugen, *vb.* be worth; be of use.

Taugenichts, *n.m.* good-for-nothing.

tauglich, *adj.* useful, qualified.

taumeln, *vb.* stagger.

taumelnd, *adj.* groggy.

Tausch, *n.m.* exchange, trade.

tauschen, *vb.* exchange.

täuschen, *vb.* deceive, delude, fool.

täuschend, *adj.* deceptive.

Tauschhandel, *n.m.* barter.

Täuschung, -en, *n.f.* deception, delusion, fallacy.

tausend, *num.* a thousand.

Tausend, -e, *n.nt.* thousand.

tausendst-, *adj.* thousandt?

Tausendstel, -, *n.nt.* thou sandth; (**ein t.**) one one thousandth.

Taxe, -n, *n.f.* tax; taxi.

taxie'ren, *vb.* appraise, estmate.

Technik, *n.f.* technique technology.

technisch, *adj.* technical.

Tee, -s, *n.m.* tea.

Teelöffel, -, *n.m.* teaspoon.

Teekanne, -n, *n.f.* tea-pot.

Teer, *n.m.* tar.

Teich, -e, *n.m.* pond, pool.

Teig, -e, *n.m.* dough, batte

Teil, -e, *n.m.* part, portion section.

teilbar, *adj.* divisible.

teilen, *vb.* divide, share.

teil-haben*, *vb.* share.

Teilhaber, -, *n.m.* partner.

Teilnahme, *n.f.* participation; sympathy.

teilnahmslos, *adj.* lethargi

teil-nehmen*, *vb.* partic

Teilnehmer, -, *n.m.* partic pant, partner.

teils, *adv.* partly.

Teilung, -en, *n.f.* partition division.

teilweise, *adv.* partly.

Teint, -s, *n.m.* complexion.

Telegramm', -e, *n.nt.* tele gram.

Telegraph', -en, -en, *n.r* telegraph.

telegraphie'ren, *vb.* tele graph.

Telephon', -e, *n.nt.* tele phone.

Telephon'buch, ˙er, *n.n* telephone directory.

Telephon'fräulein, -, *n.* telephone operator.

telephonie'ren, *vb.* tele phone.

Teller, -, *n.m.* plate.

Temperament', n.nt. ten perament, disposition; vacity.

temperament'voll, *ao* temperamental; vivacious.

Temperatur', -en, *n.f.* tem perature.

Tempo, -s, *n.nt.* speed; tempo.

Tendenz', -en, *n.f.* tendency, trend.

Tender, -, *n.m.* tender.

Tennis, *n.nt.* tennis.

Tennisschläger, -, *n.m.* tennis racket.

Tennisschuh, -e, *n.m.* sneaker.

Tenor', -e, *n.m.* tenor.

Teppich, -e, *n.m.* rug, carpet.

Termin', -e, *n.m.* fixed day, deadline.

Terpentin', *n.nt.* turpentine.

Terras'se, -n, *n.f.* terrace.

Testament', -e, *n.nt.* testament, will.

testamenta'risch, *adj.* testamentary, noted in the will.

teuer, *adj.* expensive, dear.

Teuerung, *n.f.* rising cost of living.

Teufel, -, *n.m.* devil.

teuflisch, *adj.* diabolic.

Text, -e, *n.m.* text.

Texti'lien, *n.pl.* textiles.

Textil'ware, -n, *n.f.* textile.

Thea'ter, -, *n.nt.* theater; spectacle.

Thea'terkasse, -n, *n.f.* box office.

Thea'terstück, -e, *n.nt.* play.

Thea'terwissenschaft, -en, *n.f.* dramatics.

theatra'lisch, *adj.* theatrical.

Thema, -men, *n.nt.* theme, subject, topic.

Theolo'ge. -n, -n, *n.m.* theologian.

theore'tisch, *adj.* theoretical.

Theorie', -i'en, *n.f.* theory.

Therapie', *n.f.* therapy.

Thermome'ter, -, *n.nt.* thermometer.

These, -n, *n.f.* thesis.

Thron, -e, *n.m.* throne.

Thunfisch, -e, *n.m.* tuna.

tief, *adj.* deep, low; profound.

Tiefe, -n, *n.f.* depth.

Tiefebene, -n, *n.f.* plain, lowland.

tiefgründig, *adj.* profound.

Tiefkühler, -, *n.m.* freezer.

tiefsinnig, *adj.* profound; pensive.

tieftraurig, *adj.* heartbroken.

Tier, -e, *n.nt.* animal.

Tierarzt, -e, *n.m.* veterinary.

tierisch, *adj.* animal, bestial.

Tiger, -, *n.m.* tiger.

tilgen, *vb.* obliterate; delete; pay off, amortize.

Tilgung, -en, *n.f.* liquidation, amortization.

Tinte, -n, *n.f.* ink.

Tintenfisch, -e, *n.m.* octopus.

Tip, -s, *n.m.* hint, suggestion.

tippen, *vb.* type.

Tisch, -e, *n.m.* table.

Tischdecke, -n, *n.f.* tablecloth.

Tischler, -, *n.m.* carpenter.

Tischtuch, -er, *n.nt.* tablecloth.

Titel, -, *n.m.* title.

Toast, *n.m.* toast.

toben, *vb.* rave, rage.

Tochter, -, *n.f.* daughter.

Tod, -e, *n.m.* death.

Todesfall, -e, *n.m.* (case of) death.

Todesstrafe, -n, *n.f.* capital punishment.

tödlich, *adj.* deadly, mortal; lethal.

Toilet'te, -n, *n.f.* toilet.

Toilet'tenartikel, *n.pl.* toilet articles.

tolerant', *adj.* tolerant.

Toleranz', *n.f.* tolerance.

toll, *adj.* mad, crazy.

tollkühn, *adj.* foolhardy.

Tollwut, *n.f.* rabies.

tölpelhaft, *adj.* clumsy.

Toma'te, -n, *n.f.* tomato.

Ton, -e, *n.m.* tone, sound; clay.

tonangebend, *adj.* setting the style.

Tonart, -en, *n.f.* key.

Tonband, -er, *n.nt.* magnetic tape.

Tonbandaufnahme, -n, *n.f.* tape recording.

Tonbandgerät, -e, *n.nt.* tape recorder.

tönen, *vb.* sound, resound, ring.

Tonfall, ⸚e, *n.m.* intonation, inflection.

Tonfilm, -e, *n.m.* sound movie.

Tonhöhe, -n, *n.f.* pitch.

Tonleiter, -n, *n.f.* scale.

Tonstufe, -n, *n.f.* (music) pitch.

Tonwaren, *n.pl.* earthenware.

Tonne, -n, *n.f.* ton; barrel.

Topf, ⸚e, *n.m.* pot.

Töpferware, -n, *n.f.* pottery.

Tor, -en, -en, *n.m.* fool.

Tor, -e, *n.nt.* gate, gateway; (sport) goal.

Torbogen, ⸚, *n.m.* archway.

Torheit, -en, *n.f.* folly.

töricht, *adj.* foolish.

torkeln, *vb.* lurch, stagger.

Tornister, -, *n.m.* knapsack, pack.

torpedieren, *vb.* torpedo.

Torpedo, -s, *n.m.* torpedo.

Torte, -n, *n.f.* tart, layer cake.

Törtchen, -, *n.nt.* tart.

Tortur, -en, *n.f.* torture.

tosen, *vb.* rage, roar.

tot, *adj.* dead.

total, *adj.* total.

totalitär, *adj.* totalitarian.

töten, *vb.* kill.

Totenwache, -n, *n.f.* wake.

Totschlag, ⸚e, *n.m.* (case of) manslaughter.

Toto, *n.m.* lottery.

Tour, -en, *n.f.* tour, excursion, trip.

Tourist, -en, -en, *n.m.* tourist.

Trab, *n.m.* trot.

traben, *vb.* trot.

Trabant, -en, -en, *n.m.* henchman.

Tracht, -en, *n.f.* costume.

trachten, *vb.* seek, endeavor.

Tradition, -en, *n.f.* tradition.

traditionell, *adj.* traditional.

Tragbahre, -n, *n.f.* stretcher.

tragbar, *adj.* portable; bearable.

träge, *adj.* indolent, sluggish.

tragen*, *vb.* carry, bear; wear.

Träger, -, *n.m.* carrier; girder; (lingerie) straps.

Tragik, *n.f.* tragic art; calamity.

tragisch, *adj.* tragic.

Tragödie, -n, *n.f.* tragedy.

Tragweite, -n, *n.f.* range; significance, consequence.

Trainer, -, *n.m.* coach.

trainieren, *vb.* train, work out; coach.

Trambahn, -en, *n.f.* trolley.

trampeln, *vb.* trample.

Tranchiermesser, -, *n.nt.* carving-knife.

Träne, -n, *n.f.* tear.

tränen, *vb.* water (eye).

Trank, ⸚e, *n.m.* potion.

tränken, *vb.* water (animals).

Transaktion, -en, *n.f.* transaction.

Transformator, -o'ren, *n.m.* transformer, converter.

Transfusion, -en, *n.f.* transfusion.

transpirieren, *vb.* perspire.

transponieren, *vb.* transpose.

Transport, -e, *n.m.* transport.

transportieren, *vb.* transport.

Trapez, -e, *n.nt.* trapeze.

Traube, -n, *n.f.* grape.

trauen, *vb.* (intr.) trust; (tr.) marry, join in marriage.

Trauer, *n.f.* grief; mourning.

trauern, *vb.* grieve, mourn.

trauervoll, *adj.* mournful.

Traufe, -n, *n.f.* gutter; (**vom Regen in die T.**) out of the frying pan into the fire.

Traum, ⸚e, *n.m.* dream; (**böser T.**) nightmare.

träumen, *vb.* dream; (**vor sich hin-t**) daydream.

Träumer, -, *n.m.* dreamer.

Träumerei, -en, *n.f.* daydream, reverie.

träumerisch, *adj.* fanciful, faraway.

traumhaft, *adj.* dreamlike; dreamy.

traurig, *adj.* sad.

Trauring, -e, *n.m.* wedding ring.

Trecker, -, *n.m.* tractor.

Treff, *n.nt.* clubs (cards).

treffen*, *vb.* hit; meet; (**sich t.**) meet.

treffend, *adj.* pertinent.

Treffer, -, *n.m.* hit.

trefflich, *adj.* excellent.

treiben*, *vb.* (*tr.*) drive; be engaged in, (*intr.*) drift, float.

Trend, -s, *n.m.* trend.

trennen, *vb.* separate, divide; hyphenate; (**sich t.**) part.

Trennung, -en, *n.f.* separation, division.

treppab', *adv.* down the stairs.

treppauf', *adv.* up the stairs.

Treppe, -n, *n.f.* staircase, stairs.

Tresor', -e, *n.m.* vault.

treten*, *vb.* step, tread.

treu, *adj.* true, faithful, loyal.

Treue, *n.f.* faith, loyalty; allegiance.

Treueid, -e, *n.m.* oath of allegiance.

Treuhänder, -. *n.m.* trustee.

treuherzig, *adj.* trusting, guileless.

treulos, *adj.* disloyal.

Treulosigkeit, -en, *n.f.* disloyalty.

treulich, *adv.* faithfully.

Tribü'ne, -n, *n.f.* grand stand.

Trichter, -, *n.m.* funnel.

Trick, -s, *n.m.* trick.

Trickfilm, -e, *n.m.* animated cartoon.

Tricktrack, *n.nt.* backgammon.

Trieb, -e, *n.m.* sprout, shoot; urge.

Triebfeder, -n, *n.f.* mainspring.

triebhaft, *adj.* instinctive, unrestrained.

Triebwagen, -, *n.m.* railcar.

triefen*, *vb.* drip.

triftig, *adj.* weighty.

Trikot', *n.nt.* knitted cloth.

trimmen, *vb.* trim.

trinkbar, *adj.* drinkable.

trinken*, *vb.* drink.

Trinker, -, *n.m.* drunkard.

Trinkgeld, -er, *n.nt.* tip.

Trinkspruch, -e, *n.m.* toast.

Tripper, *n.m.* gonorrhea.

Tritt, -e, *n.m.* step; kick.

Trittleiter, -n, *n.f.* stepladder.

Triumph', -e, *n.m.* triumph.

triumphie'ren, *vb.* triumph.

trivial', *adj.* trivial.

trocken, *adj.* dry.

Trockenhaube, -n, *n.f.* hair drier.

trocken-legen, *vb.* (land) drain; (baby) change the diapers.

trocknen, *vb.* dry.

trödeln, *vb.* dawdle.

Trog, -e, *n.m.* trough.

trollen, *vb.* (**sich t.**) toddle off.

Trommel, -n, *n.f.* drum.

Trommelfell, -e, *n.nt.* eardrum.

Trompe'te, -n, *n.f.* trumpet.

Tropen, *n.pl.* tropics.

Tropfen, -, *n.m.* drop.

tropfen, *vb.* drip.

Tropfer, -, *n.m.* dropper.

Trophä'e, -n, *n.f.* trophy.

tropisch, *adj.* tropical.

Trost, *n.m.* consolation, solace, comfort.

trösten, *vb.* console, comfort.

trostlos, *adj.* desolate, dreary.

trostreich, *adj.* comforting.

Trott, *n.m.* trot.

Trottel, -, *n.m.* idiot, dope.

trotz, *prep.* in spite of, despite, notwithstanding.

trotzdem, 1. *conj.* although, despite the fact that. **2.** *adv.* nevertheless.

trotzen, *vb.* defy.

trotzig, *adj.* defiant.

trübe, *adj.* dim; muddy; cloudy.

trüben, *vb.* dim.

Trübsal, *n.f.* misery, sorrow.

trübselig, *adj.* sad, gloomy.

Trübsinn, *n.m.* dejection, gloom.

trübsinnig, *adj.* gloomy.

Trubel, *n.m.* bustle, confusion.

Trüffel, -n, *n.f.* truffle.

Trug, *n.m.* deceit; delusion.

trügen*, *vb.* (*tr.*) deceive; (*intr.*) be deceptive.

trügerisch, *adj.* deceptive; illusory; treacherous.

Trugschluß, -sse, *n.m.* fallacy.

Truhe, -n, *n.f.* chest.

Trümmer, *n.pl.* ruins, debris.

Trunk, -e, *n.m.* drink; draught.

Trunkenbold, -e, *n.m.* drunkard.

Trunkenheit, *n.f.* drunkenness.

Trupp, -s, *n.m.* troop, squad.

Truppe, -n, *n.f.* troops.

Truppeneinheit, -en, *n.f.* unit, outfit.

Trust, -s, *n.m.* trust.

Truthahn, -e, *n.m.* turkey.

Tscheche, -n, -n, *n.m.* Czech.

tschechisch, *adj.* Czech.

Tschechei', *n.f.* Czechoslovakia.

Tschechoslowa'ke, -n, -n, *n.m.* Czechoslovakian.

Tschechoslowakei', *n.f.* Czechoslovakia.

tschechoslowa'kisch, *adj.* Czechoslovakian.

Tube, -n, *n.f.* tube.

Tuberkulo'se, *n.f.* tuberculosis.

Tuch, -er, *n.nt.* cloth.

tüchtig, *adj.* able, efficient.

Tüchtigkeit, *n.f.* ability, efficiency.

Tücke, -n, *n.f.* malice, perfidy.

tückisch, *adj.* malicious, treacherous.

Tugend, *n.f.* virtue.

tugendhaft, *adj.* virtuous.

tugendsam, *adj.* virtuous.

Tüll, *n.m.* tulle.

Tülle, -n, *n.f.* spout.

Tulpe, -n, *n.f.* tulip.

tummeln, *vb.* move about, romp.

Tummelplatz, -e, *n.m.* playground.

Tumor, -o'ren, *n.m.* tumor.

Tümpel, -, *n.m.* pool.

Tumult', -e, *n.m.* tumult, uproar; hubbub.

tun*, *vb.* do.

Tünche, -n, *n.f.* whitewash; (*fig.*) veneer.

Tunichtgut, -e, *n.m.* ne'er-do-well.

Tunke, -n, *n.f.* sauce, gravy.

tunken, *vb.* dunk.

Tunnel, -, *n.m.* tunnel.

tupfen, *vb.* dab.

Tür, -en, *n.f.* door; (**mit der T. ins Haus fallen***) blurt out.

Turbi'nenjäger, -, *n.m.* turbo-jet plane.

Turbi'nenpropellertriebwerk, -e, *n.nt.* turbo-prop.

Türeingang, -e, *n.m.* doorway.

Türke, -n, -n, *n.m.* Turk.

Türkei', *n.f.* Turkey.

Türkis', -e, *n.m.* turquoise.

türkisch, *adj.* Turkish.

Turm, -e, *n.m.* tower, spire, steeple; (chess) castle, rook; (**spitzer T.**) spire.

türmen, *vb.* (*tr.*) pile up; (*intr.*) beat it; (**sich t.**) rise high.

turnen, *vb.* do gymnastics.

Turner, -, *n.m.* gymnast.

Turnhalle, -n, *n.f.* gym(nasium).

Turnier', -e, *n.nt.* tournament.

tuscheln, *vb.* whisper.

Tuschkasten, -, *n.m.* paint box.

Tüte, -n, *n.f.* (paper) bag, sack.

Tüttelchen, -, *n.nt.* dot.

Typ, -en, *n.m.* type.

Type, -n, *n.f.* (printing) type.

Typhus, *n.m.* typhus, typhoid fever.

typisch, *adj.* typical.

Typographie', *n.f.* typography.

Tyrann', -en, -en, *n.m.* tyrant.

Tyrannei', *n.f.* tyranny.

tyrannisie'ren, *vb.* tyrannize, oppress.

U

U-Bahn, -en, *n.f.* (= Unter-grundbahn) subway.

übel, *adj.* bad; nasty; nauseated.

Übel, *n.nt.* evil; nuisance.

Übelkeit, *n.f.* nausea.

übel-nehmen*, *vb.* hold against, resent.

Übeltat, -en, *n.f.* offence.

Übeltäter, -, *n.m.* offender.

üben, *vb.* practice.

über, *prep.* over, about, above, across, beyond.

überall, *adv.* everywhere.

überar'beiten, *vb.* work over; (**sich ü.**) overwork.

überaus, *adv.* exceedingly.

überbelichten, *vb.* overexpose.

überbie'ten*, *vb.* outbid; surpass.

Überbleibsel, -, *n.nt.* rest, left-over.

Überblick, -e, *n.m.* survey; general view.

überbli'cken, *vb.* survey.

überbrin'gen*, *vb.* deliver.

Überbrin'ger, -, *n.m.* bearer.

überbrü'cken, *vb.* bridge.

überdau'ern, *vb.* outlive, outlast.

überdies', *adv.* furthermore.

Überdruß, *n.m.* boredom; (**bis zum Ü.**) ad nauseam.

überdrüssig, *adj.* tired of, sick of.

übereilt', *adj.* rash, hasty.

übereinan'der, *adv.* one on top of the other.

überein'-kommen*, *vb.* agree.

Überein'kommen, -, *n.nt.* agreement.

Überein'kunft, ⸗e, *n.f.* agreement.

überein'-stimmen, *vb.* agree.

Überein'stimmung, -en, *n.f.* agreement, accord.

überfah'ren*, *vb.* drive over, run over.

Überfahrt, -en, *n.f.* passage, crossing.

Überfall, ⸗e, *n.m.* raid; hold-up.

überfal'len*, *vb.* attack suddenly, hold up.

überfällig, *adj.* overdue.

überflie'gen*, *vb.* fly over; (*fig.*) scan.

über-fließen*, *vb.* overflow.

überflü'geln, *vb.* surpass.

Überfluß, ⸗sse, *n.m.* abundance.

überflüssig, *adj.* superfluous.

überflu'ten, *vb.* overflow.

überführ'ren, *vb.* transfer; transport; convict.

Überfüh'rung, -en, *n.f.* transport; transfer; (rail-road) overpass.

überfüllt', *adj.* overcrowded, jammed.

Übergabe, *n.f.* delivery; surrender.

Übergang, ⸗e, *n.m.* passage; transition.

überge'gen*, *vb.* hand over, deliver; (**sich ü.**) vomit.

über-gehen*, *vb.* go over to.

überge'hen*, *vb.* pass over, skip.

Übergewicht, *n.nt.* over-weight, preponderance; (**das Ü. bekommen***) get the upper hand.

über-greifen*, *vb.* spread; encroach.

Übergriff, -e, *n.m.* encroach-ment.

über-haben*, *vb.* be sick of, be fed up with

überhand'-nehmen*, *vb.* spread, become dominant.

überhäu'fen, *vb.* overwhelm.

überhaupt', *adv.* in general; altogether; at all.

überheb'lich, *adj.* over-bearing.

überho'len, *vb.* overhaul; drive past, pass.

überholt', *adj.* out-of-date.

überhö'ren, *vb.* purposely not hear, ignore.

überla'den, *adj.* ornate.

überlas'sen*, *vb.* give to, yield, leave to.

über-lau-fen*, *vb.* overrun; defect, desert.

überlau'fen, *adj.* overrun.

Überläufer, -, *n.m.* deserter.

überle'ben, *vb.* outlive, survive.

Überle'ben, *n.nt.* survival.

überle'gen, *vb.* reflect on, think over.

überle'gen, *adj.* superior.

überlegt', *adj.* deliberate.

Überle'gung, -en, *n.f.* deliberation, consideration.

überlie'fern, *vb.* hand over.

Überlie'ferung, -en, *n.f.* tradition.

Übermacht, *n.f.* superiority.

überman'nen, *vb.* overpower.

Übermaß, *n.nt.* excess.

übermäßig, *adj.* excessive.

Übermensch, -en, -en, *n.m.* superman.

übermit'teln, *vb.* transmit, convey.

übermorgen, *adv.* the day after tomorrow.

Übermü'dung, *n.f.* overfatigue, exhaustion.

Übermut, *n.m.* high spirits; arrogance.

übernächst, *adj.* next but one.

übernach'ten, *vb.* spend the night, stay overnight.

übernatürlich, *adj.* supernatural.

überneh'men*, *vb.* take over.

überparteilich, *adj.* nonpartisan.

überprü'fen, *vb.* examine, check.

Überprü'fung, -en, *n.f.* checking, check-up.

überque'ren, *vb.* cross.

überra'gen, *vb.* surpass.

überra'gend, *adj.* superior.

überra'schen, *vb.* surprise.

Überra'schung, -en, *n.f.* surprise.

überre'den, *vb.* persuade.

Überre'dung, -en, *n.f.* persuasion.

überreich, *adj.* abundant, profuse.

überrei'chen, *vb.* hand over, present.

Überrest, -e, *n.m.* remains, relics.

überrum'peln, *vb.* take by surprise.

Überschallgeschwindigkeit, -en, *n.f.* supersonic speed.

überschat'ten, *vb.* overshadow.

überschät'zen, *vb.* overestimate.

überschau'en, *vb.* survey, get the whole view of.

überschla'fen*, *vb.* oversleep.

Überschlag, ̈e, *n.m.* estimate.

überschla'gen*, *vb.* pass over, skip; (**sich ü.**) turn over.

Überschrift, -en, *n.f.* title, heading, headline.

Überschuhe, *n.pl.* galoshes.

Überschuß, ̈sse, *n.m.* surplus.

überschüt'ten, *vb.* overwhelm.

überschwem'men, *vb.* inundate.

Überschwem'mung, -en, *n.f.* flood.

Übersee, *n.f.* oversea(s).

Überseedampfer, -, *n.m.* transoceanic liner.

übersehbar, *adj.* capable of being taken in at a glance; foreseeable.

überse'hen*, *vb.* view; overlook, not notice, ignore.

Überse'hen, -, *n.nt.* oversight.

übersen'den*, *vb.* send, transmit; consign, remit.

überset'zen, *vb.* translate.

Überset'zung, -en, *n.f.* translation.

Übersicht, -en, *n.f.* overview; summary, outline.

übersichtlich, *adj.* clear; easily understandable.

überspannt', *adj.* eccentric.

übersprin'gen*, *vb.* skip.

übersprudelnd, *adj.* exuberant.

überste'hen*, *vb.* endure, survive.

überstei'gen*, *vb.* surpass.

überstim'men, *vb.* outvote, overrule.

Überstunde, -n, *n.f.* hour of overtime work; (*pl.*) overtime.

überstür'zen, *vb.* precipitate.

überstürzt', *adj.* headlong, precipitate.

übertrag'bar, *adj.* transferable.

übertra'gen*, *vb.* transfer, transmit; translate; **(im Radio ü.)** broadcast; **(im Fernseh ü.)** televise.

Übertra'gung, -en, *n.f.* transfer; translation; broadcast.

übertref'fen*, *vb.* surpass, excel.

übertrei'ben*, *vb.* exaggerate.

Übertrei'bung, -en, *n.f.* exaggeration.

über·tre'ten*, *vb.* go over.

übertre'ten*, *vb.* trespass, violate, infringe.

Übertre'tung, -en, *n.f.* violation, infringement.

übertrie'ben, *adj.* exaggerated, extravagant.

übervor'teilen, *vb.* get the better of (someone).

überwa'chen, *vb.* watch over, keep under surveillance, control.

Überwa'chung, -en, *n.f.* surveillance, control.

überwäl'tigen, *vb.* overpower, overwhelm.

überwei'sen*, *vb.* transfer; remit.

Überwei'sung, -en, *n.f.* remittance.

überwer'fen*, *vb.* **(sich ü.)** have a falling-out with.

überwie'gen*, *vb.* outweigh; predominate.

überwie'gend, *adj.* preponderant.

überwin'den*, *vb.* overcome, conquer.

Überwin'dung, -en, *n.f.* conquest; effort, reluctance.

überwin'tern, *vb.* hibernate.

Überzahl, *n.f.* numerical superiority.

überzäh'lig, *adj.* surplus.

überzeu'gen, *vb.* convince.

überzeu'gend, *adj.* convincing.

Überzeu'gung, -en, *n.f.* conviction.

Überzeu'gungskraft, *n.f.* forcefulness.

Überzieher, -, *n.m.* overcoat.

üblich, *adj.* customary, usual.

U-Boot, -e, *n.nt.* (= Unterseeboot) submarine.

übrig, *adj.* remaining, left over.

übrig-bleiben*, *vb.* be left over; **(es bleibt mir nichts anderes übrig)** I have no other choice.

übrig-haben*, *vb.* have left over; **(nichts ü. für)** have no use for.

übrigens, *adv.* incidentally, by the way.

Übung, -en, *n.f.* practice; exercise.

Übungsbeispiel, -e, *n.nt.* paradigm.

UdSSR, *abbr.* (= Union' der Soziali'stischen Sowjetrepubliken) Union of Soviet Socialist Republics.

Ufer, -, *n.nt.* shore, bank.

Ufereinfassung, -en, *n.f.* embankment.

uferlos, *adj.* limitless.

Uhr, -en, *n.f.* watch, clock; **(wieviel U. ist es?)** what time is it?; **(sieben U.)** seven o'clock.

Uhrmacher, -, *n.m.* watchmaker.

Uhu, -s, *n.m.* owl.

Ulk, -e, *n.m.* fun.

ulkig, *adj.* funny.

Ultra-, *cpds.* ultra.

um, *prep.* around; at (clock time); **(um . . . zu)** in order to; (**u. so mehr**) the more, all the more so.

um·adressieren, *vb.* readdress.

um·arbeiten, *vb.* rework, revise.

umar'men, *vb.* embrace.

Umar'mung, -en, *n.f.* embrace.

um·bauen, *vb.* remodel.

um·biegen*, *vb.* turn, turn around.

um·bringen*, *vb.* kill.

um·drehen, *vb.* turn around, rotate, revolve.

Umdre'hung, -en, *n.f.* turn, revolution, rotation.

um·erziehen* *vb.* reeducate.

umfah'ren*, *vb.* circumnavigate, circle.

um·fallen*, *vb.* fall over.

Umfang, *ˇe*, *n.m.* circumference; extent; volume.

umfangreich, *adj.* extensive; comprehensive; voluminous.

umfas'sen, *vb.* enclose, surround; comprise.

umfas'send, *adj.* comprehensive.

um·formen, *vb.* remodel, transform, convert.

Umfrage, -n, *n.f.* inquiry, poll.

Umgang, *n.m.* intercourse, association.

Umgangssprache, *n.f.* colloquial speech, vernacular.

umge'ben*, *vb.* surround.

Umge'bung, -en, *n.f.* surroundings, environment; vicinity.

um·gehen*, *vb.* go around, circulate; (**u. mit**) deal with, handle; (**mit dem Gedanken u.**) contemplate, plan.

umge'hen*, *vb.* evade, circumvent.

Umge'hen, -, *n.nt.* evasion.

Umge'hung, -en, *n.f.* circumvention; (*mil.*) flanking movement.

Umge'hungsstraße, -n, *n.f.* by-pass.

umgekehrt, 1. *adj.* reverse,

inverse, **2.** *adv.* the other way round.

um·gestalten, *vb.* transform, alter, modify.

umgren'zen, *vb.* enclose; circumscribe.

um·gucken, *vb.* (**sich u.**) look around.

um·haben*, *vb.* have on.

Umhang, *ˇe*, *n.m.* wrap.

umher', *adv.* around, about.

umher'gehen*, *vb.* walk around.

umher'wandern, *vb.* wander.

Umkehr, *n.f.* return; reversal.

um·kehren, *vb.* turn (back, round, inside out, upside down).

Umkehrung, -en, *n.f.* reversal, reversing.

um·kippen, *vb.* turn over, tip over.

um·kleiden, *vb.* (**sich u.**) change one's clothes.

Umkleideraum, *ˇe*, *n.m.* dressing-room.

um·kommen*, *vb.* perish.

Umkreis, -e, *n.m.* circumference; range, radius.

umkrei'sen, *vb.* circle around, rotate around.

Umlauf, *n.m.* circulation.

um·laufen*, *vb.* circulate.

um·legen, *vb.* put on; change the position, shift; change the date.

um·leiten, *vb.* divert.

Umleitung, -en, *n.f.* detour.

um·lernen, *vb.* learn anew, readjust one's views.

umliegend, *adj.* surrounding.

umrah'men, *vb.* frame.

umran'den, *vb.* edge.

um·rechnen, *vb.* convert.

umrei'ßen*, *vb.* outline.

umrin'gen, *vb.* surround.

Umriß, -sse, *n.m.* contour, outline.

um·rühren, *vb.* stir.

Umsatz, *ˇe*, *n.m.* turnover, sales.

Umsatzsteuer, -n, *n.f.* sales tax.

um·schalten, vb. switch.

Umschau, n.f. (**U. halten**) look around.

umschichtig, adv. in turns.

Umschlag, ⁼e, n.m. envelope; (book) cover; turn-over; compress.

umschließen*, vb. encircle, encompass.

umschlin'gen*, vb. embrace.

um·schreiben*, vb. rewrite.

umschrei'ben*, vb. circumscribe, paraphrase.

Umschrei'bung, -en, n.f. paraphrase.

Umschrift, -en, n.f. transcription.

Umschwung, ⁼e, n.m. change, about-face.

um·sehen*, vb. (**sich u.**) look around.

um·setzen, vb. transpose; (goods) sell.

Umsicht, n.f. circumspection.

umsichtig, adj. circumspect, prudent.

umso, adv. (**u. besser**) so much the better; (**je mehr, u. besser**) the more the better.

umsonst', adv. in vain; gratis, free of charge.

Umstand, ⁼e, n.m. circumstance, condition; (pl.) formalities, fuss; (**in anderen Umständen**) pregnant.

umständlich, adj. complicated, fussy.

Umstandskleid, -er, n.nt. maternity dress.

Umstandswort, ⁼er, n.nt. adverb.

Umstehend-, n.m.&f. bystander.

um·steigen*, vb. transfer, change.

Umsteiger, -, n.m. transfer (ticket).

um·stellen, vb. change the position of; (**sich u. auf**) readjust, convert to.

umstel'len, vb. surround.

um·steuern, vb. reverse.

um·stimmen, vb. make someone change his mind.

um·stoßen*, vb. overturn, overthrow, upset.

umstri'cken, vb. ensnare.

Umsturz, ⁼e, n.m. overthrow, revolution.

um·stürzen, vb. overturn.

umtauschbar, adj. exchangeable.

Umtausch, -e, n.m. exchange; (**vom U. ausgeschlossen**) no exchange.

um·tauschen, vb. exchange.

Umtrieb, -e, n.m. intrigue, machinations.

um·tun*, vb. (**sich nach etwas u.**) look for, apply for.

Umwälzung, -en, n.f. upheaval, revolution.

um·wandeln, vb. transform; change; convert.

um·wechseln, vb. change, convert.

Umweg, -e, n.m. detour.

Umwelt, n.f. environment.

umwer'ben*, vb. woo, court.

Umwer'bung, n.f. courtship.

um·werfen*, vb. overthrow; upset.

um·ziehen*, vb. move; (**sich u.**) change one's clothes.

umzin'geln, vb. surround.

Umzug, ⁼e, n.m. move; procession.

unabhängig, adj. independent.

Unabhängigkeit, n.f. independence.

unabkömmlich, adj. indispensable.

unablässig, adj. incessant.

unabseh'bar, adj. unforeseeable.

unabwendbar, adj. inevitable.

unachtsam, adj. inattentive; careless.

unähnlich, adj. dissimilar, unlike.

unangebracht, adj. out of place.

unangemessen, adj. unsuitable, improper.

unangenehm, adj. unpleasant, distasteful.

Unannehmlichkeit, -en, n.f. trouble.

unansehnlich, *adj.* plain, inconspicuous.

unanständig, *adj.* indecent, obscene.

unanwendbar, *adj.* inapplicable.

unappetitlich, *adj.* unappetizing; nasty.

Unart, -en, *n.f.* rudeness, bad manners.

unartig, *adj.* naughty.

unauffällig, *adj.* inconspicuous.

unaufhörlich, *adj.* incessant.

unaufmerksam, *adj.* inattentive.

Unaufmerksamkeit, -en, *n.f.* inattentiveness; inadvertence.

unaufrichtig, *adj.* insincere.

Unaufrichtigkeit, -en, *n.f.* insincerity; lie.

unausbleiblich, *adj.* inevitable.

unausgeglichen, *adj.* unbalanced, unstable.

unausgesetzt, *adj.* continual.

unausstehlich, *adj.* insufferable.

unbändig, *adj.* unruly; excessive.

unbarmherzig, *adj.* merciless.

unbeabsichtigt, *adj.* unintentional.

unbeachtet, *adj.* unnoticed; **(u. lassen*)** ignore.

unbedacht, *adj.* thoughtless.

unbedenklich, *adj.* harmless.

unbedeutend, *adj.* insignificant.

unbedingt', *adj.* absolute, unconditional.

unbefangen, *adj.* natural, naïve.

unbefleckt, *adj.* immaculate; **(u. e Empfängnis)** Immaculate Conception.

unbefriedigend, *adj.* unsatisfactory.

unbefriedigt, *adj.* dissatisfied.

unbefugt, *adj.* unauthorized.

unbegabt, *adj.* untalented, dumb.

unbegreiflich, *adj.* incomprehensible.

unbegrenzt, *adj.* limitless.

Unbehagen, *n.nt.* discomfort.

unbehaglich, *adj.* uneasy.

unbeholfen, *adj.* awkward, clumsy.

unbekannt, *adj.* unknown, unfamiliar.

unbekümmert, *adj.* unconcerned.

unbeliebt, *adj.* unpopular.

unbemerkbar, *adj.* imperceptible.

unbemerkt, *adj.* unnoticed.

unbenommen, *adj.* **(es bleibt Ihnen u.)** you are at liberty to.

unbequem, *adj.* inconvenient; uncomfortable.

unbere'chenbar, *adj.* incalculable; unreliable, erratic.

unberechtigt, *adj.* unauthorized; unjustified.

unberufen! *interj.* touch wood!

unbeschädigt, *adj.* undamaged.

unbescheiden, *adj.* immodest; selfish.

Unbescholtenheit, *n.f.* integrity.

unbeschreiblich, *adj.* indescribable.

unbeschrieben, *adj.* blank.

unbesehen, *adj.* unseen.

unbesieg'bar, *adj.* invincible.

unbesonnen, *adj.* thoughtless.

unbesorgt, *adj.* carefree, unconcerned.

unbeständig, *adj.* changeable.

unbestellbar, *adj.* undeliverable.

unbestimmt, *adj.* indefinite, vague.

unbestritten, *adj.* undisputed.

unbeträchtlich, *adj.* inconsiderable.

unbeugsam, *adj.* inflexible; obstinate.

unbewandert, *adj.* inexperienced.

unbewiesen, *adj.* not proved.

unbewohnbar, *adj.* uninhabitable.

unbewohnt, *adj.* uninhabited.

unbewußt, *adj.* unconscious; unknown.

unbezahl'bar, *adj.* priceless.

unbrauchbar, *adj.* useless.

und, *conj.* and.

Undank, *n.m.* ingratitude.

undankbar, *adj.* ungrateful.

undefinierbar, *adj.* indefinable.

undenklich, *adj.* inconceivable; **(seit u. en Zeiten)** since time out of mind.

undeutlich, *adj.* unclear, indistinct.

undicht, *adj.* leaky.

Unding, *n.nt.* absurdity, nonsense.

unduldsam, *adj.* intolerant.

undurchführbar, *adj.* not feasible.

undurchsichtig, *adj.* opaque.

uneben, *adj.* uneven.

unecht, *adj.* not genuine, false, counterfeit; artificial.

unehelich, *adj.* illegitimate.

unehrenhaft, *adj.* dishonorable.

unehrerbietig, *adj.* disrespectful.

unehrlich, *adj.* dishonest, insincere.

uneingeschränkt, *adj.* unlimited.

uneinig, *adj.* **(u. sein*)** disagree.

Uneinigkeit, -en, *n.f.* disagreement, dissension.

unempfindlich, *adj.* insensitive.

unend'lich, *adj.* infinite: **(u. klein)** infinitesimal.

Unend'lichkeit, -en, *n.f.* infinity.

unentbehrlich, *adj.* indispensable.

unentgeltlich, *adj.* gratuitous.

unentschieden, *adj.* unde-

cided; **(das Spiel ist u.)** the game is a draw.

unentschlossen, *adj.* undecided.

unentwegt, *adj.* constant.

unerfahren, *adj.* inexperienced.

Unerfahrenheit, -en, *n.f.* inexperience.

unerfreulich, *adj.* unpleasant.

unerheblich, *adj.* insignificant, irrelevent.

unerhört', *adj.* unheard of, outrageous.

unerkannt, *adj.* unrecognized.

unerkennbar, *adj.* unrecognizable.

unerklärlich, *adj.* inexplicable.

unerläßlich, *adj.* indispensable.

unerlaubt, *adj.* unlawful, illegal, illicit.

unermeß'lich, *adj.* immeasurable.

unermüdlich, *adj.* indefatigable.

unerquicklich, *adj.* unpleasant.

unerschrocken, *adj.* intrepid.

unersetzlich, *adj.* irreplaceable.

unersprießlich, *adj.* unpleasant.

unerträglich, *adj.* unbearable, insufferable.

unerwartet, *adj.* unexpected.

unerwünscht, *adj.* unwelcome.

unerzogen, *adj.* ill-bred, ill-mannered.

unfähig, *adj.* unable, incapable, incompetent.

unfair, *adj.* unfair.

Unfall, -e, *n.m.* accident.

unfaß'bar, *adj.* incomprehensible.

unfaß'lich, *adj.* incomprehensible.

unfehl'bar, *adj.* infallible.

Unfeinheit, -en, *n.f.* crudeness, crudity.

unförmig, *adj.* shapeless.

unfreiwillig, *adj.* involuntary.

unfreundlich, *adj.* unkind, unfriendly; rude.

unfruchtbar, *adj.* barren, sterile.

Unfug, *n.m.* mischief.

unfügsam, *adj.* unmanageable.

Ungar, -n, -n, *n.m.* Hungarian.

ungarisch, *adj.* Hungarian.

Ungarn, *n.nt.* Hungary.

ungastlich, *adj.* inhospitable.

ungeachtet, *prep.* notwithstanding.

ungebildet, *adj.* uneducated.

ungebührlich, *adj.* improper.

ungebunden, *adj.* free.

Ungeduld, *n.f.* impatience.

ungeduldig, *adj.* impatient.

ungeeignet, *adj.* unqualified, unsuitable.

ungefähr, 1. *adj.* approximate. **2.** *adv.* approximately, about.

ungefährlich, *adj.* harmless.

ungefällig, *adj.* unobliging, impolite.

ungeheuchelt, *adj.* sincere.

Ungeheuer, -. *n.nt.* monster.

ungeheuer, *adj.* tremendous, huge.

ungeheuerlich, *adj.* monstrous.

ungehobelt, *adj.* uncouth.

ungehörig, *adj.* improper, rude.

ungehorsam, *adj.* disobedient.

Ungehorsam, *n.m.* disobedience.

ungekünstelt, *adj.* unaffected, natural.

ungeläufig, *adj.* unfamiliar.

ungelegen, *adj.* inconvenient.

ungelenk, *adj.* clumsy.

ungelernt, *adj.* unskilled.

ungemein, *adv.* uncommonly.

ungemütlich, *adj.* uncomfortable.

ungeneigt, *adj.* disinclined.

ungeniert, *adj.* free and easy.

ungenießbar, *adj.* unedible; unbearable.

ungenügend, *adj.* insufficient; unsatisfactory.

ungerade, *adj.* uneven; (numbers) odd.

ungerecht, *adj.* unjust, unfair.

ungerechtfertigt, *adj.* unwarranted.

Ungerechtigkeit, -en, *n.f* injustice.

ungeschehen, *adj.* (**u. machen**) to undo.

ungeschickt, *adj.* clumsy, awkward.

Ungeschicklichkeit, -en, *n.f.* clumsiness.

ungeschlacht, *adj.* uncouth.

ungesetzlich, *adj.* illegal.

ungesittet, *adj.* unmannerly.

ungestört, *adj.* undisturbed.

ungestraft, 1. *adj.* unpunished. **2.** *adv.* with impunity.

ungestüm, *adj.* impetuous.

ungesund, *adj.* unhealthy; unsound.

Ungetüm, -e, *n.nt.* monster.

ungewandt, *adj.* awkward.

ungewiß, *adj.* uncertain.

Ungewißheit, -en, *n.f.* uncertainty.

Ungewitter, -. *n.nt.* thunderstorm.

ungewöhnlich, *adj.* unusual, abnormal.

ungewohnt, *adj.* unaccustomed, unfamiliar.

ungewollt, *adj.* unintentional.

ungezählt, *adj.* innumerable.

ungezügelt, *adj.* unrestrained.

ungezwungen, *adj.* easy-going.

Ungläubig-, *n.m.&f.* infidel.

unglaublich, *adj.* incredible.

unglaubwürdig, *adj.* unreliable.

ungleich, *adj.* unequal, uneven, unlike.

ungleichartig, *adj.* dissimilar.

Ungleichheit, -en, *n.f.* unequality, dissimilarity.

Unglück, -e, *n.nt.* misfortune, calamity, disaster, accident.

unglücklich, *adj.* unhappy; unfortunate.

unglücklicherweise, *adv.* unfortunately.

unglückselig, *adj.* disastrous; utterly miserable.

Ungnade, *n.f.* disfavor.

ungnädig, *adj.* ungracious.

ungültig, *adj.* invalid, void; **(für u. erklären)** annul, declare null and void.

ungünstig, *adj.* unfavorable.

unhaltbar, *adj.* untenable.

unhandlich, *adj.* unwieldy.

Unheil, *n.nt.* harm, disaster.

unheilbar, *adj.* incurable.

unheilbringend, *adj.* fatal, ominous.

unheilvoll, *adj.* ominous.

unheimlich, *adj.* scary, sinister.

unhöflich, *adj.* impolite, rude.

unhygienisch, *adj.* unsanitary.

Uniform', -en, *n.f.* uniform.

uninteressant, *adj.* uninteresting.

universal', *adj.* universal.

Universität', -en, *n.f.* university.

unkenntlich, *adj.* unrecognizable.

unklar, *adj.* unclear, obscure.

unkleidsam, *adj.* unbecoming.

Unkosten, *n.pl.* expenses, overhead.

unlängst, *adv.* recently.

unlauter, *adj.* impure; unfair.

unleserlich, *adj.* illegible.

unlieb, *adj.* disagreeable.

unliebenswürdig, *adj.* unfriendly, impolite.

unlogisch, *adj.* illogical.

unlustig, *adj.* listless.

unmanierlich, *adj.* unmannered.

unmaßgeblich, *adj.* irrelevant; unauthoritative.

unmäßig, *adj.* immoderate.

Unmenge, -n, *n.f.* enormous quantity.

Unmensch, -en, -en, *n.m.* brute.

unmenschlich, *adj.* inhuman.

unmerklich, *adj.* imperceptible.

unmittelbar, *adj.* immediate.

unmodern, *adj.* old-fashioned, out of style.

unmöglich, *adj.* impossible.

unmoralisch, *adj.* immoral.

unnachahmlich, *adj.* inimitable.

unnahbar, *adj.* inaccessible.

unnötig, *adj.* needless, unnecessary.

unnütz, *adj.* useless.

unordentlich, *adj.* disorderly, messy.

Unordnung, *n.f.* disorder.

unparteiisch, *adj.* impartial, neutral.

unpassend, *adj.* unsuitable; improper, off-color.

unpassierbar, *adj.* impassable.

unpäßlich, *adj.* unwell, indisposed.

unpersönlich, *adj.* impersonal.

unpolitisch, *adj.* nonpolitical.

unpraktisch, *adj.* impractical.

unpünktlich, *adj.* not on time.

unrecht, *adj.* wrong; **(u. haben*)** be wrong.

Unrecht, *n.nt.* wrong, harm, injustice.

unreell, *adj.* dishonest.

unregelmäßig, *adj.* irregular.

unreif, *adj.* immature.

unrein, *adj.* unclean; impure.

unrichtig, *adj.* incorrect.

Unruhe, -n, *n.f.* unrest, trouble, disturbance.

unruhig, *adj.* restless, troubled, uneasy.

unschädlich, *adj.* harmless.

unscheinbar, *adj.* insignificant.

unschicklich, *adj.* improper.

unschlüssig, *adj.* undecided.

Unschuld, *n.t.* innocence.

unschuldig, *adj.* innocent.

unselig, *adj.* unhappy, fatal.

unser, -, -e, *adj.* our.

uns(e)rer, -es, -e, *pron.* ours.

unsicher, *adj.* uncertain; unsafe.

Unsicherheit, -en, *n.f.* uncertainty, insecurity.

unsichtbar, *adj.* invisible.

Unsinn, *n.m.* nonsense.

unsinnig, *adj.* absurd, nonsensical.

Unsitte, -n, *n.f.* bad habit.

unsittlich, *adj.* immoral.

unsterblich, *adj.* immortal.

unstet, *adj.* unsteady.

Unstimmigkeit, -en, *n.f.* discrepancy, disagreement.

untauglich, *adj.* unfit.

unteilbar, *adj.* indivisible.

unten, *adv.* below, down, downstairs.

unter, *prep.* under, beneath, below; among; **(u. uns)** just between you and me.

unter-, *adj.* under, lower.

Unterarm, -e, *n.m.* forearm.

unterbewußt, *adj.* subconscious.

Unterbewußtsein, *n.nt.* subconsciousness.

unterbie'ten*, *vb.* undercut; lower.

unterblei'ben*, *vb.* not get done.

unterbre'chen*, *vb.* interrupt.

Unterbre'chung, -en, *n.f.* interruption.

unterbrei'ten, *vb.* submit.

unter-bringen*, *vb.* lodge, accommodate.

unterdes'(sen), *adv.* meanwhile.

unterdrü'cken, *vb.* suppress, oppress, repress, stifle, subdue.

unterdrückt', *adj.* downtrodden.

Unterdrü'ckung, -en, *n.f.* suppression.

untereinan'der, *adv.* among them- (our-, your-)selves.

unterernährt, *adj.* undernourished.

Unterernährung, *n.f.* malnutrition.

Unterfüh'rung, -en, *n.f.* underpass.

Untergang, ⁓e, *n.m.* downfall, decline.

unterge'ben, *adj.* subordinate.

Unterge'ben-, *n.m.&f.* subordinate.

unter-gehen*, *vb.* perish; set (sun).

untergeordnet, *adj.* subordinate.

untergra'ben*, *vb.* undermine, subvert.

Untergrundbahn, -en, *n.f.* subway.

unterhalb, *prep.* below.

Unterhalt, *n.m.* maintenance, keep.

unterhal'ten*, *vb.* maintain, support; entertain; **(sich u.)** converse.

Unterhal'tung, -en, *n.f.* maintenance; entertainment, conversation.

Unterhand'lung, -en, *n.f.* negotiation.

Unterhaus, *n.nt.* lower house (of parliament, congress).

Unterhemd, -en, *n.nt.* undershirt.

Unterhose, -n, *n.f.* underpants.

unterjo'chen, *vb.* subjugate.

Unterkunft, ⁓e, *n.f.* lodging.

Unterlage, -n, *n.f.* base, bed; evidence; bottom sheet.

unterlas'sen*, *vb.* omit, fail to do.

Unterlas'sung, -en, *n.f.* omission, default.

unterle gen, *adj.* inferior.

Unterleib, -er, *n.m.* abdomen.

unterlie'gen*, *vb.* succumb to, be overcome by.

Untermieter, -, *n.m.* subtenant.

unterneh men*, *vb.* undertake.

Unterneh'men, -, *n.nt.* enterprise.

unterneh'mend, *adj.* enterprising.

Unterneh'mer, -, *n.m.* entrepreneur, contractor.

Unterneh'mung, -en, *n.f.* undertaking.

Unteroffizier, -e, *n.m.* non-commissioned officer, sergeant.

Unterpfand, *n.nt.* pledge, security.

Unterre'dung, -en, *n.f.* discussion, parley.

Unterricht, *n.m.* instruction.

unterrich'ten, *vb.* instruct.

Unterrich'tung, *n.f.* guidance.

Unterrock, ⸚e, *n.m.* slip, petticoat.

untersa'gen, *vb.* prohibit.

Untersatz, ⸚e, *n.m.* base; saucer.

unterschät'zen, *vb.* underestimate.

unterschei'den, *vb.* distinguish, differentiate; **(sich u.)** differ.

Unterschied, -e, *n.m.* difference.

unterschiedslos, *adj.* indiscriminate.

unterschla'gen*, *vb.* embezzle, suppress.

unterschrei'ben*, *vb.* sign (one's name to).

Unterschrift, -en, *n.f.* signature.

Unterseeboot, -e, *n.nt.* submarine.

untersetzt', *adj.* chunky, thick-set.

Unterstand, ⸚e, *n.m.* dugout.

unterste'hen*, *vb.* **(sich u.)** dare.

Unterstel'lung, -en, *n.f.* innuendo, insinuation.

unterstrei'chen*, *vb.* underline, underscore.

unterstüt'zen, *vb.* support, back.

Unterstüt'zung, -en, *n.f.* support, backing.

untersu'chen, *vb.* investigate, examine.

Untersu'chung, -en, *n.f.* investigation, examination.

Untertan, (-en,) -en, *m.n.* subject.

Untertasse, -n, *n.f.* saucer.

unter-tauchen, *vb.* submerge.

Unterwäsche, *n.f.* underwear.

unterwegs', *adv.* on the way; bound for.

unterwei'sen*, *vb.* instruct.

Unterwei'sung, -en, *n.f.* instruction.

Unterwelt, *n.f.* underworld.

unterwer'fen*, *vb.* subjugate; subject to; **(sich u.)** submit (to).

Unterwer'fung, -en, *n.f.* submission.

unterwor'fen, *adj.* subject (to).

unterwür'fig, *adj.* subservient.

unterzeich'nen, *vb.* sign.

unterzie'hen*, *vb.* **(sich u.)** undergo.

untief, *adj.* shallow.

untreu, *adj.* unfaithful, disloyal.

Untreue, *n.f.* unfaithfulness, disloyalty.

untröstlich, *adj.* disconsolate.

unüberlegt, *adj.* inconsiderate, thoughtless.

unüberwindlich, *adj.* insuperable.

unumgänglich, *adj.* unavoidable.

unveränderlich, *adj.* invariable.

unverantwortlich, *adj.* irresponsible.

unverbesserlich, *adj.* incorrigible.

unverbindlich, *adj.* without obligation.

unverblümt, *adj.* blunt.

unvereinbar, *adj.* incompatible.

unvergeßlich, *adj.* unforgettable.

unvergleichlich, *adj.* incomparable.

unverheiratet, *adj.* unmarried.

unverhohlen, *adj.* frank, aboveboard.

unverkennbar, adj. unmistakable.

unvermeidlich, adj. inevitable.

unvermittelt, adj. abrupt.

unvermutet, adj. unexpected.

unverschämt, adj. shameless, impudent, nervy.

Unverschämtheit, -en, n.f. impertinence, gall.

unversehens, adv. unexpectedly.

unverständlich, adj. incomprehensible.

unverzüglich, adj. speedy, without delay.

unvollendet, adj. incomplete, unfinished.

unvollkommen, adj. incomplete, imperfect.

unvoreingenommen, adj. unbiased.

unvorher'gesehen, adj. unforeseen.

unvorsichtig, adj. careless.

unwägbar, adj. imponderable.

unwahr(haftig), adj. untrue.

Unwahrheit, -en, n.f. untruth.

unwahrnehmbar, adj. imperceptible.

unwahrscheinlich, adj. improbable.

unweigerlich, adj. unhesitating; without fail.

unwesentlich, adj. immaterial, nonessential.

unwiderlegbar, adj. irrefutable.

unwiderstehlich, adj. irresistible.

unwillkürlich, adj. involuntary.

unwirksam, adj. ineffectual.

unwissend, adj. ignorant.

unwürdig, adj. unworthy.

Unzahl, n.f. tremendous number.

unzählig, adj. countless.

Unze, -n, n.f. ounce.

Unzucht, n.f. lewdness.

unzüchtig, adj. lewd.

unzufrieden, adj. dissatisfied.

Unzufriedenheit, -en, n.f. dissatisfaction.

unzulänglich, adj. insufficient, inadequate.

unzureichend, adj. insufficient.

unzuverlässig, adj. unreliable.

Ur-, cpds. original; very old; tremendously.

uralt, adj. very old, ancient.

Uraufführung, -en, n.f. première.

Urenkel, -, n.m. great-grandson.

Urenkelin, -nen, n.f. great-granddaughter.

Urgroßeltern, n.pl. great-grandparents.

Urgroßmutter, ⁚, n.f. great-grandmother.

Urgroßvater, ⁚, n.m. great-grandfather.

Urheber, -, n.m. author, originator.

Urheberrecht, -e, n.nt. copyright.

Urin', -e, n.m. urine.

urinie'ren, vb. urinate.

Urkunde, -n, n.f. document.

Urlaub, -e, n.m. leave, furlough.

Urne, -n, n.f. urn; ballot box.

Urquell, -e, n.m. fountainhead.

Ursache, -n, n.f. cause; **(keine U.)** don't mention it.

Ursprung, ⁚e, n.m. origin.

ursprünglich, adj. original.

Urteil, -e, n.nt. judgment, sentence.

urteilen, vb. judge.

usurpie'ren, vb. usurp.

usw., abbr. (= **und so weiter**) etc., and so forth.

V

Vagabund', -en, -en, n.m. tramp.

vage, adj. vague.

Valu'ta, -ten, *n.f.* value; (foreign) currency.

Vanil'le, *n.f.* vanilla.

Variation', -en, *n.f.* variation.

Varieté', *n.nt.* variety show, vaudeville.

variie'ren, *vb.* vary.

Vase, -n, *n.f.* vase.

Vater, ∵, *n.m.* father.

Vaterland, *n.nt.* fatherland.

pväterlich, *adj.* fatherly, paternal.

vaterlos, *adj.* fatherless.

Vaterschaft, -en, *n.f.* fatherhood, paternity.

Vaterun'ser, *n.nt.* Lord's Prayer.

Veilchen, -, *n.nt.* violet.

Vene, -n, *n.f.* vein.

vene'risch, *adj.* venereal.

Ventil', -e, *n.nt.* valve.

Ventilation', *n.f.* ventilation.

Ventila'tor, -o'ren, *n.m.* ventilator, fan.

ventilie'ren, *vb.* ventilate.

verab'reden, *vb.* agree upon; **(sich v.)** make an appointment. date.

Verab'redung, -en, *n.f.* appointment, engagement, date.

verab'scheuen, *vb.* abhor, detest.

verab'schieden, *vb.* dismiss; pass (a bill); **(sich v.)** take one's leave.

verach'ten, *vb.* scorn, despise.

verach'tenswert, *adj.* despicable.

veräcbt'lich, *adj.* contemptuous.

Verach'tung, -en, *n.f.* contempt.

verallgemei'nern, *vb.* generalize.

Verallgemei'nerung, -en, *n.f.* generalization.

veral'tet, *adj.* obsolete.

Veran'da, -den, *n.f.* porch.

verän'derlich, *adj.* changeable.

verän'dern, *vb.* change.

Verän'derung, -en, *n.f.* change.

veran'kern, *vb.* anchor, moor.

veran'lassen*, *vb.* cause, motivate.

Veran'lassung, -en, *n.f.* cause, motivation.

veran'schaulichen, *vb.* illustrate.

veran'stalten, *vb.* arrange, put on.

Veran'staltung, -en, *n.f.* arrangement, performance.

verant'wortlich, *adj.* responsible.

Verant'wortlichkeit, -en, *n.f.* responsibility.

Verant'wortung, -en, *n.f.* responsibility; accounting, justification.

verant'wortungslos, *adj.* irresponsible.

verant'wortungsvoll, *adj.* carrying responsibility.

verar'beiten, *vb.* process.

verär'gern, *vb.* exasperate.

verar'men, *vb.* become poor.

Verb, -en, *n.nt.* verb.

verbal', *adj.* verbal.

Verband', -̈e, *n.m.* association; bandage, dressing.

verban'nen, *vb.* banish, exile.

Verban'nung, -en, *n.f.* banishment, exile.

verbau'en, *vb.* build badly; obstruct.

verber'gen*, *vb.* hide.

verbes'sern, *vb.* improve, correct.

Verbes'serung, -en, *n.f.* improvement, correction.

verbeu'gen, *vb.* **(sich v.)** bow.

Verbeu'gung, -en, *n.f.* bow.

verbeu'len, *vb.* dent, batter.

verbie'gen*, *vb.* bend (out of shape).

verbie'ten*, *vb.* forbid, prohibit, ban.

verbie'terisch, *adj.* prohibitive.

verbin'den*, *vb.* connect, join, combine; bandage.

verbind'lich, *adj.* binding, obligatory.

Verbin'dung, -en, *n.f.* connection, combination; (chemical) compound; (student) fraternity; **(in V. stehen mit)** be in touch with; **(sich**

in V. setzen mit) get in touch with.

verbis'sen, *adj.* suppressed; dogged.

verbit'ten*, *vb.* decline; not stand for.

verbit'tern, *vb.* embitter.

verbla'ssen, *vb.* turn pale, fade.

Verbleib', *n.m.* whereabouts.

verblei'chen*, *vb.* grow pale, fade.

verblüf'fen, *vb.* dumbfound, flabbergast.

verbo'gen, *adj.* bent.

verbor'gen, *adj.* hidden.

Verbot', *-e*, *n.nt.* prohibition.

Verbrauch', *n.m.* consumption.

verbrau'chen, *vb.* consume, use up, wear out.

Verbrau'cher, *-*, *n.m.* consumer.

Verbrauchs'steuer, *-n*, *n.f.* excise tax.

Verbre'chen, *-*, *n.nt.* crime.

Verbre'cher, *-*, *n.m.* criminal.

verbre'cherisch, *adj.* criminal.

verbrei'ten, *vb.* disseminate, propagate, diffuse.

verbrenn'bar, *adj.* combustible.

verbren'nen*, *vb.* burn; cremate.

Verbren'nung, *n.f.* burning; cremation; combustion.

verbrin'gen*, *vb.* spend (time).

verbrü'hen, *vb.* scald.

verbun'den, *adj.* indebted, obliged.

verbün'den, *vb.* ally.

Verbün'det-, *n.m.* ally, confederate.

verbür'gen, *vb.* guarantee.

Verdacht', *n.m.* suspicion.

verdäch'tig, *adj.* suspicious, suspected.

verdam'men, *vb.* damn, condemn.

verdam'menswert, *adj.* damnable.

Verdamm'nis, *n.f* (eternal) damnation.

verdammt', *adj.* damned, damn it!

Verdam'mung, -en, *n.f.* damnation.

verdam'pfen, *vb.* evaporate.

verdan'ken, *vb.* owe (something to someone), be indebted to.

verdau'en, *vb.* digest.

verdau'lich, *adj.* digestible.

Verdau'ung, *n.f.* digestion.

Verdau'ungsstörung, -en, *n.f.* indigestion.

Verdeck', *-e*, *n.nt.* deck covering; top (of an auto).

verder'ben*, *vb.* take amiss.

Verder'ben*, *vb.* perish, spoil, ruin.

Verder'ben, *n.nt.* perdition, ruin, doom.

verderb'lich, *adj.* ruinous; perishable.

verderbt', *adj.* corrupt.

verdeut'lichen, *vb.* make clear.

verdich'ten, *vb.* thicken, solidify.

verdie'nen, *vb.* earn, deserve.

Verdienst', *-e*, *n.m.* earnings.

Verdienst', *-e*, *n.nt.* merit.

verdienst'lich, *adj.* meritorious.

verdient', *adj.* deserving, deserved.

verdol'metschen, *vb.* interpret, translate.

verdop'peln, *vb.* double.

Verdop'pelung, -en, *n.f.* doubling.

verdor'ren, *vb.* wither.

verdrän'gen, *vb.* push out, displace; suppress, inhibit.

Verdrän'gung, -en, *n.f.* displacement; repression, inhibition.

verdre'hen, *vb.* twist, distort, pervert.

verdrie'ßen*, *vb.* grieve, vex, annoy.

verdrieß'lich, *adj.* morose, sulky.

Verdruß', *n.m.* vexation, irritation.

verdun'keln, *vb.* darken.

Verdun'kelung, -en, *n.f.* blackout.

verdün'nen, *vb.* thin, dilute, rarefy.

verdut'zen, vb. bewildern.

vereh'ren, vb. adore, respect, revere.

Vereh'rer, -, n.m. admirer.

Vereh'rung, n.f. adoration, reverence.

verei'digen, vb. administer an oath to.

Verei'digung, -en, n.f. swearing-in.

Verein', -e, n.m. association.

verein'bar, adj. compatible.

verein'baren, vb. come to an agreement, reconcile.

Verein'barkeit, n.f. compatibility.

Verein'barung, n.f. agreement.

verei'nen, vb. unify.

verein'fachen, vb. simplify.

verein'heitlichen, vb. standardize, make uniform.

verei'nigen, vb. unite.

Verei'nigten Staaten von Ame'rika, die, n.pl. United States of America.

Verei'nigung, -en, n.f. union, alliance, association, merger.

Verein'ten, Natio'nen, die, n.pl. United Nations.

verein'zelt, adj. isolated, individual; scattered, stray.

verei'teln, vb. thwart, foil.

verer'ben, vb. bequeath.

vererb'lich, adj. hereditary.

Verer'bung, -en, n.f. heredity.

verfah'ren*, vb. act, proceed, deal; **(sich v.)** lose one's way.

Verfah'ren, -, n.nt. procedure, process.

Verfall', n.m. decay, decline, disrepair.

verfal'len*, vb. decay, decline, deteriorate; full due, lapse.

verfäl'schen, vb. falsify, adulterate.

Verfäl'schung, -en, n.f. falsification, adulteration.

verfäng'lich, adj. captious, insidious.

verfas'sen, vb. compose, write.

Verfas'ser, -, n.m. author.

Verfas'sung, -en, n.f. composition; state, condition; constitution.

verfas'sungsmäßig, adj. constitutional.

verfas'sungswidrig, adj. unconstitutional.

verfau'len, vb. rot.

verfault', adj. putrid.

verfecht'bar, adj. defensible.

verfeh'len, vb. miss.

verfei'nern, vb. refine.

Verfei'nerung, -en, n.f. refinement.

verfer'tigen, vb. manufacture.

verfil'men, vb. film, make a movie of.

verflie'ßen*, vb. flow away, lapse.

verflu'chen, vb. curse, damn.

verflucht', adj. cursed, damned; damn it!

verfol'gen, vb. pursue, haunt, persecute.

Verfol'gung, -en, n.f. pursuit, persecution.

verfrach'ter, -, n.m. shipper.

verfrüht', adj. premature.

verfüg'bar, adj. available.

verfü'gen, vb. enact, order; **(v. über)** have at one's disposal.

Verfü'gung, -en, n.f. disposition, instruction, enactment; **(mir zur V. stehen*)** be at my disposal; **(mir zur V. stellen)** place at my disposal.

verfüh'ren, vb. lead astray, entice, pervert, seduce.

verfüh'rerisch, adj. seductive.

vergan'gen, adj. past, last.

Vergan'genheit, n.f. past.

vergäng'lich, adj. ephemeral, transitory.

Verga'ser, -, n.m. carburetor.

verge'ben*, vb. forgive; **(sich v.)** misdeal (at cards); **(sich etwas v.)** compromise oneself.

verge'bens, adv. in vain.

vergeb'lich, adj. vain, futile.

Verge'bung, n.f. forgiveness.

vergegenwär'tigen, *vb.* envisage, picture to oneself.

verge'hen*, *vb.* pass, elapse; **(sich v.)** err, sin, commit a crime.

Verge'hen, -, *n.nt.* misdemeanor.

vergel'ten*, *vb.* repay; retaliate.

Vergel'tung, -en, *n.f.* recompense; retaliation.

Vergel'tungsmaßnahme, -n, *n.f.* reprisal.

verges'sen*, *vb.* forget.

Verges'senheit, *n.f.* oblivion.

vergeß'lich, *adj.* forgetful.

vergeu'den, *vb.* squander.

vergewal'tigen, *vb.* use force on, rape.

Vergewal'tigung, -en, *n.f.* rape.

vergewis'sern, *vb.* confirm; reassure.

vergie'ßen*, *vb.* shed.

vergif'ten, *vb.* poison.

Vergiß'meinnicht, -e, *n.nt.* forget-me-not.

Vergleich', -e, *n.m.* comparison.

vergleich'bar, *adj.* comparable.

verglei'chen*, *vb.* compare.

vergnü'gen, *vb.* amuse.

Vergnü'gen, *n.nt.* fun; **(viel V.)** have a good time.

vergnügt', *adj.* in good spirits, gay.

Vergnü'gung, -en, *n.f.* pleasure, amusement, diversion.

vergöt'tern, *vb.* idolize.

vergrei'fen*, *vb.* **(sich v.)** do the wrong thing; **(sich an etwas v.)** attack, misappropriate.

vergrö'ßern, *vb.* enlarge, magnify.

Vergrö'ßerung, -en, *n.f.* enlargement.

Vergrö'ßerungsapparat, -e, *n.m.* enlarger.

Vergün'stigung, -en, *n.f.* favor; reduction.

vergü'ten, *vb.* pay back.

verhaf'ten, *vb.* arrest.

Verhaftung, -en, *n.f.* arrest.

verhal'ten*, *vb.* hold back; **(sich v.)** be, behave.

verhal'ten, *adj.* suppressed.

Verhal'ten, *n.nt.* behavior.

Verhält'nis, -se, *n.nt.* relation(ship), proportion, ratio; love affair; *(pl.)* circumstances, conditions.

verhält'nismäßig, *adj.* relative, comparative.

verhan'deln, *vb.* negotiate.

Verhand'lung, -en, *n.f.* negotiation.

Verhand'lungsweise, *n.f.* procedure.

Verhäng'nis, -se, *n.nt.* fate, destiny.

verhäng'nisvoll, *adj.* fatal, fateful.

verhar'ren, *vb.* remain, persist.

verhär'ten, *vb.* harden, stiffen.

verhaßt', *adj.* hateful, odious.

verhau'en*, *vb.* beat up; make a mess of.

verhed'dern, *vb.* **(sich v.)** get snarled, caught.

verhee'ren, *vb.* desolate.

verhee'rend, *adj.* disastrous.

verheim'lichen, *vb.* conceal.

verhei'raten, *vb.* marry off; **(sich v.)** get married.

verherr'lichen, *vb.* glorify.

verhin'dern, *vb.* prevent, hinder.

Verhin'derung, *n.f.* prevention, hindrance.

verhoh'len, *adj.* hidden, clandestine.

Verhör', -e, *n.nt.* interrogation, hearing.

verhö'ren, *vb.* interrogate.

verhun'gern, *vb.* starve to death.

verhü'ten, *vb.* prevent.

Verhü'tung, -en, *n.f.* prevention.

verir'ren, *vb.* **(sich v.)** lose one's way, go astray.

Verkauf', -e, *n.m.* sale.

verkau'fen, *vb.* sell.

Verkäu'fer, -, *n.m.* clerk, salesman.

verkäuf'lich, *adj.* saleable.

Verkehr', *n.m.* trade, traffic; relations, intercourse.

verkeh'ren, *vb.* (*tr.*) change; (*intr.*) run, go; associate, consort, frequent.

Verkehrs'ampel, -n, *n.f.* traffic light.

Verkehrs'flugzeug, -e, *n.nt.* air liner.

Verkehrs'licht, -er, *n.nt.* traffic light.

verkehrt', *adj.* hindside to, wrong, backwards.

verken'nen*, *vb.* mistake, misunderstand.

verket'ten, *vb.* link.

verkla'gen, *vb.* sue, accuse.

Verklagt'-, *n.m.&f.* defendant.

verklärt', *adj.* transfigured, radiant.

verklei'den, *vb.* disguise; panel.

verklei'nern, *vb.* make smaller; belittle.

Verklei'nerung, -en, *n.f.* diminution; disparagement.

verknüp'fen, *vb.* connect, relate.

verkom'men*, *vb.* decay, come down in the world, die.

verkom'men, *adj.* squalid, dissolute.

verkör'pern, *vb.* embody.

verkör'pert, *adj.* incarnate.

Verkör'perung, -en, *n.f.* embodiment, epitome.

verkrüp'pelt, *adj.* crippled.

verküm'mern, *vb.* wither.

verkün'd(ig)en, *vb.* announce, proclaim.

Verkün'd(ig)ung, -en, *n.f.* announcement, Annunciation.

verkür'zen, *vb.* shorten.

verla'den*, *vb.* load, ship.

Verla'der, -, *n.m.* shipper.

Verlag', **-e,** *n.m.* publishing house.

verla'gern, *vb.* shift, displace.

Verlan'gen, *vb.* demand, require, ask; (**v. nach**) desire, long for.

Verlan'gen, *n.nt.* demand, request, craving.

verlän'gern, *vb.* lengthen, prolong, extend, renew.

Verlän'gerung, -en, *n.f.* prolongation, extension, renewal.

verlas'sen*, *vb.* leave, abandon, forsake; (**sich v. auf**) depend on, rely on.

verlas'sen, *adj.* abandoned, deserted, forlorn.

verläß'lich, *adj.* dependable.

Verlauf', *n.m.* course, lapse.

verlau'fen*, *vb.* pass, elapse; (**sich v.**) get lost.

verle'ben, *vb.* pass.

verlebt', *adj.* dissipated.

verle'gen, *vb.* move, shift; block; misplace; publish.

verle'gen, *adj.* embarrassed.

Verle'ger, -, *n.m.* publisher.

Verle'gung, -en, *n.f.* transfer, removal.

verlei'hen*, *vb.* lend; confer, bestow.

Verlei'hung, -en, *n.f.* bestowal.

verlei'ten, *vb.* lead astray, inveigle.

verler'nen, *vb.* forget.

verletz'bar, *adj.* vulnerable.

verlet'zen, *vb.* hurt, offend; violate, infringe.

Verlet'zung, -en, *n.f.* injury; violation.

verleug'nen, *vb.* deny, disown.

verleum'den, *vb.* slander.

verleum'derisch, *adj.* libellous.

Verleum'dung, -en, *n.f.* libel, slander.

verlie'ben, *vb.* (**sich v.**) fall in love.

verliebt', *adj.* in love.

verlie'ren*, *vb.* lose.

verlo'ben, *vb.* affiance, betroth; (**sich v.**) get engaged.

verlobt', *adj.* engaged.

Verlobt'-, *n.m.* fiancé.

Verlobt'-, *n.f.* fiancée.

Verlo'bung, -en, *n.f.* engagement.

verlo'cken, *vb.* entice, lure.

verlö'schen*, *vb.* go out, be extinguished.

Verlust', **-e,** *n.m.* loss; (*pl.*) casualties.

verma'chen, *vb.* bequeath.

Vermächt'nis, -se, *n.nt.* bequest, legacy.

vermäh'len, *vb.* espouse.

Vermäh'lung, -en, *n.f.* espousal.

vermeh'ren, *vb.* augment, multiply, increase.

vermeid'bar, *adj.* avoidable.

vermei'den*, *vb.* avoid.

vermeint'lich, *adj.* supposed.

vermen'gen, *vb.* blend; mix up.

Vermerk', -e, *n.m.* note; entry.

vermer'ken, *vb.* note down.

vermes'sen*, *vb.* measure, survey; **(sich v.)** have the audacity.

Vermes'senheit, *n.f.* presumptuousness.

Vermes'sung, -en, *n.f.* survey.

vermie'ten, *vb.* rent (to someone).

vermin'dern, *vb.* diminish.

vermis'sen, *vb.* miss.

vermit'teln, *vb.* mediate, negotiate, arrange.

Vermitt'ler, -, *n.m.* mediator.

vermö'ge, *prep.* by virtue of.

vermö'gen*, *vb.* be able.

Vermö'gen, -, *n.nt.* fortune, wealth, estate; ability, power.

vermö'gend, *adj.* wealthy, well-to-do.

vermu'ten, *vb.* presume.

vermut'lich, *adj.* presumable.

Vermu'tung, -en, *n.f.* surmise.

vernach'lässigen, *vb.* neglect.

Vernach'lässigung, -en, *n.f.* neglect.

verneh'men*, *vb.* perceive, hear, learn; examine.

vernehm'lich, *adj.* perceptible.

Verneh'mung, -en, *n.f.* hearing.

vernei'gen, *vb.* **(sich v.)** bow.

vernei'nen, *vb.* deny.

vernei'nend, *adj.* negative.

Vernei'nung, -en, *n.f.* denial.

vernich'ten, *vb.* annihilate, destroy.

vernich'tend, *adj.* devastating.

Vernich'tung, -en, *n.f.* annihilation, destruction.

Vernunft', *n.f.* reason.

vernunft'gemäß, *adj.* rational, according to reason.

vernünf'tig, *adj.* reasonable, sensible.

veröf'fentlichen, *vb.* publish.

Veröf'fentlichung, -en, *n.f.* publication.

verord'nen, *vb.* decree, order.

Verord'nung, -en, *n.f.* decree, ordinance, edict.

verpa'cken, *vb.* pack up, wrap up.

verpas'sen, *vb.* miss.

verpes'ten, *vb.* infect.

verpfän'den, *vb.* pawn, pledge.

verpfle'gen, *vb.* care for; feed.

Verpfle'gung, -en, *n.f.* food, board.

verpflich'ten, *vb.* oblige; **(sich v.)** commit oneself.

Verpflich'tung, -en, *n.f.* obligation.

Verrat', *n.m.* treason, betrayal.

verra'ten*, *vb.* betray.

Verrä'ter, -, *n.m.* traitor.

verrä'terisch, *adj.* treacherous.

verrech'nen, *vb.* reckon up; **(sich v.)** make a mistake in figuring, miscalculate.

verrei'sen, *vb.* go away on a trip.

verreist', *adj.* away on a trip.

verren'ken, *vb.* sprain.

verrich'ten, *vb.* do, perform, carry out.

verrin'gern, *vb.* decrease.

verros'ten, *vb.* rust.

verrucht', *adj.* infamous, wicked.

verrückt', *adj.* mad, crazy.

Verruf', *n.m.* disrepute, notoriety.

verru'fen, *adj.* disreputable, notorious.

Vers, -e, *n.m.* verse.

versa'gen, *vb.* refuse; fail.

Versa'gen, *n.nt.* failure.

Versa'ger, -, *n.m.* failure, flop.

versam'meln, *vb.* assemble.

Versamm'lung, -en, *n.f.* assembly, gathering, meeting.

Versand', *n.m.* dispatch.

versäu'men, *vb.* neglect, miss.

Versäum'nis, -se, *n.nt.* omission.

verschaf'fen, *vb.* procure.

verschämt', *adj.* bashful, coy.

verschan'zen, *vb.* entrench.

verschär'fen, *adj.* intensify.

verschei'den, *vb.* expire.

verschen'ken, *vb.* give away.

verscher'zen, *vb.* throw away, lose frivolously.

verscheu'chen, *vb.* scare away.

verschi'cken, *vb.* send off.

verschie'ben*, *vb.* shift, displace; postpone.

Verschie'bung, -en, *n.f.* shift; postponement.

verschie'den, *adj.* different, distinct; various, assorted; separate.

verschie'denartig, *adj.* various; heterogeneous.

verschie'ßen*, *vb.* fire off, fade.

verschla'fen*. 1. *vb.* miss by sleeping too long; sleep off; **(sich v.)** oversleep. **2.** *adj.* sleepy.

Verschlag', ¨e, *n.m.* partition, compartment.

verschla'gen*. 1. *vb.* drive away; **(es verschlägt' mir den Atem)** it takes my breath away. **2.** *adj.* sly.

verschlech'tern, *vb.* make worse, impair; **(sich v.)** become worse, deteriorate.

Verschlech'terung, -en, *n.f.* deterioration.

verschlei'ern, *vb.* veil.

verschlep'pen, *vb.* delay; abduct.

verschleu'dern, *vb.* squander.

verschlie'ßen*, *vb.* close, lock.

verschlim'mern, *vb.* make

worse, aggravate; **(sich v.)** become worse, deteriorate.

verschlin'gen*, *vb.* devour.

verschlis'sen, *adj.* worn out, frayed.

verschlos'sen, *adj.* closed, locked; reserved, taciturn.

verschlu'cken, *vb.* swallow; **(sich v.)** swallow the wrong way, choke.

Verschluß', ¨sse, *n.m.* closure; lock, plug, stopper; fastening, fastener; (camera) shutter.

verschmach'ten, *vb.* languish.

verschmel'zen*, *vb.* fuse, merge.

Verschmel'zung, -en, *n.f.* fusion.

verschneit', *adj.* covered with snow.

Verschnitt', *n.m.* adulteration; watered spirits.

verschnupft', *adj.* having a cold.

verschol'len, *adj.* missing, never heard of again.

verscho'nen, *vb.* spare.

verschö'nern, *vb.* beautify.

verschrei'ben*, *vb.* prescribe.

verschüch'tern, *vb.* intimidate.

verschul'det, *adj.* indebted.

verschüt'ten, *vb.* spill.

verschwei'gen*, *vb.* keep quiet about.

verschwen'den, *vb.* squander, waste, dissipate.

Verschwen'der, -, *n.m.* spendthrift.

verschwen'derisch, *adj.* wasteful, extravagant, prodigal.

Verschwen'dung, -en, *n.f.* extravagance, wastefulness.

verschwie'gen, *vb.* silent, discreet, reticent.

verschwin'den*, *vb.* disappear.

Verschwin'den, *n.nt.* disappearance.

verschwommen, *adj.* blurred.

verschwö'ren*, *vb.* renounce; **(sich v.)** conspire.

Verschwö'rer, -, *n.m.* conspirator.

Verschwö'rung, -en, *n.f.* conspiracy.

verse'hen*, *vb.* provide; perform; (**sich v.**) make mistake.

Verse'hen, -, *n.nt.* oversight, error; (**aus V.**) by mistake.

versen'den*, *vb.* send off.

versen'gen, *vb.* singe, scorch.

versen'ken, *vb.* sink.

verset'zen, *vb.* move, transfer; (school) promote; pawn, hock; reply.

versi'chern, *vb.* insure, assure; affirm, assert.

Versi'cherung, -en, *n.f.* insurance, assurance.

versie'geln, *vb.* seal.

versie'gen, *vb.* dry up.

versin'ken*, *vb.* sink.

versinn'bildlichen, *vb.* symbolize.

Version', -en, *n.f.* version.

versöh'nen, *vb.* reconcile.

versöh'nend, *adj.* conciliatory.

versöhn'lich, *adj.* conciliatory.

Versöh'nung, -en, *n.f.* reconciliation.

versor'gen, *vb.* provide, supply.

Versor'gung, *n.f.* supply, maintenance.

verspä'ten, *vb.* (**sich v.**) be late.

verspä'tet, *adj.* late.

Verspä'tung, -en, *n.f.* lateness.

versper'ren, *vb.* bar, obstruct.

verspie'len, *vb.* gamble away; (**sich v.**) misplay.

verspielt', *adj.* playful.

verspot'ten, *vb.* mock, deride.

verspre'chen*, *vb.* promise; (**sich v.**) make a slip of the tongue.

Verspre'chen, -, *n.nt.* promise.

verstaat'lichen, *vb.* nationalize.

Verstand', *n.m.* mind, intellect, brains.

verstän'dig, *adj.* sensible, intelligent.

verstän'digen, *vb.* inform; (**sich v.**) make oneself understood, make an agreement.

Verstän'digung, -en, *n.f.* agreement, understanding.

verständ'lich, *adj.* understandable.

Verständ'nis, *n.nt.* understanding.

verständ'nisvoll, *adj.* understanding.

verstär'ken, *vb.* strengthen, reinforce, intensify, amplify.

Verstär'ker, -, *n.m.* amplifier.

Verstär'kung, -en, *n.f.* reinforcement.

verstau'ben, *vb.* get covered with dust.

verstäu'ben, *vb.* atomize.

verstau'chen, *vb.* sprain.

Versteck', -e, *n.nt.* hiding-place; ambush; (**V. spielen**) play hide-and-go-seek.

verste'cken, *vb.* hide.

versteckt', *adj.* hidden; veiled, oblique, ulterior.

verste'hen*, *vb.* understand.

Verstei'gerung, -en, *n.f* auction.

verstell'bar, *adj.* adjustable.

verstel'len, *vb.* adjust, change, disguise.

Verstel'lung, -en, *n.f.* adjustment; disguise, sham, hypocrisy.

versteu'ern, *vb.* pay tax on.

verstim'men, *vb.* annoy, upset.

verstimmt', *adj.* annoyed, cross; (*music*) out of tune.

verstockt', *adj.* obdurate; impenitent.

verstoh'len, *adj.* stealthy, surreptitious.

verstop'fen, *vb.* stop up, clog.

Verstop'fung, -en, *n.f.* obstruction, jam; (*med.*) constipation.

verstor'ben, *adj.* deceased.

verstört', *adj.* distracted, bewildered.

Verstoß', **⁃e**, *n.m.* violation, offence.

versto'ßen*, *vb.* expel, disown; (**v. gegen**) infringe on, offend.

verstrei'chen*, *vb.* elapse.

verstri'cken, *vb.* ensnare, enmesh.

verstüm'meln, *vb.* mutilate.

Verstüm'melung, -en, *n.f.* mutilation.

verstum'men, *vb.* become silent.

Versuch', **-e**, *n.m.* attempt; test, trial, experiment; effort.

versu'chen, *vb.* attempt, try, test; strive; entice, tempt.

versuchs'weise, *adv.* experimentally.

Versu'chung, -en, *n.f.* temptation.

versün'digen, *vb.* (**sich v.**) sin against.

versun'ken, *adj.* sunken; (**v. sein**) be absorbed, be lost.

versü'ßen, *vb.* sweeten.

verta'gen, *vb.* adjourn.

Verta'gung, -en, *n.f.* adjournment.

vertau'schen, *vb.* exchange for; mistake for; substitute.

vertei'digen, *vb.* defend, advocate.

Vertei'diger, **-**, *n.m.* defender; (*jur.*) counsel for the defense.

Vertei'digung, -en, *n.f.* defense.

vertei'len, *vb.* distribute; disperse.

Vertei'ler, **-**, *n.m.* distributor.

Vertei'lung, -en, *n.f.* distribution; dispersal.

vertie'fen, *vb.* deepen; (**sich v.**) deepen, become engrossed.

vertieft', *adj.* absorbed.

vertil'gen, *vb.* consume; exterminate.

Vertrag', **⸗e**, *n.m.* contract, treaty, pact.

vertra'gen*, *vb.* endure, tolerate, stand; (**sich v.**) agree, get along.

vertrag'lich, *adj.* contractual.

verträg'lich, *adj.* compatible, good-natured.

vertrau'en, *vb.* trust; confide in; rely on.

Vertrau'en, *n.f.* trust, confidence, faith.

vertrau'ensvoll, *adj.* confident, reliant.

Vertrau'ensvotum, *n.nt.* vote of confidence.

vertrau'lich, *adj.* confidential.

Vertrau'lichkeit, -en, *n.f.* familiarity, intimacy; (**in aller V.**) in strict confidence.

vertraut', *adj.* acquainted, familiar; intimate.

Vertraut'-, *n.m.&f.* confidant(e).

Vertraut'heit, -en, *n.f.* familiarity; intimacy.

vertrei'ben*, *vb.* drive away, expel.

Vertrei'bung, -en, *n.f.* expulsion.

vertre'ten*, *vb.* represent; act as substitute; advocate.

Vertre'ter, **-**, *n.m.* representative, agent; deputy, substitute.

Vertre'tung, -en, *n.f.* representation, agency; substitution.

Vertrieb', **-e**, *n.m.* sale, market.

Vertrie'ben-, *n.m.&f.* expellee, refugee.

Vertriebs'stelle, -n, *n.f.* distributor.

vertu'schen, *vb.* hush up.

verü'beln, *vb.* take amiss.

verü'ben, *vb.* commit.

verun'glücken, *vb.* meet with an accident; fail.

verun'reinigen, *vb.* pollute.

verun'stalten, *vb.* disfigure.

verun'zieren, *vb.* mar.

verur'sachen, *vb.* cause, bring about; result in.

verur'teilen, *vb.* condemn; (*jur.*) sentence.

Verur'teilung, *n.f.* condemnation; (*jur.*) sentence.

verviel'fachen, *vb.* multiply.

verviel'fältigen, *vb.* multiply; mimeograph; (**sich v.**) multiply.

vervoll'kommnen, *vb.* perfect.

Vervoll'kommnung, *n.f.* perfection.

vervoll'ständigen, *vb.* complete.

verwach'sen*, *vb.* grow together; become deformed.

Verwach'sung, -en, *n.f.* deformity.

verwah'ren, *vb.* keep, hold in safe-keeping.

verwahr'losen, *vb.* neglect.

Verwah'rung, *n.f.* custody.

verwal'ten, *vb.* administer, manage.

Verwal'ter, -, *n.m.* administrator.

Verwal'tung, -en, *n.f.* administration, management.

verwan'deln, *vb.* change, transform.

Verwand'lung, -en, *n.f.* change, transformation; metamorphosis.

verwandt', *adj.* related.

Verwandt'-, *n.m.&f.* relation, relative.

Verwandt'schaft, -en, *n.f.* relationship, affinity.

verwech'seln, *vb.* mistake for, confuse.

Verwechs'lung, -en, *n.f.* mistake, mix-up.

verwe'gen, *adj.* daring, bold.

verweh'ren, *vb.* prevent from; refuse.

verwei'gern, *vb.* refuse.

Verwei'gerung, -en, *n.f.* refusal.

verwei'len, *vb.* linger.

Verweis', -e, *n.m.* reprimand; **(einen V. erteilen)** reprimand.

verwei'sen*, *vb.* banish; **(v. auf)** refer to.

verwend'bar, *adj.* usable, applicable.

Verwend'barkeit, *n.f.* usability, applicability.

verwen'den(*), *vb.* use, supply; expend.

Verwen'dung, -en, *n.f.* use, application.

verwer'fen*, *vb.* reject.

verwe'sen, *vb.* putrify, decay.

verwi'ckeln, *vb.* entangle, involve, implicate.

verwi'ckelt, *adj.* involved, intricate, complicated.

Verwick'lung, -en, *n.f.* entanglement, implication; complication.

verwin'den*, *vb.* get over, overcome.

verwir'ken, *vb.* forfeit.

verwirk'lichen, *vb.* realize, materialize.

Verwirk'lichung, -en, *n.f.* realization.

verwir'ren, *vb.* confuse, bewilder, confound, puzzle, mystify.

Verwir'rung, -en, *n.f.* confusion, bewilderment, perplexity.

verwi'schen, *vb.* wipe out; smudge.

verwit'wet, *adj.* widowed.

verwor'fen, *adj.* depraved.

verwor'ren, *adj.* confused.

verwun'den, *vb.* wound.

verwun'dern, *vb.* astonish.

Verwun'dung, -en, *n.f.* wound, injury.

verwun'schen, *adj.* enchanted.

verwün'schen, *vb.* curse; bewitch.

verwüs'ten, *vb.* devastate.

verza'gen, *vb.* despair.

verzagt', *adj.* despondent.

verzäh'len, *vb.* **(sich v.)** miscount.

verzär'teln, *vb.* pamper.

verzau'bern, *vb.* bewitch.

verzeh'ren, *vb.* consume.

verzeich'nen, *vb.* register, list.

Verzeich'nis, -se, *n.nt.* list, index.

verzei'hen*, *vb.* pardon, forgive.

Verzei'hung, -en, *n.f.* pardon, forgiveness; **(ich bitte um V.)** I beg your pardon.

verzer'ren, *vb.* distort.

Verzicht', -e, *n.m.* renunciation; **(V. leisten)** renounce.

verzich'ten, *vb.* renounce, forego, waive.

verzie'hen*, *vb.* pull out of shape; (child) spoil; **(sich v.)** withdraw; vanish, disperse; (wood) warp.

verzie'ren, *vb.* embellish.

Verzie'rung, -en, *n.f.* ornament, embellishment.

verzin'sen, *vb.* pay interest; **(sich v.)** bear interest.

Verzin'sung, -en, *n.f.* interest return; payment of interest; interest rate.

verzo'gen, *adj.* moved away; (child) spoiled.

verzö'gern, *vb.* delay.

Verzö'gerung, -en, *n.f.* delay.

verzol'len, *vb.* pay duty on.

verzückt', *adj.* enraptured.

Verzug', -e, *n.m.* delay; default.

verzwei'feln, *vb.* despair.

verzwei'felt, *adj.* desperate.

Verzweif'lung, -en, *n.f.* desperation.

verzwickt', *adj.* complicated.

Vesper, -n, *n.f.* vespers.

Veterinär', -e, *n.m.* veterinary.

Vetter, -n, *n.m.* cousin.

Viadukt', -e, *n.m.* viaduct.

Vibration', -en, *n.f.* vibration.

vibrie'ren, *vb.* vibrate.

Vieh, *n.nt.* cattle.

viehisch, *adj.* brutal.

Viehzucht, *n.f.* cattle breeding.

viel, *adj.* much; (*pl.*) many.

vielbedeutend, *adj.* significant.

vieldeutig, *adj.* ambiguous.

Vieleck, -e, *n.nt.* polygon.

vielerlei, *adj.* various, many.

vielfach, *adj.* manifold.

vielfältig, *adj.* multiple.

Vielfältigkeit, *n.f.* multiplicity.

vielfarbig, *adj.* multicolored.

Vielfraß, -e, *n.m.* glutton.

Vielheit, -en, *n.f.* multiplicity.

vielleicht', *adv.* perhaps.

vielmals, *adv.* many times.

vielmehr, *adv.* rather.

vielsagend, *adj.* significant, highly suggestive.

vielseitig, *adj.* many-sided; versatile.

vielverheißend, *adj.* very promising.

vielversprechend, *adj.* very promising.

vier, *num.* four.

Viereck, -e, *n.nt.* square.

viereckig, *adj.* square.

vierfach, *adj.* fourfold.

Vierfüßler, -, *n.m.* quadruped.

vierschrötig, *adj.* thick-set.

viert-, *adj.* fourth.

vierteilen, *vb.* quarter.

Viertel, -, *n.nt.* fourth, quarter; **(ein v.)** one-fourth.

vierzehn, *num.* fourteen.

vierzig, *num.* forty.

vierzigst-, *adj.* fortieth.

Vierzigstel, -, *n.nt.* fortieth; **(ein v.)** one-fortieth.

violett', *adj.* violet.

Violi'ne, -n, *n.f.* violin.

Violinist', -en, -en, *n.m.* violinist.

Visier', -e, *n.nt.* visor; (gun) sight.

visuell', *adj.* visual.

Visum, -sa, *n.nt.* visa.

Vitalität', *n.f.* vitality.

Vize-, *cpds.* vice-.

Vogel, ¨, *n.m.* bird.

vogelartig, *adj.* birdlike.

Vogelbauer, -, *n.nt.* bird cage.

Vogelscheuche, -n, *n.f.* scarecrow.

Vogt, ¨e, *n.m.* overseer.

Vokal', -e, *n.m.* vowel.

Volant', -s, *n.m.* flounce.

Volk, ¨er, *n.nt.* people, nation.

Völkerbund, *n.m.* League of Nations.

Völkerkunde, *n.f.* ethnology; (school) social studies.

Völkermord, *n.m.* genocide.

Völkerrecht, *n.nt.* international law.

Volksabstimmung, -en, *n.f.* plebiscite, referendum.

Volkscharakter, *n.m.* national character.

Volksentscheid, *n.m.* plebiscite, referendum.

Volksgenosse, -n, -n, *n.m.* fellow countryman.

Volkskunde, *n.f.* folklore.

Volkslied, -er, *n.nt.* folk-song.

Volksmenge, *n.f.* crowd, mob.

Volksschule, -n, *n.f.* elementary school.

Volkstanz, -e, *n.m.* folk-dance.

volkstümlich, *adj.* popular.

Volkszählung, -en, *n.f.* census.

voll, *adj.* full.

Vollblut, *n.nt.* thorough-bred.

vollblütig, *adj.* full-blooded.

vollbrin'gen*, *vb.* accomplish, fulfill.

vollen'den, *vb.* finish, complete.

vollen'det, *adj.* accomplished.

vollends, *adv.* completely.

Völlerei', *n.f.* gluttony.

vollfüh'ren, *vb.* accomplish.

Vollgas, *n.nt.* full throttle.

völlig, *adj.* complete, entire.

volljährig, *adj.* of age.

vollkom'men, *adj.* perfect.

Vollkom'menheit, *n.f.* perfection.

Vollmacht, -e, *n.f.* authority, warrant, proxy, power of attorney.

vollständig, *adj.* complete.

voll·stopfen, *vb.* cram, stuff.

vollstre'cken, *vb.* execute, carry out.

Vollversammlung, *n.f.* (U.N.) General Assembly.

vollzählig, *adj.* complete.

vollzie'hen*, *vb.* execute, carry out; consummate; **(sich v.)** take place.

Volontär', -e, *n.m.* volunteer.

Volontär'arzt, -e, *n.m.* intern.

Volt, -, *n.nt.* volt.

Volu'men, -, *n.nt.* volume.

von, *prep.* of, from, by.

vor, *prep.* before; in front of; ago.

Vorabend, -e, *n.m.* eve.

Vorahnung, -en, *n.f.* premonition, foreboding.

voran', *adv.* in front of, ahead; onward.

voran'·gehen*, *vb.* precede.

voran'·kommen*, *vb.* get ahead.

Vor'anmeldung, -en, *n.f.* (telephone) **(mit V.)** person-to-person call.

Voranschlag, -e, *n.m.* estimate.

Vorarbeit', -en, *n.f.* preparatory work.

Vorarbeiter, -, *n.m.* foreman.

vorauf', *adv.* before, ahead.

voraus', *adv.* in advance, ahead; **(im v.)** in advance.

voraus'·bedingen*, *vb.* stipulate in advance.

voraus'·bestellen, *vb.* order ahead, make reservations.

voraus'·gehen*, *vb.* precede.

voraus'gesetz , adv. (v. daß) provided that.

voraus'·nehmen*, *vb.* state now, anticipate.

Voraus'sage, -n, *n.f.* prediction, forecast.

voraus'·sagen, *vb.* predict, forecast.

voraus'·setzen, *vb.* presume, presuppose.

Voraus'setzung, -en, *n.f.* supposition, assumption; prerequisite.

Voraus'sicht, *n.f.* foresight.

voraus'sichtlich, 1. *adj.* prospective. **2.** *adv.* presumably.

voraus'·zahlen, *vb.* pay in advance, advance.

Vorbedacht, *n.m.* forethought.

Vorbedeutung, -en, *n.f.* omen.

Vorbedingung, -en, *n.f.* prerequisite.

vor·behalten*, *vb.* reserve.

Vorbehalt, *n.m.* reservation.

vorbei', *adv.* over, past.

vorbelastet, *adj.* having a questionable record; **(jur.)** having a criminal record.

vor·bereiten, *vb.* prepare.

vor·bestellen, *vb.* order in advance, make reservations.

vor·beugen, *vb.* prevent.

vorbeugend, *adj.* preventive.

Vorbild, -er, *n.nt.* model.

vorbildlich, *adj.* exemplary.

vor·bringen*, *vb.* state; propose.

vorder-, *adj.* front, anterior.

Vorderfront, -en, *n.f.* frontage; *(fig.)* forefront.

Vordergrund, *n.m.* foreground.

vorderhand, *adv.* for the time being; right now.

Vordermann, ⁓er, *n.m.* person ahead of one.

Vorderseite, -n, *n.f.* front.

Vorderteil, -e, *n.nt.* front part.

vor·drängen, *vb.* **(sich v.)** elbow one's way forward.

vor·dringen*, *vb.* press forward, advance.

Vordruck, ⁓e, *n.m.* form, blank.

voreilig, *adj.* rash, hasty.

voreingenommen, *adj.* prejudiced.

Voreingenommenheit, *n.f.* partiality.

vor·enthalten*, *vb.* withhold.

vorerst, *adv.* first of all.

Vorfahr, -en, -en, *n.m.* ancestor.

vor·fahren*, *vb.* drive up; **(v. lassen*)** let pass.

Vorfahrtsrecht, -e, *n.nt.* right of way.

Vorfall, ⁓e, *n.m.* incident.

vor·fallen*, *vb.* occur.

vor·finden*, *vb.* find.

vor·führen, *vb.* show, demonstrate, produce.

Vorführung, -en, *n.f.* demonstration, show, production.

Vorgang, ⁓e, *n.m.* occurrence, process, procedure.

Vorgänger, -, *n.m.* predecessor.

vor·geben*, *vb.* pretend, feign.

Vorgefühl, -e, *n.nt.* presentiment, hunch.

vor·gehen*, *vb.* advance; come first, precede.

Vorgehen, *n.nt.* procedure, policy.

Vorgericht, -e, *n.nt.* appetizer; first course.

Vorgeschichte, *n.f.* prehistory; history, background.

vorgeschrieben, *adj.* prescribed.

vorgesehen, *adj.* planned, scheduled.

Vorgesetzt-, *n.m.&f.* superior.

vorgestern, *adv.* the day before yesterday.

vorgetäuscht, *adj.* makebelieve.

vor·greifen*, *vb.* anticipate.

vor·haben*, *vb.* plan, have in mind.

Vorhaben, *n.nt.* plan, intention.

Vorhalle, -n, *n.f.* lounge.

vor·halten*, *vb. (fig.)* reproach.

Vorhand, *n.f.* forehand.

vorhan'den, *adj.* existing, present, available.

Vorhang, ⁓e, *n.m.* curtain, drapery.

vorher, *adv.* before, beforehand, previously.

vorher'gehend, *adj.* previous.

vor·herrschen, *vb.* prevail.

vorherrschend, *adj.* prevalent, predominant.

Vorherrschaft, *n.f.* predominance.

Vorher'sage, -n, *n.f.* prediction.

vorher'·sagen, *vb.* foretell.

vorher'·sehen*, *vb.* foresee.

Vorhut, *n.f.* vanguard.

vorig, *adj.* previous, last.

Vorjahr, -e, *n.nt.* preceding year.

Vorkämpfer, -, *n.m.* pioneer, champion.

Vorkenntnis, -se, *n.f.* preliminary knowledge; rudiments.

Vorkommen, *n.nt.* occurrence.

vor·kommen*, *vb.* occur.

Vorkommnis, -se, *n.nt.* occurence.

Vorkriegs-, *cpds.* prewar.

vor·laden*, *vb.* summon.

Vorladung, -en, *n.f.* summons.

vor·lassen*, *vb.* let pass; admit.

Vorlassung, -en, *n.f.* admittance.

vorläufig. 1. *adj.* preliminary, tentative; temporary. **2.** *adv.* for the time being.

vorlaut, *adj.* flippant, fresh.

vor·legen, *vb.* show, submit, produce.

vor·lesen*, *vb.* read out loud.

Vorlesung, -en, *n.f.* reading; lecture.

Vorlesungsverzeichnis, -se, *n.nt.* university catalogue.

vorletzt, *adj.* last but one.

Vorliebe, *n.f.* preference, fondness.

vorlieb'·nehmen*, *vb.* be satisfied with.

vor·liegen*, *vb.* exist.

vorliegend, *adj.* present, at hand, in question.

vor·machen, *vb.* show how to do; **(einem etwas v.)** deceive, fool.

Vormachtstellung, -en, *n.f.* predominance.

vormalig, *adj.* former.

vormals, *adv.* heretofore.

Vormann, ·er, *n.m.* foreman.

Vormarsch, ·e, *n.m.* advance.

vor·merken, *vb.* make a note of; reserve.

Vormittag, -e, *n.m.* forenoon.

Vormund, -e, *n.m.* guardian.

vorn, *adv.* in front.

Vorname(n), -, *n.m.* first name.

vornehm, *adj.* noble, distinguished.

vor·nehmen*, *vb.* **(sich v.)** undertake, consider, take up, resolve.

vornehmlich, *adv.* chiefly.

Vorort, -e, *n.m.* suburb.

Vorortzug, ·e, *n.m.* local (train).

Vorplatz, ·e, *n.m.* hall; court.

Vorrang, *n.m.* priority, precedence.

Vorrat, ·e, *n.m.* supply, provision, stock, stockpile.

Vorratskammer, -n, *n.f.* storeroom, pantry.

vorrätig, *adj.* in stock.

Vorrecht, -e, *n.nt.* privilege, prerogative.

Vorrede, -n, *n.f.* preface.

Vorrichtung, -en, *n.f.* arrangement; contrivance, device, fixture.

vor·rücken, *vb.* move forward, advance.

Vorsatz, ·e, *n.m.* purpose, intention; *(jur.)* premeditation.

vorsätzlich, *adj.* wilful, intentional; *(jur.)* premeditated.

Vorschein, *n.m.* **(zum V. kommen*)** appear.

Vorschlag, ·e, *n.m.* proposal, proposition, suggestion.

vor·schlagen*, *vb.* propose, suggest.

vorschnell, *adj.* rash.

vor·schreiben*, *vb.* prescribe.

Vorschrift, -en, *n.f.* regulation.

vorschriftsmäßig, *adj.* as prescribed, regulation.

Vorschub, *n.m.* assistance.

Vorschule, -n, *n.f.* elementary school.

Vorschuß, ·sse, *n.m.* advance payment.

vor·schützen, *vb.* pretend, plead.

vor·sehen*, *vb.* earmark, plan, schedule; **(sich v.)** be careful.

Vorsehung, *n.f.* providence.

Vorsicht, -en, *n.f.* caution.

vorsichtig, *adj.* careful, cautious.

vorsichtshalber, *adv.* as a precaution.

Vorsichtsmaßregel, -n, *n.f.* precaution.

Vorsilbe, -n, *n.f.* prefix.

Vorsitz, -e, *n.m.* chairmanship, presidency; **(den V. führen)** preside.

Vorsitzende(r), *-n, n.m. & f.* chairman; chairwoman.

Vorsorge, *n.f.* providence.

foresight; (**V. treffen***) take precautions.

vorsorglich, *adv.* as a precaution.

Vorspeise, -n, *n.f.* appetizer.

vor·spiegeln, *vb.* deceive, delude.

Vorspiel, -e, *n.nt.* prelude.

vor·springen*, *vb.* project.

Vorsprung, ·e, *n.m.* advantage; head start; (*arch.*) ledge.

Vorstadt, ·e, *n.f.* suburb, outskirts.

vorstellbar, *adj.* conceivable.

vor·stellen, *vb.* present, introduce; (clock set ahead); (**sich v.**) imagine, picture.

Vorstellung, -en, *n.f.* presentation, introduction; imagination, idea, notion; (theater) performance, show.

Vorstoß, ·e, *n.m.* attack.

vor·stoßen*, *vb.* push forward.

vor·strecken, *vb.* stretch forward; (money) advance.

vor·täuschen, *vb.* make-believe, simulate.

Vorteil, -e, *n.m.* advantage.

vorteilhaft, *adj.* advantageous, profitable.

Vortrag, ·e, *n.m.* lecture, talk.

vor·tragen*, *vb.* lecture, recite, report.

Vortragend-, *n.m.&f.* lecturer.

vortreff'lich, *adj.* excellent.

Vortritt, *n.m.* precedence.

vorü'ber, *adv.* past, gone.

vorü'ber·gehen*, *vb.* pass.

vorü'bergehend, *adj.* temporary.

Vorurteil, -e, *n.nt.* prejudice.

Vorväter, *n.pl.* forefathers.

Vorwahl, -en, *n.f.* primary election.

Vorwand, ·e, *n.m.* pretense, pretext.

Vorwarnung, -en, *n.f.* forewarning.

vorwärts, *adv.* forward.

vorwärts·kommen*, *vb.* get ahead, make headway.

vorweg'·nehmen*, *vb.* anticipate; forestall.

vor·werfen*, *vb.* reproach.

Vorwort, *n.nt.* preface.

Vorwurf, ·e, *n.m.* reproach.

vor·zeigen, *vb.* show, produce.

vorzeitig, *adj.* premature.

vor·ziehen*, *vb.* prefer.

Vorzimmer, -, *n.nt.* antichamber, anteroom.

Vorzug, ·e, *n.m.* preference; advantage.

vorzüg'lich, 1. *adj.* excellent, exquisite. **2.** *adv.* especially.

Vorzüg'lichkeit, -en, *n.f.* excellence.

vorzugsweise, *adv.* preferably.

vulgär', *adj.* vulgar.

Vulkan', -e, *n.m.* volcano.

W

Waage, -n, *n.f.* scales.

waagerecht, *adj.* horizontal.

Waagschale, -n, *n.f.* scale.

Wabe, -n, *n.f.* honeycomb.

wach, *adj.* awake.

Wache, -n, *n.f.* watch, guard.

wachen, *vb.* be awake, stay awake; watch over.

wachhabend, *adj.* on duty.

Wachlokal, -e, *n.nt.* guardhouse, police station.

Wachposten, -, *n.m.* sentry.

Wachs, -e, *n.nt.* wax.

wachsam, *adj.* watchful, vigilant.

Wachsamkeit, *n.f.* vigilance.

wachsen*, *vb.* grow, increase.

wachsen, *vb.* wax.

Wachskerze, -n, *n.f.* candle.

Wachstum, *n.nt.* growth.

Wacht, *n.f.* guard, watch.

Wächter, -, *n.m.* watchman; keeper.

Wachtmeister, -, *n.m.* (police) sergeant.

wackelig, *adj.* shaky, wobbly.

wackeln, *vb.* shake, wobble.

wacker, *adj.* staunch, brave, stouthearted.

Wade, -n, *n.f.* calf (of the leg).

Waffe, -n, *n.f.* weapon, arm.

Waffenfabrik, -en, *n.f.* arms factory.

Waffengattung, -en, *n.f.* arm; branch of the army.

waffenlos, *adj.* unarmed, defenseless.

Waffenstill'stand, ⁀e, *n.m.* armistice, truce.

Waffel, -n, *n.f.* waffle.

waffnen, *vb.* arm.

wagemutig, *adj.* venturesome.

wagen, *vb.* dare, risk, venture.

Wagen, -, *n.m.* carriage, coach, wagon, car.

wägen(*), *vb.* consider.

Wagenheber, -, *n.m.* auto jack.

Waggon', -s, *n.m.* railroad car.

Waggon'ladung, -en, *n.f.* carload.

waghalsig, *adj.* rash, risky.

Wagnis, -se, *n.nt.* venture.

Wahl, -en, *n.f.* choice, election, vote, ballot.

wählbar, *adj.* eligible; (**nicht w.**) ineligible.

wahlberechtigt, *adj.* eligible to vote.

Wahlbezirk, -e, *n.m.* constituency.

wählen, *vb.* choose; elect, vote; (telephone) dial.

Wähler, -, *n.m.* constituent, voter.

wählerisch, *adj.* choosy, fastidious.

Wählerschaft, *n.f* electorate.

Wahlgang, ⁀e, *n.m.* ballot.

Wahlkampf, ⁀e, *n.m.* election campaign.

Wahlliste, -n, *n.f.* ticket, slate.

Wahlrecht, -e, *n.nt.* franchise, suffrage; (**W. erteilen**) enfranchise; (**W. entziehen**) disenfranchise.

Wählscheibe, -n, *n.f.* dial (on a telephone).

Wahlspruch, ⁀e, *n.m.* slogan, motto.

Wahlstimme, -n, *n.f.* vote.

Wahn, *n.m.* delusion.

Wahnsinn, *n.m.* insanity.

wahnsinnig, *adj.* insane, delirious.

wahr, *adj.* true, truthful, real; (**nicht w.?**) is it that so?

wahren, *vb.* keep, preserve.

währen, *vb.* continue, last.

während, 1. *prep.* during. **2.** *conj.* while.

wahrhaftig, *adj.* true, sincere.

Wahrheit, -en *n.f.* truth.

wahrnehmbar, *adj.* perceptible.

wahr-nehmen*, *vb.* perceive.

Wahrnehmung, -en, *n.f.* perception.

wahr-sagen, *vb.* prophesy, tell fortunes.

Wahrsager, -, *n.m.* fortuneteller.

wahrschein'lich, *adj.* probable, likely.

Währung, -en, *n.f.* currency.

Wahrzeichen, -, *n.nt.* distinctive mark, landmark.

Waise, -n, *n.f.* orphan.

Waisenhaus, ⁀er, *n.nt.* orphanage.

Wald, ⁀er, *n.m.* wood forest.

Walfisch, -e, *n.m.* whale.

Wall, ⁀e, *n.m.* rampart.

wallen, *vb.* undulate; bubble.

Wallfahrer, -, *n.m.* pilgrim.

Wallfahrt, -en, *n.f.* pilgrimage.

Walnuß, ⁀sse, *n.f.* walnut.

Walroß, -sse, *n.nt.* walrus.

walten, *vb.* rule.

Walze, -n, *n.f.* roll, roller.

walzen, *vb.* roll.

wälzen, *vb.* roll.

Walzer, -, *n.m.* waltz.

Wand, ⁀e, *n.f.* wall.

Wandel, *n.m.* change.

wandelbar, *adj.* changeable.

Wandelhalle, -n, *n.f.* lobby.

wandeln, *vb.* change; go, wander.

wandern, *vb.* hike, wander, roam.

Wanderschaft, *n.f.* travels.

Wanderung, -en, *n.f.* hike, wandering; migration.

Wandgemälde, -, *n.nt.* mural.

Wandlung, -en, *n.f.* change, transformation.

Wandschrank, -e, *n.m.* (eingebauter W.) closet.

Wandtafel, -n, *n.f.* blackboard.

Wandteppich, -e, *n.m.* tapestry.

Wange, -n, *n.f.* cheek.

wankelmütig, *adj.* fickle.

wanken, *vb.* stagger, sway.

wann, 1. *conj.* when. **2.** *adv.* when.

Wanne, -n, *n.f.* tub.

Wanze, -n, *n.f.* bedbug.

Wappen, -, *n.nt.* coat of arms.

Ware, -n, *n.f.* article, commodity, merchandise, ware; (*pl.*) goods.

Warenhandel, *n.m.* trade, commerce.

Warenhaus, -er, *n.nt.* department store.

Warenrechnung, -en, *n.f.* invoice.

warm(-), *adj.* warm.

Wärme, *n.f.* warmth, heat.

wärmen, *vb.* warm.

Wärmflasche, -n, *n.f.* hot water bottle.

warnen, *vb.* warn, caution.

Warnung, -en, *n.f.* warning.

Warte, -n, *n.f.* watch-tower, lookout.

warten, *vb.* wait.

Wärter, -, *n.m.* keeper, guard.

Warteraum, -e, *n.m.* waiting room.

Wartezeit, -en, *n.f.* wait.

Wartezimmer, -, *n.nt.* waiting room.

warum', *adv.&conj.* why.

Warze, -n, *n.f.* wart.

was, *pron.* what.

Waschanstalt, -en, *n.f.* laundry.

waschbar, *adj.* washable.

Waschbecken, -, *n.nt.* washbasin.

waschecht, *adj.* colorfast; (*fig.*) dyed in the wool.

Wäsche, *n.f.* laundry, linen.

waschen*, *vb.* wash, launder.

Wäscherei, -en, *n.f.* laundry.

Wäscheschrank, -e, *n.m.* linen closet.

Waschfrau, -en, *n.f.* laundress.

Waschlappen, -, *n.m.* face cloth.

Waschleder, *n.nt.* suede.

Waschmaschine, -n, *n.f.* washing machine.

Waschpulver, *n.nt.* soap powder.

Waschraum, -e, *n.m.* washroom.

Waschseife, -n, *n.f.* laundry soap.

Waschtisch, -e, *n.m.* washstand, washbowl.

Waschzettel, -, *n.m.* laundry list; (book) blurb; memo.

Wasser, -, *n.nt.* water.

wasserdicht, *adj.* watertight, waterproof.

Wasserfall, -e, *n.m.* waterfall.

Wasserflugzeug, -e, *n.nt.* hydroplane.

Wasserhahn, -e, *n.m.* faucet.

wässerig, *adj.* watery, aqueous.

Wasserleitung, -en, *n.f.* water main; aqueduct.

wässern, *vb.* water.

Wasserrinne, -n, *n.f.* gully, gutter.

Wasserstoff, *n.m.* hydrogen.

Wasserstoffbombe, -n, *n.f.* hydrogen bomb.

Wasserstoffsu'peroxyd, *n.nt.* hydrogen peroxide.

Wassersucht, *n.f.* dropsy.

waten, *vb.* wade.

watscheln, *vb.* waddle.

weben(*), *vb.* weave.

Webeschiffchen, -, *n.nt.* shuttle.

Webstuhl, -e, *n.m.* loom.

Wechsel, -, *n.m.* change, shift, rotation; (*comm.*) draft.

Wechselgeld, *n.nt.* change.

Wechseljahre, *n.pl.* menopause.

Wechselkurs, -e, *n.m.* rate of exchange.

wechseln, *vb.* change, exchange.

wechselnd, *adj.* intermittent.

Wechselstrom, ̈e, *n.m.* alternating current.

wecken, *vb.* wake, awaken.

Wecker, -, *n.m.* alarm clock.

wedeln, *vb.* wag.

weder, *adj.* **(w. . . . noch)** neither . . . nor.

Weg, -e, *n.m.* way, path, route.

weg, *adv.* away; gone.

wegen, *prep.* because of.

weg-fahren*, *vb.* drive away, leave.

weg-fallen*, *vb.* be omitted; not take place.

weg-gehen*, *vb.* go away, leave.

weg-kommen*, *vb.* get away; get off.

weg-lassen*, *vb.* leave out.

weg-nehmen*, *vb.* take away.

weg-räumen, *vb.* remove.

weg-schicken, *vb.* send off.

weg-schnappen, *vb.* snatch.

Wegweiser, -, *n.m.* guidepost, signpost.

Wegzehrung, -en, *n.f.* provisions for a journey.

Weh, *n.nt.* woe, pain, ache.

weh, *adj.* sore; **(w. tun*)** hurt, be sore.

wehen, *vb.* (wind) blow; (flag) wave.

Wehen, *n.pl.* labor pains.

Wehklage, -n, *n.f.* lament, lamentation.

wehklagen, *vb.* wail, lament.

Wehmut, *n.f.* sadness.

wehmütig, *adj.* sad, melancholy.

Wehr, -e, *n.nt.* dam.

Wehr, -en, *n.f.* defense, resistance.

Wehrdienst, *n.m.* military service.

wehren, *vb.* **(sich w.)** defend oneself, fight.

wehrfähig, *adj.* fit to serve (in the army).

wehrlos, *adj.* defenseless.

Wehrmacht, *n.f.* armed forces; (specifically, German army to 1945).

Wehrpflicht, *n.f.* duty to serve in armed forces; **(allgemeine W.)** compulsory military service.

weh-tun*, *vb.* hurt, be sore.

Weib, -er, *n.nt.* woman.

Weibchen, -, *n.nt.* (zool.) female.

Weibersache, -n, *n.f.* women's affair.

weiblich, *adj.* female, feminine.

weich, *adj.* soft.

Weiche, -n, *n.f.* switch.

weichen*, *vb.* give way, yield.

weichen, *vb.* soften.

weichlich, *adj.* soft; effeminate.

Weide, -n, *n.f.* pasture; willow.

weiden, *vb.* graze, **(sich w.)** feast one's eyes, gloat.

weidlich, *adv.* thoroughly.

weigern, *vb.* **(sich w.)** refuse.

Weihe, -n, *n.f.* consecration.

weihen, *vb.* consecrate.

weihevoll, *adj.* solemn.

Weiher, -, *n.m.* pond.

Weihnachten, -, *n.nt.* Christmas.

Weihnachtslied, -er, *n.nt.* Christmas carol.

Weihnachtsmann, ̈er, *n.m.* Santa Claus.

Weihrauch, *n.m.* incense.

Weihung, -en, *n.f.* consecration.

weil, *conj.* because, since.

Weile, *n.f.* while.

weilen, *vb.* stay.

Weiler, -, *n.m.* hamlet.

Wein, -e, *n.m.* wine.

Weinbauer, -, *n.m.* wine grower.

Weinberg, -e, *n.m.* vineyard.

Weinbrand, -e, *n.m.* brandy.

weinen, *vb.* cry, weep.

Weingarten, ̈, *n.m.* vineyard.

Weinlese, *n.f.* vintage.

Weinrebe, -n, *n.f.* grapevine.

Weinstock, -e, *n.m.* grape-vine.

Weinstube, -n, *n.f.* tap room.

Weintraube, -n, *n.f.* grape.

weise, *adj.* wise.

Weise, -n, *n.f.* manner, way, method.

weisen*, *vb.* show; **(von sich w.)** reject.

Weisheit, -en, *n.f.* wisdom.

weis·machen, *vb.* make someone believe, fool.

weiß, *adj.* white.

weissagen, *vb.* prophesy, tell fortunes.

Weissager, -, *n.m.* fortune teller.

Weißwaren, *n.pl.* linen goods.

Weisung, -en, *n.f.* order, direction.

weit, *adj.* far; wide, large.

weitab', *adv.* far away.

weitaus', *adv.* by far.

Weite, -n, *n.f.* width, largeness, expanse; size.

weiter, *adv.* farther, further; **(und so w.)** and so forth.

weiterhin, *adv.* furthermore.

weitgehend, *adj.* far-reaching.

weither', *adv.* from afar.

weitläufig, *adj.* lengthy, elaborate, complex.

weitreichend, *adj.* far-reaching.

weitsichtig, *adj.* far-sighted.

weittragend, *adj.* far-reaching.

weitverbreitet, *adj.* widespread.

weitverstreut, *adj.* far-flung.

Weizen, *n.m.* wheat.

welcher, -es, -e, *pron.&adj.* which, what.

welchergestalt, *adv.* in what manner.

welk, *adj.* wilted.

welken, *vb.* wilt.

Welle, -n, *n.f.* wave; *(tech.)* shaft.

wellen, *vb.* wave; *(tech.)* corrugate.

Wellenlänge, -n, *n.f.* wave length.

wellig, *adj.* wavy.

Welt, -en, *n.f.* world.

Weltall, *n.nt.* universe.

Weltanschauung, -en, *n.f.* philosophy of life.

Weltbürger, -, *n.m.* cosmopolite.

weltgeschichtlich, *adj.* historical.

weltgewandt, *adj.* sophisticated.

weltklug(ː), *adj.* worldly-wise.

Weltkrieg, -e, *n.m.* world war.

Weltkugel, -n, *n.f.* globe.

weltlich, *adj.* worldly, secular.

Weltmeister, -, *n.m.* world's champion.

Weltmeisterschaft, -en, *n.f.* world's championship.

weltnah, *adj.* worldly, realistic.

Weltraum, *n.m.* outer space.

Weltreich, -e, *n.nt.* empire.

Weltschmerz, *n.m.* world-weariness.

Weltstadt, ːe, *n.f.* metropolis.

weltweit, *adj.* world-wide.

Wende, -n, *n.f.* turn, bend.

wenden*, *vb.* turn; **(sich w. an)** appeal to.

Wendekreis, -e, *n.m.* tropic; **(W. des Krebses)** tropic of cancer; **(W. des Steinbocks)** tropic of capricorn.

wendig, *adj.* versatile, resourceful.

Wendung, -en, *n.f.* turn.

wenig, *adj.* few, little.

weniger, *adj.* fewer, less; minus.

Wenigkeit, -en, *n.f.* trifle; **(meine W.)** yours truly.

wenigstens, *adv.* at least.

wenn, *conj.* when, if.

wer, *pron.* who.

werben*, *vb.* recruit, enlist, advertise; woo.

Werbeplakat, -e, *n.nt.* poster.

Werber, -, *n.m.* suitor.

Werbung, -en, *n.f.* recruiting, advertising; courting.

Werdegang, ːe, *n.m.* development; career.

werden*, *vb.* become, get, grow.

werfen 186 GERMAN - ENGLISH

werfen*, *vb.* throw, cast; **(über den Haufen w.)** upset.

Werft, -en, *n.f.* dockyard, shipyard.

Werk, -e, *n.nt.* work, labor, deed; factory, plant.

werken, *vb.* work, operate.

Werkstatt, -en, *n.f.* plant, shop.

Werktag, -e, *n.m.* work day, weekday.

werktags, *adv.* weekdays.

Werkzeug, -e, *n.nt.* tool, instrument.

Wermut, *n.m.* vermouth.

Wert, -e, *n.m.* value, worth, merit.

wert, *adj.* worth, valued, esteemed.

Wertarbeit, -en, *n.f.* workmanship.

Wertbrief, -e, *n.m.* registered insured letter.

wertlos, *adj.* worthless, useless.

Wertlosigkeit, -en, *n.f.* worthlessness, uselessness.

Wertpapier, -e, *n.nt.* security, bond, stock.

Wertschätzung, -en, *n.f.* esteem, value.

Werturteil, -e, *n.nt.* value judgment.

Wertverminderung, -en, *n.f.* depreciation.

wertvoll, *adj.* valuable.

Wesen, -, *n.nt.* being, creature; nature, character; essence, substance.

Wesenheit, *n.f.* entity.

wesenlos, *adj.* unreal.

Wesenszug, -e, *n.m.* characteristic.

wesentlich, *adj.* essential, material; substantial, vital.

weshalb, 1. *conj.* for which reason. **2.** *adv.* why.

Wespe, -n, *n.f.* wasp.

wessen, *pron.* whose.

West, Westen, *n.m.* west.

Weste. -n, *n.f.* vest, waistcoat.

westlich, *adj.* western; to the west.

westwärts, *adv.* westward.

Wettbewerb, -e, *n.m.* competition.

Wettbewerber, -, *n.m.* competitor, contestant.

Wette, -n, *n.f.* wager, bet.

wetteifern, *vb.* compete, rival.

wetten, *vb.* wager, bet.

Wetter, *n.nt.* weather.

Wetterfahne. -n, *n.f.* weather vane.

Wettermeldung, -en, *n.f.* weather report.

Wetterverhältnisse, *n.pl.* weather conditions.

Wettkampf, -e, *n.m.* match, contest; competition.

Wettlauf, -e, *n.m.* race (on foot).

Wettläufer, -, *n.m.* runner.

Wettrennen, -, *n.nt.* race.

Wettrüsten, *n.nt.* armament race.

Wettspiel, -e, *n.nt.* match, tournament.

Wettstreit, -e, *n.m.* contest, competition; match, race.

wetzen, *vb.* hone, sharpen.

Whisky, -s, *n.m.* whiskey.

wichsen, *vb.* shine; thrash.

Wicht, -e, *n.m.* little fellow.

wichtig, *adj.* important.

Wichtigkeit, *n.f.* importance.

Wichtigtuer, -, *n.m.* busybody, pompous fellow.

Wickel, -, *n.m.* wrapping, compress; curler.

wickeln, *vb.* wind, reel; wrap; curl.

wider, *prep.* against, contrary to.

widerfah'ren*, *vb.* happen to.

Widerhall, -e, *n.m.* reverberation.

wider-hallen, *vb.* resound, reverberate.

Widerhalt, *n.m.* support.

widerle'gen, *vb.* refute, disprove.

Widerle'gung, -en, *n.f.* refutation, disproof, rebuttal.

widerlich, *adj.* distasteful, repulsive.

widernatürlich, *adj.* perverse.

widerra'ten*, *vb.* dissuade.

widerrechtlich, *adj.* illegal.

Widerrede, -n, *n.f.* contradiction.

Widerruf, -e, *n.m.* revocation; cancellation.

widerru'fen*, *vb.* revoke, repeal; retract; cancel.

Widersacher, -, *n.m.* antagonist.

Widerschein, *n.m.* reflection.

widerset'zen, *vb.* (sich w.) oppose.

Widersinn, *n.m.* absurdity.

widersinnig, *adj.* absurd, preposterous.

widerspenstig, *adj.* recalcitrant, contrary.

wider-spiegeln, *ib.* reflect.

widerspre'chen*, *vb.* contradict.

widerspre'chend, *adj.* contradictory.

Widerspruch, -e, *n.m.* contradiction, disagreement.

Widerstand, -e, *n.m.* resistance.

widerstandsfähig, *adj.* resistant, tough.

Widerstandskraft, -e, *n.f.* power of resistance, resilience.

widerstandslos, *adj.* without resistance.

widerste'hen*, *vb.* resist, withstand.

widerstre'ben, *vb.* resist; be repugnant.

Widerstre'ben, *n.nt.* reluctance.

widerstre'bend, *adj.* reluctant.

Widerstreit, -e, *n.m.* antagonism, conflict.

widerstrei'ten*, *vb.* resist, conflict with.

widerwärtig, *adj.* repugnant, repulsive.

Widerwille(n), *n.m.* distaste.

widerwillig, *adj.* unwilling, reluctant.

widmen, *vb.* dedicate, devote.

Widmung, -en, *n.f.* dedication.

widrig, *adj.* contrary.

widrigenfalls, *adv.* failing which, otherwise.

wie, 1. *conj.* how; as. **2.** *adv.* how.

wieder, *adv.* again; back, in return.

Wiederauf'bau, *n.m.* reconstruction.

Wiederauf'erstehung, *n.f.* resurrection.

Wiederauf'rüstung, -en, *n.f.* rearmament.

Wiederauf'wertung, -en, *n.f.* revaluation.

Wiederbelebung, -en, *n.f.* revival.

wiederein'-setzen, *vb.* reinstate.

wiederein'-stellen, *vb.* reinstate.

wieder-erkennen*, *vb.* recognize.

Wiedererkennung, -en, *n.f.* recognition.

wieder-erlangen, *vb.* retrieve.

wieder-erstatten, *vb.* reimburse, refund.

wieder-finden*, *vb.* recover.

Wiedergabe, -n, *n.f.* return; rendition, reproduction.

wieder-geben*, *vb.* return, restore.

Wiedergeburt, *n.f.* rebirth.

wieder-gewinnen*, *vb.* recover, regain.

Wiedergewinnung, -en, *n.f.* recovery.

wiedergut'-machen, *vb.* redress, restitute, right.

Wiedergut'machung, -en, *n.f.* restitution, redress.

wiederher'-stellen, *vb.* restore.

Wiederher'stellung, -en, *n.f.* restoration.

wiederho'len, *vb.* repeat.

Wiederho'lung, -en, *n.f.* repetition.

Wiederhören, *n.nt.* hearing again; (**auf W.**) good-bye (at the end of a telephone call).

Wiederinstand'setzung, -en, *n.f.* reconditioning.

Wiederkehr, *n.f.* return, recurrence.

wieder·kehren, *vb.* return.

Wiedersehen, *n.nt.* seeing again: **(auf W.)** good-bye.

Wiedervereinigung, *n.f.* re-unification.

wieder·verheiraten, *vb.* **(sich w.)** remarry.

wieder·versöhnen, *vb.* reconcile.

Wiederversöhnung, **-en,** *n.f.* reconciliation.

Wiege, -n, *n.f.* cradle.

wiegen, *vb.* rock.

wiegen*, *vb.* weigh.

Wiegenlied, -er, *n.nt.* lullaby.

wiehern, *vb.* neigh.

Wiese, -n, *n.f.* meadow.

wieso', *adv.* how so, why.

wild, *adj.* wild, ferocious, savage.

Wild, *n.nt.* game.

Wild-, *n.m.* savage.

Wildbret, *n.nt.* game.

Wildfang, ⸗e, *n.m.* tomboy.

Wildheit, *n.f.* ferocity, fierceness.

Wildleder, -, *n.nt.* chamois, suede.

Wildnis, -se, *n.f.* wilderness.

Wille(n), *n.m.* will.

willenlos, *adj.* irresolute, passive, shifting.

Willenskraft, *n.f.* willpower.

willensstark(⸚), *adj.* strong-willed, resolute.

willfah'ren*, *vb.* comply with, gratify.

willfährig, *adj.* complaisant.

willig, *adj.* willing, ready.

Willkom'men, *n.nt.* welcome.

Willkür, *n.f.* arbitrariness, choice.

willkürlich, *adj.* arbitrary.

wimmeln, *vb.* swarm.

wimmern, *vb.* moan.

Wimper, -n, *n.f.* eyelash.

Wind, -e, *n.m.* wind.

Winde, -n, *n.f.* reel.

Windel, -n, *n.f.* diaper.

winden*, *vb.* wind, coil; **(sich w.)** squirm.

Windhund, -e, *n.m.* greyhound.

windig, *adj.* windy.

Windmühle, -n, *n.f.* windmill.

Windpocken, *n.pl.f.* chickenpox.

Windschutzscheibe, **-n,** *n.f.* windshield.

windstill, *adj.* calm.

Windstoß, ⸗e, *n.m.* gust.

Windzug, *n.m.* draft.

Wink, -e, *n.m.* sign, wave; *(fig.)* hint, tip.

Winkel, -, *n.m.* angle, corner.

Winkelzug, ⸗e, *n.m.* dodge, subterfuge.

winken, *vb.* wave, beckon.

winseln, *vb.* whimper, wail.

Winter, -, *n.m.* winter.

Winterfrische, *n.f.* winter resort.

Wintergarten, ⸚, *n.m.* conservatory.

winterlich, *adj.* wintry.

Winzer, -, *n.m.* wine-grower.

winzig, *adj.* tiny, minute.

Wippe, -n, *n.f.* seesaw.

wir, *pron.* we.

Wirbel, -, *n.m.* whirl, whirlpool; cowlick; vertebra.

wirbeln, *vb.* whirl.

Wirbelsäule, -n, *n.f.* vertebral column, spine.

Wirbelsturm, ⸗e, *n.m.* cyclone.

Wirbeltier, -e, *n.nt.* vertebrate.

wirken, *vb.* work, effect; **(w. auf)** effect.

wirklich, *adj.* real, actual.

Wirklichkeit, *n.f.* reality.

Wirklichkeitsflucht, *n.f.* escapism.

wirklichkeitsnah, *adj.* realistic.

wirksam, *adj.* effective.

Wirksamkeit, *n.f.* effectiveness, validity; **(in W. treten*),** take effect.

Wirkung, -en, *n.f.* effect.

Wirkungskraft, *n.f.* effect, efficacy.

wirkungslos, *adj.* ineffectual.

wirkungsvoll, *adj.* effective.

wirr, *adj.* confused.

Wirrnis, -se, *n.f.* tangle, confusion.

Wirrwarr, *n.nt.* confusion, maze.

Wirt, -e, *n.m.* host; landlord; proprietor.

Wirtin, -nen, *n.f.* hostess; landlady.

Wirtschaft, -en, *n.f.* inn, tavern; household; economy.

wirtschaften, *vb.* manage; keep house.

Wirtschafterin, -nen, *n.f.* housekeeper.

wirtschaftlich, *adj.* economic(al).

Wirtschaftlichkeit, *n.f.* economy.

Wirtschaftsabkommen, -, *n.nt.* trade agreement.

Wirtschaftsprüfer, -, *n.m.* certified public accountant.

Wirtschaftswissenschaft, *n.f.* economics.

Wirtshaus, ⸚er, *n.nt.* inn.

Wisch, -e, *n.m.* scrap.

wischen, *vb.* wipe.

Wischlappen, -, *n.m.* cleaning rag.

wispern, *vb.* whisper.

Wißbegier, *n.f.* desire for knowledge; curiosity.

wissen*, *vb.* know.

Wissen, *n.nt.* learning, knowledge.

Wissenschaft, -en, *n.f.* learning, knowledge, science, scholarship.

wissenschaftlich, *adj.* scientific, scholarly.

wissenswert, *adj.* worth knowing.

wissentlich, *adv.* knowingly.

wittern, *vb.* smell; suspect.

Witterung, *n.f.* weather.

Witterungsverhältnisse, *n.pl.* weather conditions.

Witwe, -n, *n.f.* widow.

Witwer, -, *n.m.* widower.

Witz, -e, *n.m.* joke, pun, gag.

Witzbold,-e, *n.m.* joker, wise guy.

witzeln, *vb.* quip.

witzig, *adj.* witty, humorous.

witzlos, *adj.* pointless, fatuous.

wo, *adv.* where, in what place.

woan'ders, *adv.* elsewhere.

wobei', *adv.* whereby.

Woche, -n, *n.f.* week.

Wochenblatt, ⸚er, *n.nt.* weekly paper.

Wochenende, -n, *n.nt.* weekend.

Wochenschau, *n.f.* newsreel.

Wochentag, -e, *n.m.* weekday.

wöchentlich, *adj.* weekly.

wodurch', *adv.* through what; whereby.

wofern', *conj.* in so far as.

Woge, -n, *n.f.* wave, billow.

wogen, *vb.* wave, heave.

woher', *adv.* whence, from where.

wohl, *adv.* well; presumably, I suppose.

Wohl, *n.nt.* well-being, good health; **(zum W,)** here's to you.

wohlbedacht, *adj.* well-considered.

Wohlbehagen, *n.nt.* comfort.

Wohlergehen, *n.nt.* welfare.

wohlerzogen, *adj.* well brought up.

Wohlfahrt, *n.f.* welfare.

Wohlfahrtsstaat, -en, *n.m.* welfare state.

Wohlgefallen, *n.nt.* pleasure.

wohlgefällig, *adj.* pleasant, agreeable.

wohlgemerkt, *adv.* nota bene.

wohlgemut, *adj.* cheerful.

wohlgeneigt, *adj.* affectionate.

Wohlgeruch, ⸚e, *n.m.* fragrance.

wohlhabend, *adj.* prosperous, well-to-do.

wohlig, *adj.* comfortable.

wohlklingend, *adj.* melodious.

wohlriechend, *adj.* fragrant.

wohlschmeckend, *adj.* tasty.

Wohlsein, *n.nt.* good health; **(zum W.)** your health.

Wohlstand, *n.m.* prosperity.

Wohltat, -en, *n.f.* benefit; pleasure.

Wohltäter, -, *n.m.* benefactor.

wohltätig, *adj.* charitable.

Wohltätigkeit, -en. *n.f.* charity.

wohltuend, *adj.* beneficial, pleasant, soothing.

wohlweislich, *adv.* well-knowingly.

Wohlwollen, *n.nt.* benevolence, good will.

wohlwollend, *adj.* benevolent.

wohnen, *vb.* reside, live, dwell.

wohnhaft, *adj.* resident.

wohnlich, *adj.* comfortable, cozy.

Wohnort, -e, *n.m.* domicile, place of residence.

Wohnsitz, -e, *n.m.* residence.

Wohnung, -en, *n.f.* apartment, place of living.

Wohnwagen, -, *n.m.* trailer.

wölben, *vb.* (**sich w.**) arch over.

Wolf, ¨e, *n.m.* wolf.

Wolke, -n, *n.f.* cloud.

Wolkenbruch, ¨e, *n.m.* cloudburst.

wolkenlos, *adj.* cloudless.

Wolle, *n.f.* wool.

wollen, *adj.* woolen.

wollen*, *vb.* want, be willing, intend.

wollig, *adj.* fluffy, fleecy.

Wollust, *n.f.* voluptuousness, lust.

wollüstig, *adj.* lascivious.

womög'lich, *adv.* if possible.

Wonne, -n, *n.f.* delight.

wonnig, *adj.* charming, delightful.

Wort, -e *or* ¨**er,** *n.nt.* word.

Wortart, -en, *n.f.* part of speech.

Wörterbuch, ¨er, *n.nt.* dictionary.

Wörterverzeichnis, -se, *n.nt.* vocabulary.

Wortführer, -, *n.m.* spokesman.

wortgetreu, *adj.* literal, verbatim.

wortkarg, *adj.* taciturn.

Wortlaut, -e, *n.m.* wording, text.

wörtlich, *adj.* literal.

wortlos, *adj.* speechless.

wortreich, *adj.* wordy, verbose.

Wortschatz, ¨e, *n.m.* vocabulary.

Wortspiel, -e, *n.nt.* pun.

Wortwechsel, -, *n.m.* altercation.

Wrack, -s, *n.nt.* wreck.

wringer*, *vb.* wring.

Wucher, *n.m.* usury.

wucherisch, *adj.* usurious.

Wuchs, *n.m.* growth, figure, height.

Wucht, *n.f.* weight; momentum.

wühlen, *vb.* burrow, rummage; (*fig.*) agitate.

wühlerisch, *adj.* inflammatory, subversive.

wulstig, *adj.* thick.

wund, *adj.* sore, wounded.

Wunde, -n, *n.f.* wound.

Wunder, -, *n.nt.* miracle, wonder.

wunderbar, *adj.* wonderful, miraculous.

Wunderdoktor, -en, *n.m.* quack.

Wunderkind, -er, *n.nt.* child prodigy.

wunderlich, *adj.* strange.

wundern, *vb.* surprise; (**sich w.**) be surprised.

wundersam, *adj.* wondrous.

wunderschön, *adj.* lovely, exquisite.

wundervoll, *adj.* wonderful.

Wundmal, -e, *n.nt.* scar; (*pl.*) stigmata.

Wunsch, ¨e, *n.m.* wish, desire.

wünschen, *vb.* wish, desire, want.

wünschenswert, *adj.* desirable.

Würde, *n.f.* dignity.

Würdenträger, -, *n.m.* dignitary.

würdig, *adj.* worthy, dignified.

würdigen, *vb.* honor, appreciate.

Wurf, ¨e, *n.m.* throw; litter, brood.

Würfel, -, *n.m.* cube; (*pl.*) dice.

Würfelzucker, *n.m.* lump sugar.
Wurfpfeil, -e, *n.m.* dart.
würgen, *vb.* choke; retch; strangle.
Wurm, ▔er, *n.m.* worm.
wurmen, *vb.* annoy, rankle.
wurmstichig, *adj.* wormy.
Wurst, ▔e, *n.f.* sausage.
Würstchen, -, *n.nt.* **(heißes W.)** frankfurter.
Würze, -n, *n.f.* seasoning, flavor.
Wurzel, -n, *n.f.* root.
würzen, *vb.* season, spice.
würzig, *adj.* aromatic, spicy.
wüst, *adj.* waste, desolate; unkempt; wild; vulgar.
Wüste, -n, *n.f.* desert.
Wut, *n.f.* rage, fury.
wüten, *vb.* rage.
wüt.nd, *adj.* furious.

X

x-beliebig, *adj.* any old, any ... at all; **(jeder x-beliebige)** every Tom, Dick, and Harry.
X-beinig, *adj.* knock-kneed.
X-Strahlen, *n.pl.* x-rays.
Xylophon′, -e, *n.nt.* xylophone.

Y

Yacht, -en, *n.f.* yacht.

Z

Zacke, -n, *n.f.* jag; spike; (fork) prong; (dress) edging.
zacken, *vb.* indent, notch.

zackig, *adj.* jagged; notched; snappy.
zag, *adj.* faint-hearted.
zagen, *vb.* hesitate.
zaghaft, *adj.* timid.
zäh, *adj.* tough, tenacious.
zähflüssig, *adj.* viscous.
Zähigkeit, *n.f.* tenacity, perseverance.
Zahl, -en, *n.f.* number, figure.
zahlen, *vb.* pay; **(Herr Ober, bitte z.)** waiter, the check please.
zählen, *vb.* count.
Zahlenangaben, *n.pl.* figures.
zahlenmäßig, *adj.* numerical.
Zähler, -, *n.m.* meter.
Zahlkarte, -n, *n.f.* money order.
zahllos, *adj.* countless.
zahlreich, *adj.* numerous.
Zahltag, -e, *n.m.* payday.
Zahlung, -en, *n.f.* payment.
zahlungsfähig, *adj.* solvent.
Zahlungsmittel, -, *n.nt.* tender, currency.
zahlungsunfähig, *adj.* insolvent.
Zahlwort, ▔er, *n.nt.* numeral.
zahm *adj.* tame.
zähmen, *vb.* tame, domesticate.
Zahn, ▔e, *n.m.* tooth; *(tech.)* cog.
Zahnarzt, ▔e, *n.m.* dentist.
Zahnbürste, -n, *n.f.* toothbrush.
zahnen, *vb.* teeth.
Zahnfleisch, *n.nt.* gum.
Zahnheilkunde, *n.f.* dentistry.
Zahnpaste, -n, *n.f.* toothpaste.
Zahnplombe, -n, *n.f.* filling.
Zahnputzmittel, -, *n.nt.* dentrifice.
Zahnradbahn, -en, *n.f.* cog railroad.
Zahnschmerzen, *n.pl.* toothache.
Zahnstein, *n.m.* tartar.

Zahnstocher, -, *n.m.* toothpick.

Zahnweh, *n.nt.* toothache.

Zange, -n, *n.f.* pliers; forceps.

Zank, *n.m.* quarrel.

zanken, *vb.* **(sich z.)** quarrel, bicker.

Zapfen, -, *n.m.* peg, plug.

zapfen, *vb.* tap.

Zapfenstreich, *n.m.* tattoo, retreat to quarters.

zappelig, *adj.* fidgety.

zappeln, *vb.* flounder, fidget.

Zar, -en, -en, *n.m.* czar.

zart, *adj.* tender, dainty.

Zartheit, -en, *n.f.* tenderness, daintiness.

zärtlich, *adj.* tender, affectionate.

Zauber, -, *n.m.* enchantment, spell, charm, fascination.

Zauberei', *n.f.* sorcery, magic.

Zauberer, -, *n.m.* magician, wizard.

zauberhaft, *adj.* enchanting.

Zauberkraft, -e, *n.f.* magic power.

Zauberkunst, -e, *n.f.* magic.

Zauberspruch, -e, *n.m.* incantation, charm.

zaudern, *vb.* hesitate.

Zaum, -e, *n.m.* bridle.

zäumen, *vb.* bridle.

Zaun, -e, *n.m.* fence.

zausen, *vb.* tousle.

Zebra, -s, *n.nt.* zebra.

Zeche, -n, *n.f.* bill for drinks; mine, colliery.

zechen, *vb.* drink, carouse.

Zeder, -n, *n.f.* cedar.

Zeh, -en, *n.m.* toe.

Zehe, -n, *n.f.* toe.

Zehenspitze, -n, *n.f.* tip of the toe; **(auf Z.n gehen)** tiptoe.

zehn, *num.* ten.

zehnt-, *adj.* tenth.

Zehntel, -, *n.nt.* tenth; **(ein z.)** one-tenth.

zehren, *vb.* **(z. an)** wear out, consume; **(z. von)** live on.

Zeichen, -, *n.nt.* sign, mark, token.

Zeichenfilm, -e, *n.m.* animated cartoon.

zeichnen, *vb.* draw; initial; *(comm.)* subscribe.

Zeichner, -, *n.m.* draftsman.

Zeichnung, -en, *n.f.* drawing, *(comm.)* subscription.

Zeigefinger, -, *n.m.* forefinger.

zeigen, *vb.* show, indicate, point; demonstrate; exhibit.

Zeiger, -, *n.m.* (clock) hand.

Zeile, -n, *n.f.* line.

Zeit, -en, *n.f.* time.

Zeitalter, -, *n.nt.* age, era.

Zeitaufnahme, -n, *n.f.* time exposure.

Zeitdauer, *n.f.* period of time.

Zeitgeist, *n.m.* spirit of the times.

zeitgemäß, *adj.* timely.

Zeitgenosse, -n, -n, *n.m.* contemporary.

zeitgenössisch, *adj.* contemporary.

zeitig, *adj.* early.

zeitlich, 1. *adj.* temporal. **2.** *adv.* in time.

zeitlos, *adj.* timeless, ageless.

Zeitmangel, *n.m.* lack of time.

Zeitpunkt, -e, *n.m.* time, moment.

zeitraubend, *adj.* time-consuming.

Zeitraum, -e, *n.m.* period.

Zeitschrift, -en, *n.f.* magazine, journal, periodical.

Zeitspanne, -n, *n.f.* period of time.

Zeitung, -en, *n.f.* newspaper.

Zeitungsanzeige, -n, *n.f.* ad, announcement.

Zeitungsausschnitt, -e, *n.m.* newspaper clipping.

Zeitungshändler, -, *n.m.* newsdealer.

Zeitungsjunge, -n, -n, *n.m.* paper-boy.

Zeitungsnotiz, -en, *n.f.* press item.

Zeitvertreib, *n.m.* pastime.

zeitweilig, *adj.* temporary.

Zeitwort, -er, *n.nt.* verb.

Zelle, -n, *n.f.* cell.

zellig, adj. cellular.

Zellophan', n.nt. cellophane.

Zellstoff, -e, n.m. cellulose.

Zelluloid', n.nt. celluloid.

Zellulo'se, n.f. cellulose.

Zelt, -e, n.nt. tent.

zelten, vb. live in a tent, camp.

Zelter, -, n.m. camper.

Zement', -e, n.m. cement, concrete.

zensie'ren, vb. censor; (school) grade, mark.

Zensor, -'oren n.m. censor.

Zensur', -en, n.f. censorship; (school) grade, mark.

Zensus, n.m. census.

Zentime'ter, -, n.nt. centimeter.

Zentner, -, n.m. 100 German pounds.

zentral', adj. central.

Zentral'heizung, n.f. central heating.

zentralisie'ren, vb. centralize.

Zentrum, -tren, n.nt. center.

zerbre'chen*, vb. break to pieces, shatter.

zerbrech'lich, adj. fragile, frail.

zerbrö'ckeln, vb. crumble.

zerdrü'cken, vb. crush.

Zeremonie', -i'en, n.f. ceremony.

zeremoniell', adj. ceremonial.

zerfah'ren, adj. absentminded, scatter-brained.

Zerfall', n.m. ruin, decay.

zerfal'len*, vb. fall into ruin, disintegrate; **(in Teile z.)** be divided.

zerfet'zen, vb. tear into shreds.

zerflei'schen, vb. mangle.

zerfres'sen*, vb. erode, corrode.

zerge'hen*, vb. dissolve, melt.

zerglie'dern, vb. dismember, dissect.

zerklei'nern, vb. reduce to small pieces, crush; (wood) chop.

zerknaut'schen, vb. crumple.

zerknirscht', adj. contrite.

zerknül'len, vb. crumple.

zerlas'sen*, vb. dissolve, melt.

zerle'gen, vb. separate, cut up, carve.

zerlumpt', adj. ragged.

zermal'men, vb. crunch.

zermar'tern, vb. torture; **(den Kopf z.)** rack one's brain.

zermür'ben, vb. wear down.

zermür'bung, -en, n.f. attrition.

zerpflü'cken, vb. pick to pieces.

zerquet'schen, vb. squash.

Zerrbild, -er, n.nt. distorted picture, caricature.

zerrei'ßen*, vb. tear up, rend.

zerren, vb. tug, pull.

zerrin'nen*, vb. disappear, melt away.

zerrüt'ten, vb. ruin.

Zerrüt'tung, -en, n.f. ruin.

zerschla'gen*, vb. smash, shatter.

zerschmei'ßen*, vb. smash.

zerset'zen, vb. decompose.

zerset'zend, adj. subversive.

Zerset'zung, -en, n.f. decomposition; subversion.

zersprin'gen*, vb. burst.

zerstäu'ben, vb. pulverize; atomize; scatter.

zerstö'ren, vb. destroy, demolish.

zerstö'rend, adj. destructive.

Zerstö'rung, -en, n.f. destruction, demolition.

zerstreu'en, vb. scatter, divert, amuse.

zerstreut', adj. absentminded.

Zerstreu'ung, -en, n.f. scattering; relaxation, amusement.

zertei'len, vb. cut up; separate, divide.

zertren'nen, vb. sever; (dress) cut up.

zertre'ten*, vb. trample.

zertrüm'mern, *vb.* wreck, demolish.

Zerwürf'nis, -se, *n.nt.* discord, quarrel.

zerzau'sen, *vb.* tousle, rumple.

Zettel, -, *n.m.* slip of paper, note, sticker, bill.

Zeug, -e, *n.nt.* stuff, material, cloth.

Zeuge, -n, -n, *n.m.* witness.

zeugen, *vb.* testify, give evidence; beget, create, produce.

Zeugenaussage, -n, *n.f.* testimony.

Zeugnis, -se, *n.nt.* testimony, evidence; reference (for a job); (school) report card.

Zicho'rie, -n, *n.f.* chickory.

Zickzack, -e, *n.m.* zigzag.

Ziege, -n, *n.f.* (she-)goat.

Ziegel, -, *n.m.* tile.

Ziegelstein, -e, *n.m.* brick.

Ziegenbock, ᵉe, *n.m.* billygoat.

Ziegenpeter, *n.m.* mumps.

ziehen*, *vb.* (*intr.*) move, go, draw, be drafty; (*tr.*) pull, drag, draw, tug; cultivate.

Ziehharmonika, -s, *n.f.* accordion.

Ziehung, -en, *n.f.* drawing.

Ziel, -e, *n.nt.* goal, target, end, objective.

zielbewußt, *adj.* with a clear goal, resolute.

zielen, *vb.* aim.

ziellos, *adj.* aimless, erratic.

Zielscheibe, -n, *n.f.* target.

ziemen, *vb.* be fitting for; (**sich z.**) be proper.

ziemlich, 1. *adj.* suitable, fitting; pretty much of. **2.** *adv.* pretty, rather, quite.

Zier, *n.f.* ornament(ation).

Zierat, -e, *n.m.* or **-en**, *n.f.* ornament, decoration.

Zierde, -n, *n.f.* ornament; honor.

zieren, *vb.* adorn, ornament.

zierlich, *adj.* dainty.

Ziffer, -n, *n.f.* figure, numeral.

Zifferblatt, ᵉer, *n.nt.* dial, face (of a clock).

Zigaret'te, -n, *n.f.* cigarette.

Zigar're, -n, *n.f.* cigar.

Zigeu'ner, -, *n.m.* gypsy.

Zimbel, -n, *n.f.* cymbal.

Zimmer, -, *n.nt.* room.

Zimmerdecke, -n, *n.f.* ceiling.

Zimmermädchen, -, *n.nt.* chambermaid.

Zimmermann, -leute, *n.m.* carpenter.

zimperlich, *adj.* finicky, prim.

Zimt, *n.m.* cinnamon.

Zinke, -n, *n.f.* prong.

Zinn, *n.nt.* tin, pewter.

Zipfel, -, *n.m.* tip.

Zins, -en, *n.m.* interest.

Zinseszins, -en, *n.m.* compound interest.

Zinssatz, ᵉe, *n.m.* rate of interest.

Zirkel, -, *n.m.* compass (for making a circle).

zirkulie'ren, *vb.* circulate.

zirkulie'rend, *adj.* circulatory.

Zirkus, -se, *n.m.* circus.

zirpen, *vb.* chirp.

zischen, *vb.* hiss, sizzle; whiz.

ziselie'ren, *vb.* engrave, chase.

Zitadel'le, -n, *n.f.* citadel.

Zitat', -e, *n.nt.* quotation.

zitie'ren, *vb.* quote, cite.

Zitro'ne, -n, *n.f.* lemon.

zittern, *vb.* quiver, shiver, tremble.

zivil', *adj.* civil; reasonable.

Zivil', *n.nt.* civilians; civilian clothes.

Zivil'bevölkerung, -en, *n.f.* civilian population.

Zivilisation', -en, *n.f.* civilization.

zivilisie'ren, *vb.* civilize.

Zivilist', -en, -en, *n.m.* civilian.

Zobel, *n.m.* sable.

zögern, *vb.* hesitate.

Zögern, *n.nt.* hesitation.

zögernd, *adj.* hesitant.

Zölibat', *n.m.* or *nt.* celibacy.

Zoll, -, *n.m.* inch.

Zoll, ᵉe, *n.m.* tariff duty, toll.

Zollamt, ⸚er, *n.nt.* custom house.

Zollbeamt-, *n.m.* customs officer.

zollfrei, *adj.* duty free.

zollpflichtig, *adj.* subject to duty.

Zolltarif, -e, *n.m.* tariff.

Zollverein, -e, *n.m.* customs union.

Zollverschluß, *n.m.* customs seal; (unter Z.) under bond.

Zöllner, -, *n.m.* customs collector; (Bible) publican.

Zone, -, *n.f.* zone.

Zoo, -s, *n.m.* zoo.

Zoologie, *n.f.* zoology.

zoolo'gisch, *adj.* zoological.

Zorn, *n.m.* ire, wrath, anger.

zornig, *adj.* angry.

zottig, *adj.* shaggy.

zu, *adv.* too; closed.

zu, *prep.* to.

Zubehör, *n.nt.* accessories, appurtenances, trimmings.

zu-bereiten, *vb.* prepare.

Zubereitung, -en, *n.f.* preparation.

zu-bringen*, *vb.* bring to; pass, spend.

Zucht, -en, *n.f.* breed(ing), rearing, education, training, decency.

züchten, *vb.* breed, raise.

Züchter, -, *n.m.* breeder.

Zuchthaus, ⸚er, *n.nt.* penitentiary.

züchtig, *adj.* chaste, demure.

züchtigen, *vb.* chasten, chastise.

zucken, *vb.* twitch, jerk, flash.

Zucker, *n.m.* sugar.

Zuckerbäcker, -, *n.m.* confectioner.

Zuckerguß, ⸚sse, *n.m.* icing.

Zuckerkrankheit, *n.f.* diabetes.

Zuckerwerk, *n.nt.* confectionery.

Zuckung, -en, *n.f.* twitch, convulsion.

zu-decken, *vb.* cover up.

zudem', *adv.* in addition.

zudringlich, *adj.* intruding, obtrusive.

Zueignung, -en, *n.f.* dedication.

zueinan'der, *adv.* to one another.

zu-erkennen*, *vb.* award.

zuerst', *adv.* first, at first.

Zufall, ⸚e, *n.m.* chance, coincidence.

zufällig, **1.** *adj.* chance, fortuitous. **2.** *adv.* by chance.

Zuflucht, *n.f.* refuge; recourse.

Zufluchtsort, -e, *n.m.* place of refuge.

Zufluß, ⸚sse, *n.m.* flowing in, influx.

zufol'ge, *prep.* as a result of; according to.

zufrie'den, *adj.* content, satisfied.

zufrie'den-stellen, *vb.* satisfy.

zu-frieren*, *vb.* freeze over, freeze up.

zu-fügen, *vb.* inflict.

Zufuhr, -en, *n.f.* bringing in, importation, supply.

zu-führen, *vb.* bring to, import, supply.

Zug, ⸚e, *n.m.* pull, drawing, draft; stroke; feature trait; move; train; procession; trend; flight; (mil.) squad.

Zugabe, -n, *n.f.* bonus, premium, encore.

Zugang, ⸚e, *n.m.* access, approach.

zugänglich, *adj.* accessible, approachable.

zu-geben*, *vb.* give in addition; admit.

zugegebenerma'ßen, *adv.* admittedly.

zuge'gen, *adv.* present.

zugehörig, *adj.* belonging to, pertinent.

Zügel, -, *n.m.* rein; restraint.

zügellos, *adj.* unbridled, unrestrained.

zügeln, *vb.* bridle, curb, check.

zugestandenerma'ßen, *adv.* avowedly.

Zugeständnis, -se, *n.nt.* confession; concession.

zu·gestehen*, vb. confess, concede.

zugetan, adj. devoted to, fond of.

zugig, adj. drafty.

Zugkraft, n.f. pull, thrust.

zugleich', adv. at the same time.

zu·greifen*, vb. lend a hand; help oneself.

zugrun'de, adv. at the bottom, as a basis; (z. gehen*) go to ruin, perish; (z. richten) ruin, destroy.

zugun'sten, adv.&prep. for the benefit of, in favor of.

zugu'te, adv. for the benefit of.

zu·haken, vb. hook.

zu·halten*, vb. keep shut.

zuhan'den, adv. at hand.

zu·hören, vb. listen to.

Zuhörer, -, n.m. listener, auditor; (pl.) audience.

Zuhörerraum, ⸗e, n.m. auditorium.

Zuhörerschaft, -en, n.f. audience.

zu·kleben, vb. paste together.

zu·knallen, vb. slam.

zu·knöpfen, vb. button up.

zu·knüpfen, vb. tie, knot, fasten.

zu·kommen*, vb. be one's due; be proper for.

Zukunft, n.f. future.

zukünftig, adj. future.

Zulage, -n, n.f. extra pay, pay raise.

zu·langen, vb. help oneself.

zulänglich, adj. adequate.

zu·lassen*, vb. leave closed; admit; permit.

zuläs'sig, adj. permissible, admissi⸗le.

Zulauf, n./. run; (Z. haben*) be popular.

zu·laufen*, vb. run to, to.

zu·legen, vb. add; (sich etwas z.) acquire.

zulei'de, adv. (z. tun*) hurt, harm.

zuletzt', adv. at last, finally.

zulie'be, adv. for the sake of.

zu·machen, vb. shut.

zumal', 1. adv. especially; together. 2. conj. especially because.

zu·mauern, vb. wall up.

zumeist', adv. for the most part.

zu·messen*, vb. allot.

zumin'dest, adv. at least.

zumu'te, adv. (z. sein*) feel, be in a mood.

zu·muten, vb. expect, demand.

Zumutung, -en, n.f. imposition.

zunächst', adv. first of all.

Zunahme, -n, n.f. increase.

Zuname(n), -, n.m. surname, last name.

zünden, vb. ignite; (fig.) inflame.

Zünder, -, n.m. fuse.

zündend, adj. inflammatory.

Zündholz, ⸗er, n.nt. match.

Zündkerze, -n, n.f. spark plug.

Zündschlüssel, -, n.m. ignition key.

Zündstoff, -e, n.m. fuel.

Zündung, n.f. ignition; detonation.

zu·nehmen*, vb. grow, increase; (moon) wax; put on weight.

zu·neigen, vb. incline.

Zuneigung, -en, n.f. inclination; affection.

Zunft, ⸗e, n.f. guild.

Zunge, -n, n.f. tongue.

zungenfertig, adj. glib.

zunich'te, adv. to nothing, ruined; (z. machen) ruin, frustrate.

zunut'ze, adv. (z. machen) profit by, utilize.

zuo'berst, adv. at the top.

zu·packen, vb. (fig.) get to work.

zupfen, vb. pull, (wool) pick.

zu·raten*, vb. advise in favor of.

zurechnungsfähig, adj. accountable.

zurecht', adv. right, in good order.

zurecht'·finden*, vb. (sich z.) find one's way.

urecht'.machen, vb. prepare.

a.reden, vb. urge, encourage.

ureichend, adj. sufficient.

u.richten, vb. prepare; **(übel z.)** maul.

irnen, vb. be angry.

urschau'stellung, -en, n.f. display.

urück', adv. back, behind.

urück'.behalten*, vb. keep back.

urück'.bleiben*, vb. lag behind.

urück'.bringen*, vb. return.

urück'.drängen, vb. drive back.

urück'.erstatten, vb. reimburse.

urück'.fahren*, vb. drive back; recoil.

urück'.fallen*, vb. fall back; relapse.

urück'.führen, vb. lead back; trace back, attribute.

urück'.geben*, vb. return.

urück'geblieben, adj. backward.

urück'gebliebenheit, n.f. backwardness.

urück'.gehen*, vb. go back; decline.

urück'gesetzt, adj. (prices) reduced.

urück'gezogen, adj. secluded.

urück'gezogenheit, n.f. seclusion.

urück'.halten*, vb. retain; restrain; withhold.

urück'.haltend, adj. reticent.

urück'haltung, n.f. restraint.

urück'.kehren, vb. return, revert.

urück'.kommen*, vb. return.

urück'.lassen*, vb. leave behind.

urück'.legen, vb. lay aside; accomplish.

urück'.lehnen, vb. **(sich z.)** lean back, recline.

zurück'.liegen*, vb. lie in the past.

zurück'.nehmen*, vb. take back; retract.

zurück'.prallen, vb. recoil, rebound.

zurück'.rufen*, vb. recall.

zurück'.schauen, vb. look back.

zurück'.schlagen*, vb. hit back, repulse.

zurück'.schrecken, vb. be startled; shrink (from).

zurück'.sehen*, vb. look back on; reflect.

zurück'.sehnen, vb. **(sich z.)** long to return.

zurück'.setzen, vb. put back; set aside; reduce.

zurück'.stehen*, vb. stand back; (fig.) be inferior.

zurück'.stellen, vb. set back; set aside; (mil.) defer.

zurück'.stoßen*, vb. repulse.

zurück'.strahlen, vb. reflect.

zurück'.treiben*, vb. repel.

zurück'.treten*, vb. resign.

zurück'.verfolgen, vb. trace.

zurück'.versetzen, vb. put back; **(sich z.)** go back to a time.

zurück'.weichen*, vb. retreat.

zurück'.weisen*, vb. send back; reject.

Zurück'weisung, -en, n.f. rebuff.

zurück'.zahlen, vb. refund, repay.

zurück'.ziehen*, vb. pull back, withdraw; **(sich z.)** withdraw, back out.

Zuruf', -e, n.m. call; shout; acclamation.

Zusage, -n, n.f. acceptance.

zu.sagen, vb. accept; **(es sagt mir zu)** it pleases me, it agrees with me.

zusam'men, adv. together.

Zusam'menarbeit, n.f. cooperation, collaboration.

zusam'men.arbeiten, vb. cooperate, collaborate.

Zusam'menbau, n.m. assemblage.

zusam'men·brauen, *vb.* concoct.

zusam'men·brechen*, *vb.* collapse.

Zusam'menbruch, ⸚e, *n.m.* collapse.

zusam'men·drängen, *vb.* **(sich z.)** crowd together; huddle.

zusam'men·fahren*, *vb.* ride together; crash; be startled, wince.

zusam'men·fassen, *vb.* summarize, recapitulate.

zusam'menfassend, *adj.* comprehensive; summary.

Zusam'menfassung, -en, *n.f.* summary, condensation.

zusam'men·fügen, *vb.* join together.

zusam'men·gehören, *vb.* belong together.

zusam'men·geraten*, *vb.* collide.

zusam'mengesetzt, *adj.* composed; compound.

Zusam'menhang, ⸚e, *n.m.* connection, relation; context; association.

zusam'men·hängen*, *vb.* hang together, be connected, cohere.

zusam'menhängend, *adj.* coherent.

zusam'menhangslos, *adj.* disconnected, incoherent.

zusam'men·häufen, *vb.* pile up.

zusam'men·kauern, *vb.* huddle.

zusam'men·kommen*, *vb.* get together, convene.

Zusam'menkunft, ⸚e, *n.f.* meeting.

zusam'men·laufen*, *vb.* converge.

zusam'men·legen, *vb.* combine, pool, merge.

zusam'men·nehmen*, *vb.* **(sich z.)** pull oneself together.

zusam'men·passen, *vb.* go well together.

Zusam'menprall, -e, *n.m.* collision, impact.

zusam'men·pressen, *vb.* compress.

zusam'men·rechnen, *vb.* add up.

zusam'men·reißen*, *vb.* **(sich z.)** pull oneself together.

zusam'men·rotten, *vb.* **(sich z.)** band together.

zusam'men·rufen*, *vb.* summon, convene.

zusam'men·scharen, *vb.* scrape together; **(sich z.)** band together, cluster.

zusam'men·schließen*, *vb.* join together; **(sich z.)** close ranks.

Zusam'menschluß, ⸚sse, *n.m.* federation, merger.

zusam'men·schrumpfen, *vb.* shrink, dwindle.

zusam'men·setzen, *vb.* combined, compound; **(sich z.)** consist, be composed.

Zusam'mensetzung, -en, *n.f.* combination, composition.

zusam'men·stehen*, *vb.* stand together, stick together.

zusam'men·stellen, *vb.* make up, compile.

Zusam'menstellung, -en, *n.f.* composition, arrangement.

Zusam'menstoß, ⸚e, *n.m.* collision, clash.

zusam'men·stoßen*, *vb.* get together; collide, clash; crash.

zusam'men·strömen, *vb.* flow together, flock together.

zusam'men·stürzen, *vb.* collapse.

zusam'men·tragen*, *vb.* compile.

zusam'men·treffen*, *vb.* meet, encounter; coincide.

Zusam'mentreffen, -, *n.nt.* encounter; coincidence.

zusam'men·treten*, *vb.* convene.

zusam'men·tun, *vb.* put together; **(sich z.)** unite.

zusam'men·wirken, *vb.* work together, collaborate.

zusam'men·zählen, *vb.* sum up.

zusam'men·ziehen*, *vb.*

draw together; **(sich z.)** contract, constrict.

Zusam'menziehung, -en, *n.f.* contraction.

Zusatz, -̈e, *n.m.* addition.

zusätzlich, *adj.* additional, supplementary.

zuschan'den-machen, *vb.* ruin.

zu-schauen, *vb.* look on, watch.

Zuschauer, -, *n.m.* spectator.

zu-schicken, *vb.* send to, forward.

zu-schieben*, *vb.* shove towards; **(die Schuld z.)** put the blame on.

zu-schießen*, *vb.* contribute.

Zuschlag, -̈e, *n.m.* increase; additional charge.

zu-schlagen*, *vb.* strike; bang shut.

zu-schließen*, *vb.* lock.

zu-schneiden*, *vb.* cut out.

zu-schreiben*, *vb.* ascribe, attribute, impute.

Zuschrift, -en, *n.f.* communication.

Zuschuß, -̈sse, *n.m.* subsidy.

zu-sehen*, *vb.* look on, watch.

zusehends, *adv.* visibly.

zu-senden*, *vb.* send, forward.

zu-sichern, *vb.* assure, promise.

Zustand, -̈e, *n.m.* state, condition; situation.

zustan'de-bringen*, *vb.* bring about, achieve, accomplish.

zustan'de-kommen*, *vb.* come about, be accomplished.

zuständig, *adj.* competent, qualified.

Zuständigkeit, -en, *n.f.* competence; jurisdiction.

zustat'ten-kommen*, *vb.* be useful.

zu-stehen*, *vb.* be due to; become, suit; behoove.

zu-stellen, *vb.* deliver.

Zustellung, -en, *n.f.* delivery.

zu-stimmen, *vb.* agree, consent.

Zustimmung, -en, *n.f.* agreement, consent, approval.

zu-stopfen, *vb.* plug.

zu-stoßen*, *vb.* slam tight, meet with, befall.

Zustrom, *n.m.* influx.

Zutat, -en, *n.f.* ingredient.

zu-teilen, *vb.* allot, assign allocate.

zu-trauen, *vb.* believe someone capable of doing.

Zutrauen, *n.nt.* confidence.

zu-treffen*, *vb.* prove right, apply.

zutreffend, *adj.* correct, applicable.

Zutritt, -e, *n.m.* admittance, admission.

Zutun, *n.nt.* assistance.

zuverlässig, *adj.* reliable, trustworthy.

Zuversicht, *n.f.* confidence, trust.

zuversichtlich, *adj.* confident, sure.

zuviel', *adv.* too much.

zuvor', *adv.* beforehand.

zuvor'derst, *adv.* up front.

zuvör'derst, *adv.* first of all.

zuvor'-kommen*, *vb.* anticipate, forestall.

zuvor'kommend, *adj.* obliging, polite.

Zuvor'kommenheit, *n.f.* civility.

Zuwachs, *n.m.* increase, rise, growth.

zu-wandern, *vb.* immigrate.

zuwe'ge-bringen*, *vb.* bring about, achieve.

zuwei'len, *adv.* at times.

zu-weisen*, *vb.* assign, apportion, allot.

Zuweisung, -en, *n.f.* assignment, allocation.

zu-wenden*, *vb.* turn towards; bestow upon.

Zuwendung, -en, *n.f.* donation.

zuwi'der, 1. *adv.* abhorrent, repugnant. **2.** *prep.* contrary to.

zuwi'der-handeln, *vb.* act contrary to, disobey.

zu-zahlen, *vb.* pay extra.
zu-ziehen*, *vb.* pull closed; **(sich etwas z.)** contract, incur.
Zuzug, *n.m.* move, influx.
zuzüglich, *adv.* plus.
Zwang, *n.m.* compulsion, coercion, duress; constraint.
zwanglos, *adj.* unrestrained, informal, casual.
Zwangsarbeit, *n.f.* forced labor; hard labor.
zwangsläufig, *adv.* necessarily.
zwangsräumen, *vb.* evict.
Zwangsverschleppt-, *n.m. &f.* displaced person.
zwangsweise, *adv.* forcibly.
Zwangswirtschaft, *n.f.* controlled economy.
zwanzig *num.* twenty.
zwanzigst-, *adj.* twentieth.
Zwanzigstel, -, *n.nt.* twentieth; **(ein z.)** one-twentieth.
zwar, *adv.* to be sure (means that a *but* is coming); **(und z.)** namely, to give further details.
Zweck, -e, *n.m.* purpose, end, aim.
zweckdienlich, *adj.* expedient.
zweckmäßig, *adj.* expedient.
Zwecke, -n, *n.f.* tack.
zwecks, *prep.* for the purpose of.
zwei, *num.* two.
zweideutig, *adj.* ambiguous.
Zweideutigkeit, -en, *n.f.* ambiguity.
zweierlei, *adj.* of two kinds.
zweifach, *adj.* twofold.
zweifältig, *adj.* twofold, double.
Zweifel, -, *n.m.* doubt.
zweifelhaft, *adj.* doubtful.
zweifellos, *adj.* doubtless.
zweifeln, *vb.* doubt.
Zweifler, -, *n.m.* doubter, sceptic.
Zweig, -e, *n.m.* branch, bough, twig.
Zweikampf, -e, *n.m.* duel.
zweimal, *adv.* twice.
zweimalig, *adj.* repeated, done twice.

zweimonatlich, *adj.* bimonthly.
Zweirad, -er, *n.nt.* bicycle.
zweiseitig, *adj.* two-sided, bilateral.
Zweisitzer, -, *n.m.* two-seater, roadster.
zweit-, *adj.* second.
zweitbest-, *adj.* second-best.
zweiteilig, *adj.* two-piece; bipartite.
zweitens, *adv.* in the second place, secondly.
zweitklassig, *adj.* second-class.
Zwerchfell, -e, *n.nt.* diaphragm.
Zwerg, -e, *n.m.* dwarf; midget.
zwergenhaft, *adj.* dwarfish, diminutive.
Zwetschge, -n, *n.f.* plum.
zwicken, *vb.* pinch.
Zwickmühle, -n, *n.f.* dilemma, jam.
Zwieback, -e *or* **-e,** *n.m.* zwieback, rusk.
Zwiebel, -n, *n.f.* onion.
zwiefach, *adj.* double.
Zwiegespräch, -e, *n.nt.* dialogue.
Zwielicht, *n.nt.* twilight.
zwielichtig, *adj.* shady.
Zwiespalt, -e, *n.m.* discrepancy; discord; schism.
zwiespältig, *adj.* discrepant, conflicting.
Zwilling, -e, *n.m.* twin.
zwingen*, *vb.* force, compel.
zwingend, *adj.* compelling.
Zwinger, -, *n.m.* cage; (dog) kennel.
zwinkern, *vb.* wink.
Zwirn, -e, *n.m.* thread; twine.
Zwirnfaden, -, *n.m.* thread.
zwischen, *prep.* between, among.
Zwischenakt, -e, *n.m.* entr'acte; interval.
Zwischenbemerkung, -en, *n.f.* incidental remark, interruption.
Zwischendeck, -e, *n.nt.* steerage.
Zwischending, -e, *n.nt.*

something halfway between, mixture, cross.

zwischendurch', *adv.* in between; now and then.

Zwischenfall, ⁼e, *n.m.* incident.

Zwischenhändler, -, *n.m.* jobber.

Zwischenlandung, -en, *n.f.* stopover.

Zwischenraum, ⁼e, *n.m.* space in between; interval.

Zwischenruf, -e, *n.m.* interjection, interruption.

Zwischenspiel, -e, *n.nt.* interlude, intermezzo.

Zwischenstock, ⁼e, *n.m.* mezzanine.

Zwischenzeit, *n.f.* interval, interim.

Zwist, -e, *n.m.* quarrel, discord.

zwitschern, *vb.* twitter, chirp.

Zwitter, -, *n.m.* hybrid.

zwo, *num.* two (used especially on the telephone to avoid having *zwei* misunderstood as *drei*).

zwot-, *adj.* second.

zwölf, *num.* twelve.

Zwölffin'gerdarm, ⁼e, *n.m.* duodenum.

zwölft-, *adj.* twelfth.

Zwölftel, -, *n.nt.* twelfth; **(ein z.)** one-twelfth.

Zyklon', -e, *n.m.* cyclone.

Zyklotron, -e, *n.nt.* cyclotron.

Zyklus, **-klen**, *n.m.* cycle.

Zylin'der, -, *n.m.* cylinder; top hat.

Zyniker, -, *n.m.* cynic.

zynisch, *adj.* cynical.

Zypres'se, -n, *n.f.* cypress.

Zyste, -n, *n.f.* cyst.

ENGLISH - GERMAN

A

a, *art.* ein, -, -e.

abandon, *vb.* verlas'sen*.

abandoned, *adj.* verlas'sen; (*depraved*) verwor'fen.

abandonment, *n.* Aufgeben *nt.*

abash, *vb.* beschä'men.

abate, *vb.* nach·lassen*.

abatement, *n.* Vermin'derung, -en *f.*

abbess, *n.* Äbtis'sin, -nen *f.*

abbey, *n.* Abtei', -en *f.*, Kloster, ⁼ *nt.*

abbot, *n.* Abt, ⁼e *m.*

abbreviate, *vb.* ab·kürzen.

abbreviation, *n.* Abkürzung, -en *f.*

abdicate, *vb.* ab·danken.

abdication, *n.* Abdankung, -en *f.*

abdomen, *n.* Unterleib, -er *m.*

abdominal, *adj.* Leib- (*cpds.*).

abduct, *vb.* entfüh'ren.

abduction, *n.* Entfüh'rung, -en *f.*

abductor, *n.* Entfüh'rer, - *m.*

aberration, *n.* Abweichung, -en *f.*

abet, *vb.* an·treiben*, helfen*.

abetment, *n.* Beistand, ⁼e *m.*

abettor, *n.* Helfershelfer, - *m.*

abeyance, *n.* Schwebezustand, ⁼e *m.*

abhor, *vb.* verab'scheuen.

abhorrence, *n.* Abscheu, -e *m.*

abhorrent, *adj.* zuwi'der.

abide, *vb.* (*dwell*) wohnen; (*remain*) bleiben*; (*tolerate*) leiden*.

abiding, *adj.* dauernd.

ability, *n.* Fähigkeit, -en *f.*

abject, *adj.* elend, niedrig, unterwür'fig.

abjure, *vb.* ab·schwören* entsa'gen.

ablative, *n.* Ablativ, -e *m.*

ablaze, *adj.* in Flammen.

able, *adj.* fähig, tüchtig; (**to be a.**) können*.

able-bodied, *adj.* kräftig.

ablution, *n.* Abwaschung -en *f.*

ably, *adv.* fähig, tüchtig.

abnormal, *adj.* ungewöhnlich, abnorm'.

abnormality, *n.* Mißbildung -en *f.*, Abnormität', -en *f.*

aboard, *adv.* an Bord.

abode, *n.* Wohnsitz, -e *m.*, Wohnung, -en *f.*

abolish, *vb.* ab·schaffen.

abolition, *n.* Aufhebung, -en *f.*

abominable, *adj.* abscheulich.

abominate, *vb.* verab'scheuen.

abomination, *n.* Abscheu, -e *m.*

aboriginal, *adj.* ursprünglich, Ur- (*cpds.*).

aborigine, *n.* Ureinwohner, - *m.*

abort, *vb.* fehl·gebären*, ab·treiben*.

abortion, *n.* Fehlgeburt, -en *f.*, Abtreibung, -en *f.*

abortive, *adj.* mißglückt'.

abound, *vb.* im Überfluß vorhanden sein.

about, 1. *adv.* (*approximately*) etwa, ungefähr; (*around*) herum', umher'; (**be a. to**) im Begriff sein. **2.** *prep.* (*around*) um; (*concerning*) über.

about-face, *n.* Kehrtwendung *f.*

above, 1. *adj.* obig. **2.** *adv.* oben. **3.** *prep.* über.

aboveboard, *adj.* offen, unverhoh'len.

abrasion, *n.* Abschaben *nt.*, Abschleifen *nt.*

abrasive, 1. *n.* Schleifmittel,

nt. **2.** *adj.* abschabend, abschleifend.

abreast, *adv.* nebeneinan'der, Seite an Seite.

abridge, *vb.* ab·kürzen.

abridgment, *n.* Abkürzung, -en *f.*

abroad, *adv.* im Ausland.

abrupt, *adj.* schroff.

abruptness, *n.* Schroffheit, -en *f.*

abscess, *n.* Eitergeschwulst, -e *f.*

abscond, *vb.* durch·brennen*.

absence, *n.* Abwesenheit, -en *f.*

absent, *adj.* abwesend.

absentee, *n.* Abwesend- *m.*

absent-minded, *adj.* zerstreut'.

absinthe, *n.* Absinth' -e *m.*

absolute, *adj.* absolut', unbedingt'.

absoluteness, *n.* Unbedingt'heit, -en *f.*

absolution, *n.* Absolution', -en *f.*

absolve, *vb.* frei·sprechen*, entla'sten

absorb, *vb.* auf·saugen, absorbie'ren.

absorbed, *adj. (fig.)* vertieft'.

absorbent, 1. *n.* Absorbie'rungsmittel.- *nt.* **2.** *adj.* aufsaugend.

absorbing, *adj.* aufsaugend; *(interesting)* packend.

absorption, *n.* Absorption', -en *f.*

abstain, *vb.* sich enthal'ten*.

abstemious, *adj.* enthalt'sam.

abstinence, *n.* Enthalt'samkeit, -en *f.*

abstract, 1. *n. (book, article)* Auszug. -e *m.* **2.** *adj.* abstrakt'. **3.** *vb.* abstrahie'ren.

abstraction, *n.* Abstraktion', -en *f.*

abstruse, *adj.* abstrus'.

absurd, *adj.* unsinnig.

absurdity, *n.* Unsinnigkeit, -en *f.*

abundance, *n.* Überfluß, -sse *m.*

abundant, *adj.* überreich.

abuse, 1. *vb.* mißbrau'chen; **2.** *n.* Mißbrauch, -e *m.*

abusive, *adj.* mißbräuchlich, beschimp'fend.

abut, *vb.* an·grenzen.

abutment, *n.* Angrenzung, -en *f.*

abyss, *n.* Abgrund, -e *m.*

academic, *adj.* akade'misch.

academy, *n.* Akademie', -mi·en *f.*, Hochschule, -n *f.*

acanthus, *n.* Akan'thus, -se *m.*

accede, *vb.* ein·willigen.

accelerate, *vb.* beschleunigen.

acceleration, *n.* Beschleu'nigung. -en *f.*

accelerator, *n.* Gashebel, -m.

accent, 1. *n.* Akzent', -e *m.* **2.** *vb.* beto'nen.

accentuate, *vb.* beto'nen.

accept, *vb.* an·nehmen*.

acceptability, *n.* Annehmbarkeit, -en *f.*

acceptable, *adj.* annehmbar.

acceptance, *n.* Annahme, -n *f.*

access, *n.* Zugang, -e *m.*

accessible, *adj.* zugänglich.

accessory, 1. *n. (person)* Mithelfer, - *m.; (thing)* Zubehör *nt.* **2.** *adj.* zusätzlich.

accident, *n.* Unfall, -e *m.; (chance)* Zufall, -e *m.*

accidental, *adj.* zufällig.

acclaim, 1. *n.* Beifall, -e *m.* **2.** *vb.* Beifall rufen*.

acclamation, *n.* Zuruf, -e *m.*, Beifall. -e *m.*

acclimate, *vb.* akklamatisie'ren.

accommodate, *vb.* an·passen, *(lodge)* unter·bringen*.

accommodating, *adj.* entge'genkommend.

accommodation, *n.* Anpassung, -en *f.*, *(lodging)* Unterkunft, -e *f.*

accompaniment, *n.* Begleitung, -en *f.*

accompanist, *n.* Beglei'ter, - *m.*

accompany, *vb.* beglei'ten.

accomplice, *n.* Mittäter, - *m.*

accomplish, vb. leisten.

accomplished, adj. vollen'-det.

accomplishment, n. Leistung, -en f.

accord, n. Einvernehmen, - nt.

accordance, n. Überein'-stimmung, -en f.

accordingly, adv. demgemäß.

according to, prep. laut, gemäß'.

accordion, n. Ziehharmonika, -s f.

accost, vb. an'sprechen*.

account, n. (comm.) Konto, -ten nt., (narrative) Bericht', -e m.

accountable, adj. verant'-wortlich.

accountant, n. Buchhalter, - m.

accounting, n. Buchführung, -en f.

accredit, vb. akkreditie'ren, beglau'bigen.

accrual, n. Zuwachs m.

accrue, vb. an'wachsen*.

accumulate, vb. (sich) an'-häufen.

accumulation, n. Anhäu-fung, -en f.

accumulator, n. Ansammler, - m., Akkumula'tor, -to'ren m.

accuracy, n. Genau'igkeit, -en f.

accurate, adj. genau'.

accursed, adj. verflucht'.

accusation, n. Anklage, -n f.

accusative, 1. n. Akkusativ, -e m. **2.** adj. anklagend.

accuse, vb. an'klagen.

accused, n. Angeklagt- m. & f.

accuser, n. Ankläger, - m.

accustom, vb. gewöh'nen.

accustomed, adj. gewohnt', gewöhnt'; **(become a. to)** sich gewöh'nen an.

ace, n. As, -se nt.

acetate, n. Acetat', -e nt.

acetic, adj. ace'tisch.

acetylene, n. Acetylen' nt.

ache, 1. n. Schmerz, -en m. **2.** vb. weh tun*, schmerzen.

achieve, vb. errei'chen.

achievement, n. Leistung, -en f.

acid, 1. n. Säure, -n f. **2.** adj. sauer.

acidify, vb. in Säure ver-wandeln.

acidity, n. Säuerlichkeit, -en f.

acknowledge, vb. an'er-kennen*, bestä'tigen.

acme, n. Höhepunkt, -e m.

acne, n. Akne, -n f.

acolyte, n. Altar'diener, - m.

acorn, n. Eichel, -n f.

acoustics, n. Aku'stik f.

acquaint, vb. bekannt'ma-chen.

acquaintance, n. Bekannt'-schaft, -en f.

acquainted, adj. bekannt', vertraut'.

acquiesce, vb. ein'willigen, ruhig hin'nehmen*.

acquiescence, n. Einwilli-gung, -en f.

acquire, vb. erwer'ben*.

acquisition, n. Erwer'bung, -en f.

acquisitive, adj. gewinn'-süchtig.

acquit, vb. frei'sprechen*.

acquittal, n. Freispruch, -e m.

acre, n. Morgen, - m.

acreage, n. Flächeninhalt nach Morgen.

acrimonious, adj. scharf, bitter.

acrimony, n. Bitterkeit, -en f.

acrobat, n. Akrobat', -en, -en m.

across, 1. prep. über. **2.** adv. hinü'ber, herü'ber.

act, 1. n. (deed) Tat, -en f.; (drama) Akt, -e m.; (law) Gesetz', -e nt. **2.** vb. han-deln; (stage) spielen; (be-have) sich beneh'men*.

acting, 1. n. (stage) Schau-spielkunst, -e f. **2.** adj. stellvertretend.

action, n. Handlung, -en f.

activate, vb. aktivie'ren.

activation, n. Aktivie'rung, -en f.

active, adj. tätig, aktiv'.

activity, *n.* Tätigkeit, -en *f.*

actor, *n.* Schauspieler, - *m.*

actress, *n.* Schauspielerin, -nen *f.*

actual, *adj.* tatsächlich.

actuality, *n.* Wirklichkeit, -en *f.*

actually, *adv.* wirklich.

actuary, *n.* Gerichts'schreiber, - *m.;* Versi'cherungsthema'tiker, - *m.*

acumen, *n.* Scharfsinn *m.*

acute, *adj.* scharf, scharfsinnig, akut'; *(angle)* spitz.

acuteness, *n.* Schärfe, -n *f.,* Scharfsinnigkeit *f.*

adage, *n.* Sprichwort, *er nt.*

adamant, *adj.* hartnäckig.

adapt, *vb.* an·passen, bearbeiten.

adaptability, *n.* Anpassungsfähigkeit, -en *f.*

adaptable, *adj.* anpassungsfähig.

adaptation, *n.* Anwendung, -en *f.,* Bear'beitung, -en *f.*

adapter, *n.* Bear'beiter, - *m.*

add, *vb.* hinzu'·fügen, addie'ren.

adder, *n.* Natter, -n *f.*

addict, *n.; drug a.* Rauschgiftsüchtig- *m.&f.; alcohol a.* Alkoholsüchtig- *m.&f.*

addition, *n.* Zusatz, *e m.*

additional, *adj.* zusätzlich.

address, 1. *n. (on letters, etc.)* Adres'se, -n *f.; (speech)* Ansprache, -n *f.* **2.** *vb. (a letter)* adressie'ren; *(a person)* an·sprechen*.

addressee, *n.* Empfäng'er, - *m.*

adenoid, *n.* Nasenwucherung *f.; (pl.)* Poly'pen *pl.*

adept, *adj.* erfah'ren, geschickt'.

adequacy, *n.* Angemessenheit, -en *f.*

adequate, *adj.* angemessen.

adhere, *vb.* haften, fest·halten*.

adherence, *n.* Festhalten *n.*

adherent, *n.* Anhäng·er, - *m.*

adhesive, 1. *n.* Klebemittel, - *nt.* **2.** *adj.* anhaftend; *a.* **tape,** Leukoplast' *n.nt.*

adieu, *interj.* lebewohl'!, ade'!

adjacent, *adj.* angrenzend.

adjective, *n.* Eigenschaftswort, *er nt.,* Adjektiv, -e *nt.*

adjoin, *vb.* an·grenzen.

adjourn, *vb.* verta'gen.

adjournment, *n.* Verta'gung, -en *f.*

adjunct, **1.** *n.* Zusatz, *e m.* **2.** *adj.* zusätzlich.

adjust, *vb.* passend machen, berich'tigen, aus·gleichen*.

adjuster, *n.* Ausgleicher, - *m.*

adjustment, *n.* Ausgleichung, -en *f.*

adjutant, *n.* Adjutant', -en, -en *m.*

administer, *vb.* verwal'ten; ertei'len.

administration, *n.* Verwal'tung, -en *f.*

administrative, *adj.* Verwal'tungs- *(cpds.).*

administrator, *n.* Verwal'ter, - *m.*

admirable, *adj.* bewun'dernswert.

admiral, *n.* Admiral', -e *m.*

admiralty, *n.* Admiralität', -en *f.*

admiration, *n.* Bewun'derung *f.*

admire, *vb.* bewun'dern.

admirer, *n.* Vereh'rer, - *m.*

admissible, *adj.* zulässig.

admission, *n. (entrance)* Eintritt, -e *m.; (confession)* Zugeständnis, -se *nt.*

admit, *vb. (permit)* zu·lassen*; *(concede)* zu·gestehen*.

admittance, *n.* Zutritt, -e *m.*

admittedly, *adv.* zugegebenerma'ßen.

admixture, *n.* Beimischung, -en *f.*

admonish, *vb.* ermah'nen.

admonition, *n.* Ermah'nung, -en *f.*

adolescence, *n.* das heranwachsende Alter, Jugendzeit, -en *f.*

adolescent, 1. *n.* der heranwachsende Junge, das

heran'wachsende Mädchen.
2. *adj.* jugendlich.

adopt, *vb.* adoptie'ren, an-nehmen*.

adoption, *n.* Adoption', -en *f.*

adorable, *adj.* reizend, entzück'end.

adoration, *n.* Vereh'rung *f.*, Anbetung *f.*

adore, *vb.* vereh'ren, anbeten.

adorn, *vb.* schmücken, zieren.

adornment, *n.* Verzie'rung, -en *f.*

adrift, *adv.* treibend, Wind und Wellen preisgegeben.

adroit, *adj.* geschickt'.

adulation, *n.* Schmeichelei', -en *f.*

adult, 1. *n.* Erwach'sen-*m.&f.* **2.** *adj.* erwach'sen.

adulterate, *vb.* verfäl'schen.

adultery, *n.* Ehebruch, *e m.*

advance, 1. *n.* Fortschritt, -e *m.*; *(mil.)* Vormarsch, *e m.*; *(pay)* Vorschuß, *sse m.*; **(in a.)** im voraus'. **2.** *vb.* Fortschritte machen; *(mil.)* vorrücken; *(pay)* voraus'zahlen; *(promote)* beför'dern.

advanced, *adj.* fortgeschrittten, modern'.

advancement, *n.* Förderung, -en *f.*, Beför'derung, -en *f.*

advantage, *n.* Vorteil, -e *m.*

advantageous, *adj.* vorteilhaft.

advent, *n.* Ankunft, *e f.*; *(eccl.)* Advent' *m.*

adventure, *n.* Abenteuer, -*nt.*

adventurer, *n.* Abenteurer, -*m.*

adventurous, *adj.* abenteuerlich.

adverb, *n.* Adverb', -en *nt.*, Umstandswort, *er nt.*

adverbial, *adj.* adverbial'.

adversary, *n.* Gegner, - *m.*

adverse, *adj.* ungünstig, nachteilig.

adversity, *n.* Mißgeschick, -e *nt.*

advertise, *vb.* an'zeigen, annoncie'ren, Rekla'me machen.

advertisement, *n.* Annon'ce, -n *f.*, Inserat', -e *nt.*, Rekla'me, -n *f.*

advertiser, *n.* Inserent', -en *m.*, Anzeiger, - *m.*

advertising, *n.* Rekla'me, -n *f.*

advice, *n.* Rat *m.*

advisability, *n.* Ratsamkeit *f.*

advisable, *adj.* ratsam.

advise, *vb.* raten*, bera'ten*.

advisedly, *adv.* absichtlich.

adviser, *n.* Bera'ter, - *m.*

advocacy, *n.* Befür'wortung *f.*

advocate, 1. *n.* Anwalt, *e m.* **2.** *vb.* vertei'digen, befür'worten.

aerate, *vb.* mit Luft vermen'gen.

aerial, 1. *n.* Anten'ne, -n *f.* **2.** *adj.* Luft- *(cpds.)*.

aeronautics, *n.* Aeronau'tik *f.*

aesthetic, *adj.* ästhe'tisch.

aesthetics, *n.* Ästhe'tik *f.*

afar, *adv.* von ferne.

affability, *n.* Freundlichkeit *f.*

affable, *adj.* freundlich.

affair, *n.* Angelegenheit, -en *f.*; Affä're, -n *f.*

affect, 1. *n.* Affekt', -e *m.* **2.** *vb.* wirken auf.

affectation, *n.* Affektiert'heit, -en *f.*

affected, *adj.* betrof'fen; *(unnatural)* affektiert'.

affection, *n.* Zuneigung, -en *f.*, Liebe, -n *f.*

affectionately, *adv.* *(letter)* mit herzlichen Grüßen.

affidavit, *n.* eidesstattliche Erklä'rung, -en *f.*

affiliate, *vb.* an'gliedern.

affiliation, *n.* Angliederung, -en *f.*

affinity, *n.* Verwandt'schaft, -en *f.*

affirm, *vb.* *(declare)* erklä'ren; *(confirm)* bestä'tigen; *(say yes to)* beja'hen.

affirmation, *n.* Bestä'tigung, -en *f.*; Beja'hung, -en *f.*

affirmative, *adj.* beja'hend.

affix, 1. *n.* *(gram.)* Affix, -e

nt. 2. vb. an'heften; (add on) bei'fügen.

afflict, vb. plagen.

affliction, n. Plage, -n f., Leid nt.

affluence, n. Reichtum, ⸗er m.

affluent, adj. reich.

afford, vb. gewäh'ren; (have the means to) sich leisten.

affront, 1. n. Belei'digung, -en f. **2.** vb. belei'digen.

afield, adv. (far a.) weit entfernt'.

afire, adv. in Flammen.

afraid, adj. bange; (be a. of) sich fürchten vor.

Africa, n. Afrika, nt.

African, 1. n. Afrika'ner, -m. **2.** adj. afrika'nisch.

aft, adv achtern.

after, 1. prep. nach, hinter. **2.** conj. nachdem'.

aftermath, n. Nachernte, -n f.

afternoon, n. Nachmittage, -e m.

afterward(s), adv. hinter'her', nachher.

again, adv. wieder, noch einmal.

against, prep. gegen.

age, 1. n. Alter, - nt.; (era) Zeitalter, - nt. **2.** vb. altern.

aged, adj. bejahrt'.

ageless, adj. zeitlos.

agency, n. Vertre'tung, -en f., Agentur', -en f.

agenda, n. Tagesordnung, -en f.

agent, n. Vertre'ter, - m.

aggrandizement, n. Machterweiterung, -en f.

aggravate, vb. verschlim'mern, erschwe'ren.

aggravation, n. Verschlim'merung, -en f.

aggregate, 1. n. Aggregat', -e nt. **2.** adj. Gesamt- (cpds.).

aggregation, n. Anhäufung, -en f.

aggression, n. Angriff, -e m., Aggression', -en f.

aggressive, adj. aggresiv'.

aggressiveness, n. Angriffslust f.

aggressor, n. Angrei'fer, - m.

aghast, adj. entsetzt'.

agile, adj. flink, behen'd(e).

agility, n. Behen'digkeit f.

agitate, vb. bewe'gen beun'ruhigen.

agitation, n. Bewe'gung, -en f., Beun'ruhigung, -en f.

agitator, n. Hetzredner, - m.

agnostic, 1. n. Agno'stiker, - m.. **2.** adj. agno'stisch.

ago, adv. vor.

agony, n. Qual, -en f.

agree, vb. überein'stimmen.

agreeable, adj. angenehm.

agreement, n. Überein'stimmung, -en f.

agricultural, adj. landwirtschaftlich.

agriculture, n. Landwirtschaft f.

ahead, adv. voraus'; (straight a.) gera'de aus.

aid, n. Hilfe, -n f. **2.** vb. helfen*.

aide, n. Adjutant', -en, -en m.

ail, vb. kranken.

ailment, n. Krankheit, -en f.

aim, 1. n. (goal) Ziel, -e nt.; (purpose) Zweck, -e m. **2.** vb. zielen.

aimless, adj. ziellos.

air, 1. n. Luft, ⸗e f. **2.** vb. lüften.

air base, n. Luftstützpunkt, -e m.

airborne, adj. in der Luft; (a. troops) Luftlandetruppen pl.

air-condition, vb. klimatisie'ren, mit Klima-Anlage verse'hen*.

air-conditioned, adj. klimatisiert', mit Klima-Anlage verse'hen.

air-conditioning, n. Klima-Anlage, -n f.

aircraft, n. Flugzeug, -e nt.

aircraft carrier, n. Flugzeuträger, -, m., Flugzeugmut'terschiff, -e nt.

air line, n. Luftlinie, -n f.

air liner, n. Verkehrs'flugzeug, -e, nt.

air mail, n. Luftpost f.

airplane, n. Flugzeug, -e nt.

airport, n. Flughafen, ⸗ m.

air pressure, *n.* Luftdruck. -e *m.*

air raid, *n.* Luftangriff, -e *m.*

airsick, *adj.* luftkrank (*).

airtight, *adj.* luftdicht.

airy, *adj.* luftig.

aisle, *n.* Gang, *-e *m.*; (*church*) Chorgang, *-e *m.*

ajar, *adj.* angelehnt, halb offen.

akin, *adj.* verwandt'.

alarm, 1. *n.* Alarm', -e *m.* **2.** *vb.* alarmie'ren, beun'ruhi-gen.

albino, *n.* Albi'no, -s *m.*

album, *n.* Album, -ben *nt.*

albumen, *n.* Eiweißstoff, -e *m.*, Albu'men *nt.*

alcohol, *n.* Alkohol, -e *m.*

alcoholic, 1. *n.* Alkoho'liker, - *m.* **2.** *adj.* alkoho'lisch.

alcove, *n.* Alko'ven, - *m.*

ale, *n.* englisches Bier, Ale *nt.*

alert, 1. *n.* Alarm', -e *m.* Vorwarnung, -en *f.* **2.** *adj.* aufmerksam **3.** *vb.* alarmie'-ren.

alfalfa, *n.* Alfal'fa *nt.*

algebra, *n.* Algebra *f.*

algebraic, *adj.* algebra'isch.

alias, *adv.* alias.

alibi, *n.* Alibi, -s *nt.*

alien, 1. *n.* Ausländer, - *m.* **2.** *adj.* fremd, ausländisch.

alienate, *vb.* entfrem'den.

alight, *vb.* sich nieder-lassen*; (*dismount*) ab'steigen*.

align, *vb.* aus'richten, (*ally*) zusam'men-tun*.

alike, *adj.* gleich.

alive, *adj.* leben'dig; (**be a.**) leben.

alkali, *n.* Alka'li *nt.*

alkaline, *adj.* alka'lisch.

all, *adj.* aller, -es, -e; (**above a.**) vor allem; (**a. at once**) auf einmal; (**a. the same**) gleich; (**a. of you**) Sie alle; (**not at a.**) gar nicht.

allay, *vb.* beru'higen, stillen.

allegation, *n.* Behaup'tung, -en *f.*

allege, *vb.* an'führen, behaup'ten.

allegiance, *n.* Treue *f.*, Gehor'sam *m.*

allegory, *n.* Allegorie', -i'en *f.*; Sinnbild, -er *nt.*

allergy, *n.* Allergie', -i'en *f.*

alleviate, *vb.* erleich'tern, lindern.

alley, *n.* Gasse, -n *f.*; Durch-gang, *-e *m.*; (**blind a.**) Sackgasse, -n *f.*

alliance, *n.* Bündnis, -se *nt.*; Allianz', -en *f.*

allied, *adj.* verbün'det; (*re-lated*) verwandt'.

alligator, *n.* Alliga'tor, -to'-ren *m.*

allocate, *vb.* zu-teilen.

allot, *vb.* zu'weisen*; zu-teilen.

allotment, *n.* Zuweisung, -en *f.*

allow, *vb.* erlau'ben, gestat'-ten.

allowance, *n.* (*money*) Taschengeld, -er *nt.*; (*per-mission*) Erlaub'nis, -se *f.*; (**make a.s for**) Rücksicht nehmen auf.

alloy, *n.* Legie'rung, -en *f.* **2.** *vb.* legie'ren.

all right, *interj.* gut, schön, in Ordnung.

allude, *vb.* hin'weisen*, an'-spielen.

allure, 1. *n.* Charme *m.* **2.** *vb.* verlock'en.

allusion, *n.* Anspielung, -en *f.*

ally, 1. *n.* Verbün'det- *m.*, Alliiert'- *m.* **2.** *vb.* verbün'-den.

almanac, *n.* Almanach, -e *m.*

almighty, *adj.* allmäch'tig.

almond, *n.* Mandel, -n *f.*

almost, *adv.* beinahe, fast.

alms, *n.* Almosen, - *nt.*

aloft, *adv.* hochoben; empor'.

alone, *adj.* allein'; (**leave a.**) in Ruhe lassen*.

along, 1. *adv.* entlang'; (**come a.**) mit-kommen*. **2.** *prep.* entlang', längs.

alongside, *prep.* neben.

aloof, 1. *adj.* gleichgültig. **2.** *adv.* abseits.

aloud, *adv.* laut.

alpaca, *n.* Alpa'ka, -s *nt.*

alphabet, *n.* Alphabet', -e *nt.*

alphabetical, *adj.* alphabe'tisch.

alphabetize, *vb.* alphabeti-sie'ren.

Alps, *n.pl.* Alpen *pl.*

already, *adv.* schon.

also, *adv.* auch.

altar, *n.* Altar', -e *m.*

alter, *vb.* ändern.

alteration, *n.* Änderung, -en *f.*

alternate, 1. *n.* Stellvertreter, - *m.* **2.** *adj.* alternativ'. **3.** *vb.* ab·wechseln.

alternating current, *n.* Wechselstrom, -e *m.*

alternative, 1. *n.* Alternati've, -n *f.* **2.** *adj.* alternativ'.

although, *conj.* obwohl', obgleich'.

altitude, *n.* Höhe, -n *f.*

alto, *n.* Altstimme, -n *f.*

altogether, *adv.* völlig, ganz und gar; alles in allem.

altruism, *n.* Altruis'mus *m.*

alum, *n.* Alaun', -e *m.*

aluminum, *n.* Alumi'nium *nt.*

always, *adv.* immer.

amalgamate, *vb.* amalgamie'ren.

amass, *vb.* an·sammeln.

amateur, *n.* Amateur', -e *m.*

amaze, *vb.* erstau'nen.

amazement, *n.* Erstau'nen *nt.*

amazing, *adj.* erstaun'lich.

ambassador, *n.* Botschafter, - *m.*, Gesandt' -e *m.*

amber, *n.* Bernstein, -e *m.*

ambiguity, *n.* Zweideutigkeit, -en *f.*

ambiguous, *adj.* zweideutig.

ambition, *n.* Ehrgeiz *m.*, Ambition', -en *f.*

ambitious, *adj.* ehrgeizig.

ambulance, *n.* Krankenwagen, - *m.*, Krankenauto, -s *nt.*

ambush, 1. *n.* Hinterhalt *m.* **2.** *vb.* aus dem Hinterhalt überfallen*.

ameliorate, *vb.* verbes'sern.

amenable, *adj.* zugänglich.

amend, *vb.* verbes'sern, ergän'zen.

amendment, *n.* Gesetz'-

---

abänderung, -en *f.*, Verfas'sungszusatz, "e *m.*

amenity, *n.* Annehmlichkeit, -en *f.*

America, *n.* Ame'rika *nt.*

American, 1. *n.* Amerika'ner, - *m.* **2.** *adj.* amerika'nisch.

amethyst, *n.* Amethyst', -e *m.*

amiable, *adj.* liebenswürdig.

amicable, *adj.* freundschaftlich.

amid, *prep.* inmit'ten.

amidships, *adv.* mittschiffs.

amiss, *adj.* los, schief; **(take a.)** übel·nehmen*.

amity, *n.* Freundschaft, -en *f.*

ammonia, *n.* Ammoniak *nt.*; **(household a.)** Salmiakgeist *m.*

ammunition, *n.* Munition', -en *f.*

amnesia, *n.* Amnesie' *f.*

amnesty, *n.* Amnestie', -i'en *f.*

amoeba, *n.* Amö'be, -n *f.*

among, *prep.* unter, zwischen, bei.

amorous, *adj.* verliebt'.

amortize, *vb.* tilgen, amortisie'ren.

amount, 1. *n.* (*sum*) Betrag', "e *m.*; (*large a.*) Menge, -n *f.* **2.** *vb.* **(a. to)** betra'gen*.

ampere, *n.* Ampere, - *(pron.* Ampär') *nt.*

amphibian, 1. *n.* Amphi'bie, -n *f.* **2.** *adj.* amphi'bisch.

amphibious, *adj.* amphi'bisch.

amphitheater, *n.* Amphi'theater, - *nt.*

ample, *adj.* reichlich.

amplify, *vb.* (*enlarge*) erwei'tern; (*make louder*) verstär'ken; (*state more fully*) ausführ'licher dar·stellen.

amputate, *vb.* amputie'ren.

amuse, *vb.* belus'tigen, amüsie'ren.

amusement, *n.* Unterhal'tung, -en *f.*; Belus'tigung, -en *f.*

an, *art.* ein, -, -e.

anachronism, *n.* Ana-chronis'mus, -men *m.*

analogical, *adj.* analo'gisch.

analogous, *adj.* analog'.

analogy, *n.* Analogie', -i'en *f.*

analysis, *n.* Analy'se, -n *f.*

analyst, *n.* Analy'tiker, - *m.*

analytic, *adj.* analy'tisch.

analyze, *vb.* analysie'ren.

anarchy, *n.* Anarchie', -i'en *f.*

anatomy, *n.* Anatomie', -i'en *f.*

ancestor, *n.* Vorfahr, -en, -en, *m.*

ancestral, *adj.* Stamm- (*cpds.*).

ancestry, *n.* Abstammung, -en *f.*

anchor, 1. *n.* Anker, - *m.* **2.** *vb.* veran'kern.

anchovy, *n.* Sardel'le, -n *f.*

ancient, *adj.* alt, uralt.

and, *conj.* und.

anecdote, *n.* Anekdo'te, -n *f.*

anemia, *n.* Blutarmut *f.*

anemic, *adj.* blutarm.

anesthesia, *n.* Anästhesie' *f.*

anesthetic, 1. *n.* Narko'se, -n *f.,* Betäu'bungsmittel, - *nt.* **2.** *adj.* betäu'bend, narko'tisch.

anew, *adv.* aufs neue, von neuem.

angel, *n.* Engel, - *m.*

anger, *n.* Zorn *m.,* Ärger *m.*

angle, 1. *n.* (*geom.*) Winkel, - *m.;* (*point of view*) Gesichts-punkt, -e *m.* **2.** *vb.* (*fish*) angeln.

angry, *adj.* böse, ärgerlich; (**be a.**) sich ärgern.

anguish, *n.* Qual, -en *f.*

angular, *adj.* eckig.

animal, 1. *n.* Tier, -e *nt.* **2.** *adj.* tierisch.

animate, *vb.* bele'ben.

animated, *adj.* lebhaft.

animated cartoon, *n.* Trick-film, -e *m.*

animation, *n.* Lebhaftig-keit, -en *f.*

animosity, *n.* Erbit'terung, -en *f.*

annals, *n.pl.* Anna'len *pl.*

ankle, *n.* Fessel, -n *f.;* Fessel-gelenk, -e *nt.*

annex, 1. *n.* Anhang, -e *m.;* (*building*) Nebengebäude, - *nt.* **2.** *vb.* annektie'ren.

annexation, *n.* Annektie'-rung, -en *f.*

annihilate, *vb.* vernich'ten.

anniversary, *n.* Jahrestag, -e *m.*

annotate, *vb.* mit Anmer-kungen verse'hen*, annotie'-ren.

announce, *vb.* an-kündigen, bekannt'geben*.

announcement, *n.* Be-kannt'machung, -en *f.*

announcer, *n.* Ansager, - *m.*

annoy, *vb.* beläs'tigen, ärgern.

annoyance, *n.* Ärger *m.;* Beläs'tigung, -en *f.*

annual, 1. *n.* Jahrbuch, -er *nt.* **2.** *adj.* jährlich.

annuity, *n.* Jährliche Rente, -n *f.*

annul, *vb.* annullie'ren.

anoint, *vb.* salben.

anomaly, *n.* Anomalie', -i'en *f.*

anonymous, *adj.* anonym'.

another, *adj.* (*different*) ein ander-; (*additional*) noch ein; (**one a.**) sich, einan'der.

answer, 1. *n.* Antwort, -en *f.* **2.** *vb.* antworten, beant'-worten.

answerable, *adj.* beant'-wortbar; verant'wortlich.

ant, *n.* Ameise, -n *f.*

antagonism, *n.* Widerstreit, -e *m.*

antagonist, *n.* Widersacher, - *m.,* Gegner, - *m.*

antagonistic, *adj.* wider-strei'tend.

antagonize, *vb.* vor den Kopf stoßen*.

antarctic, 1. *n.* Antark'tis, *f.* **2.** *adj.* antark'tisch.

antecedent, 1. *n.* (*gram.*) Bezie'hungswort, -er *nt.* **2.** *adj.* vorher'gehend.

antelope, *n.* Antilo'pe, -n *f.*

antenna, *n.* (*radio*) Anten'-ne, -n *f.;* (*insect*) Fühler, - *m.*

anterior, *adj.* vorder-.

anteroom, *n.* Vorzimmer, -*nt.*

anthem, Hymne, -n *f.;* (**national a.**) National'hymne, -n *f.*

anthology, *n.* Anthologie', -i'en *f.*

anthracite, *n.* Anthrazit' *m.*

anthropologist, *n.* Anthropolo'ge, -n, -n *m.*

anthropology, *n.* Anthropologie' -i'en *f.*

antiaircraft, *adj.* Flak-(*cpds.*).

antibody, *n.* Antikörper, - *m.*

antic, *n.* Posse, -n *f.;* Mätzchen, - *nt.*

anticipate, *vb.* vorweg'nehmen*; erwar'ten.

anticipation, *n.* Erwar'tung, -en *f.*

anticlimax, *n.* enttäu'schende Wendung, -en *f.*

antidote, *n.* Gegengift, -e *nt.*

antiquated, *adj.* veral'tet.

antique, *adj.* antik'.

antiquity, *n.* Anti'ke *f.;* Altertum, *-*er *nt.*

antiseptic, 1. *n.* antisep'tisches Mittel *nt.* **2.** *adj.* antisep'tisch.

antisocial, *adj.* antisozial'.

antitoxin, *n.* Gegengift, -e *nt.*

antlers, *n.pl.* Geweih', -e *nt.*

anvil, *n.* Amboß, -sse *m.*

anxiety, *n.* Angst, -e *f.;* Besorg'nis, -se *f.*

anxious, *adj.* besorgt'; ängstlich.

any, *adj.* irgendein, -, -e; irgendwelcher, -es, -e; jeder, -es, -e; (**not a.**) kein, -, -e.

anybody, *pron.* jemand, irgendjemand; (**not . . . a.**) niemand.

anyhow, *adv.* sowieso'.

anyone, *pron.* jemand, irgendjemand; (**not . . . a.**) niemand.

anything, *pron.* etwas, irgendetwas; (**not . . . a.**) nichts.

anyway, *adv.* sowieso'.

anywhere, *adv.* (*location*) irgendwo; (*direction*) irgendwohin'.

apart, *adv.* abseits, beisei'te; (**a. from**) abgesehen von; (**take a.**) auseinan'der-nehmen*.

apartment*, *n.* Mietswohnung, en *f.*

ape, *n.* Affe, -n, -n *m.* **2.** *vb.* nach'affen.

aperture, *n.* Öffnung, -en *f.*

apex, *n.* Gipfel, - *m.*

aphorism, *n.* Aphoris'mus, -men *m.*

apiece, *adv.* (**ten dollars a.**) je zehn Dollar.

apologetic, *adj.* entschul'digend.

apologize, *vb.* sich entschul'digen.

apology, *n.* Entschul'digung, -en *f.*

apoplexy, *n.* Schlaganfall, -e *m.*

apostle, *n.* Apos'tel, - *m.*

appall, *vb.* entset'zen.

apparatus, *n.* Apparat', -e *m.;* Ausrüstung, -en *f.*

apparel, *n.* Kleidung, -en *f.*

apparent, *adj.* (*visible*) sichtbar; (*clear*) klar; (*obvious*) offensichtlich; (*probable*) scheinbar.

apparition, *n.* Erschei'nung, -en *f.;* Gespenst', -er, *nt.*

appeal, 1. *n.* (*request*) Bitte, -n *f.;* (*charm*) Reiz, -e *m.;* (*law*) Beru'fung, -en *f.* **2.** *vb.* (*law*) Beru'fung einlegen, appellie'ren; (*a. to, turn to*) sich wenden* an; (*a. to, please*) gefal'len*.

appear, *vb.* (*seem*) scheinen*; (*come into view*) erschei'nen*.

appearance, *n.* Erschei'nung, -en *f.,* Anschein, -e *m.*

appease, *vb.* beschwich'tigen.

appeasement, *n.* Beschwich'tigung, -en *f.*

appendage, *n.* Anhang, -e *m.*

appendectomy, *n.* Blinddarmoperation, -en *f.*

appendicitis, *n.* Blinddarmentzündung, -en *f.*

appendix, *n.* Anhang, -e *m.;* (*med.*) Blinddarm, -e *m.*

appetite, *n.* Appetit' *m.*

appetizer, *n.* Vorgericht, -e *nt.*

appetizing, *adj.* appetit'lich; lecker.

applaud, *vb.* applaudie'ren, Beifall klatschen.

applause, *n.* Beifall, -e *m.*

apple, *n.* Apfel, = *m.*

applesauce, *n.* Apfelmus *nt.*

appliance, *n.* Gerät', -e *nt.*

applicable, *adj.* anwendbar.

applicant, *n.* Bewer'ber, - *m.*

application, *n.* (*request*) Bewer'bung, -en *f.*; (*use*) Anwendung, -en *f.*

appliqué, *adj.* **(a. work)** Applikations'stickerei, -en *f.*

apply, *vb.* (*make use of*) anwenden*; (*request*) sich bewer'ben*.

appoint, *vb.* ernen'nen*.

appointment, *n.* (*to a position*) Ernen'nung, -en *f.*; (*doctor's*) Anmeldung, -en *f.*; (*date*) Verab'redung, -en *f.*

apportion, *vb.* proportional'vertei'len; zu·teilen.

appraisal, *n.* Abschätzung, -en *f.*

appraise, *vb.* ab·schätzen.

appreciable, *adj.* beträcht'lich.

appreciate, *vb.* schätzen; an·erkennen*.

appreciation, *n.* Anerkennung, -en *f.*

apprehend, *vb.* (*grasp*) erfas'sen; (*arrest*) verhaf'ten; (*fear*) befürch'ten.

apprehension, *n.* (*worry*) Besorg'nis, -se *f.*; (*arrest*) Verhaf'tung, -en *f.*

apprehensive, *adj.* besorgt'.

apprentice, *n.* Lehrling, -e *m.*

apprise, *vb.* benach'richtigen.

approach. 1. *n.* (*nearing*) Annäherung, -en *f.*; (*access*) Zugang, =e *m.* **2.** *vb.* (*come nearer*) sich nähern; (*turn to*) sich wenden* an.

approachable, *adj.* zugäng'lich.

approbation, *n.* Geneh'migung, -en *f.*

appropriate. 1. *adj.* angemessen, passend. **2.** *vb.*

(*seize*) sich an·eignen; (*vote funds*) bewilligen.

appropriation, *n.* (*seizure*) Aneignung, -en *f.*; (*approval*) Bewil'ligung, -en *f.*

approval, *n.* Zustimmung, -en *f.*, Einwilligung, -en *f.*

approve, *vb.* zu·stimmen, geneh'migen.

approximate. 1. *vb.* sich nähern. **2.** *adj.* annähernd.

approximately, *adv.* ungefähr, etwa.

approximation, *n.* Annäherung, -en *f.*

apricot, *n.* Apriko'se, -n *f.*

April, *n.* April' *m.*

apron, *n.* Schürze, -n *f.*

apropos. 1. *adj.* treffend. **2.** *prep.* hinsichtlich.

apt, *adj.* (*fitting*) passend; (*likely*) geneigt'; (*able*) fähig.

aptitude, *n.* Fähigkeit, -en *f.*

aquarium, *n.* Aqua'rium, -ien *nt.*

aquatic, *adj.* Wasser- (*cpds.*).

aqueduct, *n.* Wasserleitung, -en *f.*

Arab. 1. *n.* Araber, - *m.* **2.** *adj.* ara'bisch.

Arabian, *adj.* ara'bisch.

Arabic, *adj.* ara'bisch.

arable, *adj.* bestell'bar.

arbiter, *n.* Schlichter, - *m.*

arbitrary, *adj.* willkürlich.

arbitrate, *vb.* schlichten.

arbitration, *n.* Schlichtung, -en *f.*

arbitrator, *n.* Schlichter, - *m.*

arbor, *n.* Laube, -n *f.*

arc, *n.* Bogen, -(=) *m.*

arcade, *n.* Arka'de, -n *f.*

arch, *n.* Bogen, -(=) *m.*; (*instep*) Spann, -e *m.*

archaeology, *n.* Altertumskunde *f.*, Archäologie' *f.*

archaic, *adj.* archa'isch, altertümlich.

archbishop, *n.* Erzbischof, =e *m.*

archdiocese, *n.* Erzdiözese, -n *f.*

archduke, *n.* Erzherzog, =e *m.*

archer, n. Bogenschütze, -n, -n m.

archery, n. Bogenschießen nt.

architect, n. Architekt', en, -en m.

architectural, adj. architekto'nisch.

architecture, n. Architektur', -en f.

archives, n. Archiv', -e nt.

archway, n. Torbogen, ⁼ m.

arctic, 1. n. Arktis f. **2.** adj. arktisch.

ardent, adj. eifrig, inbrünstig.

ardor, n. Eifer m., Inbrunst f.

arduous, adj. mühsam.

area, n. Fläche, -n f., Gebiet', -e nt.

arena, n. Are'na, -nen f.

Argentina, n. Argenti'nien nt.

argue, vb. argumentie'ren; (quarrel) sich streiten*.

argument, n. Argument', -e nt.

argumentative, adj. streitsüchtig.

aria, n. Arie, -n f.

arid, adj. dürr, trocken.

arise, vb. auf·stehen*, sich erhe'ben*; (come into being) entste'hen*.

aristocracy, n. Aristokratie', -i'en f.

aristocrat, n. Aristokrat', -en, -en m.

aristocratic, adj. aristokra'tisch.

arithmetic, n. Rechnen nt., Arithme'tik f.

ark, n. Arche, -n f.; (Noah's a.) Arche Noah.

arm, 1. n. Arm, -e m.; (weapon) Waffe, -n f. **2.** vb. bewaff'nen, rüsten.

armament, n. Bewaff'nung, -en f.; (weapons) Waffen pl.

armchair, n. Lehnstuhl, ⁼e m.

armful, n. Menge, -n f.

armhole, n. Armloch, ⁼er nt.

armistice, n. Waffenstillstand m.

armor, n. Rüstung, -en f., Panzer, - m.

armored, adj. gepan'zert; Panzer- (cpds.).

armory, n. Exerzier'halle, -n f.; Waffenfabrik, -en f.

armpit, n. Achselhöhle, -n f.

arms, n.pl. Waffen pl.

army, n. Heer, -e nt., Armee', -me'en f.

aroma, n. Aro'ma, -s nt.

aromatic, adj. würzig.

around, 1. adv. herum'; (approximately) etwa, ungefähr. **2.** prep. um.

arouse, vb. (excite) erre'gen; (waken) wecken.

arraign, vb. richterlich vorführen.

arrange, vb. arrangie'ren, ein·richten; (agree) vereinbaren.

arrangement, n. Anordnung, -en f.

array, 1. n. Anordnung, -en f.; (fig.) Menge, -n f. **2.** vb. ordnen.

arrears, n.pl. Schulden pl.; (in a.) in Rückstand.

arrest, 1. n. (law) Verhaftung, -en f. **2.** vb. (law) verhaf'ten; (stop) an·halten*.

arrival, n. Ankunft, ⁼e f.

arrive, vb. an·kommen*.

arrogance, n. Anmaßung, -en f., Arroganz, -en f.

arrogant, adj. anmaßend, arrogant'.

arrow, n. Pfeil, -e m.

arsenal, n. Waffenlager, - nt.

arsenic, n. Arsen' nt.

arson, n. Brandstiftung, -en f.

art, n. Kunst, ⁼e f.

arterial, adj. Arte'rien- (cpds.); (a. highway) Hauptverkehrs'straße, -n f.

arteriosclerosis, n. Arte'rienverkalkung, -en f.

artery, n. Arte'rie, -ien f., Pulsader, -n f.

artful, adj. kunstvoll; (sly) schlau.

arthritis, n. Arthri'tis f.

artichoke, n. Artischock'e, -n f.

article, n. Arti'kel, - m.

articulate, 1. vb. (utter)

atikulie′ren; (*join*) zusam′-
men-fügen. **2.** *adj.* deutlich.

articulation, *n.* Artikulie′-
rung. -en *f.*

artifice, *n.* List, -en *f.*

artificial, *adj.* künstlich.

artificiality, *n.* Künstlich-
keit, -en *f.*

artillery, *n.* Artillerie′, -i′en
f.

artisan, *n.* Handwerker, - *m.*

artist, *n.* Künstler, - *m.*

artistic, *adj.* künstlerisch.

artistry, *n.* Künstlertum *nt.*

artless, *adj.* kunstlos.

as, *conj.& adv.* (*when*) wie,
als; (*because*) da; (**a. if**) als
ob; (**with X a. Hamlet**)
mit X als Hamlet; (**a. big
a.**) so groß wie; (**just a. big
a.**) ebenso groß wie; (**he a.
well a. I**) er sowohl wie ich.

asbestos, *n.* Asbest′. -e *m.*

ascend, *vb.* (*intr.*) steigen*;
(*tr.*) besti′gen*.

ascent, *n.* Aufstieg, -e *m.*

ascertain, *vb.* fest-stellen.

ascetic, 1. *n.* Asket′. -en, -en
m. **2.** *adj.* aske′tisch.

ascribe, *vb.* zu-schreiben*.

ash, *n.* Asche, -n *f.*; (*tree*)
Esche, -n *f.*

ashamed, *adj.* beschämt′;
(**be a.**) sich schämen.

ashen, *adj.* aschgrau.

ashes, *n.pl.* Asche *f.*

ashore, *adv.* an Land.

ash tray, *n.* Aschenbecher, -
m., Aschbecher, - *m.*

Asia, *n.* Asien *nt.*

Asiatic, 1. *n.* Asiat′, -en, -en
m. **2.** *adj.* asia′tisch.

aside, *adv.* beisei′te; (**a.
from**) außer.

ask, *vb.* (*question*) fragen;
(*request*) bitten*; (*demand*)
verlangen.

asleep, *adj.* schlafend; (**be
a.**) schlafen*.

asparagus, *n.* Spargel, - *m.*

aspect, *n.* Anblick, -e *m.*;
(*fig.*) Gesichts′punkt, -e *m.*

aspersion, *n.* Verleum′dung,
-en *f.*

asphalt, *n.* Asphalt, -e *m.*

asphyxiate, *vb.* ersti′cken.

aspirant, Anwärter, - *m.*

aspirate, 1. *n.* Hauchlaut, -e
m., **2.** *adj.* aspiriert′. **3.**
vb. aspirie′ren.

aspiration, *n.* Aspiration′,
-en *f.*, Bestre′bung, -en *f.*

aspire, *vb.* streben.

aspirin, *n.* Aspirin′ *nt.*

ass, *n.* Esel, - *m.*

assail, *vb.* an-greifen*.

assailable, *adj.* angreifbar.

assailant, *n.* Angreifer, - *m.*

assassin, *n.* Attentä′ter, - *m.*,
Mörder, - *m.*

assassinate, *vb.* ermor′den.

assassination, *n.* Ermor′-
dung, -en *f.*, Attentat′, -e *nt.*

assault, 1. *n.* Angriff, -e *m.*;
(*law*) tätliche Belei′digung.
-en *f.* **2.** *vb.* an-greifen*.

assay, 1. *n.* Probe, -n *f.* **2.**
vb. prüfen.

assemblage, *n.* Versamm′-
lung, -en *f.*

assemble, *vb.* versam′meln;
(*tech.*) montie′ren.

assembly, *n.* Versamm′lung,
-en *f.*; (*tech.*) Monta′ge, -n *f.*

assent, 1. *n.* Zustimmung,
-en *f.* **2.** *vb.* zu-stimmen.

assert, *vb.* behaup′ten.

assertion, *n.* Behaup′tung,
-en *f.*

assertive, *adj.* bestimmt′.

assess, *vb.* ein-schätzen.

assessor, *n.* Steuerab-
schätzer, - *m.*

asset, *n.* Vorzug, -̈e *m.*;
(*comm.*) Guthaben, - *nt.*

asseverate, *vb.* beteu′ern.

assiduous, *adj.* emsig.

assign, *vb.* zu-teilen, zu-
weisen*; (*homework*) aufgeben*.

assignable, bestimm′bar.

assignation, *n.* Anweisung,
-en *f.*; (*tryst*) Stelldichein, -
nt.

assignment, *n.* Anweisung,
-en *f.*; (*homework*) Aufgabe,
-n *f.*

assimilate, *vb.* an-gleichen*,
assimilie′ren.

assimilation, *n* Angleichung, -en *f.*, Assimilie′rung,
-en *f.*

assimilative, *adj.* angleichend.

assist, *vb.* unterstüt'zen, helfen*.

assistance, *n.* Unterstüt'zung, -en *f.*, Hilfe, -n *f.*

assistant, 1. *n.* Gehil'fe, -n *m.*, Assistent', -en, -en *m.* 2. *adj.* Hilfs- (*cpds.*) stellvertretend.

associate, 1. *n.* Partner, - *m.* 2. *vb.* verkeh'ren, assoziie'ren.

association, *n.* Verbin'dung, -en *f.*, Verei'nigung, -en *f.*

assonance, *n.* Assonanz', -en *f.*

assort, *vb.* sortie'ren.

assorted, *adj.* verschie'den.

assortment, *n.* Auswahl, -en *f.*

assuage, *vb.* beschwich'tigen.

assume, *vb.* an·neh'men*; (*arrogate*) sich an·ma'ßen.

assuming, *adj.* anmaßend; (**a. that**) angenommen, daß.

assumption, *n.* Annahme, -n *f.*; (*eccles.*) Himmelfahrt *f.*

assurance, *n.* Versi'cherung, -en *f.*, Zusicherung, -en *f.*

assure, *vb.* versi'chern, zu·sichern.

assured, *adj.* sicher, zuversichtlich.

aster, *n.* Aster, -n *f.*

asterisk, *n.* Sternchen, - *nt.*

asthma, *n.* Asthma *nt.*

astigmatism, *n.* Astigmatis'mus, -men *m.*

astonish, *vb.* erstau'nen; (**be astonished**) staunen.

astonishment, *n.* Erstau'nen, - *nt.*

astound, *vb.* erstau'nen.

astray, *adj.* irre; (**go a.**) sich verir'ren, auf Abwege gera'ten*.

astringent, *adj.* gefäß'spannend, hautstraffend, adstringie'rend.

astrology, *n.* Astrologie', -i'en *f.*

astronomy, *n.* Astronomie', -i'en *f.*

astute, *adj.* scharf (∘), schlau.

asylum, *n.* (*refuge*) Asyl', -e *nt.*; (*institution*) Anstalt, -en *f.*

at, *prep.* an; (**at home**) zu Hause.

atheist, *n.* Atheist', -en, -en *m.*

athlete, *n.* Athlet', -en, -en *m.*, Sportler, - *m.*

athletic, *adj.* athle'tisch, sportlich.

athletics, *n.* Sport, -e *m.*

Atlantic, 1. *n.* Atlan'tik *m.* 2. *adj.* atlan'tisch.

Atlantic Ocean, *n.* Atlan'tik *m.*

atlas, *n.* Atlas, -lan'ten *m.*

atmosphere, *n.* Atmosphä're, -n *f.*

atmospheric, *adj.* atmosphä'risch.

atoll, *n.* Atoll', -e *nt.*

atom, *n.* Atom', -e *nt.*

atomic, *adj.* atomar'; Atom'- (*cpds.*).

atomize, *vb.* atomisie'ren.

atone, *vb.* büßen, sühnen.

atonement, *n.* Buße, -n *f.*, Sühne, -n *f.*

atrocious, *adj.* entsetz'lich, grausam.

atrocity, *n.* Grausamkeit, -en *f.*

atrophy, *n.* Atrophie', -i'en *f.*

attach, *vb.* an·heften, -ei·fügen; (*attribute*) bei·messen*.

attaché, *n.* Attaché, -s *m.*

attachment, *n.* Beifügung, -en *f.*; (*device*) Vorrichtung, -en *f.*, Zubehör *nt.*; (*liking*) Zuneigung, -en *f.*

attack, 1. *n.* Angriff, -e *m.* 2. *vb.* an·greifen*.

attain, *vb.* errei'chen.

attainable, *adj.* erreich'bar.

attainment, *n.* Errun'genschaft, -en *f.*

attempt, 1. *n.* Versuch', -e *m.* 2. *vb.* versu'chen.

attend, *vb.* (*meeting*) bei·wohnen; (*lecture*) besu'chen, hören; (*patient*) behan'deln; (*person*) beglei'ten.

attendance, *n.* Anwesenheit, -en *f.*, Besuch', -e *m.*

attendant, 1. *n.* Beglei'ter,

- *m.* **2.** *adj.* begleiʼtend.
anweesend.

attention, *n.* Aufmerksamkeit, -en *f.;* **(a.!)** Achtung!,
(pay a.) aufʼpassen.

attentive, *adj.* aufmerksam.

attenuate, *vb.* verdünʼnen,
verminʼdern; *(jur.)* mildern.

attest, *vb.* bezeuʼgen.

attic, *n.* Dachboden, = *m.*
Boden. = *m.*

attire, **1.** *n.* Kleidung, -en *f.*
2. *vb.* kleiden.

attitude, *n.* Haltung, -en *f.*

attorney, *n.* Anwalt, =e *m.*

attract, *vb.* anʼziehen*.

attraction, *n.* Anziehungskraft, =e *f.*

attractive, *adj.* anziehend.

attribute, **1.** *n.* Eigenschaft,
-en *f.* **2.** *vb.* zuʼschreiben*.

attribution, *n.* Beimessung,
-en *f.*

auction, *n.* Versteiʼgerung,
-en *f.*, Auktionʼ, -en *f.*

auctioneer, *n.* Versteiʼgerer
- *m.*, Auktionaʼtor, -toʼren *m.*

audacious, *adj.* kühn.

audacity, *n.* Kühnheit, -en *f.*

audible, *adj.* hörbar.

audience, *n.* Zuhörerschaft,
-en *f.*, Publikum, -ka *nt.; (of
a king)* Audienzʼ, -en *f.*

audit, **1.** *n.* Rechnungssprüfung, -en *f.* **2.** *vb.*
prüfen.

audition, *n.* Vorführungsprobe, -n *f.*

auditor, *n.* Hörer, - *m.;
(comm.)* Rechnungsprüfer, - *m.*

auditorium, *n.* Zuhörerraum, =e *m.*, Auditoʼrium,
-rien *nt.*

augment, *vb.* vermehʼren.

augur, **1.** *n.* Augurʼ, -en, -en
m. **2.** *vb.* weissagen.

August, *n.* Augustʼ *m.*

aunt, *n.* Tante, -n *f.*

auspices, *n.pl.* Auspiʼzien.

auspicious, *adj.* günstig.

austere, *adj.* streng.

austerity, *n.* Enthaltʼsamkeit, -en *f.*

Austria, *n.* Österreich *nt.*

Austrian, **1.** *n.* Österreicher,
- *m.* **2.** *adj.* österreichisch.

authentic, *adj.* authenʼtisch.

authenticate, *vb.* beglauʼbigen.

authenticity, *n.* Echtheit,
-en *f.*

author, *n.* Verfasʼser - *m.*

authoritarian, *adj.* autoritärʼ.

authoritative, *adj.* maßgebend.

authority, *n.* Autoritätʼ, -en
f.

authorization, *n.* Vollmacht,
=e *f.*

authorize, *vb.* bevollʼmächtigen.

auto, *n.* Auto, -s *nt.*

autobiography, *n.* Selbstbiographie -iʼen *f.*

autocracy, *n.* Autokratieʼ,
-iʼen *f.*

autocrat, *n.* Autokratʼ, -en,
-en *m.*.

autograph, *n.* Autogrammʼ, -e *nt.*

automatic, *adj.* automaʼtisch.

automaton, *n.* Automatʼ,
en, -en *m.*

automobile, *n.* Kraftwagen,
- *m.*

automotive, *adj.* Auto-
(cpds.).

autonomous, *adj.* autonomʼ.

autonomy, *n.* Autonomieʼ,
-iʼen *f.*

autopsy, *n.* Leichenöffnung,
-en *f.*

autumn, *n.* Herbst, -e *m.*

auxiliary, *adj.* Hilfs- *(cpds.).*

avail, **1.** *n.* Nutzen *m.* **2.** *vb.*
nützen; **(a. oneself of)**
benutʼzen.

available, *adj.* vorhanʼden.

avalanche, *n.* Lawiʼne, -n *f.*

avarice, *n.* Geiz, =e *m.*

avaricious, *adj.* geizig.

avenge, *vb.* rächen.

avenue, *n.* Alleeʼ, -eʼn *f.*

average, **1.** *n.* Durchschnitt,
-e *m.* **2.** *adj.* durchschnittlich; Durchschnitts- *(cpds.).*

averse, *adj.* abgeneigt.

aversion, *n.* Abneigung, -en
f.

aviation, *n.* Luftfahrt *f.*

aviator, *n.* Flieger, - *m.*

aviatrix, *n.* Fliegerin, -nen *f.*

avid, *adj.* begie'rig.

avocation, *n.* Nebenberuf, -e *m.*

avoid, *vb.* vermei'den*.

avoidable, *adj.* vermeid'lich.

avoidance, *n.* Vermei'dung, -en *f.*

avow, *vb.* geste'hen*.

avowal, *n.* Geständ'nis, -se *nt.*

await, *vb.* erwar'ten.

awake, *adj.* wach.

awaken, *vb.* (*tr.*) wecken; (*intr.*) erwach'en.

award, **1.** *n.* Preis, -e *m.*; (*jur.*) Urteil, -e *nt.* **2.** *vb.* zu·erkennen*.

aware, *adj.* bewußt'.

away, *adv.* weg, fort.

awe, *n.* Ehrfurcht *f.*

awful, *adj.* schrecklich.

awhile, *adv.* eine Weile.

awkward, *adj.* (*clumsy*) un·geschickt'; (*embarrassing*) peinlich.

awning, *n.* Marki'se, -n *f.*

awry, *adj.* schief.

axe, *n.* Axt, ⁓e *f.*

axiom, *n.* Axiom', -e *nt.*

axis, *n.* Achse, -n *f.*

axle, *n.* Achse, -n *f.*

azure, *adj.* azur'blau.

B

babble, **1.** *n.* Geschwätz' *nt.* **2.** *vb.* schwatzen.

baboon, *n.* Pavian, -e *m.*

baby, *n.* Baby, -s *nt.*, Säugling. -e *m.*

bachelor, *n.* Junggeselle, -n, -n *m.*

back, **1.** *n.* Rücken. - *m.*, Kreuz, -e *nt.*; (*chair*) Lehne, -n *f.* **2.** *vb.* rückwärts·fahren*; (*support*) unterstüt'zen. **3.** *adj.* hinter-. **4.** *adv.* zurück'.

backbone, *n.* Rückgrat, -e

backfire, *n.* Fehlzündung, -en *f.*

background, *n.* Hintergrund, ⁓e *m.*

backing, *n.* Unterstüt'zung, -en *f.*

backward, **1.** *adj.* zurück'-geblieben, rückständig. **2.** *adv.* rückwärts.

backwards, *adv.* rückwärts; (*wrongly*) verkehrt'.

bacon, *n.* Speck *m.*

bacterium, *n.* Bakte'rium, -rien *nt.*

bad, *adj.* (*not good*) schlecht; (*serious*) schlimm; (**too b.**) schade.

bag, *n.* Sack, ⁓e *m.*; (*paper*) Tüte, -n *f.*; (*luggage*) Koffer, - *m.*; (*woman's purse*) Tasche, -n *f.*

baggage, *n.* Gepäck' *nt.*

baggy, *adj.* bauschig.

bail, *n.* Kaution', -en *f.*, Bürgschaft, -en *f.*

bail out, *vb.* (*set free*) Kaution' stellen für; (*empty out water*) schöpfen, aus·schöpfen; (*make a parachute jump*) ab·springen*

bake, *vb.* backen*

baking, *n.* Backen *nt.*

baking soda, *n.* doppelkohlensaures Natron.

balance, **1.** *n.* (*equilibrium*) Gleichgewicht *nt.*; (*remainder*) Rest, -e *m.*; (*trade*) Bilanz', -en *f.* **2.** *vb.* balancie'ren; (*make come out equal*) aus·gleichen*

balcony, *n.* Balkon', -s *m.*

bald, *adj.* kahl; (**b. head**) Glatzkopf, ⁓e *m.*; (**b. spot**) Glatze, -n *f.*

balk, *vb.* (*hinder*) verhin'dern; (**b. at nothing**) vor nichts zurück'scheuen.

ball, *n.* (*for throwing, game, dance*) Ball, ⁓e *m.*; (*spherical object, bullet*) Kugel, - *f.*

ballerina, *n.* Balleri'na, -nen *f.*

ballot, *n.* (*paper*) Stimmzettel, - *m.*; (*voting*) Wahl, -en *f.*

ballroom, n. Tanzsaal, -säle m.

balm, n. Balsam, -e m.

balmy, adj. sanft.

balsam, n. Balsam, -e m.

Baltic Sea, n. Ostsee f.

bamboo, n. Bambus, -se m.

ban, 1. n. Bann, -e m. **2.** vb. bannen, verbie'ten*.

banal, adj. banal.

banana, n. Bana'ne, -n f.

band, n. Band, -er nt.; (gang) Bande, -n f.; (music) Musik'kapelle, -n f.

bandage, 1. n. Verband', -e m. **2.** vb. verbin'den*.

bandanna, n. Kopftuch, -er nt., Halstuch, -er nt.

bandit, n. Bandit', -en, -en m.

baneful, adj. giftig, verderb'lich.

bang, 1. n. Knall, -e m. **2.** vb. knallen.

banish, vb. verban'nen.

banishment, n. Verban'nung, -en f.

banister, n. Treppengeländer, - nt.

bank, 1. n. Bank, -en f.; (river) Ufer, - nt.; (slope) Böschung, -en f.

bankbook, n. Kontobuch, -er nt.

banker, n. Bankier', -s m.

banking, n. Bankgeschäft, -e nt.

bank note, n. Banknote, -n f.

bankrupt, adj. bankrott'.

bankruptcy, n. Konkurs', -e m.

banner, n. Banner, - nt.

banquet, n. Festessen, - nt.

banter, 1. n. Scherz, -e m. **2.** vb. scherzen.

baptism, n. Taufe, -n f.

baptismal, adj. Tauf- (cpds.).

Baptist, n. Baptist', -en, -en m.

baptistery, n. Taufkapelle, -n f., Taufstein, -e m.

baptize, vb. taufen.

bar, 1. n. Stange, -n f.; (for drinks) Bar, -s f.; (jur.) Gericht, -e nt. **1.** vb. ausschließen*.

barb, n. Widerhaken, - m.

barbarian, 1. n. Barbar', -en, -en m. **2.** adj. barba'risch.

barbarism, n. Barbarei', -en f.

barbarous, adj. barba'risch.

barber, n. Herrenfriseur, -e m.

barbiturate, n. Barbitur'säurepräparat, -e nt.

bare, 1. adj. bloß, nackt. **2.** vb. entblö'ßen.

barefoot, adj. barfuß.

barely, adv. kaum.

bargain, 1. n. Gele'genheitskauf, -e m. **2.** vb. feilschen, handeln.

barge, 1. n. Schleppkahn, -e m., Leichter, - m. **2.** vb. stürmen.

baritone, n. Bariton, -e m.

barium, n. Barium nt.

bark, 1. n. (tree) Rinde, -n f.; (boat) Barke, -n f.; (dog) Bellen nt. **2.** vb. bellen.

barley, n. Gerste, -n f., Graupen pl.

barn, n. (hay, grain) Scheune, -n f.; (animals) Stall, -e m.

barnacle, n. Entenmuschel, -n f.

barnyard, n. Bauernhof, -e m.

barometer, n. Barome'ter, - nt.

barometric, adj. barome'trisch.

baron, n. Baron', -e m.

baroness, n. Barones'se, -n f.

baroque, 1. n. Barock', nt. **2.** adj. barock'.

barracks, n. Kaser'ne, -n f.

barrage, n. Sperre, -n f.; (mil.) Sperrfeuer, - nt.

barrel, n. Faß, -sser nt.

barren, adj. unfruchtbar, dürr.

barricade, 1. n. Barrika'de, -n f. **2.** vb. verbarrikadie'ren.

barrier, n. Schranke, -n f.

barroom, n. Schankstube, -n f.

bartender, n. Barmixer, - m

barter, 1. n. Tauschhandel, m. **2.** vb. tauschen.

base, 1. *n.* der unterste Teil, -e *m.*; (*geom.*) Grundlinie, -n *f.*; (*mil.*) Stützpunkt, -e *m.* **2.** *vb.* basie'ren. **3.** *adj.* niederträchtig.

baseball, *n.* Baseball, -e *m.*

baseboard, *n.* Waschleiste, -n *f.*

basement, *n.* Keller, - *m.*

baseness, *n.* Niederträchtigkeit, -en *f.*

bashful, *adj.* schüchtern.

bashfulness, *n.* Schüchternheit, -en *f.*

basic, *adj.* grundlegend.

basin, *n.* Becken, - *nt.*

basis, *n.* Grundlage, -n *f.*, Basis, -sen *f.*

basket, *n.* Korb, "e *m.*

bass, *n.* (*singer*) Baß, "sse *m.*; (*fish*) Barsch, -e *m.*

bassinet, *n.* Korbwiege, -n *f.*

bassoon, *n.* Fagott', -e *nt.*

bastard, *n.* uneheliches Kind *nt.*, Bastard, -e *m.*

baste, *vb.* (*thread*) heften; (*roast*) begie'ßen*.

bat, *n.* Fledermaus, "e, *f.*; (*sport*) Schlagholz, "er *nt.*

batch, *n.* Shub, -e *m.*

bath, *n.* Bad, "er *nt.*

bathe, *vb.* baden.

bather, *n.* Badend- *m.&f.*

bathrobe, *n.* Bademantel, - *m.*

bathroom, *n.* Badezimmer, - *nt.*

bathtub, *n.* Badewanne, -n *f.*

baton, *n.* Taktstock, "e *m.*

battalion, *n.* Bataillon', -e *nt.*

batter, 1. *n.* (*one who bats*) Schläger, - *m.*; (*cooking*) Teig, -e *m.* **2.** *vb.* schlagen*.

battery, *n.* Batterie', -i'en *f.*

battle, 1. *n.* Schlacht, -en *f.* **2.** *vb.* kämpfen.

battlefield, *n.* Schlachtfeld, -er *nt.*

battleship, *n.* Schlachtschiff, -e *nt.*

bawl, *vb.* brüllen.

bay, 1. *n.* (*geography*) Bucht, -en *f.*; (*plant*) Lorbeer, -en *m.*; (**at b.**) in Schach. **2.**

adj. (*color*) rotbraun. **3.** *vb.* bellen.

bayonet, *n.* Bajonett', -e *nt.*

bazaar, *n.* Bazar', -e *m.*

be, *vb.* sein*.

beach, *n.* Strand, -e *m.*

beachhead, *n.* Landekopf, "e *m.*

beacon, *n.* Leuchtfeuer, - *nt.*

bead, *n.* Perle, -n *f.*; (*drop*) Tropfen, - *m.*

beading, *n.* Perlstickerei, -en *f.*

beak, *n.* Schnabel, " *m.*

beaker, *n.* Becher, - *m.*

beam, 1. *n.* (*construction*) Balken, - *m.*; (*light*) Strahl, -en *m.* **2.** *vb.* strahlen, glänzen.

beaming, *adj.* strahlend.

bean, *n.* Bohne, -n *f.*

bear, 1. *n.* (*animal*) Bär, -en, -en *m.* **2.** *vb.* (*carry*) tragen*; (*endure*) ertra'gen*; (*give birth to*) gebä'ren*.

bearable, *adj.* erträg'lich.

beard, *n.* Bart, "e *m.*

bearer, *n.* Überbrin'ger, - *m.*

bearing, *n.* (*behavior*) Haltung, -en *f.*; (*affect*) Bezug', "e *m.*; (*machinery*) Lager, - *nt.*

beast, *n.* Vieh *nt.*, Tier, -e *nt.*, Bestie, - *f.*

beat, 1. *n.* Schlag, -e *m.*; (*music*) Takt, -e *m.* **2.** *vb.* schlagen*.

beaten, *adj.* geschla'gen.

beatify, *vb.* selig-sprechen*.

beating, *n.* (*punishment*) Prügel *pl.*, Schläge *pl.*; (*defeat*) Niederlage, -n *f.*

beatitudes, *n.pl.* (*biblical*) Seligpreisungen *pl.*

beau, *n.* Vereh'rer, - *m.*

beautiful, *adj.* schön.

beautify, *vb.* verschö'nern.

beauty, *n.* Schönheit, -en *f.*

beauty parlor, *n.* Schönheitssalon, -s *m.*, Frisiersalon, -s *m.*

beaver, *n.* Biber, - *m.*

because, *conj.* weil; (**b. of**) wegen.

beckon, *vb.* winken.

become, *vb.* werden*.

becoming, *adj.* kleidsam.

bed, *n.* Bett, -en *nt.; (garden)* Beet, -e *nt.*

bedbug, *n.* Wanze, -n *f.*

bedding, *n.* Bettzeug *nt.*

bedroom, *n.* Schlafzimmer, - *nt.*

bedspread, *n.* Bettdecke, -n *f.*

bee, *n.* Biene, -n *f.*

beef, *n.* Rindfleisch *nt.*

beefsteak, *n.* Beefsteak, -s *nt.*

beehive, *n.* Bienenstock, ⸗e *m.*

beer, *n.* Bier, -e *nt.*

beet, *n.* Bete, -n *f.,* Runkelrübe, -n *f.,* rote Rübe, -n *f.*

beetle, *n.* Käfer, - *m.*

befall, *vb.* zu·stoßen*.

befit, *vb.* gezie′men.

befitting, *adj.* schicklich; (be b.) sich schicken.

before, 1. *adv. (time)* vorher; *(place)* voran′. **2.** *prep.* vor. **3.** *conj.* ehe, bevor′.

beforehand, *adv.* vorher.

befriend, *vb.* sich an·freunden mit.

befuddle, *vb.* verwir′ren.

beg, *vb.* betteln; *(implore)* bitten*.

beggar, *n.* Bettler, - *m.*

begin, *vb.* an·fangen*, begin′nen*.

beginner, *n.* Anfänger, - *m.*

beginning, *n.* Anfang, ⸗e *m.*

begrudge, *vb.* mißgön′nen.

beguile, *vb.* bestrick′en.

behalf, *n.* (on b. of) zugun′sten von, im Namen von.

behave, *vb.* sich beneh′men*.

behavior, *n.* Beneh′men, *nt.*

behead, *vb.* enthaup′ten.

behind, 1. *adv.* hinten, zurück. **2.** *prep.* hinter.

behold, 1. *vb.* sehen*. **2.** *interj.* sieh(e) da.

beige, *adj.* beigefarben.

being, *n.* Sein *nt.,* Wesen, *nt.*

belated, *adj.* verspä′tet.

belch, *vb.* rülpsen.

belfry, *n.* Glockenturm, ⸗e *m.*

Belgian, 1. *n.* Belgier, - *m.* **2.** *adj.* belgisch.

Belgium, *n.* Belgien *nt.*

belie, *vb.* Lügen strafen.

belief, *n.* Glaube(n), - *m.*

believable, *adj.* glaubhaft.

believe, *vb.* glauben.

believer, *n.* Gläubig- *m.&f.*

belittle, *vb.* bagatellisie′ren.

bell, *n. (small)* Klingel, -n *f.; (large)* Glocke, -n *f.*

bellboy, *n.* Hotel′boy, -s *m.*

belligerence, *n.* Kriegslust, ⸗e *f.;* Kriegszustand, ⸗e *m.*

belligerent, *adj.* kriegerisch, kriegsführend.

bellow, *vb.* brüllen.

bellows, *n.* Blasebalg, ⸗e *m.*

belly, *n.* Bauch, ⸗e *m.*

belong, *vb.* gehö′ren.

belongings, *n.pl.* Habseligkeiten *pl.*

beloved, *adj.* geliebt′.

below, 1. *adv.* unten. **2.** *prep.* unter.

belt, *n.* Gürtel, - *m.*

bench, *n.* Bank, ⸗e *f.*

bend, *vb.* biegen*.

beneath, 1. *adv.* unten. **2.** *prep.* unter.

benediction, *n.* Segen, - *m.*

benefactor, *n.* Wohltäter, - *m.*

benefactress, *n.* Wohltäterin, -nen *f.*

beneficent, *adj.* wohltätig.

beneficial, *adj.* wohltuend, nützlich.

beneficiary, *n.* Begün′stigt- *m.&f.;* Nutzniesser, - *m.*

benefit 1. *n.* Wohltat, -en *f.; (advantage)* Nutzen, - *m.,* Vorteil, -e *m.*. **2.** *vb.* nützen; (b. from) Nutzen ziehen* aus.

benevolence, *n.* Wohlwollen *nt.*

benevolent, *adj.* wohlwollend.

benign, *adj.* gütig.

bent, *adj.* gebeugt′; *(out of shape)* verbo′gen.

benzine, *n.* Benzin′ *nt.*

bequeath, *vb.* verma′chen.

bequest, *n.* Vermächt′nis, -se *nt.,* Legat′, -e *nt.*

berate, *vb.* aus·schelten*.

bereave, *vb.* berau′ben.

bereavement, *n.* Verlust durch Tod.

berry, *n.* Beere, -n *f.*

berth, n. Bettplatz, -e m.

beseech, vb. an·flehen.

beset, vb. bedrän'gen.

beside, prep. neben; **(b. one-self)** außer sich.

besides, 1. adv. außerdem. 2. prep. außer.

besiege, vb. bela'gern.

best, 1. adj. best-. 2. vb. übertref'fen*.

bestial, adj. bestia'lisch, tierisch.

bestow, vb. verlei'hen*

bestowal, n. Verlei'hung, -en f.

bet, 1. n. Wette, -n f. 2. vb. wetten.

betake oneself, vb. sich auf·machen.

betoken, vb. bezeich'nen.

betray, vb. verra'ten*.

betrayal, n. Verrat' m.

betroth, vb. verlo'ben; **(be b. ed)** sich verlo'ben.

betrothal, n. Verlo'bung, -en f.

better, 1. adj. besser. 2. vb. verbes'sern.

between, prep. zwischen.

bevel, 1. n. schräger An-schnitt, -e m. 2. vb. schräg ab·schneiden*.

beverage, n. Getränk', -e nt.

bewail, vb. bekla'gen.

beware, vb. sich hüten.

bewilder, vb. verwir'ren.

bewilderment, n. Verwir'-rung, -en f.

bewitch, vb. bezau'bern; verzau'bern.

beyond, 1. adv. jenseits. 2. prep. jenseits. über.

biannual, adj. halbjährlich.

bias, n. Vorurteil, -e nt.

bib, n. Lätzchen, - nt.

Bible, n. Bibel, -n f.

Biblical, adj. biblisch.

bibliography, n. Bibliog-raphie', -i'en f.

bicarbonate, n. (of soda) doppelkohlensaures Natron nt.

biceps, n. Bizeps, -e m.

bicker, vb. sich zanken.

bicycle, n. Fahrrad, *er nt.

bicyclist, n. Radfahrer, - m.

bid, 1. n. Angebot, -e nt. 2. vb. bieten*.

bide, vb. ab·warten.

biennial, adj. zweijährlich.

bier, n. Bahre -n f.

bifocal, adj. bifokal'.

big, adj. groß (größer, größt-).

bigamist, n. Bigamist', -en, -en m.

bigamous, adj. biga'misch.

bigamy, n. Bigamie', -i'en f.

bigot, n. Frömmler, - m.

bigoted, adj. bigott'.

bigotry, n. Frömmelei', -en f.

bilateral, adj. zweiseitig.

bile, n. Galle, -n f.

bilingual, adj. zweisprachig.

bilious, adj. gallig.

bill, n. (bird) Schnabel, = m.; (banknote) Geldschein, -e m.; (sum owed) Rechnung, -en f.; (legislative) Geset'zesvor-lage, -n f.

billboard, n. Rekla'meschild, -er nt.

billet, 1. n. Quartier', -e nt. 2. vb. ein·quartieren.

billfold, n. Brieftasche, -n f.

billiards, n. Billard, -s nt.

billion, n. Billion', -en f.

bill of fare, n. Speisekarte, -n f.

bill of health, n. Gesund'-heitsattest, -e nt.

bill of lading, n. Frachtbrief, -e m.

bill of sale, n. Kaufkon-trakt, -e m.

billow, 1. n. Woge, -n f. 2. vb. wogen.

bimonthly, adj. zweimo'-natlich.

bin, n. Kasten, = m.

bind, vb. binden*; verbin-den*.

bindery, n. Buchbinderei', -en f.

binding, 1. n. (book) Ein-band, *e m.; (ski) Bindung, -en f. 2. adj. bindend.

binocular, n. Fernglas, *er nt.

biochemistry, n. Biochemie' f.

biographer, n. Biograph', -en, -en m.

biographical, *adj.* biogra'-phisch.

biography, *n.* Biographie', -i'en *f.*

biological, *adj.* biolo'gisch.

biology, *n.* Biologie', -i'en *f.*

bipartisan, *adj.* die Regierungs- und die Oppositionspartei vertretend.

bird, *n.* Vogel. ⁼ *m.*

birth, *n.* Geburt'. -en *f.*

birthday, *n.* Geburts'tag, -e *m.*

birthmark, *n.* Muttermal, -e *nt.*

birthplace, *n.* Geburts'ort, -e *m.*

birth rate, *n.* Gebur'tenziffer, -n *f.*

birthright, *n.* Erstgeburtsrecht, -e *nt.*; angestammtes Recht *nt.*

biscuit, *n.* Biskuit', -e *nt.*; Keks, -e *m.*

bisect, *vb.* halbie'ren.

bishop, *n.* Bischof, ⁼e, *m.*

bismuth, *n.* Wismut *nt.*

bison, *n.* Bison, -s *m.*

bit, *n.* (*piece*) Bißchen, - *nt.*; (**a. b. of**) ein bißchen; (*harness*) Gebiß, -sse *nt.*

bitch, *n.* Hündin, -nen *f.*

bite, 1. *n.* Bissen, - *m.* **2.** *vb.* beißen*.

biting, *adj.* beißend.

bitter, *adj.* bitter.

bitterness, *n.* Bitterkeit, -en *f.*

biweekly, *adj.* zweiwöchentlich.

black, *adj.* schwarz(⁼).

blackberry, *n.* Brombeere, -n *f.*

blackbird, *n.* Amsel, -n *f.*

blackboard, *n.* Wandtafel, -n *f.*

blacken, *vb.* schwärzen.

blackmail, 1. *n.* Erpres'-sung, -en *f.* **2.** *vb.* erpres'-sen.

black market, *n.* Schwarzmarkt, ⁼e *m.*

blackout, *n.* Verdun'kelung, -en *f.*

blacksmith, *n.* Schmied, -e *m.*

bladder, *n.* Blase, -n *f.*

blade, *n.* (*knife*) Klinge, -n *f.*; (*grass*) Halm, -e *m.*

blame, 1. *n.* Schuld, -en *f.* **2.** *vb.* beschul'digen.

blanch, *vb.* bleichen; bleich werden*.

bland, *adj.* mild.

blank, 1. *n.* (*form*) Formular', -e *nt.* **2.** *adj.* unbeschrieben, leer.

blanket, *n.* Decke, -n *f.*, Wolldecke, -n *f.*

blaspheme, *vb.* lästern.

blasphemer, *n.* Gottesläster- er, - *m.*

blasphemous, *adj.* gottesläs-terlich.

blasphemy, *n.* Gottesläs-terung, -en *f.*, Blasphemie', -i'en *f.*

blast, 1. *n.* (*of wind*) Windstoß, ⁼e *m.*; (*explosion*) Explosion', -en *f.* **2.** *vb.* sprengen.

blatant, *adj.* laut, aufdring-lich.

blaze, 1. *n.* Flamme, -n *f.* **2.** *vb.* lodern, leuchten.

bleach, *vb.* bleichen.

bleak, *adj.* öde.

bleed, *vb.* bluten.

blemish, *n.* Makel, - *m.*

blend, 1. *n.* Mischung, -en *f.* **2.** *vb.* mischen.

bless, *vb.* segnen.

blessed, *adj.* gese'gnet, selig.

blessing, *n.* Segen, - *m.*

blight, 1. *n.* (*bot.*) Brand, ⁼e *m.* **2.** (*fig.*) verei'teln.

blind, 1. *adj.* blind. **2.** *vb.* blenden.

blindfold, 1. *n.* Augenbinde, -n *f.* **2.** *vb.* die Augen verbin'den*.

blindness, *n.* Blindheit, -en *f.*

blink, *vb.* blinken, blinzeln.

blinker, *n.* Scheuklappe, -n *f.*; (*signal*) Blinklicht, -e *nt.*

bliss, *n.* Glückseligkeit, -en *f.*

blissful, *adj.* glückselig.

blister, *n.* Blase, -n *f.*

blithe, *adj.* fröhlich.

blizzard, *n.* Schneesturm, ⁼e *m.*

bloat, *vb.* blähen.

bloc, *n.* Block, ≃e *m.*

block, 1. *n. (wood)* Holzblock, ≃e *m.; (city)* Häuserblock, ≃e *m.* **2.** *vb.* sperren.

blockade, *n.* Blocka'de, -n *f.*

blond, *adj.* blond.

blood, *n.* Blut *nt.*

bloodhound, *n.* Bluthund, -e *m.*

blood plasma, *n.* Plasma, -men *nt.*

blood poisoning, *n.* Blutvergiftung, -en *f.*

blood pressure, *n.* Blutdruck, *m.*

bloodshed, *n.* Blutvergießen *nt.*

bloodshot, *adj.* blutunterlaufen.

bloody, *adj.* blutig.

bloom, 1. *n.* Blüte, -n *f.* **2.** *vb* blühen.

blossom, 1. *n.* Blüte -n *f.*

blot, 1. *n.* Fleck, -e *m.* **2.** *vb.* beflec'ken, *(ink)* löschen.

blotter, *n.* Löschpapier, -e *nt.*

blouse, *n.* Bluse, -n *f.*

blow, 1. *n.* Schlag, ≃e *m.*, Stoß, ≃e *m.* **2.** *vb.* blasen*.

blowout, *n.* Reifenpanne, -n *f.*

blubber, 1. *n.* Walfischspeck *m.* **2.** *vb.* flennen.

blue, *adj.* blau.

bluebird, *n.* Blaukehlchen, *nt.*

blueprint, *n.* Blaudruck, -e *m.; (fig.)* Plan, ≃e *m.*

bluff, 1. *n. (cliff)* Klippe, -n *f.,* schroffer Felsen, - *m.; (cards)* Bluff, -s *m.* **2.** *adj.* schroff. **3.** *vb.* bluffen.

bluffer, *n.* Bluffer, - *m.*

bluing, *n.* Waschblau *nt.*

blunder, 1. *n.* Fehler, - *m.* **2.** *vb.* Fehler machen.

blunderer, *n.* Tölpel, - *m.*

blunt, *adj.* stumpf; *(fig)* unverblümt.

blur, 1. *n.* Verschwommenheit *f.* **2.** *vb (intr.)* verschwim'men*; *(tr.)* trüben.

blurred, *adj.* verschwommen.

blush, 1. *n.* Errö'ten *nt.* **2.** *vb* erröten.

bluster, *vb.* toben; *(swagger)* prahlen.

boar, *n.* Eber, - *m.*

board, 1. *n. (plank)* Brett, -er *nt.,* Bord, -e *nt.; (food) (committee)* Ausschuß, ≃ss *m.; (council)* Behör'de, -n *f.; (ship)* Bord, -e *nt.* **2.** *vb.* an Bord gehen*.

boarder, *n.* Kostgänger, - *m.*

boarding house, *n.* Pension', -en *f.*

boast, 1. *n.* Angeberei', -en *f.* **2.** *vb.* prahlen, an'geben*.

boaster, *n.* Angeber, - *m.*

boastful, *adj.* angeberisch.

boastfulness, *n.* Angeberei', -en *f.*

boat, *n.* Boot, -e *nt.,* Schiff, -e *nt.*

bob, 1. *n. (hair)* Bubikopf *m.* **2.** *vb.* baumeln; *(hair)* kurz schneiden*.

bobby pin, *n.* Haarklammer, -n *f.*

bodice, *n.* Oberteil -e *nt.*

bodily, *adj.* leiblich.

body, *n.* Körper, - *m.,* Leib, -er *m.*

bodyguard, *n.* Leibwache, -n *f.*

bog, *n.* Sumpf, ≃e *m.* **2.** *vb.* **(b. down)** stecken bleiben*.

Bohemian, 1. *n.* Böhme, -n, -n *m.* **2.** *adj.* böhmisch.

boil, 1. *n. (med.)* Furun'kel, -n *f.* **2.** *vb.* kochen.

boiler, *n.* Kessel, - *m.*

boisterous, *adj.* ungestüm.

bold, *adj.* kühn.

boldface, *n.* Fettdruck, -e *m.*

boldness, *n.* Kühnheit, -en *f.*

Bolivian, 1. *n.* Bolivia'ner, - *m.* **2.** *adj.* bolivia'nisch.

bolster, 1. *n.* Polster, - *nt.* **2.** *vb. (support)* unterstüt'zen.

bolster up, *vb.* stärken.

bolt, 1. *n. (lock)* Riegel, - *m.; (screw with nut)* Schraube, -n *f.; (lightning)* Blitz, -e *m.* **2.** *vb. (lock)* verrie'geln; *(dash, of persons)* davon'stürzen, *(of horses)* durch'gehen*.

bomb, 1. *n.* Bombe, -n *f.* **2.** *vb.* bomben.

bombard, *vb.* bombardie'ren.

bombardier, *n.* Bombardier', -e *m.*

bombardment, *n.* Beschie'ßung, -en *f.*

bomber, *n.* Bombenflugzeug, -e *nt.*

bombproof, *adj.* bombensicher.

bombshell, *n.* Bombe, -n *f.*

bombsight, *n.* Bombenzielvorrichtung, -en *f.*

bonbon, *n.* Fondant', -s *m.*

bond, *n.* Band, -e *nt.*, Fessel, -n *f.*; (*law*) Bürgschaft, -en *f.*; (*stock exchange*) Obligation', -en *f.*

bondage, *n.* Knechtschaft, -en *f.*

bone, *n.* Knochen, - *m.*; (*fish*) Gräte, -n *f.*

bonfire, *n.* Freudenfeuer, - *nt.*

bonnet, *n.* Damenhut, -e *m.*

bonus, *n.* Extrazahlung, -en *f.*; Tantie'me, -n *f.*

bony, *adj.* knochig.

book, 1. *n.* Buch, -er *nt.* **2.** *vb.* buchen.

bookcase, *n.* Bücherschrank, -e *m.*

bookkeeper, *n.* Buchhalter, - *m.*

bookkeeping, *n.* Buchführung, -en *f.*

booklet, *n.* Broschü're, -n *f.*

bookseller, *n.* Buchhändler, - *m.*

bookstore, *n.* Buchhandlung, -en *f.*

boom, 1. *n.* Baum, -e *m.*; (*econ.*) Hochkonjunktur, -en *f.* **2.** *vb.* brummen dröhnen.

boon, *n.* Geschenk', -e *nt.*; (*fig.*) Segen, - *m.*

boor, *n.* Grobian, -e *m.*

boorish, *adj.* grob(-).

boost, 1. *n.* (*increase*) Aufschwung, -e *m.*; (*push*) Antrieb, -e *m.* **2.** *vb.* (*increase*) steigern; (*push*) nachhelfen*.

boot, *n.* Stiefel, - *m.*

bootblack, *n.* Schuhputzer, -

booth, *n.* Bude, -n *f.*; (*telephone*) Fernsprechzelle, -n *f.*

border, 1. *n.* Grenze, -n *f.* **2.** *vb.* grenzen an.

borderline, *n.* Grenze, -n *f.*

bore, 1. *n.* (*hole*) Bohrloch, -er *nt.*; (*cylinder*) Bohrung, -en *f.*; (*person*) langweiliger Mensch, -en, -en *m.* **2.** *vb.* bohren; (*annoy*) langweilen.

boredom, *n.* Langeweile *f.*

boric, *adj.* Bor- (*cpds.*).

boring, *adj.* langweilig.

born, *adj.* gebo'ren.

borough, *n.* Stadtteil, -e *m.*

borrow, *vb.* borgen, leihen*.

bosom, *n.* Busen, - *m.*

boss, *n.* Chef, -s *m.*

bossy, *adj.* herrschsüchtig.

botanical, *adj.* bota'nisch.

botany, *n.* Bota'nik *f.*

both, *adj.&pron.* beide.

bother, 1. *n.* Verdruß' *m.* **2.** *vb.* belä'stigen; (*disturb*) stören.

bothersome, *adj.* lästig.

bottle, *n.* Flasche, -n *f.*

bottom, *n.* Grund, -e *m.*

bottomless, *adj.* bodenlos.

boudoir, *n.* Boudoir', -e *m.*

bough, *n.* Ast, -e *m.*, Zweig, -e *m.*

bouillon, *n.* Kraftbrühe, -n *f.*

boulder, *n.* Felsblock, -e *m.*

boulevard, *n.* Boulevard', -s *m.*

bounce, *vb.* springen*.

bound, 1. *n.* (*jump*) Sprung, -e *m.*; (b.s.) Grenzen *pl.* **2.** *vb.* (*jump*) springen*; (*limit*) begren'zen. **3.** *adj.* (*tied*) gebun'den; (**duty b.**) verpflich'tet; (**b. for**) unterwegs' nach.

boundary, *n.* Grenze, -n *f.*

bound for, *adj.* unterwegs' nach.

boundless, *adj.* grenzenlos.

bounty, *n.* Freigebigkeit, -en *f.*

bouquet, *n.* Blumenstrauß, -e *m.*

bourgeois, *adj.* bürgerlich.

bout, *n.* (*boxing*) Boxkampf, -e *m.*

bovine, *adj.* Rinder- (*cpds.*)

bow, 1. n. (for arrows, violin) Bogen, - m.; (greeting) Verbeu'gung, -en f.; (hair, dress) Schleife, -n f.; (of boats) Bug, -e m. **2.** vb. sich verbeu'gen.

bowels, n.pl. Eingeweide pl.

bowl, 1. n. Schüssel -n f.; Schale, -n f. **2.** vb. kegeln.

bowlegged, adj. o-beinig.

bowler, n. Kegelspieler, - m.; (hat) Melo'ne, -n f.

bowling, n. Kegeln nt.

box, 1. n. (small) Schachtel, -n f.; (large) Kasten. = m.; (theater) Loge, -n f.; (letter b.) Briefkasten. = m. **2.** vb. (sport) boxen.

boxcar, n. Güterwagen, - m.

boxer, n. Boxer, - m.

boxing, n. Boxen nt.

box office, n. Thea'terkasse, -n f.

boy, n. Junge -n, -n m.; Bube, -n, -n m.

boycott, 1. n. Boykott', -e m. **2.** vb. boykotti'ren.

boyhood, n. Jugend, -en f.

boyish, adj. jungenhaft, jung.

brace, 1. n. Klammer, -n f.; Stütze, -n f. **2.** vb. ab-steifen.

bracelet, n. Armband, -er nt.

bracket, n. Klammer, -n f.; (typography) Klammer, -n f.; (group) Gruppe, -n f.

brag, vb. prahlen, an'geben*.

braggart, n. Angeber, - m.

braid, 1. n. Flechte, -n f. **2.** vb. flechten*.

brain, n. Gehirn', -e nt.

brake, 1. n. Bremse, -n f. **2.** vb. bremsen.

bran, n. Kleie, -n f.

branch, n. Ast, =e m., Zweig, -e m.

brand, 1. n. (sort) Sorte, -n f.; (mark) Marke, -n f. **2.** vb. brandmarken.

brandish, vb. schwingen*.

brandy, n. Weinbrand, -e m.; Kognak, -s m.

brash, adj. dreist.

brass, n. Messing nt.

brassiere, n. Büstenhalter, - m.

brat, n. Balg, =e m.

bravado, n. Bravour' f., Schneid m.

brave, adj. tapfer.

bravery, n. Tapferkeit -en f.

brawl, n. Rauferei', -en f.

brawn, n. Muskelkraft, =e f.

bray, 1. n. Eselsgeschrei nt. **2.** vb. schrein*.

brazen, adj. ehern; (insolent) unverschämt

Brazil, n. Brasi'lien nt.

Brazilian, 1. n. Brasilia'ner, - m. **2.** adj. brasilia'nisch.

breach, n. Bruch, =e m.

bread, n. Brot. -e nt.

breadth, n. Breite, -n f.

break, 1. n. Bruch, =e m.; Pause, -n f. **2.** vb. brechen*.

breakable, adj. zerbrech'-lich.

breakfast, n. Frühstück, -e nt.

breakneck, adj. halsbrech-erisch.

breakwater, n. Mole. -n f.

breast, n. Brust, =e f.

breath, n. Atem, - m.

breathe, vb. atmen.

breathing, n. Atmen nt.

breathless, adj. atemlos.

breeches, n. Kniehose -n f.

breed, 1. n. Zucht, -en f. **2.** vb. (beget) erzeu'gen; (raise) züchten; (educate) erzie'-hen*.

breeder, n. Züchter, - m.

breeding, n. Erzie'hung, -en f.

breeze, n. Brise, -n f.

breezy, adj. luftig.

brevity, n. Kürze, -n f.

brew, 1. n. Gebräu, -e nt. **2.** vb. brauen.

brewer, n. Brauer, - m.

brewery, n. Brauerei', -en f.

briar, n. Dornbusch, =e m.; Bruyèreholz nt.

bribe, vb. beste'chen*.

briber, n. Beste'cher, - m.

bribery, n. Beste'chung, -en f.

brick, n. Backstein, -e m.; Ziegelstein, -e m.

bricklayer, n. Maurer, - m.

bridal, *adj.* Hochzeits(*cpds.*).

bride, *n.* Braut, ≈e *f.*

bridegroom, *n.* Bräutigam, -e *m.*

bridesmaid, *n.* Brautjungfer, -n *f.*

bridge, 1. *n.* Brücke, -n *f.*; (*game*) Bridge *nt.* **2.** *vb.* überbrü'cken.

bridle, *n.* Zaum, ≈e *m.*

brief, *adj.* kurz(≈).

brief case, *n.* Aktenmappe, -n *f.*

bright, *adj.* hell; (*smart*) gescheit'.

brighten, *vb.* erhel'len.

brightness, *n.* Klarheit, -en *f.*

brilliance, *n.* Glanz. -e *m.*

brilliant, *adj.* glänzend; (*smart*) hochbegabt.

brim, *n.* (*cup*) Rand, ≈er *m.*; (*hat*) Krempe, -n *f.*

brine, *n.* Salzwasser, - *nt.*, Sole, -n *f.*

bring, *vb.* bringen*.

brink, *n.* Rand, ≈er *m.*

briny, *adj.* salzig.

brisk, *adj.* lebhaft.

brisket, *n.* (*meat*) Bruststück, -e *nt.*

briskness, *n.* Lebhaftigkeit, -en *f.*

bristle, 1. *n.* Borste, -n *f.* **2.** *vb.* sich sträuben.

Britain, *n.* Britan'nien *nt.*

British, *adj.* britisch.

Briton, *n.* Brite, -n, -n *m.*

brittle, *adj.* brüchig, spröde.

broad, *adj.* breit, weit.

broadcast, 1. *n.* Rundfunksendung, -en *f.*, Übertra'gung, -en *f.* **2.** *vb.* senden, im Radio übertra'gen*.

broadcaster, *n.* Rundfunksprecher, - *m.*

broadcloth, *n.* feiner Wäschestoff *m.*

broaden, *vb.* erwei'tern.

broadly, *adv.* allgemein'.

broadminded, *adj.* großzügig, tolerant'.

brocade, *n.* Brokat', -e *m.*

broil, *vb.* grillen.

broiler, *n.* Bratrost, -e *m.*

broke, *adj.* pleite.

broken, *adj.* gebro'chen; kaputt'.

broker, *n.* Makler, - *m.*

brokerage, *n.* (*business*) Maklergeschäft. -e *nt.*; (*charge*) Maklergebühr, -en *f.*

bronchial, *adj.* bronchial'.

bronchitis, *n.* Bronchi'tis *f.*

bronze, *n.* Bronze, -n *f.*

brooch, *n.* Brosche, -n *f.*

brood, 1. *n.* Brut, -en *f.* **2.** *vb.* brüten.

brook, *n.* Bach, ≈e *m.*

broom, *n.* Besen, - *m.*

broomstick, *n.* Besenstiel, -e *m.*

broth, *n.* Brühe, -n *f.*

brothel, *n.* Bordell', -e *nt.*

brother, *n.* Bruder, ≈ *m.*

brotherhood, *n.* Brüderschaft, -en *f.*

brother-in-law, *n.* Schwager, ≈ *m.*

brotherly, *adj.* brüderlich.

brow, *n.* Stirn, -en *f.*

brown, *adj.* braun.

browse, *vb.* schmökern.

bruise, 1. *n.* Quetschung, -en *f.*; **2.** *vb.* quetschen, stoßen*.

brunette, *n.* Brünet'te, -n *f.*

brunt, *n.* (**bear the b.**) die Hauptlast tragen*.

brush, 1. *n.* Bürste, -n *f.*; (*artist*) Pinsel, - *m.* **2.** *vb.* bürsten.

brusque, *adj.* brüsk.

brutal, *adj.* brutal'.

brutality, *n.* Brutalität', -en *f.*

brutalize, *vb.* verro'hen.

brute, *n.* Unmensch, -en, -en *m.*

bubble, 1. *n.* Luftblase, -n *f.* **2.** *vb.* sprudeln.

buck, 1. *n.* Bock, ≈e *m.* **2.** *vb.* bocken; (*fig.*) sich gegen etwas auf bäumen.

bucket, *n.* Eimer, - *m.*

buckle, 1. *n.* Schnalle, - *f.* **2.** *vb.* (*fasten*) schnallen; (*bend*) sich krümmen, biegen*.

buckwheat, *n.* Buchweizen *m.*

bud, 1. *n.* Knospe, -n *f.* **2.** *vb.* knospen.

budge, *vb.* sich rühren.

budget, n. Etat', -s m.

buffalo, n. Büffel. - m.

buffer, n. Puffer. - m.; (**b. state**) Pufferstaat. -en m.

buffet, 1. n. Büfett', -e, Buffet', -s nt. 2. vb. schlagen*.

bug, n. Käfer. - m.

bugle, n. Signal'horn. -er nt.

build, vb. bauen.

builder, n. Baumeister, - m.

building, n. Gebäu'de, - nt.

bulb, n. Knolle, -n f.; (electric) Glühbirne, -n f.

bulge, 1. n. Ausbuchtung. -en f. 2. vb. sich ausbuchten.

bulk, n. Umfang m., Hauptteil, -e m.

bulky, adj. umfangreich.

bull, n. Bulle, -n, -n m.

bulldog, n. Bulldogge, -n f.

bullet, n. Kugel, -n f.

bulletin, n. Bericht'. -e nt.

bully, 1. n. Kraftmeier, - m. 2. vb. kraftmeiern.

bulwark, n. Bollwerk, -e nt.

bum, 1. n. (fam.) Lump, -en, -en m. 2. vb. (fam.) pumpen.

bumblebee, n. Hummel, -n f.

bump, 1. n. Stoß, -e m. 2. vb. stoßen*.

bumper, n. Stoßstange, -n f.

bun, n. Brötchen, - nt.

bunch, n. Büschel, - nt.

bundle, n. Bündel, - nt.

bungle, vb. pfuschen.

bunion, n. Entzün'dung am großen Zeh.

bunny, n. Kanin'chen, - nt.

buoy, n. Boje, -n f.

buoyant, adj. schwimmend, tragfähig; (fig.) lebhaft.

burden, 1. n. Last, -en f. 2. vb. belas'ten.

burdensome, adj. beschwerlich.

bureau, n. Büro'. -s nt.; (furniture) Kommo'de, -n f.

burglar, n. Einbrecher, - m.

burglary, n. Einbruch, -e m.

burial, n. Begräb'nis, -se nt.

burlap, n. grobe Leinwand f.

burly, adj. stämmig.

burn, 1. n. Verbren'nung.

-en f. 2. vb. (intr.) brennen*, (tr.) verbren'nen*

burner, n. Brenner. - m.

burrow, 1. n. (of an animal) Bau, -e m. 2. vb. sich eingraben*.

burst, 1. n. Krach, -e m.; Explosion', -en f. 2. vb. (intr.) platzen; (tr.) sprengen.

bury, vb. begra'ben*; eingraben*.

bus, n. Bus, -se m.

bush, n. Busch, -e m.

bushel, n. Scheffel, - m.

bushy, adj. buschig.

business, n. Geschäft', -e nt.

businesslike, adj. geschäftsmäßig.

businessman, n. Geschäftsmann, -er or -leute m.

businesswoman, n. Geschäfts'frau, -en f.

bust, 1. n. Büste, -n f. 2. vb. (fam.) kaputt' machen.

bustle, n. Geschäf'tigkeit, -en f.

busy, adj. beschäf'tigt; geschäf'tig.

but, 1. prep. außer. 2. conj. aber.

butcher, n. Fleischer, - m., Metzger, - m., Schlächter, - m., Schlachter, - m.

butler, n. Diener, - m.

butt, 1. n. (gun) Kolben, - m.; (aim) Ziel, -e nt. 2. vb. mit dem Kopf stoßen*.

butter, n. Butter f.

butterfly, n. Schmetterling, -e m.

buttermilk, n. Buttermilch f.

buttocks, n.pl. Gesäß', - nt.

button, n. Knopf, -e m.

buttonhole, n. Knopfloch, -er nt.

buttress, 1. n. Stütze, -n f.; (arch.) Strebepfeiler, - m. 2. vb. stützen.

buxom, adj. drall.

buy, vb. kaufen.

buyer, n. Käufer, - m.

buzz, vb. summen.

buzzard, n. Bussard, -e m.

buzzer, n. Klingel, -n f.

by, *prep.* von; *(through)* durch; *(near)* bei.

by-and-by, *adv.* später.

bygone, *adj.* vergan'gen.

by-pass, *n.* Umge'hungs-straße, -n *f.*

by-product, *n.* Neben-produkt, -e *nt.*

bystander, *n.* Zuschauer, - *m.*

byway, *n.* Nebenweg, -e *m.*

C

cab, *n.* *(taxi)* Taxe, -n *f.,* Taxi, -s *nt.;* *(locomotive)* Führerstand, -e *m.*

cabaret, *n.* Kabarett', -e *nt.*

cabbage, *n.* Kohl *m.*

cabin, *n.* Kabi'ne, -n *f.*

cabinet, *n.* Kabinett', -e *nt.*

cabinetmaker, *n.* Kunst-tischler, - *m.*

cable, 1. *n.* Kabel, - *nt.* **2.** *vb.* kabeln.

cablegram, *n.* Kabel, - *nt.*

cache, *n.* Versteck', -e *nt.*

cackle, *vb.* gackern.

cactus, *n.* Kaktus, -te'en *m.*

cad, *n.* Schuft, -e *m.*

cadaver, *n.* Leichnam, -e *m.*

cadet, *n.* Kadett', -en, -en *m.*

cadence, *n.* Tonfall, -e *m.;* Kadenz', -en *f.*

cadmium, *n.* Kadmium *nt.*

café, *n.* Cafe', -s *nt.;* Kondi-torei', -en *f.*

caffeine, *n.* Koffein', -e *nt.*

cage, *n.* Käfig, -e *m.*

cajole, *vb.* beschwat'zen.

cake, *n.* Kuchen, - *m.*

calamity, *n.* Unglück, -e *nt.*

calcium, *n.* Kalzium *nt.*

calculable, *adj.* bere'chen-bar.

calculate, *vb.* berech'nen.

calculating machine, *n.* Rechenmaschine, -n *f.*

calculation, *n.* Berech'nung, -en *f.*

calculus, *n.* Differential'-rechnung, -en *f.*

caldron, *n.* Kessel, - *m.*

calendar, *n.* Kalen'der, - *m.*

calf, *n.* Kalb, ·er *nt.*

calfskin, *n.* Kalbleder, - *nt.*

caliber, *n.* Kali'ber, - *nt.*

calico, *n.* Kattun', -e *m.*

calipers, *n.pl.* Greifzirkel, - *m.*

calisthenics, *n.pl.* Leibes-übungen *pl.*

call, 1. *n.* Ruf, -e *m.;* *(tele-phone)* Anruf, -e *m.* **2.** *vb.* rufen*.

calling card, *n.* Visi'-tenkarte, -n *f.*

callous, *adj.* schwielig; *(un-feeling)* gefühl'los.

callus, *n.* Schwiele, -n *f.*

calm, 1. *adj.* ruhig. **2.** *vb.* beru'higen.

calmness, *n.* Ruhe *f.*

caloric, *adj.* kalo'risch.

calorie, *n.* Kalorie', -i'en *f.*

Calvary, *n.* Kalva'rienberg *m.*

calve, *vb.* kalben.

cambric, *n.* Batist', -e *m.*

camel, *n.* Kamel', -e *nt.*

cameo, *n.* Kame'e, -n *f.*

camera, *n.* Kamera, -s *f.,* Photoapparat, -e *m.*

camouflage, 1. *n.* Tarnung -en *f.;* **(natural c.)** Mimikry *f.,* Schutzfarbe, -n *f.* **2.** *vb.* tarnen.

camp, 1. *n.* Lager, - *nt.* **2.** *vb.* lagern.

campaign, 1. *n.* Feldzug, -e *m.;* Kampag'ne, -n *f.* **2.** *vb.* *(political)* Wahlreden hal-ten*.

camper, *n.* Zelter, - *m.*

camping, *n.* Zelten *nt.*

camphor, *n.* Kampfer *m.*

campus, *n.* Universitäts'-gelände, - *nt.,* College-Ge-lände, - *nt.*

can, 1. *n.* *(tin)* Büchse, -n *f.;* *(large)* Kanne, -n *f.* **2.** *vb.* *(preserve)* ein-machen; *(be able)* können*.

Canada, *n.* Kanada *nt.*

Canadian, 1. *n.* Kana'dier, - *m.* **2.** *adj.* Kana'disch.

canal, *n.* Kanal', -e *m.*

canapé, *n.* Cocktailgebäck *nt.*

canary, *vb.* Kana'rienvogel, - *m.*

cancel, *vb.* entwer'ten, rückgängig machen, auf·heben*.

cancellation, *n.* Aufhebung, -en *f.*, Entwer'tung, -en *f.*

cancer, *n.* Krebs, -e *m.*

candelabrum, *n.* Armleuchter, - *m.*

candid, *adj.* offen, ehrlich.

candidacy, *n.* Kandidatur', -en *f.*

candidate, *n.* Kandidat', -en, -en *m.*

candied, *adj.* kandiert'.

candle, *n.* Kerze, -n *f.*

candlestick, *n.* Leuchter, - *m.*

candor, *n.* Offenheit, -en *f.*

cane, *n.* Stock, *-e m.*; (*sugar*) Rohr, -e *nt.*

canine, *adj.* Hunde- (*cpds.*).

canister, *n.* Blechbüchse, -n *f.*

canker, *n.* Krebs, -e *m.*

canned, *adj.* eingemacht; Büchsen- (*cpds.*).

cannibal, *n.* Kanniba'le, -n, -n *m.*

canning, *n.* Einmachen *nt.*

cannon, *n.* Kano'ne, -n *f.*

cannot, *vb.* nicht können*.

canny, *adj.* schlau, umsichtig.

canoe, *n.* Kanu', -s *nt.*

canon, *n.* (*rule, song*) Kanon, -s *m.*; (*person*) Domherr, -n, -en *m.*

canonical, *adj.* kano'nisch.

canonize, *vb.* kanonisie'ren.

can opener, *n.* Büchsenöffner, - *m.*

canopy, *n.* Baldachin, -e *m.*

cant, *n.* Heuchelei', -en *f.*

cantaloupe, *n.* Melo'ne, -n *f.*

canteen, *n.* Kanti'ne, -n *f.*

canvas, *n.* (*material*) Segeltuch *nt.*; (*painter's*) Leinwand *f.*

canvass, 1. *n.* Stimmenprüfung -en *f.* **2.** *vb.* untersu'chen, prüfen.

canyon, *n.* Schlucht, -en *f.*

cap, *n.* Mütze, -n *f.*

capability, *n.* Fähigkeit, -en *f.*

capable, *adj.* fähig.

capacious, *adj.* geräu'mig.

capacity, *n.* (*content*) Inhalt

m.; (*ability*) Fähigkeit, -en *f.*; (*quality*) Eigenschaft, -en *f.*

cape, *n.* (*clothing*) Umhang, *-e m.*; (*geogr.*) Kap, -s *nt.*

caper, 1. *n.* Luftsprung, *-e m.* **2.** *vb.* Luftsprünge machen.

capital, 1. *n.* (*money*) Kapital', -ien *nt.*; (*city*) Hauptstadt, *-e f.* **2.** *adj.* kapital'.

capitalism, *n.* Kapitalis'mus *m.*

capitalist, *n.* Kapitalist', -en, -en *m.*

capitalistic, *adj.* kapitali'stisch.

capitalization, *n.* Kapitalisie'rung, -en *f.*

capitalize, *vb.* kapitalisie'ren.

capitulate, *vb.* kapitulie'ren.

capon, *n.* Kapaun', -e *m.*

caprice, *n.* Laune, -n *f.*

capricious, *adj.* launenhaft.

capsize, *vb.* kentern.

capsule, *n.* Kapsel, -n *f.*

captain, *n.* Kapitän', -e *m.*; (*army*) Hauptmann, -leute *m.*

caption, *n.* Überschrift, -en *f.*

captious, *adj.* verfäng'lich.

captivate, *vb.* fesseln.

captive, 1. *n.* Gefan'gen, - *m.&f.* **2.** *adj.* gefan'gen.

captivity, *n.* Gefan'genschaft, -en *f.*

captor, *n.* Fänger, - *m.*

capture, 1. *n.* Gefan'gennahme, -n *f.* **2.** *vb.* (*person*) fangen*; (*city*) ero'bern.

car, *n.* Wagen, - *m.*; Auto, -s *nt.*

carafe, *n.* Karaf'fe, -n *f.*

caramel, *n.* Karamel' *nt.*

carat, *n.* Karat', -e *nt.*

caravan, *n.* Karawa'ne, -n *f.*

caraway, *n.* Kümmel *m.*

carbide, *n.* Karbid' *nt.*

carbine, *n.* Karabi'ner, - *m.*

carbohydrate, *n.* Kohlehydrat, -e *nt.*

carbon, *n.* Kohlenstoff, -e *m.*

carbon dioxide, *n.* Kohlendioxyd *nt.*

carbon monoxide, *n.* Kohleoxyd' *nt.*

carbon paper, *n.* Kohle-papier, -e *nt.*

carbuncle, *n.* Karbun'kel, - *m.;* (*gem*) Karfun'kel, - *m.*

carburetor, *n.* Verga'ser, - *m.*

carcass, *n.* Kada'ver, - *m.*

card, *n.* Karte, -n *f.*

cardboard, *n.* Pappe, -n *f.*

cardiac, *adj.* Herz- (*cpds.*).

cardinal, 1. *n.* Kardinal', -e *m.* **2.** *adj.* hauptsächlich.

care, 1. *n.* (*worry*) Sorge, -n *f.;* (*prudence*) Vorsicht *f.;* (*accuracy*) Sorgfalt *f.;* (**take c. of**) sorgen für. **2.** *vb.* (*attend*) sorgen für; (*c. for like*) gern mögen*; (**c. about**) sich kümmern um.

careen, *vb.* wild fahren*.

career, *n.* Karrie're, -n *f.*

carefree, *adj.* sorglos.

careful, *adj.* (*prudent*) vorsichtig; (*accurate*) sorgfältig.

carefulness, *n.* (*prudence*) Vorsicht *f.;* (*accuracy*) Sorgfalt *f.*

careless, *adj.* (*imprudent*) unvorsichtig; (*inaccurate*) unsorgfältig, nachlässig.

carelessness, *n.* (*imprudence*) Unvorsichtigkeit, -en *f.;* (*inaccuracy*) Nachlässigkeit, -en *f.*

caress, 1. *n.* Liebkosung, -en *f.* **2.** *vb.* liebkosen, streicheln.

caretaker, *n.* Verwal'ter, - *m.*

cargo, *n.* Ladung, -en *f.,* Fracht, -en *f.*

caricature, 1. *n.* Karikatur', -en *f.* **2.** *vb.* karikie'ren.

caries, *n.* Karies *f.*

carload, *n.* Waggon'ladung, -en *f.*

carnal, *adj.* fleischlich.

carnation, *n.* Nelke, -n *f.*

carnival, *n.* Karneval, -s *m.*

carnivorous, *adj.* fleischfressend.

carol, 1. *n.* Weihnachtslied, -er *nt.* **2.** *vb.* singen*.

carouse, *vb.* zechen.

carousel, *n.* Karussell', -s *nt.*

carpenter, *n.* (*construction*)

Zimmermann, -leute *m.;* (*finer work*) Tischler, - *m.*

carpet, *n.* Teppich, -e *m.*

carriage, *n.* (*vehicle*) Wagen, - *m.;* (*posture*) Haltung, -en *f.*

carrier, *n.* Träger, - *m.*

carrot, *n.* Mohr'rübe, -n *f.*

carry, *vb.* tragen*; (**c. on,** *intr.*) fort·fahren*; (**c. on,** *tr.*) fort·setzen; (**c. out**) aus·führen; (**c. through**) durch·führen.

cart, *n.* Karren, - *m.*

cartage, *n.* Transport', -e *m.*

cartel, *n.* Kartell', -e *nt.*

cartilage, *n.* Knorpel, - *m.*

carton, *n.* Karton', -s *m.*

cartoon, *n.* Karikatur', -en *f.*

cartridge, *n.* Patro'ne, -n *f.*

carve, *vb.* schneiden*; (*wood*) schnitzen; (*meat*) zerle'gen, tranchie'ren.

carving, *n.* Schnitzwerk, -e *nt.*

case, *n.* Fall, ∺e *m.*

cash, 1. *n.* Bargeld, -er *nt.* **2.** *vb.* ein·lösen. **3.** *adj.* bar.

cashier, *n.* Kassie'rer, - *m.*

cashmere, *n.* Kaschmir, -e *m.*

casing, *n.* Hülle, -n *f.*

casino, *n.* Kasi'no, -s *nt.*

cask, *n.* Tonne, -n *f.,* Faß, ∺sser *nt.*

casket, *n.* Sarg, ∺e *m.*

casserole, *n.* Schmorpfanne, -n *f.*

cast, 1. *n.* (*theater*) Rollenverteilung, -en *f.* **2.** *vb.* (*throw*) werfen*; (*metal*) gießen*.

caste, *n.* Kaste, -n *f.*

castigate, *vb.* züchtigen.

castle, *n.* Schloß, ∺sser *nt.*

castoff, *adj.* abgelegt.

castor oil, *n.* Rizinusöl, -e *nt.*

casual, *adj.* (*accidental*) zufällig; (*nonchalant*) zwanglos.

casualness, *n.* Zwanglosigkeit, -en *f.*

casualty, *n.* Opfer, - *nt.;* (*casualties*) Verlus'te *pl.*

cat, *n.* Katze, -n *f.*; *(tomcat)* Kater. - *m.*

cataclysm, *n.* Sündflut, -en *f.*

catacomb, *n.* Katakom'be, -n *f.*

catalogue, *n.* Katalog', -e *m.*

catapult, *n.* Katapult', -e *m.*

cataract, *n.* (*eye*) Katarakt', -e *m.*, grauer Star, -e *m.*

catarrh, *n.* Katarrh', -e *m.*

catastrophe, *n.* Katastro'phe, -n *f.*

catch, *vb.* fangen*; (*sickness, train*) bekom'men*.

catcher, *n.* Fänger. - *m.*

catechism, *n.* Katechis'mus, -men *m.*

categorical, *adj.* katego'risch.

category, *n.* Kategorie', -i'en *f.*

cater, *vb.* versor'gen.

caterpillar, *n.* Raupe, -n *f.*

cathartic, l *n.* Abführmittel,- *nt.* 2. *adj.* abführend.

cathedral, *n.* Kathedra'le, -n *f.*; Dom, -e *m.*

cathode, *n.* Katho'de, -n *f.*

Catholic, 1. *n.* Katholik', -en, -en *m.* 2. *adj.* katho'lisch.

Catholicism, *n.* Katholizis'mus, -men *m.*

catsup, *n.* Ketchup *nt.*

cattle, *n.* Vieh *nt.*

cauliflower, *n.* Blumenkohl, -e *m.*

cause, 1. *n.* (*origin*) Ursache, -n *f.*; (*idea*) Sache, -n *f.* 2. *vb.* verur'sachen.

caustic, *adj.* beißend.

cauterize, *vb.* aus·brennen*.

cautery, *n.* Ausbrennen *nt.*

caution, 1. *n.* Vorsicht, -en *f.* 2. *vb.* warnen.

cautious, *adj.* vorsichtig.

cavalcade, *n.* Kavalka'de, -n *f.*

cavalier, *n.* Kavalier', -e *m.*

cavalry, *n.* Kavallerie', -i'en *f.*

cave, *n.* Höhle, -n *f.*

cavern, *n.* Höhle, -n *f.*

caviar, *n.* Kaviar *m.*

cavity, *n.* Loch, ✦er *nt.*; Höhle, -n *f.*

cease, *vb.* (*:ntr.*) auf·hören, (*tr.*) ein·stellen.

cedar, *n.* Zeder, -n *f.*

cede, *vb.* ab·treten*.

ceiling, *n.* Zimmerdecke, -n *f.*; (*fig.*) Höchstgrenze, -n *f.*

celebrate, *vb.* feiern.

celebrated, *adj.* berühmt'.

celebration, *n.* Feier, -n *f.*

celebrity, *n.* Berühmt'heit, -en *f.*

celery, *n.* Sellerie *m.*

celestial, *adj.* himmlisch.

celibacy, *n.* Zölibat', *nt.*, Ehelosigkeit *f.*

celibate, *adj.* ehelos.

cell, *n.* Zelle, -n *f.*

cellar, *n.* Keller. - *m.*

cellist, *n.* Cellist', -en, -en *m.*

cello, *n.* Cello, -s *nt.*

cellophane, *n.* Zellophan' *nt.*

celluloid, *n.* Zelluloid' *nt.*

cellulose, *n.* Zellstoff, -e *m.*

Celtic, *adj.* keltisch.

cement, 1. *n.* Zement', -e *m.* 2. *vb.* zementie'ren.

cemetery, *n.* Friedhof, ✦e *m.*

censor, 1. *n.* Zensor, -o'ren *m.* 2. *vb.* zensie'ren.

censorship, *n.* Zensur', -en *f.*

censure, *n.* Tadel, - *m.*, Verweis', -e *m.*

census, *n.* Volkszählung, -en *f.*, Zensus, - *m.*

cent, *n.* Cent, -s *m.*

centenary, *n.* Hundertjahr'feier, -n *f.*

centennial, 1. *n.* Hundertjahr'feier, -n *f.* 2. *adj.* hundertjährig.

center, *n.* Mitte, -n *f.*; Mittelpunkt, -e *m.*; Zentrum, -tren *nt.*

centigrade, *n.* (**c. thermometer**) Celsiusthermometer, - *nt.*; (**10 degrees c.**) 10 Grad Celsius.

central, *adj.* zentral'.

centralize, *vb.* zentralisie'ren.

century, *n.* Jahrhun'dert, -e *nt.*

ceramic, *adj.* kera'misch.

ceramics, *n.* Kera'mik, -en *f.*

cereal, *n.* Getrei'de - *nt.*; Getreidespeise, -n *f.*

cerebral, *adj.* Gehirn-(*cpds.*).

ceremonial, *adj.* zeremoni-ell'.

ceremonious, *adj.* feierlich.

ceremony, *n.* Zeremonie', -i'en *f.*; Feierlichkeit, -en *f.*

certain, *adj.* sicher.

certainty, *n.* Gewißheit, -en *f.*

certificate, *n.* Beschei'nigung, -en *f.*; Urkunde, -n *f.*

certification, *n.* Beschei'nigung, -en *f.*

certify, *vb.* beschei'nigen, beglau'bigen, bezeu'gen.

cervix, *n.* Gebär'mutterhals *m.*

cessation, *n.* Aufhören *nt.*

cesspool, *n.* Senkgrube, -n *f.*

chafe, *vb.* reiben*.

chagrin, *n.* Kummer, - *m.*

chain, 1. *n.* Kette, -n *f.* **2.** *vb.* an·ketten, fesseln.

chain reaction, *n.* Kettenreaktion, -en *f.*

chair, *n.* Stuhl, ⸚e *m.*

chairman, *n.* Vorsitzend- *m.*

chalice, *n.* Kelch, -e *m.*

chalk, *n.* Kreide, -n *f.*

chalky, *adj.* kreidig.

challenge, 1. *n.* Heraus'forderung, -en *f.* **2.** *vb.* heraus·fordern, auf·fordern.

challenger, *n.* Heraus'forderer, - *m.*

chamber, *n.* Kammer, -n *f.*; (*pol.*) Haus, ⸚er *nt.*

chambermaid, *n.* Zimmermädchen, - *nt.*

chamber music, *n.* Kammermusik *f.*

chamois, *n.* (*animal*) Gemse, -n *f.*; (*leather*) Wildleder *nt.*

champagne, *n.* Sekt, -e *m.*, Champag'ner, - *m.*

champion, *n.* Kämpfer, - *m.*; (*sport*) Meister, - *m.*

championship, *n.* Meisterschaft, -en *f.*

chance, 1. *n.* Zufall, ⸚e *m.*; (*expectation*) Aussicht, -en *f.*; (*occasion*) Gele'genheit, -en *f.* **2.** *vb.* wagen. **3.** *adj.* zufällig.

chancel, *n.* Altar'platz, ⸚e *m.*

chancellery, *n.* Kanzlei', -en *f.*

chancellor, *n.* Kanzler, - *m.*

chandelier, *n.* Kronleuchter, - *m.*

change, 1. *n.* Verän'derung, -en *f.*; (*alteration*) Änderung, -en *f.*; (*variety*) Abwechslung, -en *f.*; (*small coins*) Kleingeld *nt.*; (*money due*) Rest *m.* **2.** *vb.* verän'dern; (*alter*) ändern; (*money*) wechseln.

changeability, *n.* Unbeständigkeit, -en *f.*

changeable, *adj.* unbeständig.

channel, *n.* Fahrwasser *nt.*, Kanal', ⸚e *m.*; (*radio*) Frequenz'band, ⸚er *nt.*

chant, 1. *n.* Gesang', ⸚e *m.* **2.** *vb.* singen*.

chaos, *n.* Chaos *nt.*

chaotic, *adj.* chao'tisch.

chap, 1. *n.* Bursche, -n, -n *m.*, Kerl, -e *m.* **2.** *vb.* (**become c. ed**) auf·springen*.

chapel, *n.* Kapel'le, -n *f.*

chaplain, *n.* Geistlich- *m.*; (*mil.*) Feldgeistlich- *m.*

chapter, *n.* Kapi'tel, - *nt.*

char, *vb.* verkoh'len.

character, *n.* Charak'ter, -te're *m.*

characteristic, *adj.* charakteris'tisch.

characterization, *n.* Charakterisie'rung, -en *f.*

characterize, *vb.* charakterisie'ren.

charcoal, *n.* Holzkohle, -n *f.*

charge, 1. *n.* (*load*) Ladung, -en *f.*; (*attack*) Angriff, -e *m.*; (*price*) Preis, -e *m.*; (*custody*) Obhut, -en *f.* **2.** *vb.* (*load*) laden*; (*set a price*) berech'nen; (*put on one's account*) an·schreiben* lassen*.

chariot, *n.* Wagen, - *m.*

charitable, *adj.* wohltätig, nachsichtig.

charity, *n.* Wohltätigkeit, -en *f.*, Nächstenliebe *f.*

charlatan, *n.* Scharlatan, -e *m.*

charm 1. *n.* Charme *m.*; Liebreiz, -e *m*·; (*magic say-*

ing) Zauberspruch, ~e *m.* **2.** *vb.* bezau'bern.

charming, *adj.* bezau'bernd, reizend.

chart, *n.* (*map*) Karte, -n *f.*; (*graph*) Tabel'le, -n *f.*

charter, *n.* Urkunde. -n *f.*

charwoman, *n.* Putzfrau, -en *f.*

chase, 1. *n.* Jagd, -en *f.* **2.** *vb.* jagen.

chasm, *n.* Abgrund, ~e *m.*

chassis, *n.* Fahrgestell, -e *nt.*

chaste, *adj.* züchtig, Keusch.

chasten, *vb.* züchtigen.

chastise, *vb.* züchtigen.

chastity, *n.* Keuschheit *f.*

chat, 1. *n.* Plauderei' -en *f.* **2.** *vb.* plaudern.

chateau, *n.* Château', -s *nt.*

chatter, 1. *n.* Geschwätz' *nt.* **2.** *vb.* schwatzen; (*teeth*) klappern.

chauffeur, *n.* Fahrer, - *m.*, Chauffeur', -e *m.*

cheap, *adj.* billig, (*fig.*) ordinär'.

cheapen, *vb.* im Wert herab'setzen.

cheapness, *n.* Billigkeit, -en *f.*

cheat, *vb.* betrü'gen*; (*harmless*) schummeln.

check, 1. *n.* (*restraint*) Hemmnis, -se *nt.*; (*verification*) Kontrol'le, -n *f.*, Überprü'fung, -en *f.*; (*clothes, language*) Kontroll'marke, n *f.*; (*bank*) Scheck, -s *m.*; (*bill*) Rechnung, -en *f.* **2.** *vb.* (*verify*) kontrollie'ren, überprü'fen; (*luggage*) auf·geben* ab·geben*; (*mark*) ab·haken.

checkerboard, *n.* Damebrett, -er *nt.*

checkers, *n.* Damespiel, -e *nt.*

cheek, *n.* Backe, -n *f.*, Wange, -n *f.*

cheer, 1. *n.* Beifallsruf, -e *m.* **2.** *vb.* Beifall rufen*; (**c. up**) auf·muntern.

cheerful, *adj.* fröhlich.

cheerfulness, *n.* Fröhlichkeit *f.*

cheery, *adj.* heiter.

cheese, *n.* Käse *m.*

cheesecloth, *n.* grobe Gaze, -n *f.*

chef, *n.* Küchenchef, -s *m.*

chemical, 1. *n.* chemisches Präparat', -e *nt.*; (**c.s**) Chemikal'ien *pl.* **2.** *adj.* chemisch.

chemist, *n.* Chemiker, - *m.*

chemistry, *n.* Chemie' *f.*

chenille, *n.* Chenille', -n *f.*

cherish, *vb.* schätzen.

cherry, *n.* Kirsche, -n *f.*

cherub, *n.* Cherub, -s or -im or -i'nen *m.*

chess, *n.* Schach *nt.*, Schachspiel, -e *nt.*

chessboard, *n.* Schachbrett, -er *nt.*

chessman, *n.* Schachfigur, -en *f.*

chest, *n.* (*box*) Kiste, -n *f.*, Truhe, -n *f.*; (*body*) Brust *f.*

chestnut, *n.* Kasta'nie, -n *f.*

chevron, *n.* Dienstgradabzeichen, - *nt.*

chew, *vb.* kauen.

chic, *adj.* schick; elegant'.

chick, *n.* Küken, - *nt.*

chicken, *n.* Huhn, ~er *nt.*

chicken pox, *n.* Windpocken *pl.*

chicory, *n.* Zicho'rie, -n *f.*

chide, *vb.* schelten*.

chief, 1. *n.* Oberhaupt, ~er *nt.* **2.** *adj.* hauptsächlich; Haupt- (*cpds.*)

chieftain, *n.* Häuptling, -e *m.*

chiffon, *n.* Chiffon', -s *m.*

child, *n.* Kind, -er *nt.*

childbirth, *n.* Niederkunft *f.*

childhood, *n.* Kindheit, -en *f.*

childish, *adj.* kindisch.

childishness, *n.* Kindhaftigkeit, -en *f.*

childless, *adj.* kinderlos.

childlike, *adj.* kindlich.

chill, 1. *n.* Frost, ~e *m.*; (*fever*) Schauer, - *m.* **2.** *vb.* auf Eis stellen.

chilliness, *n.* Kühle *f.*

chilly, *adj.* kühl.

chime, 1. *n.* (*chimes*) Glockenspiel, -e *nt.* **2.** *vb.* läuten.

chimney, *n.* Schornstein, -e *m.*

chimpanzee, *n.* Schimpan'se, -n, -n *m.*

chin, *n.* Kinn, -e *nt.*

China, *n.* China *nt.*

china, *n.* Porzellan', -e *nt.*

chinchilla, *n.* Chinchil'la, -s *m.*

Chinese, 1. *n.* Chine'se, -n, -n *m.;* Chine'sing, -nen *f.* **2.** *adj.* chine'sisch.

chintz, *n.* Chintz, -e *m.*

chip, 1. *n.* Splitter, - *m.* **2.** *vb.* ab'brechen*; ab'splittern.

chiropodist, *n.* Fußpfleger, - *m.*

chiropractor, *n.* Chiroprak'tiker, - *m.*

chirp, 1. *n.* Gezirp' *nt.* **2.** *vb.* zirpen.

chisel, 1. *n.* (*stone, metal*) Meißel, - *m.;* (*wood*) Beitel, - *m.* **2.** *vb.* meißeln.

chivalrous, *adj.* ritterlich.

chivalry, *n.* Ritterlichkeit, -en *f.*

chive, *n.* Schnittlauch, *m.*

chloride, *n.* Chlorid', -e *nt.*

chlorine, *n.* Chlor, -s *nt.*

chloroform, *n.* Chloroform' *nt.*

chocolate, *n.* Schokola'de, -n *f.*

choice, *n.* Wahl, -en *f.;* (*selection*) Auswahl, *f.*

choir, *n.* Chor, -e *m.*

choke, *vb.* erwür'gen, erstick'en.

choker, *n.* Halsband, -er *nt.*

cholera, *n.* Cholera *f.*

choose, *vb.* wählen.

chop, 1. *n.* (*meat*) Kotelett', -s *nt.* **2.** *vb.* hacken.

choppy, *adj.* (*sea*) unruhig.

choral, *adj.* Chor- (*cpds.*).

chord, *n.* (*string*) Saite, -n *f.;* (*harmony*) Akkord', -e *m.*

chore, *n.* Alltagsarbeit, -en *f.*

choreographer, *n.* Choreograph', -en, -en *m.*

choreography, *n.* Choreographie', -i'en *f.*

chorus, *n.* Chor, -e *m.;* Refrain', -s *m.*

Christ, *n.* Christus *m.*

christen, *vb.* taufen.

Christendom, *n.* Christenheit *f.*

christening, *n.* Taufe, -n *f.*

Christian, 1. *n.* Christ, -en, en *m.* **2.** *adj.* christlich.

Christianity, *n.* Christentum *nt.*

Christmas, *n.* Weihnachten *nt.*

chrome, chromium, *n.* Chrom *nt.*

chronic, *adj.* chronisch.

chronicle, *n.* Chronik, -en *f.*

chronological, *adj.* chronolo'gisch.

chronology, *n.* Chronologie', -i'en *f.*

chrysanthemum, *n.* Chrysanthe'me, -n *f.*

chubby, *adj.* dicklich.

chuckle, *vb.* vergnügt'lachen.

chug, *vb.* daher'keuchen.

chunk, *n.* Stück, -e *nt.*

church, *n.* Kirche, -n *f.*

churchyard, *n.* Kirchhof, -e *m.*

churn, 1. *n.* Butterfaß, -sser *nt.* **2.** *vb.* buttern; (*fig.*) auf-wühlen.

chute, *n.* (*mail*) Postschacht, e *m.;* (*laundry*) Wäscheschacht, -e *m.*

cider, *n.* Apfelwein, -e *m.*

cigar, *n.* Zigar're, -n *f.*

cigarette, *n.* Zigaret'te, -n *f.*

cinch, *n.* Sattelgurt, -e *m.;* (*fam.*) Kleinigkeit, -en *f.*

cinder, *n.* Asche, -n *f.*

cinema, *n.* Kino, -s *nt.*

cinnamon, *n.* Zimt *m.*

cipher, *n.* (*number*) Ziffer, -n *f.;* (*zero*) Null, -en *f.;* (*code*) Chiffre, -n *f.*

circle, *n.* Kreis, -e *m.*

circuit, *n.* (*course*) Umkreis, -e *m.;* (*elec.*) Stromkreis, -e *m.;* (**short c.**) Kurzschluß, -sse *m.*

circuitous, *adj.* umwegig.

circular, 1. *n.* Rundschreiben, - *nt.* **2.** *adj.* kreisförmig.

circulate, *vb.* zirkulie'ren.

circulation, *n.* (*blood*) Kreislauf, -e *m.;* (*paper*) Auflage, -n *f.;* (*money*) Umlauf, -e *m.*

circulatory, *adj.* zirkulie'rend.

circumcise, *vb.* beschnei-den*.

circumcision, n. Beschnei'dung, -en f.

circumference, n. Umfang, -e m.

circumlocution, n. Umschrei'bung, -en f.

circumscribe, vb. (geom.) umschrei'ben*; (delimit) begren'zen.

circumspect, adj. umsichtig.

circumstance, n. Umstand, -e m.; (pl.) Verhält'nisse pl.

circumstantial, adj. eingehend; (c. evidence) Indi'zienbeweis, -e m.

circumvent, vb. umge'hen*.

circumvention, n. Umge'hung, -en f.

circus, n. Zirkus, -se m.

cirrhosis, n. Zirrho'se, -n f.

cistern, n. Zister'ne, -n f.

citadel, n. Zitadel'le, -n f.

citation, n. Auszeichnung, -en f.; (law) Vorladung, -en f.

cite, vb. an·führen, zitie'ren; (law) vor·laden*.

citizen, n. Bürger, - m.

citizenship, n. Staatsangehörigkeit, -en f.

city, n. Stadt, -e f.

civic, adj. Bürger- (cpds.).

civil, adj. bürgerlich; (law) zivil'rechtlich; (polite) höflich.

civilian, 1. n. Zivilist' -en, -en m. **2.** adj. bürgerlich.

civility, n. Höflichkeit, -en f.

civilization, n. Zivilisation', -en f.

civilize, vb. zivilisie'ren.

civilized, adj. zivilisiert'.

clad, adj. geklei'det.

claim, 1. n. Anspruch, -e m. **2.** vb. bean'spruchen, fordern.

claimant, n. Bean'spruchend- m. & f.

clairvoyance, n. Hellsehen nt.

clairvoyant, 1. n. Hellseher, - m. **2.** adj. hellseherisch.

clammy, adj. feuchtkalt.

clamor, 1. n. Geschrei' nt. **2.** vb. schreien*.

clamp, 1. n. Klammer, -n f. **2.** vb. fest-klammern.

clandestine, adj. heimlich.

clap, vb. klatschen.

claret, n. Rotwein, -e m.

clarification, n. Klarstellung, -en f.

clarify, vb. klar·stellen.

clarinet, n. Klarinet'te, -n f.

clarity, n. Klarheit, -en f.

clash, 1. n. Zusam'menstoß, -e m. **2.** vb. zusam'menstoßen*; (fig.) sich nicht vertra'gen*.

clasp, 1. n. Schnalle, -n f.; (hands) Händedruck m. **2.** vb. fest·schnallen; (grasp) umfas'sen; (embrace) umar'men.

class, n. Klasse, -n f.; (period of instruction) Stunde, -n f.

classic, classical, adj. klassisch.

classicism, n. Klassizis'mus, -men m.

classification, n. Klassifizie'rung, -en f.

classify, vb. klassifizie'ren.

classmate, n. Klassenkamerad, -en, -en m.

classroom, n. Klassenzimmer, - nt.

clatter, 1. n. Geklap'per nt. **2.** vb. klappern.

clause, n. Satzteil, -e m.; (main c.) Hauptsatz, -e m.; (subordinate c.) Nebensatz, -e m.; (law) Klausel, -n f.

claw, n. Kralle, -n f., Klaue, -n f. vb. krallen.

clay, n. Ton, -e m., Lehm, -e m.

clean, 1. vb. sauber machen, reinigen. **2.** adj. sauber.

clean-cut, adj. sauber.

cleaner, n. (the c.s) Reinigung, -en f.

cleanliness, cleanness, n. Sauberkeit f.

cleanse, vb. reinigen.

clear, 1. vb. klären; (profit) rein verdie'nen; (weather) sich auf·klären. **2.** adj. klar.

clearance, n. (enough space) Raum m.; (sale) Räumung,

-en f.; (approval) Gutheißung f.

clearing, n. Lichtung, -en f.

clearness, n. Klarheit, -en f.

cleat, n. (naut.) Klampe, -n f.; (on boots) Krampe, -n f.

cleavage, n. Spaltung, -en f.

cleave, vb. spalten*.

cleaver, n. Fleischerbeil, -e nt.

clef, n. Notenschlüssel, - m.

cleft, **1.** n. Spalte, -n f. **2.** adj. gespal'ten.

clemency, n. Milde f.

clench, vb. zusam'menpressen; (fist) ballen.

clergy, n. Geistlichkeit f.

clergyman, n. Geistlich-, m.

clerical, adj. (eccles.) geistlich, klerikal'; (writing) Schreib- (cpds.).

clerk, n. Schreiber,- m.; (salesc.) Verkäu'fer,- m., Verkäu'ferin, -nen f.

clever, adj. klug(¨), geschickt', schlau.

cleverness, n. Klugheit, -en f., Geschick'lichkeit, -en f.

clew, n. (object) Knäuel, - nt.; (fact) Anhaltspunkt, -e m., Schlüssel, - m.

cliché, n. Klischee', -s nt.

click, **1.** n. Klicken nt.; (language) Schnalzlaut, -e m. **2.** vb. klicken, knacken.

client, n. Kunde, -n, -n m., Klient', -en, -en m.

clientele, n. Kundschaft, -en f.

cliff, n. Klippe, -n f.

climate, n. Klima, -s or a'te nt.

climatic, adj. klima'tisch.

climax, n. Höhepunkt -e m.

climb, vb. (intr.) steigen*', klettern; (tr.) erstei'gen*.

climber, n. Kletterer, - m.

clinch, vb. fest-machen; (fig.) den Ausschlag geben*.

cling, vb. sich an-klammern.

clinic, n. Klinik, -en f.

clinical, adj. klinisch.

clip, **1.** n. Klammer, -n f.; (jewelry) Schmucknadel, -n f. **2.** vb. beschnei'den*.

clippers, n.pl. Schere, -n f.;

(barber) Haarschneidemaschine, -n, f.

clipping, n. (newspaper) Zeitungsausschnitt, -e m.

clique, n. Clique, -n f.

cloak, n. Mantel, ¨ m.

cloakroom, n. Gardero'be, -n f.

clock, n. Uhr, -en f.

clod, n. Klumpen, - m.

clog, **1.** n. Holzschuh, -e m. **2.** vb. verstop'fen.

cloister, n. Kloster, ¨ nt.; (arch.) Kreuzgang, ¨e m.

close, **1.** adj. (narrow) eng, knapp; (near) nahe(¨). **2.** vb. schließen*, zu-machen.

closeness, n. Enge, -n f., Nähe, -n f.

closet, n. Wandschrank, ¨e m.

clot, **1.** n. Klumpen, - m. **2.** vb. gerin'nen*.

cloth, n. Tuch, ¨er nt., Stoff, -e m.

clothe, vb. kleiden.

clothes, n.pl. Kleider pl.

clothing, n. Kleidung, -en f.

cloud, n. Wolke, -n f.

cloudburst, n. Wolkenbruch, ¨e m.

cloudiness, n. Bewölkt'heit f.

cloudy, adj. bewölkt', trübe.

clove, n. Gewürz'nelke, -n f.

clover, n. Klee m.

clown, n. Clown, -s m.

cloy, vb. übersät'tigen.

club, n. (group) Klub, -s m.; (stick) Keule, -n f.

clubs, n. (cards) Treff nt.

clue, n. Anhaltspunkt, -e m., Schlüssel, - m.

clump, n. Klumpen, - m.

clumsiness, n. Ungeschicklichkeit, -en f.

clumsy, adj. ungeschickt.

cluster, **1.** n. Büschel, - m. **2.** vb. sich zusam'menscharen.

clutch, **1.** n. (auto) Kupplung, -en f. **2.** vb. packen.

clutter, vb. umher'streuen.

coach, **1.** n. Kutsche, -n f.; (train) Eisenbahnwagen,- m.; (sports) Trainer, - m.; (tutor) Privat'lehrer, - m.

2. vb. (sports) trainie'ren; (tutor) Privat'stunden geben*.

coagulate, vb. gerin'nen*.

coagulation, n. Gerin'nen nt.

coal, n. Kohle, -n f.

coalesce, vb. verschmel'zen*.

coalition, n. Koalition', -en f.

coarse, adj. grob(*).

coarsen, vb. vergrö'bern.

coarseness, n. Grobheit, -en f.

coast, n. Küste, -n f.

coastal, adj. Küsten- (cpds.)

coaster, n. Küstenfahrer, - m.

coat, n. (suit) Jacke, -n f.; (overcoat) Mantel, ⸚ m.

coating, n. Überzug, ⸚ m.

coat of arms, n. Wappen, - nt.

coax, vb. überre'den.

cobalt, n. Kobalt m.

cobblestone, n. Kopfstein, -e m.

cobweb, n. Spinngewebe, - nt.

cocaine, n. Kokain' nt.

cock, **1.** n. Hahn, ⸚e m. **2.** vb. (gun) spannen.

cockeyed, adj. schielend; (crazy) verrückt'.

cockpit, n. Führersitz, -e m.

cockroach, n. Küchenschabe, -n f.

cocktail, n. Cocktail, -s m.

cocky, adj. frech.

cocoa, n. Kaka'o, -s m.

coconut, n. Kokosnuß, ⸚sse f.

cocoon, n. Kokon', -s m.

cod, n. Kabeljau, -e m.

C. O. D., adv. per Nachnahme.

coddle, vb. verpäp'peln.

code, n. (law) Kodex, -dizes m.; (secret) Kode, -s m.

codeine, n. Kodein' nt.

codfish, n. Kabeljau, -e m.

codify, vb. kodifizie'ren.

cod-liver oil, n. Lebertran m.

coeducation, n. Koeduka- tion' f.

coerce, vb. zwingen*.

coercion, n. Zwang m.

coexist, vb. koexistie'ren.

coffee, n. Kaffee m.

coffin, n. Sarg, ⸚e m.

cog, n. Zahn, ⸚e m.; (c. railway) Zahnradbahn, -en f.

cogent, adj. zwingend.

cogitate, vb. nach·denken*.

cognizance, n. Kenntnis, -se f.

cognizant, adj. bewußt'.

cogwheel, n. Zahnrad, ⸚er nt.

cohere, vb. zusam'men- hängen*.

coherent, adj. zusam'men- hängend.

cohesion, n. Kohäsion' f.

cohesive, adj. kohärent'.

cohort, n. Kohor'te, -n f.

coiffure, n. Frisur', -en f.

coil, **1.** n. Rolle, -n f.; (elec.) Spule, -n f. **2.** vb. auf- rollen; (rope) auf·schießen.

coin, **1.** n. Münze, -n f. **2.** vb. prägen.

coinage, n. Prägung, -en f.

coincide, vb. zusam'men- treffen*.

coincidence, n. Zufall, ⸚e m.

coincident, adj. gleichzeitig.

coincidental, adj. zufällig.

cold, **1.** n. Kälte, -n f.; (med.) Erkäl'tung, -en f. **2.** adj. kalt(*).

cold-blooded, adj. kaltblü- tig.

collaborate, vb. zusam'men- arbeiten, mit·arbeiten.

collaboration, n. Mitarbeit f.

collaborator, n. Mitarbeiter, - m.

collapse, **1.** n. Zusam'men- bruch ⸚e m. **2.** vb. zusam'- men·brechen*.

collar, n. Kragen, - m.

collarbone, n. Schlüsselbein, -e nt.

collate, vb. verglei'chen*.

collateral, **1.** n. (econ.) Deckung f. **2.** adj. kollate- ral'.

colleague, n. Kolle'ge, -n, -n m.

collect, vb. sammeln; (money) ein·kassieren.

collection, n. Sammlung, -en f.; (church) Kollek'te, -n f.

collective, *adj.* kollektiv'.

collector, *n.* (*art*) Sammler, - *m.*; (*tickets*) Schaffner, - *m.* (*tax*) Steuereinnehmer, - *m.*

college, *n.* College, -s *nt.*

collegiate, *adj.* College- (*cpds.*).

collide, *vb.* zusam'menstoßen*.

collision, *n.* Zusam'menstoß, *∗*e *m.*

colloquial, *adj.* umgangssprachlich.

colloquialism, *n.* umgangssprachlicher Ausdruck, *∗*e *m.*

collusion, *n.* Kollusion', -en *f.*

Cologne, *n.* Köln *nt.*

colon, *n.* (*typogr.*) Doppelpunkt, -e *m.*, Kolon, -s *or* Kola *nt.*; (*med.*) Dickdarm, *∗*e *m.*, Kolon, -s *or* Kola *nt.*

colonel, *n.* Oberst, -en, -en, *m.*

colonial, *adj.* kolonial'.

colonist, *n.* Siedler, - *m.*, Kolonist', -en. -en *m.*

colonization, *n.* Kolonisation', -en *f.*

colonize, *vb.* kolonisie'ren.

colony, *n.* Kolonie', -i'en *f.*

color, 1. *n.* Farbe, -n *f.* 2. *vb.* färben.

colored, *adj.* farbig.

colorful, *adj.* farbenreich.

coloring, *n.* Färbung, -en *f.*

colorless, *adj.* farblos.

colossal, *adj.* kolossal'.

colt, *n.* Fohlen, - *nt.*

column, *n.* (*arch.*) Säule, -n *f.*; (*typogr.*) Spalte, -n *f.*; (*mil.*) Kolon'ne, -n *f.*

columnist, *n.* Zeitungsartikelschreiber, - *m.*

coma, *n.* Koma *nt.*

comb, 1. *n.* Kamm, *∗*e *m.* 2. *vb.* kämmen.

combat, 1. *n.* Kampf, *∗*e *m.* 2. *vb.* bekäm'pfen.

combatant, *n.* Kämpfer, - *m.*

combination, *n.* Kombination', -en *f.*

combine, *vb.* verbin'den*, verei'nigen, zusam'mensetzen, kombinie'ren.

combustible, *adj.* (ver)-brenn'bar.

combustion, *n.* Verbren'-nung *f.*

come, *vb.* kommen*.

comedian, *n.* Komiker, - *m.*

comedienne, *n.* Komikerin, -nen *f.*

comedy, *n.* Komö'die, -n *f.*

come in, *interj.* herein'!

comely, *adj.* hübsch.

comet, *n.* Komet', -en, -en *m.*

comfortable, *adj.* behag'-lich, bequem'.

comforter, *n.* Steppdecke, -n *f.*

comfort, 1. *n.* Behag'lichkeit, -en *f.*, Bequem'lichkeit, -en *f.* 2. *vb.* trösten.

comic, comical, *adj.* komisch.

comma, *n.* Komma, -s *or* -ta *nt.*

command, 1. *n.* Befehl', -e *m.* 2. *vb.* befeh'len*.

commandeer, *vb.* requirie'ren.

commander, *n.* Befehls'-haber, - *m.*; (*navy*) Fregat'tenkapitän, -e *m.*

commander in chief, *n.* Oberbefehlshaber, - *m.*

commandment, *n.* Gebot', -e *nt.*

commemorate, *vb.* geden'-ken*.

commemoration, *n.* Gedächt'nisfeier, -n *f.*

commemorative, *adj.* Gedächt'nis- (*cpds.*).

commence, *vb.* begin'nen*.

commencement, *n.* Anfang, *∗*e *m.*; (*college*) akade'mische Abschlußfeier, -n *f.*

commend, *vb.* (*praise*) loben; (*recommend*) empfeh'len*.

commendable, *adj.* lobenswert.

commendation, *n.* Lob *nt.*, Auszeichnung, -en *f.*

commensurate, *adj.* angemessen.

comment, 1. *n.* Bemerkung, -en *f.* 2. *vb.* bemer'ken.

commentary, n. Kommentar', -e m.

commentator, n. Kommenta'tor, -o'ren m.

commerce, n. Handel m.

commercial, adj. kommerziell', kaufmännisch; (cpds.) Handels-.

commercialism, n. Handelsgeist m.

commercialize, vb. in den Handel bringen*.

commiserate, vb. bemit'leiden.

commissary, n. Kommissar', -e m.; (store) Militärversor'gungsstelle, -n f.

commission, 1. n. (committee) Kommission', -en f.; (percentage) Provision', -en f.; (assignment) Auftrag, ⸗e m. **2.** vb. beauf'tragen; (mil.) das Offiziers'patent verlei'hen*.

commissioner, n. Beauf'tragt- m.

commit, vb. (give over) anvertrauen; (crime) bege'hen*; (oneself) sich verpflich'ten.

commitment, n. Verpflich'tung, -en f.

committee, n. Ausschuß, ⸗sse m.

commodity, n. Ware, -n f.

common, adj. allgemein', gewöhn'lich; (vulgar) ordinär'.

commonness, n. Häufigkeit f.

commonplace, 1. n. Gemein'platz, ⸗e m. **2.** adj. abgedroschen.

commonwealth, n. Commonwealth nt.

commotion, n. Aufruhr m.

communal, adj. Gemein'de- (cpds.).

commune, 1. n. Gemein'de, -n f. **2.** vb. Kommunizie'ren.

communicable, adj. mitteilbar; (med.) ansteckbar.

communicant, n. Kommunikant', -en, -en m.

communicate, vb. mitteilen.

communication, n. Mitteilung, -en f.

communicative, adj. mitteilsam.

communion, n. Gemein'schaft f.; (eccl.) Abendmahl nt.; (Catholic) Kommunion', -en f.

communiqué, n. Kommuniqué', -s nt.

communism, n. Kommunis'mus m.

communist, 1. n. Kommunist', -en, -en m. **2.** adj. kommunis'tisch.

communistic, adj. kommunis'tisch.

community, n. Gemein'de, -n f. Gemein'schaft, -en f.

commutation, n. Austausch m.; (law) Milderung f.

commute, vb. täglich von der Vorstadt in die Stadt fahren und zurück; (law) herab'setzen.

compact, 1. n. (cosmetics) Puderdose, -n f. **2.** adj. kompakt'.

compactness, n. Kompakt'heit f.

companion, n. Beglei'ter, - m.

companionable, adj. gesel'lig.

companionship, n. Kamerad'schaft, -en f.

company, n. Gesell'schaft, -en f., Firma, -men f.

comparable, adj. vergleich'bar.

comparative, 1. n. (gram.) Komparativ, -e m. **2.** adj. verhält'nismäßig.

compare, vb. verglei'chen*.

comparison, n. Vergleich', -e m.

compartment, n. Abtei'lung, -en f., Fach, ⸗er nt.; (train) Abteil, -e nt.

compass, n. (naut.) Kompaß, ⸗sse m.; (geom.) Zirkel, - m.

compassion, n. Mitleid nt.. Erbar'men nt.

compassionate, adj. mitleidig.

compatible, adj. verträg'lich.

compatriot, n. Landsmann, -leute m.

compel, vb. zwingen*.

compensate, vb. entschä'digen, kompensie'ren.

compensation, n. Entschä'digung, -en f., Kompensa'tion', -en f.

compete, vb. wetteifern, konkurrie'ren.

competence, n. (ability) Fähigkeit, -en f.; (field of responsibility) Zuständigkeit, -en f.

competent, adj. (able) fähig; (responsible) zuständig.

competition, n. Wettbewerb, -e m., ¡Konkurrenz', -en f.

competitive, adj. auf Konkurrenz' eingestellt.

competitor, n. Mitbewerber, - m., Konkurrent', -en, -en m.

compile, vb. zusam'mentragen*.

complacency, n. Selbstzufriedenheit f.

complacent, adj. selbstzufrieden.

complain, vb. sich bekla'gen, sich beschwe'ren.

complaint, n. Klage, -n f., Beschwer'de, -n f.

complement, 1. n. Ergän'zung, -en f. 2. vb. ergän'zen.

complete, 1. vb. vollen'den. 2. adj. vollständig, fertig.

completely, adv. völlig.

completion, n. Vollen'dung, -en f.

complex, 1. n. Komplex', -e m. 2. adj. komplex', weitläufig.

complexion, n. (type) Natur' f.; (skin) Teint, -s m.

complexity, n. Weitläufigkeit, -en f.

compliance, n. Bereit'willigkeit f., Einwilligen nt.

compliant, adj. bereit'willig, nachgiebig.

complicate, vb. (make more complex) verwi'ckeln; (make harder) erschwe'ren.

complicated, adj. kompliziert', verwi'ckelt.

complication, n. Komplika'tion', -en f.

compliment, 1. n. Kompliment', -e nt. 2. vb. beglück'wünschen.

complimentary, adj. schmeichelhaft; (free) Frei'(cpds.).

comply, vb. ein·willigen, sich fügen.

component, n. Bestand'teil, -e m.

compose, vb. zusam'mensetzen; (music) komponie'ren.

composer, n. Komponist', -en, -en m.

composite, adj. zusam'mengesetzt.

composition, n. Zusam'mensetzung, -en f.; (school) Aufsatz, *e m.; (mus.) Komposition', -en f.

composure, n. Fassung f.

compote, n. Kompott', -e nt.

compound, 1. n. Mischung, -en f.; (gram.) Kompo'situm, -ta nt.; (chem.) Verbin'dung, -en f.; (mil.) eingezäunte Lagerabteilung, -en f. 2. adj. zusam'mengesetzt; (c. interest) Zinseszins m. 3. vb. zusam'mensetzen.

comprehend, vb. verste'hen*, begrei'fen*.

comprehensible, adj. verständ'lich.

comprehension, n. Fassungsvermögen, - nt.

comprehensive, adj. umfas'send.

compress, 1. n. Kompres'se, -n f. 2. vb. zusam'menpressen.

compressed, adj. Press'(cpds.).

compression, n. Kompression', -en f.

comprise, vb. umfas'sen, enthal'ten*.

compromise, 1. n. Kompromiss', -sse m. 2. vb. einen Kompromiß schließen*; (embarrass) kompromittie'ren.

compulsion, n. Zwang m.

compulsive, *adj.* Zwangs- (*cpds.*).

compulsory, *adj.* obligato'risch.

compunction, *n.* Beden'ken, - *nt.*

computation, *n.* Berech'nung, -en *f.*

compute, *vb.* rechnen, berech'nen.

comrade, *n.* Kamerad', -en, -en *m.*

concave, *adj.* konkav'.

conceal, *vb.* verste'cken, verheim'lichen.

concealment, *n.* Versteck', -e *nt.*, Verheim'lichung, -en *f.*

concede, *vb.* zu'gestehen*.

conceit, *n.* Einbildung, -en *f.*

conceited, *adj.* eingebildet.

conceivable, *adj.* vorstellbar.

conceivably, *adv.* unter Umständen.

conceive, *vb.* begrei'fen*, sich vor'stellen; (*child*) empfan'gen*.

concentrate, *vb.* konzentrie'ren.

concentration camp, *n.* Konzentrations'lager, - *nt.*

concept, *n.* Begriff', -e *m.*

concern, 1. *n.* (*affair*) Angelegenheit, -en *f.*; (*interest*) Interes'se, -n *nt.*; (*firm*) Konzern', -e *m.*; (*worry*) Sorge, -n *f.* **2.** *vb.* an'gehen*.

concerning, *prep.* hinsichtlich.

concert, *n.* Konzert', -e *nt.*

concession, *n.* Konzession', -en *f.*

concierge, *n.* Portier', -s *m.*

conciliate, *vb.* versöh'nen, schlichten.

conciliation, *n.* Versöh'nung, -en *f.*, Schlichtung, -en *f.*

conciliator, *n.* Schlichter, - *m.*

conciliatory, *adj.* versöh'nend.

concise, *adj.* knapp, gedrängt'.

conciseness, *n.* Gedrängt'heit *f.*

conclude, *vb.* schließen*.

conclusion, *n.* Abschluß, ᵗsse *m.*, Schluß, ᵗsse *m.*

conclusive, *adj.* entschei'dend.

concoct, *vb.* zusam'menbrauen.

concoction, *n.* Gebräu', -e *nt.*

concomitant, *adj.* beglei'tend.

concord, *n.* Eintracht *f.*

concourse, *n.* Sammelplatz, ᵗe *m.*

concrete, 1. *n.* Zement' *m.* **2.** *adj.* konkret'.

concubine, *n.* Konkubi'ne, -n *f.*

concur, *vb.* überein'stimmen.

concurrence, *n.* Zustimmung, -en *f.*

concurrent, *adj.* (*simultaneous*) gleichzeitig; (*agreeing*) überein'stimmend.

concussion, *n.* Erschüt'terung, -en *f.*; (*brain*) Gehirn'erschütterung, -en *f.*

condemn, *vb.* verur'teilen; (*disapprove*) mißbil'ligen.

condemnable, *adj.* strafbar; nichtswürdig.

condemnation, *n.* Verur'teilung *f.*; Mißbilligung *f.*

condensation, *n.* Kondensation', -en *f.*; (*summary*) Zusam'menfassung, -en *f.*

condense, *vb.* kondensie'ren; (*summarize*) zusam'menfassen.

condenser, *n.* Kondensa'tor, -o'ren *m.*

condescend, *vb.* sich herab'lassen*.

condescending, *adj.* herab'lassend.

condescension, *n.* Herab'lassung, -en *f.*

condiment, *n.* Gewürz', -e *nt.*

condition, 1. *n.* (*stipulation*) Bedin'gung, -en *f.*; (*state*) Zustand, ᵗe *m.* **2.** *vb.* bedin'gen; (*training*) in Form bringen*.

conditional, *adj.* abhängig.

conditionally, *adv.* unter gewissen Bedingungen.

condolence, *n.* Beileid *nt.*

condone, *vb.* entschul'digen.

conducive, *adj.* förderlich.

conduct, 1. *n.* Betra'gen *nt.*
2. *vb.* leiten; *(behave)* sich
betra'gen*; *(music)* dirigie'-
ren.

conductor, *n.* Leiter, - *m.;*
(train) Schaffner, - *m.; (music)* Dirigent', -en, -en *m.*

conduit, *n.* Leitungsrohr, -e
nt.

cone, *n.* Kegel, - *m.; (pine)*
Tannenzapfen, - *m.*

confection, *n.* Konfekt', -e
nt.

confectioner, *n.* Zuckerbäcker, - *m.*

confectionery, *n.* Zuckerwerk *nt.*

confederacy, *n.* Bündnis, -se
nt.; (conspiracy) Verschwö'-
rung, -en *f.*

confederate, 1. *n.* Helfershelfer, - *m.* **2.** *adj.* verbün'-
det.

confederation, *n.* Staatenbund, -e *m.*

confer, *vb. (bestow)* verlei'-
hen*; *(counsel)* berat'schlagen.

conference, *n.* Bespre'chung,
-en *f.,* Konferenz', -en *f.*

confess, *vb.* zu·gestehen*;
(eccles.) beichten.

confession, *n.* Geständ'nis,
-se *nt.; (eccles.)* Beichte, -n *f.*

confessional, *n.* Beichtstuhl,
·e *m.*

confessor, *n.* Beken'ner, -
m.; **(father c.)** Beichtvater,
·· *m.*

confidant, *n.* Vertraut'- *m.*

confidante, *n.* Vertraut'- *f.*

confide, *vb.* vertrau'en; sich
an·vertrauen.

confidence, *n. (trust)* Vertrau'en *nt.; (assurance)* Zuversicht *f.*

confident, *adj.* zuversichtlich.

confidential, *adj.* vertrau'-
lich.

confidentially, *adv.* unter
uns.

confine, *vb.* beschrän'ken;
(imprison) ein·sperren.

confirm, *vb.* bestä'tigen;
(church) konfirmie'ren.

confirmation, *n.* Bestä'-
tigung, -en *f.; (church)* Konfirmation', -en *f.*

confiscate, *vb.* beschlag'-
nahmen, konfiszie'ren.

confiscation, *n.* Beschlag'-
nahme, -n *f.*

conflagration, *n.* Brand, ·e
m., Feuersbrunst *f.*

conflict, 1. *n.* Konflikt', -e
m. **2.** *vb.* in Widerspruch
stehen*, nicht überein'-
stimmen.

conform, *vb.* sich an·passen.

conformation, *n.* Anpassung, -en *f.; (shape)* Gestal'-
tung, -en *f.*

conformer, conformist, *n.*
Mitmacher, - *m.*

conformity, *n.* Überein'-
stimmung, -en *f.*

confound, *vb. (make confused)* verwir'ren; **(c. A
with B)** A mit B verwech'-
seln; **(c. it!)** zum Donnerwetter!

confront, *vb.* gegenü'ber-
stellen, konfrontie'ren.

confuse, *vb. (make confused)*
verwir'ren; **(c. A with B)**
A mit B verwech'seln.

confusion, *n.* Verwir'rung,
-en *f.;* Durcheinan'der *nt.,*
Verwechs'lung, -en *f.*

congeal, *vb.* erstar'ren.

congenial, *adj.* sympa'-
thisch.

congenital, *adj.* angeboren.

congestion, *n.* Stauung, -en
f.

conglomerate, 1. *n.* Anhäufung, -en *f.* **2.** *vb.* zusam'men·ballen.

conglomeration, *n.* Anhäu-
fung, -en *f.*

congratulate, *vb.* gratulie'-
ren, beglück'wünschen.

congratulation, *n.* Glückwunsch, ·e *m.*

congratulatory, *adj.* Glück-
wunsch- *(cpds.)*

congregate, *vb.* sich versam'-
meln.

congregation, *n. (church)*
Gemein'de, -n *f.*

congress, *n.* Kongreß', -sse
m.

congressional, *adj.* Kongreß'- (*cpds.*).

conjecture, 1. *n.* Mutmaßung, -en *f.* 2. *vb.* mutmaßen.

conjugal, *adj.* ehelich.

conjugate, *vb.* konjugie'ren.

conjugation, *n.* Konjugation', -en *f.*

conjunction, *n.* Zusam'mentreffen, -*nt.*; (*gram.*) Bindewort, "er *nt.*, Konjunktion', -en *f.*

conjunctive, *adj.* verbin'dend.

conjunctivitis, *n.* Bindehautentzündung, -en *f.*

conjure, *vb.* zaubern.

connect, *vb.* verbin'den*.

connection, *n.* Verbin'dung, -en *f.*

connive, *vb.* in heimlichem Einverständnis stehen*.

connoisseur, *n.* Kenner, - *m.*

connotation, *n.* Nebenbedeutung, -en *f.*, Beiklang, "e *m.*

connote, *vb.* in sich schließen*.

conquer, *vb.* ero'bern.

conqueror, *n.* Ero'berer, - *m.*

conquest, *n.* Ero'berung, -en *f.*

conscience, *n.* Gewis'sen, - *nt.*

conscientious, *adj.* gewis'senhaft.

conscious, *adj.* bewußt, bei Bewußt'sein.

consciousness, *n.* Bewußt'sein *nt.*

conscript, *n.* Dienstpflichtig- *m.*

conscription, *n.* Militär'dienstpflicht *f.*

consecrate, *vb.* weihen.

consecration, *n.* Weihung, -en *f.*

consecutive, *adj.* aufeinan'derfolgend.

consensus, *n.* allgemeine Meinung, -en *f.*

consent, 1. *n.* Zustimmung, -en *f.* 2. *vb.* zu'stimmen.

consequence, *n.* Folge, -n *f.*

consequent, *adj.* folgend.

consequential, *adj.* folgenreich.

consequently, *adv.* folglich.

conservation, *n.* Bewah'rung, -en *f.*; Konservie'rung, -en *f.*

conservative, *adj.* konservativ'.

conservatism, *n.* Konservatis'mus *m.*

conservatory, *n.* (*music*) Konservato'rium, -rien *nt.*; (*plants*) Treibhaus, "er *nt.*

conserve, *vb.* bewah'ren.

consider, *vb.* betrach'ten; (*take into account*) berück'sichtigen.

considerable, *adj.* beträcht'lich.

considerate, *adj.* rücksichtsvoll.

consideration, *n.* (*thought*) Erwä'gung, -en *f.*; (*kindness*) Rücksicht, -en *f.*; (**in c. of**) in Anbetracht.

consign, *vb.* übersen'den*.

consignment, *n.* Übersen'dung, -en *f.*

consist, *vb.* beste'hen*.

consistency, *n.* Folgerichtigkeit *f.*; (*substance*) Konsistenz' *f.*

consistent, *adj.* folgerichtig, konsequent'.

consolation, *n.* Trost *m.*

console, *vb.* trösten.

consolidate, *vb.* festigen, konsolidie'ren.

consommé, *n.* Bouillon', -s *f.*

consonant, *n.* Konsonant', -en, -en *m.*

consort, 1. *n.* Gemahl', -e *m.*; Gemah'lin, -nen *f.* 2. *vb.* verkeh'ren.

conspicuous, *adj.* auffällig.

conspiracy, *n.* Verschwö'rung, -en *f.*

conspirator, *n.* Verschwö'rer, - *m.*

conspire, *vb.* sich verschwö'ren*.

constancy, *n.* Standhaftigkeit *f.*

constant, *adj.* bestän'dig, konstant'.

constantly, *adv.* dauernd.

constellation, *n.* Konstella-tion', -en *f.*

consternation, *n.* Bestür'-zung, -en *f.*

constipated, *adj.* verstopft'.

constipation, *n.* Verstop'-fung, -en *f.*

constituency, *n.* *(people)* Wählerschaft, -en *f.*; *(place)* Wahlbezirk, -e *m.*

constituent, *n.* Bestand'teil, -e *m.*; *(voter)* Wähler, - *m.*

constitute, *vb.* *(make up)* aus·machen; *(found)* grün-den.

constitution, *n.* Konstitu-tion', -en *f.*; *(government)* Verfas'sung, -en *f.*

constitutional, *adj.* konsti-tutionell'.

constrain, *vb.* zwingen*.

constrict, *vb.* zusam'men-ziehen*.

construct, *vb.* konstruie'ren.

construction, *n.* Konstruk-tion', -en *f.*

constructive, *adj.* positiv.

construe, *vb.* aus·legen.

consul, *n.* Konsul, -n, *m.*

consular, *adj.* konsula'risch.

consulate, *n.* Konsulat', -e *nt.*

consult, *vb.* zu Rate ziehen*; konsultie'ren.

consultant, *n.* Bera'ter, - *m.*

consultation, *n.* Konferenz', -en *f.*; *(med.)* Konsultation', -en *f.*

consume, *vb.* verzeh'ren, verbrau'chen.

consumer, *n.* Verbrau'cher, - *m.*

consummate, 1. *vb.* vollen'-den. **2.** *adj.* vollen'det.

consummation, *n.* Vollzie'-hung, -en *f.*

consumption, *n.* Verbrauch' *m.*; *(med.)* Schwindsucht *f.*

consumptive, *adj.* schwind-süchtig.

contact, 1. *n.* Kontakt', -e *m.* **2.** *vb.* sich in Verbin'-dung setzen mit.

contagion, *n.* Ansteckung, -en *f.*

contagious, *adj.* ansteckend.

contain, *vb.* enthal'ten*.

container, *n.* Behäl'ter, - *m.*

contaminate, *vb.* verun'-reinigen.

contemplate, *vb.* betrach'-ten.

contemplation, *n.* Betrach'-tung, -en *f.*

contemplative, *adj.* nach-denklich.

contemporary, 1. *n.* Zeit-genosse, -n, -n *m.* **2.** *adj.* zeitgenössisch.

contempt, *n.* Verach'tung, -en *f.*

contemptible, *adj.* verach'-tenswert.

contemptuous, *adj.* ver-ächt'lich.

contend, *vb.* *(assert)* be-haup'ten; *(fight)* streiten*.

contender, *n.* Streiter, - *m.*

content, 1. *n.* Inhalt *m.* **2.** *adj.* zufrie'den.

contented, *adj.* zufrie'den.

contention, *n.* *(assertion)* Behaup'tung, -en *f.*; *(fight)* Streit, -e *m.*

contentment, *n.* Zufrie'-denheit *f.*

contest, 1. *n.* Wettstreit, -e *m.*; *(advertising)* Preisaus-schreiben, - *nt.* **2.** *vb.* bestrei'ten*.

contestant, *n.* Bewer'ber, - *m.*

context, *n.* Zusam'menhang, ‑e *m.*

continent, 1. *n.* Kontinent, -e *m.* **2.** *adj.* enthalt'sam.

continental, *adj.* kontinen-tal'.

contingency, *n.* Eventuali-tät', -en *f.*

continual, *adj.* dauernd.

continuation, *n.* Fortset-zung, -en *f.*

continue, *vb.* *(tr.)* fort-setzen; *(intr.)* fort·fahren*.

continuity, *n.* Fortdauer *f.*

continuous, *adj.* fortdau-ernd.

contort, *vb.* verdre'hen.

contortion, *n.* Verdre'hung, -en *f.*

contour, *n.* Umriß, -sse *m.*

contraband, *n.* Schmuggel-ware, -n *f.*

contract, 1. n. Vertrag', -e m. 2. vb. vertrag'lich ab- schließen*; (disease) sich zu'ziehen*.

contraction, n. Zusam' menziehung, -en f.

contractor, n. Bauunter- nehmer, - m.

contradict, vb. widerspre'- chen*.

contradiction, n. Wider- spruch, -e m.

contradictory, adj. wider- spre'chend.

contralto, n. Altstimme, -n f.

contraption, n. Vorrichtung, -en f.

contrary, 1. n. Gegenteil, -e nt. 2. adj. (opposite) entge' gengesetzt; (obstinate) wider- spenstig.

contrast, 1. n. Gegensatz, -e m. 2. vb. entge'gen- setzen.

contribute, vb. bei'tragen*.

contribution, n. Beitrag, -e m.

contributor, n. Beiträger, - m.

contributory, adj. mitwir- kend.

contrite, adj. zerknirscht'.

contrivance, n. Vorrichtung, -en f.

contrive, vb. fertig bringen*, erfin'den*.

control, 1. n. Kontrol'le, -n f. 2. vb. beherr'schen.

controllable, adj. kontrol- lier'bar.

controller, n. Überprü'fer, - m.

controversial, adj. strittig.

controversy, n. Streitfrage, -n f.

contusion, n. Quetschung, -en f.

convalesce, vb. gene'sen*.

convalescence, n. Konva- leszenz' f.

convalescent, adj. gene'- send.

convene, vb. zusam'men- kommen*.

convenience, n. Annehm- lichkeit, -en f.

convenient, adj. bequem', geeig'net.

convent, n. Nonnenkloster, - nt.

convention, n. Versamm'- lung, -en f., Tagung, -en f.; (contract) Abkommen, - nt.; (tradition) Konvention', -en f.

conventional, adj. konven- tionell'.

converge, vb. zusam'men- laufen*.

convergence, n. Konver- genz', -en f.

convergent, adj. konvergie'- rend.

conversant with, adj. bewan'dert in.

conversational, adj. Ge- sprächs'- (cpds.).

converse, 1. n. Kehrseite, -n f. 2. vb. sich unterhal'- ten*. 3. adj. umgekehrt.

convert, 1. n. Konvertit', -en, -en m. 2. vb. (belief, goods, money) konvertie'ren; (missionary) bekeh'ren.

converter, n. Bekeh'rer, - m.; (elec.) Transforma'tor, -o'ren m.

convertible, 1. n. (auto) Kabriolett', -s nt. 2. adj. konvertier'bar.

convex, adj. konvex'.

convey, vb. beför'dern, über- mit'teln.

conveyance, n. (vehicle) Be- för'derungsmittel, - nt.; (tradition) Übermitt'lung, -en f.

conveyor, n. Beför'derer, - m.

convict, 1. n. Sträfling, -e m. 2. vb. überfüh'ren.

conviction, n. Schuldig- sprechung, -en f.; (belief) Überzeu'gung, -en f.

convince, vb. überzeu'gen.

convincing, adj. überzeu'- gend.

convivial, adj. gesel'lig.

convocation, n. Versamm'- lung, -en f.

convoy, 1. n. Geleit'zug, -e m. 2. vb. gelei'ten.

convulse, vb. in Zuckungen

versetzen; **(be c.d)** sich krümmen.

convulsion, n. Krampf, =e m.

convulsive, adj. krampfhaft.

cook, 1. n. Koch, =e m.; Köchin, -nen f. 2. vb. kochen.

cookbook, n. Kochbuch, =er nt.

cookie, n. Keks, -e m.

cool, 1. adj. kühl. 2. vb. ab·kühlen.

coolness, n. Kühle f.

coop, n. Hühnerkorb, =e m.

cooperate, vb zusam'men·arbeiten.

cooperation, n. Zusam'menarbeit, -en f.

cooperative, 1. n. Konsum'verein, -e m. 2. adj. hilfsbereit.

coordinate, 1. adj. bei·geordnet, koordiniert'. 2. vb. bei·orden, koordinie'ren.

coordination, n. Beiordnung, -en f.; Koordination', -en f.

coordinator, n. Organisations'planer, - m.

cop, n. Schupo, -s m.

cope, vb. sich ab·mühen.

copious, adj. reichlich.

copper, n. Kupfer nt.

copy, 1. n. Abschrift, -en f., Kopie', -i'en f.; (book) Exemplar', -e nt. 2. vb. abschreiben*, kopie'ren.

copyright, n. Urheberrecht, -e nt.

coquette, 1. n. Koket'te, -n f. 2. adj. kokett'.

coral, n. Koral'le, -n f.

cord, n. Schnur, =e f.

cordial, adj. herzlich.

cordiality, n. Herzlichkeit f.

cordovan, n. Korduanleder, - nt.

core, n. (fruit) Kernhaus, =er nt.; (heart) Kern, -e m.

cork, n. (material) Kork m.; (stopper) Korken, - m.

corkscrew, n. Korkenzieher, - m

corn, n. (grain) Getrei'de nt.; (maize) Mais m.; (foot) Hühnerauge, -n nt.

corn-plaster, n. Hühneraugenpflaster, - nt.

cornea, n. Hornhaut, =e f.

corner, n. Ecke, -n f.

cornet, n. Kornett', - f.

cornice, n. Gesims', -e nt.

cornstarch, n. Maize'na nt.

coronation, n. Krönung, -en f.

coronet, n. Adelskrone, -n f.

corporal, 1. n. (mil.) Gefreit- m. 2. adj. körperlich.

corporate, adj. körperschaftlich.

corporation, n. Körperschaft, -en f.; (comm.) Aktiengesellschaft, -en f.

corps, n. Korps, - nt.

corpse, n. Leichnam, -e m.

corpulent, adj. korpulent'.

corpuscle, n. Körperchen, - nt.

correct, 1. adj. richtig, korrekt'. 2. vb. verbes'sern, berich'tigen, korrigie'ren.

correction, n. Verbes'serung, -en f., Berich'tigung, -en f.

corrective, adj. korrektiv'.

correctness, n. Korrekt'heit, -en f.

correlate, vb. aufeinan'der bezie'hen*.

correlation, n. Korrelation', -en f.

correspond, vb. entspre'chen*; (agree) überein'·stimmen; (letters) korrespondie'ren.

correspondence, n. Entspre'chung, -en f.; (agreement) Überein'stimmung, -en f.; (letters) Korrespondenz, -en f.

correspondent, n. Korrespondent', -en, -en m.

corridor, n. Korridor, -e m.

corroborate, vb. bestä'tigen.

corroboration, n. Bestä'tigung, -en f.

corrode, vb. korrodie'ren.

corrosion, n. Korrosion', -en f.

corrupt, vb. wellen.

corrupt, 1. vb. korrumpie'ren. 2. adj. korrupt'.

corrupter, n. Verfüh'rer, - m.

corruptible, *adj.* verführ'-bar.

corruption, *n.* Korruption', -en *f.*

corsage, *n.* Blume oder Blumen zum Anstecken.

corset, *n.* Korsett', -s *nt.*

cortège, *n.* Leichenzug, "e *m.*

cosmetic. 1. *n.* kosme'tisches Mittel, - *nt.* **2.** *adj.* kosme'tisch.

cosmic, *adj.* kosmisch.

cosmopolitan, *adj* kosmo-poli'tisch.

cosmos, *n.* Kosmos *m.*

cost. 1. *n* Preis, -e *m.;* Kosten *pl.* **2.** *vb.* kosten.

costliness, *n.* Kostspielig-keit, -en *f.*

costly, *adj.* kostspielig.

costume, *n* (*fancy*) Kostüm', -e *nt.;* (*native*) Tracht, -en *f.*

cot, *n.* Feldbett. -en *nt.*

cottage, *n.* Häuschen, - *nt.;* Landhaus, "er *nt.*

cotton, *n.* Baumwolle *f.*

couch, *n.* Couch, -es *f.*

cough, 1 *n.* Husten *m.* **2.** *vb.* husten.

could, *vb.* (*was able*) konnte; (*would be able*) könnte.

council, *n.* Rat, "e *m.*

counsel. 1. *n.* Rat, "e *m ;* (*lawyer*) Anwalt, "e *m.* **2.** *vb.* bera'ten*, raten*.

counselor, *n.* Bera'ter, - *m.*

count. 1. *n.* Gesamt'zahl, -en *f.;* (*noble*) Graf, -en, -en *m.* **2.** *vb.* zählen.

countenance, *n.* Gesicht', -er *nt*

counter. 1. *n.* Zähler, - *m.;* (*store*) Ladentisch, -e *m.* **2.** *adv.* (**c. to**) entge'gen.

counteract, *vb.* entge'gen-arbeiten.

counterattack. 1. *n* Gegenangriff, -e *m.* **2.** *vb.* einen Gegenangriff machen.

counterbalance, 1. *n.* Gegengewicht, -e *nt.* **2.** *vb.* auf'wiegen*.

counterfeit. 1. *n.* Falsch'geld, -er *nt.* **2.** *adj.* gefälscht'. **3.** *vb.* fälschen.

countermand, *vb.* widerru'fen*.

counteroffensive, *n.* Gegenoffensive, -n *f.*

counterpart, *n.* Gegenstück, -e *nt.*

countess, *n.* Gräfin, -nen *f.*

countless, *adj.* zahllos.

country, *n.* Land, "er *nt.*

countryman, *n.* Landsmann, -leute *m.*

countryside, *n.* Landschaft, -en *f.*

county, *n.* Grafschaft, -en *f.*

coupé, *n.* geschlossenes Zweisitzer-Auto, -s *nt.*

couple. 1. *n.* Paar, -e *nt.* **2.** *vb.* koppeln.

coupon, *n.* Coupon', -s *m.*

courage, *n.* Mut *m.*

courageous, *adj.* mutig.

courier, *n.* Kurier', -e *m.*

course, *n.* Lauf, "e *m.;* (*race*) Rennbahn, -en *f.;* (*nautical*) Kurs, -e *m.;* (*school*) Kursus, Kurse *m.;* (*food*) Gang, "e *m.;* (**of c.**) natür'lich.

court. 1. *n.* Hof, "e *m.* **2** *vb.* den Hof machen.

courteous, *adj.* höflich.

courtesan, *n.* Kurtisa'ne, -n *f.*

courtesy, *n.* Höflichkeit, -en *f.*

courthouse, *n.* Gerichts'gebäude, - *nt.*

courtier, *n.* Höfling, -e *m.*

courtly, *adj.* höfisch.

courtmartial, *n.* Kriegsgericht, -e *nt.*

courtroom, *n.* Gerichts'saal, -säle *m.*

courtship, *n.* Freien *nt.*

courtyard, *n.* Hof, "e *m.*

cousin, *n.* Vetter, -n *m.;* Cousi'ne, -n *f.*

covenant, *n.* Vertrag', "e *m.*

cover. 1. *n.* Deckel, - *m.* **2.** *vb.* bede'cken; (**c. up**) zu'decken.

covering, *n.* Bede'ckung, -en *f.*

covet, *vb.* begeh'ren.

covetous, *adj.* begie'rig.

cow, *n.* Kuh, "e *f.*

coward, *n.* Feigling, -e *m.*

cowardice, *n.* Feigheit, -en *f.*

cowardly, *adj.* feige.

cowboy, *n.* Cowboy, -s *m.*

cower, *vb.* kauern.

cowhide, *n.* Rindsleder, - *nt.*

coy, *adj.* spröde.

cozy, *adj.* behag'lich.

crab, *n.* Taschenkrebs, -e *m.*

crack, 1. *n.* Spalt, -e *m.*, Sprung, *e m.*, Riß, -sse *m.* 2. *vb.* brechen*, springen*.

cracker, *n.* Salzkeks, -e *m.*

cradle, *n.* Wiege, -n *f.*

craft, *n.* Kunstfertigkeit, -en *f.*; (*ship*) Schiff, -e *nt.*

craftsman, *n.* Handwerker, - *m.*

craftsmanship, *n.* Kunstfertigkeit, -en *f.*

crafty, *adj.* gewiegt'.

cram, *vb.* voll'stopfen*; (*exam*) pauken.

cramp, *n.* Krampf, *e m.*

crane, *n.* Kran, *e m.*; (*bird*) Kranich, -e *m.*

crank, 1. *n.* (*handle*) Kurbel, -n *f.*; (*crackpot*) Sonderling, -e *m.* 2. *vb.* an'kurbeln.

cranky, *adj.* mißvergnügt.

cranny, *n.* Ritze, -n *f.*

crash, 1. *n.* Krach *m.*; (*collision*) Zusam'menstoß, *e m.*; (*plane*) Absturz, *e m.* 2. *vb.* krachen; zusam'men-stoßen*; ab'stürzen.

crate, *n.* Kiste, -n *f.*

crater, *n.* Krater, - *m.*

crave, *vb.* verlan'gen nach.

craving, *adj.* gieriges Verlan'gen, - *nt.*

crawl, *vb.* kriechen*; (*swimming*) kraulen.

crayon, *n.* Buntstift, -e *m.*

crazed, *adj.* wahnsinnig.

crazy, *adj.* verrückt'.

creak, *vb.* knarren.

cream, *n.* Sahne *f.*, Rahm *m.*; (*cosmetic*) Creme, -s *f.*, Krem, -s *m.*

creamery, *n.* Molkerei', -en *f.*

creamy, *adj.* sahnig.

crease, 1. *n.* Falte, -n *f.* 2. *vb.* falten.

create, *vb.* schaffen*, erschaf'fen*; erzeu'gen.

creation, *n.* Erschaf'fung, -en *f.*; Schöpfung, -en *f.*

creative, *adj.* schöpferisch.

creator, *n.* Schöpfer, - *m.*

creature, *n.* Geschöpf', -e *nt.*; Wesen, - *nt.*

credentials, *n.pl.* Beglau'bigungsschreiben, - *nt.*

credibility, *n.* Glaubwürdigkeit *f.*

credible, *adj.* glaubwürdig.

credit, 1. *n.* Verdienst', - *nt.*; (*comm.*) Kredit', -e *m.* 2. *vb.* gut'schreiben*.

creditable, *adj.* anerkennenswert.

creditor, *n.* Gläubig- *m.*

credo, *n.* Glaubensbekenntnis, -se *nt.*

credulity, *n.* Leichtgläubigkeit *f.*

credulous, *adj.* leichtgläubig.

creed, *n.* Glaubensbekenntnis, -se *nt.*

creek, *n.* Bach, *e m.*

creep, *vb.* kriechen*.

cremate, *vb.* ein'äschern.

cremation, *n.* Einäscherung, -en *f.*

crematory, *n.* Krematorium, -rien *nt.*

crepe, *n.* Krepp *m.*

crescent, *n.* Mondsichel, -n *f.*

crest, *n.* Kamm, *e m.*

crestfallen, *adj.* geknickt'.

cretonne, *n.* Kretonn'e, -s *m.*

crevasse, *n.* Gletscherspalte, -n *f.*

crevice, *n.* Riß, -sse *m.*

crew, *n.* Mannschaft, -en *f.*

crib, *n.* Krippe, -n *f.*; (*bed*) Kinderbett, -en *nt.*

cricket, *n.* Grille, -n *f.*

crime, *n.* Verbre'chen, - *nt.*

criminal, 1. *n.* Verbre'cher, - *m.* 2. *adj.* verbre'cherisch.

criminology, *n.* Kriminalis'tik *f.*

crimson, *adj.* karmin'rot.

cringe, *vb.* sich krümmen.

cripple, 1. *n.* Krüppel, - *m.* 2. *vb.* zum Krüppel machen; lähmen.

crippled, *adj.* verkrüp'pelt, gelähmt'.

crisis, *n.* Krise, -n *f.*

crisp, adj. (weather, vegetables) frisch; (bread, etc.) knusprig.

criterion, n. Krite'rium, -rien nt.

critic, n. Kritiker, - m.

critical, adj. kritisch.

criticism, n. Kritik', -en f.

criticize, vb. kritisie'ren

croak, vb. krächzen.

crochet, vb. häkeln.

crock, n. Steintopf, -e m.

crockery, n. Steingut nt.

crocodile, n. Krokodil', -e nt.

crook, n. (bend) Biegung, -en f.; (cheater) Schwindler, - m.

crooked, adj. (not straight) krumm, schief; (dishonest) unehrlich, betrü'gerisch.

croon, vb. summen; (jazz) Schlager singen*.

crop, n. Ernte, -n f.; (riding) Peitsche, -n f.

croquet, n. Kroket'spiel, -e nt.

croquette, n. Kroket'te, -n f.

cross, 1. n. Kreuz, -e nt.; (mixture) Kreuzung, -en f. **2.** vb. kreuzen.

cross-eyed, adj. (be c.) schielen.

crossing, n. Kreuzung, -en f.

crossroads, n.pl. Scheideweg, -e m.; Kreuzung, -en f.

cross section, n. Querschnitt, -e m.

crossword puzzle, n. Kreuzworträtsel, - nt.

crotch, n. (trousers) Schritt, -e m.; (tree) Gabelung, -en f.

crouch, vb. kauern.

croup, n. Krupp m.

crouton, n. Crouton', -s m.

crow, 1. n. Krähe, -n f. **2.** vb. krähen.

crowd, 1. n. Menge, -n f. **2.** vb. drängeln.

crown, 1. n. Krone, -n f. **2.** vb. krönen.

crucial, adj. entschei'dend.

crucible, n. Schmelztiegel, - m.

crucifix, n. Kruzifix, -e nt.

crucifixion, n. Kreuzigung, -en f.

crucify, vb. kreuzigen.

crude, adj. roh, grob(").

crudeness, n. Grobheit, -en f., Unfeinheit, -en f.

crudity, n. Roheit, -en f., Unfeinheit, -en f.

cruel, adj. grausam.

cruelty, n. Grausamkeit, -en f.

cruise, 1. n. Seereise, -n f. **2.** vb. kreuzen.

cruiser, n. Kreuzer, - m.

crumb, n. Krümel, - m.

crumble, vb. zerbrö'ckeln.

crumple, vb. zerknül'len.

crusade, n. Kreuzzug, -e m.

crusader, n. Kreuzzügler, - m.

crush, 1. n. (crowd) Gedrän'ge nt. **2.** vb. zerdrü'cken.

crust, n. Kruste, -n f.

crustacean, n. Krustentier, -e nt.

crusty, adj. knusprig.

crutch, n. Krücke, -n f.

cry, 1. n. Schrei, -e m. **2.** vb. schreien*; (weep) weinen.

crying, adj. (urgent) dringend.

cryptic, adj. geheim'.

cryptography, n. Geheim'schrift, -en f.

crystal, 1. n. Kristall', -e nt. **2.** adj. kristal'len.

crystalline, adj. kristal'len.

crystallize, vb. kristallisie'ren.

cub, n. Junge- nt.

cube, n. Würfel, - m.

cubic, adj. würfelförmig, kubisch; Kubik'- (cpds.).

cubicle, n. kleiner Schlafraum, -e m..

cuckoo, n. Kuckuck, -e m.

cucumber, n. Gurke, -n f.

cud, n. Wiedergekäut- nt.; (chew the c.) wieder·käuen.

cuddle, vb. herzen.

cudgel, n. Keule, -n f.

cue, n. Stichwort, -er nt.

cuff, n. (sleeve) Manschet'te, -n f.; (trousers) Hosenaufschlag, -e m.

cuisine, n. Küche, -n f.

culinary, adj. kulina'risch.

cull, vb. pflücken.

culminate, vb. gipfeln.

culmination, *n.* Höhepunkt, -e *m.*

culpable, *adj.* schuldhaft.

culprit, *n.* Täter, - *m.*

cult, *n.* Kult. -e *m.*

cultivate, *vb.* kultivie'ren.

cultivated, *adj.* kultiviert'.

cultivation, *n.* Kultivie'-rung *f.*

cultural, *adj.* kulturell'.

culture, *n.* Kultur', -ren *f.*

cultured, *adj.* kultiviert'.

cumbersome, *adj.* schwer-fällig.

cumulative, *adj.* kumulativ'.

cunning. 1. *n.* List, -en *f.*
2. *adj.* listig; *(sweet)* goldig.

cup, *n.* Tasse, -n *f.*

cupboard, *n.* Schrank, ⸗e *m.*

cupidity, *n.* Begier'de, -n *f.*

cupola, *n.* Kuppel, -n *f.*

curable, *adj.* heilbar.

curator, *n.* Kura'tor, -o'ren *m.*

curb. 1. *n.* *(sidewalk)* Bord-stein, -e *m.; (harness)* Zügel, - *m.* **2.** *vb.* zügeln

curdle, *vb.* gerin'nen*.

cure. 1. *n.* Kur, -en *f.; (medicine)* Heilmittel, - *nt.*
2. *vb.* heilen.

curfew, *n.* Polizei'stunde, -n *f.*

curio, *n.* Kuriosität', -en *f.*

curiosity, *n.* Neu ierde *f.*

curious, *adj.* neugierig.

curl. 1. *n.* Locke, -n *f.* **2.** *vb.* locken, kräuseln.

curly, *adj.* lockig, kraus.

currant, *n.* Johan'nisbeere, -n *f.; (dried)* Korin'the, -n *f.*

currency, *n.* Währung, -en *f.*

current. 1. *n.* Strom, ⸗e *m.* **2.** *adj.* laufend.

currently, *adv.* zur Zeit.

curriculum, *n.* Lehrplan, ⸗e *m.*

curry, *n.* Curry *nt.*

curse. 1. *n.* Fluch, ⸗e *m.* **2.** *vb. (intr.)* fluchen, *(tr.)* verflu'chen.

cursed, *adj.* verflucht'.

curse-word, *n.* Schimpfwort, ⸗er *nt.*

cursory, *adj.* flüchtig.

curt, *adj.* kurz angebunden.

curtail, *vb.* ein-schränken.

curtain, *n.* Gardi'ne, -n *f.; (drapes)* Vorhang, ⸗e *m.*

curtsy, *n.* Knicks. -e *m.*

curvature, *n.* Krümmung, -en *f.*

curve, *n.* Kurve, -n *f.*

cushion, *n.* Kissen, - *nt.*

custard, *n.* Eierpudding, -s *m.*

custodian, *n.* Hausmeister, - *m.*

custody, *n.* Verwah'rung *f.*

custom, *n.* Sitte, -n *f.,* Brauch, ⸗e *m.; (habit)* Gewohn'heit, -en *f.*

customary, *adj.* gebräuch'-lich.

customer, *n.* Kunde, -n, -n *m.*

custom house, *n.* Zollamt, ⸗er *nt.*

customs, *n.* Zoll, ⸗e *m.*

customs officer, *n.* Zoll-beamt- *m.*

cut. 1. *n.* Schnitt, -e *m.; (wound)* Schnittwunde, -n *f.; (salary)* Kürzung, -en *f.; (taxes)* Senkung, -en *f.* **2.** *vb.* schneiden*; kürzen; sen-; *(class)* schwänzen.

cut glass, *n.* geschlif'fenes Glas *nt.*

cute, *adj.* niedlich, süß, goldig.

cuticle, *n.* Nagelhaut, ⸗e *f.*

cutlet, *n.* Kotelett', -s *nt.*

cutlery, *n.* Stahlwaren *pl.*

cutter, *n.* Zuschneider, - *m.; (boat)* Kutter, - *m.*

cycle. 1. *n.* Kreislauf, ⸗e *m.;* Zyklus, -klen *m.* **2.** *vb.* radeln.

cyclist, *n.* Radfahrer, - *m.*

cyclone, *n.* Wirbelsturm, ⸗e *m.*

cyclotron, *n.* Zyklotron, - *nt.*

cylinder, *n.* Zylin'der, - *m.*

cylindrical, *adj.* zylin'drisch.

cymbal, *n.* Zimbel, -n *f.*

cynic, *n.* Zyniker, - *m.*

cynical, *adj.* zynisch.

cynicism, *n.* Zynis'mus, -men *m.*

cypress, *n.* Zypres'se, -n *f.*

cyst, *n.* Zyste, -n *f.*

D

dab, *vb.* tupfen.

dabble, *vb.* sich dilettantenhaft mit einer Sache ab·geben*.

daffodil, *n.* Narzis'se, -n *f.*

dagger, *n.* Dolch. -e *m.*

dahlia, *n.* Dahlie, -n *f.*

daily, 1. *n.* (*newspaper*) Tageszeitung, -en *f.* 2. *adj.* täglich.

daintiness, *n.* Zartheit, -en *f.*

dainty, *adj.* zart, delikat', zierlich.

dairy, *n.* Milchwirtschaft, -en *f.*, Molkerei' -en *f.*

dairyman, *m.* Milchhändler, - *m.*

dais, *n.* Podium, -ien *nt.*

daisy, *n.* Margeri'te, -n *f.*

dale, *n.* Tal, -er *nt.*

dally, *vb.* tändeln; (*dawdle*) trödeln.

dam, 1. *n.* Damm, -e *m.* 2. *vb.* ein·dämmen.

damage, 1. *n.* Schaden, -e *m.*; (*damages, law*) Schadenersatz *m.* 2. *vb.* schädigen; beschä'digen.

damask, *n.* Damast, -e *m.*

damn, *vb.* verdam'men; (*curse*) verflu'chen.

damnation, *n.* Verdam'mung, -en *f.*

damp, *adj.* feucht.

dampen, *vb.* (*moisten*) ein·feuchten; (*quiet*) dämpfen; (*fig.*) nieder·schlagen*.

dampness, *n.* Feuchtigkeit, -en *f.*

dance, 1. *n.* Tanz, -e *m.* 2. *vb.* tanzen.

dancer, *n.* Tänzer, - *m.*

dancing, *n.* Tanzen *nt.*

dandelion, *n.* Löwenzahn *m.*

dandruff, *n.* Kopfschuppen *pl.*

dandy, 1. *n.* Geck, -en, -en *m.* 2. *adj.* prima.

Dane, *n.* Däne, -n, -n *m.*

danger, *n.* Gefahr', -en *f.*

dangerous, *adj.* gefähr'lich.

dangle, *vb.* baumeln; baumeln lassen*.

Danish, *adj.* dänisch.

dapper, *adj.* klein und elegant'.

dare, *vb.* wagen.

daredevil, *n.* Draufgänger, - *m.*

daring, *adj.* gewagt'.

dark, 1. *n.* Dunkel *nt.*; Dunkelheit, -en *f.* 2. *adj.* dunkel.

darken, *vb.* verdun'keln.

darkness, *n.* Dunkel *nt.*; Dunkelheit, -en *f.*

darling, 1. *n.* Liebling, -e *m.* 2. *adj.* goldig.

darn, *vb.* (*socks*) stopfen.

dart, 1. *n.* Wurfpfeil, -e *m.* 2. *vb.* fliezen*.

dash, 1. *n.* (pen) Strich, -e *m.*; (*sport*) Lauf, -e *m.* 2. *vb.* (*intr.*) sich stürzen; (*tr.*) stoßen*, schleudern.

dashboard, *n.* Armatu'renbrett, -er *nt.*

dashing, *adj.* schneidig.

data, *n.pl.* Angaben *pl.*

date, 1. *n.* Datum, -ten *nt.*; (*appointment*) Verab'redung, -en *f.*; (*fruit*) Dattel, -n *f.* 2. *vb.* datie'ren; aus·gehen* mit.

daub, *vb.* schmieren.

daughter, *n.* Tochter, - *f.*

daughter-in-law, *n.* Schwiegertochter, - *f.*

daunt, *vb.* entmu'tigen.

dauntless, *adj.* kühn.

dawdle, *vb.* trödeln.

dawn, 1. *n.* Morgendämmerung, -en *f.* 2. *vb.* dämmern.

day, *n.* Tag, -e *m.*

daybreak, *n.* Tagesanbruch *m.*

daydream, 1. *n.* Träumerei', -en *f.* 2. *vb.* vor sich hin träumen; sinnie'ren.

daylight, *n.* Tageslicht *nt.*

daze, 1. *n.* Benom'menheit *f.* 2. *vb.* betäu'ben.

dazzle, *vb.* blenden.

deacon, *n.* Diakon', -e *m.*

dead, *adj.* tot.

deaden, *vb.* dämpfen.

dead end, *n.* Sackgasse, -n *f.*

deadline, *n.* Termin', -e *m.*

deadlock, *n.* Stockung, -en *f.*

deadly, *adj.* tötlich.

deaf, *adj.* taub.

deafen, *vb.* betäu'ben.

deafness, *n.* Taubheit *f.*

deal, 1. *n.* Anzahl *f.;* (*business*) Geschäft', -e *nt.* **2.** *vb.* (*cards*) geben*; (**d. with**) behan'deln; (**d. in**) handeln mit.

dealer, *n.* Händler, - *m.;* (*cards*) Geber, - *m.*

dean, *n.* Dekan', -e *m.*

dear, *adj.* lieb, teuer.

dearly, *adv.* sehr.

dearth, *n.* Mangel, - *m.*

death, *n.* Tod *m.;* Todesfall, -e *m.*

deathless, *adj.* unsterblich.

debase, *vb.* ernie'drigen.

debatable, *adj.* bestreit'bar.

debate, 1. *n.* Debat'te, -n *f.* **2.** *vb.* debattie'ren.

debauch, 1. *n.* Orgie, -n *f.* **2.** *vb.* verfüh'ren.

debenture, *n.* Obligation', -en *f.*

debilitate, *vb.* entkräf'ten.

debit, *n.* Debet, -s *nt.*

debonair, *adj.* zuvor'kommend; heiter und sorglos.

debris, *n.* Trümmer *pl.*

debt, *n.* Schuld, -en *f.*

debtor, *n.* Schuldner, - *m.*

debunk, *vb.* mit etwas aufräumen, den Nimbus rauben.

debut, *n.* Debüt', -s *nt.*

debutante, *n.* Debütan'tin, -nen *f.*

decade, *n.* Jahrzehnt', -e *nt.*

decadence, *n.* Dekadenz' *f.*

decadent, *adj.* dekadent'.

decanter, *n.* Karaf'fe, -n *f.*

decapitate, *vb.* enthaup'ten.

decay, 1. *n.* Verfall' *m.;* Verwe'sung, -en *f.* **2.** *vb.* verfal'len*; verwe'sen.

deceased, *adj.* verstor'ben.

deceit, *n.* Täuschung, -en *f.;* Betrug', -e *m.*

deceitful, *adj.* falsch; betrü'gerisch.

deceive, *vb.* täuschen; betrü'gen*.

December, *n.* Dezem'ber *m.*

decency, *n.* Anständigkeit, -en *f.*

decent, *adj.* anständig.

decentralization, *n.* Dezentralisation', -en *f.*

decentralize, *vb.* dezentralisie'ren.

deception, *n.* Täuschung, -en *f.*

deceptive, *adj.* irreführend; täuschend.

decide, *vb.* entschei'den*; sich entschlie'ßen*.

decimal, 1. *n.* Dezimal'bruch, -e *m.* **2.** *adj.* Dezimal'- (*cpds.*).

decimate, *vb.* dezimie'ren.

decipher, *vb.* entzif'fern.

decision, *n.* Entschei'dung, -en *f.;* Beschluß', -sse *m.*

decisive, *adj.* entschei'dend.

deck, *n.* (*ship*) Deck, -s *nt.;* (*cards*) Spiel, -e *nt.*

declaration, *n.* Erklä'rung, -en *f.*

declarative, *adj.* erklä'rend; (**d. sentence**) Aussagesatz, -e *m.*

declare, *vb.* erklä'ren, behaup'ten; (*customs*) deklarie'ren.

declension, *n.* Deklination', -en *f.*

decline, 1. *n.* Niedergang *m.* **2.** *vb.* neigen; (*refuse*) ab·lehnen; (*gram.*) deklinie'ren.

décolleté, *n.* Dekolleté', -s *nt.*

decompose, *vb.* (*tr.*) zerset'zen; (*intr.*) verwe'sen.

decomposition, *n.* Zerset'zung, -en *f.;* Verwe'sung, -en *f.*

décor, *n.* Ausstattung, -en *f.*

decorate, *vb.* schmücken, dekorie'ren.

decoration, *n.* Dekoration', -en *f.*

decorative, *adj.* dekorativ'.

decorator, *n.* Dekorateur', -e *m.;* (**interior d.**) Innenarchitekt, -en *m.*

decorous, *adj.* schicklich.

decorum, *n.* Schicklichkeit *f.*

decoy, 1. *n.* Lockvogel, - *m.* **2.** *vb.* locken.

decrease, 1. *n.* Abnahme, -n *f.* 2. *vb.* (*tr.*) verrin'gern; (*intr.*) ab·nehmen*.

decree, 1. *n.* Erlaß', -sse *m.* 2. *vb.* verord'nen.

decrepit, *adj.* gebrech'lich, klapprig.

decry, *vb.* mißbil'ligen, ta-deln.

dedicate, *vb.* widmen.

dedication, *n.* Widmung, -en *f.*

deduce, *vb.* folgern.

deduct, *vb.* ab·ziehen*.

deduction, *n.* Abzug, ·e *m.*; (*logic*) Folgerung, -en *f.*

deductive, *adj.* deduktiv'.

deed, *n.* Tat, -en *f.*; (*document*) Urkunde, -n *f.*

deem, *vb.* denken*; halten* für.

deep, *adj.* tief.

deepen, *vb.* vertie'fen.

deer, *n.* Reh, -e *nt.*; Hirsch, -e *m.*

deerskin, *n.* Rehleder, - *nt.*; Hirschleder, - *nt.*

deface, *vb.* entstel'len.

defamation, *n.* Verleum'dung, -en *f.*

defame, *vb.* in schlechten Ruf bringen*.

default, 1. *n.* Versäum'nis, -se *nt.*; Unterlas'sung, -en *f.* 2. *vb.* im Verzug'sein*.

defeat, 1. *n.* Niederlage, -n *f.* 2. *vb.* besie'gen.

defect, 1. *n.* Fehler, - *m.*, Defekt', -e *m.* 2. *vb.* über-laufen*.

defection, *n.* Versa'gen *nt.*; Treubruch, ·e *m.*

defective, *adj.* fehlerhaft.

defend, *vb.* vertei'digen.

defendant, *n.* Angeklagt-*m.&f.*

defender, *n.* Vertei'diger, - *m.*, Beschüt'zer, - *m.*

defense, *n.* Vertei'digung, -en *f.*

defenseless, *adj.* wehrlos.

defensible, *adj.* verfecht'bar, zu vertei'digen.

defensive, 1. *n.* Defensi've, -n *f.* 2. *adj.* defensiv'.

defer, *vb.* (*put off*) auf·schie-ben*; (*yield*) nach·geben*.

deference, *n.* Achtung *f.*

deferential, *adj.* ehrerbietig.

defiance, *n.* Heraus'forde-rung, -en *f.*; Trotz *m.*

defiant, *adj.* trotzig, heraus'-fordernd.

deficiency, *n.* Mangel, ·· *m.*

deficient, *adj.* unzureichend.

deficit, *n.* Defizit, -e *nt.*

defile, 1. *n.* Engpaß, -sse *m.* 2. *vb.* (*march*) defilie'ren; (*soil*) besu'deln.

definite, *adj.* bestimmt'.

definition, *n.* Definition', -en *f.*

definitive, *adj.* definitiv'.

deflate, *vb.* die Luft heraus'-lassen*.

deflation, *n.* Deflation', -en *f.*

deflect, *vb.* ab·wenden*.

deform, *vb.* entstel'len.

deformity, *n.* Verwachs'ung, -en *f.*

defraud, *vb.* betrü'gen*.

defray, *vb.* bestrei'ten*.

defrost, *vb.* entfros'ten.

deft, *adj.* geschickt'.

defy, *vb.* trotzen.

degenerate, 1. *adj.* de-generiert'. 2. *vb.* entar'ten.

degeneration, *n.* Degenera-tion' *f.*

degradation, *n.* Ernie'dri-gung, -en *f.*

degrade, *vb.* ernie'drigen.

degree, *n.* Grad, -e *m.*

deify, *vb.* vergött'lichen.

deign, *vb.* geru'hen.

deity, *n.* Gottheit, -en *f.*

dejected, *adj.* niederge-schlagen.

dejection, *n.* Trübsinn *m.*

delay, 1. *n.* Verzö'gerung, -en *f.* 2. *vb.* auf·schieben*, verzö'gern.

delectable, *adj.* ergötz'lich.

delegate, 1. *n.* Delegier't-*m.&f.* 2. *vb.* delegie'ren.

delegation, *n.* Abordnung, -en *f.*, Delegation', -en *f.*

delete, *vb.* aus·streichen*.

deliberate, 1. *vb.* erwä'gen*. 2. *adj.* bedäch'tig; (*on pur-pose*) absichtlich.

deliberation, *n.* Überle'-

gung, -en f., Erwä'gung, -en f.

delicacy, n. (food) Delikates'se, -n f.; (fig.) Feinheit, -en f.

delicate, adj. delikat'.

delicious, adj. köstlich.

delight, 1. n. Entzü'cken, -nt. **2.** vb. entzü'cken.

delightful, adj. entzü'ckend.

delineate, vb. dar-stellen.

delinquency, n. Verge'hen, - nt.; Unterlas'sung, -en f.

delinquent, 1. n. Kriminell'- m.&f.; (**juvenile d.**) Jugendverbrecher,- m. **2.** adj. verbre'cherisch, kriminell'; (in default) säumig.

delirium, n. Deli'rium, -rien nt.

delirious, adj. im Fieberwahnsinn; wahnsinnig.

deliver, vb. (set free) erlö'sen; (hand over) überge'ben*, ab-liefern.

deliverance, n. Erlö'sung, -en f., Befrei'ung, -en f.

delivery, n. Lieferung, -en f.; (childbirth) Entbin'dung, -en f.

delude, vb. täuschen, verlei'ten.

deluge, 1. n. Überschwem'mung, -en f.; (Bible) Sintflut f. **2.** vb. überflu'ten.

delusion, n. Täuschung, -en f., Wahn m.

de luxe, adj. Luxus- (cpds.).

delve, vb. graben*; (fig.) sich vertie'fen.

demand, 1. n. Forderung, -en f.; (claim) Anspruch -e m.; (econ.) Nachfrage f. **2.** vb. fordern, verlan'gen; fragen.

demean (oneself), vb. sich entwür'digen.

demeanor, n. Betra'gen nt.

demerit, n. (school) Tadel, - m.

demilitarize, vb. entmilitarisie'ren.

demobilization, n. Demobilisie'rung, -en f.

demobilize, vb. demobilisie'ren.

democracy, n. Demokratie', -n f.

democrat, n. Demokrat' -en, -en m.

democratic, adj. demokra'tisch.

demolish, vb. ab-reißen* zerstö'ren.

demolition, n. Zerstö'rung, -en f.

demon, n. Dämon, -o'nen m.

demonstrable, adj. nach-weisbar.

demonstrate, vb. zeigen vor-führen, demonstrie'ren.

demonstration, n. Beweis'-e m., Darlegung, -en f., Kundgebung, -en f.

demonstrative, adj. demonstrativ'.

demonstrator, n. Demonstrie'rend- m.&f.

demoralize, vb. demoralisie'ren.

demote, vb. degradie'ren.

demur, vb. Einwendungen machen.

demure, adj. züchtig.

den, n. Höhle, -n f.

denaturalize, vb. denaturalisie'ren.

denial, n. Vernei'nung, -en f.

Denmark, n. Dänemark nt.

denomination, n. (money) Nennwert, -e m.; (church) Sekte, -n f.

denominator, n. Nenner, - m.

denote, vb. kennzeichnen.

dénouement, n. Ausgang, -e m.

denounce, vb. denunzie'ren.

dense, adj. dicht.

density, n. Dichte f.

dent, n. Einbuchtung, -en f.

dental, adj. Zahn- (cpds.).

dentifrice, n. Zahnputzmittel, - nt.

dentist, n. Zahnarzt, -e m.

dentistry, n. Zahnheilkunde f.

denture, n. künstliches Gebiß', -sse nt.

denunciation, n. Denunzie'rung, -en f.

deny, vb. leugnen, vernei'nen.

deodorant, n. Desodorisie'rungsmittel, - nt.

depart, vb. ab·fahren*; (deviate) ab·weichen*.

department, n. Abtei'lung, -en f.; (government) Ministe'rium. -rien nt.

departmental, adj. Abtei'lungs- (cpds.).

departure, n. Abfahrt, -en f.; (deviation) Abweichung, -en f.

depend, vb. ab·hängen*; (rely) sich verlas'sen*.

dependability, n. Verläß'lichkeit f.

dependable, adj. zuverlässig.

dependence, n. Abhängigkeit f.

dependent, 1. n. Angehörig- m.&f. 2. adj. abhängig.

depict, vb. dar·stellen*.

depiction, n. Darstellung, -en f.

deplete, vb. erschöp'fen.

deplorable, adj. bekla'genswert.

deplore, vb. bekla'gen.

deport, vb. deportie'ren.

deportation, n. Deporta'tion', -en f.

deportment, n. Betra'gen nt.

depose, vb. ab·setzen.

deposit, 1. n. Anzahlung, -en f.; (bank) Einzahlung, -en f.; (ore, etc.) Lager, - nt. 2. vb. ein·zahlen; hinterle'gen.

deposition, n. (eidesstattliche) schriftliche Aussage, -n f.

depositor, n. Einzahler, - m., Bankkunde, -n, -n m.

depot, n. Lager, - nt.; Depot'. -s nt.; (railroad) Kleinbahnhof, -e m.

depravity, n. Verwor'fenheit f.

deprecate, vb. mißbilligen.

depreciate, vb. (tr.) entwer·ten, den Wert mindern; (intr.) im Wert sinken*.

depreciation, n. Wertminderung f.

depress, vb. deprimie'ren.

depression, n. Depression', -en f.

deprivation, n. Berau'bung, -en f.

deprive, vb. berau'ben.

depth, n. Tiefe, -n f.

deputy, n. (substitute) Stellvertreter, - m.; (parliament) Abgeordnet- m.&f.

derail, vb. entglei'sen lassen*; (be d.ed) entglei'sen.

deranged, adj. geistesgestört.

derelict, 1. n. Wrack, -s or -e nt. 2. adj. nachlässig.

dereliction, n. Vernach'lässigung, -en f.

deride, vb. verspot'ten.

derision, n. Hohn m.

derisive, adj. spöttisch.

derivation, n. Ableitung, -en f.

derivative, adj. abgeleitet.

derive, vb. ab·leiten.

derogatory, adj. abfällig.

derrick, n. Ladebaum, -e m.; (oil) Bohrturm, -e m.

descend, vb. herab'steigen*; (ancestry) ab·stammen.

descendant, n. Nachkomme, -n, -n m.

descent, n. Abstieg, -e m.

describe, vb. beschrei'ben*.

description, n. Beschrei'bung, -en f.

descriptive, adj. beschrei'bend.

desecrate, vb. entwei'hen.

desert, 1. n. Wüste, -n f.; (merit) Verdienst', -e nt. 2. vb. verlas'sen*.

deserter, n. Fahnenflüchtig- m.&f., Deserteur', -e m.

desertion, n. (law) böswilliges Verlas'sen nt.; (army) Desertion', -en f., Fahnenflucht f.

deserve, vb. verdie'nen.

deserving, adj. verdienst'voll.

design, 1. n. Entwurf', -e m., Muster, - nt.; (aim) Absicht, -en f. 2. vb. entwer'fen*; beab'sichtigen.

designate, vb. bezeich'nen, bestim'men.

designation, n. Bezeich'nung, -en f., Bestim'mung, -en f.

designer, *n.* Konstrukteur', -e *m.*; *(fashion)* Modeschöpfer, - *m.*

desirability, *n.* Erwünscht'heit, -en *f.*

desirable, *adj.* wünschenswert.

desire, 1. *n.* Verlan'gen, - *nt.*, Wunsch, "e *m.* **2.** *vb.* verlan'gen, wünschen.

desperado, *n.* Bandit', -en, -en *m.*, Despera'do, -s *m.*

desperate, *adj.* verzwei'felt.

desperation, *n.* Verzweif'lung, -en *f.*

despicable, *adj.* verach'tenswert, gemein'.

despise, *vb.* verach'ten.

despite, *prep.* trotz.

despondent, *adj.* verzagt'.

despot, *n.* Despot', -en, -en *m.*

despotic, *adj.* despo'tisch.

despotism, *n.* Gewalt'herrschaft *f.*

dessert, *n.* Nachtisch, -e *m.*

destination, *n.* Bestim'mung *f.*; Bestim'mungsort, -e *m.*

destine, *vb.* bestim'men.

destiny. *n.* Schicksal, -e *nt.*

destitute, *adj.* mittellos.

destitution, *n.* Armut *f.*, Not, "e *f.*

destroy, *vb.* zerstö'ren.

destroyer, *n.* Zerstö'rer, - *m.*

destruction, *n.* Zerstö'rung, -en *f.*

destructive, *adj.* zerstö'rend.

desultory, *adj.* flüchtig.

detach, *vb.* ab·trennen; *(mil.)* ab·kommandieren.

detachment, *n.* *(mil.)* Abtei'lung, -en *f.*; Objektivität' *f.*

detail, *n.* Einzelheit, -en *f.*

detain, *vb.* ab·halten*; festhalten*; auf·halten*.

detect, *vb.* entde'cken, ermit'teln.

detection, *n.* Entde'cken *nt.*; Ermitt'lung, -en *f.*

detective, *n.* Detektiv', -e *m.*

detention, *n.* Haft *f.*

deter, *vb.* ab·halten*, hindern.

detergent, *n.* chemisches Seifenmittel, - *nt.*

deteriorate, *vb.* sich verschlech'tern.

deterioration, *n.* Verschlech'terung, -en *f.*

determination, *n.* Bestim'mung, -en *f.*; *(resolve)* Entschlos'senheit *f.*

determine, *vb.* bestim'men.

determined, *adj.* entschlos'sen.

detest, *vb.* verab'scheuen.

detonate, *vb.* explodie'ren.

detonation, *n.* Explosion', -en *f.*

detour, *n.* Umweg, -e *m.*; *(traffic)* Umleit.ung, -en *f.*

detract, *vb.* ab·zie'hen*; **(d. from)** schmälern.

detriment, *n.* Nachteil, -e *m.*, Schaden, " *m.*

detrimental, *adj.* nachteilig.

devaluate, *vb.* ab·werten.

devastate, *vb.* verwüs'ten.

devastation, *n.* Verwüs'tung, -en *f.*

develop, *vb.* entwi'ckeln.

developer, *n.* Entwick'ler, - *m.*

development, *n.* Entwick'lung, -en *f.*

deviate, *vb.* ab·weichen*.

deviation, *n.* Abweichung, -en *f.*

device, *n.* Vorrichtung, -en *f.*

devil, *n.* Teufel, - *m.*

devilish, *adj.* teuflisch.

devious, *adj.* abweichend.

devise, *vb.* ersin'nen*.

devoid, *adj.* **(d. of)** leer an, ohne.

devote, *vb.* widmen.

devoted, *adj.* erge'ben.

devotee, *n.* Verfech'ter, - *m.*

devotion, *n.* Hingebung *f.*; *(religious)* Andacht, -en *f.*

devour, *vb.* verschlin'gen*.

devout, *adj.* andächtig, fromm.

dew, *n.* Tau *m.*

dewy, *adj.* betaut'.

dexterity, *n.* Gewandt'heit, -en *f.*

dexterous, *adj.* gewandt'.

diabetes, *n.* Zuckerkrankheit *f.*

diabolic, *adj.* teuflisch.

diadem, *n.* Diadem', -e *nt.*

diagnose, *vb.* diagnostizie'ren.

diagnosis, *n.* Diagno'se, -n *f.*

diagnostic, *adj.* diagnos'tisch.

diagonal, **1.** *n.* Diagona'le, -n *f.* **2.** *adj.* diagonal', schräg.

diagram, *n.* graphische Darstellung, -en *f.*

dial, **1.** *n.* Zifferblatt, *er nt.; (telephone)* Wählscheibe, -n *f.* **2.** *vb. (telephone)* wählen.

dialect, *n.* Dialekt', -e *m.,* Mundart, -en *f.*

dialogue, *n.* Dialog', -e *nt.*

diameter, *n.* Durchmesser, - *m.*

diametrical, *adj.* diametral'.

diamond, *n.* Diamant', -en, -en *m.; (cards)* Karo *nt.*

diaper, *n.* Windel, -n *f.*

diaphragm, *n.* Zwerchfell, -e *nt.*

diarrhea, *n.* Durchfall *m.*

diary, *n.* Tagebuch, *er nt.*

diathermy, *n.* Diathermie' *f.*

diatribe, *n.* Schmähschrift, -en *f.*

dice, *n.pl.* Würfel, - *m.*

dicker, *vb.* feilschen.

dictate, *vb.* diktie'ren.

dictation, *n.* Diktat', -e *nt.*

dictator, *n.* Dikta'tor, -o'ren *m.*

dictatorial, *adj.* diktato'risch.

dictatorship, *n.* Diktatur', -en *f.*

diction, *n.* Aussprache, -n *f.*

dictionary, *n.* Wörterbuch, *er nt.,* Lexikon, -ka *nt.*

didactic, *adj.* didak'tisch.

die, **1.** *n. (gaming cube)* Würfel, - *m.; (stamper)* Prägestempel, - *m.* **2.** *vb.* sterben*.

diet, *n.* Diät', -en *f.; (government)* Parlament', -e *nt.*

dietary, *adj.* diät'gemäß.

dietetic, *adj.* diäte'tisch.

dietitian, *n.* Diät'planer, - *m.*

differ, *vb.* sich unterschei'-

den*, ab·weichen*, verschiedener Meinung sein*.

difference, *n.* Unterschied, -e *m.*

different, *adj.* verschie'den, ander-.

differential, **1.** *n.* Unterschied, - *m.; (d. gear)* Differential', -e *nt.,* Ausgleichsgetriebe, - *nt.* **2.** *adj.* differential'.

differentiate, *vb.* unterschei'den*.

desirous, *adj.* begie'rig.

desist, *vb.* ab·lassen*.

desk, *n.* Schreibtisch, -e *m.*

desolate, *adj.* trostlos. **2.** *vb.* verhee'ren.

desolation, *n.* Verwüs'tung, -en *f.;* Trostlosigkeit *f.*

despair, **1.** *n.* Verzweif'lung, -en *f.* **2.** *vb.* verzwei'feln.

despatch, **1.** *n.* Absendung, -en *f.* **2.** *vb.* ab·senden*, eilig weg·schicken.

difficult, *adj.* schwer, mühsam, schwierig.

difficulty, *n.* Schwierigkeit, -en *f.*

diffident, *adj.* zurück'haltend, schüchtern.

diffuse, **1.** *adj.* weitverbreitet, diffus'. **2.** *vb.* verbrei'ten.

diffusion, *n.* Diffusion', -en *f.*

dig, *vb.* graben*.

digest, *vb.* verdau'en.

digestible, *adj.* verdau'lich.

digestion, *n.* Verdau'ung *f.*

digestive, *adj.* Verdau'ungs-*(cpds.).*

digitalis, *n.* Digita'lis *nt.*

dignified, *adj.* würdig.

dignify, *vb.* ehren, aus·zeichnen.

dignitary, *n.* Würdenträger, - *m.*

dignity, *n.* Würde *f.*

digress, *vb.* ab·schweifen.

digression, *n.* Abschweifung, -en *f.*

dike, *n.* Deich, -e *m.*

dilapidated, *adj.* baufällig.

dilate, *vb.* aus·dehnen.

dilemma, *n.* Dilem'ma, -s *nt.*

dilettante, n. Dilettant', -en, -en m.

diligence, n. Fleiß m.

diligent, adj. fleißig.

dill, n. Dill m.

dilute, vb. verdün'nen.

dilution, n. Verdün'nung, -en f.

dim, 1. adj. trübe, dunkel. **2.** vb. trüben; (auto lights) ab·blenden.

dimension, n. Ausmaß, -e nt., Dimension'. -en f.

diminish, vb. vermin'dern.

diminution, n. Vermin'derung, -en f.

diminutive, 1. n. Diminutiv'. -e nt. **2.** adj. winzig.

dimness, n. Dunkelheit f.

dimple, n. Grübchen, - nt.

din, n. Lärm m.

dine, vb. speisen.

diner, dining-car, n. Speisewagen, - m.

dingy, adj. schäbig.

dinner, n. (noon) Mittagessen, - nt.; (evening) Abendessen, - nt.

dinosaur, n. Dinosau'rier, - m.

diocese, n. Diöze'se. -n f.

dip, vb. tauchen, ein·tauchen; sich senken.

diphtheria, n. Diphtherie' f.

diploma, n. Diplom', -e nt.

diplomacy, n. Diplomatie', -en f.

diplomat, n. Diplomat', -en, -en m.

diplomatic, adj. diploma'tisch.

dipper, n. Schöpflöffel, - m., Schöpfkelle, -n f.; **(Big D.)** Großer Bär m.; **(Little D.)** Kleiner Bär m.

dire, adj. gräßlich.

direct, 1. adj. direkt'. **2.** vb. führen; an·weisen*; leiten.

direct current, n. Gleichstrom, -e m.

direction, n. (leadership) Leitung, -en f., Führung, -en f.; (instruction) Anweisung, -en f.; (course) Richtung, -en f.

directional, adj. Leitungs-, Richtungs- (cpds.).

directive, 1. adj. leitend; Richtung gebend. **2.** n. Direkti've, -n f.

directness, n. Gerad'heit f., Offenheit f.

director, n. Leiter, - m., Direk'tor, o'ren m.

directory, n. (addresses) Adreß'buch. ⸱er nt.; **(telephone d.)** Telephon'buch. ⸱er nt.

dirigible, n. Luftschiff, -e nt.

dirt, n. Schmutz m.

dirty, adj. schmutzig.

disability, n. Unfähigkeit f.; Körperbehinderung, -en f.

disable, vb. untauglich machen.

disabled, adj. untauglich; kriegsversehrt.

disadvantage, n. Nachteil, -e m.

disagree, vb. anderer Meinung sein*; (food) nicht bekom'men*.

disagreeable, adj. unangenehm.

disagreement, n. Uneinigkeit, -en f., Widerspruch, ⸱e m.

disappear, vb. verschwin'den*.

disappearance, n. Verschwin'den nt.

disappoint, vb. enttäu'schen.

disappointment, n. Enttäu'schung, -en f.

disapproval, n. Mißbilligung, -en f.

disapprove, vb. mißbilligen.

disarm, vb. entwaff'nen, ab·rüsten.

disarmament, n. Abrüstung, -en f.

disarray, n. Unordnung f.

disaster, n. Unglück, -e nt., Katastro'phe. -n f.

disastrous, adj. verhee'rend.

disavow, vb. ab·leugnen.

disband, vb. auf·lösen.

disburse, vb. aus·zahlen.

discard, vb. ab·legen.

discern, vb. unterschei'den*.

discerning, adj. scharfsinnig.

discernment, n. Scharfsinn m., Einsicht f.

discharge, 1. n. Entlas'sung, -en f.; (medicine) Ausscheidung, -en f. 2. vb. entlas'sen*; aus·scheiden*; (gun) ab·feuern.

disciple, n. Jünger, - m.

disciplinary, adj. maßregelnd.

discipline, 1. n. Disziplin' f. 2. vb. schulen, disziplinie'ren.

disclaim, vb. ab·leugnen; verzich'ten.

disclose, vb. enthül'len.

disclosure, n. Enthül'lung, -en f.

discomfort, n. Unbehagen nt.

disconcert, vb. in Verwir'rung bringen*.

disconnect, vb. los·lösen; (elec.) aus·schalten.

discontent, 1. n. Unzufriedenheit f. 2. adj. unzufrieden.

discontinue, vb. ein·stellen.

discord, n. Mißklang, ∗e m.; (fig.) Uneinigkeit, -en f.

discount, 1. n. Rabatt' m. 2. vb. ab·ziehen*.

discourage, vb. entmu'tigen.

discouragement, n. Entmu'tigung, -en f.

discourse, 1. n. Gespräch', -e nt.; Abhandlung, -en f. 2. vb. sprechen*.

discourteous, adj. unhöflich.

discourtesy, n. Unhöflichkeit, -en f.

discover, vb. entde'cken.

discovery, n. Entde'ckung, -en f.

discredit, 1. n. Nichtachtung f. 2. vb. nicht glauben; in schlechten Ruf bringen*.

discreet, adj. diskret'.

discrepancy, n. Zwiespalt, -e m.

discretion, n. Diskretion' f.; Beson'nenheit f.

discriminate, vb. unterschei'den*; diskriminie'ren.

discrimination, n. Diskriminie'rung, -en f.

discuss, vb. diskutie'ren.

discussion, n. Diskussion', -en f.

disdain, vb. verach'ten.

disdainful, adj. verächt'lich.

disease, n. Krankheit, -en f.

disembark, vb. landen.

disembarkation, n. Landung, -en f.

disenchantment, n. Enttäu'schung, -en f., Ernüch'terung f.

disengage, vb. los·lösen.

disentangle, vb. entwir'ren.

disfavor, n. Mißfallen nt.; Ungnade f.

disfigure, vb. entstel'len.

disgrace, 1. n. Schande, -n f., Unehre f. 2. vb. schänden, blamie'ren.

disgraceful, adj. schändlich.

disgruntled, adj. mürrisch.

disguise, 1. n. Verklei'dung, -en f. 2. vb. verklei'den.

disgust, 1. n. Ekel m. 2. vb. an·ekeln.

disgusting, adj. ekelhaft, widerlich.

dish, n. Schüssel, -n f.; (food) Gericht', -e nt.

dishcloth, n. Abwaschtuch, ∗er nt.

dishearten, vb. entmu'tigen.

dishonest, adj. unehrlich.

dishonesty, n. Unehrlichkeit, -en f.

dishonor, 1. n. Schande, -n f. 2. vb. enteh'ren.

dishonorable, adj. unehrenhaft.

dishtowel, n. Geschirr'handtuch, ∗er nt.

disillusion, 1. n. Enttäu'schung, -en f. 2. vb. enttäu'schen.

disinfect, vb. desinfizie'ren.

disinfectant, n. Desinfizie'rungsmittel, - nt.

disinherit, vb. enter'ben.

disintegrate, vb. zerfal'len*.

disinterested, adj. gleichgültig.

disjointed, adj. unzusammenhängend.

disk, n. Scheibe, -n f.

dislike, 1. n. Abneigung, -en f. 2. vb. nicht mögen*.

dislocate, vb. aus·renken.

dislodge, vb. los·reißen*, vertrei'ben*.

disloyal, adj. treulos.

disloyalty, n. Untreue, -n f.

dismal, adj. jämmerlich.

dismantle, vb. demontie'ren.

dismay, **1.** n. Bestür'zung, -en f. **2.** vb. erschre'cken.

dismember, vb. zerstü'ckeln.

dismiss, vb. entlas'sen*; fallen lassen*.

dismissal, n. Entlas'sung, -en f.

dismount, vb. ab·steigen*.

disobedience, n. Ungehorsam m.

disobedient, adj. ungehorsam.

disobey, vb. nicht gehor'chen.

disorder, n. Unordnung f.

disorderly, adj. unordentlich, liederlich.

disorganize, vb. in Unordnung bringen*.

disown, vb. verleug'nen.

disparage, vb. herab'setzen.

disparity, n. Ungleichheit, -en f.

dispassionate, adj. leidenschaftslos.

dispatch, **1.** n. Absendung, -en f. **2.** vb. ab·senden*; eilig weg·schicken.

dispatcher, n. Absender, m.

dispel, vb. vertrei'ben*.

dispensable, adj. entbehr'lich.

dispensary, n. Arznei'ausgabestelle, -n f.

dispensation, n. Befrei'ung, -en f.

dispense, vb. aus·geben*; (d. with) verzich'ten auf.

dispersal, n. Vertei'lung, -en f.

disperse, vb. vertei'len.

displace, vb. verdrän'gen.

displaced person, n. Zwangsverschleppt- m.&f. D.P., -s m.

display, **1.** n. Aufwand m.; (window) Schaufensterauslage, -n f. **2.** vb. entfal'ten, zeigen.

displease, vb. mißfal'len*.

displeasure, n. Mißfallen nt.

disposable, adj. verfüg'bar.

disposal, n. Verfü'gung, -en f.

dispose, vb. bestim'men.

disposition, n. Verfü'gung, -en f.; (character) Anlage f.

dispossess, vb. enteig'nen.

disproof, n. Widerle'gung, -en f.

disproportion, n. Mißverhältnis, -se nt.

disproportionate, adj. unverhältnismäßig.

disprove, vb. widerle'gen.

disputable, adj. bestreit'bar

dispute, **1** n. Streit, -e m. **2.** vb. bestrei'ten*.

disqualification, n. Disqualifizie'rung, -en f.

disqualify, vb. disqualifizie'ren.

disregard, **1.** n. Nichtbeachtung f. **2.** vb. nicht beach'ten.

disrepair, n. Verfall' m.

disreputable, adj. verru'fen.

disrespect, n. Nichtachtung f., Mißachtung f.

disrespectful, adj. unehrerbietig, unhöflich.

disrobe, vb. entklei'den.

disrupt, vb. auseinan'der-reißen*.

dissatisfaction, n. Unzufriedenheit, -en f.

dissatisfy, vb. nicht befrie'digen.

dissect, vb. zerglie'dern; (med.) sezie'ren.

disseminate, vb. verbrei'ten.

dissension, n. Uneinigkeit, -en f.

dissent, **1.** n. Meinungsverschiedenheit, -en f. **2.** vb. anderer Meinung sein*.

dissertation, n. Dissertation', -en f.

dissimilar, adj. unähnlich.

dissipated, adj. ausschweifend, verlebt'.

dissipation, n. Ausschweifung, -en f.

dissociate, vb. trennen.

dissolute, adj. verkom'men.

dissolution, n. Auflösung, -en f.

dissolve, vb. auf·lösen.

dissonance, n. Dissonanz', -en f.

dissonant, adj. dissonant'.

dissuade, vb. ab·raten*.

distance, n. Entfer'nung, -en f., Abstand, -e m.

distant, adj. entfernt'; (fig.) zurück'haltend.

distaste, n. Widerwille(n), -m., Abneigung, -en f.

distasteful, adj. widerwär-tig, widerlich.

distemper, n. (dog) Staupe f.

distend, vb. aus·dehnen.

distill, vb. destillie'ren.

distillation, n. Destillation', -en f.

distiller, n. Destillateur', -e m.

distillery, n. Branntwein-brennerei,-en f.

distinct, adj. deutlich; (dif-ferent) verschie'den.

distinction, n. (difference) Unterschied, -e m.; (ele-gance) Vornehmheit f.; (honor) Auszeichnung, -en f.

distinctive, adj. kennzeich-nend.

distinctness, n. Deutlich-keit f.

distinguish, vb. (differenti-ate) unterschei'den*; (honor) aus·zeichnen.

distinguished, adj. (famous) berühmt'; (elegant) vor-nehm.

distort, vb. verzer'ren.

distract, vb. ab·lenken.

distraction, n. Ablenkung, -en f.

distress, 1. n. Not, "e f. 2. vb. betrü'ben.

distribute, vb. vertei'len.

distribution, n. Vertei'lung, -en f.

distributor, n. Vertei'ler, -m.; (agent) Vertriebs'stelle, -n f.

district, n. Bezirk', -e m.

distrust, 1. n. Mißtrauen nt. 2. vb. mißtrau'en.

distrustful, adj. mißtrau-isch.

disturb, vb. stören, beun'-ruhigen.

disturbance, n. Störung, -en f., Unruhe, -n f.

ditch, n. Graben, = m.

diva, n. Diva, -s f.

divan, n. Diwan, -e m.

dive, 1. n. Kopfsprung, "e m. 2. vb. tauchen.

diver, n. Taucher, - m.

diverge, vb. auseinan'der·-gehen*.

divergence, n. Divergenz'. -en f.

divergent, adj. divergie'rend.

diverse, adj. verschie'den.

diversion, n. Ablenkung, -en f.; (pastime) Zeitvertreib, -e m.

diversity, n. Mannigfaltig-keit, en f.

divert, vb. ab·lenken, um·-leiten.

divest, vb. entklei'den.

divide, vb. teilen.

dividend, n. Dividen'de, -n f.

divine, adj. göttlich.

divinity, n. Gottheit, -en f.; (study) Theologie', -i'en f.

divisible, adj. teilbar.

division, n. Teilung, -en f.; (mil.) Division', -en f.

divorce, 1. n. Scheidung, -en f. 2. vb. (get d.d) sich scheiden lassen*; (d. a per-son) sich von einem Mens-chen scheiden lassen*.

divorcée, n. geschie'dene Frau, -en f.

divulge, vb. enthül'len.

dizziness, n. Schwindel m.

dizzy, adj. schwindlig.

do, vb. tun*, machen.

docile, adj. fügsam.

dock, n. Dock, -s nt.

docket, n. Gerichts'kalender, - m.; Geschäfts'ordnung, -en f.

doctor, n. Doktor, -o'ren m.; (physician) Arzt, "e m.

doctorate, n. Doktorat', -e nt.

doctrine, n. Lehre, -n f.; Grundsatz, "e m.

document, n. Urkunde, -n f., Dokument', -e nt.

documentary, *adj.* urkund-lich, dokumenta'risch.

documentation, *n.* Doku-mentation', -en *f.*

dodge, *vb.* aus·weichen*.

doe, *n.* Reh, -e *nt.*

doeskin, *n.* Rehleder *nt.*

dog, *n.* Hund, -e *m.*

dogma, *n.* Dogma, -men *nt.*

dogmatic, *adj.* dogma'tisch.

dogmatism, *n.* Dogma'tik *f.*

dole, 1. *n.* Arbeitslosenun-terstützung, -en *f.;* (**be on the d.**) stempeln gehen*. **2.** *vb.* (**d. out**) vertei'len.

doleful, *adj.* kummervoll.

doll, *n.* Puppe, -n *f.*

dollar, *n.* Dollar, -s *m.*

domain, *n.* Bereich', -e *m.*

dome, *n.* Dom, -e *m.*, Kup-pel, -n *f.*

domestic, *adj.* häuslich; (**d. policy**) Innenpolitik *f.*

domesticate, *vb.* zähmen.

domicile, *n.* Wohnort, -e *m.*

dominance, *n.* Herrschaft, -en *f.*

dominant, *adj.* vorherr-schend.

dominate, *vb.* beherr'schen.

domination, *n.* Herrschaft, -en *f.*

domineer, *vb.* tyrannisie'ren.

dominion, *n.* Domi'nion, -s *nt.*

domino, *n.* Domino, -s *m.*

don, *vb.* an·ziehen*; (**hat**) auf·setzen.

donate, *vb.* stiften.

donation, *n.* Gabe, -n *f.*, Schenkung, -en *f.*

done, *adj.* (*food*) gar.

donkey, *n.* Esel, - *m.*

doom, *n.* Verder'ben *nt.*

door, *n.* Tür, -en *f.*

doorman, *n.* Portier', -e *m.*

doorway, *n.* Türeingang, -e *m.*

dope, *n.* (*drug*) Rauschgift, -e *nt.;* (*fool*) Trottel, - *m.*

dormant, *adj.* ruhend, la-tent'.

dormitory, *n.* (*room*) Schlaf-saal, -säle *m.;* (*building*) Studentenheim, -e *nt.*

dosage, *n.* Dosie'rung, -en *f.*

dossier, *n.* Akte, -n *f.*

dose, *n.* Dosis, -sen *f.*

dot, *n.* Punkt, -e *m.*

double-cross, *vb.* hinterge'-hen*.

double, 1. *n.* Doppelgänger, - *m.* **2.** *adj.* doppelt.

double-breasted, *adj.* zwei-reihig.

doubt, 1. *n.* Zweifel, - *m.* **2.** *vb.* zweifeln, bezwei'feln.

doubtful, *adj.* zweifelhaft.

doubtless, *adj.* zweifellos.

dough, *n.* Teig, -e *m.*

douse, *vb.* begie'ßen; (*fire*) löschen.

dove, *n.* Taube, -n *f.*

dowdy, *adj.* schlampig.

down, 1. *n.* Flaum *m.;* (*material*) Daune, -n *f.* **2.** *vb.* nieder·werfen*, (*fig.*) besie'-gen. **3.** *adv.* unten, nieder, ab; hin-, herun'ter, hin-, herab'

downcast, *adj.* niederge-schlagen.

downfall, *n.* Untergang, -e *m.*

downhearted, *adj.* betrübt'.

downhill, *adv.* bergab'.

down payment, *n.* Anzah-lung, -en *f.*

downpour, *n.* Regenguß, -sse *m.*

downstairs, *adv.* unten.

downtown, 1. *n.* Geschäfts'-viertel, - *nt.* **2.** *adv.* (*direction*) in die Stadt; (*location*) in der Stadt.

downward, *adv.* nach unten.

dowry, *n.* Mitgift, -en *f.*

doze, *vb.* dösen.

dozen, *n.* Dutzend, -e *nt.*

drab, *adj.* (*color*) bräunlich gelb; (*dull*) farblos.

draft, 1. *n.* (*plan*) Entwurf', -e *m.;* (*money*) Wechsel, - *m.;* (*air*) Zug, -e *m.;* (*military service*) militä'rische Dienstpflicht *f.* **2.** *vb.* ent-wer'fen*; (*mil.*) ein·ziehen*.

draftee, *n.* Rekrut', -en, -en *m.*

draftsman, *n.* Zeichner, - *m.*

drafty, *adj.* zugig.

drag, *vb.* schleppen, schleifen.

dragon, *n.* Drache, -n, -n *m.*

drain, 1. *n.* Abfluß, -sse *m.*

2. *vb.* ab·laufen lassen*; entwäs'sern.

drainage, *n.* Abfluß, «sse *m.*; Entwäs'serung, -en *f.*

dram, *n.* Drachme, -n *f.*

drama, *n.* Drama, -men *nt.*; Schauspiel, -e *nt.*

dramatic, *adj.* drama'tisch.

dramatics, *n.* Thea'terwissenschaft, -en *f.*

dramatist, *n.* Drama'tiker, - *m.*

dramatize, *vb.* dramatisie'ren.

drape, **1.** *n.* Vorhang, «e *m.* **2.** *vb.* drape'ren.

drapery, *n.* Vorhang, «e *m.*; Behang', «e *m.*

drastic, *adj.* drastisch.

draught, see draft.

draw, *vb.* (*pull*) ziehen*; (*picture*) zeichnen; (**d.up**) ab·fassen.

drawback, *n.* Nachteil, -e *m.*; Schattenseite, -n *f.*

drawbridge, *n.* Zugbrücke, -n *f.*

drawer, *n.* Schublade, -n *f.*

drawing, *n.* (*picture*) Zeichnung, -en *f.*; (*lottery*) Ziehung, -en *f.*

drawl, *vb.* langsam und ausgedehnt sprechen*.

dread, **1.** *n.* Furcht *f.*, Angst, «e *f.* **2.** *vb.* fürchten.

dreadful, *adj.* furchtbar.

dream, **1.** *n.* Traum, «e *m.* **2.** *vb.* träumen.

dreamy, *adj.* träumerisch, verträumt'.

dreary, *adj.* trostlos.

dredge, **1.** *n.* Bagger, - *m.* **2.** *vb.* baggern.

dregs, *n.pl.* Bodensatz, «e *m.*; (*fig.*) Abschaum, «e *m.*

drench, *vb.* durchnäs'sen.

dress, **1.** *n.* Kleid, -er *nt.* **2** *vb.* an·ziehen*; kleiden.

dresser, *n.* Kommo'de, -n *f.*

dressing, *n.* (*food*) Soße, -n *f.*; (*med.*) Verband', «e *m.*

dressing gown, *n.* Schlafrock, «e *m.*, Morgenrock, «e *m.*

dressmaker, *n.* Schneiderin, -nen *f.*

drier, *n.* (*hair*) Trocken-

---

haube, -n *f.*; (*clothes*) Trockenautomat, -en, -en *m.*

drift, **1.** *n.* (*snow*) Schneewehe, -n *f.*; (*tendency*) Richtung, -en *f.*, Strömung, -en *f.* **2.** *vb.* treiben*.

drill, **1.** *n.* (*tool*) Drillbohrer, - *m.*; (*practice*) Schulung, -en *f.*; (*mil.*) Exerzie'ren *nt.* **2.** *vb.* bohren; schulen; exerzie'ren.

drink, **1.** *n.* Getränk', -e *nt.* **2.** *vb.* trinken*.

drinkable, *adj.* trinkbar.

drip, *vb.* tropfen.

drive, **1.** *n.* (*ride*) Spazier'fahrt, -en *f.*; (*energy*) Schwungkraft *f.* **2.** *vb.* treiben*; (*auto*) fahren*.

driver, *n.* Fahrer, - *m.*

driveway, *n.* Auffahrt, -en *f.*

drizzle, **1.** *n.* Sprühregen, - *m.* **2.** *vb.* nieseln.

drone, **1.** *n.* (*bee*) Drohne, -n *f.*; (*hum*) Gesum'me *nt.* **2.** *vb.* summen.

droop, *vb.* herab'·hängen*.

drop, **1.** *n.* Tropfen, - *m.* **2.** *vb.* (*fall*) fallen*; (*let fall*) fallen' lassen*.

dropper, *n.* Tropfer, -n *m.*

dropsy, *n.* Wassersucht *f.*

drought, *n.* Dürre, -n *f.*, Trockenheit, -en *f.*

drown, *vb.* (*intr.*) ertrin'ken*; (*tr.*) erträn'ken.

drowsiness, *n.* Schläfrigkeit *f.*

drowsy, *adj.* schläfrig.

drudgery, *n.* Plackerei', -en *f.*

drug, *n.* Droge, -n *f.*, Medikament', -e *nt.*

druggist, *n.* Drogist', -en, -en *m.*, Apothe'ker, - *m.*

drug store, *n.* Drogerie' -i'en *f.*, Apothe'ke, -n *f.*

drum, *n.* Trommel, -n *f.*

drummer, *n.* Trommler, - *m.*

drumstick, *n.* Trommelschlegel, - *m.*; (*fowl*) Geflü'gelschlegel, - *m.*

drunk, *adj.* betrun'ken; (**get d.**) sich betrin'ken*.

drunkard, *n.* Trinker, - *m.*: Trunkenbold, -e *m.*

drunken, *adj.* betrun'ken.

drunkenness, *n.* Trunken-heit *f.*

dry, 1. *adj.* trocken. **2.** *vb.* trocknen.

dry cell, *n.* Trockenelement, -e *nt.*

dry-cleaner, *n.* Reinigung, -en *f.*

dry-cleaning, *n.* chemische Reinigung, -en *f.*

dry goods, *n.pl.* Texti'lien *pl.*

dryness, *n.* Trockenheit, -en *f.*

dual, *adj.* Doppel- (*cpds.*).

dubious, *adj.* zweifelhaft.

duchess, *n.* Herzogin, -nen *f.*

duchy, *n.* Herzogtum, ⸗er *nt.*

duck, 1. *n.* Ente, -n *f.* **2.** *vb.* sich ducken.

duct, *n.* Rohr, -e *nt.*; Kanal', ⸗e *m.*

due, *adj.* schuldig; fällig.

duel, *n.* Duell', -e *nt.*

dues, *n.pl.* Gebüh'ren *pl.*, Beitrag, ⸗e *m.*

duet, *n.* Duett', -e *nt.*

duffle bag, *n.* Seesack, ⸗e *m.*

duke, *n.* Herzog, ⸗e *m.*

dull, *adj.* (*not sharp*) stumpf; (*boring*) langweilig.

dullness, *n.* Stumpfheit *f.*; Langweiligkeit *f.*

duly, *adv.* gebüh'rend.

dumb, *adj.* stumm; (*stupid*) dumm(⸗), blöde.

dumbwaiter, *n.* Drehauf-zug, ⸗e *m.*

dumfound, *vb.* verblüf'fen.

dummy, *n.* (*posing as some-one*) Strohmann, ⸗er *m.*; (*window-display*) Schaufen-sterpuppe, -n *f.*; (*bridge*) Tisch *m.*; (*theater*) Statist', -en, -en *m.*

dump, 1. *n.* Abladeplatz, ⸗e *m.*; (*refuse*) Schuttablade, -n *f.* **2.** *vb.* ab-laden*.

dumpling, *n.* Kloß, ⸗e *m.*

dun, 1. *adj.* graubraun. **2.** *vb.* zur Zahlung mahnen.

dunce, *n.* Schafskopf, ⸗e *m.*, Dummkopf, ⸗e *m.*

dune, *n.* Düne, -n *f.*

dung, *n.* Dung *m.*

dungarees, *n.pl.* Arbeitshose, -n *f.*

dungeon, *n.* Kerker, - *m.*

dunk, *vb.* tunken.

dupe, 1. *vb.* düpie'ren. **2.** *n.* Düpiert'- *m.&f.*

duplex, *adj.* Doppel- (*cpds.*).

duplicate, *vb.* verdop'peln, kopie'ren.

duplication, *n.* Verdop'-pelung, -en *f.*

duplicity, *n.* Duplizität', -en *f.*

durable, *adj.* dauerhaft.

durability, *n.* Dauerhaftig-keit *f.*

duration, *n.* Dauer *f.*

duress, *n.* Zwang *m.*

during, *prep.* Während.

dusk, *n.* Abenddämmerung, -en *f.*

dust, 1. *n.* Staub *m.* **2.** *vb.* ab-stauben.

dusty, *adj.* staubig.

Dutch, *adj.* holländisch.

Dutchman, *n.* Holländer, - *m.*

dutiful, *adj.* pflichtgetreu.

duty, *n.* Pflicht, -en *f.*; (*tax*) Zoll, ⸗e *m.*

dwarf, *n.* Zwerg, -e *m.*

dwell, *vb.* wohnen.

dweller, *n.* Bewoh'ner, - *m.*

dwelling, *n.* Wohnung, -en *f.*; Wohnsitz, -e *m.*

dwindle, *vb.* schrumpfen.

dye, 1. *n.* Farbe, -n *f.*; Farb-stoff, -e *m.* **2.** *vb.* färben.

dyer, *n.* Färber, - *m.*

dyestuff, *n.* Farbstoff, -e *m.*

dynamic, *adj.* dyna'misch.

dynamite, *n.* Dynamit' *nt.*

dynamo, *n.* Dyna'mo, -s *m.*

dynasty, *n.* Dynastie', -i'en *f.*

dysentery, *n.* Ruhr *f.*

dyspepsia, *n.* Dyspepsie' *f.*

E

each, *adj.* jeder, -es, -e.

each other, *pron.* einan'der.

eager, *adj.* eifrig.

eagerness, *n.* Eifer *m.*

eagle, n. Adler, - m.

ear, n. Ohr, -en nt.

earache, n. Ohrenschmerzen pl.

eardrum, n. Trommelfell, -e nt.

earl, n. Graf, -en, -en m.

early, adj. früh.

earmark, 1. n. Anzeichen, - nt. 2. vb. bestim'men; (be e.ed) vorgesehen sein*.

earn, vb. verdie'nen.

earnest, adj. ernst.

earnestness, n. Ernst m.

earnings, n.pl. Einnahmen pl.

earring, n. Ohrring, -e m.

earth, n. Erde, -n f.

earthenware, n. Steingut nt.

earthly, adj. irdisch.

earthquake, n. Erdbeben, - nt.

earthy, adj. erdig; (fig.) derb.

ease, 1. n. Leichtigkeit, -en f.; (comfort) Behag'lichkeit, -en f. 2. vb. erleich'tern, lindern.

easel, n. Staffelei', -en f.

easiness, n. Leichtigkeit, -en f.

east, 1. n. Osten m.; Orient m. 2. adj. östlich; Ost- (cpds.).

Easter, n. Ostern nt.

easterly, adj. östlich.

eastern, adj. östlich.

eastward, adv. ostwärts.

easy, adj. leicht.

easygoing, adj. gutmütig, ungezwungen.

eat, vb. essen*.

eatable, adj. eßbar.

eaves, n.pl. Dachrinne, -n f.

ebb, 1. n. Ebbe, -n f. 2. vb. ab·nehmen*.

ebony, n. Ebenholz, =er nt.

eccentric, adj. exzen'trisch.

eccentricity, n. Exzentrizi-tät', -en f.

ecclesiastic, adj. kirchlich, geistlich.

ecclesiastical, adj. kirchlich, geistlich.

echelon, n. Staffel, -n f.

echo, 1. n. Echo, -s nt. 2. vb. wider·hallen.

eclipse, n. Finsternis, -se f.

economic, adj. wirtschaft-lich.

economical, adj. sparsam.

economics, n. Volkswirt-schaft f., National'ökonomie f.

economist, n. Volkswirt-schaftler, - m.

economize, vb. haus·halten*.

economy, n. Wirtschaft f.; Sparsamkeit f.

ecstasy, n. Verzü'ckung, -en f.

eczema, n. Ekzem', -e nt.

eddy, n. Strudel, - m.

edge, n. Rand, =er m.; (knife etc.) Schneide, -n f.

edible, adj. eßbar.

edict, n. Verord'nung, -en f., Edikt', -e nt.

edifice, n. Gebäu'de, - nt.

edify, vb. erbau'en.

edit, vb. heraus'geben*.

edition, n. Ausgabe, -n f., Auflage, -n f.

editor, n. Heraus'geber, - m.

editorial, 1. n. Leitartikel, - m. 2. adj. Redaktions'- (cpds.).

educate, vb. (bring up) erzie'-hen*; (train) aus·bilden.

education, n. (upbringing) Erzie'hung f.; (training) Ausbildung f.; (culture) Bil-dung f.

educational, adj. erzie'-herisch.

educator, n. Erzie'her, - m.; Pädago'ge, -n, -n m.

eel, n. Aal, -e m.

effect, n. Wirkung, -en f.

effective, adj. wirkungsvoll.

effectiveness, n. Wirksam-keit f.

effectual, adj. wirksam.

effeminate, adj. verweich'-licht.

effervescence, n. Sprudeln nt.

effete, adj. entkräf'tet.

efficiency, n. Leistungsfä-higkeit f., Tüchtigkeit f., Wirksamkeit f.

efficient, adj. leistungsfähig, tüchtig, wirksam.

effigy, n. Abbild, -er nt.

effort, *n.* Mühe, -n *f.*; *(exertion)* Anstrengung, -en *f.*; *(attempt)* Versuch, -e *m.*

effrontery, *n.* Frechheit, -en *f.*

effusive, *adj.* überschwenglich.

egg, *n.* Ei, -er *nt.*

eggplant, *n.* Aubergi'ne, -n *f.*

ego, *n.* Ich *nt.*

egoism, *n.* Egois'mus *m.*

egotism, *n.* Egotis'mus *m.*

egotist, *n.* Egoist', -en, -en *m.*

Egypt, *n.* Ägyp'ten *nt.*

Egyptian, **1.** *n.* Ägyp'ter, *m.* **2.** *adj.* ägyp'tisch.

eight, *num.* acht.

eighteen, *num.* achtzehn.

eighteenth, **1.** *adj.* achtzehnt-. **2.** *n.* Achzehntel, *nt.*

eighth, **1.** *adj.* acht-. **2.** *n.* Achtel, -e *nt.*

eightieth, **1.** *adj.* achtzigst-. **2.** *n.* Achtzigstel, -*nt.*

eighty, *num.* achtzig.

either, **1.** *pron. & adj.* jeder, -es, -e; beides, *pl.* beide. **2.** *conj.* (**e ... or**) entweder ... oder. **3.** *adv.* (**not . . . e.**) auch nicht, auch kein, -, -e.

ejaculation, *n.* Ausruf, -e *m.*

eject, *vb.* hinaus'werfen*; vertrei'ben*.

ejection, *n.* Hinaus'werfen *nt.*

eke out, *vb.* sich durch·helfen*.

elaborate, **1.** *adj.* weitläufig; kunstvoll. **2.** *vb.* ins einzelne gehen*.

elapse, *vb.* verge'hen*.

elastic, **1.** *n.* Gummiband, -*er nt.* **2.** *adj.* elas'tisch.

elasticity, *n.* Elastizität' *f.*

elate, *vb.* erfreu'en.

elated, *adj.* hocherfreut.

elation, *n.* Freude, -n *f.*

elbow, *n.* Ellbogen, - *m.*

elder, **1.** *n.* (*tree*) Holun'der, - *m.*; (*church*) Ältest- *m.* **2.** *adj.* älter.

elderly, *adj.* ältlich.

eldest, *adj.* ältest-.

elect, *vb.* wählen.

election, *n.* Wahl, -en *f.*

elective, *adj.* Wahl- (*cpds.*).

electorate, *n.* Wählerschaft, -en *f.*

electric, electrical, *adj.* elek'trisch.

electrician, *n.* Elek'triker, - *m.*

electricity, *n.* Elektrizität' *f.*

electrocution, *n.* Tötung durch elektrischen Strom; Hinrichtung auf dem elektrischen Stuhl.

electrode, *n.* Elektro'de, -n *f.*

electrolysis, *n.* Elektroly'se *f.*

electron, *n.* Elektron, -o'nen *nt.*

electronic, *adj.* Elektro'nen- (*cpds.*).

electronics, *n.* Elektro'nen-wissenschaft *f.*

elegance, *n.* Eleganz' *f.*

elegant, *adj.* elegant'.

elegy, *n.* Elegie', -i'en *f.*

element, *n.* Element', -e *nt.*

elemental, elementary, *adj.* elementar'.

elephant, *n.* Elefant', -en, -en *m.*

elephantine, *adj.* elefan'tenartig.

elevate, *vb.* erhö'hen.

elevation, *n.* Erhö'hung, -en *f.*; Höhe, -n *f.*

elevator, *n.* Fahrstuhl, -*e m.*

eleven, *num.* elf.

eleventh, **1.** *adj.* elft-. **2.** *n.* Elftel, - *nt.*

elf, *n.* Kobold, -e *m.*

elfin, *adj.* koboldartig.

elicit, *vb.* heraus'holen; -wir'ken.

eligibility, *n.* Qualifiziert'heit *f.*

eligible, *adj.* qualifiziert'.

eliminate, *vb.* besei'tigen, aus·scheiden*.

elimination, *n.* Besei'tigung, -en *f.*; Ausscheidung, -en *f.*

elixir, *n.* Elixier', -e *nt.*

elk, *n.* Elch, -e *m.*

elm, *n.* Ulme, -n *f.*

elocution, *n.* Redekunst, -*e f.*

elongate, *vb.* verlän'gern.

elope, *vb.* mit einem Mädchen

oder einem Jungen durch-·
brennen*.

eloquence, *n.* Bered'samkeit
f.

eloquent, *adj.* redegewandt.

else, *adv.* anders, sonst.

elsewhere, *adv.* anderswo.

elucidate, *vb.* erläu'tern.

elude, *vb.* entge'hen*.

elusive, *adj.* nicht greifbar;
aalglatt.

emaciated, *adj.* abgezehrt.

emanate, *vb.* aus·strömen.

emancipate, *vb.* emanzipie'-
ren.

emancipation, *n.* Emanzi-
pation', -en *f.*

emancipator, *n.* Befrei'er, -
m.

emasculate, *vb.* entman'nen.

embalm, *vb.* ein·balsamieren.

embankment, *n.* Ufoeran-
lage, -n *f.*

embargo, *n.* Embar'go, -s *nt.*

embark, *vb.* ein·schiffen.

embarrass, *vb.* in Verle'genheit bringen*.

embarrassed, *adj.* verle'gen.

embarrassment, *n.* Verle'-
genheit, -en *f.*

embassy, *n.* Botschaft, -en *f.*

embellish, *vb.* aus·schmück-
en.

embellishment, *n.* Aus-
schmückung, -en *f.*

embezzle, *vb.* unterschla'-
gen*.

embitter, *vb.* verbit'tern.

emblem, *n.* Wahrzeichen, -
nt., Emblem', -e *nt.*

embody, *vb.* verkör'pern.

embrace, *vb.* umar'men.

embroider, *vb.* sticken.

embroidery, *n.* Stickerei',
-en *f.*

embroil, *vb.* verwi'ckeln.

embryo, *n.* Embryo, -s *m.*

emerald, *n.* Smaragd', -e *m.*

emerge, *vb.* hervor·treten*,
auf·tauchen.

emery, *n.* Schmirgel *m.*

emetic, *n.* Brechmittel, - *nt.*

emigrant, *n.* Auswanderer, -
m.

emigrate, *vb.* aus·wandern.

emigration, *n.* Auswanderung, -en *f.*

eminence, *n.* (*hill*) Anhöhe,
-n *f.*; (*distinction*) Auszeichnung, -en *f.*; (*title*) Emi-
nenz', -en *f.*

eminent, *adj.* erha'ben.

emissary, *n.* Gesandt' - *m.&*
f.

emit, *vb.* von sich geben*.

emotion, *n.* Gefühl', -e *nt.*;
Erre'gung, -en *f.*

emotional, *adj.* gefühls'-
mäßig; erreg'bar.

emperor, *n.* Kaiser, - *m.*

emphasis, *n.* Nachdruck *m.*

emphasize, *vb.* beto'nen,
hervor·heben*.

emphatic, *adj.* nachdrücklich.

empire, *n.* Kaiserreich, -e *nt.*

empirical, *adj.* empi'risch.

employ, *vb.* an·stellen, beschäf'tigen.

employee, *n.* Arbeitnehmer,
- *m.*, Angestellt- *m.&f.*

employer, *n.* Arbeitgeber, -
m.

employment, *n.* Anstellung,
-en *f.*; Beschäf'tigung, -en
f.

empower, *vb.* ermäch'tigen.

empress, *n.* Kaiserin, -nen *f.*

emptiness, *n.* Leere *f.*

empty, *adj.* leer.

emulate, *vb.* nach·eifern.

emulsion, *n.* Emulsion', -en
f.

enable, *vb.* ermög'lichen;
(**e.ing act**) Ermäch'tigungs-
gesetz, -e *nt.*

enact, *vb.* (*law*) erlas'sen;
(*role*) spielen.

enactment, *n.* Verord'nung,
-en *f.*

enamel, *n.* Emai'lle *f.*

enamor, *vb.* (**be e.ed of**) in
jemand verliebt' sein*; (**become e.ed of**) sich in jemand verlie'ben.

encamp, *vb.* sich lagern.

encampment, *n.* Lager, - *nt.*

encephalitis, *n.* Gehirn'-
entzündung, -en *f.*

enchant, *vb.* entzü'cken;
bezau'bern.

enchantment, *n.* Bezau'-
berung *f.*; Zauber *m.*

encircle, *vb.* umrin'gen.

enclose, vb. ein·schließen*; (letter) bei·fügen.

enclosure, n. Einzäunung, -en f.; (letter) Beilage, -n f.

encompass, vb. umschlie'ßen*, ein·schließen*.

encounter, vb. treffen', begeg'nen.

encourage, vb. ermu'tigen.

encouragement, n. Ermu'tigung, -en f.

encroach upon, vb. sich ein·drängen.

encyclical, n. Enzy'klika, -ken f.

encyclopedia, n. Konversations'lexikon, -ka nt.; Enzyklopädie', -i'en f.

end, 1. n. Ende, -n nt.; (purpose) Zweck, -e m.; (goal) Ziel, -e nt. **2.** vb. been'den, vollen'den, been'digen.

endanger, vb. gefähr'den.

endear, vb. lieb, teuer, wert machen.

endearment, n. Zärtlichkeit, -en f.

endeavor, vb. sich bemü'hen, streben.

ending, n. Ende, -n nt., Schluß, *sse m.

endless, adj. endlos.

endocrine, adj. endokrin'.

endorse, vb. gut·heißen*; (check) girie'ren.

endorsement, n. Billigung, -en f.; (check) Giro nt.

endow, vb. aus·statten; stiften.

endowment, n. Ausstattung, -en f.; Stiftung, -en f.

endurance, n. Ausdauer f.

endure, vb. (last) dauern; (bear) ertra'gen*.

enema, n. Klistier', -e nt.

enemy, n. Feind, -e m.

energetic, adj. tatkräftig.

energy, n. Tatkraft, *e f., Energie', -n f.

enfold, vb. ein·hüllen.

enforce, vb. durch·setzen; auf·schwingen*.

enforcement, n. Durchführung, -en f., Durchsetzung, -en f.

engage, vb. (hire) an·stellen;

(affiance) verlo'ben; (rent) mieten.

engaged, adj. (busy) beschäf'tigt; (affianced) verlobt'.

engagement, n. (date) Verab'redung, -en, f.; (betrothal) Verlo'bung, -en f.

engaging, adj. anziehend.

engender, vb. hervor'·bringen*.

engine, n. Maschi'ne, - f.; Motor, -o'ren, m.; Lokomoti've, -n f.

engineer, n. Ingenieur', -e m.; (locomotive) Lokomotiv'führer, - m.; (mil.) Pionier', -e m.

engineering, n. Ingenieur'wesen nt.

England, n. England nt.

English, adj. englisch.

Englishman, n. Engländer, - m.

Englishwoman, n. Engländerin, -nen f.

engrave, vb. gravie'ren.

engraver, n. Graveur, -e m.

engraving, n. Kupferstich, -e m.

engross, vb. in Anspruch nehmen*.

enhance, vb. erhö'hen.

enigma, n. Rätsel, - nt.

enigmatic, adj. rätselhaft, dunkel.

enjoin, vb. (command) befeh'len*; (forbid) verbie'ten*.

enjoy, vb. genie'ßen*, sich erfreu'en

enjoyable, adj. erfreu'lich, angenehm, nett.

enjoyment, n. Freude, -n f., Genuß', *sse m.

enlarge, vb. vergrö'ßern.

enlargement, n. Vergrö'ßerung, -en f.

enlarger, n. Vergrö'ßerungsapparat, -e m.

enlighten, vb. auf·klären.

enlightenment, n. Aufklärung f.

enlist, vb. ein·spannen; (mil.) sich freiwillig melden.

enlisted man, n. Soldat', -en, -en m.

enlistment, n. freiwillige Meldung zum Militärdienst.

enliven, vb. bele'ben.

enmity, n. Feindschaft, -en f.

ennui, n. Langeweile f.

enormity, n. Ungeheuer'lichkeit, -en f.

enormous, adj. ungeheuer, enorm'.

enough, adv. genug', genü'gend.

enrage, vb. rasend machen.

enrapture, vb. entzü'cken.

enrich, vb. berei'chern.

enroll, vb. als Mitglied ein··tragen.*

enrollment, n. Eintragung (f.) als ·· glied; Mitgliederzahl, ·· f.

ensen· le, n. Ensem'ble, -s nt.

enshrine, vb. als Heiligtum verwah'ren.

ensign, n. (rank) Fähnrich, -e m.; (flag) Fahne. -n f.

enslave, vb. verskla'ven, knechten.

ensnare, vb. verstri'cken.

ensue, vb. folgen.

entail, vb. ein·schließen*.

entangle, vb. verwi'ckeln.

enter, vb. ein·treten*, ein·dringen*.

enterprise, n. Unterneh'men, - nt.

enterprising, adj. unterneh'mend.

entertain, vb. unterhal'ten*.

entertainment, n. Unterhal'tung, -en f.

enthrall, vb. bezau'bern.

enthusiasm, n. Begeis'terung f.

enthusiastic, adj. begeis'tert.

entice, vb verlo'cken.

entire, adj. ganz, gesamt'.

entirety, n. Ganz- nt., Ganzheit f., Gesamt'heit f.

entitle, vb. berech'tigen; (name) beti'teln.

entity, n. Wesenheit f.

entrails, n.pl. Eingeweide pl.

entrain, vb. den Zug bestei'gen*.

entrance, n. Eingang, ··e m.

entrant, n. Teilnehmer, - m.

entrap, vb. in einer Falle fangen*; verstri'cken.

entreat, n. an·flehen.

entreaty, n. Gesuch', -e nt.

entrench, vb. verschan'zen.

entrepreneur, n. Unternehmer, - m.

entrust, vb. an·vertrauen.

entry, n. Eintritt, -e m.; (writing) Eintragung, -en f.

enumerate, vb. auf·zählen.

enumeration, n. Aufzäh'lung, -en f.

enunciate, vb. aus·sprechen*.

enunciation, n. Aussprache, -n f.

envelop, vb. ein·hüllen.

envelope, n. Umschlag, ··e m., Kuvert', -s nt.

enviable, adj. benei'denswert.

envious, adj. neidisch.

environment, n. Umge'bung, -en f., Umwelt f.

environs, n. Umge'bung, -en f.

envisage, vb. vergegenwär'tigen.

envoy, n. Gesandt'- m.

envy, n. Neid m.

eon, n. Äon', -en m.

ephemeral, adj. vergäng'lich.

epic, 1. n. Epos, -pen nt. 2. adj. episch.

epicure, n. Feinschmecker, - m.

epidemic, 1. n. Epidemie', i'en f. 2. adj. epide'misch.

epidermis, n. Epider'mis f.

epigram, n. Epigramm', -e nt.

epilepsy, n. Epilepsie' f.

episode, n. Episo'de, -n f.

epistle, n. Schreiben, - nt.

epitaph, n. Epitaph', -e nt.

epithet, n. Beiwort, ··er nt.

epitome, n. Kurzfassung, -en f.; (fig.) Verkör'perung, -en f.

epitomize, vb. zusam'men·fassen; bezeich'nend sein für.

epoch, n. Epo'che, -n f.

equal, 1. adj. gleich. 2. vb gleichen*.

equality, n. Gleichheit f.

equalize, *vb.* gleich·machen; aus·gleichen*.

equanimity, *n.* Gleichmut *m.*

equate, *vb.* gleich·setzen.

equation, *n.* Gleichung. -en *f.*

equator, *n.* Äqua'tor *m.*

equatorial, *adj.* äquatorial.

equestrian, *n.* Reiter, - *m.*

equilateral, *adj.* gleichseitig.

equilibrium, *n.* Gleichgewicht *nt.*

equinox, *n.* Tag- und Nachtgleiche, -n *f.*

equip, *vb.* aus·rüsten.

equipment, *n.* Ausrüstung, -en *f.*

equitable, *adj.* gerecht', billig.

equity, *n.* Billigkeit *f.*; Billigkeitsrecht *nt.*; (*mortgage, etc.*) Rückkaufswert, -e *m.*

equivalent, *adj.* gleichwertig.

equivocal, *adj.* zweideutig.

equivocate, *vb.* zweideutig sein*.

era, *n.* Zeitalter, - *nt.*

eradicate, *vb.* aus·rotten.

erase, *vb.* aus·radieren.

erasure, *n.* Ausradierung, -en *f.*

erect, 1. *adj.* gera'de. **2.** *vb.* errich'ten.

erection, *n.* Errich'tung, -en *f.*

erectness, *n.* Gerad'heit *f.*

ermine, *n.* Hermelin' *m.*

erode, *vb.* erodie'ren, zerfres'sen*.

erosion, *n.* Erosion', -en *f.*

erotic, *adj.* ero'tisch.

err, *vb.* irren.

errand, *n.* Besor'gung, -en *f.*

errant, *adj.* wandernd; abwegig.

erratic, *adj.* verirrt'; ziellos.

erroneous, *adj.* irrtümlich.

error, *n.* Fehler, - *m.*; Irrtum, ¤er *m.*

erudite, *adj.* gelehrt'.

erudition, *n.* Gelehr'samkeit *f.*

erupt, *vb.* hervor'·brechen*, aus·brechen*.

eruption, *n.* Ausbruch, ¤e *m.*

escalator, *n.* Rolltreppe, -n *f.*

escapade, *n.* Streich, -e *m.*

escape, 1. *n.* Flucht *f.* **2.** *vb.* entkom'men*, entge'hen*.

escapism, *n.* Wirklichkeitsflucht *f.*

escort, 1. *n.* Beglei'ter, - *m.* **2.** *vb.* beglei'ten.

escutcheon, *n.* Wappenschild, -er *nt.*

esophagus, *n.* Speiseröhre, -n *f.*

esoteric, *adj.* esote'risch.

especial, *adj.* beson'der-.

especially, *adv.* beson'ders.

espionage, *n.* Spiona'ge *f.*

espousal, *n.* Vermäh'lung, -en *f.*; (**e. of**) Eintreten für *nt.*

espouse, *vb.* vermäh'len; (**e. a cause**) ein·treten* für.

essay, 1. *n.* Essay, -s *m.* **2.** *vb.* versu'chen.

essence, *nt.* Wesen *nt.*, Wesenlich- *nt.*

essential, *adj.* wesentlich.

establish, *vb.* fest·setzen; errich'ten; ein·richten.

establishment, *n.* Einrichtung, -en *f.*; Betrieb', -e *m.*

estate, *n.* (*inheritance*) Nachlaß, ¤sse *m.*; (*possessions*) Vermö'gen *nt.*; (*condition*) Zustand, ¤e *m.*, Stand, ¤e *m.*

esteem, 1. *n.* Achtung *f.* **2.** *vb.* achten, schätzen.

estimable, *adj.* schätzenswert.

estimate, 1. *n.* Kostenanschlag, ¤e *m.* **2.** *vb.* schätzen.

estimation, *n.* Achtung *f.*; (*view*) Ansicht, -en *f.*

estrange, *vb.* entfrem'den.

etch, *vb.* ätzen.

etching, *n.* Radie'rung, -en *f.*

eternal, *adj.* ewig.

eternity, *n.* Ewigkeit, -en *f.*

ether, *n.* Äther *m.*

ethereal, *adj.* äthe'risch.

ethical, *adj.* ethisch, sittlich, mora'lisch.

ethics, *n.* Ethik *f.*

etiquette, *n.* Etiket'te *f.*

etymology, n. Etymologie', -j'en f.

eucalyptus, n. Eukalyp'tus tun m.

eugenic, adj. euge'nisch.

eugenics, n. Eugene'tik f.

eulogize, vb. lobpreisen*.

eulogy, n. Lobrede, -n f.

eunuch, n. Eunuch', -en, -en m.

euphonious, adj. wohlklingend.

Europe, n. Euro'pa nt.

European, 1. n. Europä'er, - m. **2.** adj. europä'isch.

euthanasia, n. Gnadentod m., Euthanasie' f.

evacuate, vb. evakuie'ren.

evade, vb. aus-weichen*, vermei'den*.

evaluate, vb. ab-schätzen, den Wert berech'nen.

evaluation, n. Abschätzung, -en f., Wertbestimmung, -en f.

evangelist, n. Evangelist', -en, -en m.

evaporate, vb. verdam'pfen.

evaporation, n. Verdam'pfung f.

evasion, n. Umge'hen, - nt.

evasive, adj. ausweichend.

eve, n. Vorabend, -e m.

even, 1. adj. gleich, gera'de, eben. **2.** adv. eben, sogar', selbst.

evening, n. Abend, -e m.

evenness, n. Ebenheit, -en f.; Gleichheit, -en f.; Gleichmut m.

event, n. Ereig'nis, -se nt.

eventful, adj. ereig'nisreich.

eventual, adj. (approximate) etwaig; (final) schließlich.

ever, adv. je, jemals.

evergreen, adj. immergrün.

everlasting, adj. ewig.

every, adj. jeder, -es, -e.

everybody, pron. jeder m.; alle pl.

everyday, adj. Alltags- (cpds.).

everyone, pron. jeder m.; alle pl.

everything, pron. alles.

everywhere, adv. überall'.

evict, vb. aus-weisen*; zwangsräumen.

eviction, n. Ausweisung, -en f.; Zwangsräumung, -en f.

evidence, n. Beweis', -e m.; Augenschein m.; (law) Beweis'material, -ien nt.; (give e.) aus-sagen.

evident, adj. klar, deutlich.

evidently, adv. offenbar.

evil, 1. n. Bös- nt. **2.** adj. böse, übel.

evince, vb. offenba'ren.

evoke, vb. hervor'-rufen*.

evolution, n. Evolution', -en f.

evolve, vb. entwi'ckeln.

ewe, n. Mutterschaf, -e nt.

exact, 1. adj. genau'. **2.** vb. erzwin'gen*.

exaggerate, vb. übertrei'ben*.

exaggeration, n. Übertrei'bung, -en f.

exalt, vb. erhö'hen, verherr'lichen.

exaltation, n. Erhö'hung f.; Erre'gung, -en f.

examination, n. Prüfung, -en f., Exa'men, - nt.; Untersu'chung, -en f.

examine, vb. prüfen; untersu'chen.

example, n. Beispiel, -e nt.

exasperate, vb. reizen, verär'gern.

exasperation, n. Gereizt'heit, f.

excavate, vb. aus-graben*.

excavation, n. Ausgrabung, -en f.; Aushöhlung, -en f.

exceed, vb. übertref'fen*.

exceedingly, adv. außerordentlich.

excel, vb. sich aus-zeichnen.

excellence, n. Vorzüg'lichkeit, -en f.

Excellency, n. Excellenz', -en f.

excellent, adj. ausgezeich'net.

except, 1. vb. aus-schließen*. **2.** prep. außer, ausgenommen; (e. for) außer.

exception, n. Ausnahme, -n f.

exceptional, adj. außerge-wöhnlich.

excerpt, n. Auszug, ⸗e m.

excess, n. Übermaß nt.

excessive, adj. übermäßig.

exchange, 1. n. Tausch m.; **(rate of e.)** Wechselkurs m.; **(foreign e.)** Valu'ta f.; (student) Austausch m.; **(stock e.)** Börse, -n f. **2.** vb. tau-schen; wechseln; aus'tau-schen; (goods) um'tauschen.

exchangeable, adj. aus-tauschbar; umtauschbar.

excise, 1. n. Verbrauchs'-steuer, -n f. **2.** vb. heraus'-schneiden*.

excite, vb. auf'regen, erre'-gen; **(get e.d)** sich auf'-regen.

excitement, n. Erre'gung, -en f.; Aufregung, -en f.

exclaim, vb. aus'rufen*.

exclamation, n. Ausruf, -e m.

exclamation point or mark, n. Ausrufungszeichen, - nt.

exclude, vb. aus'schließen*.

exclusion, n. Ausschluß, ⸗sse m.

exclusive, adj. ausschließ-lich; **(e. of)** abgesehen von; (select) exklusiv'.

excommunicate, vb. exkom-munizie'ren.

excommunication, n. Ex-kommunikation', -en f.

excrement, n. Exkrement', -e nt.

excruciating, adj. qualvoll.

excursion, n. Ausflug, ⸗e m.

excusable, adj. entschuld'-bar.

excuse, vb. entschul'digen, verzei'hen*.

execute, vb. aus'führen; (legal killing) hin'richten.

execution, n. Ausführung, -en f.; (legal killing) Hin-richtung, -en f.

executioner, n. Scharf-richter, - m.

executive, 1. n. Mann in leitender Stellung; (gov't.) Exekuti've f. **2.** adj. vollzie'-hend, ausübend.

executor, n. Testaments'-vollstrecker, - m.

exemplary, adj. musterhaft.

exemplify, vb. als Beispiel dienen.

exempt, 1. adj. befreit'. **2.** vb. befrei'en.

exercise, 1. n. Übung, -en f.; (carrying out) Ausübung, -en f.; (physical) Bewe'gung, -en f. **2.** vb. üben; aus'üben; bewe'gen.

exert, vb. aus'üben; **(e. one-self)** sich an'strengen.

exertion, n. Anstrengung, -en f.

exhale, vb. aus'atmen.

exhaust, 1. n. (auto) Aus-puff, -e m. **2.** vb. erschöp'-fen.

exhaustion, n. Erschöp'-fung, -en f.

exhaustive, adj. erschöp'-fend.

exhibit, 1. n. Ausstellung, -en f. **2.** vb. aus'stellen; zeigen.

exhibition, n. Ausstellung, -en f.

exhibitionism, n. Exhibi-tionis'mus m.

exhilarate, vb. auf'heitern.

exhort, vb. ermah'nen.

exhortation, n. Ermah'nung, -en f.

exhume, vb. aus'graben*.

exigency, n. Dringlichkeit, -en f.

exile, 1. n. Verban'nung, -en f. **2.** vb. verban'nen.

exist, vb. beste'hen*, existie'-ren.

exodus, n. Auszug, ⸗e m.; Auswanderung, -en f.

exonerate, vb. entlas'ten.

exorbitant, adj. übermäßig.

exotic, adj. exo'tisch.

expand, vb. aus'dehnen, aus'-breiten, erwei'tern.

expanse, n. Ausdehnung, -en f., Weite, -n f.

expansion, n. Ausdehnung, -en f., Ausbreitung, -en f.; Expansion' f.

expansive, adj. umfas'send.

expatriate, n. Emigrant', -en, -en m.

expect, vb. erwar'ten.

expectancy, n. Erwar'tung, -en f.

expectation, n. Erwar'tung, -en f.

expectorate, vb. (aus·)spucken.

expediency, n. Zweckmäßigkeit, -en f.

expedient, adj. zweckmäßig.

expedite, vb. beschleu'nigen.

expedition, n. Expediti'on', -en f.

expel, vb. vertrei'ben*.

expend, vb. (money) aus·geben*; (energy) auf·wenden*.

expenditure, n. Ausgabe, -n f., Aufwand m.

expense, n. Ausgabe, -n f.; Kosten pl., Unkosten pl.; (on an e. account) auf Spesen.

expensive, adj. teuer, kostspielig.

experience, 1. n. Erfah'rung, -en f. 2. vb. erfah'ren*.

experienced, adj. erfah'ren.

experiment, 1. n. Versuch', -e m., Experiment', -e nt. 2. vb. experimentie'ren.

experimental, adj. Versuchs'- (cpds.).

experimentally, adv. versuchs'weise.

expert, 1. n. Sachverständig- m., Exper'te, -n, -n m. 2. adj. erfah'ren.

expiate, vb. büßen.

expiration, n. (breath) Ausatmung, -en f.; (end) Ablauf m.

expire, vb. (breathe out) aus·atmen; (die) verschei'den; (end) ab·laufen*.

explain, vb. erklä'ren.

explanation, n. Erklä'rung, -en f.

explanatory, adj. erklä'rend.

expletive, 1. n. Füllwort, ·er nt.; Ausruf, -e m. 2. adj. ausfüllend.

explicit, adj. ausdrücklich.

explode, vb. explodie'ren.

exploit, vb. aus·beuten, aus·nutzen.

exploitation, n. Ausbeutung, -en f., Ausnutzung, -en f.

exploration, n. Erfor'schung, -en f.

exploratory, adj. untersu'chend, erkun'dend.

explore, vb. erfor'schen, untersu'chen.

explorer, n. Forscher, - m., Forschungsreisend- m.

explosion, n. Explosi'on', -en f.

explosive, 1. n. Sprengstoff, -e m. 2. adj. explosiv'.

exponent, n. Exponent', -en, -en m.

export, 1. n. Export', -e m., Ausfuhr f. 2. vb. exportie'ren, aus·führen.

exportation, n. Ausfuhr f.

expose, vb. aus·setzen; (photo) belich'ten; (disclose) enthül'len.

exposé, n. Darlegung, -en f.; (disclosure) Enthül'lung, -en f.

exposition, n. Darlegung, -en f.; (exhibit) Ausstellung, -en f.

expository, adj. erklä'rend.

exposure, n. Aussetzung, -en f.; (photo) Belich'tung, -en f.; (photo) Belich'tung, -en f.; Bloßstellung, -en f.

expound, vb. aus·legen, erklä'ren.

express, 1. n. (train) Schnellzug, ·e m. 2. vb. aus·drücken. 3. adj. ausdrücklich.

expression, n. Ausdruck, ·e m.

expressive, adj. ausdrucksvoll.

expropriate, vb. enteig'nen.

expulsion, n. Vertrei'bung, -en f., Entlas'sung, -en f.

expurgate, vb. reinigen.

exquisite, adj. vorzüg'lich.

extant, adj. vorhan'den.

extemporaneous, adj. aus dem Stegreif.

extend, vb. (intr.) sich erstre'cken, reichen; (tr.) aus·dehnen.

extension, n. Ausdehnung, -en f.; Verlän'gerung, en f.

extensive, adj. umfangreich.

extent, *n.* Umfang, ~em.

exterior, *adj.* äußer-, äußerlich.

exterminate, *vb.* aus-rotten, vernich'ten.

extermination, *n.* Ausrottung, -en *f.,* Vernich'tung, -en *f.*

external, *adj.* äußer-; auswärtig.

extinct, *adj.* ausgestorben.

extinction, *n.* Aussterben *nt.*

extinguish, *vb.* aus-löschen.

extol, *vb.* loben, preisen*.

extort, *vb.* ab-zwingen*.

extortion, *n.* Erpres'sung, -en *f.*

extra, *adj.* extra, beson'der-.

extra-, (*cpds.*) außer-.

extract, 1. *n.* Auszug, ~e *m.,* Extrakt', -e *m.* **2.** *vb.* heraus'-ziehen*, heraus'-holen.

extraction, *n.* Ausziehen *nt.;* (*race*) Herkunft, ~e *f.* Abstammung, -en *f.*

extradite, *vb.* aus-liefern.

extradition, *n.* Auslieferung, -en *f.*

extraneous, *adj.* fremd.

extraordinary, *adj.* außergewöhnlich.

extravagance, *n.* Verschwen'dung, -en *f.,* Extravaganz', -en *f.*

extravagant, *adj.* verschwen'derisch; übertrie'ben.

extravaganza, *n.* phantas'tische, überspann'te Komposition', -en *f.*

extreme, *adj.* äußerst-.

extremely, *adv.* äußerst, höchst.

extremity, *n.* Äußerst- *nt.;* (*limbs*) Gliedmaßen *pl.*

extricate, *vb.* heraus-winden*.

exuberant, *adj.* überschwenglich.

exult, *vb.* frohlo'cken.

exultant, *adj.* frohlo'ckend.

eye, *n.* Auge, -n *n.*

eyeball, *n.* Augapfel, ~ *m.*

eyebrow, *n.* Augenbraue, -n *f.*

eyeglasses, *n.pl.* Brille, -n *f.*

eyelash, *n.* Augenwimper, -n *f.*

eyelet, *n.* Öse, -n *f.*

eyelid, *n.* Augenlid, -er *nt.*

eyesight, *n.* Augensicht *f.;* Augen *pl.*

F

fable, *n.* Fabel, -n *f.*

fabric, *n.* Stoff, -e *m.*

fabricate, *vb.* her-stellen; (*lie*) erdich'ten.

fabrication, *n.* Herstellung, -en *f.;* (*lie*) Erdich'tung, -en *f.*

fabulous, *adj.* sagenhaft.

façade, *n.* Fassa'de, -n *f.*

face, 1. *n.* Gesicht', -er *nt.;* (*surface*) Oberfläche, -n *f.* **2.** *vb.* ins Gesicht'sehen*; (*be opposite*) gegenü'ber-liegen*.

facet, *n.* Facet'te, -n *f.*

facetious, *adj.* scherzhaft.

face value, *n.* Nennwert, -e *m.*

facial, 1. *n.* Gesichts'massage, -n *f.* **2.** *adj.* Gesichts'- (*cpds.*).

facile, *adj.* gewandt'.

facilitate, *vb.* erleich'tern.

facility, *n.* (*ease*) Leichtigkeit *f.;* (*skill*) Geschick'lichkeit *f.;* (*possibility*) Möglichkeit, -en *f.*

facing, *n.* (*clothing*) Besatz' *m.*

facsimile, *n.* Faksi'mile, -s *nt.*

fact, *n.* Tatsache, -n *f.*

faction, *n.* Faktion', -en *f.*

factor, *n.* Faktor, -o'ren *m.*

factory, *n.* Fabrik', -en *f.*

factual, *adj.* auf Tatsachen beschränkt'; Tatsachen- (*cpds.*).

faculty, *n.* Fähigkeit, -en *f.,* Gabe, -n *f.;* (*college*) Fakultät', -en *f.*

fad, *n.* Mode, -n *f.*

fade, *vb.* verblas'sen.

fail, *vb.* versa'gen; (*school*)

durch·fallen*; **(f. to do)** nicht tun*.

failure, *n.* Versa'gen *nt.,* Mißerfolg, -e *m.; (bankruptcy)* Bankrott', -e *m.*

faint, 1. *adj.* schwach 2. *vb.* in Ohnmacht fallen*.

fair, 1. *n.* Messe, -n *f.,* Jahrmarkt, ⸚e *m.* 2. *adj.* *(weather)* heiter; *(blond)* blond; *(just)* gerecht'.

fairness, *n.* Gerech'tigkeit, -en *f.*

fairy, *n.* Fee, Fe'en *f.*

fairy tale, *n.* Märchen, - *nt.*

faith, *n. (trust)* Vertrau'en *nt.; (belief)* Glaube(n), - *m.*

faithful, *adj.* treu.

faithfulness, *n.* Treue *f.*

faithless, *adj.* treulos.

fake, 1. *adj.* falsch 2. *vb.* vor·täuschen.

faker, *n.* Schwindler, - *m.*

falcon, *n.* Falke, -n, -n *m.*

fall, 1. *n.* Fall, ⸚e *m.,* Sturz, ⸚e *m.; (autumn)* Herbst, -e *m.* 2. *adj.* fallen*.

fallacious, *adj.* trügerisch.

fallacy, *n.* Trugschluß ⸚sse *m.*

fallible, *adj.* fehlbar.

fallow, *adj.* brach.

false, *adj.* falsch.

falsehood, *n.* Lüge, -n *f.*

falseness, *n.* Falschheit, -en *f.*

falsetto, *n.* Falsett', -e *nt.*

falsification, *n.* Verfäl'schung, -en *f.*

falsify, *vb.* verfäl'schen.

falter, *vb.* straucheln, stocken.

fame, *n.* Ruhm *m.*

famed, *adj.* berühmt'.

familiar, *adj.* vertraut'.

familiarity, *n.* Vertraut'heit, -en *f.;* Vertrau'lichkeit, -en *f.*

familiarize, *n.* vertraut'machen.

family, *n.* Fami'lie, -n *f.*

famine, *n.* Hungersnot, ⸚e *f.*

famished, *adj.* ausgehungert.

famous, *adj.* berühmt'.

fan, 1. *n.* Fächer, - *m.;* Ventila'tor, -o'ren *m.; (enthusiast)* Vereh'rer, - *m.,* Anhänger, - *m.* 2. *vb.* fächern.

fanatic, 1. *n.* Fana'tiker, - *m.* 2. *adj.* fana'tisch.

fanatical, *adj.* fana'tisch.

fanaticism, *n.* Fanatis'mus *m.*

fanciful, *adj.* phantas'tisch

fancy, 1. *n. (imagination)* Einbildung, -en *f.; (mood)* Laune, -n *f.; (liking)* Vorliebe *f.* 2. *adj.* apart', ausgefallen; Luxus- (*cpds.*). 3. *vb.* sich ein·bilden.

fanfare, *n.* Fanfa're, -n *f.;* *(fig.)* Getu'e *nt.*

fang, *n.* Fang, ⸚e *m.*

fantastic, *adj.* phantas'tisch.

fantasy, *n.* Phantasie', -i'en *f.*

far, *adj.* weit fern.

faraway, *adj.* entfernt'; *(fig.)* träumerisch.

farce, *n.* Farce, -n *f.*

fare, 1. *n. (passenger)* Fahrgeld, -er *nt.; (price)* Fahrpreis -e *m.; (food)* Kost *f.* 2. *vb.* gehen*.

farmer, *n.* Landwirt, -e *m.* Farmer, - *m.,* Bauer, (-n), -n *m.*

farm, 1. *n.* landwirtschaftlicher Betrieb', -e *m.,* Farm, -en *f.* 2. *vb.* Landwirtschaft betrei'ben*, Landwirt sein*

farina, *n.* Griessmehl *nt.*

far-fetched, *adj.* gesucht'.

farewell, 1. *n.* Abschied, -e *m.;* Abschieds- (*cpds.*). 2. *interj.* lebe wohl! leben Sie wohl!

farmhouse, *n.* Farmhaus, ⸚er *nt.;* Bauernhaus, ⸚er *nt.*

farming, *n.* Landwirtschaft *f.;* Ackerbau *m.*

farmyard, *n.* Bauernhof, ⸚e *m.*

far-sighted, *adj.* weitsichtig.

farther, *adj.* weiter.

farthest, *adj.* weitest-.

fascinate, *vb.* faszinie'ren, bezau'bern.

fascination, *n.* Faszination *f.,* Zauber *m.*

fascism, *n.* Faschis'mus *m.*

fascist, 1. *n.* Faschist', -en, -en *m.* 2. *adj.* faschis'tisch.

fashion, *n.* Mode, -n *f.;* *(manner)* Art, -en *f.*

fashionable, *adj.* modern', schick.

fast, 1. *n.* Fasten *nt.* **2.** *adj.* (*speedy*) schnell; (**be f.,** of a clock) vor'gehen*; (*firm*) fest. **3.** *vb.* fasten.

fasten, *vb.* fest·machen.

fastener, fastening, *n.* Ver-schluß', ·sse *m.*

fastidious, *adj.* wählerisch; eigen.

fat, 1. *n.* Fett, -e *nt.* **2.** *adj.* fett, dick.

fatal, *adj.* tötlich; verhäng'-nisvoll.

fatality, *n.* Verhäng'nis, -se *nt.;* Todesfall, ·e *m.*

fate, *n.* Schicksal, -e *nt.*

fateful, *adj.* schicksals-schwer; verhäng'nisvoll.

father, *n.* Vater, · *m.*

fatherhood, *n.* Vaterschaft, -en *f.*

father-in-law, *n.* Schwie-gervater, · *m.*

fatherland, *n.* Vaterland *nt.*

fatherless, *adj.* vaterlos.

fatherly, *adj.* väterlich.

fathom, 1. *n.* Klafter, -n *f.* **2.** *vb.* loten; (*fig.*) ergrün'den.

fatigue, 1. *n.* Ermü'dung *f.* **2.** *vb.* ermü'den.

fatten, *vb.* mästen.

fatty, *adj.* fettig.

faucet, *n.* Wasserhahn, ·e *m.*

fault, *n.* Fehler, - *m.;* (**it's my f.**) es ist meine Schuld.

faultless, *adj.* fehlerlos, ma-kellos.

faulty, *adj.* fehlerhaft.

favor, 1. *n.* Gunst, -en *f.;* (**do a f.**) einen Gefallen tun*. **2.** *vb.* begün'stigen, bevor'zugen; (*a sore limb*) schonen.

favorable, *adj.* günstig.

favorite, 1. *n.* Liebling, -e *m.;* (*sport*) Favorit', -en, -en *m.* **2.** *adj.* Lieblings- (*cpds.*).

favoritism, *n.* Begün'sti-gung *f.*

fawn, *n.* Rehkalb, ·er *nt.*

faze, *vb.* in Verle'genheit bringen*.

fear, 1. *n.* Furcht *f.,* Angst, ·e *f.* **2.** *vb.* fürchten.

fearful, *adj.* (*afraid*) furcht-sam; (*terrible*) furchtbar.

fearless, *adj.* furchtlos.

fearlessness, *n.* Furchtlosig-keit *f.*

feasible, *adj.* durchführbar.

feast, 1. *n.* Fest, -e *nt.,* Fest-mahl, -e *nt.*

feat, *n.* Tat, -en *f.;* Kunst-stück, -e *nt.*

feather, *n.* Feder, -n *f.*

feature, *n.* (*quality*) Eigen-schaft, -en *f.;* (*face*) Gesichts-zug, ·e *m.;* (*distinguishing mark*) Kennzeichen, - *nt.*

February, *n.* Februar *m.*

feces, *n.pl.* Exkremen'te *pl.*

federal, *adj.* bundesstaat-lich; Bundes- (*cpds.*).

federation, *n.* Staatenbund, -e *m.,* Föderation', -en *f.;* Bundesstaat, -en *m.*

fee, *n.* Gebühr', -en *f.*

feeble, *adj.* schwach(·).

feeble-minded, *adj.* schwachsinnig.

feebleness, *n.* Schwäche, -n *f.*

feed, 1. *n.* Futter, - *nt.* **2.** *vb.* füttern.

feel, *vb.* fühlen.

feeling, *n.* Gefühl', -e *nt.*

feign, *vb.* vor'geben*, heu-cheln.

felicitate, *vb.* beglück'wün-schen.

felicity, *n.* Glück *nt.*

fell, *vb.* fällen.

fellow, *n.* Kerl, -e *m.,* Bur-sche, -n, -n *m.;* (*member*) Mitglied, -er *nt.*

fellowship, *n.* Gemein'schaft, -en *f.*

felony, *n.* Gewalt'verbrechen, - *nt.*

felt, *n.* Filz, -e *m.*

female, 1. *n.* (*human*) Frau, -en *f.;* (*animal*) Weibchen, - *nt.* **2.** *adj.* weiblich.

feminine, *adj.* weiblich, femini'.

femininity, *n.* Weiblichkeit *f.*

fence, 1. *n.* Zaun, ·e *m.* **2.** *vb.* ein·zäunen; (*sport*) fech-ten*.

fencing, *n.* Fechten *nt.*

fender, n. (auto) Kotflügel, - m.

ferment, vb. gären*.

fermentation, n. Gärung, -en f.

fern, n. Farnkraut, *er nt.

ferocious, adj. wild.

ferocity, n. Wildheit f.

ferry, n. Fähre, -n f.

fertile, adj. fruchtbar.

fertility, n. Fruchtbarkeit f.

fertilization, n. Befruchtung, -en f.

fertilize, vb. befruch'ten; düngen.

fertilizer, n. Dünger m. Kunstdünger m.

fervent, adj. inbrünstig.

fervid, adj. brennend.

fervor, n. Inbrunst f., Eifer m.

fester, vb. eitern.

festival, n. Fest, -e nt.

festive, adj. festlich.

festivity, n. Festlichkeit, -en f.

festoon, n. Girlan'de, -n f.

fetch, vb. holen.

fetching, adj. reizend.

fête, n. Fest, -e nt.

fetid, adj. stinkend.

fetish, n. Fetisch, -e m.

fetters, n.pl. Fesseln pl.

fetus, n. Foetus, -se m.

feud, n. Feindschaft, -en f.; (historical) Fehde, -n f.

feudal, adj. feudal'.

feudalism, n. Feudalis'mus m.

fever, n. Fieber, - nt.

feverish, adj. fieberhaft.

few, adj. wenig; (a f.) ein paar.

fiancé, n. Verlobt'- m.

fiancée, n. Verlobt'- f.

fiasco, n. Fias'ko, -s nt.

fib, n. Lüge, -n f.

fiber, n. Faser, -n f.

fickle, adj. wankelmütig.

fickleness, n. Wankelmütigkeit f.

fiction, n. Erdich'tung f.; (novel writing) Prosadichtung, -en f.

fictional, adj. erdich'tet.

fictitious, adj. fingiert'.

fiddle, 1. n. Geige, -n f. **2.** vb. geigen.

fidelity, n. Treue f.

fidget, vb. zappeln.

field, n. Feld, -er nt.

fiend, n. Teufel, - m.

fiendish, adj. teuflisch.

fierce, adj. wild.

fiery, adj. feurig.

fife, n. Querpfeife, -n f.

fifteen, num. fünfzehn.

fifteenth, 1. adj. fünfzehnt-. **2.** n. Fünfzehntel, - nt.

fifth, 1. adj. fünft-. **2.** n. Fünftel, - nt.

fiftieth, 1. adj. fünfzigst-. **2.** n. Fünfzigstel, - nt.

fifty, num. fünfzig.

fig, n. Feige, -n f.

fight, 1. n. Kampf, *e m.; (brawl) Schlägerei', -en f.; (quarrel) Streit, -e m. **2.** vb. kämp'fen; bekämp'fen.

fighter, n. Kämpfer, - m.

figment, n. Fiktion', en f.

figurative, adj. bildlich; (f. meaning) übertra'gene Bedeu'tung, -en f.

figure, 1. n. Figur', -en f., Gestalt', -en f.; (number) Zahl, -en f. **2.** vb. rechnen; berech'nen.

figurehead, n. Galionsfigur, -en f.; (fig.) Repräsentations'figur, -en f.

figure of speech, n. Redewendung, -en f.

figurine, n. Porzellan'figur, -en f.

filament, n. Faser, -n f. Faden, * m.

file, 1. n. (tool) Feile, -n f.; (row) Reihe, -n f.; (papers etc.) Akte, -n f.; (cards) Kartothek', -en f. **2.** vb. (tool) feilen; (papers) einordnen.

filigree, n. Filigran', -e nt.

fill, vb. füllen.

fillet, n. Filet', -s nt.

filling, n. (tooth) Plombe, -n f.

filling station, n. Tankstelle, -n f.

film, 1. n. Film, -e m. **2.** vb. filmen.

filmy, *adj.* mit einem Häut-
chen bedeckt; duftig.

filter, 1. *n.* Filter. - *m.*
2. *vb.* filtrie'ren.

filth, *n.* Dreck *m.*

filthy, *adj.* dreckig; (*fig.*)
unanständig.

fin, *n.* Flosse, -n *f.*

final, *adj* endgültig.

finale, *n.* Fina'le, -s *nt.*

finalist, *n.* Teilnehmer (-, *m.*)
in der Schlußrunde.

finality, *n.* Endgültigkeit *f.*

finance, 1. *n.* Finanz', -en
f.; (*study*) Finanz'wesen *nt.*;
(**f.s**) Finan'zen *pl.* 2. *vb.*
financie'ren.

financial, *adj.* finanziell'.

financier, *n.* Finanz'mann,
-er, *m.*

find, *vb.* finden*.

findings, *n.pl.* Tatbestand,
-e, *m.*

fine, 1. *n.* Geldstrafe, -n *f.*
2. *adj.* fein. 3. *vb.* zu einer
Geldstrafe verur'teilen.

fine arts, *n.* Kunstwissenschaft *f.*

finery, *n.* Putz *m.*

finesse, *n.* Fines'se, -n *f.*

finger, *n.* Finger. - *m.*

fingernail, *n.* Fingernagel,
m.

fingerprint, *n.* Fingerabdruck, -e *m.*

finicky, *adj.* zimperlich

finish, 1. *n.* Ende, -n *nt.*;
Abschluß, -sse. 2. *vb.* been'-
den, vollen'den.

finite, *adj.* endlich.

fir, *n.* Fichte, -n *f.*

fire, 1. *n.* Feuer, - *nt.* 2. *vb.*
(*shoot*) feuern; (*dismiss*)
entlas'sen*.

firearm, *n.* Feuerwaffe *n f.*

fire engine, *n.* Feuerspritze,
-n *f.*

fire escape, *n.* Feuerleiter, -n
f.

fire extinguisher, *n.* Feuer-
löscher, - *m.*

fireman, *n.* Feuerwehrmann,
-er *m.*

fireplace, *n.* Kamin', -e *m.*

fireproof, *adj.* feuerfest.

fireworks, *n.* Feuerwerk, -e
nt.

firm, 1. *n.* Firma, -men *f.*
2. *adj.* fest.

firmness, *n.* Festigkeit *f.*

first, 1. *adj.* erst. 2. *adv.*
zuerst'.

first aid, *n.* erste Hilfe *f.*

first-class, *adj.* erstklassig,
erster Klasse.

fiscal, *adj.* fiska'lisch.

fish, 1. *n.* Fisch, -e *m.* 2.
vb. fischen, angeln.

fisherman, *n.* Fischer, -*m.*,
Angler, - *m.*

fishing, *n.* Angeln *nt.*

fission, *n.* Spaltung, -en *f.*;
(**nuclear f.**) Kernspaltung *f.*

fissure, *n.* Spalt, -e *m.*

fist, *n.* Faust, -e *f.*

fit, 1. *n.* (*attack*) Anfall, -e
m. 2. *adj.* in Form. 3. *vb.*
passen; (*adapt*) an·passen.

fitful, *adj.* unregelmäßig.

fitness, *n.* Tauglichkeit *f.*;
Gesund'heit *f.*

fitting, 1. *n.* Anprobe, -n *f.*
2. *adj.* passend.

five, *num.* fünf.

fix, 1. *n.* (*predicament*)
Verle'genheit, -en *f.* 2. *vb.*
fest·setzen; (*prepare*) zu-
bereiten; (*repair*) reparie'ren.

fixation, *n.* Fixie'rung, -en *f.*

fixed, *adj.* (*repaired*) heil;
(*set*) fest.

fixture, *n.* Vorrichtung, -en
f.; Zubehör *nt.*

flabby, *adj.* schlaff.

flag, 1. *n.* Fahne, -n *f.*, Flagge,
-n *f.*

flagpole, *n.* Fahnenstange,
-n *f.*

flagrant, *adj.* schreiend.

flagship, *n.* Flaggschiff, -e
nt.

flair, *n.* Flair *nt.*

flake, *n.* Flocke, -n *f.*

flamboyant, *adj.* flammend;
(*fig.*) überla'den.

flame, 1. *n.* Flamme, -n *f.* 2.
vb. flammen.

flank, 1. *n.* Flanke, -n *f.*
2. *vb.* flankie'ren.

flannel, *n.* Flanell', -e *m.*

flap, 1. *n.* Klappe, -n *f.*;
(*wings*) Flügelschlag, *e m.*
2. *vb.* flattern.

flare, 1. *n.* Leuchtsignal, -e *nt.* **2.** *vb.* flackern.

flash, 1. *n.* Lichtstrahl, -en *m.* **2.** *vb.* auf·flammen.

flashlight, *n.* Taschenlampe, -n *f.*

flashy, *adj.* auffällig; (*clothes, etc.*) laut.

flask, *n.* Flasche, -n *f.*

flat, 1. *n.* Mietswohnung, -en *f.* **2.** *adj.* flach, platt.

flatcar, *n.* offener Güterwagen, - *m.*

flatness, *n.* Flachheit, -en *f.*

flatten, *vb.* flach machen.

flatter, *vb.* schmeicheln.

flattering, *adj.* schmeichelhaft.

flattery, *n.* Schmeichelei', -en *f.*

flaunt, *vb.* zur Schau stellen.

flavor, 1. *n.* (*taste*) Geschmack', -e *m.*; (*odor*) Geruch', -e *m.* **2.** *vb.* würzen.

flavoring, *n.* Geschmack', -e *m.*; Essenz', -en *f.*

flavorless, *adj.* fade.

flaw, *n.* Fehler, - *m.*, Makel, - *m.*

flawless, *adj.* fehlerfrei, makellos.

flax, *n.* Flachs *m.*

flay, *vb.* schinden *f.*

flea, *n.* Floh, -e *m.*

fleck, *n.* Fleck, -e *m.*

flee, *vb.* fliehen*, flüchten.

fleece, *n.* Vlies, -e *nt.*

fleecy, *adj.* wollig.

fleet, *n.* Flotte, -n *f.*

fleeting, *adj.* flüchtig.

Fleming, *n.* Flame, -n, -n *m.*

Flemish, *adj.* flämisch.

flesh, *n.* Fleisch *nt.*

fleshy, *adj.* fleischig.

flex, *vb.* biegen*; beugen.

flexibility, *n.* Biegsamkeit *f.*

flexible, *adj.* biegsam, flexi'bel.

flicker, *vb.* flackern.

flier, *n.* Flieger, - *m.*

flight, *n.* Flug, -e *m.*; (*escape*) Flucht, -en *f.*

flimsy, *adj.* dünn; lose.

flinch, *vb.* zurück'zucken.

fling, *vb.* schleudern.

flint, *n.* Feuerstein, -e *m.*

flip, *vb.* schnellen.

flippant, *adj.* vorlaut.

flirt, 1. *n.* Flirt, -s *m.* **2.** *vb.* flirten, kokettie'ren.

flirtation, *n.* Flirt, s *m.*

float, 1. *n.* Floß, -e *nt.* **2.** *vb.* treiben*, schwimmen*.

flock, *n.* Herde, - *f.*, Schar, -en *f.*

flog, *vb.* peitschen.

flood, 1. *n.* Flut, -en *f.*; Überschwem'mung, -en *f.* **2.** *vb.* überschwem'men.

floodlight, *n.* Scheinwerfer, - *m.*

floor, *n.* Fußboden, - *m.*; (*story*) Stockwerk, -e *nt.*

floorwalker, *n.* Abteilungsaufseher (, - *m.*) in einem Warenhaus.

flop. 1. *n.* (*thud*) Plumps *m.*; (*failure*) Reinfall, -e *m.* **2.** *vb.* plumpsen; rein·gallen*.

floral, *adj.* Blumen- (*cpds.*).

florid, *adj.* gerö'tet.

florist, *n.* Blumenhändler, - *m.*

flounce, 1. *n.* Volant', -s *m.* **2.** *vb.* tänzeln.

flounder, 1. *n.* Flunder, -n *f.* **2.** *vb.* taumeln.

flour, *n.* Mehl *nt.*

flourish, *vb.* (*grow*) gedei'hen*, blühen; (*shake*) schwenken.

flow, *vb.* fließen*.

flower, 1. *n.* Blume, -n *f.* **2.** *vb.* blühen.

flowerpot, *n.* Blumentopf, -e *m.*

flowery, *adj.* blumig.

fluctuate, *vb.* schwanken.

fluctuation, *n.* Schwankung, -en *f.*

flue, *n.* Rauchfang, -e *m.*

fluency, *n.* Geläu'figkeit *f.*

fluent, *adj.* fließend.

fluffy, *adj.* flaumig, wollig.

fluid, 1. *n.* Flüssigkeit, -en *f.* **2.** *adj.* flüssig.

fluidity, *n.* flüssiger Aggregat'zustand *m.*; Flüssigsein *nt.*

fluorescent, *adj.* fluoreszie'rend.

fluoroscope, *n.* Leuchtschirm, -e *m.*, Fluroskop', -e *nt.*

flurry, *n.* Wirbel, - *m.*

flush, 1. n. Röte f.; (fig.) Flut f. **2.** vb. errö'ten; (wash out) aus·spülen; (toilet) auf·ziehen*.

flute, n. Flöte, -n f.

flutter, vb. flattern.

flux, n. Fluss m.; Strömen nt.

fly, 1. n. Fliege, -n f. **2.** vb. fliegen*.

foam, 1. n. Schaum, -e m. **2.** vb. schäumen.

focal, adj. fokal'.

focus, 1. n. Brennpunkt, -e m. **2.** vb. (scharf, richtig) ein·stellen.

fodder, n. Futter nt.

foe, n. Feind, -e m.

fog, n. Nebel m.

foggy, adj. neblig.

foil, 1. n. Rapier', -e nt. **2.** vb. verei'teln.

foist, vb. unterschie'ben*.

fold, 1. n. Falte, -n f. **2.** vb. falten.

folder, n. (for papers) Mappe, -n f.; Hefter, - m.; (brochure) Broschü're, -n f., Prospekt', -e m.

foliage, n. Laub nt.

folio, n. Folio, -lien nt.

folk, n. Volk, -er nt.

folklore, n. Volkskunde f.

folks, n.pl. Leute pl.

follow, vb. folgen.

follower, n. Anhänger, - m.

folly, n. Torheit, -en f.

foment, vb. schüren.

fond, adj. (be f. of) gern haben*.

fondle, vb. liebkosen.

fondness, n. Vorliebe f.

food, n. Nahrung f., Essen nt.

foodstuffs, n. Nahrungsmittel pl.

fool, 1. n. Narr, -en, -en m. **2.** vb. täuschen, zum Narren halten*.

foolhardiness, n. Tollkühnheit, -en f.

foolhardy, adj. tollkühn.

foolish, adj. dumm, närrisch.

foolproof, adj. narrensicher.

foot, n. Fuss, -e m.

footage, n. Länge in Fuß gemessen.

football, n. Fußball, -e m.

foothills, n.pl. Vorgebirge nt.

foothold, n. Halt m.

footing, n. Stand m.; Boden m.

footlights, n.pl. Rampenlicht, -er nt.

footnote, n. Fußnote, -n f.

footprint, n. Fußstapfe, -n f.

footstep, n. Fußstapfe, -n f.

for, 1. prep. für. **2.** conj. denn.

forage, 1. n. Futter nt. **2.** vb. furagie'ren.

foray, n. Überfall, -e m.

forbearance, n. Enthal'tung f.; Nachsicht f.

forbid, vb. verbie'ten*.

forbidding, adj. abschreckend.

force, 1. n. Kraft, -e f., Gewalt', -en f. **2.** vb. zwingen*.

forceful, adj. kräftig, wirkungsvoll.

forcefulness, n. Überzeu'gungskraft f.

forceps, n. Zange, -n f.

forcible, adj. kräftig, heftig, mit Gewalt'.

ford, n. Furt, -en f.

fore, adv. vorn.

forearm, n. Unterarm, -e m.

forebears, n.pl. Vorfahren pl.

foreboding, n. Vorahnung, -en f.

forecast, 1. n. Voraus'sage, -n f. **2.** vb. voraus'sagen.

forecaster, n. Wetterprophet, -en, -en m.

foreclosure, n. Zwangsvollstreckung, -en f.

forefather, n. Vorfahr, -en, -en m.

forefinger, n. Zeigefinger, - m.

forefront, n. Vordergrund m.

foreground, n. Vordergrund m.

forehead, n. Stirn, -en f.

foreign, adj. fremd, ausländisch.

foreigner, n. Ausländer, - m.

foreman, n. Vorarbeiter, - m.

foremost, adj. vorderst-.

forenoon, n. Vormittag, -e m.

forerunner, n. Vorläufer, - m.

foresee, vb. vorher'sehen*.

foreshadow, vb. ahnen lassen*.

foresight, n. Voraus'sicht f.

forest, n. Wald, -er m.

forestall, vb. verhin'dern, vorweg'nehmen*.

forester, n. Förster, - m.

forestry, n. Forstwirtschaft f.

foretaste, n. Vorgeschmack, -"e m.

foretell, vb. vorher'sagen, prophezei'en.

forever, adv. ewig.

forevermore, adv. für, auf immer und ewig.

forewarn, vb. vorher warnen.

foreword, n. Vorwort, -e nt.

forfeit, vb. verwir'ken, einbüßen.

forfeiture, n. Verwir'kung f., Einbuße f.

forgather, vb. sich versam'meln.

forge, 1. n. Schmiede, -n f. **2.** vb. schmieden; (falsify) fälschen.

forger, n. Fälscher, - m.

forgery, n. Fälschung, -en f.

forget, vb. verges'sen*.

forgetful, adj. vergeß'lich.

forgive, vb. verge'ben*, verzei'hen*.

forgiveness, n. Verge'bung f.

forgo, vb. verzich'ten auf.

fork, n. Gabel, -n f.

forlorn, adj. verlas'sen.

form, 1. n. Form, -en f.; (blank) Formular', -e nt. **2.** vb. bilden, formen.

formal, adj. formell'; offiziell'.

formaldehyde, n. Formaldehyd', -e nt.

formality, n. Formalität', -en f.; Förmlichkeit, -en f.

format, n. Format', -e nt.

formation, n. Gestal'tung, -en f.; (mil.) Formation', -en f.

former, adj. ehemalig, früher; (the f.) jener, -es, -e.

formerly, adv. früher.

formidable, adj. beacht'lich.

formless, adj. formlos.

formula, n. Formel, -n f.

formulate, vb. formulie'ren.

formulation, n. Formulie'rung, -en f.

forsake, vb. verlas'sen*.

fort, n. Feste, -n f.

forte, n. Stärke, -n f.

forth, adv. fort; (and so f.) un so weiter.

forthcoming, adj. angekündigt.

forthright, adj. offen, ehrlich.

fortieth, 1. adj. vierzigst-. **2.** n. Vierzigstel, - nt.

fortification, n. Befesti'gungswerk, -e nt.

fortify, vb. stärken, befestigen.

fortissimo, adj. fortis'simo.

fortitude, n. seelische Stärke f., Mut m.

fortnight, n. vierzehn Tage pl.

fortress, n. Festung, -en f.

fortuitous, adj. zufällig.

fortunate, adj. glücklich.

fortune, n. Glück nt.; (money) Vermö'gen, - nt.

fortune-teller, n. Wahrsager, - m.

forty, adj. vierzig.

forum, n. Forum, -ra nt.

forward, adv. vorwärts.

forwardness, n. Dreistigkeit f.

fossil, n. Fossil', -ien nt.

foster, vb. (nourish) nähren; (raise) auf'ziehen*; Pflege- (cpds.).

foul, adj. schmutzig.

found, vb. gründen.

foundation, n. (building) Fundament', -e nt.; (fund) Stiftung, -en f.

founder, n. Gründer, - m.

foundling, n. Findling, -e m.

foundry, n. Gießerei', -en f.

fountain, n. Springbrunnen, - m.

fountainhead, n. Urquell, -e m.

fountain pen, n. Füllfederhalter, - m.

four, num. vier.

fourteen, num. vierzehn.

fourteenth, 1. adj. vier-zehnt-. **2.** n. Vierzehntel, -e nt.

fourth, 1. adj. viert-. **2.** n. Viertel, -e nt.

fowl, n. Geflü'gel nt.; Huhn, -er nt.

fox, n. Fuchs, -e m.·

foxglove, n. Fingerhut, -e m.

foxhole, n. Schüt'zenloch, -er nt.

foxy, adj. schlau.

foyer, n. Foyer', -s nt.

fracas, n. Keilerei', -en f.

fraction, n. (number) Bruch-stück, -e nt.; (part) Bruch-teil, -e nt.; (f.s.) Bruchrech-nung f.

fracture, 1. n. Bruch, -e m. **2.** vb. brechen*.

fragile, adj. zerbrech'lich.

fragment, n. Bruchstück, -e nt.

fragmentary, adj. frag-menta'risch.

fragrance, n. Duft, -e m.

fragrant, adj. wohlriechend.

frail, adj. zerbrech'lich, schwach(-).

frailty, n. Schwachheit, -en f.

frame, 1. n. Rahmen, - m. **2.** vb. (shape) formen; (en-close) ein'rahmen.

framework, n. Rahmen, - m.

France, n. Frankreich nt.

franchise, n. Wahlrecht, -e nt.

frank, adj. frei, offen.

frankfurter, n. Frankfurter Würstchen, - nt.

frankly, adv. ehrlich gesagt'.

frankness, n. Offenheit f.

frantic, adj. wahnsinnig.

fraternal, adj. brüderlich.

fraternity, n. Brüderlich-keit f.; (students) Studen'-tenverbindung, -en f.

fraternize, vb. fraternisie'-ren.

fraud, n. Betrug' m.

fraudulent, adj. betrü'-gerisch.

fraught, adj. voll.

fray, n. Tumult', -e m.; Schlägerei', -en f.

freak, 1. n. Mißgeburt, -en f.; Kurio'sum, -sa nt. **2.** adj. monströs', bizarr'.

freckle, n. Sommersprosse, -n f.

freckled, adj. sommerspros-sig.

free, 1. adj. frei; kostenlos. **2.** vb. befrei'en; frei'lassen*.

freedom, n. Freiheit, -en f.

freeze, vb. (be cold) frieren*; (turn to ice) (intr.) gefrie'-ren*, (tr.) gefrie'ren lassen*; (food) tief kühlen.

freezer, n. Tiefkühler, - m.; (in refrigerator) Gefrier'-fach, -er nt.

freezing, adj. eisig.

freight, n. Fracht, -en f.; Frachtgut nt.

freightage, n. Frachtspesen pl.

freighter, n. Frachter, - m.

French, adj. franzö'sisch.

Frenchman, n. Franzo'se, -n, -n m.

Frenchwoman, n. Franzö'-sin, -nen f.

frenzied, adj. rasend.

frenzy, n. Raserei', -en f.

frequency, n. Häufigkeit, -en f.; (physics) Frequenz', -en f.

frequent, adj. häufig.

fresh, adj. frisch; (impudent) frech.

freshen, vb. erfri'schen.

freshman, n. Student' im ersten College-Jahr.

freshness, n. Frische f.

fresh water, n. Süßwasser nt.

fret, vb. nervös' sein*, ner-vös' werden*.

fretful, adj. nervös', unruhig.

fretfulness, n. Reizbarkeit f.

friar, n. Bettelmönch, -e m.

fricassee, n. Frikassee', -s nt.

friction, n. Reibung, -en f.

Friday, n. Freitag, -e m.

friend, n. Freund, -e m.; Freundin, -nen f.

friendless, adj. freundlos.

friendliness, n. Freundlich-keit, -en f.

friendly, adj. freundlich.

friendship, n. Freundschaft, -en f.

frigate, n. Fregat'te, -n f.

fright, n. Angst, ⁼e f.; Schreck m.

frighten, vb. ängstigen, erschre'cken; **(be f.ed)** erschre'cken*.

frightful, adj. schrecklich.

frigid, adj. kalt(⁼); **(sexual)** frigid'.

frill, n. Krause, -n f.

fringe, n. Franse, -n f.; Rand, ⁼er m.

frisky, adj. lebhaft.

fritter, n. eine Art Pfannkuchen.

frivolous, adj. leichtsinnig, frivol'.

frivolity, n. Frivolität', -en f.

frivolousness, n. Leichtsinnigkeit, -en f.

frock, n. Kleid, -er nt.; **(monk)** Kutte, -n f.

frog, n. Frosch, ⁼e m.

frolic, vb. ausgelassen sein*.

from, prep. von, aus.

front, n. Vorderseite, -n f.; **(mil.)** Front, -en f.; **(in f.)** vorn; **(in f. of)** vor.

frontage, n. Vorderfront, -en f.

frontal, adj. frontal.

frontier, n. Grenze, -n f.

frost, n. Frost, ⁼e m.

frostbite, n. Frostbeule, -n f.

frosting, n. Kuchenglasur, -en f.

frosty, adj. frostig.

froth, n. Schaum, ⁼e m.

frown, vb. die Stirn runzeln.

frugal, adj. sparsam, frugal'.

frugality, n. Sparsamkeit f.

fruit, n. Frucht, ⁼e f., Obst nt.

fruitful, adj. fruchtbar.

fruition, n. Reife f.

fruitless, adj. unfruchtbar; **(fig.)** vergeb'lich.

frustrate, vb. verdrän'gen; **(nullify)** verei'teln.

frustration, n. Verdrän'gung, -en f.; Verei'telung, -en f.

fry, vb. braten*.

fryer, n. junges Brathuhn, ⁼er nt.

frying pan, n. Bratpfanne, -n f.

fuchsia, n. Fuchsie, -n f.

fuel, n. Brennstoff, -e m.

fugitive, n. Flüchtling, -e m.

fugue, n. Fuge, -n f.

fulcrum, n. Drehpunkt, -e m.

fulfill, vb. erfül'len.

fulfillment, n. Erfül'lung, -en f.

full, adj. voll.

full dress, n. Frack, ⁼e m.; Gala-Uniform, -en f.

fullness, n. Fülle f.

fully, adv. völlig.

fumble, vb. umher'tappen.

fume, 1. n. Dampf, ⁼e m., Dunst, ⁼e m. 2. vb. dampfen, dunsten; **(fig.)** wüten.

fumigate, vb. aus-räuchern.

fumigator, n. Räucherapparat, -e m.

fun, n. Vergnü'gen nt., Spaß m., Jux m.

function, 1. n. Funktion', -en f. 2. vb. funktionie'ren.

functional, adj. sachlich.

fund, n. Fond, -s m.

fundamental, adj. grundlegend.

funeral, n. Begräb'nis, -se nt., Beer'digung, -en f.

funereal, adj. düster.

fungicide, n. Pilzvernichtungsmittel, - nt.

fungus, n. Fungus, - m.

funnel, n. Trichter, - m.; **(smoke-stack)** Schornstein, -e m.

funny, adj. komisch, drollig.

fur, n. Pelz, -e m.

furious, adj. wütend.

furlough, n. Urlaub, -e m.

furnace, n. Ofen, ⁼ m.

furnish, vb. möblie'ren.

furnishings, n.pl. Ausstattung, -en f.

furniture, n. Möbel pl.

furor, n. Aufsehen nt.

furrier, n. Pelzhändler, - m.

furrow, n. Furche, -n f.

furry, adj. pelzartig.

further, 1. vb. fördern. 2. adj. weiter, ferner.

furtherance, n. Förderung, -en f.

furthermore, adv. ausserdem, überdies'.

fury, n. Wut f.; Zorn m.; (mythology) Furie, -n f.

fuse, 1. n. (elec.) Sicherung, -en f.; (explosives) Zünder, - m. 2. vb. verschmel'zen*.

fuselage, n. Rumpf, *e m.

fusillade, n. Gewehr'feuer nt.

fusion, n. Verschmel'zung, -en f.; Fusion', -en f.

fuss, n. Aufheben nt., Umstand, *e m.

fussy, adj. umständlich, genau', betu'lich.

futile, adj. vergeb'lich, nutzlos.

futility, n. Nutzlosigkeit f.

future, 1. n. Zukunft f. 2. adj. zukünftig.

futurity, n. Zukunft f.

fuzz, n. Flaum m.

fuzzy, adj. flaumig.

G

gab, vb. schwatzen.

gabardine, n. Gabardine m.

gable, n. Giebel, - m.

gadget, n. Vorrichtung, -en f.

gag, 1. n. Knebel, - m.; (joke) Witz, -e m. 2. vb. knebeln.

gaiety, n. Ausgelassenheit f.

gain, 1. n. Gewinn', -e m. 2. vb. gewin'nen*.

gainful, adj. einträglich.

gait, n. Gang, -e m.

gala, adj. festlich.

galaxy, n. Milchstrasse, -n f.

gale, n. Sturm, *e m.

gall, 1. n. (bile) Galle, -n f.; (insolence) Unverschämtheit, -en f. 2. vb. ärgern.

gallant, adj. aufmerksam, galant'.

gallantry, n. Höflichkeit, -en f., Galanterie', -i'en f.

gall bladder, n. Gallenblase, -n f.

gallery, n. Galerie', -i'en f.

galley, n. (ship) Galee're, -n f.; (kitchen) Kombü'se, -n f.; (typogr.) Setzschiff, -e nt.

Gallic, adj. gallisch.

gallivant, vb. bummeln.

gallon, n. Gallo'ne, -n f.

gallop, 1. n. Galopp', -s m. 2. vb. galoppie'ren.

gallows, n.pl. Galgen, - m.

gallstone, n. Gallenstein, -e m.

galore, adv. in Hülle un Fülle.

galosh, n. Überschuh, -e m.

gamble, 1. n. (game) Glücksspiel n.; (risk) Risiko, -s nt. 2. vb. um Geld spielen; riskie'ren.

gambler, n. Glücksspieler, - m.

gambling, n. Glücksspiel, -e nt.

game, 1. n. Spiel, -e nt.; (hunting) Wild nt., Wildbret nt. 2. adj. beherzt'; (lame) lahm.

gander, n. Gänserich, -e m.

gang, n. Bande, -n f.

gangplank, n. Laufplanke, -n f.

gangrene, n. Gangrän', -e nt.

gangrenous, adj. gangränös', brandig.

gangster, n. Gangster, - m.

gangway, n. Laufplanke, -n f.

gap, n. Lücke, -n f.; Spalte, -n f.

garage, n. Gara'ge, -n f.

garb, n. Gewand', *er nt.

garbage, n. Abfall, *e m., Müll m.

garble, vb. entstel'len, verzer'ren.

garden, n. Garten, * m.

gardener, n. Gärtner, - m.

gardenia, n. Garde'nia, -ien f.

gargle, vb. gurgeln.

gargoyle, n. Wasserspeier, - m.

garish, adj. grell.

garland, n. Girlan'de, -n f.

garlic, n. Knoblauch m.

garment, n. Kleidungsstück, -e nt.

garner, vb. auf-speichern.

garnet, n. Granat', -e m.

garnish, vb. garnie'ren.

garret, n. Dachstube, -n f.

garrison, n. Garnison', -en f.

garrulous, adj. schwatzhaft.

garter, n. Strumpfband, -er nt.; Hosenband, -er nt.; Sockenhalter, - m.

gas, n. Gas, -e nt.; (gasoline) Benzin' nt.

gaseous, adj. gasförmig.

gash, 1. n. klaffende Wunde, -n f. **2.** vb. eine tiefe Wunde schlagen*.

gasket, n. (Hanf-)Dichtung f.

gas mask, n. Gasmaske, -n f.

gasoline, n. Benzin' nt.

gasp, vb. keuchen; nach Luft schnappen.

gastric, adj. gastrisch.

gastritis, n. Magenschleimhautentzündung, -en f.

gastronomical, adj. gastrono'misch.

gate, n. Tor, -e nt., Pforte, -n f.

gateway, n. Einfahrt, -en f., Tor, -e nt.

gather, vb. sammeln, pflücken; (infer) schließen*.

gathering, n. Versamm'lung, -en f.

gaudiness, n. auffälliger Protz m.

gaudy, adj. protzig.

gauge, 1. n. (measurement) Maß, -e nt.; (instrument) Messer, - m., Zeiger, - m.; (railway) Spurweite, -n f. **2.** vb. ab·messen*.

gaunt, adj. hager.

gauntlet, n. Handschuh, -e m.

gauze, n. Gaze, -n f.

gavel, n. Hammer, - m.

gawky, adj. linkisch.

gay, adj. fröhlich, heiter.

gaze, vb. starren.

gazelle, n. Gazel'le, -n f.

gazette, n. Zeitung, -en f.

gazetteer, n. geogra'phisches Namensverzeichnis, -se, nt.

gear, n. Zahnrad, -er nt.; (auto) Gang, -e m.; (equipment) Zeug nt.

gearing, n. Getrie'be, - nt.

gearshift, n. Schalthebel, m.

gelatin, n. Gelati'ne, -n f.

gelatinous, adj. gallertartig.

geld, vb. kastrie'ren.

gelding, n. Wallach, -e m.

gem, n. Edelstein, -e m.

gender, n. Geschlecht', -er nt., Genus, -nera nt.

gene, n. Gen, -e nt.

genealogical, adj. genealo'gisch.

genealogy, n. Genealogie', -i'en f.

general, 1. n. General', -e m. **2.** adj. allgemein.

generality, n. Allgemein'heit, -en f.

generalization, n. Verallgemei'nerung, -en f.

generalize, vb. verallgemei'nern.

generally, adv. (in general) im allgemei'nen; (usually) gewöhn'lich, meistens.

generate, vb. erzeu'gen.

generation, n. Generation', -en f.

generator, n. Genera'tor, -o'ren m.

generic, adj. Gattungs- (cpds.).

generosity, n. Großzügigkeit f.

generous, adj. großzügig, freigebig.

genetic, adj. gene'tisch.

genetics, n. Verer'bungslehre f.

Geneva, n. Genf nt.

genial, adj. freundlich, froh.

geniality, n. Freundlichkeit f.

genital, adj. genital'.

genitals, n. Geschlechts'organe pl.

genitive, n. Genitiv, -e m.

genius, n. Genie', -s nt.

genocide, n. Völkermord m.

genre, n. Genre, -s nt.

genteel, adj. vornehm.

gentile, 1. n. Nichtjude, -n, -n m. **2.** adj. nichtjüdisch.

gentility, n. Vornehmheit f.

gentle, adj. sanft, mild.

gentleman, *n.* Gentleman, -men *m.*

gentleness, *n.* Sanftheit *f.*

gentry, *n.* niederer Adel *m.*

genuflect, *vb.* das Knie beugen.

genuine, *adj.* echt.

genuineness, *n.* Echtheit *f.*

genus, *n.* Geschlecht', -er *nt.*, Gattung, -en *f.*

geographer, *n.* Geograph', -en, -en *m.*

geographical, *adj.* geogra'phisch.

geography, *n.* Geographie' *f.*, Erdkunde *f.*

geometric, *adj.* geome'trisch.

geometry, *n.* Geometrie' *f.*

geopolitics, *n.* Geopolitik' *f.*

geranium, *n.* Gera'nie, -n *f.*

germ, *n.* Keim, -e *m.*; Bakte'rie, -n *f.*

German, **1.** *n.* Deutsch- *m.&f.* **2.** *adj.* deutsch.

germane, *adj.* zur Sache gehö'rig.

Germanic, *adj.* germa'nisch.

German measles, *n.* Röteln *pl.*

Germany, *n.* Deutschland *nt.*

germicide, *n.* keimtötendes Mittel, - *nt.*

germinal, *adj.* Keim- (*cpds.*).

germinate, *vb.* keimen.

gestate, *vb.* aus·tragen*.

gestation, *n.* Gestation', -en *f.*

gesticulate, *vb.* gestikulie'ren.

gesticulation, *n.* Gebär'de, -n *f.*

gesture, *n.* Gebär'de, -n *f.*, Geste, -n *f.*

get, *vb.* (*receive*) bekom'men*, kriegen; (*fetch*) holen; (*become*) werden*; (*arrive*) an·kommen*; (**g. to**) hin·kommen*; (**g. up**) auf·stehen*; (**g. in**) ein·steigen*; (**g. out**) aus·steigen*.

geyser, *n.* Geiser, - *m.*

ghastly, *adj.* grauenhaft.

ghost, *n.* Geist, -er *m.*, Gespenst', -er *nt.*

giant, **1.** *n.* Riese, -n, -n *m.* **2.** *adj.* riesenhaft.

gibberish, *n.* Kauderwelsch *nt.*

gibbon, *n.* Gibbon, -s *m.*

giblets, *n.* Geflü'gelklein *nt.*

giddy, *adj.* schwindlig.

gift, *n.* Gabe, -n *f.*, Geschenk', -e *nt.*

gifted, *adj.* begabt'.

gigantic, *adj.* riesenhaft.

giggle, *vb.* kichern.

gigolo, *n.* Eintänzer, - *m.*

gild, *vb.* vergol'den.

gill, *n.* Kieme, -n *f.*

gilt, *n.* Vergol'dung, -en *f.*

gimlet, *n.* Handbohrer, - *m.*

gin, *n.* Gin, -s *m.*; (*cotton*) Entker'nungsmaschine, -n *f.*

ginger, *n.* Ingwer *m.*

gingerly, *adv.* sachte.

gingham, *n.* Kattun', -e *m.*

giraffe, *n.* Giraf'fe, -n *f.*

gird, *vb.* gürten.

girder, *n.* Träger, - *m.*

girdle, *n.* Gürtel, - *m.*; Strumpfbandgürtel, - *m.*

girl, *n.* Mädchen, - *nt.*

girlish, *adj.* mädchenhaft.

girth, *n.* Umfang, ⸚e *m.*

gist, *n.* Kern, -e *m.*

give, *vb.* geben*.

given name, *n.* Vorname(n), - *m.*

gizzard, *n.* Geflü'gelmagen, ⸚ *m.*

glacé, *adj.* glaciert'.

glacial, *adj.* Eis- (*cpds.*).

glacier, *n.* Gletscher, - *m.*

glad, *adj.* froh.

gladden, *vb.* erfreu'en.

gladiolus, *n.* Schwertlilie, -n *f.*

gladly, *adv.* gern.

gladness, *n.* Freude, -n *f.*

glamor, *n.* äußerer Glanz *m.*; beste'chende Schönheit *f.*

glamorous, *adj.* äußerlich beste'chend, blendend.

glance, **1.** *n.* Blick, -e *m.* **2.** *vb.* blicken.

gland, *n.* Drüse, -n *f.*

glandular, *adj.* Drüsen- (*cpds.*).

glare, **1.** *n.* blendendes Licht *nt.* **2.** *vb.* blenden; (*look*) starren; (**g. at**) an·starren.

glaring, *adj.* grell.

glass, *n.* Glas, ⸚er *m.*

lasses, *n.pl.* Brille, -n *f.*

lassware, *n.* Glasware, -n *f.*

lassy, *adj.* glasig.

laucoma, *n.* Glaukom', -e *nt.*

laze, 1. *n.* Glasur', -en *f.* 2. *vb.* glasie'ren.

lazier, *n.* Glaser, - *m.*

leam, 1. *n.* Lichtstrahl, -en *m.* 2. *vb.* strahlen, glänzen.

lee, *n.* Freude, -n *f.*

leeful, *adj.* fröhlich.

len, *n.* enges Tal, -er *nt.*

lib, *adj.* zungenfertig.

lide, 1. *n.* Gleitflug, -e *m.* 2. *vb.* gleiten*.

lider, *n.* Segelflugzeug, -e *nt.*

limmer, 1. *n.* Schimmer, - *m.* 2. *vb.* schimmern.

limpse, *n.* flüchtiger Blick, -e *m.*

lint, *n.* Lichtschimmer, - *m.*

listen, *vb.* glänzen.

litter, 1. *n.* Glanz *m.* 2. *vb.* glitzern.

loat, *vb.* sich weiden; schadenfroh sein*.

lobal, *adj.* global'.

lobe, *n.* Erdkugel, -n *f.*; Globus, -se *m.*

lobular, *adj.* kugelförmig.

lobule, *n.* Kügelchen, - *nt.*

loom, *n.* Düsterheit *f.*; (*fig.*) Trübsinn *m.*

loomy, *adj.* düster; trübsinnig.

lorification, *n.* Verherr'lichung *f.*

lorify, *vb.* verherr'lichen.

lorious, *adj.* ruhmvoll, glorreich.

lory, *n.* Ruhm *m.*; Herrlichkeit *f.*

loss, *n.* Glanz *m.*

lossary, *n.* Glossar', -e *nt.*

lossy, *adj.* glänzend.

love, *n.* Handschuh, -e *m.*

low, 1. *n.* Glühen *nt.* 2. *vb.* glühen.

lucose, *n.* Traubenzucker *m.*

lue, 1. *n.* Leim *m.* 2. *vb.* leimen.

lum, *adj.* mürrisch.

lumness, *n.* Mürrischkeit *f.*

glut, 1. *n.* Überfluß *m.* 2. *vb.* übersät'tigen.

glutinous, *adj.* leimig.

glutton, *n.* Vielfraß, -e *m.*

gluttonous, *adj.* gefrä'ßig.

glycerine, *n.* Glyzerin' *nt.*

gnarled, *adj.* knorrig.

gnash, *vb.* knirschen.

gnat, *n.* Schnake, -n *f.*

gnaw, *vb.* knabbern.

go, *vb.* gehen*; (*become*) werden*; (g. without) entbeh'ren.

goad, 1. *n.* Treibstock, -e *m.* 2. *vb.* an'stacheln.

goal, *n.* Ziel, -e *nt.*; (*soccer*) Tor, -e *nt.*

goal-keeper, *n.* Torwart, -er *m.*

goat, *n.* Ziege, -n *f.*, Geiß, -en *f.*; (billy g.) Ziegenbock, -e *m.*

goatee, *n.* Spitzbart, -e *m.*

goatskin, *n.* Ziegenleder *nt.*

gobble, *vb.* verschlin' gen*.

go-between, *n.* Vermitt'ler, - *m.*

goblet, *n.* Kelchglas, -er *nt.*

goblin, *n.* Kobold, -e *m.*

god, *n.* Gott, -er *m.*

godchild, *n.* Patenkind, -er *nt.*

goddess, *n.* Göttin, -nen *f.*

godfather, *n.* Patenonkel, - *m.*

godless, *adj.* gottlos.

godlike, *adj.* gottähnlich.

godly, *adj.* göttlich.

godmother, *n.* Patentante, -n *f.*

godsend, *n.* Gottesgabe, -n *f.*

Godspeed, *n.* Lebewohl' *nt.*

go-getter, *n.* Draufgänger, - *m.*

goiter, *n.* Kropf, -e *m.*

gold, *n.* Gold *nt.*

golden, *adj.* golden.

goldfinch, *n.* Stieglitz, -e *m.*

goldfish, *n.* Goldfisch, -e *m.*

goldsmith, *n.* Goldschmied, -e *m.*

golf, *n.* Golf *nt.*

gondola, *n.* Gondel, -n *f.*

gondolier, *n.* Gondelführer, - *m.*

gone, *adv.* weg.

gong, *n.* Gong, -s *m.*

gonorrhea, *n.* Tripper *m.*

good, *adj.* gut (besser, best-).

goods, *n.pl.* Waren *pl.*

good-by, *interj.* auf Wiedersehen.

Good Friday, *n.* Karfrei'tag *m.*

good-hearted, *adj.* gutherzig.

good-humored, *adj.* gutmütig.

good-looking, *adj.* gutaussehend.

good-natured, *adj.* gutmütig.

goodness, *n.* Güte *f.*

good will, *n.* Wohlwollen *nt.*

goose, *n.* Gans. ⸗e *f.*

gooseberry, *n.* Stachelbeere, -n *f.*

gooseneck, *n.* Gänsehals, ⸗e *m.*

goose step, *n.* Stechschritt *m.*

gore, **1.** *n.* Blut *nt.* **2.** *vb.* aufspießen.

gorge, *n.* (*anatomical*) Gurgel, -n *f.*; (*ravine*) Schlucht, -en *f.*

gorgeous, *adj.* prachtvoll.

gorilla, *n.* Goril'la, -s *m.*

gory, *adj.* blutig.

gospel, *n.* Evange'lium, -ien *nt.*

gossamer, **1.** *n.* hauchdünner Stoff *m.* **2.** *adj.* hauchdünn.

gossip, **1.** *n.* Klatsch *m.* **2.** *vb.* klatschen.

Gothic, **1.** *n.* Gotik *f.* **2.** *adj.* gotisch.

gouge, **1.** *n.* Hohleisen, - *nt.* **2.** *vb.* aushöhlen.

gourd, *n.* Kürbis, -se *m.*

gourmand, *n.* Vielfraß, ⸗e *m.*

gourmet, *n.* Feinschmecker, - *m.*

govern, *vb.* regie'ren.

governess, *n.* Erzie'herin, -nen *f.*

government, *n.* Regie'rung, -en *f.*

governmental, *adj.* Regie'rungs- (*cpds.*).

governor, *n.* Gouverneur', -e *m.*

governorship, *n.* Gouverneurs'amt, ⸗er *nt.*

gown, *n.* Kleid, -er *nt.*

grab, *vb.* greifen*.

grace, *n.* Anmut *f.*; (*mercy*) Gnade *f.*

graceful, *adj.* anmutig.

graceless, *adj.* unbeholfen.

gracious, *adj.* gnädig, gütig.

grade, **1.** *n.* Grad, -e *m.* Rang, ⸗e *m.*; (*mark*) Zensur' -en *f.*; (*class*) Klasse, -n *f.*; (*rise*) Steigung, -en *f.* **2.** *vb.* bewer'ten; (*smooth*) ebnen.

grade crossing, *n.* Bahnübergang, ⸗e *m.*

gradual, *adj.* allmäh'lich.

graduate, *vb.* graduie'ren.

graft, **1.** *n.* Beste'chung, -en *f.*, Korruption' *f.* **2.** *vb.* (*bot.*) propfen.

grail, *n.* Gral *m.*

grain, *n.* Körnchen, - *nt.*; (*wheat, etc.*) Getrei'de *nt.*; (*wood*) Maserung, -en *f.*

gram, *n.* Gramm, - *nt.*

grammar, *n.* Gramma'tik, -en *f.*

grammar school, *n.* Grundschule, -n *f.*

grammatical, *adj.* gramma'tisch.

gramophone, *n.* Grammophon', -e *nt.*

granary, *n.* Kornspeicher, - *m.*

grand, *adj.* großartig.

grandchild, *n.* Enkelkind, -er *nt.*

granddaughter, *n.* Enkelin, -nen *f.*

grandeur, *n.* Erha'benheit *f.*

grandfather, *n.* Großvater, ⸗ *m.*

grandiloquent, *adj.* schwülstig.

grandiose, *adj.* grandios'.

grandmother, *n.* Großmutter, ⸗ *f.*

grandparents, *n. pl* Großeltern *pl.*

grandson, *n.* Enkel, - *m.*

grandstand, *n.* Tribü'ne, -n *f.*

granite, *n.* Granit' *m.*

grant, **1.** *n.* finanziel'le Beihilfe, -n *f.*; Stipen'dium, -en *nt.* **2.** *vb.* gewäh'ren.

granular, *adj.* körnig.

granulated sugar, *n.* Streuzucker *m.*

granulation, *n.* Körnung *f.*

granule, *n.* Körnchen *nt.*

grape, *n.* Weintraube, -n *f.*

grapefruit, *n.* Pampelmu'se, -n *f.*

grapevine, *n.* Weinstock, ⸚e *m.*; (*rumor*) Amtstratsch *m.*

graph, *n.* graphische Darstellung, -en *f.*, Diagramm', -e *nt.*

graphic, *adj.* graphisch.

graphite, *n.* Graphit', -e *m.*

graphology, *n.* Graphologie' *f.*

grapple, 1. *n.* Enterhaken, - *m.* **2.** *vb.* packen; ringen*.

grasp, 1. *vb.* n. Griff, -e *m.*; (*mental*) Fassungsvermögen *nt.* **2.** *vb.* ergrei'fen*.

grasping, *adj.* habgierig.

grass, *n.* Gras, ⸚er *nt.*; (*lawn*) Rasen, - *m.*

grasshopper, *n.* Heuschrecke, -n *f.*

grassy, *adj.* grasartig.

grate, 1. *n.* Rost *m.* **2.** *vb.* (*cheese, etc.*) reiben*, (*irritate*) irritie'ren.

grateful, *adj.* dankbar.

grater, *n.* Reibe, -n *f.*

gratify, *vb.* befrie'digen.

grating, *n.* Gitter, - *nt.*

gratis, *adj.* gratis.

gratitude, *n.* Dankbarkeit, -en *f.*

gratuitous, *adj.* unentgeltlich.

gratuity, *n.* Geschenk', -e *nt.*; (*tip*) Trinkgeld, -er *nt.*

grave, 1. *n.* Grab, ⸚er *nt.* **2.** *adj.* schwerwiegend.

gravel, *n.* Kies *m.*

graveyard, *n.* Friedhof, ⸚e *m.*

gravitate, *vb.* angezogen werden*; gravitie'ren.

gravity, *n.* Schwerkraft *f.*; Ernst *m.*

gravure, *n.* Gravü're, -n *f.*

gravy, *n.* Soße, -n *f.*

gray, *adj.* grau.

graze, *vb.* grasen, weiden.

grease, 1. *n.* Fett, -e *nt.* **2.** *vb.* fetten; schmieren.

greasy, *adj.* fettig, schmierig.

great, *adj.* groß (größer, größt-).

greatness, *n.* Größe, -n *f.*

Greece, *n.* Griechenland *nt.*

greed, *n.* Gier *f.*, Habsucht *f.*

greediness, *n.* Gier *f.*, Habsucht *f.*

greedy, *adj.* gierig, habsüchtig.

Greek, 1. *n.* Grieche, -n, -n *m.* **2.** *adj.* griechisch.

green, *adj.* grün.

greenery, *n.* Grün *nt.*

greenhouse, *n.* Gewächs'haus, ⸚er *nt.*, Treibhaus, ⸚er *nt.*

greet, *vb.* begrü'ßen.

greeting, *n.* Gruß, ⸚e *m.*

gregarious, *adj.* gesel'lig.

grenade, *n.* Grana'te, -n *f.*

grenadine, *n.* Granat'apfellikör *m.*

greyhound, *n.* Windhund, -e *m.*

grid, *n.* Gitter, - *nt.*; (*elec.*) Stromnetz, -e *nt.*

griddle, *n.* Bratpfanne, -n *f.*

grief, *n.* Kummer *m.*

grievance, *n.* Beschwer'de, -n *f.*

grieve, *vb.* (*intr.*) trauern; (*tr.*) betrü'ben.

grievous, *adj.* schmerzlich; (*serious*) schwerwiegend.

grill, *n.* Grill, -s *m.*

grim, *adj.* grimmig.

grimace, *n.* Grimas'se, -n *f.*, Fratze, -n *f.*

grime, *n.* Ruß *m.*

grimy, *adj.* schmutzig.

grin, 1. *n.* Grinsen *nt.* **2.** *vb.* grinsen.

grind, *vb.* mahlen*.

grindstone, *n.* Schleifstein, -e *m.*

grip, 1. *n.* Griff, -e *m.*; (*suitcase*) Koffer, - *m.* **2.** *vb.* fassen.

gripe, 1. *n.* (*complaint*) Ärgernis, -se *nt.* **2.** *vb.* (*complain*) nörgeln.

grippe, *n.* Grippe, -n *f.*

gristle, *n.* Knorpel, - *m.*

grit, 1. *n.* Kies *m.*; (*courage*) Mut *m.* **2.** *vb.* (**g. one's teeth**) die Zähne zusammen·beissen*.

grizzled, adj. grau.

groan, 1. n. Stöhnen nt. **2.** vb. stöhnen.

grocer, n. Kolonial'warenhändler, - m.

groceries, n.pl. Kolonial'waren pl.

grocery store, n. Kolonial'warengeschäft, -e nt., Lebensmittelgeschäft, -e nt.

grog, n. Grog, -s m.

groggy, adj. benom'men; (be g.) taumeln.

groin, n. Leistengegend f.

groom, n. Reitknecht, -e m.; (footman) Diener, - m.; (bridegroom) Bräutigam -e m.

groove, n. Rinne, -n f.

grope, vb. tappen.

gross, 1. n. Gros, -se nt. **2.** adj. grob(∗); (weight) brutto.

grossness, n. Kraßheit, -en f.

grotesque, adj. grotesk'.

grotto, n. Grotte, -n f.

grouch, 1. n. Griesgram, -e m. **2.** vb. verdrieß'lich sein∗.

ground, 1. n. Grund, ∗e m., Boden m.; Gebiet', -e nt. **2.** vb. (elec.) erden.

groundless, adj. grundlos.

groundwork, n. Grundlage, -n f.

group, 1. n. Gruppe, -n f. **2.** vb. gruppie'ren.

grouse, n. schottisches Schneehuhn, ∗er nt.

grove, n. Hain, -e m.

grovel, vb. kriechen∗, speichelleckerisch sein∗.

grow, vb. wachsen∗.

growl, vb. knurren.

grown, adj. erwach'sen.

grown-up, 1. n. Erwach'sen- m.&f. **2.** adj. erwach'sen.

growth, n. Wachstum nt.; (med.) Gewächs', -e nt.

grub, 1. n. Larve, -n f.; (food) Fressa'lien pl. **2.** vb. wühlen.

grudge, n. Groll m.

gruel, n. dünne Hafergrütze f.

gruesome, adj. schauerlich.

gruff, adj. bärbeißig.

grumble, vb. murren,

grumpy, adj. mürrisch.

grunt, 1. n. Grunzen, - nt. **2.** vb. grunzen.

guarantee, 1. n. Garantie', -i'en f. **2.** vb. garantie'ren.

guarantor, n. Bürge, -n, -n m.

guaranty, n. Sicherheit, -en f.; Bürgschaft, -en f.

guard, 1. n. Wache, -n f.; **2.** vb. bewa'chen.

guarded, adj. vorsichtig.

guardian, n. Vormund, -e m.

guerrilla, n. Partisan', (-en,) -en m.

guess, vb. raten∗.

guesswork, n. Raterei' f.

guest, n. Gast, ∗e m.

guidance, n. Leitung f., Führung f.

guide, 1. n. Führer, - m. **2.** vb. führen, leiten.

guidebook, n. Reiseführer, - m.

guidepost, n. Wegweiser, - m.

guild, n. Gilde, -n f.

guile, n. Arglist f.

guillotine, n. Guilloti'ne, -n f.

guilt, n. Schuld f.

guiltless, adj. schuldlos.

guilty, adj. schuldig.

guinea fowl, n. Perlhuhn, ∗er nt.

guinea pig, n. Meerschweinchen, - nt.

guise, n. Art, -en f.; (clothes) Aussehen nt.

guitar, n. Gitar're, -n f.

gulf, n. Golf, -e m.

gull, n. Möwe, -n f.

gullet, n. Kehle, -n f.

gullible, adj. leichtgläubig.

gully, n. Wasserrinne, -n f.

gulp, vb. schlucken.

gum, n. Gummi, -s nt.; (teeth) Zahnfleisch nt.; (chewing g.) Kaugummi, -s nt.

gummy, adj. gummiartig, klebrig.

gun, n. (small) Gewehr', -e nt.; (large) Geschütz', -e nt.

gunboat, n. Kano'nenboot, -e nt.

gunner, n. Kanonier', -e m.

gunpowder, n. Schießpulver nt.

gunshot, n. Schuß,-sse m.

gurgle, vb. gluckern.

gush, vb. hervor'quellen.

gusher, n. sprudelnde Petroleumquelle, -n f.

gusset, n. Zwickel, - m.

gust, n. Windstoß, -e m.

gustatory, adj. Geschmacks'- (cpds.).

gusto, n. Schwung m.

gusty, adj. windig.

guts, n. Eingeweide pl.; (courage) Mumm m.

gutter, n. (street) Rinnstein, -e m., Gosse,-n f.; (house) Dachtraufe, -n f.

guttural, adj. guttural'.

guy, n. Kerl, -e m.

guzzle, vb. saufen*.

gymnasium, n. Turnhalle, -n f.

gymnast, n. Turner, - m.

gymnastic, adj. gymnas'tisch.

gymnastics, n. Gymnas'tik f.

gynecologist, n. Frauenarzt, -e m., Gynäkolo'ge, -n -n m.

gynecology, n. Gynäkologie' f.

gypsum, n. Gips m.

gypsy, n. Zigeu'ner, - m.

gyrate, vb. kreiseln.

gyroscope, n. Kreiselkompaß, -sse m.

H

haberdashery, n. Geschäft' für Herrenartikel.

habit, n. Gewohn'heit, -en f.; Kleidung, -en f.

habitable, adj. bewohn'bar.

habitat, n. Wohnbereich, -e m.

habitual, adj. gewöhn'lich; Gewohn'heits- (cpds.).

habitué, n. Stammgast, -e m.

hack, 1. n. Droschke, -n f.;

(horse) Klepper, - m.   2. vb. hacken.

hacksaw, n. Metall'säge, -n f.

hag, n. Vettel, -n f.

haggard, adj. abgehärmt.

haggle, vb. feilschen.

Hague, n. Den Haag m.

hail, 1. n. Hagel m.   2. vb. hageln; (greet) begrü'ßen. 3. interj. heil!

hailstone, n. Hagelkorn, -er nt.

hailstorm, n. Hagelwetter, - nt.

hair, n. Haar, -e nt.

haircut, n. Haarschnitt, -e m.; (get a h.) sich die Haare schneiden lassen*.

hairdo, n. Frisur, -en f.

hairdresser, n. Friseur', - m., Friseu'se, -n f.

hairline, n. Haaransatz, -e m.; Haarstrich, -e m.

hairpin, n. Haarnadel, -n f.

hair-raising, adj. haarsträubend.

hairy, adj. haarig.

hale, adj. kräftig.

half, 1. n. Hälfte, -n f.   2. adj. halb.

half-breed, n. Mischling, -e m.

half-brother, n. Stiefbruder, - m.

half-hearted, adj. lauwarm.

half-mast, n. Halbmast m.

halfway, adv. halbwegs.

half-wit, n. Narr, -en -en m.

halibut, n. Heilbutt, -e m.

hall, n. (auditorium) Halle, -n f.; (large room) Saal, Säle m.; (corridor) Gang, -e m., Korridor, -e m.; (front h.) Diele, -n f.

hallmark, n. Stempel der Echtheit m.

hallow, vb. heiligen.

Halloween, n. Abend (m.) vor Allerhei'ligen.

hallucination, n. Wahnvorstellung, -en f., Halluzination', -en f.

hallway, n. Gang, -e m., Korridor, -e m.

halo, n. Heiligenschein, -e m.

halt, 1. n. Halt, -e m.; (fig.)

Stillstand *m.* **2.** *vb.* an-halten*. **3.** *interj.* haltl

halter, *n.* (*horse*) Halfter,-*nt.*; (*female clothing*) Oberteil eines Bade- oder Luftan-zuges.

halve, *vb.* halbie'ren.

ham, *n.* Schinken, - *m.*

Hamburg, *n.* Hamburg *nt.*

hamlet, *n.* Flecken, - *m.*

hammer, 1. *n.* Hammer,-*m.* **2.** *vb.* hämmern.

hammock, *n.* Hängematte,-n *f.*

hamper, 1. *n.* Korb,=e *m.* **2.** *vb.* hemmen.

hamstring, *vb.* lähmen.

hand, 1. *n.* Hand, =e *f.* **2.** *vb.* reichen.

handbag, *n.* Handtasche, -n *f.*

handbook, *n.* Handbuch, =er *nt.*

handcuffs, *n.pl.* Handschel-len *pl.*

handful, *n.* Handvoll *f.*

handicap, 1. *n.* Handikap, -s *nt.*; Hindernis, -se *nt.* **2.** *vb.* hemmen.

handicraft, *n.* Handwerk *nt.*

handiwork, *n.* Handarbeit, -en *f.*, handwork *nt.*

handkerchief, *n.* Taschen-tuch, =er *nt.*

handle, 1. *n.* Henkel, - *m.*, Griff, -e *m.* **2.** *vb.* hand-haben.

hand-made, *adj.* handgear-beitet.

handout, *n.* Almosen, - *nt.*

handsome, *adj.* gutaussehend; ansehnlich.

hand-rail, *n.* Gelän'der, - *nt.*

handwriting, *n.* Handschrift, -en *f.*

handy, *adj.* handlich; (skilled) geschickt'.

handy man, *n.* Fakto'tum, -s *nt.*

hangar, *n.* Schuppen, - *m.*

hanger, *n.* Aufhänger, - *m.*; (*clothes*) Kleiderbügel, - *m.*

hanger-on, *n.* Schmarot'zer, - *m.*

hanging, *n.* Hinrichtung (- en *f.*) durch Hängen.

hangman, *n.* Henker, - *m.*

hangnail, *n.* Niednagel, = *m.*

hangout, *n.* Stammlokal, -e *nt.*

hang-over, *n.* Kater, - *m.*, Katzenjammer *m.*

haphazardly, *adv.* aufs Gera-tewohl'.

happen, *vb.* sich ereig'nen, gesche'hen*, passie'ren.

happening, *n.* Ereig'nis, -se *nt.*

happiness, *n.* Glück *nt.*

happy, *adj.* glücklich.

happy-go-lucky, *adj.* sorg-los.

harangue, 1. *n.* marktschrei-erische Ansprache, -n *f.* **2.** *vb.* eine marktschreierische Ansprache halten*.

harass, *vb.* plagen.

harbinger, *n.* Vorbote, -n, -n *m.*

harbor, *n.* Hafen, = *m.*

hard, *adj.* (*not soft*) hart(=); (*not easy*) schwer, schwierig.

hard-boiled, *adj.* hartge-kocht; (*fig.*) abgebrüht.

hard coal, *n.* Anthrazit', -e *m.*

harden, *vb.* (*intr.*) hart wer-den*; (*tr.*) ab'härten.

hard-headed, *adj.* praktisch, realis'tisch.

hard-hearted, *adj.* hart-herzig.

hardly, *adv.* kaum.

hardness, *n.* Härte, -n *f.*

hardship, *n.* Not, =e *f.*; (*ex-ertion*) Anstrengung, -en *f.*

hardware, *n.* Eisenwaren *pl.*

hardwood, *n.* Hartholz *nt.*

hardy, *adj.* rüstig.

hare, *n.* Hase, -n, -n *m.*

harem, *n.* Harem, -s *m.*

hark, *vb.* horchen.

Harlequin, *n.* Harlekin, -e *m.*

harm, 1. *n.* Schaden, = *m.*; Unrecht, -e *nt.* **2.** *vb.* scha-den; Unrecht zu'fügen.

harmful, *adj.* schädlich.

harmless, *adj.* harmlos.

harmonic, *adj.* harmo'nisch.

harmonica, *n.* Harmo'nika, -s *f.*

harmonious, *adj.* harmo'nisch.

harmonize, *vb.* harmonisie'ren.

harmony, *n.* Harmonie' . -i'en *f.;* (*fig.*) Eintracht *f.*

harness, 1. *n.* Geschirr', -e *nt.* **2.** *vb.* ein·spannen.

harp, *n.* Harfe, -n *f.*

harpoon, 1. *n.* Harpu'ne, -n *f.* **2.** *vb.* harpunie'ren.

harpsichord, *n.* Spinett', -e *nt.*

harrow, 1. *n.* Egge, -n *f.* **2.** *vb.* eggen.

harry, *vb.* plündern; plagen.

harsh, *adj.* rauh; streng.

harshness, *n.* Rauheit *f.;* Strenge *f.*

harvest, 1. *n.* Ernte, -n *f.* **2.** *vb.* ernten.

hassock, *n.* geposterter Hocker, - *m.*

haste, *n.* Eile *f.*

hasten, *vb.* eilen; sich beei'len.

hasty, *adj.* eilig.

hat, *n.* Hut, ⸗e *m.*

hatch, 1. *n.* Luke, -n *f.* **2.** *vb.* aus·brüten.

hatchet, *n.* Beil, -e *nt.*

hate, 1. *n.* Haß *m.* **2.** *vb.* hassen.

hateful, *adj.* verhaßt'; widerlich.

hatred, *n.* Haß *m.*

haughtiness, *n.* Hochmut *m.*

haughty, *adj.* hochmütig.

haul, *vb.* schleppen.

haunch, *n.* Keule, -n *f.*

haunt, *vb.* verfol'gen.

have, *vb.* haben*; **(I h. it made)** ich lasse* es machen; **(I h. him make it)** ich lasse* ihn es machen.

haven, *n.* Hafen, ⸗ *m.;* Zufluchtsort, -e *m.*

havoc, *n.* Verwüs'tung, -en *f.*

hawk, *n.* Habicht, -e *m.*

hawser, *n.* Trosse, -n *f.*

hay, *n.* Heu *nt.*

hay fever, *n.* Heuschnupfen, - *m.*

hayloft, *n.* Heuboden, ⸗ *m.*

haystack, *n.* Heuhaufen, - *m.*

hazard, 1. *n.* Risiko. -s *nt.* **2.** *vb.* riskie'ren.

hazardous, *adj.* gewagt'.

haze, *n.* Dunst, ⸗e *m.*

hazel, *adj.* haselnußbraun.

hazelnut, *n.* Haselnuß, ⸗sse' *f.*

hazy, *adj.* dunstig, unklar.

he, *pron.* er.

head, *n.* Kopf, ⸗e *m.;* Haupt, ⸗er *nt.*

headache, *n.* Kopfschmerzen *pl.*

headfirst, *adv.* Hals über Kopf.

headgear, *n.* Kopfbedeckung, -en *f.*

heading, *n.* Überschrift, -en *f.,* Rubrik', -en *f.*

headlight, *n.* Scheinwerfer, - *m.*

headline, *n.* Überschrift, -en *f.;* (*newspaper*) Schlagzeile, -n *f.*

headlong, *adj.* überstürzt'.

headmaster, *n.* Schuldirektor, -en *m.*

head-on, *adv.* direkt von vorn.

headquarters, *n.pl.* Hauptquartier, -e *nt.*

headstone, *n.* (*grave*) Grabstein, -e *m.;* (*arch.*) Eckstein, -e *m.*

headstrong, *adj.* dickköpfig.

headwaters, *n.pl.* Quelle, -n *f.*

headway, *n.* **(make h.)** vorwärts kommen*.

heal, *vb.* heilen.

health, *n.* Gesund'heit, -en *f.*

healthful, *adj.* gesund'(⸗).

healthy, *adj.* gesund'(⸗).

heap, 1. *n.* Haufen, - *m.* **2.** *vb.* häufen.

hear, *vb.* hören.

hearing, *n.* Gehör' *nt.;* (*jur.*) Verhör', -e *nt.*

hearsay, *n.* Hörensagen *nt.*

hearse, *n.* Leichenwagen - *m.*

heart, *n.* Herz(en), - *nt.*

heartache, *n.* Herzenskummer *m.*

heart-breaking, *adj.* herzzerbrechend.

heartbroken, *adv.* tieftraurig.

heartburn, *n.* Sodbrennen, -*nt.*

heartfelt, *adj.* aufrichtig.

hearth, *n.* Kamin', -e *m.*

heartless, *adj.* herzlos.

heart-rending, *adj.* herzzerreißend.

heart-sick, *adj.* niedergeschlagen.

heart-to-heart, *adj.* freimütig.

hearty, *adj.* herzhaft.

heat, 1. *n.* Hitze *f.*, Wärme *f.*; (*house*) Heizung *f.* 2. *vb.* heiß machen, erhit'zen; (*house*) heizen.

heated, *adj.* geheizt'; (*fig.*) hitzig.

heater, *n.* Heizvorrichtung, -en *f.*

heathen, 1. *n.* Heide, -n, -n *m.* 2. *adj.* heidnisch.

heather, *n.* Heidekraut -, *f.*

heat-stroke, *n.* Hitzschlag, ⁼e *m.*

heat wave, *n.* Hitzewelle, -n *f.*

heave, *vb.* heben*; wogen; (*utter*) ausstoßen*.

heaven, *n.* Himmel - *m.*

heavenly, *adj.* himmlisch.

heavy, *adj.* schwer; (*fig.*) heftig.

heavyweight, *n.* Schwergewicht *nt.*

Hebrew, 1. *n.* Hebrä'er, - *m.* 2. *adj.* hebrä'isch.

hectic, *adj.* hektisch.

hedge, *n.* Hecke, -n *f.*

heckle, *vb.* hecheln.

hedgehog, *n.* Igel, - *m.*

hedge-hop, *vb.* (*mil.*) im Tiefflug an'fliegen*.

hedgerow, *n.* Baumhecke, -n *f.*

hedonism, *n.* Hedonis'mus *m.*

heed, *vb.* beach'ten.

heedless, *adj.* achtlos.

heel, *n.* (*shoes*) Absatz, ⁼e *m.*; (*foot*) Ferse, -n *f.*; (*scoundrel*) Schuft, -e *m.*

heifer, *n.* junge Kuh, ⁼e *f.*

height, *n.* Höhe, -n *f.*; (*person*) Größe, -n *f.*

heighten, *vb.* erhö'hen.

heinous, *adj.* abscheu'lich, verrucht'.

heir, *n.* Erbe, -n, -n *m.*

heirloom, *n.* Erbstück, -e *nt.*

helicopter, *n.* Hubschrauber, - *m.*

heliotrope, *n.* Heliotrop', -e *nt.*

helium, *n.* Helium *nt.*

hell, *n.* Hölle, -n *f.*

Hellenic, *adj.* helle'nisch.

Hellenism, *n.* Hellenis'mus *m.*

hello, *interj.* guten Tag (Morgen, Abend); (*call for attention*) hallo.

helm, *n.* Steuerruder, - *nt.*

helmet, *n.* Helm, -e *m.*

helmsman, *n.* Steuermann, ⁼er *m.*

help, 1. *n.* Hilfe *f.* 2. *vb.* helfen*.

helper, *n.* Helfer, - *m.*

helpful, *adj.* hilfreich, hilfsbereit.

helpfulness, *n.* Hilfsbereitschaft *f.*

helping, *n.* Portion', -en *f.*

helpless, *adj.* hilflos.

helter-skelter, *adv.* hol'terdiepol'ter.

hem, 1. *n.* Saum, ⁼e *m.* 2. *vb.* säumen.

hematite, *n.* Hematit', -e *m.*

hemisphere, *n.* Halbkugel, -n *f.*

hemlock, *n.* Schierling *m.*

hemoglobin, *n.* Hämoglobin' *nt.*

hemophilia, *n.* Bluterkrankheit *f.*

hemorrhage, *n.* Bluterguß, ⁼sse *m.*

hemorrhoid, *n.* Hämorrhoi'de, -n *f.*

hemp, *n.* Hanf *m.*

hemstitch, *n.* Hohlsaum, ⁼e *m.*

hen, *n.* Henne, -n *f.*

hence, *adv.* (*time*) von nun an; (*place*) von hier aus; (*therefore*) daher, deshalb, deswegen, also.

henceforth, *adv.* von nun an.

henchman, *n.* Trabant', -en, -en *m.*

henna, *n.* Henna *f.*

henpecked, *adj.* unter dem Pantof'fel stehend.

hepatic, *adj.* Leber- (*cpds.*).

hepatica, *n.* Hepa'tika, -ken *f.*

her, 1. *pron.* sie, ihr. **2.** *adj.* ihr, -, -e.

heraldic, *adj.* heral'disch.

heraldry, *n.* Wappenkunde *f.*

herb, *n.* Kraut, -er *nt.*, Gewürz'kraut, -er *nt.*

herculean, *adj.* herku'lisch.

herd, *n.* Herde, -n *f.*

here, *adv.* (*in this place*) hier; (*to this place*) hierher'; (**from h.**) hierhin'.

hereabout, *adv.* hier.

hereafter, 1. *n.* Leben (*nt.*) nach dem Tode. **2.** *adv.* in Zukunft.

hereby, *adv.* hiermit.

hereditary, *adj.* erblich.

heredity, *n.* Erblichkeit *f.*; Vererb'ung, -en *f.*

herein, *adv.* hierbei, hiermit.

heresy, *n.* Ketzerei', -en *f.*

heretic, 1. *n.* Ketzer, - *m.* **2.** *adj.* ketzerisch.

heritage, *n.* Erbe *nt.*

hermetic, *adj.* herme'tisch.

hermit, *n.* Einsiedler, - *m.*

hernia, *n.* Bruch, -e *m.*

hero, *n.* Held, -en, -en *m.*

heroic, *adj.* heldenhaft.

heroin, *n.* Heroin' *nt.*

heroine, *n.* Heldin, -nen *f.*

heroism, *n.* Heldenmut *m.*

heron, *n.* Reiher, - *m.*

herring, *n.* Hering, -e *m.*

herringbone, *n.* Heringsgräte, -n *f.*

hers, *pron.* ihrer, -s, -e.

hesitancy, *n.* Zöge:n *nt.*

hesitant, *adj.* zögernd.

hesitate, *vb.* zögern.

hesitation, *n.* Zögern *nt.*

heterodox, *adj.* heterodox'.

heterogeneous, *adj.* heterogen'.

hew, *vb.* hauen*.

hexagon, *n.* Sechseck, -e *nt.*

heyday, *n.* Blütezeit, -en *f.*

hi *interj.* hallo.

hibernate, *vb.* überwin'tern.

hibernation, *n.* Überwin'terung, -en *f.*

hibiscus, *n.* Hibis'kus, -ken *m.*

hiccup, *n.* Schluckauf *m.*

hickory, *n.* Hickoryholz, -er *nt.*

hide, 1. *n.* Haut, -e *f.*; Fell, -e *nt.* **2.** *vb.* verber'gen*, verste'cken; verheim'lichen.

hideous, *adj.* gräßlich.

hide-out, *n.* Schlupfwinkel, - *m.*

hierarchy, *n.* Rangordnung, -en *f.*, Hierachie', -i'en *f.*

hieroglyphic, *adj.* hieroglyphisch.

high, *adj.* hoch, hoh- (höher, höchst); (*tipsy*) beschwipst'.

highbrow, *adj.* intellektuell'.

high-handed, *adj.* anmaßend.

highland, *n.* Hochland, -er *nt.*

highlight, *n.* Höhepunkt, -e *m.*

highly, *adv.* höchst.

high-minded, *adj.* edelmütig.

Highness, *n.* Hoheit, -en *f.*

high school, *n.* höhere Schule, -n *f.*

high seas, *n.* hohe See *f.*

high-strung, *adj.* nervös, kribbelig.

high tide, *n.* Flut, -en *f.*

highway, *n.* Landstraße, -n *f.*, Chaussee', -n *f.*

hike, 1. *n.* Wanderung, -en *f.* **2.** *vb.* wandern.

hilarious, *adj.* ausgelassen.

hilarity, *n.* Ausgelassenheit *f.*

hill, *n.* Hügel, - *m.*

hilt, *n.* Heft, -e *nt.*

him, *pron.* ihn; ihm.

hind, *adj.* hinter-.

hinder, *vb.* hindern; verhindern.

hindmost, *adj.* letzt-, hinterst-.

hindrance, *n.* Hindernis, -se *nt.*; (*disadvantage*) Nachteil, -e *m.*

hinge, *n.* Scharnier, -e *nt.*

hint, 1. *n.* Wink, -e *m.* **2.** *vb.* an'deuten.

hinterland, *n.* Hinterland *nt.*

hip, *n.* Hüfte, -n *f.*

hippopotamus, *n.* Nilpferd, -e *nt.*

hire, *vb.* mieten; (*persons*) an·stellen.

his, 1. *adj.* sein, -, -e. **2.** *pron.* seiner, -es, -e.

hiss, *vb.* zischen.

historian, *n.* Histo'riker, - *m.*

historic, historical, *adj.* histo'risch.

history, *n.* Geschich'te, -en *f.*

hit, 1. *n.* Stoß, *-e* m., Schlag, *-e* m.; (*success*) Treffer, - *m.* **2.** *vb.* stoßen*, schlagen*, treffen*.

hitch, 1. *n.* (*knot*) Knoten, - *m.*; (*obstacle*) Hindernis, -se *nt.* **2.** *vb.* fest·machen.

hitchhike, *vb.* per Anhalter fahren*.

hive, *n.* Bienenstock, *-e* *m.*

hives, *n.* Nesselsucht *f.*

hoard, 1. *n.* Vorrat, *-e* *m.* **2.** *vb.* hamstern.

hoarse, *adj.* heiser.

hoax, *n.* Schabernack, - *e m.*

hobble, *vb.* humpeln.

hobby, *n.* Liebhaberei', -en *f.*

hobgoblin, *n.* Kobold, -e *m.*

hobnob with, *vb.* mit jemand auf vertrau'tem Füße stehen*.

hobo, *n.* Landstreicher, - *m.*

hockey, *n.* Hockey *nt.*

hocus-pocus, *n.* Ho'kuspo'kus *m.*

hod, *n.* Traggestell, -e *nt.*

hodgepodge, *n.* Mischmasch, -e *m.*

hoe, 1. *n.* Hacke,-n *f.* **2.** *vb.* hacken.

hog, *n.* Schwein, -e *nt.*

hogshead, *n.* Oxhoft, -e *nt.*

hoist, *vb.* hoch·ziehen*, hissen.

hold, 1. *n.* Halt *m.*; (*ship*) Laderaum*, *-e* *m.* **2.** *vb.* halten*; (*contain*) enthal'ten*; (**h. up**) auf·halten*.

holder, *n.* Halter, - *m.*

holdup, *n.* Überfall, *-e m.*

hole, *n.* Loch, *-er nt.*

holiday, *n.* Feiertag, -e *m.*, Festtag, -e *m.*

holiness, *n.* Heiligkeit *f.*

Holland, *n.* Holland *nt.*

hollow, *adj.* hohl.

holly, *n.* Stechpalme, -n *f.*

hollyhock, *n.* Malve, -n *f.*

holocaust, *n.* Brandopfer, - *nt.*, Großfeuer, - *nt.*

holster, *n.* Pisto'lenhalter, - *m.*

holy, *adj.* heilig.

holy day, *n.* Kirchenfeiertag, -e *m.*

Holy See, *n.* der Heilige Stuhl *m.*

Holy Spirit, *n.* der Heilige Geist *m.*

Holy Week, *n.* Karwoche *f.*

homage, *n.* Huldigung, -en *f.*

home, 1. *n.* Heim, -e *nt.*; (**h. town**) Heimat, -en *f.*; (*place of residence*) Wohnort, -e *m.*; (*house*) Haus, *-er nt.*; (*institution*) Heim, -e *nt.* **2.** *adv.* (*location*) zu Hause, daheim'; (*direction*) nach Hause, heim.

homeland, *n.* Heimatland, *-er nt.*

homeless, *adj.* heimatlos; obdachlos.

homelike, *adj.* behag'lich.

homely, *adj.* häßlich.

home-made, *adj.* selbstgefertigt.

home rule, *n.* Selbstverwaltung *f.*

homesick, be, *vb.* Heimweh haben*.

homesickness, *n.* Heimweh *nt.*

homestead, *n.* Fami'liensitz, -e *m.*

homeward, *adv.* heimwärts.

homework, *n.* Hausaufgabe, -n *f.*, Schularbeiten *pl.*

homicide, *n.* Mord, -e *m.*

homogeneous, *adj.* homogen'.

homogenize, *vb.* homogeni·sie'ren.

homonym, *n.* Homonym', -e *nt.*

homosexual, *adj.* homosexuell'.

hone, *n.* Wetzstein, -e *m.*

honest, *adj.* ehrlich, aufrichtig.

honesty, *n.* Ehrlichkeit, -en *f.*

honey, n. Honig m.
honey-bee, n. Honigbiene, -n f.
honeycomb, n. Honigwabe. -n f.
honeymoon, n. Hochzeitsreise, -n f., Flitterwochen pl.
honeysuckle, n. Geißblatt nt.
honor, 1. n. Ehre, -n f. 2. vb. ehren; honorie'ren.
honorable, adj. ehrbar, ehrenvoll.
honorary, adj. Ehren- (cpds.).
hood, n. Haube, -n f., (monk) Kapu'ze, -n f.
hoodlum, n. Rowdy, -s m.
hoodwink, vb. übertöl'peln.
hoof, n. Huf, -e nt.
hook, 1. n. Haken, - m. 2. vb. zu·haken; (catch) fangen*.
hoop, n. Reifen, - m.
hoot, vb. schreien*.
hop, 1. n. (plant) Hopfen m.; (jump) Sprung, -e m. 2. vb. hüpfen, springen*.
hope, 1. n. Hoffnung, -en f. 2. vb. hoffen.
hopeful, adj. hoffnungsvoll.
hopeless, adj. hoffnungslos.
hopelessness, n. Hoffnungslosigkeit f.
horde, n. Horde, -n f.
horizon, n. Horizont', -e m.
horizontal, adj. waagerecht, horizontal'.
hormone, n. Hormon', -e nt.
horn, n. Horn, -er nt.
hornet, n. Hornis'se, -n f.
horny, adj. hornig, hörnern.
horoscope, n. Horoskop', -e nt.
horrible, adj. grauenhaft.
horrid, adj. gräßlich.
horrify, vb. entset'zen.
horror, n. Grauen nt.
horse, n. Pferd, -e nt.
horseback, on, adv. zu Pferde.
horsehair, n. Roßhaar, -e nt.
horseman, n. Reiter, - m.
horsemanship, n. Reitkunst f.
horse-power, n. Pferdestärke, -n f.

horseradish, n. Meerrettich, -e m.
horseshoe, n. Hufeisen, - nt.
horticulture, n. Gartenbau m.
hose, n. (tube) Schlauch, -e m.; (stocking) Strumpf, -e m.
hosiery, n. Strumpfwaren pl.
hospitable, adj. gastfreundlich, gastfrei.
hospital, n. Krankenhaus, -er nt.
hospitality, n. Gastfreundschaft, Gastfreiheit f.
hospitalization, n. Krankenhausaufenthalt m.
hospitalize, vb. ins Krankenhaus stecken; (be h.d) im Krankenhaus liegen müssen*.
host, n. Gastgeber, - m.; (innkeeper) Wirt, -e m.; (crowd) Menge, -n f.; (Eucharist) Hostie f.
hostage, n. Geisel, -n m.
hostel, n. Herberge, -n f.; (youth h.) Jugendherberge, -n f.
hostess, n. Gastgeberin, -nen f.
hostile, adj. feindlich.
hostility, n. Feindseligkeit, -en f., Krieg, -e m.
hot, adj. heiß.
hotbed, n. Mistbeet, -e nt.; (fig.) Brutstätte, -n f.
hot dog, n. Bockwurst, -e f.
hotel, n. Hotel', -s nt.
hothouse, n. Treibhaus, -er nt.
hound, n. Hund, -e m.
hour, n. Stunde, -n f.
hourglass, n. Stundenglas, -er nt.
hourly, adj. stündlich.
house, n. Haus, -er nt.
housefly, n. Stubenfliege, -n f.
household, n. Haushalt, -e m.
housekeeper, n. Haushälterin, -nen f.
housekeeping, n. Haushaltung f.
housemaid, n. Hausmädchen. - nt.

housewife, n. Hausfrau, -en f.

housework, n. Hausarbeit, -en f.

hovel, n. Hütte, -n f.

hover, vb. schweben.

how, adv. wie.

however, 1. conj. aber, doch, jedoch'. 2. adv. wie . . . auch.

howitzer, n. Haubit'ze, -n f.

howl, 1. n. Gebrüll' nt. 2. vb. brüllen.

hub, n. Nabe, -n f.; (fig.) Mittelpunkt, -e m.

hubbub, n. Tumult', -e m.

huckleberry, n. Heidelbeere, -n f.

huddle, vb. zusam'men-kauern, sich zusam'men-drängen.

hue, n. Färbung, -en f.

hug, 1. n. Umar'mung, -en f. 2. vb. umar'men.

huge, adj. sehr groß, unge-heuer.

hull, n. Hülse, -n f.; (fruit) Schale, -n f.; (ship) Rumpf, ⁓e m.

hum, 1. n. (people) Gemur'mel nt.; (insects) Summen nt. 2. vb. murmeln; summen.

human, adj. menschlich.

humane, adj. human', menschlich.

humanism, n. Humanis'mus m.

humanitarian, adj. mensch-enfreundlich.

humanity, n. (mankind) Menschheit f.; (humaneness) Menschlichkeit f.

humble, adj. demütig, be-schei'den.

humbug, n. Schwindel m., Quatsch m.

humdrum, adj. langweilig, eintönig.

humid, adj. feucht.

humidity, n. Feuchtigkeit f.

humidor, n. Tabakstopf, ⁓e m.

humiliate, vb. demütigen.

humiliation, n. Demüti-gung, -en f.

humility, n. Demut f.

humor, n. Humor' m.; (mood) Laune, -n f.

humorist, n. Humorist', -en, -en m.

humorous, adj. humor'voll, witzig.

hump, n. Buckel, - m., Höcker, - m.

hunch, 1. n. Höcker, - m., Buckel, - m.; (suspicion) Ahnung, -en f., Riecher, - m. 2. vb. krümmen.

hunchback, 1. n. Buckel m.; (person) Bucklig- m.&f. 2. adj. bucklig.

hundred, num. hundert.

hundredth, 1. adj. hun-dertst-. 2. n. Hundertstel, -nt.

Hungarian, 1. n. Ungar, -n, -n m. 2. adj. ungarisch.

Hungary, n. Ungarn nt.

hunger, n. Hunger m.

hungry, adj. hungrig.

hunt, 1. n. Jagd, -en f. 2. vb. jagen.

hunter, n. Jäger, - m.

hunting, n. Jagd, -en f.

hurdle, 1. n. Hürde, -n f. 2. vb. hinü'berspringen*.

hurl, vb. schleudern.

hurrah, interj. (h. for him) er lebe hoch!

hurricane, n. Orkan', -e m.

hurry, vb. eilen, sich beei'len.

hurt, vb. weh tun*, verlet'zen.

hurtful, adj. schädlich.

husband, n. Mann, ⁓er m., Gatte, -n -n m.

husbandry, n. Lantwirt-schaft f.; (management) Wirt-schaften nt.

hush, 1. n. Stille f. 2. vb. zum Schweigen bringen*. 3. interj. still!

husk, 1. n. Hülse, -n f. 2. vb. enthül'sen.

husky, adj. (hoarse) rauh; (strong) stark(⁓).

hustle, vb. rührig sein*.

hut, n. Hütte, -n f.

hyacinth, n. Hyazin'the, -n f.

hybrid, adj. hybrid'.

hydrangea, n. Horten'sie, -n f.

hydrant, *n.* Hydrant', -en, -en *m.*

hydraulic, *adj.* hydrau'lisch.

hydrochloric acid, *n.* Salzsäure *f.*

hydroelectric, *adj.* hydroelek'trisch.

hydrogen, *n.* Wasserstoff *m.*

hydrogen bomb, *n.* Wasserstoffbombe, -n *f.*

hydrophobia, *n.* krankhafte Wasserscheu *f.*

hydroplane, *n.* Wasserflugzeug, -e *nt.*

hydrotherapy, *n.* Hydrotherapie' *f.*

hyena, *n.* Hyä'ne, -n *f.*

hygiene, *n.* Hygie'ne *f.*

hygienic, *adj.* hygie'nisch.

hymn, *n.* Hymne, -n *f.*, Choral', -e *m.*, Kirchenlied, -er *nt.*

hymnal, *n.* Gesang'buch, -er *nt.*

hyperacidity, *n.* Hyperacidität', *f.*

hyperbole, *n.* Hyper'bel, -n *f.*

hypercritical, *adj.* überkritisch.

hypersensitive, *adj.* überempfindlich.

hypertension, *n.* übernormaler Blutdruck *m.*

hyphen, *n.* Bindestrich, -e *m.*

hyphenate, *vb.* trennen.

hypnosis, *n.* Hypno'se, -n *f.*

hypnotic, *adj.* hypno'tisch.

hypnotism, *n.* Hypnotis'mus *m.*

hypnotize, *vb.* hypnotisie'ren.

hypochondria, *n.* Schwermut *f.*

hypochondriac, **1.** *n.* Hypochon'der, - *m.* **2.** *adj.* schwermütig.

hypocrisy, *n.* Heuchelei', -en *f.*

hypocrite, *n.* Heuchler, - *m.*

hypocritical, *adj.* heuchlerisch.

hypodermic, *n.* Spritze, -n *f.*

hypothesis, *n.* Hypothe'se, -n *f.*

hypothetical, *adj.* hypothe'tisch.

hysteria, hysterics, *n.* Hysterie' *f.*

hysterical, *adj.* hyste'risch.

I

I, *pron.* ich.

ice, *n.* Eis *nt.*

iceberg, *n.* Eisberg, -e *m.*

ice-box, *n.* Eisschrank, -e *m.*

ice cream, *n.* Eis *nt.*, Sahneneis *nt.*

ice skate, **1.** *n.* Schlittschuh, -e *m.* **2.** *vb.* Schlittschuh laufen*.

icing, *n.* Zuckerguß, -sse *m.*

icon, *n.* Iko'ne, -n *f.*

icy, *adj.* eisig.

idea, *n.* Idee', -de'en *f.*, Gedan'ke(n), - *m.*

ideal, **1.** *n.* Ideal', -e *nt.* **2.** *adj.* ideal'.

idealism, *n.* Idealis'mus *m.*

idealist, *n.* Idealist', -en, -en *m.*

idealistic, *adj.* idealis'tisch.

idealize, *vb.* idealisie'ren.

identical, *adj.* iden'tisch.

identifiable, *adj.* identifizier'bar.

identification, *n.* Identifizie'rung, -en *f.*; (*card*) Ausweis, -e *m.*

identify, *vb.* identifizie'ren.

identity, *n.* Identität', -en *f.*

ideology, *n.* Ideologie', -i'en *f.*

idiocy, *n.* Blödsinn *m.*

idiom, *n.* Idiom', -e *nt.*

idiot, *n.* Idiot', -en, -en *m.*

idiotic, *adj.* idio'tisch, blödsinnig.

idle, *adj.* müßig; arbeitslos.

idleness, *n.* Müßigkeit *f.*

idol, *n.* Götzenbild, -er *nt.*

idolatry, *n.* Abgötterei', -en *f.*

idolize, *vb.* vergöt'tern.

if, *conj.* wenn; (**as if**) als ob.

ignite, *vb.* an-zünden.

ignition, *n.* Zündung *f.*

ignition key, n. Zündschlüssel, - m.

ignominious, adj. schmachvoll.

ignoramus, n. Nichtswisser, - m.

ignorance, n. Unwissenheit f.

ignorant, adj. unwissend.

ignore, vb. überse'hen*, unbeachtet lassen*.

ill, adj. krank(·).

illegal, adj. illegal, ungesetzlich.

illegible, adj. unleserlich.

illegitimate, adj. ungesetzlich; (unmarried) unehelich.

illicit, adj. unerlaubt.

illiteracy, n. Analphabe'tentum nt.

illiterate, 1. n. Analphabet', -en, -en m. **2.** adj. des Lesens und Schreibens unkundig.

illness, n. Krankheit, -en f.

illogical, adj. unlogisch.

illuminate, vb. beleuch'ten, erleuch'ten.

illumination, n. Beleuch'tung, -en f.

illusion, n. Illusion', -en f.

illusive, illusory, adj. trügerisch, illuso'risch.

illustrate, vb. erläu'tern; (with pictures) illustrie'ren.

illustration, n. Erläu'terung, -en f.; (picture) Illustration', -en f.

illustrative, adj. erläu'ternd.

illustrious, adj. berühmt'.

image, n. Abbild, -er nt.

imaginable, adj. denkbar.

imaginary, adj. scheinbar, imaginär'.

imagination, n. Einbildung, -en f., Vorstellung, -en f.

imaginative, adj. phantasievoll.

imagine, vb. sich ein·bilden, sich vor·stellen.

imbecile, adj. schwachsinnig.

imitate, vb. nach·ahmen, imitie'ren.

imitation, n. Nachahmung, -en f., Imitation', -en f.

immaculate, adj. unbefleckt, makellos, blitzsauber; (i.

conception) unbefleckte Empfäng'nis f.

immaterial, adj. unwesentlich.

immature, adj. unreif.

immediate, adj. unmittelbar.

immediately, adv. sofort'.

immense, adj. unermeßlich.

immerse, vb. unter·tauchen, versen'ken.

immigrant, n. Einwanderer, - m.

immigrate, vb. ein·wandern.

imminent, adj. bevor'stehend.

immobile, adj. unbeweglich.

immobilize, vb. unbeweglich machen.

immoderate, adj. unbescheiden.

immodest, adj. unbescheiden, anstößig.

immoral, adj. unsittlich, unmoralisch.

immorality, n. Unsittlichkeit, -en f.

immortal, adj. unsterblich.

immortality, n. Unsterblichkeit f.

immortalize, vb. unsterblich machen.

immune, adj. immun'.

immunity, n. Immunität', -en f.

immunize, vb. immunisie'ren.

impact, n. Zusam'menprall m.; (fig.) Auswirkung, -en f.

impair, vb. verrin'gern, verschlechtern.

impart, vb. zu·kommen lassen*.

impartial, adj. unparteiisch.

impatience, n. Ungeduld f.

impatient, adj. ungeduldig.

impeach, vb. an·klagen, beschul'digen.

impeachment, n. Anklage, -n f.; Beschul'digung, -en f.; (U.S.) Verhandlung gegen einen Beamten vor dem Kongreß.

impede, vb. behin'dern.

impediment, n. Behin'derung, -en f.; (speech 1.) Sprachfehler, - m.

impel, vb. an·treiben*, zwin·gen*

impenetrable, adj. undurch·dringlich.

imperative, 1. n. Imperativ, -e m. 2. adj. zwingend.

imperceptible, adj. unmerklich, unwahrnehmbar.

imperfect, 1. n. Imperfekt, -e nt. 2. adj. unvollkommen, fehlerhaft.

imperfection, n. Unvollkommenheit, -en f., Fehler, - m.

imperial, adj. kaiserlich.

imperialism, n. Imperialismus m.

impersonal, adj. unpersönlich.

impersonate, vb. verkör·pern; (theater) dar·stellen.

impersonation, n. Verkör·perung, -en f.; (theater) Darstellung, -en f.

impersonator, n. Imita·tor, -o'ren m.; (swindler) Hochstapler, - m.

impertinence, n. Frechheit, -en f., Unverschämtheit, -en f.

impertinent, adj. frech, unverschämt.

impervious, adj. unzugänglich; (fig.) gefühl·los.

impetuous, adj. ungestüm.

impetus, n. Anstoß m., Antrieb m.

implement, 1. n. Werkzeug, -e nt. 2. vb. durch·führen.

implicate, vb. verwi'ckeln.

implication, n. implizier'ter Gedan'ke(n), - m.; Verwick'lung, -en f.; (by i.) impli'cite.

implicit, adj. inbegriffen, stillschweigend.

implied, adj. miteinbegriffen, 'mplore, vb. an·flehen.

imply, vb. in sich schliessen*, impli'cite sagen, an·deuten.

impolite, adj. unhöflich.

import, 1. n. Einfuhr f., Import', -e m.; (meaning) Bedeu'tung, -en f. 2. vb. ein·führen, importie'ren.

importance, n. Wichtigkeit f.

important, adj. wichtig, bedeu'tend.

importation, n. Einfuhr f.

impose, vb. auf·erlegen.

imposition, n. Belas'tung, -en f.

impossibility, n. Unmöglichkeit, -en f.

impossible, adj. unmöglich.

impotence, n. Unfähigkeit, -en f.; (med.) Impotenz, -en f.

impotent, adj. unfähig; (med.) impotent.

impoverish, vb. arm machen; (fig.) aus·saugen.

impregnable, adj. uneinnehmbar.

impregnate, vb durchdrin'gen*; (make pregnant) schwängern.

impresario, n. Impresa'rio, -s m.

impress, vb. (imprint) prägen, ein·prägen; (affect) beein'drucken.

impression, n. Druck, -e m.; (copy) Abdruck, -e m.; (fig.) Eindruck, -e m.

impressive, adj. eindrucksvoll.

imprison, vb. ein·sperren.

imprisonment, n. Haft f.

improbable, adj. unwahrscheinlich.

impromptu, adv. aus dem Stegreif.

improper, adj. unrichtig, unschicklich.

improve, vb. verbes'sern.

improvement, n. Verbes'serung, -en f.; Besserung f.

improvise, vb. improvisie'ren.

impudent, adj. frech.

impulse, n. Impuls', -e m.

impulsive, adj. impulsiv'.

impunity, n. (with i.) ungestraft.

impure, adj. unrein.

impurity, n. Unreinheit, -en f.

in, prep. in.

inadvertent, adj. achtlos, unaufmerksam.

inalienable, *adj.* unver-äußerlich.

inane, *adj.* leer, geistlos.

inaugural, *adj.* Antritts-(*cpds.*).

inaugurate, *vb.* ins Amt ein·führen.

inauguration, *n.* Einwei-hung, -en *f.*; Amtseinfüh-rung, -en *f.*

incandescent, *adj.* glühend; Glüh- (*cpds.*).

incandescence, *n.* Glühen *nt.*

incantation, *n.* Beschwö-rung *f.*, Zauberspruch. ·e *m.*

incapacitate, *vb.* unfähig machen.

incapacity, *n.* Unfähigkeit, -en *f.*

incarcerate, *vb.* ein·kerkern.

incarnate *adj.* verkör'pert, fleischgeworden.

incarnation, *n.* Verkör'-perung, -en *f.*, Fleischwer-dung *f.*

incendiary, *adj.* Brand-(*cpds.*); aufwieglerisch.

incense, *n.* Weihrauch *m.*

incentive, *n.* Anreiz, -e *m.*, Antrieb, -e *m.*

inception, *n.* Begin'nen *nt.*

incessant, *adj.* unaufhörlich.

incest, *n.* Blutschande *f.*

inch, *n.* Zoll. - *m.*

incidence, *n.* Vorkommen *nt.*

incident, *n.* Vorfall, ·e *m.*

incidental, *adj.* zufällig.

incidentally, *adv.* übrigens.

incision, *n.* Einschnitt, -e *m.*

incisor, *n.* Schneidezahn, ·e *m.*

incite, *vb.* an·regen, an·stacheln.

inclination, *n.* Neigung, -en *f.*

incline, *vb* neigen; (**be i.d**) geneigt sein*.

inclose, *vb.* ein·schließen*.

include, *vb.* ein·schließen*.

including, *prep.* einschließ-lich.

inclusive, *adj.* einschließlich.

incognito, *adv.* inkog'nito.

income, *n.* Einkommen, - *nt.*

incomparable, *adj.* unver-gleichlich.

inconsiderate, *adj.* unüber-legt, rücksichtslos.

inconvenience, *n.* Mühe, -n *f.*, Belas'tung, -en *f.*

inconvenient, *adj.* mühsam, ungelegen.

incorporate, *vb.* verei'nigen; auf·nehmen*.

incorrigible, *adj.* unverbes-serlich.

increase, 1. *n.* Zunahme, -n *f.* **2.** *vb.* zu·nehmen*, wach-sen*.

incredible, *adj.* unglaublich.

incredulity, *n.* Zweifel. - *m.*

incredulous, *adj.* zweifelnd.

increment, *n.* Zunahme, -n *f.*

incriminate, *vb.* belas'ten, beschul'digen.

incrimination, *n.* Beschul'-digung, -en *f.*, Belas'tung, -en *f.*

incrust, *vb.* überkrus'ten.

incubator, *n.* Brutapparat, -e *m.*

incumbent, 1. *n.* Amtsin-haber, - *m.*; **2.** *adj.* ver-pflich'tend.

incur, *vb.* auf sich laden*.

incurable, *adj.* unheilbar.

indebted, *adj.* verschul'det.

indeed, *adv.* in der Tat.

indefatigable, *adj.* uner-müdlich.

indefinite, *adj.* unbestimmt.

indefinitely, *adv.* endlos.

indelible, *adj.* unauslösch-lich.

indemnify, *vb.* sicher·stellen; entschä'digen.

indemnity, *n.* Sicherstel-lung, -en *f.*; Entschä'digung, -en *f.*

indent, *vb.* zacken; (*para-graph*) ein·rücken; (*damage*) verbeu'len.

indentation, *n.* Einkerbung, -en *f.*; (*paragraph*) Einrück-ung, -en *f.*; (*damage*) Ver-beu'lung, -en *f.*

indigestion, *n.* Verdau'ungs-störung, -en *f.*

induct, *vb.* ein·führen; (*phys-*

ics) induzie'ren; *(mil.)* ver-ei'digen.

induction, *n.* Einführung, -en *f.; (physics)* Induktion', -en *f.; (mil.)* Verei'digung, -en *f.*

indulge, *vb.* nach·sehen*; frönen.

indulgence, *n.* Nachsicht, -en, *f.* Langmut *m.,* Frönen *nt.; (eccles.)* Ablaß, ·sse *m.*

indulgent, *adj.* nachsichtig, langmütig.

ineligible, *adj.* nicht wähl-bar; nicht in Frage kom-mend.

infatuate, *vb.* betö'ren, hin-reißen*.

independence, *n.* Unabhän-gigkeit *f.*

independent, *adj.* unabhän-gig.

index, *n.* Verzeich'nis, -se *nt.,* Regi'ster, - *nt.;* **(i. finger)** Zeigefinger, - *m.*

India, *n.* Indien *nt.*

Indian, **1.** *n.* Inder, - *m.;* **(American I.)** India'ner, - *m.* **2.** *adj.* indisch; india'-nisch.

indicate, *vb.* zeigen, an-deuten.

indication, *n.* Hinweis, -e *m.,* Anzeichen, - *nt.*

indicative, **1.** *n.* Indikativ, -e *m.* **2.** *adj.* bezeich'nend.

indicator, *n.* Zeiger, - *m.,* Indika'tor, -o'ren *m.; (sign)* Zeichen, - *nt.*

indict, *vb.* an·klagen.

indictment, *n.* Anklage, -n *f.*

indifference, *n.* Gleichgül-tigkeit *f.*

indifferent, *adj.* gleichgül-tig.

indignant, *adj.* entrüs'tet.

indignation, *n.* Entrüs'-tung, -en *f.*

indignity, *n.* Unwürdigkeit, -en *f.; (insult)* Belei'digung, -en *f.*

indirect, *adj.* indirekt.

indiscreet, *adj.* indiskret.

indiscretion, *n.* Indiskre-tion', -en *f.*

indispensable, *adj.* unab-kömmlich.

indisposed, *adj.* unpäßlich; *(disinclined)* abgeneigt.

indisposition, *n.* Unpäß-lichkeit, -en *f.;* Abneigung, -en *f.*

individual, **1.** *n.* Einzeln-*m.,* Indi'duum, -duen *nt.* **2.** *adj.* einzeln, individuell'.

individuality, *n.* Indivi-dualität', -en *f.*

indivisible, *adj.* unteilbar.

indoctrinate, *vb.* schulen.

indolent, *adj.* träge.

Indonesia, *n.* Indone'sien *nt.*

indoor, *adj.* Haus-, Zimmer-*(cpds.).*

indoors, *adv.* zu Hause, drinnen.

indorse, *vb.* gut·heißen*; *(check)* girie'ren.

induce, *vb.* veran'lassen; *(elec.)* induzie'ren.

inductive, *adj.* induktiv'.

industrial, *adj.* industriell', Industrie- *(cpds.).*

industrialist, *n.* Industriell'-*m.*

industrious, *adj.* fleißig.

industry, *n.* Industrie', -i'en *f.; (hard work)* Fleiß *m.*

inept, *adj.* ungeschickt, un-fähig.

inert, *adj.* träge.

inertia, *n.* Trägheit, -en *f.*

inevitable, *adj.* unvermeid-lich.

infallible, *adj.* unfehlbar.

infamous, *adj.* berüch'tigt.

infamy, *n.* Niedertracht, -en *f.,* Schande, -n *f.*

infancy, *n.* Kindheit, -en *f.; (fig.)* Anfang, ·e *m.*

infant, *n.* Säugling, -e *m.*

infantile, *adj.* kindlich, kind-isch.

infantry, *n.* Infanterie', -i'en *f.*

infantryman, *n.* Infante-rist', -en, -en *m.*

infect, *vb.* an·stecken.

infected, *adj.* entzün'det.

infection, *n.* Entzün'dung, -en *f.*

infectious, *adj.* ansteckend.

infer, *vb.* folgern, an·neh·men*.

inference, *n.* Folgerung, -en *f.*, Annahme, -n *f.*

inferior, *adj.* minderwertig, unterle'gen.

inferiority, *n.* Minderwertigkeit, -en *f.*, Unterle'genheit *f.*

infernal, *adj.* höllisch.

inferno, *n.* Hölle *f.*; Fegefeuer *nt.*

infest, *vb.* heim·suchen.

infidel, *n.* Ungläubig- *m.&f.*

infidelity, *n.* Untreue *f.*

infiltrate, *vb.* ein·dringen*, infiltrie'ren.

infinite, *adj.* unendlich.

infinitesimal, *adj.* unendlich klein; winzig.

infinitive, *n.* Infinitiv, -e *m.*

infinity, *n.* Unendlichkeit, -en *f.*

infirm, *adj.* schwach(×).

infirmary, *n.* Schul- oder Studen'tenkrankenhaus, ×er *nt.*

infirmity, *n.* Schwachheit, -en *f.*

inflame, *vb.* entzün'den.

inflammable, *adj.* entzünd'bar, feuergefährlich.

inflammation, *n.* Entzün'dung, -en *f.*

inflate, *vb.* auf·blasen*; (*tires*) auf·pumpen.

inflation, *n.* Inflation', -en *f.*

inflection, *n.* Biegung, -en *f.*; (*voice*) Tonfall, ×e *m.*; (*gram.*) Beugung, -en *f.*

inflict, *vb.* zu·fügen.

infliction, *n.* Last, -en *f.*

influence, **1.** *n.* Einfluß, ×sse *m.* **2.** *vb.* beein'flussen.

influential, *adj.* einflußreich.

influenza, *n.* Grippe, -n *f.*

inform, *vb.* benach'richtigen, mit·teilen; (**i. on**) denunzie'ren.

informal, *adj.* zwanglos, nicht formell'.

information, *n.* Auskunft, ×e *f.*

infringe, *vb.* übertre'ten*; (*jur.*) verlet'zen.

infuriate, *vb.* wütend machen, rasend machen, erbo'sen.

---

ingenious, *adj.* erfin'derisch, genial'.

ingenuity, *n.* Findigkeit *f.*, Genialität' *f.*

ingredient, *n.* Bestand'teil, -e *m.*; (*cooking*) Zutat, -en *f.*

inhabit, *vb.* bewoh'nen.

inhabitant, *n.* Bewoh'ner, - *m.*, Einwohner, - *m.*

inhale, *vb.* ein·atmen.

inherent, *adj.* angeboren, eigen.

inherit, *vb.* erben.

inheritance, *n.* Erbe *nt.*; Erbschaft, -en *f.*

inhibit, *vb.* hindern, ab·halten*.

inhibition, *n.* Hemmung, -en *f.*

inhuman, *adj.* unmenschlich.

inimitable, *adj.* unnach·ahmlich.

iniquity, *n.* Ungerechtigkeit, -en *f.*; Schändlichkeit, -en *f.*

initial, **1.** *n.* Anfangsbuchstabe, -n, -n *m.* **2.** *adj.* anfänglich; Anfangs- (*cpds.*).

initiate, *vb.* ein·führen, ein·weihen.

initiation, *n.* Einführung, -en *f.*, Einweihung, -en *f.*

initiative, *n.* Initiati've, -n *f.*

inject, *vb.* ein·spritzen.

injection, *n.* Einzspritzung, -en *f.*

injunction, *n.* gerichtlicher Unterlas'sungsbefehl, -e *m.*

injure, *vb.* verlet'zen.

injurious, *adj.* schädlich; (*fig.*) nachteilig.

injury, *n.* Verlet'zung, -en *f.*, Schaden, × *m.*

injustice, *n.* Ungerechtigkeit, -en *f.*

ink, *n.* Tinte, -n *f.*

inland, **1.** *n.* Binnenland, ×er *nt.* **2.** *adj.* inländisch.

inlet, *n.* kleine Bucht, -en *f.*

inmate, *n.* Insasse, -n, -n *m.*

inn, *n.* Gasthaus, ×er *nt.*, Wirtshaus, ×er *nt.*

inner, *adj.* inner-.

innermost, *adj.* innerst-.

innocence, *n.* Unschuld *f.*

innocent, *adj.* unschuldig.

innovation, *n.* Neuerung, -en *f.*

innuendo, *n.* Unterstel'lung, -en *f.*

innumerable, *adj.* zahllos.

inoculate, *vb.* ein·impfen.

inoculation, *n.* Einimpfung, -en *f.*

inquest, *n.* gerichtliche Untersuchung, -en *f.*

inquire, *vb.* fragen, sich erkun'digen.

inquiry, *n.* Nachfrage, -n *f.*, Erkun'digung, -en *f.*

inquisition, *n.* Untersu'chung, -en *f.*; (*eccles.*) Inquisition', -en *f.*

inquisitive, *adj.* neugierig.

insane, *adj.* wahnsinnig.

insanity, *n.* Wahnsinn *m.*

inscribe, *vb.* ein·zeichnen, ein·schreiben*.

inscription, *n.* Inschrift, -en *f.*

insect, *n.* Insekt', -en *nt.*

insecticide, *n.* Insek'tenpulver, - *nt.*

insensible, *adj.* gefühl'los.

insensitive, *adj.* unempfindlich.

inseparable, *adj.* unzertrennlich.

insert, 1. *n.* Beilage, -n *f.* **2.** *vb.* ein·fügen, ein·setzen.

insertion, *n.* Einsatz,⸗e *m.*

inside. 1. *n.* Innenseite, -n *f.*, Inner·ei. **2.** *adj.* inner⸗. **3.** *adv.* innen, drinnen.

insidious, *adj.* hinterlistig.

insight, *n.* Einsicht, -en *f.*

insignia, *n.pl.* Abzeichen, - *nt.*; Insig'nien *pl.*

insignificance, *n.* Bedeu'tungslosigkeit *f.*

insignificant, *adj.* bedeu'tungslos.

insinuate, *vb.* an·spielen auf; (**i. oneself**) sich ein·schmeicheln.

insinuation, *n.* Anspielung, -en *f.*

insipid, *adj.* fade.

insist, *vb.* beste'hen*, behar'ren.

insistence, *n.* Beste'hen *nt.*, Behar'ren *nt.*

insistent, *adj.* beharr'lich, hartnäckig.

insolence, *n.* Unverschämtheit, -en *f.*

insolent, *adj.* unverschämt.

insomnia, *n.* Schlaflosigkeit *f.*

inspect, *vb.* besich'tigen.

inspection, *n.* Besich'tigung, -en *f.*

inspector, *n.* Inspek'tor, -o'ren *m.*

inspiration, *n.* Eingebung, -en *f.*, Inspiration', -en *f.*

inspire, *vb.* an·feuern, begeis'tern.

install, *vb.* ein·bauen; (*fig.*) ein·führen.

installation, *n.* Installation', -en *f.*

installment, *n.* Rate, -n *f.*; (**i. plan**) Ratenzahlung, -en *f.*

instance, *n.* (*case*) Fall, ⸗e *m.*; (*example*) Beispeil, -e *nt.*; (*law*) Instanz', -en *f.*; (**for i.**) zum Beispiel.

instant, 1. *n.* Augenblick, -e *m.* **2.** *adj.* augenblicklich.

instantaneous, *adj.* sofortig.

instantly, *adv.* sofort', auf der Stelle.

instead, *adv.* statt dessen, dafür; (**i. of**) statt, anstatt'.

instigate, *vb.* veran'lassen, an·stacheln.

instill, *vb.* ein·flößen.

instinct, *n.* Instinkt', -e *m.*

instinctive, *adj.* unwillkürlich, instinktiv'.

institute, 1. *n.* Institut', -e *nt.* **2.** *vb.* ein·leiten, an·ordnen.

institution, *n.* Einrichtung, -en *f.*; Institut', -e *nt.*, Anstalt, -en *f.*

instruct, *vb.* unterrich'ten, an·weisen*.

instruction, *n.* Anweisung, -en *f.*; (*school*) Unterricht *m.*

instructive, *adj.* lehrreich.

instructor, *n.* Lehrer, - *m.*

instructress, *n.* Lehrerin, -nen *f.*

instrument, *n.* Werkzeug, -e *nt.*, Instrument', -e *nt.*

instrumental, *adj.* behilf'lich; *(music)* Instrumental'- *(cpds.).*

insufferable, *adj.* unerträglich.

insufficient, *adj.* ungenügend.

insulate, *vb.* isolie'ren.

insulation, *n.* Isolie'rung, -en *f.*

insulator, *n.* Isola'tor, -o'ren *m.*

insulin, *n.* Insulin' *nt.*

insult, 1. *n.* Belei'digung, -en *f.* **2.** *vb.* belei'digen.

insurance, *n.* Versi'cherung, -en *f.*

insure, *vb.* versi'chern.

insurgent, 1. *n.* Aufständisch- *m.* **2.** *adj.* aufständisch.

insurrection, *n.* Aufstand, ⸗e *m.*

intact, *adj.* intakt'.

intangible, *adj.* nicht greifbar.

integral, 1. *n.* (*math.*) Integral', -e *nt.* **2.** *adj.* unerläßlich.

integrate, *vb.* integrie'ren.

integrity, *n.* Unbescholtenheit *f.*

intellect, *n.* Verstand' *m.*, Intellekt' *m.*

intellectual, 1. *n.* Intellektuell- *m.&f.* **2.** *adj.* intellektuell'.

intelligence, *n.* Intelligenz' *f.*

intelligent, *adj.* intelligent'.

intelligentsia, *n.* geistige Oberschicht *f.*

intelligible, *adj.* verständ'lich.

intend, *vb.* beab'sichtigen.

intense, *adj.* angespannt, intensiv'.

intensify, *vb.* verstär'ken.

intensive, *adj.* intensiv'.

intent, 1. *n.* Absicht, -en *f.* **2.** *adj.* erpicht'.

intention, *n.* Absicht, -en *f.*

intentional, *adj.* absicht'lich.

inter, *vb.* beer'digen.

intercede, *vb.* dazwi'schentreten*.

intercept, *vb.* ab'fangen*.

intercourse, *n.* Verkehr' *m.*, Umgang *m.*

interest, 1. *n.* Interes'se, -n *nt.*; (*comm.*) Zins, -en *m.* **2.** *vb.* interessie'ren.

interesting, *adj.* interessant'.

interfere, *vb.* sich einmischen; ein'greifen*.

interference, *n.* Einmischung, -en *f.*; (*radio*) Störung, -en *f.*

interim, 1. *n.* Zwischenzeit, -en *f.* **2.** *adj.* Interims-(*cpds.*).

interior, 1. *n.* Inner- *nt.* **2.** *adj.* inner-; Innen- (*cpds.*).

interject, *vb.* dazwi'schenwerfen*.

interjection, *n.* Ausruf, -e *m.*; (*gram.*) Interjektion', -en *f.*

interlude, *n.* Zwischenspiel, -e *nt.*

intermarry, *vb.* untereinander heiraten.

intermediary, 1. *n.* Vermitt'ler, - *m.* **2.** *adj.* Zwischen- (*cpds.*).

intermediate, *adj.* Zwischen-(*cpds.*).

interment, *n.* Begräb'nis, -se *nt.*

intermission, *n.* Unterbre'chung, -en *f.*; (*theater*) Pause, -n *f.*

intermittent, *adj.* wechselnd, perio'disch.

intern, *vb.* internie'ren.

internal, *adj.* inner-, innerlich.

international, *adj.* international'.

internationalism, *n.* Internationalis'mus *m.*

interne, *n.* Volontär'arzt, ⸗e *m.*

interpose, *vb.* ein'fügen.

interpret, *vb.* interpretie'ren; (*language*) dolmetschen.

interpretation, *n.* Interpretation', -en *f.*, Auslegung, -en *f.*

interpreter, *n.* Dolmetscher, - *m.*

interrogate, *vb.* aus·fragen; (*law*) verneh'men*, verhö'ren.

interrogation, *n.* Verhör', -e *nt.*

interrogative, 1. *n.* Fragewort, "er *nt.* **2.** *adj.* fragend, Frage- (*cpds.*).

interrupt, *vb.* unter·bre'chen*.

interruption, *n.* Unterbre'chung, -en *f.*

intersect, *vb.* (*intr.*) sich schneiden*, sich kreuzen; (*tr.*) durchschnei'den, durchkreu'zen.

intersection, *n.* Kreuzung, -en *f.*

intersperse, *vb.* durchset'zen.

interval, *n.* Abstand, "e *m.*

intervene, *vb.* dazwi'schen-kommen*, sich ein·mischen.

intervention, *n.* Dazwi'-schentreten *nt.,* Einmischung, -en *f.*

interview, 1. *n.* Interview, -s *nt.* **2.** *vb.* interview'en

intestine, *n.* Darm, "e *m.*

intimacy, *n.* Vertrau'lich-keit, -en *f.*

intimate, *adj.* vertraut', innig.

intimidate, *vb.* ein·schüch-tern.

intimidation, *n.* Einschüch-terung, -en *f.*

into, *prep.* in.

intolerant, *adj.* intolerant.

intonation, *n.* Tonfall, "e *m.*

intoxicate, *vb.* berau'schen.

intoxication, *n.* Rausch, "e *m.*

intravenous, *adj.* intravenös'.

intrepid, *adj.* furchtlos.

intricacy, *n.* Kompliziert'-heit, -en *f.*

intricate, *adj.* verwi'ckelt; kompliziert'.

intrigue, 1. *n.* Intri'ge, -n *f.* **2.** *vb.* intrige'ren.

intrinsic, *adj.* innerlich; wahr.

introduce, *vb.* ein·führen, ein·leiten; (*persons*) vor··stellen.

introduction, *n.* Einführung, -en *f.*, Einleitung, -en *f.*; Vorstellung, -en *f.*

introductory, *adj.* einleitend.

introvert, *n.* nach innen gekehr'ter Mensch, -en -en *m.*

intrude, *vb.* ein·dringen*.

intruder, *n.* Eindringling -e *m.*

intuition, *n.* Intuition', -en *f.*

inundate, *vb.* überschwem'-men.

invade, *vb.* ein·dringen*, ein·fallen*.

invader, *n.* Angreifer, - *m.*

invalid, 1. *n.* Invali'de, -n, -n *m.* **2.** *adj.* ungültig.

invariable, *adj.* unveränderlich.

invasion, *n.* Invasion', -en *f.*

inveigle, *vb.* verlei'ten.

invent, *vb.* erfin'den*.

invention, *n.* Erfin'dung, -en *f.*

inventive, *adj.* erfin'derisch.

inventor, *n.* Erfin'der, - *m.*

inventory, *n.* Inventar', -e *nt.;* Inventur', -en *f.*

inverse, *adj.* umgekehrt.

invertebrate, *adj.* ohne Wirbelsäule.

invest, *vb.* investie'ren, an·legen.

investigate, *vb.* untersu'chen.

investigation, *n.* Untersu'ch-ung, -en *f.*

investment, *n.* Kapitals'-anlage, -n *f.*

inveterate, *adj.* eingefleischt.

invigorate, *vb.* bele'ben, erfri'schen.

invincible, *adj.* unbesiegbar.

invisible, *adj.* unsichtbar.

invitation, *n.* Einladung, -en *f.*, Aufforderung, -en *f.*

invite, *vb.* ein·laden*, auf·fordern.

invocation, *n.* Anrufung, -en *f.;* (*eccles.*) Bittgebet, -e *nt.*

invoice, *n.* Warenrechnung, -en *f.*

invoke, *vb.* an·rufen*; erbit'-ten.

involuntary, adj. unfreiwillig.

involve, vb. ein·schließen*;
verwi'ckeln.

involved, adj. verwi'ckelt.

invulnerable, adj unver-
letzlich; uneinnehmbar.

inward, adj. inner-, innerlich.

inwardly, adv. innerlich.

iodine, n. Jod nt.

Iran, n. Iran' m.

Iraq, n. Irak' m.

irate, adj. zornig.

Ireland, n. Irland nt.

iridium, n. Iri'dium nt.

iris, n. Iris f.; (flower) Schwertlilie, -n f.

Irish, adj. irisch.

Irishman, n. Irländer, - m..
Ire, -n, -n m.

Irishwoman, n. Irländerin,
-nen f.

irk, vb. ärgern.

iron, 1. n. Eisen nt.; (flati.)
Bügeleisen,- nt.   **2.** adj.
eisern. **3.** vb. bügeln.

ironical, adj. spöttisch, iro'-
nisch.

irony, n. Spott m., Ironie' f.

irrational, adj. irrational'.

irrefutable, adj. unwiderlegbar.

irregular, adj. unregelmäßig.

irregularity, n. Unregel-
mäßigkeit, -en f.

irrelevant, adj. belang'los;
unanwendbar.

irresistible, adj. unwiderstehlich.

irresponsible, adj. unverantwortlich.

irreverent, adj. unehrerbietig.

irrevocable, adj. unwider-
ruflich.

irrigate, vb. bewäs'sern.

irrigation, n. Bewäs'serung,
-en f.

irritability, n. Reizbarkeit f.

irritable, adj. reizbar.

irritant, n. Reizfaktor, -en
m.

irritate, vb. reizen, irritie'ren.

irritation, n. Reizung, -en f.;
Ärger m.

island, n. Insel, -n f.

isolate, vb. isolie'ren.

isolation, n. Isolie'rung, -e
willig.

isolationist, n. Isolationist
-en, -en m.

Israel, n. Israel nt.

Israeli, 1. n. Israe'li, -s n
2. adj. israe'lisch.

Israelite, 1. n. Israelit', -e
-en m. **2.** adj. israeli'tisch

issuance, n Ausgabe, -n

issue, 1. n. Ausgabe, -n f
Problem', -e nt.; (result
Ergeb'nis, -se nt. **2.** vb. aus
geben*, aus·stellen.

isthmus, n. Isthmus, -me
m.

it, pron. es.

Italian, 1. n. Italie'ner,
m. **2.** adj. italie'nisch.

Italic, adj. ita'lisch.

italics, n Kursiv'schrift

Italy, n. Ita'lien nt.

itch, 1. n. Jucken nt. **2.** v
jucken.

item, n. Arti'kel, - m., Po
sten, - m.

itemize, vb. auf·zählen.

itinerary, n. Reiseroute, -n

ivory, n. Elfenbein nt.

ivy, n. Efeu m.

J

jab, 1. n. Stoß, ″e m., Stic
-e m. **2.** vb. stoßen

jack, n. (auto) Wagenheber
m.; (card) Bube, -n, -n n

jack-of-all-trades, n. Han
Dampf in allen Gassen n

jackal, n. Schakal', -e m.

jackass, n. Esel, - m.

jacket, n. Jacke, -n f.

jack-knife, n. Klappmesser,
nt

jade, n. Jade m.

jaded, adj. ermat'tet.

jagged, adj. zackig.

jail, n. Gefäng'nis, -se nt.

jailer, n. Gefäng'niswärter,
m.

jam, 1. n. Marmela'de, -nf

Konfitü're, -n *f.*; (*trouble*) **Klemme,** -n *f.* **2.** *vb.* klemmen.

jangle, *vb.* rasseln.

janitor, *n.* Pförtner, - *m.*, Hausmeister, - *m.*

January, *n.* Januar *m.*

Japan, *n.* Japan *nt.*

Japanese. 1. *n.* Japa'ner, - *m.* **2.** *adj.* japa'nisch.

jar, 1. *n.* Krug, ⸚e *m.*, Glas, ⸚er *nt.* **2.** *vb.* rütteln.

jargon, *n.* Jargon', -s *m.*

jasmine, *n.* Jasmin', -e *m.*

jaundice, *n.* Gelbsucht *f.*

jaunt, *n.* kurze Reise, -n *f.*

javelin, *n.* Speer, -e *m.*

jaw, *n.* Kiefer, - *m.*

jay, *n.* Eichelhäher, - *m.*

jaywalk, *vb.* quer über eine Straßenkreuzung gehen*.

jazz, *n.* Jazz *m.*

jealous, *adj.* eifersüchtig.

jealousy, *n.* Eifersucht *f.*

jeer, *vb.* spotten.

jelly, *n.* Gelee', -s *nt.*

jeopardize, *vb.* gefähr'den.

jeopardy, *n.* Gefahr', -en *f.*

jerk, 1. *n.* Ruck, -e *m.* **2.** *vb.* ruckartig bewe'gen.

jerky, *adj.* ruckartig.

jersey, *n.* Jersey, -s *nt.*

Jerusalem, *n.* Jeru'salem *nt.*

jest, 1. *n.* Scherz, -e *m.* **2.** *vb.* scherzen.

jester, *n.* Spaßmacher, - *m.*; (**court j.**) Hofnarr, -en, -en *m.*

Jesuit. 1. *n.* Jesuit', -en, -en *m.* **2.** *adj.* jesui'tisch; Jesui'ten- (*cpds.*).

Jesus Christ, *n.* Jesus Christus *m.*

jet, *n.* Strahl, -en *m.*; (*tech.*) Düse, -n *f.*; (*plane*) Düsenflugzeug, -e *nt.*; (*mineral*) Pechkohle, -n *f.*

jetsam, *n.* Strandgut *nt.*; über Bord geworfenes Gut *nt.*

jetty, *n.* Mole, -n *f.*

Jew, *n.* Jude, -n, -n *m.*

jewel, *n.* Juwel', -en *nt.*, Edelstein, -e *m.*

jeweler, *n.* Juwelier', -e *m.*

jewelry, *n.* Schmucksachen *pl.*, Schmuck *m.*

Jewish, *adj.* jüdisch.

jib, *n.* Klüver, - *m.*

jibe, *vb.* (*sailing*) halsen; (*agree*) sich decken.

jiffy, *n.* Nu *m.*

jig, *n.* Gigue *f.*

jilt, *vb.* sitzen lassen*.

jingle, *vb.* klingeln.

job, *n.* Stellung, -en *f.*; Aufgabe, -n *f.*

jobber, *n.* Zwischenhändler, - *m.*

jockey, *n.* Jockey, -s *m.*

jocular, *adj.* scherzhaft.

jog, *vb.* schubsen.

joggle, *vb.* (*tr.*) stubsen; (*inter.*) wackeln.

join, *vb.* verbin'den*; (*club, etc.*) bei'treten*.

joint, 1. *n.* Gelenk', -e *nt.* **2.** *adj.* gemein'sam.

joist, *n.* Querbalken, - *m.*

joke. 1. *n.* Witz, -e *m.*, Scherz, -e *m.*, Spaß, ⸚e *m.* **2.** *vb.* einen Witz machen, scherzen.

joker, *n.* Witzbold, -e *m.*; (*cards*) Joker, - *m.*

jolly, *adj.* heiter.

jolt, 1. *n.* Stoß, ⸚e *m.* **2.** *vb.* rütteln.

jonquil, *n.* gelbe Narzis'se, -n *f.*

jostle, *vb.* stoßen*.

journal, *n.* Journal', -e *nt.*; (*diary*) Tagebuch, ⸚er *nt.*; (*newspaper*) Zeitung, -en *f.*; (*periodical*) Zeitschrift, -en *f.*

journalism, *n.* Zeitungswesen *nt.*

journalist, *n.* Journalist', -en, -en *m.*

journey, *n.* Reise, -n *f.*

journeyman, *n.* Gesel'le, -n, -n *m.*

jovial, *adj.* jovial'.

jowl, *n.* Backe, -n *f.*

joy, *n.* Freude, -n *f.*

joyful, *adj.* freudig.

joyous, *adj.* freudig.

jubilant, *adj.* frohlockend.

jubilee, *n.* Jubilä'um, -ä'en *nt.*

Judaism, *n.* Judentum *nt.*

judge, 1. *n.* Kenner, - *m.*; *(law)* Richter, - *m.* 2. *vb.* beur'teilen; *(law)* richten, Recht sprechen*.

judgment, *n.* Urteil, -e *nt.*; *(law also:)* Rechtsspruch, *e *m.*

judicial, *adj.* richterlich; Gerichts'- *(cpds.).*

judiciary, 1. *n.* Justiz'gewalt *f.*; Richterstand *m.* 2. *adj.* richterlich.

judicious, *adj.* weise, klug.

jug, *n.* Krug, *e *m.*

juggle, *vb.* jonglie'ren.

juggler, *n.* Jongleur', -e *m.*

juice, *n.* Saft, *e *m.*

juicy, *adj.* saftig.

July, *n.* Juli *m.*

jumble, *n.* Durcheinan'der *nt.*

jump, 1. *n.* Sprung, *e *m.* 2. *vb.* springen*.

junction, *n.* Verbin'dung, -en *f.*; *(railroad)* Knotenpunkt, -e *m.*

juncture, *n.* Zusam'mentreffen, - *nt.*

June, *n.* Juni *m.*

Jungle, *n.* Dschungel, - *m.* or *nt.* (or -n *f.*).

junior, *adj.* jünger.

juniper, *n.* Wachol'der, - *m.*

junk, *n.* Altwaren *pl.*; *(fig.)* Kram *m.*

junket, *n. (food)* Milchpudding *m.*; *(trip)* Reise, -n *f.*

jurisdiction, *n.* Rechtsprechung, -en *f.*; Gerichts'barkeit *f.*; Zuständigkeit *f.*

jurisprudence, *n.* Rechtswissenschaft *f.*

jurist, *n.* Rechtsgelehrt- *m.*

juror, *n.* Geschwo'ren- *m.&f.*

jury, *n.* Geschwo'ren- *pl.*

just, 1. *adj.* gerecht'. 2. *adv.* gera'de, eben.

justice, *n.* Gerech'tigkeit *f.*

justifiable, *adj.* berech'tigt.

justification, *n.* Rechtfertigung, -en *f.*, Berech'tigung, -en *f.*

justify, *vb.* rechtfertigen.

jut, *vb.* hervor'·stehen*.

jute, *n.* Jute *f.*

juvenile, *adj.* jugendlich.

K

kale, *n.* Grünkohl *m.*

kaleidoscope, *n.* Kaleidoskop', -e *nt.*

kangaroo, *n.* Känguruh', -s *nt.*

karat, *n.* Karat', -e *nt.*

keel, *n.* Kiel, -e *m.*

keen, *adj.* scharf; *(fig.)* eifrig.

keep, 1. *n. (lodging)* Unterhalt *m.* 2. *vb.* behal'ten*, bewah'ren; *(animals, etc.)* halten*; **(k. doing something)** etwas immer wieder tun*; **(k. on doing something)** etwas weiter tun*.

keeper, *n.* Wärter, - *m.*, Wächter, - *m.*

keepsake, *n.* Andenken, - *nt.*

keg, *n.* Faß, *sser *nt.*

kennel, *n.* Hundezwinger, - *m.*

kerchief, *n.* Halstuch, *er *nt.*; Kopftuch, *er *nt.*

kernel, *n.* Kern, -e *m.*; *(grain)* Korn, *er *nt.*

kerosene, *n.* Kerosin' *nt.*

ketchup, *n.* Ketchup *m.*

kettle, *n.* Kessel, - *m.*

kettledrum, *n.* Kesselpauke, -n *f.*

key, *n.* Schlüssel, - *m.*; *(piano)* Taste, -n *f.*; *(musical structure)* Tonart, -en *f.*

keyhole, *n.* Schlüsselloch, *er *nt.*

khaki, *n.* Khaki *m.*

kick, 1. *n.* Stoß, *e *m.*, Tritt, -e *m.* 2. *vb.* stoßen*, treten*.

kid, 1. *n. (goat)* Zicklein, - *nt.*; *(child)* Kind, -er *nt.* 2. *vb.* necken, rein·legen.

kidnap, *vb.* gewalt'sam entfüh'ren.

kidnaper, *n.* Kinderräuber, - *m.*

kidnaping, *n.* Kinderraub *m.*

kidney, *n.* Niere, -n *f.*

kidney bean, *n.* Schminkbohne, -n *f.*

kill, *vb.* töten, um·bringen*.

killer, *n.* Mörder, - *m.*

kiln, *n.* Brennofen, *» m.*

kilocycle, *n.* Kilohertz, - *nt.*

kilogram, *n.* Kilo, - *nt.*

kilometer, *n.* Kilome'ter, - *nt.*

kilowatt, *n.* Kilowatt, - *nt.*

kilt, *n.* Kilt, -s *m.*

kimono, *n.* Kimo'no, -s *m.*

kin, *n.* Verwandt'schaft, -en *f.*

kind, 1. *n.* Art, -en *f.*, Sorte, -n *f.* **2.** *adj.* gütig, freundlich.

kindergarten, *n.* Kindergarten, *» m.*

kindle, *vb.* an-zünden, entzün'den.

kindly, *adj.* freundlich.

kindness, *n.* Güte *f.*, Freundlichkeit *f.*

kindred, *adj.* verwandt'.

king, *n.* König, -e *m.*

kingdom, *n.* Königreich, -e *nt.*

kink, *n.* Knoten, - *m.*

kiosk, *n.* Kiosk, -e *m.*

kiss, 1. *n.* Kuß, *»sse m,* **2.** *vb.* küssen.

kitchen, *n.* Küche, -n *f.*

kite, *n.* Drachen, - *m.; (bird)* Milan, -e *m.*

kitten, *n.* Kätzchen, - *nt.*

kleptomaniac, *n.* Kleptoma'ne, -n, -n *m.*

knack, *n.* Talent', -e *nt.*

knapsack, *n.* Rucksack, *»e m.*

knead, *vb.* kneten.

knee, *n.* Knie, Kni'e *nt.*

kneel, *vb.* knien.

knickers, *n.pl.* Kniehose, -n *f.*

knife, *n.* Messer, - *nt.*

knight, *n.* Ritter, - *m.; (chess)* Springer, - *m.*

knit, *vb.* stricken; *(fig.)* verknüp'fen.

knock, 1. *n.* Klopfen *nt.* **2.** *vb.* klopfen.

knot, 1. *n.* Knoten, - *m.; (wood)* Knorren, - *m.* **2.** *vb.* knoten.

knotty, *adj.* knotig; *(wood)* knorrig; *(fig.)* schwierig.

know, *vb. (facts)* wissen*; *(people, places, things)* kennen*.

knowledge, *n.* Kenntnis, -se *f.;* Wissen *nt.*

knuckle, *n.* Knöchel, - *m.*

Korea, *n.* Kore'a *nt.*

L

label, *n.* Etiket'te, -n *f.*

labor, 1. *n.* Arbeit, -en *f.; (workers)* Arbeiterschaft *f.; (birth)* Wehen *pl.* **2.** *vb.* arbeiten.

laboratory, *n.* Laborato'rium, -rien *nt.*

laborer, *n.* Arbeiter, - *m.*

laborious, *adj.* arbeitsam, mühselig.

labor union, *n.* Gewerk'schaft, -en *f.*

labyrinth, *n.* Labyrinth', -e *nt.*

lace, *n.* Spitze, -n *f.*

lacerate, *vb.* auf-reißen*.

laceration, *n.* Riß, -sse *m.*

lack, 1. *n.* Mangel, *» m.* **(I l. something)** es fehlt, **2.** *vb.* Mangel leiden* an; mangelt mir an etwas.

lackadaisical, *adj.* schwunglos, unlustig.

laconic, *adj.* lako'nisch.

lacquer, 1. *n.* Lack, -e *m.* **2.** *vb.* lackie'ren.

lacy, *adj.* spitzenartig; Spitzen- *(cpds.).*

lad, *n.* Knabe, -n, -n *m.*

ladder, *n.* Leiter, -n *f.*

ladle, *n.* Schöpflöffel, - *m.*

lady, *n.* Dame, -n *f.*

ladybug, *n.* Mari'enkäfer, - *m.*

lag, *n.* Verzö'gerung, -en *f.*

lag behind, *vb.* zurück'-bleiben*.

lagoon, *n.* Lagu'ne, -n *f.*

lair, *n.* Lagerstatt, *»e f.;* Höhle, -n *f.*

laity, *n.* Laienstand *m.*, Laien *pl.*

lake, *n.* See, Se'en *m.*

lamb, *n.* Lamm, ⸗er *nt.*

lame, *adj.* lahm.

lament, 1. *n.* Wehklage, -n *f.* **2.** *vb.* bekla'gen.

lamentable, *adj.* bekla'genswert.

lamentation, *n.* Wehklage, -n *f.*

laminate, *vb.* (*metal*) auswalzen, plattie'ren; **(l.d wood)** Furnier'holz *nt.*

lamp, *n.* Lampe, -n *f.*

lance, 1. *n.* Lanze, -n *f.* **2.** *vb.* durchsto'ßen*; (*med.*) mit der Lanzet'te öffnen.

land, 1. *n.* (*country*) Land, ⸗er *nt.*; (*ground*) Grund und Boden *m.* **2.** *vb.* landen.

landing, *n.* Landung, -en *f.*; (*stairs*) Treppenabsatz, ⸗e *m.*

landlady, *n.* Wirtin, -nen *f.*; Hausbesitzerin, -nen *f.*

landlord, *n.* Wirt, -e *m.*; Hausbesitzer, - *m.*

landmark, *n.* Markstein, -e *m.*

landscape, *n.* Landschaft, -en *f.*

landslide, *n.* Erdrutsch, -e *m.*; (*election*) überwäl'tigender Wahlsieg, -e *m.*

lane, *n.* Pfad, -e *m.*; (*boat*) Fahrrinne, -n *f.*; (*auto*) Fahrbahn, -en *f.*

language, *n.* Sprache, -n *f.*

languid, *adj.* energie'los, schlaff.

languish, *vb.* schmachten.

lanky, *adj.* baumlang.

lanolin, *n.* Lanolin' *nt.*

lantern, *n.* Later'ne, -n *f.*

lap, 1. *n.* Schoß ⸗e *m.*; (*sport*) Runde, -n *f.* **2.** *vb.* übereinan'der·legen.

lapel, *n.* Revers', - *m.*

lapin, *n.* Kanin'chenpelz *m.*

lapse, 1. *n.* (*error*) Lapsus, - *m.*; Verse'hen, - *nt.*; (*time*) Zwischenzeit, -en *f.* **2.** *vb.* verstrei'chen*.

larceny, *n.* Diebstahl, ⸗e *m.*

lard, *n.* Schweinefett *nt.*

large, *adj.* groß (größer, größt-); weit; umfangreich.

largely, *adv.* größtenteils.

largo, *n.* Largo, -s *nt.*

lariat, *n.* Lasso, -s *nt.*

lark, *n.* Lerche, -n *f.*; (*fun*) Vergnü'gen *nt.*

larkspur, *n.* Rittersporn *m.*

larva, *n.* Larve, -n *f.*

laryngitis, *n.* Kehlkopfentzündung, -en *f.*

larynx, *n.* Kehlkopf, ⸗e *m.*

lascivious, *adj.* wollüstig.

lash, 1. *n.* Peitsche, -n *f.*; Peitschenhieb, -e *m.*; (*eye*) Wimper, -n *f.* **2.** *vb.* peitschen.

lass, *n.* Mädchen, - *nt.*

lasso, *n.* Lasso, -s *nt.*

last, 1. *n.* Leisten, - *m.* **2.** *adj.* letzt-. **3.** *vb.* dauern.

lasting, *adj.* dauernd, anhaltend, bestän'dig.

latch, 1. *n.* Klinke, -n *f.* **2.** *vb.* ein·klinken.

late, *adj.* spät, verspä'tet; (*dead*) verstor'ben.

lately, *adv.* in letzter Zeit.

latent, *adj.* latent.

lateral, *adj.* seitlich.

lath, *n.* Latte, -n *f.*

lathe, *n.* Drehbank, ⸗e *f.*

lather, *n.* Schaum *m.*

Latin, 1. *n.* (*language*) Latein' *nt.*; (*person*) Romane, -n, -n *m.* **2.** *adj.* latei'nisch; roma'nisch.

latitude, *n.* Breite, -n *f.*

latrine, *n.* Latri'ne, -n *f.*

latter, 1. *adj.* letzter-. **2.** *pron.* **(the l.)** dieser, -es, -e.

lattice, *n.* Gitterwerk *nt.*

laud, *vb.* loben, preisen*.

laudable, *adj.* lobenswert.

laudanum, *n.* Laudanum *nt.*

laudatory, *adj.* Lob- (*cpds.*).

laugh, 1. *n.* Lachen *nt.* **2.** *vb.* lachen.

laughable, *adj.* lächerlich.

laughter, *n.* Geläch'ter *nt.*

launch, 1. *n.* Barkas'se, -n *f.* **2.** *vb.* (*throw*) schleudern; (*boat*) vom Stapel lassen*.

launching, *n.* Stapellauf, ⸗e *m.*

launder, *vb.* waschen*.

laundress, *n.* Waschfrau, -en *f.*

laundry, *n.* (*clothes*) Wäsche *f.*; (*establishment*) Wäscherei', -en *f.*

laundryman, n. Wäscherei'-angestellt- m.

laurel, n. Lorbeer, -en m.

lava, n. Lava f.

lavatory, n. Waschraum -e m.

lavender, n. Laven'del m.

lavish, adj. üppig.

law, n. (individual) Gesetz', -e nt.; (system) Recht nt.

lawful, adj. gesetz'lich, recht-mäßig.

lawless, adj. gesetz'los; (fig.) zügellos.

lawn, n. Rasen m.

lawsuit, n. Prozeß', -sse m.

lawyer, n. Rechtsanwalt, -e m.; Jurist', -en, -en m.

lax, adj. lax.

laxative, n. Abführmittel, - nt.

laxity, n. Laxheit f.

lay, 1. adj. Laien- (cpds.); 2. vb. legen.

layer, n. Schicht, -en f.

layman, n. Laie, -n, -n m.

lazy, adj. faul.

lead, 1. n. Führung f., Lei-tung f.; (metal) Blei nt. 2. vb. führen, leiten.

leaden, adj. bleiern.

leader, n. Führer, - m., Leiter, - m.

leadership, n. Führung f.

lead pencil, n. Bleistift, -e m.

leaf, n. Blatt, -er nt.

leaflet, n. Broschü're, -n f., Flugblatt, -er nt.

league, n. Bund, -e m., Bündnis, -se nt.

League of Nations, n. Völ-kerbund m.

leak, 1. n. Leck, -e nt. 2. vb. lecken.

leakage, n. Durchsickern nt.

leaky, adj. leck, undicht.

lean, 1. adj. mager. 2. vb. lehnen.

leap, 1. n. Sprung, -e m. 2. vb. springen*.

leap year, n. Schaltjahr, -e nt.

learn, vb. lernen; erfah'ren*.

learnèd, adj. gelehrt'.

learning, n. Wissen nt., Bildung f.

lease, 1. n. Mietvertrag, -e m., Pacht, -en f. 2. vb. mieten, pachten.

leash, n. Leine f.

least, adj. (slightest) geringst'-; (smallest) kleinst-; (at l., in any case) wenigstens; (at l., surely this much) mindestens, zum mindesten.

leather, 1. n. Leder, - nt. 2. adj. ledern.

leathery, adj. ledern.

leave, 1. n. (farewell) Ab-schied, -e m.; (permission) Erlaub'nis, -se f.; (furlough) Urlaub, -e m. 2. vb. (de-part) ab·fahren*; (go away) fort·gehen*; (abandon) ver-las'sen*; (let) lassen*.

leaven, n. Sauerteig, -e m.

lecherous, adj. lüstern.

lecture, 1. n. Vortrag, -e m.; (academic) Vorlesung, -en f. 2. vb. einen Vortrag halten*; eine Vorlesung hal-ten*.

lecturer, n. Vortragend- m.

ledge, n. Felsvorsprung, -e m.; Sims, -e m.

ledger, n. Hauptbuch, -er nt.

lee, n. Lee f.

leech, n. Blutegel, - m.

leek, n. Lauch, -e m.

leer, vb. begehr'lich schielen.

leeward, adv. leewärts.

left, 1. n. (pol.) Link- f. 2. adj. link-; (l. over) übrig-geblieben. 3. adv. links.

leftist, adj. links orientiert'.

left-over, n. Überbleibsel, - nt., Rest, -e m.

leg, n. Bein, -e nt.

legacy, n. Vermächt'nis, -se nt., Erbschaft, -en f.

legal, adj. gesetz'lich, gesetz'-mäßig.

legalize, vb. legalisie'ren.

legation, n. Gesandt'schaft, -en f.

legend, n. Legen'de, -n f.

legendary, adj. legendär'.

legible, adj. leserlich.

legion, n. Legion', -e f.

legislate, vb. Gesetze geben*.

legislation, n. Gesetz'ge-bung f.

legislator   314   ENGLISH - GERMAN

legislator, *n.* Gesetz′geber, - *m.*

legislature, *n.* gesetz′gebende Gewalt′ *f.;* gesetz′gebende Versamm′lung, -en *f.*

legitimate, *adj.* legitim′.

leisure, *n.* Muße *f.*

leisurely, *adj.* gemäch′lich.

lemon, *n.* Zitro′ne, -n *f.*

lemonade, *n.* Limona′de, -n *f.*

lend, *vb.* leihen*.

length, *n.* Länge, -n *f.;* *(time)* Dauer *f.*

lengthen, *vb.* verlän′gern.

lengthwise, *adv.* der Länge nach.

lengthy, *adj.* langwierig.

lenient, *adj.* mild, nachsichtig.

lens, *n.* Linse, -n *f.;* *(photo)* Objektiv′, -e *nt.*

Lent, *n.* Fastenzeit *f.*

Lenten, *adj.* Fasten- *(cpds.).*

lentil, *n.* Linse, -n *f.*

leopard, *n.* Leopard′, -en, -en *m.*

leper, *n.* Aussätzig- *m.&f.*

leprosy, *n.* Aussatz *m.*

lesion, *n.* Verlet′zung, -en *f.*

less, *adj.* weniger.

lessen, *vb.* *(tr.)* vermin′dern; *(intr.)* nach·lassen*.

lesser, *adj.* *(size)* kleiner; *(degree)* gerin′ger.

lesson, *n.* Lehre, -n *f.;* *(school)* Lehrstunde, -n *f.;* *(assignment)* Aufgabe, -n *f.*

lest, *conj.* damit′ . . . nicht.

let, *vb.* *(allow)* lassen*; *(lease)* vermie′ten.

letdown, *n.* Enttäu′schung, -en *f.*

lethal, *adj.* tödlich.

lethargic, *adj.* teilnahmslos, lethar′gisch.

lethargy, *n.* Teilnahmslosigkeit *f.,* Lethargie′ *f.*

letter, *n.* *(alphabet)* Buchstabe(n), - *(or* -n, -n) *m.;* *(communication)* Brief, -e *m.*

letterhead, *n.* Briefkopf, ″e *m.*

lettuce, *n.* Kopfsalat, -e *m.*

leukemia, *n.* Leukämie′ *f.*

levee, *n.* Damm, ″e *m.*

level, **1.** *n.* Stand, ″e *m.,*

Niveau′, -s *nt.* **2.** *adj.* eben, gera′de; flach. **3.** *vb.* ebnen; gleich·machen.

lever, *n.* Hebel, - *m.*

levity, *n.* Leichtsinn *m.*

levy, **1.** *n.* Abgabe, -n *f.,* Steuer, -n *f.* **2.** *vb.* erheben.

lewd, *adj.* unzüchtig.

lexicon, *n.* Lexikon, -ka *nt.*

liability, *n.* Verant′wortlichkeit, -en *f.;* Verpflich′tung, -en *f.*

liable, *adj.* verant′wortlich; *(law)* haftbar.

liaison, *n.* Verbin′dung, -en *f.;* Liaison′, -s *f.*

liar, *n.* Lügner, - *m.*

libel, *n.* Verleum′dung, -en *f.*

libelous, *adj.* verleum′derisch.

liberal, **1.** *n.* Liberal′- *m.* **2.** *adj.* liberal′.

liberalism, *n.* Liberalis′mus *m.*

liberality, *n.* Freigebigkeit *f.;* Freisinnigkeit *f.*

liberate, *vb.* befrei′en.

liberation, *n.* Befrei′ung, -en *f.*

libertine, *n.* Lüstling, -e *m.*

liberty, *n.* Freiheit, -en *f.*

libido, *n.* Libido *f.*

librarian, *n.* Bibliothekar′, -e *m.;* Bibliotheka′rin, -nen *f.*

library, *n.* Bibliothek′, -en *f.,* Bücherei′, -en *f.*

libretto, *n.* Libret′to, -s *nt.*

license, *n.* Erlaub′nis, -se *f.;* Geneh′migung, -en *f.;* **(driver's l.)** Führerschein, -e *m.*

lick, *vb.* lecken.

licorice, *n.* Lakrit′ze, -n *f.*

lid, *n.* Deckel, - *m.;* *(eye)* Lid, -er *nt.*

lie, **1.** *n.* Lüge, -n *f.* **2.** *vb.* *(tell untruths)* lügen*; *(recline)* liegen*; **(l. down)** sich (hin·) legen.

lien, *n.* dinglich gesi′chertes Anrecht *nt.*

lieutenant, *n.* Leutnant, -s *m.*

life, *n.* Leben, - *nt.*

lifeboat, *n.* Rettungsboot, -e *nt.*

lifeguard, *n.* Bademeister, - *m.*

life insurance, *n.* Lebensversicherung, -en *f.*

lifeless, *adj.* leblos.

life preserver, *n.* Rettungsring, -e *m.; (vest)* Schwimmweste, -n *f.*

lifetime, *n.* Lebenszeit, -en *f.*

lift, **1.** *n.* Fahrstuhl, ⸗e *m.* **2.** *vb.* heben*.

ligament, *n.* Sehne, -n *f.*

ligature, *n.* Ligatur', -en *f.*

light, **1.** *n.* Licht, -er *nt.* **2.** *adj. (color)* hell; *(weight)* leicht. **3.** *vb. (fire)* an'zünden; *(illuminate)* beleuch'ten.

lighten, *vb.* leichter machen; *(fig.)* erleich'tern; *(lightning)* blitzen.

lighter, *n. (cigar, cigarette)* Feuerzeug, e *nt.*

lighthouse, *n.* Leuchtturm, ⸗e *m.*

lightness, *n. (color)* Helligkeit *f.; (ease)* Leichtfertigkeit *f.*

lightning, *n.* Blitz, -e *m.*

like, **1.** *adj.* gleich. **2.** *vb.* gern haben*, (gern) mögen*; **(I l. it)** es gefällt* mir; **(I l. to do it)** ich tue es gern. **3.** *prep.* wie; **(l. this, l. that)** so.

likeable, *adj.* angenehm, liebenswert.

likelihood, *n.* Wahrschein'lichkeit, -en *f.*

likely, *adj.* wahrschein'lich.

liken, *vb.* verglei'chen*.

likeness, *n.* Ähnlichkeit, -en *f.*

likewise, *adv.* ebenso.

lilac, *n.* Flieder *m.*

lilt, *n.* wiegender Rhythmus *m.*

lily, *n.* Lilie, -n *f.*

lily of the valley, *n.* Maiglöckchen, - *nt.*

limb, *n.* Glied, -er *nt.*

limber, *adj.* biegsam.

limbo, *n.* Vorhölle *f.*

lime, *n.* Kalk *m.; (fruit)* Limo'ne, -n *f.*

limelight, *n.* Rampenlicht, -er *nt.*

limestone, *n.* Kalstein *m.*

limit, **1.** *n.* Grenze, -n *f.;*

Höchstgrenze, -n *f.* **2.** *vb.* begren'zen, beschrän'ken.

limitation, *n.* Begren'zung, -en *f.,* Beschrän'kung, -en *f.*

limited, *adj.* begrenzt'; beschränkt'.

limitless, *adj.* unbegrenzt.

limousine, *n.* Limousi'ne -n *f.*

limp, **1.** *adj.* schlaff. **2.** *vb.* hinken.

linden, *n.* Linde, -n *f.*

line, *n.* Linie, -n *f.; (mark)* Strich, -e *m.; (row)* Reihe, -n *f.; (writing)* Zeile, -n *f.; (rope)* Leine, -n *f.*

lineage, *n.* Geschlecht', -er *nt.*

lineal, *adj.* in gerader Linie.

linear, *adj.* linear'.

linen, **1.** *n.* Leinen, - *nt.; (household)* Wäsche *f.* **2.** *adj.* leinen.

liner, *n. (boat)* Ozeandampfer, - *m.*

linger, *vb.* verwei'len.

lingerie, *n.* Damenunterwäsche *f.*

linguist, *n.* Sprachwissenschaftler, - *m.,* Linguist', -en, -en *m.*

linguistic, *adj.* sprachlich; sprachwissenschaftlich, linguis'tisch.

linguistics, *n.* Sprachwissenschaft, -en *f.,* Linguis'tik *f.*

liniment, *n.* Einreibemittel, - *nt.*

lining, *n.* Futter, - *nt.*

link, **1.** *n. (bond)* Band, -e *nt.; (chain)* Glied, -er *nt.* **2.** *vb.* verbin'den*; verket'ten.

linoleum, *n.* Lino'leum *nt.*

linseed oil, *n.* Leinöl *nt.*

lint, *n.* Fussel, -n *f.*

lion, *n.* Löwe, -n, -n *m.*

lip, *n.* Lippe, -n *f.*

lip-stick, *n.* Lippenstift, -e *m.*

liquefy, *vb.* flüssig machen.

liqueur, *n.* Likör', -e *m.*

liquid, **1.** *n.* Flüssigkeit, -en *f.* **2.** *adj.* flüssig.

liquidate, *vb.* liquidie'ren.

liquidation, *n.* Liquidation', -en *f.*

liquor 316 ENGLISH-GERMAN

liquor, *n.* Alkohol *m.*, Spirituo'sen *pl.*

lira, *n.* Lira, -re *f.*

lisp, *vb.* lispeln.

lisle, *n.* Baumwollfaden *m.*

list, 1. *n.* Liste, -n *f.*, Verzeich'nis, -se *nt.*; *(ship)*
Schlagseite *f.* **2.** *vb.* verzeich'nen.

listen, *vb.* zu·hören, horchen.

listless, *adj.* lustlos.

litany, *n.* Litanei' *f.*

liter, *n.* Liter, -nt.

literal, *adj.* buchstäblich,
wörtlich.

literary, *adj.* litera'risch.

literacy, *n.* Lesen und Schreiben Können *nt.*

literate, *adj.* des Lesens und
Schreibens kundig.

literature, *n.* Literatur', -en
f.

lithe, *adj.* geschmei'dig.

lithograph, 1. *n.* Lithographie', -i'en *f.* **2.** *vb.*
lit'ographie'ren.

litigant, *n.* Rechtsstreit-
führer, - *m.*

litigation, *n.* Rechtsstreit,
-e *m.*

litter, 1. *n.* *(rubbish)* Abfall,
·e *m.*; *(stretcher)* Tragbahre,
-n *f.*; *(puppies, kittens, etc.)*
Wurf, **·e** *m.* **2.** *vb.* Sachen
herum'liegen lassen*.

little, *adj.* *(size)* klein;
(amount) wenig; **(a l.)** ein
bißchen, ein wenig.

liturgical, *adj.* litur'gisch.

liturgy, *n.* Liturgie', -i'en *f.*

live, 1. *adj.* leben'dig. **2.**
vb. *(be alive)* leben; *(dwell)*
wohnen.

livelihood, *n.* Lebensunterhalt *m.*

lively, *adj.* lebhaft.

liven, *vb.* bele'ben.

liver, *n.* Leber, -n *f.*

livery, *n.* Livree', -n *f.*

livestock, *n.* Viehbestand *m.*

livid, *adj.* aschfahl.

living, 1. *n.* Leben *nt.*;
Lebensweise *f.* **2.** *adj.*
lebend.

lizard, *n.* Eidechse, -n *f.*

lo, *interj.* siehe!

load, 1. *n.* Ladung, -en *f.*;

(burden) Last, -en *f.* **2.** *vb.*
laden*.

loaf, 1. *n.* Laib, -e *m.* **2.**
vb. faulenzen.

loafer, *n.* Faulenzer, - **·n.**

loam, *n.* Lehm *m.*

loan, 1. *n.* Anleihe, -n *f.*
2. *vb.* leihen*.

loath, *adj.* abgeneigt.

loathe, *vb.* verab'scheuen.

loathing, *n.* Abscheu *f.*

loathsome, *adj.* widerlich,
ekelhaft.

lobby, *n.* Wandelhalle, -n *f.*;
(political) Interes'sengruppe,
-n *f.*

lobe, *n.* Lappen, - *m.*

lobster, *n.* Hummer, - *m.*

local, 1. *n.* *(train)* Vorortzug, **·e** *m.* **2.** *adj.* örtlich,
lokal'.

locale, *n.* Schauplatz, **·e** *m.*

locality, *n.* Ort, -e *m.*

localize, *vb.* lokalisie'ren.

locate, *vb.* finden*; **(be l.d)**
liegen*.

location, *n.* Lage, -n *f.*

lock, 1. *n.* Schloß, -sser *nt.*;
(canal) Schleuse, -n *f.*; *(hair)*
Locke, -n *f.* **2.** *vb.* ab-
schließen*.

locker, *n.* Schrank, **·e** *m.*

locket, *n.* Medaillon', -s *nt.*

lockjaw, *n.* Kieferkrampf
m.

locksmith, *n.* Schlosser, - *m.*

locomotion, *n.* Fortbewe-
gung, -en *f.*

locomotive, *n.* Lokomoti've,
-n *f.*

locust, *n.* Heuschrecke, -n *f.*

lode, *n.* Erzader, -n *f.*

lodge, 1. *n.* Häuschen, -
(intr.) *nt.*; *(fraternal)* Loge,
-n *f.* **2.** *vb.* logie'ren; *(tr.)*
beherbergen.

lodger, *n.* Untermieter, - *m.*

lodging, *n.* Unterkunft, **·e** *f.*

loft, *n.* Boden, **·** *m.*; *(ware-
house)* Speicher, - *m.*

lofty, *adj.* erha'ben.

log, *n.* Holzklotz, **·e** *m.*; *(tree
trunk)* Baumstamm, **·e** *m.*;
(ship's l.) Logbuch, **·er** *nt.*

loge, *n.* Loge, -n *f.*

logic, *n.* Logik *f.*

logical, *adj.* logisch.

loin, *n.* Lende, -n *f.*

loiter, vb. herum'·stehen*.

London, n. London nt.

lone, lonely, lonesome, adj. einsam.

loneliness, n. Einsamkeit f.

long, 1. adj. lang("). **2.** vb. sich sehnen.

longevity, n. Langlebigkeit f.

longing, 1. n. Sehnsucht f. **2.** adj. sehnsüchtig.

longitude, n. Länge f.

longitudinal, adj. Längen-(cpds.).

long-lived, adj. langlebig.

long playing record, n. Langspielplatte, -n f.

look, 1. n. Blick, -e m.; (appearance, **l.s**) Aussehen nt. **2.** vb. sehen*, schauen, blicken, gucken; **(l. at)** an·sehen*, ·schauen, ·blicken, ·gucken; **(l. good, etc.)** gut (etc.) aus·sehen*; **(l. out, be careful)** auf·passen.

loom, n. Webstuhl m.

looking glass, n. Spiegel, - m.

loop, n. Schlaufe, -n f.

loophole, n. Schlupfloch, ⸚er nt.

loose, adj. lose, locker.

loosen, vb. lockern.

loot, 1. n. Beute f. **2.** vb. plündern.

lop off, vb. ab·schlagen*.

lopsided, adj. schief.

loquacious, adj. schwatzhaft.

lord, n. Herr, -n, -en m.; (title) Lord, -s m.

lordship, n. Herrschaft, -en f.

lose, vb. verlie'ren*.

loss, n. Verlust', -e m.

lot, n. Los, -e nt.; (quantity) Menge, -n f.; (ground) Grundstück, -e nt.

lotion, n. Lotion', -en f.

lottery, n. Lotterie', -i'en f.

lotus, n. Lotosblume, -n f.

loud, adj. laut; (color) grell.

loud-speaker, n. Lautsprecher, - m.

lounge, 1. n. Vorhalle, -n f. **2.** vb. herum'·lungern.

louse, n. Laus, ⸚e f.

lout, n. Lümmel, - m.

louver, n. Lattenfenster, - nt.

lovable, adj. liebenswert.

love, 1. n. Liebe, -n f. **2.** vb. lieben; **(fall in l.)** sich verlie'ben.

lovely, adj. lieblich, reizend.

lover, n. Liebhaber, - m.

low, adj. niedrig, tief; (nasty) gemein'.

lowbrow, adj. unintellektuell, ungeistig.

lower, 1. adj. tiefer, niedriger; gemei'ner. **2.** vb. herun'ter·lassen*; herab'·setzen, senken.

lowly, adj. beschei'den.

loyal, adj. treu.

loyalist, n. Regie'rungstreu, -m.

loyalty, n. Treue f., Loyalität' f.

lozenge, n. Pastil'le, -n f.

lubricant, n. Schmiermittel, - nt.

lubricate, vb. schmieren.

lucid, adj. klar.

luck, n. Glück nt., Zufall, ⸚e m.

lucky, adj. glücklich; **(be l.)** Glück haben*.

lucrative, adj. gewinn'bringend.

ludicrous, adj. lächerlich.

lug, vb. schleppen.

luggage, n. Gepäck' nt.

lukewarm, adj. lukewarm.

lull, 1. n. Pause, -n f. **2.** vb. beru'higen; **(l. to sleep)** ein·schläfern.

lullaby, n. Wiegenlied, -er nt.

lumbago, n. Hexenschuß m.

lumber, n. Holz nt.

luminous, adj. leuchtend.

lump, n. Klumpen, - m., (skin) Beule, -n f.

lumpy, adj. klumpig.

lunacy, n. Irrsinn m.

lunar, adj. Mond- (cpds.).

lunatic, 1. n. Irrsinnig- m. **2.** adj. irrsinnig.

lunch, 1. n. leichtes Mittagessen, - nt. **2.** vb. zu Mittag essen*.

luncheon, n. leichtes Mittagessen, - nt.

lung, *n.* Lunge, -n *f.*

lunge, *vb.* vorstoßen*.

lurch, *vb.* torkeln; **(leave in the l.)** sitzen lassen*.

lure, *vb.* locken.

lurid, *adj.* grell; (*fig.*) grausig.

lurk, *vb.* lauren.

luscious, *adj.* saftig, lecker.

lush, *adj.* saftig, üppig.

lust, 1. *n.* Wollust *f.* **2.** *vb.* gelüs'ten.

luster, *n.* Glanz *m.*

lustful, *adj.* lüstern.

lustrous, *adj.* glänzend.

lusty, *adj.* munter; kräftig.

lute, *n.* Laute, -n *f.*

Lutheran, 1. *n.* Luthera'ner, - *m.* **2.** *adj.* luthe'risch.

luxuriant, *adj.* üppig.

luxurious, *adj.* verschwen'derisch.

luxury, *n.* Luxus *m.*

lying, *adj.* lügnerisch.

lymph, *n.* Lymphe, -n *f.*

lynch, *vb.* lynchen.

lyre, *n.* Leier, -n *f.*

lyric, *adj.* lyrisch.

lyricism, *n.* Lyrik *f.*

M

macabre, *adj.* maka'ber.

macaroni, *n.* Makkaro'ni *pl.*

machine, *n.* Maschi'ne, -n *f.*

machine gun, *n.* Maschi'nengewehr, -e *nt.*

machinery, *n.* Mechanis'mus *m.;* Maschi'nen *pl.*

machinist, *n.* Maschinist', -en, -en *m.*

mackerel, *n.* Makre'le, -n *f.*

mackinaw, *n.* kurzer wollener Mantel, = *m.*

mad, *adj.* verrückt'; (*angry*) böse.

madam, *n.* gnädige Frau *f.*

madden, *vb.* verrückt' machen.

magazine, *n.* Magazin', -e *nt.,* Zeitschrift, -en *f.*

magic, 1. *n.* Zauberkunst, "e *f.* **2.** *adj.* magisch.

magician, *n.* Zauberer, - *m.*

magistrate, *n.* Polizei'richter, -e *m.*

magnanimous, *adj.* großzügig.

magnate, *n.* Magnat', -en, -en *m.*

magnesium, *n.* Magne'sium *nt.*

magnet, *n.* Magnet', (-en), -en *m.*

magnetic, *adj.* magne'tisch.

magnificence, *n.* Herrlichkeit *f.,* Pracht *f.*

magnificent, *adj.* großartig, prächtig.

magnify, *vb.* vergrö'ßern.

magnitude, *n.* Größe, -n *f.*

mahogany, *n.* Mahago'ni *nt.*

maid, *n.* Dienstmädchen, - *nt.;* (**old m.**) alte Jungfer, -n *f.*

maiden, *adj.* Jungfern- (*cpds.*); (**m. name**) Mädchenname(n), - *m.*

mail, 1. *n.* Post *f.* **2.** *vb.* mit der Post schicken; zur Post bringen*.

mail-box, *n.* Briefkasten, = *m.*

mailman, *n.* Postbote, -n *m.,* Briefträger, - *m.*

maim, *vb.* verstüm'meln.

main, *adj.* hauptsächlich.

mainland, *n.* Festland *nt.*

mainspring, *n.* Triebfeder, -n *f.*

maintain, *vb.* aufrecht·erhalten*; (*assert*) behaup'ten.

maintenance, *n.* Aufrechterhaltung *f.,* Instand'haltung *f.*

maize, *n.* Mais *m.*

majestic, *adj.* majestä'tisch.

majesty, *n.* Majestät', -en *f.*

major, 1. *n.* Major', -e *m.* **2.** *adj.* größer; Haupt- (*cpds.*); (*music*) Dur *nt.,* (**A-major**) A-dur.

majority, *n.* Mehrzahl, -en *f.,* Mehrheit, -en *f.,* Majorität, -en *f.*

make, *vb.* machen; (*manu-*

facture) her-stellen; (*compel*) zwingen*.

make-believe. 1. *n.* Vorspiegelung, -en *f.* **2.** *adj.* vorgetäuscht. **3.** *vb.* vortäuschen.

maker, *n.* Hersteller, - *m.*

makeshift, *n.* Notbehelf *m.*

make-up, *n.* Struktur*, -en *f.*; Aufmachung, -en *f.*; (*face*) Schminke *f.*, Make-up *nt.*

malady, *n.* Krankheit, -en *f.*

malaria, *n.* Mala'ria *f.*

male. 1. *n.* (*human*) Mann, «er *m.*; (*animal*) Männchen, - *nt.* **2.** *adj.* männlich.

malevolent, *adj.* böswillig.

malice, *n.* Bosheit, -en *f.*

malicious, *adj.* boshaft.

malignant, *adj.* bösartig.

malnutrition, *n.* Unterernährung *f.*

malt, *n.* Malz *nt.*

maltreat, *vb.* mißhan'deln.

mammal, *n.* Säugetier, -e *nt.*

man, *n.* Mann, «er *m.*; (*human being*) Mensch, -en, -en *m.*

manage, *n.* handhaben; (*administer*) verwal'ten; (*direct*) leiten.

management, *n.* Verwal'tung, -en *f.*; Leitung, -en *f.*

manager, *n.* Leiter, - *m.*; Unterneh'mer, - *m.*

mandate, *n.* Mandat', -e *nt.*

mandatory, *adj.* unerläßlich.

mandolin, *n.* Mandoli'ne, -n *f.*

mane, *n.* Mähne, -n *f.*

maneuver. 1. *n.* Manö'ver, - *nt.* **2.** *vb.* manövrie'ren.

manganese, *n.* Mangan' *nt.*

manger, *n.* Krippe, -n *f.*

mangle, *vb.* zerflei'schen; (*laundry*) mangeln.

manhood, *n.* Mannesalter *nt.*; Mannhaftigkeit *f.*

mania, *n.* Manie', -i'en *f.*

maniac, *n.* Wahnsinnig- *m.*

manicure. 1. *n.* Maniku're, -n *f.* **2.** *vb.* maniku'ren.

manifest. 1. *adj.* offenkundig. **2.** *vb.* bekun'den.

manifesto, *n.* Manifest', -e *nt.*

manifold, *adj.* mannigfaltig.

manipulate, *vb.* manipulie'ren.

mankind, *n.* Menschheit *f.*

manly, *adj.* mannhaft.

manner, *n.* Art, -en *f.*, Weise, -n *f.*; Manier', -en *f.*

mannerism, *n.* Manieris'mus *m.*

mansion, *n.* Haus, «er *nt.*

manslaughter, *n.* Totschlag, «e *m.*

mantelpiece, *n.* Kamin'sims, -e *m.*

mantle, *n.* Mantel, « *m.*

manual. 1. *n.* Handbuch, «er *nt.* **2.** *adj.* Hand- (*cpds.*).

manufacture. 1. *n.* Herstellung, -en *f.* **2.** *vb.* herstellen.

manufacturer, *n.* Fabrikant', -en, -en *m.*

manure, *n.* Mist *m.*

manuscript, *n.* Handschrift, -en *f.*, Manuskript', -e *nt.*

many, *adj. pl.* viele.

map, *n.* Landkarte, -n *f.*; (*of a small area*) Plan, «e *m.*

maple, *n.* Ahorn, -e *m.*

mar, *vb.* verun'zieren.

marble, *n.* Marmor, -e *m.*

march. 1. *n.* Marsch, «e *m.* **2.** *vb.* marschie'ren.

March, *n.* März *m.*

mare, *n.* Stute, -n *f.*

margarine, *n.* Margari'ne *f.*

margin, *n.* (*edge*) Rand, «er *m.*; (*latitude*) Spielraum, «er *m.*

marginal, *adj.* Rand- (*cpds.*).

marinate, *vb.* marinie'ren.

marine, *adj.* Meeres-, See- (*cpds.*).

mariner, *n.* Seemann, -leute *m.*

marionette, *n.* Marionet'te, -n *f.*

marital, *adj.* ehelich.

maritime, *adj.* Schiffahrts-, Seemanns- (*cpds.*).

mark. 1. *n.* Zeichen, - *nt.*; (*school*) Zensur', -en *f.*, Note, -n *f.* **2.** *vb.* kennzeichnen.

market, *n.* Markt, «e *m.*

market place, Marktplatz, "e m.

marmalade, n. Oran'gen-marmelade, -n f.

maroon, 1. adj. rotbraun. **2.** vb. aus·setzen.

marquee, n. Überda'chung, -en f.

marquis, n. Marquis', - m.

marriage, n. Heirat, -en f.; (ceremony) Trauung, -en f.; (institution) Ehe, -n f.; (matrimony) Ehestand f.

marrow, n. Mark nt.

marry, vb. heiraten; (join in marriage) trauen; **(getm.ed)** heiraten, sich verhei'raten; **(m. off)** verhei'raten.

marsh, n. Marsch, -en f.

marshal, n. Marschall, "e m.

martial, adj. kriegerisch; Kriegs- (cpds.).

martyr, n. Märtyrer, - m.

martyrdom, n. Märtyrer-tum nt.

marvel, 1. n. Wunder, - nt. **2.** vb. **(m. at)** bewun'dern.

marvelous, adj. wunderbar.

mascara, n. Augenwimpern-tusche f.

mascot, n. Maskot'te, -n f.

masculine, adj. männlich, maskulin.

mash, 1. n. Brei, -e m. **2.** vb. zersto'ßen*.

mask, 1. n. Maske, -n f. **2.** vb. maskie'ren.

mason, n. Maurer, - m.

masquerade, n. Maskera'de, -n f.

mass, n. Masse, -n f., (church) Messe, -n f.

massacre, 1. n. Gemet'zel, - nt. **2.** vb. nieder·metzeln.

massage, 1. n. Massa'ge, -n f. **2.** vb. massie'ren.

masseur, n. Masseur', -e m.

massive, adj. massiv'.

mass meeting, n. Massen-versammlung, -en f.

mast, n. Mast, -en m.

master, 1. n. Meister, - m.; Herr, -n, -en m. **2.** vb. be-herr'schen.

masterpiece, n. Meister-stück, -e nt.

mastery, n. Beherr'schung f.; Herrschaft f.

mat, n. Matte, -n f.

match, 1. n. (light) Streich-holz, "er nt.; (contest) Wett-kampf, "e m.; (marriage) Heirat, -en f., Partie', -i'en f. **2.** vb. passen zu; sich messen* mit.

mate, 1. n. (spouse) Ehe-mann, "er m.; Ehefrau, -en f.; (naut.) Maat, -e m. **2.** vb. sich paaren.

material, 1. n. Material', -ien nt.; (cloth) Stoff, -e m. **2.** adj. materiell'; wesent-lich.

materialism, n. Materialis'-mus m.

materialize, vb. sich ver-wirk'lichen.

maternal, adj. mütterlich.

maternity, n. Mutterschaft f.

mathematical, adj. mathe-ma'tisch.

mathematics, n. Mathe-matik' f.

matinee, n. Nachmittags-vorstellung, -en f.

matrimony, n. Ehestand m.

matron, n. Matro'ne, -n f.

matter, 1. n. Stoff, -e m., Mate'rie, -n f.; (fig.) Sache, -n f., Angelegenheit, -en f. **2.** vb. von Bedeu'tung sein*; aus·machen; **(it doesn't m.)** es macht nichts.

mattress, n. Matrat'ze, -n f.

mature, 1. adj. reif. **2.** vb. reifen; (fall due) fällig wer-den*.

maturity, n. Reife f.; Fälligkeit f.

maul, vb. übel zu·richten.

mausoleum, n. Mausole'um, -le'en nt.

maxim, n. Grundsatz, "e m.

maximum, 1. n. Maximum, -ma nt. **2.** adj. höchst- (cpds.).

may, vb. (be permitted) dürfen*; **(he m. come)** er wird viel-leicht kommen; **(that m. be)** das kann, mag sein.

May, n. Mai m.

maybe, adv. vielleicht'.

mayhem, *n.* Mord und Totschlag *m.*

mayonnaise, *n.* Mayonnai'se, -n *f.*

mayor, *n.* Bürgermeister, - *m.*

maze, *n.* Wirrwarr *nt.*

me, *pron.* mir; mich.

meadow, *n.* Wiese, -n *f.*

meager, *adj.* dürftig.

meal, *n.* Mahlzeit, -en *f.*; (*flour*) Mehl *nt.*

mean, **1.** *n.* (*average*) Durchschnitt, -e *m.* **2.** *adj.* mittler-, durchschnittlich; Mittel-, Durchschnitts- (*cpds.*); (*nasty*) gemein'. **3.** *vb.* (*signify*) bedeu'ten; (*intend to say*) meinen.

meaning, *n.* Bedeu'tung, -en *f.*, (*sense*) Sinn, -e *m.*

means, *n.* Mittel *pl.*

meantime, meanwhile, *n.* Zwischenzeit *f.*; (**in the m.**) inzwi'schen, unterdes'sen.

measles, *n.* Masern *pl.*

measure, **1.** *n.* Maß, -e *nt.*; (*fig.*) Maßnahme, -n *f.* **2.** *vb.* messen*.

measurement, *n.* Maß, -e *nt.*

measuring, *n.* Messen *nt.*

meat, *n.* Fleisch *nt.*

mechanic, *n.* Mecha'niker, - *m.*

mechanical, *adj.* mecha'nisch.

mechanism, *n.* Mechanis'mus, -men *m.*

mechanize, *vb.* mechanisie'ren.

medal, *n.* Orden, - *m.*

meddle, *vb.* sich ein·mischen.

mediaeval, *adj.* mittelalterlich.

median, *n.* Mittelwert, -e *m.*

mediate, *vb.* vermit'teln.

mediator, *n.* Vermitt'ler, - *m.*

medical, *adj.* ärztlich, medizi'nisch.

medicate, *vb.* medizi'nisch behan'deln.

medicine, *n.* Medizin', -en *f.*

mediocre, *adj.* mittelmäßig.

mediocrity, *n.* Mittelmäßigkeit *f.*

meditate, *vb.* nach·denken*.

meditation, *n.* Nach·lenken *nt.*

Mediterranean, *adj.* Mittelmeer- (*cpds.*).

Mediterranean Sea, *n.* Mittelmeer *nt.*

medium, **1.** *n.* Mittel, - *nt.*; Medium, -ien *nt.* **2.** *adj.* mittler-.

medley, *n.* (*music*) Potpourri, -s *nt.*

meek, *adj.* sanft.

meekness, *n.* Sanftmut *f.*

meet, *vb.* treffen*; sich treffen*; begeg'nen*.

meeting, *n.* Versamm'lung, -en *f.*, Zusam'menkunft, *e f.*, Tagung, -en *f.*; (*encounter*) Begeg'nung, -en *f.*

melancholy, **1.** *n.* Schwermut *f.*, Melancholie' *f.* **2.** *adj.* schwermütig, melancho'lisch.

mellow, *adj.* gereift'.

melodious, *adj.* wohlklingend, melo'disch.

melodrama, *n.* Melodrama, -men *nt.*

melody, *n.* Melodie', -i'en *f.*

melon, *n.* Melo'ne, -n *f.*

melt, *vb.* schmelzen*.

member, *n.* Mitglied, -er *nt.*

membership, *n.* Mitgliedschaft *f.*

membrane, *n.* Membra'ne, -n *f.*

memento, *n.* Andenken, - *nt.*

memoirs, *n.pl.* Memoi'ren *pl.*

memorable, *adj.* denkwürdig.

memorandum, *n.* Memoran'dum, -den *nt.*

memorial, **1.** *n.* Denkmal, *e*er *nt.*; Andenken, - *nt.* **2.** *adj.* Gedenk- (*cpds.*).

memorize, *vb.* auswendig lernen.

memory, *n.* (*retentiveness*) Gedächt'nis, -se *nt.*; (*remembrance*) Erin'nerung, -en *f.*

menace, **1.** *n.* drohende Gefahr', -en *f.* **2.** *vb.* drohen, bedro'hen.

menagerie, n. Menagerie', -l'en f.

mend, vb. aus-bessern.

menial, adj. niedrig.

menopause, n. Wechseljahre pl.

menstruation, n. Regel f., Menstruation' f.

mental, adj. geistig.

mentality, n. Mentalität', -en f.

menthol, n. Menthol' nt.

mention, 1. n. Erwäh'nung, -en f. **2.** vb. erwäh'nen.

menu, n. Menü', -s nt.; Speisekarte, -n f.

mercantile, adj. kaufmännisch.

mercenary, adj. gewinnsüchtig.

merchandise, n. Ware, -n f.

merchant, n. Kaufmann, -leute m.; Geschäfts'mann, -leute m.

merchant marine, n. Handelsmarine, -n f.

merciful, adj. barmher'zig, gütig, gnädig.

merciless, adj. unbarmherzig, schonungslos.

mercury, n. Quecksilber nt.

mercy, n. Gnade f., Mitleid nt., Erbar'men nt.

mere, adj. bloß, nichts als.

merely, adv. nur, bloß.

merge, vb. verschmel'zen*.

merger, n. Zusam'menschluß, -sse m.; Fusion', -en f.

meringue, n. Baiser', -s nt.

merit, 1. n. Verdienst', -e nt.; Wert, -e m.; Vorzug, -e m. **2.** vb. verdie'nen.

meritorious, adj. verdienst'lich.

mermaid, n. Nixe, -n f.

merriment, n. Fröhlichkeit, -en f.

merry, adj. fröhlich, lustig.

merry-go-round, n. Karussell', -s nt.

mesh, n. Netz, -e nt.

mess, n. Durcheinan'der nt.; Unordnung f.; Schlamas'sel nt.; (mil.) Eßsaal, -säle m.

message, n. Botschaft, -en f., Nachricht, -en f.

messenger, n. Bote, -n, -n m.

messy, adj. unordentlich, schlampig.

metabolism, n. Stoffwechsel m.

metal, n. Metall', -e nt.

metallic, adj. metal'len.

metamorphosis, n. Metamorpho'se, -n f.

metaphysics, n. Metaphysik' f.

meteor, n. Meteor', -e m.

meteorite, n. Meteorit', -e m.

meteorology, n. Meteorologie' f.

meter, n. (unit of measure) Meter, - nt. or m.; (recording device) Zähler, - m.

method, n. Metho'de, -n f.

meticulous, adj. sorgfältig.

metric, adj. metrisch.

metropolis, n. Großstadt, -e f.

metropolitan, adj. zur Großstadt gehö'rend.

mettle, n. Mut m.

Mexican, 1. n. Mexika'ner, - m. **2.** adj. mexika'nisch.

Mexico, n. Mexiko nt.

mezzanine, n. Zwischenstock m.

microbe, n. Mikro'be, -n f.

microfilm, n. Mikrofilm, -e m.

microphone, n. Mikrophon', -e nt.

microscope, n. Mikroskop', -e nt.

mid, adj. Mittel- (cpds.): (in m. air) mitten in der Luft.

middle, 1. n. Mitte, -n f. **2.** adj. mittler-.

middle-aged, adj. in mittlerem Alter.

Middle Ages, n. Mittelalter nt.

middle class, n. Mittelstand, -e m.

midget, n. Lilliputa'ner, - m.

midnight, n. Mitternacht f.

midwife, n. Hebamme, -n f.

mien, n. Miene, n f.

might, n. Macht, -e f.

mighty, adj. mächtig.

migraine, *n.* Migrä'ne *f.*

migrate, *vb.* wandern.

migration, *n.* Wanderung *f.*

migratory, *adj.* wandernd. Zug- (*cpds.*).

mildew, *n.* Schimmel *m.*

mildness, *n.* Milde *f.*

mile, *n.* Meile, -n *f.*

mileage, *n.* Meilenzahl *f.*

militant, *adj.* kriegerisch.

militarism, *n.* Militaris'mus *m.*

military, 1. *n.* Militär', -s *nt.* **2.** *adj.* milit'ärisch.

militia, *n.* Miliz', -en *f.*

milk, 1. *n.* Milch, *f.* **2.** *vb.* melken*.

milkman, *n.* Milchmann, *-*er *m.*

milky, *adj.* milchig.

mill, 1. *n.* Mühle, -n *f.*; (*factory*) Fabrik', -en *f.* **2.** *vb.* mahlen*.

miller, *n.* Müller, - *m.*

millimeter, *n.* Millime'ter, - *nt.*

millinery, *n.* Putzwaren *pl.*

million, *n.* Million', -en *f.*

millionaire, *n.* Millionär', -e *m.*

mimic, 1. *n.* Schauspieler, - *m.* **2.** *vb.* nach·ahmen.

mince, *vb.* klein schneiden*; **(he doesn t m. his words)** er nimmt kein Blatt vor den Mund.

mind, 1. *n.* Geist *m.*, Verstand' *m.*, Sinn *m.* **2.** *vb.* (*obey*) gehor'chen; (*watch over*) auf·passen auf; **(never m.)** das macht nichts.

mindful, *adj.* eingedenk.

mine, 1. *n.* Bergwerk, -e *nt.*; (*mil.*) Mine, -n *f.* **2.** *pron.* meiner, -es, -e. **3.** *vb.* ab·bauen; (*mil.*) Minen legen.

miner, *n.* Bergarbeiter, - *m.*

mineral, 1. *n.* Mineral', -e *nt.* **2.** *adj.* minera'lisch.

mingle, *vb.* mischen.

miniature, *n.* Miniatur', -en *f.*

minimal, *adj.* minimal'; Mindest-, Minimal- (*cpds.*).

minimize, *vb.* herab'setzen.

minimum, *n.* Minimum, -ma *nt.*

mining, *n.* Bergbau *m.*

minister, *n.* (*government*) Mini'ster, - *m.*; (*church*) Pfarrer, - *m.*, Pastor, -o'ren *m.*, Geistlich-*m.*

ministry, *n.* (*government*) Ministe'rium, -rien *nt.*; (*church*) Geistlicher Stand *m.*

mink, *n.* Nerz, -e *m.*

minnow, *n.* Elritze, -n *f.*

minor, 1. *n.* Minderjährig-*m.&f.* **2.** *adj.* gering'; (*music*) Moll *nt.*, **(A-minor)** a-Moll.

minority, *n.* Minderzahl, -en *f.*, Minderheit, -en *f.*, Minorität', -en *f.*

minstrel, *n.* Spielmann, -leute *m.*

mint, 1. *n.* (*plant*) Minze -n *f.*; (*coin factory*) Münze, -n *f.* **2.** *vb.* münzen.

minus, *prep.* minus, weniger.

minute, 1. *n.* Minu'te, -n *f.* **2.** *adj.* winzig.

miracle, *n.* Wunder, - *nt.*

miraculous, *adj.* wie ein Wunder.

mirage, *n.* Luftspiegelung, -en *f.*

mire, *n.* Sumpf, *-*e *m.*; Schlamm *m.*

mirror, *n.* Spiegel, - *m.*

mirth, *n.* Fröhlichkeit *f.*

misappropriate, *vb.* verun'treuen.

misbehave, *vb.* sich schlecht beneh'men*.

miscellaneous, *adj.* divers'.

mischief, *n.* Unfug *m.*

mischievous, *adj.* schelmisch.

misconstrue, *vb.* mißdeuten.

misdemeanor, *n.* Verge'hen, - *nt.*

miser, *n.* Geizhals, *-*e *m.*

miserable, *adj.* jämmerlich, kläglich.

miserly, *adj.* geizig.

misery, *n.* Elend *nt.*, Jammer *m.*

misfit, *n.* Blindgänger, - *m.*

misfortune, *n.* Unglück, -e *nt.*, Pech *nt.*

misgiving, *n.* Beden'ken, - *nt.*

mishap, *n.* Unglück, -e *nt.*

mislay, *vb.* verle'gen.

mislead, *vb.* irre-führen.

misplace, *vb.* verle'gen.

mispronounce, *vb.* falsch aus'sprechen*.

miss, 1. *n.* Fehlschlag, ᵉe *m.* **2.** *vb.* verfeh'len; (*feel the lack of*) vermis'sen; (*fail to obtain*) verpas'sen.

Miss, *n.* Fräulein.- *nt.*

missile, *n.* Wurfgeschoß, -sse *nt.*; **(guided m.)** ferngesteuertes Rake'tengeschoß, -sse *nt.*

mission, *n.* Mission', -en *f.*

missionary, 1. *n.* Missionar', -e *m.* **2.** *adj.* Missionars'- (*cpds.*).

misspell, *vb.* falsch buchstabie'ren.

mist, *n.* (*fog*) Nebel, - *m.*; (*haze*) Dunst, ᵉe *m.*

mistake, 1. *n.* Fehler, - *m.*, Irrtum, ᵉer *m.* **2.** *vb.* verken'nen*.

mistaken, *adj.* falsch; irrig **(be m.)** sich irren.

mister, *n.* Herr, -n, -en *m.*

mistletoe, *n.* Mispel, -n *f.*

mistreat, *vb.* mißhan'deln.

mistress, *n.* Herrin, -nen *f.*; (*of the house*) Hausfrau, -en *f.*; (*of a pet*) Frauchen, - *nt.*; (*lover*) Geliebt'- *f.*

mistrust, 1. *n.* Mißtrauen *nt.* **2.** *vb.* mißtrau'en.

misty, *adj.* neblig; dunstig.

misunderstand, *vb.* mißverstehen*.

misuse. 1. *n.* Mißbrauch, ᵉe *m.* **2.** *vb.* mißbrau'chen.

mite, *n.* Bißchen *nt.*; (*bug*) Milbe, -n *f.*

mitigate, *vb.* mildern.

mitten, *n.* Fausthandschuh, -e *m.*

mix, *vb.* mischen.

mixture, *n.* Mischung, -en *f.*

mix-up, *n.* Verwir'rung, -en *f.*; Verwechs'lung, -en *f.*

moan, *n.* stöhnen.

mob, *n.* Menschenmenge, -n *f.*; Pöbel *m.*

mobile, *adj.* beweg'lich; mobilisiert'.

mobilization, *n.* Mobil'machung, -en *f.*

mobilize, *vb.* mobilisie'ren.

mock, *vb.* (*tr.*) verspot'ten; (*intr.*) spotten.

mockery, *n.* Spott *m.*, Hohn *m.*

mode, *n.* (*way*) Art und Weise *f.*; (*fashion*) Mode, -n *f.*

model, 1. *n.* Vorbild, -er *nt.*, Muster, - *nt.*; Modell', -e *nt.* **2.** *vb.* modellie'ren.

moderate, 1. *adj.* mäßig, gemä'ßigt. **2.** *vb.* mäßigen; vermit'teln.

moderation, *n.* Mäßigung *f.*

modern, *adj.* modern'.

modernize, *vb.* modernisie'ren.

modest, *adj.* beschei'den.

modesty, *n.* Beschei'denheit *f.*

modify, *vb.* modifizie'ren.

modish, *adj.* modisch.

modulate, *vb.* modulie'ren.

moist, *adj.* feucht.

moisten, *vb.* befeuch'ten.

moisture, *n.* Feuchtigkeit *f.*

molar, *n.* Backenzahn ᵉe *m.*

molasses, *n.* Melas'se *f.*; Sirup *m.*

mold. 1. *n.* Form, -en *f.*; (*mildew*) Schimmel *m.* **2.** *vb.* formen; schimmelig werden*.

moldy, *adj.* schimmelig.

mole, *n.* (*animal*) Maulwurf, ᵉe *m.*; (*mark*) Muttermal, -e *nt.*

molecule, *n.* Molekül', -e *nt.*

molest, *vb.* belās'tigen.

molten, *adj.* flüssig.

moment, *n.* Augenblick, -e *m.*, Moment', -e *m.*; (*factor*) Moment', -e *nt.*

momentary, *adj.* augenblick'lich, momentan'.

momentous, *adj.* folgenschwer.

monarch, *n.* Monarch', -en, -en *m.*

monarchy, *n.* Monarchie'- -i'en *f.*

monastery, *n.* Kloster, ᵉ *nt.*

Monday, *n.* Montag, -e *m.*

monetary, adj. Geld- (cpds.).

money, n. Geld, -er nt.

money changer, n. Geldwechsler, - m.

money order, n. Postanweisung, -en f.

mongrel, n. Bastard, -e m.

monitor, n. (man) Abhörer, - m.; (apparatus) Kontroll'gerät, -e nt.

monk, n. Mönch, -e m.

monkey, n. Affe, -n, -n m.

monocle, n. Mono'kel, - nt.

monologue, n. Monolog', -e m.

monopolize, vb. monopolisie'ren.

monopoly, n. Monopol', -e nt.

monotone, n. einförmiger Ton, ⸗e m.

monotonous, adj. eintönig, monoton'.

monotony, n. Eintönigkeit f., Monotonie' f.

monster, n. Ungeheuer, - nt.

monstrosity, n. Ungeheuerlichkeit, -en f.

monstrous, adj. ungeheuerlich, haarsträubend.

month, n. Monat, -e m.

monthly, **1.** n. Monatsschrift, -en f. **2.** adj. monatlich.

monument, n. Denkmal, ⸗er nt.

monumental, adj. monumental'.

mood, n. Stimmung, -en f.; Laune, -n f.

moody, adj. launisch; schwermütig.

moon, n. Mond, -e m.

moonlight, n. Mondschein m.

moor, **1.** n. Moor, -e nt. **2.** vb. veran'kern.

mooring, n. Ankerplatz, ⸗e m.

moot, adj. strittig.

mop, n. Mop, -s m.

moral, **1.** n. Moral', -en f. **2.** adj. sittlich, mora'lisch.

morale, n. Stimmung, -en f.; Moral' f.

moralist, n. Moralist', -en, -en m.

morality, n. Sittlichkeit f., Moral' f.; Sittenlehre f.

morbid, adj. morbid'.

more, adv. mehr.

moreover, adv. außerdem.

morgue, n. Leichenhaus, ⸗er nt.

morning, n. Morgen, - m., m.; Vormittag, -e m.

moron, n. Schwachsinnigm.&f.

morose, adj. verdrieß'lich.

morphine, n. Morphium nt.

morsel, n. Bissen, - m.

mortal, adj. sterblich; tödlich.

mortality, n. Sterblichkeit f.

mortar, n. (vessel) Mörser, - m.; (building material) Mörtel m.

mortgage, n. Hypothek', -en f.

mortician, n. Leichenbestatter, - m.

mortify, vb. kastei'en; demütigen.

mortuary, n. Leichenhalle, -n f.

mosaic, n. Mosaik', -e nt.

mosquito, n. Mücke, -n f.

moss, n. Moos, -e nt.

most, adj. meist-.

mostly, adv. meistens, hauptsächlich.

moth, n. Motte, -n f.

mother, n. Mutter, ⸗ f.

mother-in-law, n. Schwiegermutter, ⸗ f.

motif, n. Motiv', -e nt.

motion, n. Bewe'gung, -en f.; (parliament) Antrag, ⸗e m.

motionless, adj. bewe'gungslos.

motion picture, n. Film, -e m.

motivate, vb. veran'lassen, motivie'ren.

motivation, n. Motivie'rung, -en f.

motive, n. Beweg'grund, ⸗e m.

motor, n. Motor, -o'ren m.

motorboat, n. Motorboot, -e nt.

motorcycle, n. Motorrad, ⸗er nt.

motorist, *n.* Kraftfahrer, - *m.*

motto, *n.* Motto, -s *nt.*

mound, *n.* Erdhügel, - *m.*

mount, *vb.* (*get on*) bestei'gen*; (*put on*) montie'ren.

mountain, *n.* Berg, -e *m.*

mountaineer, *n.* Bergbewohner, - *m.*; Bergsteiger, - *m.*

mountainous, *adj.* bergig, gebir'gig.

mourn, *vb.* (*intr.*) trauern; (*tr.*) betrau'ern.

mournful, *adj.* trauervoll.

mourning, *n.* Trauer *f.*

mouse, *n.* Maus, ⸗e *f.*

mouth, *n.* Mund, ⸗er *m.*; (*river*) Mündung, -en *f.*

mouthpiece, *n.* (*instrument*) Mundstück, -e *nt.*; (*spokesman*) Wortführer, - *m.*

movable, *adj.* beweg'lich.

move, 1. *n.* (*household goods*) Umzug, ⸗e *m.*; (*motion*) Bewe'gung, -en *f.*; (*games*) Zug. 2. *vb.* um·ziehen*; bewe'gen, sich bewe'gen; ziehen*; (*parliamentary*) bean'tragen.

movement, *n.* Bewe'gung, -en *f.*; (*music*) Satz, ⸗e *m.*

movie, *n.* Kino, -s *nt.*; Film, -e *m.*

moving, *n.* Umzug, ⸗e *m.* 2. *adj.* ergrei'fend.

mow, *vb.* mähen.

Mr., *n.* Herr *m.*

Mrs., *n.* Frau *f.*

much, *adj.* viel.

mucilage, *n.* Klebstoff, -e *m.*

muck, *n.* Schlamm *m.*

mucous, *adj.* schleimig.

mucus, *n.* Nasenschleim *m.*

mud, *n.* Schlamm *m.*, Dreck *m.*

muddy, *adj.* schlammig, trübe.

muff, 1. *n.* Muff, -e *m.* 2. *vb.* vermas'seln.

muffle, *vb.* (*wrap up*) einhüllen; (*silence*) dämpfen.

muffler, *n.* (*scarf*) Schal, -s *m.*; (*auto*) Auspufftopf, ⸗e *m.*

mug, *n.* Krug, ⸗e *m.*

mulatto, *n.* Mulat'te, -n, -n *m.*

mule, *n.* Esel. - *m.*

multiple, *adj.* vielfältig.

multiplication, *n.* Multiplikation', -en *f.*

multiply, *vb.* (*math.*) multiplizie'ren; (*increase*) vervielfältigen.

multitude, *n.* Menge, -n *f.*

mummy, *n.* Mumie, -n *f.*

mumps, *n.* Ziegenpeter *m.*

Munich, *n.* München *nt.*

municipal, *adj.* städtisch.

munificent, *adj.* freigebig.

munition, *n.* Munition', -en *f.*

mural, *n.* Wandgemälde, - *nt.*

murder, 1. *n.* Mord, -e *m.* 2. *vb.* morden, ermor'den.

murderer, *n.* Mörder, - *m.*

murmur, 1. *n.* Germur'mel, - *nt.* 2. *vb.* murmeln.

muscle, *n.* Muskel, -n *m.*

muscular, *adj.* muskulös; Muskel- (*cpds.*).

muse, 1. *n.* Muse, -n *f.* 2. *vb.* nach·denken*.

museum, *n.* Muse'um, -se'en *nt.*

mushroom, *n.* Pilz, -e *m.*

music, *n.* Musik' *f.*

musical, *adj.* musika'lisch.

musical comedy, *n.* Operet'te, -n *f.*

musician, *n.* Musiker, - *m.*

muslin, *n.* Musselin', -e *m.*

must, *vb.* müssen*.

mustache, *n.* Schnurrbart, - *m.*

mustard, *n.* Senf *m.*, Mostrich *m.*

muster, 1. *n.* Musterung, -en *f.* 2. *vb.* mustern.

musty, *adj.* muffig.

mutation, *n.* Mutation', -en *f.*

mute, *adj.* stumm.

mutilate, *vb.* verstüm'meln.

mutiny 1. *n.* Meuterei', -en *f.* 2. *vb.* meutern.

mutter, *vb.* murmeln.

mutton, *n.* Hammelfleisch *nt.*

mutual, *adj.* gegenseitig, gemein'sam.

muzzle, *n.* (*gun*) Mündung, -en *f.*; (*animal's mouth*) Maul, ⁓er *nt.*; (*mouth covering*) Maulkorb, ⁓e *m.*

my, *adj.* mein, -, -e.

myopia, *n.* Kurzsichtigkeit *f.*

myriad, 1. *n.* Myria'de, -n *f.*; (*fig.*) Unzahl, -en *f.* **2.** *adj.* unzählig.

myrtle, *n.* Myrte, -n *f.*

mysterious, *adj.* geheim'-nisvoll.

mystery, *n.* Geheim'nis, -se *nt.*; Rätsel, - *nt.*

mystic, 1. *n.* Mystiker, - *m.* **2.** *adj.* mystisch; Geheim'-(*cpds.*).

mystify, *vb.* verwir'ren; ver-dun'keln.

myth, *n.* Sage, -n *f.*; Mythus, -then *m.*

mythical, *adj.* sagenhaft, mythisch.

mythology, *n.* Mythologie', -i'en *f.*

N

nag, 1. *n.* Gaul, ⁓e *m.* **2.** *vb.* herum'⁓nörgeln; keifen.

nail, 1. *n.* Nagel, ⁓ *m.* **2.** *vb.* nageln.

naïve, *adj.* naiv', unbefangen.

naked, *adj.* nackt.

name, 1. *n.* Name(n), - *m.* **2.** *vb.* nennen*.

namely, *adv.* nämlich.

namesake, *n.* Namensvet-ter, -n *m.*

nap, 1. *n.* (*sleep*) Nicker-chen, - *nt.*, Nachmittags-schläfchen, - *nt.*; (*cloth*) Noppe, -n *f.* **2.** *vb.* ein'nicken.

naphtha, *n.* Naphtha *nt.*

napkin, *n.* Serviet'te, -n *f.*; (**sanitary n.**) Binde, -n *f.*

narcissus, *n.* Narzis'se, -n *f.*

narcotic, 1. *n.* Rauschgift, -e *nt.* **2.** *adj.* narko'tisch.

narrate, *vb.* erzäh'len.

narrative, 1. *n.* Erzäh'lung, -en *f.* **2.** *adj.* erzäh'lend.

narration, *n.* Erzäh'lung, -en *f.*

narrow, *adj.* (*tight, confined*) eng; (*not broad*) schmal(⁓, -).

nasal, *adj.* nasal'.

nasty, *adj.* häßlich.

natal, *adj.* Geburts'- (*cpds.*).

nation, *n.* Nation', -en *f.*, Volk, ⁓er *nt.*

national, *adj.* Staatsange-hörig- *m.&f.* **2.** *adj.* na-tional'.

nationalism, *n.* Nationalis'-mus *m.*

nationality, *n.* Staatsange-hörigkeit, -en *f.*, Nationa-lität', -en *f.*

nationalization, *n.* Ver-staat'lichung, -en *f.*

nationalize, *vb.* verstaat'-lichen.

native, 1. *n.* Eingeboren- *m.&f.*, Einheimisch- *m.&f.* **2.** *adj.* gebür'tig, einheimisch.

nativity, *n.* Geburt', -en *f.*

natural, *adj.* natür'lich.

naturalist, *n.* Natur'for-scher, - *m.*, Naturalist', -en, -en *m.*

naturalize, *vb.* naturalisie'-ren.

naturalness, *n.* Natür'lich-keit *f.*

nature, *n.* Natur', -en *f.*; (*essence*) Wesen *nt.*

naughty, *adj.* unartig.

nausea, *n.* Übelkeit *f.*

nauseous, *adj.* ekelerregend.

nautical, *adj.* nautisch.

naval, *adj.* See-, Schiffs-, Mari'ne- (*cpds.*).

nave, *n.* Kirchenschiff, -e *nt.*

navel, *n.* Nabel, - *m.*

navigable, *adj.* schiffbar.

navigate, *vb.* schiffen, steu-ern.

navigation, *n.* Schiffahrt *f.*, Navigation' *f.*

navigator, *n.* Seefahrer, - *m.*; (*airplane*) Orter, - *m.*

navy, *n.* Mari'ne *f.*; Flotte, -n *f.*

navy yard, *n.* Mari'newerft, -en *f.*

near, 1. *prep.* in der Nähe von. **2.** *adj.* nahe (näher, nächst-).

nearby, 1. *adj.* naheliegend, nahe gele'gen. 2. *adv.* in der Nähe.

nearly, *adv.* beinahe, fast.

near-sighted, *adj.* kurzsichtig.

neat, *adj.* sauber.

neatness, *n.* Sauberkeit *f.*

nebula, *n.* Nebelfleck, -e *m.*

nebulous, *adj.* nebelhaft.

necessary, *adj.* nötig, notwendig.

necessity, *n.* Notwendigkeit, -en *f.*

neck, *n.* Hals, ̶e *m.*

necklace, *n.* Halskette, -n *f.*

necktie, *n.* Schlips, -e *m.*, Krawat'te, -n *f.*

nectar, *n.* Nektar *m.*

need, 1. *n.* Not, ̶e *f.*; Bedürf'nis, -se *nt.* 2. *vb.* benö'tigen, brauchen.

needful, *adj.* notwendig.

needle, *n.* Nadel, -n *f.*

needless, *adj.* unnötig.

needy, *adj.* notleidend.

negative, 1. *n.* (photo) Negativ, -e *nt.* 2. *adj.* vernei'nend, negativ.

neglect, 1. *n.* Vernach'lässigung, -en *f.* 2. *vb.* vernach'lässigen.

negligee, *n.* Negligé', -s *nt.*

negligent, *adj.* nachlässig, fahrlässig.

negligible, *adj.* gering'fügig.

negotiate, *vb.* verhan'deln.

negotiation, *n.* Verhand'lung, -en *f.*

Negro, *n.* Neger, - *m.*

neighbor, *n.* Nachbar, (-n,) -n *m.*

neighborhood, *n.* Nachbarschaft, -en *f.*

neither, 1. *pron.* keiner, -es, -e (von beiden). 2. *conj.* (n. . . . nor) weder . . . noch.

neon, *n.* Neon *nt.*

nephew, *n.* Neffe, -n, -n *m.*

nepotism, *n.* Nepotis'mus *m.*

nerve, *n.* Nerv, -en *m.*; (effrontery) Dreistigkeit *f.*

nervous, *adj.* nervös'.

nest, *n.* Nest, -er *nt.*

nestle, *vb.* nisten, *(fig.)* sich an·schmiegen.

net, 1. *n.* Netz, -e *nt.* 2. *adj.* netto.

network, *n.* Netz, -e *nt.*

neuralgia, *n.* Neuralgie' *f.*

neurology, *n.* Neurologie' *f.*

neurotic, *adj.* neuro'tisch.

neutral, *adj.* neutral', unparteiisch.

neutrality, *n.* Neutralität' *f.*

never, *adv.* nie, niemals.

nevertheless, *adv.* dennoch, trotzdem.

new, *adj.* neu.

news, *n.* Nachrichten *pl.*; (item of n.) Nachricht, -en *f.*

newsboy, *n.* Zeitungsjunge, -n, -n *m.*

newscast, *n.* Nachrichtensendung, -en *f.*

newspaper, *n.* Zeitung, -en *f.*

newsreel, *n.* Wochenschau *f.*

next, *adj.* nächst-.

nibble, *vb.* knabbern.

nice, *adj.* nett, hübsch.

nick, *n.* Kerbe, -n *f.*

nickel, *n.* Nickel *nt.*

nickname, *n.* Spitzname(n), -m.

nicotine, *n.* Nikotin' *nt.*

niece, *n.* Nichte, -n *f.*

niggardly, *adj.* knauserig.

night, *n.* Nacht, ̶e *f.*

nightingale, *n.* Nachtigall, -en *f.*

night club, *n.* Nachtlokal, -e *nt.*

nightly, *adj.* nächtlich, jede Nacht.

nightgown, *n.* Nachthemd, -en *nt.*

nightmare, *n.* böser Traum, ̶e *m.*, Alpdruck *m.*

nimble, *adj.* flink.

nine, *num.* neun.

nineteen, *num.* neunzehn.

nineteenth, 1. *adj.* neunzehnt-. 2. *n.* Neunzehntel *nt.*

ninetieth, 1. *adj.* neunzigst-. 2. *n.* Neunzigstel *nt.*

ninety, *num.* neunzig.

ninth, 1. *adj.* neunt-. 2. *n.* Neuntel, - *nt.*

nip, 1. *n.* Zwick, -e *m.*;

(*drink*) Schlückchen, - *nt.*
2. *vb.* zwicken.

nipple, *n.* Brustwarze, -n *f.;*
(*baby's bottle*) Sauger, - *m.*

nitrate, *n.* Nitrat', -e *nt.*

nitrogen, *n.* Stickstoff *m.*

no, 1. *adj.* kein, -, -e. 2.
interj. nein.

nobility, *n.* Adel *m.*

noble, *adj.* (*rank*) adlig;
(*character*) edel.

nobleman, *n.* Adlige, -n *m.*

nobody, *pron.* niemand, keiner.

nocturnal, *adj.* nächtlich.

nocturne, *n.* Noktur'ne, -n
f.

nod, *vb.* nicken.

noise, *n.* Geräusch', -e *nt.;*
Lärm *m.*

noiseless, *adj.* geräusch'los.

noisy, *adj.* laut.

nomad, *n.* Noma'de, -n. -n *m.*

nominal, *adj.* nominal'.

nominate, *vb.* ernen'nen*;
(*candidate*) auf·stellen.

nomination, *n.* Ernen'nung,
-en *f.;* Kandidatur', -en *f.*

nominee, *n.* Kandidat', -en,
-en *m.*

nonchalant, *adj.* zwanglos,
nonchalant'.

noncombatant, *n.* Nicht-
kämpfer, - *m.*

non-commissioned officer,
n. Unteroffizier, -e *m.*

noncommittal, *adj.* nicht-
verpflich'tend.

nondescript, *adj.* unbestimm-
bar.

none, *pron.* keiner, -es, -e.

nonpartisan, *adj.* unparteiisch.

nonsense, *n.* Unsinn *m.*

nonstop, *adj.* durchgehend.

noodle, *n.* Nudel, -n *f.*

nook, *n.* Ecke, -n *f.;* Winkel, -
m.

noon, *n.* Mittag *m.*

noose, *n.* Schlinge, -n *f.*

nor, *conj.* noch.

normal, *adj.* normal', gewöhn'lich.

north, 1. *n.* Norden *m.* 2.
adj. nördlich; Nord- (*cpds.*).

northeast, 1. *n.* Nordost'en

m. 2. *adj.* nordöst'lich;
Nordost- (*cpds.*).

northeastern, *adj.* nordöst'-
lich.

northern, *adj.* nördlich.

North Pole, *n.* Nordpol *m.*

northwest, 1. *n.* Nordwes'-
ten *m.* 2. *adj.* nordwest'lich;
Nordwest- (*cpds.*).

Norway, *n.* Norwegen *nt.*

Norwegian, 1. *n.* Norweger, - *m.* 2. *adj.* norwegisch.

nose, *n.* Nase, -n *f.*

nosebleed, *n.* Nasenbluten
nt.

nose dive, *n.* Sturz, ¬e *m.;*
(*airplane*) Sturzflug, ¬e *m.*

nostalgia, *n.* Heimweh *nt.;*
Sehnsucht *f.*

nostril, *n.* Nasenloch, ¬er *nt.*,
Nüster, -n *f.*

not, *adv.* nicht; (**n. a., n.
any**) kein, -, -e.

notable, *adj.* bemer'kenswert.

notary, *n.* Notar', -e *m.*

notation, *n.* Aufzeichnung,
-en *f.*

notch, 1. *n.* Kerbe, -n *f.*
2. *vb.* ein·kerben.

note, 1. *n.* Notiz', -en *f.;*
(*comment*) Anmerkung, -en
f.; (*music*) Note, -n *f.;* (*letter*) kurzer Brief, -e *m.* 2.
vb. bemer'ken.

note-book, *n.* Notiz'buch,
¬er *nt.*, Heft, -e *nt.*

noted, *adj.* bekannt'.

noteworthy, *adj.* beach'tenswert.

nothing, *pron.* nichts.

notice, 1. *n.* (*attention*)
Beach'tung, -en *f.;* (*poster*)
Bekannt'machung, -en *f.;*
(*announcement*) Anzeige, -n
f.; (*give n.*) kündigen. 2.
vb. beach'ten; bemer'ken.

noticeable, *adj.* bemer'kenswert; (*conspicuous*) auffällig.

notification, *n.* Benach'-
richtigung, -en *f.*

notify, *vb.* benach'richtigen.

notoriety, *n.* Verruf' *m.*,
Verru'fenheit *f.*

notion, *n.* Vorstellung, -en

f., Idee', -de'en *f.*; **(n.s,** articles) Kurzwaren *pl.*

notorious, *adj.* berüch'tigt.

notwithstanding, 1. *prep.* ungeachtet, trotz. **2.** *adv.* nichtsdestoweniger.

noun, *n.* Hauptwort, ⸚er *nt.*, Substantiv, -e *nt.*

nourish, *vb.* nähren; ernäh'ren.

nourishment, *n.* Nahrung, -en *f.*

novel, 1. *n.* Roman', -e *m.* **2.** *adj.* neu.

novelist, *n.* Roman'schriftsteller, - *m.*

novelty, *n.* Neuheit, -en *f.*

November, *n.* Novem'ber *m.*

novena, *n.* Nove'ne, -n *f.*

novice, *n.* Neuling, -e *m.*

novocaine, *n.* Novocain' *nt.*

now, *adv.* jetzt, nun.

nowhere, *adv.* nirgends.

nozzle, *n.* Düse, -n *f.*; (*gun*) Mündung, -en *f.*

nuance, *n.* Nuan'ce, -n *f.*

nuclear, *adj.* Kern- (*cpds.*).

nucleus, *n.* Kern, -e *m.*

nude, *adj.* nackt.

nugget, *n.* Klumpen, - *m.*

nuisance, *n.* Ärgernis, -se *nt.*; (**be a n.**) ärgerlich, lästig sein*.

nullify, *vb.* annullie'ren, aufheben*.

number, 1. *n.* Zahl, -en *f.*; (*figure*) Ziffer, -n *f.*; (*magazine, telephone, house*) Nummer, -n *f.*; (*amount*) Anzahl, -en *f.* **2.** *vb.* numerie'ren; (*amount to*) sich belau'fen auf.

numerical, *adj.* zahlenmäßig.

numerous, *adj.* zahlreich.

nun, *n.* Nonne, -n *f.*

nuptial, *adj.* Hochzeits-, Ehe- (*cpds.*).

nurse, 1. *n.* Krankenschwester, -n *f.* **2.** *vb.* pflegen; (*suckle*) stillen.

nursery, *n.* Kinderzimmer, - *nt.*; (*plants*) Pflanzschule, -n *f.*

nurture, *vb.* ernäh'ren, nähren; (*fig.*) hegen.

nut, *n.* Nuß, ⸚sse *f.*

nutcracker, *n.* Nußknacker, - *m.*

nutrition, *n.* Ernäh'rung *f.*

nutritious, *adj.* nahrhaft.

nylon, *n.* Nylon *nt.*

nymph, *n.* Nymphe, -n *f.*

O

oak, *n.* Eiche, -n *f.*

oar, *n.* Ruder, - *nt.*

oasis, *n.* Oa'se, -n *f.*

oath, *n.* (*pledge*) Eid, -e *m.*, Schwur, ⸚e *m.*; (*curse*) Fluch, ⸚e *m.*

oatmeal, *n.* Hafergrütze *f.*

oats, *n.* Hafer *m.*; Haferflocken *pl.*

obedience, *n.* Gehor'sam *m.*

obedient, *adj.* gehor'sam.

obeisance, *n.* Ehrerbietung, -en *f.*

obese, *adj.* fettleibig.

obey, *vb.* gehor'chen, befol'gen.

obituary, *n.* Nachruf, -e *m.*

object, 1. *n.* Gegenstand, ⸚e *m.*; (*aim*) Ziel, -e *nt.*; (*purpose*) Zweck, -e *m.*; (*gram.*) Objekt', -e *nt.* **2.** *vb.* einwenden*, Einspruch erhe'ben*.

objection, *n.* Einwand, ⸚e *m.*, Einspruch, ⸚e *m.*

objectionable, *adj.* widerwärtig.

objective, 1. *n.* Ziel, -e *nt.*; (*photo*) Objektiv', -e *nt.* **2.** *adj.* sachlich, objektiv'.

obligation, *n.* Verpflich'tung, -en *f.*

obligatory, *adj.* obligato'risch.

oblige, *vb.* verpflich'ten; jemandem gefäl'lig sein*.

obliging, *adj.* gefäl'lig.

oblique, *adj.* schief, schräg.

obliterate, *vb.* aus·radieren, vernich'ten.

oblivion, *n.* Verges'senheit *f.*

oblong, *adj.* länglich; rechteckig.

obnoxious, *adj.* widerlich.

obscene, *adj.* unanständig, obszön'.

obscure, *adj.* dunkel.

obsequious, *adj.* unterwür'tig.

observance, *n.* Beach'tung, -en *f.; (celebration)* Feier *f.*

observation, *n.* Beob'achtung, -en *f.*

observatory, *n.* Sternwarte, -n *f.*

observe, *vb.* beob'achten; befol'gen.

observer, *n.* Beob'achter, - *m.*

obsession, *n.* fixe Idee', -de'en *f.*

obsolete, *adj.* veral'tet, überholt'.

obstacle, *n.* Hindernis, -se *nt.*

obstetrical, *adj.* geburts'hilflich.

obstetrician, *n.* Geburts'helfer, - *m.*

obstinate, *adj.* hartnäckig.

obstreperous, *adj.* lautmäulig.

obstruct, *vb.* versper'ren, hindern.

obstruction, *n.* Hindernis, -se *nt.*

obtain, *vb.* erhal'ten*, bekom'men*.

obviate, *vb.* besei'tigen.

obvious, *adj.* selbstverständlich, offensichtlich.

occasion, *n.* Gele'genheit, -en *f.*

occasional, *adj.* gele'gentlich.

Occident, *n.* Abendland *nt.*

occidental, *adj.* abendländisch.

occult, *adj.* verbor'gen, okkult'.

occupant, *n.* Inhaber, - *m.,* Insasse, -n, -n *m.,* Bewohner, - *m.*

occupation, *n. (profession)* Beruf', -e *m.; (mil.)* Beset'zung, -en *f.; (o. forces)* Besat'zung, -en *f.*

occupy, *vb. (take up)* einnehmen*; *(keep busy)* beschäf'tigen; *(mil.)* beset'zen.

occur, *vb.* vor·kommen*, gesche'hen*, passie'ren.

occurrence, *n.* Ereig'nis, -se *nt.*

ocean, *n.* Ozean, -e *m.*

o clock, *n.* Uhr *f.*

octagon, *n.* Achteck, -e *nt.*

octave, *n.* Okta've, -n *f.*

Oct ber, *n.* Okto'ber *m.*

octopus, *n.* Tintenfisch, -e *m.*

ocular, *adj.* Augen- *(cpds.).*

oculist, *n.* Augenarzt, ⸗e *m.*

odd, *adj. (numbers)* ungerade; *(queer)* merkwürdig.

oddity, *n.* Merkwürdigkeit, -en *f.*

odds, *n.pl.* Chance, -n *f.; (probability)* Wahrschein'lichkeit, -en *f.; (advantage)* Vorteil, -e *m.*

odious, *adj.* verhaßt'.

odor, *n.* Geruch', ⸗e *m.*

of, *prep.* von.

off, *adv.* ab.

offend, *vb.* verlet'zen, beleidigen.

offender, *n.* Missetäter, - *m.*

offense, *n. (crime)* Verge'hen, - *nt.; (offensive)* Offensi've, -n *f.; (insult)* Kränkung, -en *f.*

offensive, 1. *n.* Offensi've, -n *f.* **2.** *adj.* anstößig.

offer, 1. *n.* Angebot, -e *nt.* **2.** *vb.* an·bieten*.

offering, *n.* Opfer, - *nt.,* Spende, -n *f.*

offhand, *adj.* beiläufig.

office, *n.* Amt, ⸗er *nt.; (room)* Büro', -s *nt.; (doctor's, dentist's o.)* Praxis *f.*

officer, *n.* Offizier', -e *m.; (police)* Polizist', -en, -en *m.*

official, 1. *n.* Beamt'- *m.* **2.** *adj.* amtlich, offiziell'.

officiate, *vb.* amtie'ren.

offspring, *n.* Abkömmling, -e *m.*

often, *adv.* oft, häufig.

oil, 1. *n.* Öl, -e *nt.; (petroleum)* Petro'leum *nt.* **2.** *vb.* ölen.

oily, *adj.* ölig, fettig.

ointment, *n.* Salbe, -n *f.*

old, *adj.* alt(⸗).

old-fashioned, *adj.* altmodisch.

olive, n. Oli've, -n f.

omelet, n. Omelett', -e nt.

omen, n. Omen nt.

ominous, adj. unheilvoll.

omission, n. Versäum'nis, -se nt., Überse'hen, - nt.

omit, vb. aus·lassen*, unter·las'sen*.

omnibus, n. Omnibus, -se m.

omnipotent, adj. allmäch'tig.

on, prep. auf, an.

once, adv. einmal.

one, 1. pron. man, einer, -e, -e. 2. adj. ein, -, -e. 3. num. eins.

one-sided, adj. einseitig.

one-way, adj. Einbahn- (cpds.).

onion, n. Zwiebel, -n f.

only, 1. adj. einzig. 2. adv. nur.

onslaught, n. Angriff, -e m.

onward, adv. vorwärts.

ooze, vb. hervor'quellen*.

opacity, n. Undurchsichtigkeit f.

opal, n. Opal', -e m.

opaque, adj. undurchsichtig.

open, 1. adj. offen. 2. adv. offen, offen. 3. vb. öffnen, auf·machen; (inaugurate) eröff'nen.

opening, 1. n. (hole) Öffnung, -en f.; (inauguration) Eröff'nung, -en f. 2. adj. eröff'nend.

opera, n. Oper, -n f.

opera-glasses, n. Opernglas, -er nt.

operate, vb. operie'ren.

operatic, adj. Opern- (cpds.).

operation, n. Verfah'ren, - nt.; Unterneh'men, - nt.; (med.) Operation', -en f.

operator, n. Bedie'ner, - m. (of a machine); (telephone) Telefon'fräulein, - nt., Vermitt'lung f.; (manager) Manager, - m.

operetta, n. Operet'te, -n f.

ophthalmic, adj. Augen- (cpds.).

opinion, n. Meinung, -en f., Ansicht, -en f.

opponent, n. Gegner, - m.

opportunism, n. Opportunis'mus m.

opportunity, n. günstige Gele'genheit, -en f., Chance, -n f.

oppose, vb. sich widerset'zen.

opposite, 1. n. Gegenteil, -e nt.; (contrast) Gegensatz, -e m. 2. adj. entge'gengesetzt. 3. adv. gegenü'ber.

opposition, n. Opposition', -en f.

oppress, vb. unterdrü'cken.

oppression, n. Unterdrü'ckung, -en f.

oppressive, adj. tyran'nisch; bedrü'ckend, drü'ckend.

oppressor, n. Unterdrü'cker, - m.

optic, adj. optisch.

optician, n. Optiker, - m.

optics, n. Optik f.

optimism, n. Optimis'mus m.

optimistic, adj. optimis'tisch.

option, n. Wahl, -en f.; (privilege of buying) Vorkaufsrecht, -e nt.

optional, adj. freigestellt, fakultativ'.

optometry, n. praktische Augenheilkunde f.

opulence, n. Üppigkeit f.

opulent, adj. üppig.

or, conj. oder.

oracle, n. Ora'kel, - nt.

oral, adj. mündlich.

orange, 1. n. Apfelsi'ne, -n f., Oran'ge, -n f. 2. adj. orange'farbig; (pred. adj. only) orange'.

oration, n. Rede, -n f.

orator, n. Redner, - m.

oratory, n. Redekunst f.

orbit, n. Bahn, -en f.; Gestirns'-, Plane'tenbahn f.

orchard, n. Obstgarten, -e m.

orchestra, n. (large) Orches'ter, - nt.; (small) Kapel'le, -n f.

orchid, n. Orchide'e, -n f.

ordain, vb. in den geistlichen Stand auf·nehmen*.

ordeal, n. Qual, -en f.

order, 1. n. (command)

Befehl', -e *m.*; *(neatness)* Ordnung *f.*; *(decree)* Erlaß, -sse *m.*, Verord'nung, -en *f.*; *(fraternity, medal)* Orden, -m. **2.** *vb.* **(command)** befeh'len*; **(put in o.)** ordnen; *(decree)* verord'nen.

orderly, *adj.* ordentlich; geord'net.

ordinance, *n.* Verord'nung, -en *f.*

ordinary, *adj.* gewöhn'lich.

ore, *n.* Erz, -e *nt.*

organ, *n.* Organ', -e *nt.*; *(music)* Orgel, -n *f.*

organdy, *n.* Organ'dy *m.*

organic, *adj.* orga'nisch.

organism, *n.* Organis'mus, -men *m.*

organist, *n.* Organist', -en *m.*

organization, *n.* Organisation', -en *f.*

organize, *vb.* organisie'ren.

orgy, *n.* Orgie, -n *f.*

orient, *vb.* orientie'ren.

Orient, *n.* Orient *m.*

Oriental, *adj.* orienta'lisch.

orientation, *n.* Orientie'rung, -en *f.*

origin, *n.* Ursprung, ⸗e *m.*

original, *adj.* ursprünglich; *(novel)* originell'.

originality, *n.* Originalität', -en *f.*

ornament, **1.** *n.* Verzie'rung, -en *f.*, Schmuck *m.* **2.** *vb.* verzie'ren, schmücken.

ornamental, *adj.* dekorativ'.

ornate, *adj.* überla'den.

ornithology, *n.* Vogelkunde *f.*

orphan, *n.* Waise, -n *f.*

orphanage, *n.* Waisenhaus, ⸗er *nt.*

orthodox, *adj.* orthodox'.

orthography, . *n.* Rechtschreibung, -en *f.*, Orthographie', -i'en *f.*

orthopedic, *adj.* orthopä'disch.

oscillate, *vb.* schwingen*.

osmosis, *n.* Osmo'se *f.*

ostensible, *adj.* augenscheinlich.

ostentation, *n.* Schaustellung *f.*

ostentatious, *adj.* ostentativ'.

ostracize, *vb.* ächten.

ostrich, *n.* Strauß, -e *m.*

other, *adj.* ander-.

otherwise, *adv.* sonst.

ouch, *interj.* au!

ought, *vb.* sollte; **(o. to have)** hätte . . . sollen.

ounce, *n.* Unze, -n *f.*

our, *adj.* unser, -, -e.

ours, *pron.* unserer, -es, -e.

oust, *vb.* enthe'ben* *(eines Amtes).*

out, *adv.* aus, hin-, heraus'.

out of, *prep.* aus.

outbreak, *n.* Ausbruch, ⸗e *m.*

outburst, *n.* Ausbruck, ⸗e *m.*

outcast, *n.* Ausgestoßen-m.&f.

outcome, *n.* Ergeb'nis, -se *nt.*

outdoors, *adv.* draußen, im Freien.

outer, *adj.* äußer-.

outfit, **1.** *n.* Ausrüstung, -en *f.*; *(mil.)* Einheit, -en *f.* **2.** *vb.* aus'rüsten.

outgrowth, *n.* Folge, -n *f.*

outing, *n.* Ausflug, ⸗e *m.*

outlandish, *adj.* bizarr'.

outlaw, **1.** *n.* Gesetz'los- *m.* **2.** *vb.* verbie'ten*.

outlet, *n.* Abfluß, ⸗sse *m.*; *(fig.)* Ventil', -e *nt.*; *(elec.)* Steckdose, -n *f.*

outline, **1.** *n.* Umriß, -sse *m.*, Kontur', -en *f.*; *(summary)* Übersicht, -en *f.* **2.** *vb.* umrei'ßen*.

outlive, *vb.* überle'ben, überdau'ern.

out-of-date, *adj.* veral'tet, überholt'.

outpost, *n.* Vorposten, - *m.*

output, *n.* Leistung, -en *f.*, Produktion', -en *f.*

outrage, *n.* Frevel, - *m.*

outrageous, *adj.* unerhört'.

outrank, *vb.* einen höheren Rang bekleiden.

outright, *adj.* uneingeschränkt.

outrun, *vb.* hinter sich lassen*.

outside, **1.** *n.* Außenseite, -n *f.*; Außenwelt *f.* **2.** *adj.*

äußer-.   **3.** *adv.* draußen.
4. *prep.* außer, außerhalb.

outskirts, *n.* Außenbezirke *pl.*

outward, *adj.* äußerlich.

oval, *adj.* oval.

ovary, *n.* Eierstock, ≈e *m.*

ovation, *n.* Huldigung, -en *f.*

oven, *n.* Ofen, ≈ *m.*

over, 1. *prep.* über. **2.** *adv.* über; hin-, herü'ber; (*past*) vorbei'.

overbearing, *adj.* anmaßend.

overcoat, *n.* Mantel, ≈ *m.*, Überzieher, - *m.*

overcome, *vb.* überwin'den*.

overdue, *adj.* überfällig.

overflow, 1. *n.* Überf'uß, ≈sse *m.* **2.** *vb.* über'fließen*.

overhaul, *vb.* überho'len.

overhead, 1. *n.* laufende Unkosten *pl.* **2.** *adv.* oben.

overlook, *vb.* überse'hen*.

overnight, *adv.* über Nacht.

overpass, *n.* Unterfüh'rung, -en *f.*

overpower, *vb.* überwäl'tigen.

overrule, *vb.* überstim'men.

overrun, *vb.* überlau'fen*; (*flood*) überflu'ten.

oversee, *vb.* beauf'sichtigen.

oversight, *n.* Überse'hen, - *nt.*

overt, *adj.* offen.

overtake, *vb.* ein-holen.

overthrow, 1. *n.* Sturz *m.* **2.** *vb.* stürzen; um-werfen*.

overtime, *n.* Überstunden *pl.*

overture, *n.* (*music*) Ouvertü're, -n *f.*; Annäherung, -en *f.*

overturn, *vb.* um-stürzen.

overweight, *n.* Übergewicht *nt.*

overwhelm, *vb.* überwäl'tigen.

overwork, *vb.* überar'beiten.

owe, *vb.* schulden.

owing, *adj.* schuldig; **(o. to)** dank.

owl, *n.* Eule, -n *f.*

own, 1. *adj.* eigen. **2.** *vb.* besit'zen*.

owner, *n.* Besitz'er, - *m.*, Eigentümer, - *m.*, Inhaber, - *m.*

ox, *n.* Ochse, -n, -n *m.*

oxygen, *n.* Sauerstoff *m.*

oyster, *n.* Auster, -n *f.*

P

pace, *n.* Schritt, -e *m.*; (*fig.*) Tempo, -pi *nt.*

pacific, *adj.* friedlich.

Pacific Ocean, *n.* Stiller Ozean *m.*

pacifier, *n.* (*baby's*) Schnuller, - *m.*

pacifism, *n.* Pazifis'mus *m.*

pacifist, *n.* Pazifist', -en, -en *m.*

pacify, *vb.* beschwich'tigen.

pack, 1. *n.* Bündel, - *nt.*; (*gang*) Bande, -n *f.*; (*cards*) Kartenspiel, -e *nt.*; (*animals*) Rudel, - *nt.* **2.** *vb.* packen.

package, *n.* Paket', -e *nt.*

packing, *n.* Dichtung, -en *f.*

pact, *n.* Pakt, -e *m.*

pad, 1. *n.* Polster, - *nt.*; (*paper*) Block, -s *m.* **2.** *vb.* polstern.

padding, *n.* Polsterung, -en *f.*

paddle, 1. *n.* Paddel, - *nt.* **2.** *vb.* paddeln.

padlock, *n.* Vorlegeschloß, ≈sser *nt.*

pagan, *adj.* heidnisch.

page, 1. *n.* (*book*) Seite, -n *f.*; (*servant*) Page, -n, -n *m.* **2.** *vb.* suchen lassen.

pageant, *n.* prunkvoller Aufzug, ≈e *m.*

pail, *n.* Eimer, - *m.*

pain, 1. *n.* Schmerz, -en *m.* **2.** *vb.* schmerzen.

painful, *adj.* schmerzlich, schmerzhaft.

painstaking, *adj.* sorgfältig.

paint, 1. *n.* Farbe, -n *f.* **2.** *vb.* malen.

painter, *n.* Maler, - *m.*

painting, *n.* Bild, -er *nt.*, Malerei', -en *f.*

pair, *n.* Paar, -e *nt.*

palace, n. Schloß, ·sser nt., Palast', ·e m.

palatable, adj. schmackhaft.

palate, n. Gaumen, - m.

palatial, adj. palast'artig.

pale, adj. blaß(·, -).

paleness, n. Blässe f.

palette, n. Palet'te, -n f.

pall, vb. schal werden*.

pallbearer, n. Sargträger, - m.

palm, n. (tree) Palme, -n f.; (hand) Handfläche, -n f.

palpitate, vb. klopfen.

paltry, adj. armselig.

pamper, vb. verzär'teln.

pamphlet, n. Broschü're, -n f.

pan. 1. n. Pfanne, -n f. **2.** vb. herun'ter·machen.

panacea, n. Universal'mittel, - nt.

pancake, n. Pfannkuchen, - m.

pane, n. Glasscheibe, -n f.

panel, n. (wood) Einsatzstück, -e nt., Täfelung f.; (group of men) Diskussionsgruppe, -n f.; (dashboard) Armatu'renbrett, -er nt.

pang, n. plötzlicher Schmerz, -en m.

panic, n. Panik f.

panorama, n. Panora'ma, -men nt.

pant, vb. keuchen, schnaufen.

panther, n. Panther, - m.

pantomime, n. Pantomi'me, -n f.

pantry n. Speisekammer, -n f.

pants, n. Hose, -n f.

papal, adj. päpstlich.

paper. 1. n. Papier', -e nt.; (news) Zeitung, -en f. **2.** adj. papieren; Papier'- (cpds.)

paper-hanger, n. Tapezie'rer, - m.

par, n. Pari nt.

parachute, n. Fallschirm, -e m.

parade, n. Para'de, -n f.

paradise, n. Paradies' nt.

paradox, n. Paradox', -e m.

paraffin, n. Paraffin', -e nt.

paragraph, n. Paragraph', -en, -en m.; (typing) Absatz, ·e m.

parallel. 1. n. Paralle'le, -n f. **2.** adj. parallel'.

paralysis, n. Lähmung, -en f.

paralyze, vb. lähmen.

paramount, adj. oberst-.

paraphrase, vb. umschrei'ben*.

parasite, n. Schmarot'zer, - m.

parcel, n. Päckchen, - nt.; Paket', -e nt.

parch, vb. dörren.

parchment, n. Pergament', -e nt.

pardon. 1. n. Verzei'hung, -en f.; (legal) Begna'digung, -en f. **2.** vb. verzei'hen*; begna'digen.

pare, vb. schälen.

parents, n.pl. Eltern pl.

parentage, n. Herkunft, ·e f.

parenthesis, n. Klammer, -n f.

parish, n. Kirchspiel, -e nt., Gemein'de, -n f.

Paris, n. Paris' nt.

Parisian. 1. n. Pari'ser, - m. **2.** adj. pari'sisch.

park. 1. n. Park, -s m. **2.** vb. parken.

parkway, n. Ausfallstrasse, -n f.

parliament, n. Parlament', -e nt.

parliamentary, adj. parlamenta'risch.

parlor, n. gute Stube, -n f., Salon', -s m.

parochial, adj. Pfarr-, Gemein'de- (cpds.); (fig.) ·e·schränkt'.

parody, n. Parodie, -i'en f.

parrot, n. Papagei', -en m.

parsimony, n. Geiz m.

parsley, n. Petersi'lie f.

parson, n. Geistlich-m.

part. 1. n. Teil, -e m.; (hair) Scheitel, - m.; (theater) Rolle -n f. **2.** vb. trennen.

partake, vb. teil·nehmen*.

partial, adj. Teil- (cpds.); partei'isch.

partiality, n. Voreingenommenheit f.

participant, *n.* Teilnehmer, - *m.*

participate, *vb.* teil·nehmen*.

participation, *n.* Teilnahme *f.*

participle, *n.* Partizip', -ien *nt.*

particle, *n.* Teilchen, - *nt.*

particular, *adj.* beson'der-.

parting, *n.* Abschied, -e *m.*

partisan, 1. *n.* Anhänger, -m., Partisan', (-en,)-en *m.* 2. *adj.* partei'isch.

partition, *n.* Teilung, -en *f.*; (*wall*) Scheidewand, ¨e *f.*

partly, *adv.* teilweise, teils.

partner, *n.* Teilhaber, - *m.*; (*games*) Partner, - *m.*

part of speech, *n.* Redeteil, -e *m.*, Wortart, -en *f.*

party, *n.* (*pol.*) Partei', -en *f.*; (*social*) Gesell'schaft, -en *f.*

pass, 1. *n.* (*mountain*) Paß, ¨sse *m.*; (*identification*) Ausweis, -e *m.* 2. *vb.* vorü'ber-gehen*; (*car*) überho'len; (*exam*) beste'hen*; (*to hand*) reichen.

passable, *adj.* (*roads*) befahr'bar; (*fig.*) erträg'lich, passa'bel.

passage, *n.* Durchgang, ¨e *m.*, Durchfahrt, -en *f.*; (*steamer*) Überfahrt, -en *f.*; (*law*) Annahme, -n *f.*

passenger, *n.* Passagier', -e *m.*

passer-by, *n.* Passant', -en, -en *m.*

passion, *n.* Leidenschaft, -en *f.*; (*Christ*) Passion' *f.*

passionate, *adj.* leidenschaftlich.

passive, 1. *n.* Passiv *nt.* 2. *adj.* passiv.

passport, *n.* Paß, ¨sse *m.*

past, 1. *n.* Vergan'genheit *f.* 2. *adj.* vergan'gen, früher. 3. *adv.* vorbei', vorü'ber.

paste, 1. *n.* Paste, -n *f.*; (*mucilage*) Klebstoff, -e *m.* 2. *vb.* kleben.

pasteurize, *vb.* pasteurisie'ren.

pastime, *n.* Zeitvertreib *m.*

pastor, *n.* Pfarrer, - *m.*

pastry, *n.* Gebäck' *nt.*

pastry shop, *n.* Bäckerei', -en *f.*

pasture, *n.* Weide, -n *f.*

pat, 1. *n.* Klaps, -e *m.* 2. *vb.* einen leichten Schlag geben*.

patch, 1. *n.* Flicken, - *m.* 2. *vb.* flicken.

patchwork, *n.* Flickwerk, -e *nt.*

patent, *n.* Patent', -e *nt.*

patent leather, *n.* Lackleder *nt.*

paternal, *adj.* väterlich.

path, *n.* Weg, -e *m.*, Pfad, -e *m.*

pathetic, *adj.* rührend, armselig.

pathology, *n.* Pathologie' *f.*

patience, *n.* Geduld' *f.*

patient, 1. *n.* Patient', -en, -en *m.* 2. *adj.* gedul'dig.

patio, *n.* Patio, -s *m.*

patriarch, *n.* Patriarch', -en, -en *m.*

patriot, *n.* Patriot', -en, -en *m.*

patriotic, *adj.* patrio'tisch.

patriotism, *n.* Patriotis'mus *m.*

patrol, 1. *n.* Streife, -n *f.* 2. *vb.* patrouillie'ren.

patrolman, *n.* Polizist', -en, -en *m.*

patron, *n.* Schutzherr, -en *m.*; (*client*) Kunde, -n *m.*

patronage, *n.* Schirmherrschaft *f.*

patronize, *vb.* begün'stigen.

pattern, *n.* Muster, - *nt.*; (*sewing*) Schnittmuster, - *nt.*

pauper, *n.* Arm- *m.&f.*

pause, *n.* Pause, -n *f.*

pave, *vb.* pflastern.

pavement, *n.* Pflaster, - *nt.*

pavillion, *n.* Pavillon, -s *m.*

paw, *n.* Pfote, -n *f.*

pawn, 1. *n.* Pfand, ¨er *nt.*; (*chess*) Bauer, (-n,)-n *m.* 2. *vb.* pfänden.

pay, 1. *n.* Bezah'lung *f.*, Gehalt', ¨er *nt.* 2. *vb.* bezah'len.

payment, n. Bezah'lung f.; (installment) Rate, -n f.

pea, n. Erbse, -n f.

peace, n. Friede(n), - m.

peaceful, adj. friedlich.

peach, n. Pfirsich, -e m.

peacock, n. Pfau, -e m.

peak, n. Gipfel, - m.

peal, vb. läuten, dröhnen.

peanut, n. Erdnuß, »sse f.

pear, n. Birne, -n f.

pearl, n. Perle, -n f.

peasant, n. Bauer, (-n,) -n m.

pebble, n. Kieselstein, -e m.

peck, vb. picken.

peculiar, adj. merkwürdig, beson'der-.

peculiarity, n. Beson'derheit, -en f.

pedal, n. Pedal', -e nt.

pedant, n. Pedant', -en, -en m.

peddler, n. Hausie'rer, - m.

pedestal, n. Sockel, - m.

pedestrian, n. Fußgänger, - m.

pediatrician, n. Kinderarzt, »e m.

pedigree, n. Stammbaum, »e m.

peek, vb. gucken.

peel, 1. n. Schale, -n f. 2. vb. schälen.

peep, vb. (look) lugen; (chirp) piepsen.

peer, n. Ebenbürtig- m.

peg, n. Pflock, »e m.; Stift, -e m.

pelt, 1. n. Fell, -e nt. 2. vb. bewer'fen*; nieder-prasseln.

pelvis, n. Becken, - nt.

pen, 1. n. Feder, -n f.; (sty) Stall, »e m. 2. vb. schreiben*.

penalty, n. Strafe, -n f.

penchant, n. Hang m.

pencil, n. Bleistift, -e m.

pendant, n. Anhänger, - m.

penetrate, vb. (tr.) durchdrin'gen*; (intr.) ein-dringen*.

penetration, n. Eindringen nt., Durchdrin'gung f.

penicillin, n. Penicillin' nt.

peninsula, n. Halbinsel, -n f.

penitent, adj. reuig.

penitentiary, n. Zuchthaus, »er nt.

pen-knife, n. Federmesser, - nt.

penniless, adj. mittellos.

penny, n. Pfennig, -e m.

pension, n. Pension', -en f.

pensive, adj. nachdenklich.

people, n. Leute pl., Menschen pl.; (nation) Volk, »er nt.

pepper, n. Pfeffer m.

perambulator, n. Kinderwagen, - m.

perceive, vb. wahr-nehmen*.

per cent, n. Prozent', -e nt.

percentage, n. Prozent'satz, »e m.; Provision', -en f.

perceptible, adj. wahrnehmbar.

perception, n. Wahrnehmung, -en f.

perch, 1. n. (fish) Barsch, -e m.; (pole) Stange, -n f. 2. vb. sich nieder-setzen.

peremptory, adj. endgültig, diktato'risch.

perennial, 1. n. (plant) Staude, -n f. 2. adj. alljähr'lich.

perfect, 1. n. (gram.) Perfekt, -e nt. 2. adj. vollkom'men, perfekt'. 3. vb. vervoll'kommnen.

perfection, n. Vollkom'menheit f.

perforate, vb. durchlö'chern.

perforation, n. Durchlö'cherung, -en f.

perform, vb. aus-führen; (drama) auf-führen.

performance, n. Ausführung, -en f.; (accomplishment) Leistung, -en f.; (drama) Aufführung, -en f., Vorstellung, -en f.

perfume, n. Parfüm', -s nt.

perfunctory, adj. oberflächlich, mecha'nisch.

perhaps, adv. vielleicht'.

peril, n. Gefahr', -en f.

perimeter, n. Umfang, »e m.

period, n. Zeitraum, »e m.; Perio'de, -n f.; (punctuation) Punkt, -e m.

periodic, adj. perio'disch.

periphery, *n.* Umkreis, -e *m.*, Peripherie', -i'en *f.*

perish, *vb.* unter·ge'hen*; verder'ben*.

perishable, *adj.* verderb'lich.

perjure oneself, *vb.* Meineid bege'hen*.

perjury, *n.* Meineid, -e *m.*

permanent, 1. *n.* (*hair*) Dauerwelle, -n *f.* **2.** *adj.* beständ'dig.

permissible, *adj.* zulässig.

permission, *n.* Erlaub'nis, -se *f.*

permit, 1. *n.* Erlaub'nisschein, -e *m.* **2.** *vb.* erlau'ben, zu·las'sen*.

perpendicular, *adj.* senkrecht.

perpetrate, *vb.* bege'hen*.

perpetual, *adj.* ewig.

perplex, *vb.* verwir'ren.

perplexity, *n.* Verwir'rung, -en *f.*

persecute, *vb.* verfol'gen.

persecution, *n.* Verfol'gung, -en *f.*

perseverance, *n.* Beharr'lichkeit *f.*

persevere, *vb.* behar'ren.

persist, *vb.* behar'ren, beste'hen*.

persistent, *adj.* beharr'lich.

person, *n.* Mensch, -en, -en *m.*, Person', -en *f.*

personal, *adj.* persön'lich.

personality, *n.* Persön'lichkeit, -en *f.*

personnel, *n.* Personal' *nt.*

perspective, *n.* Perspekti've, -n *f.*

perspiration, *n.* Schweiß *m.*

perspire, *vb.* schwitzen.

persuade, *vb.* überre'den.

persuasive, *adj.* überzeu'gend.

pertain, *vb.* betref'fen*.

pertinent, *adj.* zugehörig.

perturb, *vb.* beun'ruhigen.

perverse, *adj.* verkehrt', widernatürlich; pervers'.

perversion, *n.* Verdre'hung, -en *f.*

pervert, 1. *n.* perver'ser Mensch, -en, -en *m.* **2.** *vb.* verdre'hen; verfüh'ren.

pessimism, *n.* Pessimis'mus *m.*

pestilence, *n.* Pest *f.*

pet, 1. *n.* Liebling, -e *m.*; (*animal*) Haustier, -e *nt.* **2.** *vb.* streicheln.

petal, *n.* Blütenblatt, ⸱er *nt.*

petition, *n.* Eingabe, -n *f.*, Antrag, ⸱e *m.*

petrify, *vb.* verstei'nern; (**be p.d**) wie gelähmt' sein*.

petrol, *n.* Benzin' *nt.*

petroleum, *n.* Petro'leum *nt.*

petticoat, *n.* steifer Unterrock, ⸱e *m.*

petty, *adj.* gering'fügig; kleinlich.

petulant, *adj.* mürrisch.

pew, *n.* Kirchenstuhl, ⸱e *m.*

phantom, *n.* Phantom', -e *nt.*

pharmacist, *n.* Apothe'ker, - *m.*

pharmacy, *n.* Apothe'ke, -n *f.*

phase, *n.* Phase, -n *f.*

pheasant, *n.* Fasan', -e(n) *m.*

phenomenal, *adj.* erstaun'lich.

phenomenon, *n.* Erscheinung, -en *f.*, Phänomen', -e *nt.*

philanthropy, *n.* Menschenliebe *f.*, Wohltätigkeit, -en *f.*

philately, *n.* Briefmarkenkunde *f.*

philosopher, *n.* Philosoph', -en, -en *m.*

philosophical, *adj.* philosophisch.

philosophy, *n.* Philosophie', -i'en *f.*

phlegm, *n.* Phlegma *nt.*; (*med.*) Schleim *m.*

phlegmatic, *adj.* phlegma'tisch.

phobia, *n.* krankhafte Angst *f.*, Phobie', -i'en *f.*

phonetic, *adj.* phone'tisch.

phonetics, *n.* Phone'tik *f.*

phonograph, *n.* Grammophon', -e *nt.*

phosphorus, *n.* Phosphor *m.*

photogenic, *adj.* photogen'.

photograph, *n.* Photographie', -i'en *f.*, Lichtbild, -er *nt.*

photographer, *n.* Photo- graph', -en, -en *m.*

photography, *n.* Photo- graphie' *f.*

photostat, **1.** *n.* Photo- kopie', -i'en *f.* **2.** *vb.* photo- kopie'ren.

phrase, 1. *n.* Satz, ⸗e *m.;* Redewendung, -en *f.* **2.** *vb.* aus·drücken.

physical, *adj.* körperlich, physisch.

physician, *n.* Arzt, ⸗e *m.*

physicist, *n.* Physiker, - *m.*

physics, *n.* Physik' *f.*

physiology, *n.* Physiologie' *f.*

physiotherapy, *n.* Physio- therapie' *f.*

physique, *n.* Körperbau *m.*

pianist, *n.* Klavier'spieler, - *m.*, Pianist', -en, -en *m.*

piano, *n.* Klavier', -e *nt.*

piccolo, *n.* Piccoloflöte, -n *f.*

pick, 1. *n.* Spitzhacke, -n *f.* **2.** *vb.* (*gather*) pflücken (*select*) aus·wählen.

picket, 1. *n.* Holzpfahl, ⸗e *m.;* (*striker*) Streikposten, - *m.* **2.** *vb.* Streikposten stehen*.

pickle, *n.* saure Gurke *f.*

pickpocket, *n.* Taschendieb, -e *m.*

picnic, *n.* Picknick, -s *nt.*

picture, 1. *n.* Bild, -er *nt.* **2.** (*fig.*) Vorstellung, -en *f.* **2.** *vb.* dar·stellen; sich vor·stel- len.

picturesque, *adj.* malerisch.

pie, *n.* eine Art Backwerk *f.*

piece, *n.* Stück, -e *nt.*

pier, *n.* Pier, -s *m.*

pierce, *vb.* durchboh'ren.

piety, *n.* Frömmigkeit *f.*

pig, *n.* Schwein, -e *nt.;* (*young*) Ferkel, - *nt.*

pigeon, *n.* Taube, -n *f.*

pigment, *n.* Pigment'. -e *nt.*

pile, 1. *n.* (*heap*) Haufen, - *m.;* (*post*) Pfahl, ⸗e *m.* **2.** *vb.* auf·häufen.

pilfer, *vb.* stehlen*.

pilgrim, *n.* Pilger, - *m.*

pilgrimage, *n.* Wallfahrt, -en *f.*

pill, *n.* Pille, -n *f.*

pillage, 1. *n.* Plünderung, -en *f.* **2.** *vb.* plündern.

pillar, *n.* Säule, -n *f.*

pillow, *n.* Kissen, - *nt.*

pillowcase, *n.* Kissenbezug, ⸗e *m.*

pilot, *n.* Pilot', -en, -en *m.;* (*ship*) Lotse, -n, -n *m.*

pimple, *n.* Pickel, - *m.*

pin, 1. *n.* Stecknadel, -n *f.* **2.** *vb.* stecken.

pinch, 1. *n.* (*of salt, etc.*) Prise, -n *f.* **2.** *vb.* kneifen*, zwicken.

pine, 1. *n.* Fichte, -n *f.;* Kiefer, -n *f.* **2.** *vb.* sich sehnen.

pineapple, *n.* Ananas, -se *f.*

ping-pong, *n.* Tischtennis *nt.*

pink, *adj.* rosa.

pinnacle, *n.* Gipfel, - *m.*

pint, *n.* etwa ein halber Liter.

pioneer, *n.* Pionier', -e *m.*

pious, *adj.* fromm(·, -).

pipe, *n.* Rohr, -e *nt.;* Röhre, -n *f.;* (*smoking*) Pfeife, -n *f.*

piquant, *adj.* pikant'.

pirate, *n.* Seeräuber, - *m.*

pistol, *n.* Pisto'le, -n *f.*

piston, *n.* Kolben, - *m.*

pit, *n.* (*stone*) Kern, -e *m.;* (*hole*) Grube, -n *f.*

pitch, 1. *n.* (*tar*) Pech *nt.;* (*resin*) Harz, -e *nt.;* (*throw*) Wurf, ⸗e *m.;* (*music*) Ton- höhe, -n *f.* **2.** *vb.* (*throw*) werfen*; (*a tent*) auf·schla- gen*.

pitcher, *n.* (*jug*) Krug, ⸗e *m.;* (*thrower*) Ballwerfer beim Baseball *m.*

pitchfork, *n.* Heugabel, -n *f.*, Mistgabel, -n *f.;* (*music*) Stimmgabel, -n *f.*

pitfall, *n.* Falle, -n *f.*

pitiful, *adj.* erbärm'lich.

pitiless, *adj.* erbar'mungslos.

pity, *n.* Mitleid *nt.*, Erbar'- men *nt.*

pivot, *n.* Drehpunkt, -e *m.*

placard, *n.* Plakat', -e *nt.*

placate, *vb.* beschwich'tigen.

place, 1. *n.* Platz, ⸗e *m.*, Ort, -e *m.* **2.** *vb.* setzen,

stellen, legen; unter·brin-
gen*.

placid, *adj.* gelas'sen.

plagiarism, *n.* Plagiat' *nt.*

plague, 1. *n.* Seuche, -n *f.*
2. *vb.* plagen.

plain, 1. *n.* Ebene, -n *f.*
2. *adj.* eben; (*fig.*) einfach,
schlicht.

plaintiff, *n.* Kläger, - *m.*

plan, 1. *n.* Plan, ⸗e *m.* 2.
vb. planen.

plane, 1. *n.* (*geom.*) Fläche,
-n *f.*; (*tool*) Hobel, - *m.*; (*airplane*) Flugzeug, -e *nt.* 2.
vb. hobeln.

planet, *n.* Planet', -en, -en
m.

planetarium, Planeta'rium,
-ien *nt.*

plank, *n.* Brett, -er *nt.*,
Planke, -n *f.*

plant, 1. *n.* Pflanze, -n *f.*;
(*factory*) Fabrik', -en *f.*; (*installation*) Werk, -e *nt.* 2.
vb. pflanzen.

planter, *n.* Pflanzer, - *m.*

plasma, *n.* Plasma, -men *nt.*

plaster, *n.* Gips *m.*; (*med.*)
Pflaster, - *nt.*; (*walls*) Ver-
putz' *m.*

plastic, 1. *n.* Kunststoff, -e
m. 2. *adj.* plastisch.

plate, *n.* Platte, -n *f.*; (*dish*)
Teller, - *m.*

plateau, *n.* Hochebene, -n
f., Plateau', -s *nt.*

platform, *n.* Plattform, -en
f.; (*train*) Bahnsteig, -e *m.*

platinum, *n.* Platin *nt.*

platitude, *n.* Plattheit, -en *f.*

platoon, *n.* Zug, ⸗e *m.*

platter, *n.* Servier'platte, -n
f.

plausible, *adj.* einleuchtend.

play, 1. *n.* Spiel, -e *nt.*;
(*theater*) Thea'terstück, -e
nt. 2. *vb.* spielen.

player, *n.* (*game*) Mitspieler,
m.; (*theater*) Schauspieler, -
m.; (*music*) Spieler, - *m.*

playful, *adj.* spielerisch.

playground, *n.* Spielplatz,
⸗e *m.*

playmate, *n.* Spielgefährte,
-n, -n *m.*

playwright, *n.* Drama'tiker, -
m.

plea, *n.* Bitte, -n *f.*; (*excuse*)
Vorwand, ⸗e *m.*; (*jur.*) Plädoyer', -s *nt.*

plead, *vb.* bitten*, plädie'ren.

pleasant, *adj.* angenehm.

please, 1. *vb.* gefal'len*.
2. *interj.* bitte.

pleasing, *adj.* angenehm.

pleasure, *n.* Vergnü'gen *nt.*
Freude, -n *f.*

pleat, *n.* Falte, -n *f.*

plebiscite, *n.* Volksabstimmung, -en *f.*

pledge, 1. *n.* Gelüb'de, - *nt.*
2. *vb.* gelo'ben.

plentiful, *adj.* reichlich.

plenty, *n.* Fülle *f.*; (**p. of**)
reichlich, genug'.

pleurisy, *n.* Rippenfellentzündung, -en *f.*

pliable, pliant, *adj.* biegsam.

pliers, *n.* Zange, -n *f.*, Kneifzange, -n *f.*

plight, *n.* schwierige Lage,
-n *f.*

plot, 1. *n.* Stück Erde *nt.*;
(*story*) Handlung, -en *f.*;
(*intrigue*) Komplott', -e *nt.*
2. *vb.* intrigie'ren; (*plan*)
entwer'fen*.

plow, 1. *n.* Pflug, ⸗e *m.* 2.
vb. pflügen.

pluck, 1. *n.* Mut *m.* 2. *vb.*
rupfen.

plug, 1. *n.* Stöpsel, - *m.*,
Pfropfen, - *m.*; (*spark p.*)
Zündkerze, -n *f.*; (*fire p.*)
Feuerhydrant, -en, -en *m.*
2. *vb.* zu·stopfen.

plum, *n.* Pflaume, -n *f.*

plumage, *n.* Gefie'der *nt.*

plumber, *n.* Klempner, - *m.*

plume, *n.* Feder, -n *f.*

plump, *adj.* dicklich.

plunder, 1. *n.* Beute *f.*,
Raub *m.* 2. *vb.* plündern.

plunge, *vb.* tauchen, stürzen.

plural, *n.* Mehrzahl, -en *f.*
Plural, -e *m.*

plus, *prep.* plus.

plutocrat, *n.* Plutokrat', -en,
-en *m.*

pneumatic, *adj.* pneuma'-
tisch.

pneumonia, *n.* Lungenentzündung, -en *f.*

poach, *vb.* (*hunt illegally*) wildern; (*eggs*) pochie'ren.

pocket, *n.* Tasche, -n *f.*

pocket-book, *n.* Handtasche, -n *f.*

pod, *n.* Schote, -n *f.*

podiatry, *n.* Fußheilkunde *f.*

poem, *n.* Gedicht', -e *nt.*

poet, *n.* Dichter. - *m.*

poetic, *adj.* dichterisch, poe'tisch.

poetry, *n.* Dichtung, -en *f.*, Poesie' *f.*

poignant, *adj.* treffend.

point, **1.** *n.* Punkt, -e *m.* **2.** *vb.* zeigen, hin·weisen*.

pointed, *adj.* spitz.

pointless, *adj.* sinnlos, witzlos.

poise, *n.* Schwebe *f.*; (*assuredness*) sicheres Auftreten *nt.*

poison, **1.** *n.* Gift, -e *nt.* **2.** *vb.* vergif'ten.

poisonous, *adj.* giftig.

poke, *vb.* stoßen*.

Poland, *n.* Polen *nt.*

polar, *adj.* polar'.

pole, *n.* (*post*) Pfahl, *e *m.*; (*rod*) Stange, -n *f.*; (*electrical, geographic*) Pol, -e *m.*

Pole, *n.* Pole, -n, -n *m.*

police, *n.* Polizei' *f.*

policeman, *n.* Polizist', -en, -en *m.*

policy, *n.* Politik' *f.*; (*insurance*) Poli'ce, -n *f.*

polish, **1.** *n.* Politur', -en *f.*; (**shoe p.**) Schuhkrem, -s *f.* **2.** *vb.* polie'ren, putzen.

Polish, *adj.* polnisch.

polite, *adj.* höflich.

politeness, *n.* Höflichkeit, -en *f.*

politic, political, *adj.* poli'tisch.

politician, *n.* Poli'tiker, - *m.*

politics, *n.* Politik' *f.*

poll, **1.** *n.* Wahl, -en *f.*, Abstimmung, -en *f.* **2.** *vb.* befra'gen.

pollen, *n.* Blütenstaub *m.*

pollute, *vb.* verun'reinigen.

polonaise, *n.* Polonä'se, -n *f.*

polygamy, *n.* Polygamie' *f.*

pomp, *n.* Pomp *m.*

pompous, *adj.* prunkvoll; (*fig.*) hochtrabend.

poncho, *n.* Poncho, -s *m.*

pond, *n.* Teich, -e *m.*

ponder, *vb.* (*tr.*) erwä'gen; (*intr.*) nach·denken*.

ponderous, *adj.* schwerfällig.

pontiff, *n.* Papst, *e *m.*

pontoon, *n.* Schwimmer, - *m.*

pony, *n.* Pony, -s *nt.*

pool, **1.** *n.* (*pond*) Tümpel, - *m.*; (**swimming p.**) Schwimmbad, *er *nt.*; (*group*) Interes'sengemeinschaft, -en *f.* **2.** *vb.* zusam'men·legen.

poor, *adj.* arm(·).

pop, **1.** *n.* Knall, -e *m.*; (*father*) Papi, -s *m.* **2.** *vb.* knallen.

pope, *n.* Pabst, *e *m.*

popular, *adj.* volkstümlich; beliebt'.

popularity, *n.* Beliebt'heit *f.*

population, *n.* Bevöl'kerung, -en *f.*

porcelain, *n.* Porzellan', -e *nt.*

porch, *n.* Veran'da, -den *f.*

pore, *n.* Pore, -n *f.*

pork, *n.* Schweinefleisch *nt.*

pornography, *n.* Pornographie' *f.*

porous, *adj.* porös'.

port, *n.* Hafen, * *m.*; (*wine*) Port *m.*

portable, *adj.* tragbar.

portal, *n.* Portal', -e *nt.*

portend, *vb.* Unheil verkün'den.

porter, *n.* Gepäck'träger, - *m.*

portfolio, *n.* Mappe, -n *f.*; Portefeuille' *nt.*

porthole, *n.* Luke, -n *f.*

portion, *n.* Teil, -e *m.*; (*serving*) Portion', -en *f.*

portrait, *n.* Porträt', -s *nt.*

portray, *vb.* schildern.

Portugal, *n.* Portugal *nt.*

Portuguese, **1.** *n.* Portugie'se, -n, -n *m.* **2.** *adj.* portugie'sisch.

pose, **1.** *n.* Haltung, -en *f.*, Pose, -n *f.* **2.** *vb.* stellen; (**p. as**) sich aus·geben* für.

position, *n.* Stellung, -en *f.*

positive, *adj.* positiv.

possess, *vb.* besit'zen*.

possession, *n.* Besitz, -e *m.*, Eigentum, *"er nt.*

possessive, *adj.* besitz'gierig.

possessor, *n.* Besit'zer, - *m.*, Eigentümer, - *m.*

possibility, *n.* Möglichkeit, -en *f.*

possible, *adj.* möglich.

possibly, *adv.* möglicherweise.

post, **1.** *n.* (*pole*) Pfahl, *"e m.;* (*place*) Posten, - *m.;* (*mail*) Post *f.* **2.** *vb.* aufstellen; zur Post geben*.

postage, *n.* Porto *nt.*

postal, *adj.* Post- (*cpds.*).

post-card, *n.* Postkarte, -n *f.*

poster, *n.* Plakat' -e *nt.*

posterior, *adj.* hinter-; Hinter- (*cpds.*).

posterity, *n.* Nachwelt *f.*

post-mark, *n.* Poststempel, - *m.*

postman, *n.* Postbote, -n, -n *m.*, Briefträger, - *m.*

post office, *n.* Post *f.*, Postamt, *"er nt.*

postpone, *vb.* auf-schieben*, verschie'ben*.

postscript, *n.* Nachschrift, -en *f.*

posture, *n.* Haltung, -en *f.*

pot, *n.* Topf, *"e m.*

potassium, *n.* Kalium *nt.*

potato, *n.* Kartof'fel, -n *f.*

potent, *adj.* stark(").

potential, **1.** *n.* Möglichkeit, -en *f.* **2.** *adj.* möglich.

potion, *n.* Trank, *"e m.*

pottery, *n.* Töpferware, -n *f.*

pouch, *n.* Tasche, -n *f.*, Beutel, - *m.*

poultry, *n.* Geflü'gel *nt.*

pound, **1.** *n.* Pfund, -e *nt.* **2.** *vb.* hämmern, schlagen*.

pour, *vb.* gießen*.

poverty, *n.* Armut *f.*

powder, **1.** *n.* Pulver, - *nt.;* (*cosmetic*) Puder, - *m.* **2.** *vb.* pudern.

power, *n.* Macht, *"e f.*

powerful, *adj.* mächtig.

powerless, *adj.* machtlos.

practicable, *adj.* durchführbar.

practical, *adj.* praktisch.

practice, **1.** *n.* Übung, -en *f.;* (*carrying out*) Ausübung *f.;* (*custom*) Gewohn'heit, -en *f.;* (*doctor*) Praxis. -xen *f.* **2.** *vb.* üben; (*carry out*) ausüben.

practitioner, *n.* Vertre'ter, - *m.;* (*med.*) praktischer Arzt *"e m.*

prairie, *n.* Prairie', i'en *f.*

praise, **1.** *n.* Lob, -e *nt.* **2.** *vb.* loben.

prank, *n.* Streich, -e *m.*

pray, *vb.* beten.

prayer, *n.* Gebet', -e *nt.*

preach, *vb.* predigen.

preacher, *n.* Prediger, - *m*

precarious, *adj.* heikel.

precaution, *n.* Vorsichtsmaßregel, -n *f.*

precede, *vb.* voran'-gehen*

precedence, *n.* Vorrang *m*

precedent, *n.* Präzedenz'fall, *"e m.*

precept, *n.* Vorschrift, -en *f*

precinct, *n.* Bezirk', -e *m.*

precious, *adj.* kostbar.

precipice, *n.* Abgrund, *"e m*

precipitate, **1.** *adj.* überstürzt'. **2.** *vb.* überstür'zen

precise, *adj.* genau.

precision, *n.* Genau'igkeit *f.* Präzision' *f.*

preclude, *vb.* aus-schließen*

precocious, *adj.* frühreif altklug(").

predecessor, *n.* Vorgänger, - *m.*

predestination, *n.* Prädestination' *f.*

predicament, *n.* Dilem'ma -s *nt.*

predicate, **1.** *n.* Prädikat' -e *nt.* **2.** *vb.* begrün'den.

predict, *vb.* voraus'-sagen.

predisposed, *adj.* geneigt; (*med.*) anfällig.

predominant, *adj.* vorherrschend.

predominate, *vb.* vorherrschen.

prefabricated, *adj.* Fertig-(*cpds.*).

preface, *n.* Vorwort, -e *nt.*

prefer, *vb.* vor-ziehen*.

preferable, *adj.* vorzuziehend; (**is p.**) ist vorzuziehen

preferably, *adv.* vorzugs-weise.

preference, *n.* Vorzug *m.,* Vorliebe *f.*

prefix, *n.* Vorsilbe, -n *f.,* Präfix, -e *nt.*

pregnancy, *n.* Schwanger-schaft, -en *f.*

pregnant, *adj.* schwanger.

prehistoric, *adj.* vorge-schichtlich, prähisto'risch.

prejudice, *n.* Vorurteil, -e *nt.*

prejudiced, *adj.* voreinge-nommen.

preliminary, *adj.* einleitend.

prelude, *n.* Einleitung, -en *f.,* Vorspiel, -e *nt.*

premature, *adj.* vorzeitig.

premeditate, *vb.* vorher überle'gen,

premeditated, *adj.* vorbe-dacht; mit Vorbedacht.

premier, *n.* Minis'terpräsi-dent, -en, -en *m.*

première, *n.* Urauffürung, -en *f.*

premise, *n.* Prämis'se, -n *f.*

premium, *n.* Prämie, -n *f.*

premonition, *n.* Vorahnung, -en *f.*

prenatal, *adj.* vorgeburtlich.

preparation, *n.* Vorberei-tung, -en *f.;* (*of food*) Zuber-eitung, *f.*

preparatory, *adj.* vorberei-tend; Vorbereitungs- (*cpds.*).

prepare, *vb.* vor·bereiten; (*food*) zu·bereiten.

preponderant, *adj.* über-wie'gend.

preposition, *n.* Präposition', -en *f.*

preposterous, *adj.* widersin-nig.

prerequisite, *n.* Vorbedin-gung, -en *f.*

prerogative, *n.* Vorrecht, -e *nt.*

prescribe, *vb.* vor·schreiben*; (*med.*) verschrei'ben*.

prescription, *n.* Rezept', -e *nt.*

presence, *n.* Anwesenheit *f.,* Gegenwart *f.*

present, 1. *n.* (*time*) Gegen-wart *f.;* (*gram.*) Präsens *nt.;*

(*gift*) Geschenk', -e *nt.* **2.** *adj.* anwesend, gegenwärtig. **3.** *vb.* dar·bieten*; (*intro-duce*) vor·stellen; (*arms*) präsentie'ren.

presentable, *adj.* präsenta'-bel.

presentation, *n.* Darstel-lung, -en *f.;* Vorstellung, -en *f.*

presently, *adv.* gleich.

preservation, *n.* Erhal'tung *f.*

preservative, *n.* Konservie'-rungsmittel, - *nt.*

preserve, *vb.* bewah'ren, er-hal'ten*; (*food*) konservie'-ren, ein·machen.

preside, *vb.* den Vorsitz führen.

presidency, *n.* Vorsitz, -e *m.;* Präsident'schaft *f.*

president, *n.* Präsident', -en, -en *m.*

press, 1. *n.* Presse *f.* **2.** *vb.* pressen, drücken; (*iron*) bügeln.

pressing, *adj.* dringend.

pressure, *n.* Druck *m.*

pressure cooker, *n.* Dampf-kochtopf, ·e *m.*

prestige, *n.* Prestige' *nt.*

presume, *vb.* an·nehmen*; voraus'·setzen.

presumptuous, *adj.* an-maßend.

presuppose, *vb.* voraus'·set-zen.

pretend, *vb.* vor·geben*.

pretense, *n.* Vorwand, ·e *m.*

pretentious, *adj.* prätentiös'.

pretext, *n.* Vorwand, ·e *m.*

pretty, 1. *adj.* hübsch, niedlich. **2.** *adv.* ziemlich.

prevail, *vb.* vor·herrschen; (*win*) siegen; (**p. upon**) überre'den.

prevalent, *adj.* vorherrsch-end.

prevent, *vb.* verhin'dern, verhü'ten.

prevention, *n.* Verhin'de-rung *f.,* Verhü'tung, -en *f.*

preventive, *adj.* Verhü'-tungs-, Präventiv'- (*cpds.*).

preview, *n.* Vorschau *f.,* Vorangzeige, -n *f.*

previous, *adj.* vorher'gehend.

prey, *n.* Raub *m.*, Beute *f.*

price, *n.* Preis, -e *m.*

priceless, *adj.* unbezahl'bar.

prick, *vb.* stechen*.

pride, *n.* Stolz *m.*, Hochmut *m.*

priest, *n.* Priester, - *m.*, Pfarrer, - *m.*

prim, *adj.* spröde, prüde.

primary, *adj.* primär'.

prime, 1. *n.* Blüte *f.* **2.** *adj.* Haupt- (*cpds.*); erstklassig; **(p. number)** Primzahl, -en *f.*

prime minister, *n.* Premier'-minister, - *m.*

primitive, *adj.* primitiv'.

prince, *n.* (*king's son*) Prinz, -en, -en *m.*; (*other ruler*) Fürst, -en, -en *m.*

princess, *n.* Prinzes'sin, -nen *f.*

principal, 1. *n.* (*school*) Schuldirektor, -o'ren *m.* **2.** *adj.* hauptsächlich, Haupt- (*cpds.*).

principle, *n.* Prinzip', -en *nt.*, Grundsatz, -e *m.*

print, 1. *n.* Druck, -e *m.* **2.** *vb.* drucken.

printing, *n.* Buchdruck *m.*

printing-press, *n.* Drucker-presse, -n *f.*

priority, *n.* Vorrang *m.*, Priorität', -en *f.*

prism, *n.* Prisma, -men *nt.*

prison, *n.* Gefäng'nis, -se *nt.*

prisoner, *n.* Gefan'gen - *m.&f.*

privacy, *n.* ungestörtes Allein'sein *nt.*

private, 1. *n.* (*mil.*) Soldat', -en, -en *m.* **2.** *adj.* privat', -en, -en *m.*

privation, *n.* Berau'bung, -en *f.*; Not, -e *f.*

privilege, *n.* Vorrecht, -e *nt.*, Privileg', -ien *nt.*

privy, 1. *n.* Abort, -e *m.* **2.** *adj.* geheim'.

prize, 1. *n.* Preis, -e *m.* **2.** *vb.* schätzen.

probability, *n.* Wahrschein'lichkeit, -en *f.*

probable, *adj.* wahrschein'lich.

probation, *n.* Probezeit, -en *f.*; (*jur.*) Bewäh'rungsfrist *f.*

probe, *vb.* sondie'ren.

problem, *n.* Problem', -e *nt.*

procedure, *n.* Verfah'ren *nt.*

proceed, *vb.* (*go on*) fort-fahren*; (*act*) verfah'ren*.

process, *n.* Verfah'ren, - *nt.*

procession, *n.* Prozession', -en *f.*

proclaim, *vb.* aus-rufen*, verkün'den.

proclamation, *n.* Bekannt'-machung, -en *f.*, Proklama-tion', -en *f.*

procrastinate, *vb.* zögern.

procure, *vb.* besor'gen, ver-schaf'fen.

prodigy, *n.* Wunder, - *nt.*; **(infant p.)** Wunderkind, -er *nt.*

produce, *vb.* (*show*) vor-legen, vor'führen; ´(*create*) erzeu'gen, her-stellen, pro-duzie'ren.

product, *n.* Erzeug'nis, -se *nt.*, Produkt', -e *nt.*

production, *n.* Herstellung, -en *f.*, Produktion', -en *f.*

productive, *adj.* produktiv'.

profane, *adj.* profan'.

profanity, *n.* Fluchen *nt.*

profess, *vb.* beken'nen*; (*pretend*) vor-geben*.

profession, *n.* Bekennt'nis, -se *nt.*; (*calling*) Beruf', -e *m.*

professional, *adj.* berufs'-mäßig.

professor, *n.* Profes'sor, -o'ren *m.*

proficient, *adj.* erfah'ren, beschla'gen.

profile, *n.* Profil', -e *nt.*

profit, 1. *n.* Gewinn' *m.* **2.** *vb.* profitie'ren.

profitable, *adj.* einträglich; (*fig.*) vorteilhaft.

profiteer, *n.* Schieber, - *m.*

profound, *adj.* tief, tiefsin-nig.

profundity, *n.* Tiefe *f.*; Tiefgründigkeit *f.*

profuse, *adj.* überreich.

program, *n.* Programm', -e *nt.*

progress, 1. *n.* Fortschritt, -e *m.* **2.** *vb.* fort-schreiten*.

progressive, adj. fortschrittlich.

prohibit, vb. verbie'ten*; verhin'dern.

prohibition, n. Verbot', -e nt.

prohibitive, adj. verbie'terisch.

project, 1. n. Projekt', -e nt. **2.** vb. (plan) projizie'ren; (stick out) vor·springen* nt.

projectile, n. Geschoß', -sse nt.

projection, n. Projektion', -en f.

projector, n. Projek'tor, -o'ren m.

prolific, adj. fruchtbar.

prologue, n. Prolog', -e m.

prolong, vb. verlän'gern, aus·dehnen.

prominent, adj. prominent'.

promiscuous, adj. unterschiedslos; sexuell' zügellos.

promise, 1. n. Verspre'chen, - nt. **2.** vb. verspre'chen*.

promote, vb. fördern; (in rank) beför'dern.

promotion, n. Förderung f.; Beför'derung, -en f.

prompt, adj. prompt.

promulgate, vb. verkün'den.

pronoun, n. Fürwort, "er nt., Prono'men, -mina nt.

pronounce, aus·sprechen*.

pronunciation, n. Aussprache, -n f.

proof, n. Beweis, -e m.; (printing) Korrektur'bogen, = m.; (photo) Abzug, "e m.

prop, 1. n. Stütze, -n f. **2.** vb. stützen.

propaganda, n. Propagan'da f.

propagate, vb. fort·pflanzen; verbrei'ten.

propel, vb. an·treiben*.

propeller, n. Propel'ler, - m.

proper, adj. passend, angebracht.

property, n. Besitz' m., Eigentum nt.

prophecy, n. Prophezei'ung, -en f.

prophesy, vb. prophezei'en.

prophet, n. Prophet', -en, -en m.

prophetic, adj. prophe'tisch.

propitious, adj. günstig.

proponent, n. Verfech'ter, - m.

proportion, n. Verhält'nis, -se nt., Proportion', -en f., Ausmaß, -e nt.

proportionate, adj. angemessen.

proposal, n. Vorschlag, "e m.; (marriage) Heiratsantrag, "e m.

propose, vb. vor·schlagen*; (intend) beab'sichtigen; einen Heiratsantrag machen.

proposition, n. Vorschlag, "e m.; (logic) Lehrsatz, "e m.

proprietor, n. Inhaber, - m., Eigentümer, - m.

propriety, n. Anstand m.

prosaic, adj. prosa'isch.

prose, n. Prosa f.

prosecute, vb. verfol'gen; (jur.) an·klagen.

prospect, n. Aussicht, -en f.

prospective, adj. voraus'sichtlich.

prosper, vb. gedei'hen*.

prosperity, n. Wohlstand m.

prosperous, adj. blühend, wohlhabend.

prostitute, n. Prostituiert'-f.

prostrate, 1. adj. hingestreckt. **2.** vb. zu Boden werfen*.

protect, vb. schützen, beschüt'zen.

protection, n. Schutz m.

protective, adj. Schutz-(cpds.).

protector, n. Beschüt'zer, - m.

protégé, n. Protegé', -s m.

protein, n. Protein' nt.

protest, 1. n. Einspruch, "e m., Protest', -e m. **2.** vb. Einspruch erhe'ben*, protestie'ren.

Protestant, 1. n. Protestant', -en, -en m. **2.** adj. protestan'tisch.

Protestantism, n. Protestantis'mus m.

protocol, *n.* Protokoll', -e *nt.*

proton, *n.* Proton, -o'nen *nt.*

protrude, *vb.* hervor'·ste-hen*

protuberance, *n.* Auswuchs ·e *m.*, Buckel, - *m.*

proud, *adj.* stolz.

prove, *vb.* bewei'sen*.

proverb, *n.* Sprichwort, ·er *nt.*

proverbial, *adj.* sprichwört-lich.

provide, *vb.* **(p. for)** sorgen für; **(p. with)** versor'gen mit, verse'hen mit.

provided, *adv.* voraus'gesetzt daß.

providence, *n.* Vorsehung *f.;* Vorsorge *f.*

province, *n.* Provinz', -en *f.*

provincial, *adj.* provinziell'.

provision, *n.* (*stipulation*) Bestim'mung, -en *f.;* (*food*) Proviant' *m.;* (*stock*) Vorrat, ·e *m.*

provocation, *n.* Provoka-tion', -en *f.*

provoke, *vb.* provozie'ren; (*call forth*) hervor'·ruten*.

prowess, *n.* Tüchtigkeit *f.*

prowl, *vb.* umher'·schlei-chen*.

proximity, *n.* Nähe *f.*

proxy, *n.* (*thing*) Vollmacht, -en *f.;* (*person*) Stellvertre-ter, - *m.*

prudence, *n.* Vorsicht *f.;* Klugheit *f.*

prudent, *adj.* klug(·); um-sichtig.

prune, *n.* Backpflaume, -n *f.*

pry, *vb.* (*break open*) auf-brechen*; (*peer about*) he-rum'·schnüffeln.

psalm, *n.* Psalm, -en *m.*

pseudonym, *n.* Pseudonym', -e *nt.*

psychiatrist, *n.* Psychia'-ter, - *m.*

psychiatry, *n.* Psychiatrie' *f.*

psychoanalysis, *n.* Psycho-analy'se, -n *f.*

psychological, *adj.* psycho-lo'gisch.

psychology, *n.* Psychologie' *f.*

psychosis, *n.* Psycho'se, -n *nt.*

ptomaine, *n.* Ptomain', -e *nt.*

public, 1. *n.* Öffentlichkeit *f.* **2.** *adj.* öffentlich.

publication, *n.* Veröf'fent-lichung, -en *f.,* Publikation', -en *f.*

publicity, *n.* Rekla'me *f.,* Propagan'da *f.*

publish, *vb.* veröf'fentlichen, publizie'ren; (*make known*) bekannt'·machen.

publisher, *n.* Heraus'geber, - *m.,* Verle'ger, - *m.*

pudding, *n.* Pudding, -s *m.*

puddle, *n.* Pfütze, -n *f.*

puff, 1. *n.* (*wind*) Windstoß, ·e *m.;* (*smoke*) Rauchwolke, -n *f.;* (*powder*) Puderquaste, -n *f.* **2.** *vb.* blasen*; paffen.

pull, 1. *n.* Zugkraft *f.,* An-ziehungskraft *f.;* (*influence*) Bezie'hung, -en *f.* **2.** *vb.* ziehen*.

pulley*, *n.* Flaschenzug, ·e *m.*

pulmonary, *adj.* Lungen-(*cpds.*).

pulp, *n.* Brei *m.;* (*fruit*) Fruchtfleisch *nt.*

pulpit, *n.* Kanzel, -n *f.*

pulsate, *vb.* pulsie'ren.

pulse, *n.* Puls, -e *m.*

pump, 1. *n.* Pumpe, -n *f.;* (*shoe*) Pump -s *m.* **2.** *vb.* pumpen.

pumpkin, *n.* Kürbis, -se *m.*

pun, *n.* Wortspiel, -e *nt.*

punch, 1. *n.* Schlag, ·e *m.,* Stoß, ·e *m.;* (*drink*) Punsch *m.* **2.** *vb.* schlagen*, stos-sen*; (*make holes*) lochen.

punctual, *adj.* pünktlich.

punctuate, *vb.* interpunk-tie'ren.

punctuation, *n.* Interpunk-tion' *f.*

puncture, 1. *n.* Loch, ·er *nt.;* (*tire*) Reifenpanne, -n *f.;* (*med.*) Punktion', -en *f.* **2.** *vb.* durchste'chen*.

pungent, *adj.* stechend, beißend.

punish, *vb.* strafen, bestra'-fen.

punishment, *n.* Strafe, -n *f.*

puny, *adj.* mickrig.

pupil, *n.* Schüler, - *m.*; Schülerin, -nen *f.*

puppet, *n.* Marionet'te, -n *f.*

puppy, *n.* junger Hund, -e *m.*

purchase, 1. *n.* Kauf, -e *m.*, Einkauf, -e *m.* 2. *vb.* kaufen, erwer'ben*.

pure, *adj.* rein.

purée, *n.* Püree', -s *nt.*

purgative, *n.* Abführmittel, - *nt.*

purge, 1. *n.* Säuberungsaktion, -en *f.* 2. *vb.* säubern.

purify, *vb.* reinigen, läutern.

puritanical, *adj.* purita'nisch.

purity, *n.* Reinheit *f.*, Echtheit *f.*

purple, *adj.* purpurn; lila.

purport, 1. *n.* Sinn *m.* 2. *vb.* den Anschein erwecken als ob.

purpose, *n.* Zweck, -e *m.*; Absicht, -en *f.*

purposely, *adv.* absichtlich.

purse, *n.* (handbag) Handtasche, -n *f.*; Geldbeutel, - *m.*

pursue, *vb.* verfol'gen.

pursuit, *n.* Verfol'gung, -en *f.*

push, 1. *n.* Stoß, -e *m.* (fig.) Energie', -i'en *f.* 2. *vb.* stossen*, schieben*.

put, *vb.* setzen; stellen; legen.

putrid, *adj.* faul, verfault'.

puzzle, 1. *n.* Rätsel, - *nt.*; (game) Puzzle, -s *nt.* 2. *vb.* verwir'ren, zu denken ge-ben*.

pyjamas, *n.pl.* Pyja'ma, -s *m.*

pyramid, *n.* Pyrami'de, -n *f.*

Q

quadrangle, *n.* Viereck, -e *nt.*

quadruped, *n.* Vierfüßler, - *m.*

quail, *n.* Wachtel, -n *f.*

quaint, *adj.* seltsam; altmodisch.

quake, 1. *n.* Beben *nt.* 2. *vb.* beben, zittern.

qualification, *n.* Befä'higung, -en *f.*, Qualifikation', -en *f.*; (reservation) Einschränkung, -en *f.*

qualified, *adj.* geeig'net; (limited) eingeschränkt.

qualify, *vb.* qualifizie'ren; (limit) ein·schränken.

quality, *n.* (characteristic) Eigenschaft, -en *f.*; (grade) Qualität', -en *f.*

qualm, *n.* Beden'ken *nt.*

quandary, *n.* Dilem'ma *nt.*

quantity, *n.* Menge, -n *f.*, Quantität', -en *f.*

quarantine, *n.* Quaranta'ne *f.*

quarrel, 1. *n.* Streit *m.*, Zank *m.* 2. *vb.* streiten*, sich streiten*, sich zanken.

quarry, *n.* Steinbruch, -e *m.*

quarter, 1. *n.* Viertel, - *nt.* 2. *vb.* ein·quartieren.

quarterly, 1. *n.* Vierteljah'resschrift, -en *f.* 2. *adj.* vierteljähr'lich.

quartet, *n.* Quartett', -e *nt.*

queen, *n.* Königin, -nen *f.*

queer, *adj.* merkwürdig, sonderbar.

quell, *vb.* unterdrü'cken.

quench, *vb.* löschen, stillen.

query, 1. *n.* Frage, -n *f.* 2. *vb.* fragen.

quest, *n.* Suche, -n *f.*

question, 1. *n.* Frage, -n *f.* 2. *vb.* fragen, befra'gen; an·zweifeln.

questionable, *adj.* fraglich, fragwürdig.

question mark, *n.* Fragezeichen, - *nt.*

questionnaire, *n.* Fragebogen, - *m.*

quick, *adj.* schnell, rasch.

quiet, 1. *adj.* leise, ruhig, still. 2. *vb.* beru'higen.

quilt, *n.* Steppdecke, -n *f.*

quinine, *n.* Chinin' *nt.*

quintet, *n.* Quintett', -e *nt.*

quip, 1. *n.* witziger Seitenhieb, -e *m.*, spitze Bemer'-

kung, -en *f.* **2.** *vb.* witzeln.

quit, *vb.* (*leave*) verlas'sen*; (*stop*) auf·hören; (*resign*) kündigen.

quite, *adj.* ziemlich; (*completely*) ganz, völlig.

quiver, 1. *n.* Köcher, - *m.* **2.** *vb.* beben, zittern.

quiz, 1. *n.* Quiz *m.;* (*school*) Klassenarbeit, -en *f.* **2.** *vb.* aus·fragen.

quorum, *n.* beschluß'fähige Versamm'lung *f.*

quota, *n.* Quote, -n *f.*

quotation, *n.* Zitat', -e *nt.;* (*price*) Notie'rung, -en *f.*

quotation mark, *n.* Anführungsstrich, -e *m.,* Anführungszeichen, - *nt.*

quote, *vb.* an·führen, zitie'ren.

R

rabbi, *n.* Rabbi'ner, - *m.*

rabbit, *n.* Kanin'chen, - *nt.*

rabble, *n.* Volksmenge *f.,* Pöbel *m.*

rabid, *adj.* fana'tisch.

rabies, *n.* Tollwut *f.*

race, 1. *n.* (*contest*) Rennen, - *nt.,* Wettrennen, - *nt.;* (*breed*) Rasse, -n *f.* **2.** *vb.* rennen*, um die Wette rennen*.

race-track, *n.* Rennbahn, -en *f.*

rack, 1. *n.* (*torture*) Folterbank, -e *f.;* (*feed*) Futtergestell, -e *nt.;* (*luggage*) Ständer, - *m.;* (*train*) Gepäcknetz, -e *nt.* **2.** *vb.* foltern.

racket, *n.* (*tennis*) Schläger, - *m.;* (*uproar*) Krach *m.;* (*crime*) Schiebung, -en *f.*

radar, *n.* Radar *nt.*

radiance, *n.* Glanz *m.,* Strahlen *nt.*

radiant, *adj.* strahlend.

radiate, *vb.* aus·strahlen.

radiation, *n.* Ausstrahlung, -en *f.*

radiator, *n.* Heizkörper, - *m.;* (*auto*) Kühler, - *m.*

radical, *adj.* radikal'.

radio, *n.* Rundfunk *m.;* Rundfunkgerät, -e *nt.;* Radio, -s *nt.*

radioactive, *adj.* radioaktiv'; (**r. fall-out**) radioaktiver Niederschlag, -e *m.*

radish, *n.* Radies'chen, - *nt.;* (*white*) Rettich, -e *m.;* (**horse r.**) Meerrettich, -e *m.*

radium, *n.* Radium *nt.*

radius, *n.* Radius, -ien *m.*

raffle, 1. *n.* Lotterie', -i'en *f.* **2.** *vb.* (**r. off**) aus·losen.

raft, *n.* Floß, -e *nt.*

rag, *n.* Lumpen, - *m.,* Lappen, - *m.*

rage, 1. *n.* Wut *f.;* (*fashion*) Schrei *m.* **2.** *vb.* wüten, rasen.

ragged, *adj.* zerlumpt'; (*jagged*) zackig.

raid, 1. *n.* Überfall, -e *m.,* Razzia, -ien *f.* **2.** *vb.* überfal'len*, plündern.

rail, *n.* Schiene, -n *f.*

railing, *n.* Gelän'der, - *nt.*

railroad, *n.* Eisenbahn, -en *f.*

rain, 1. *n.* Regen *m.* **2.** *vb.* regnen.

rainbow, *n.* Regenbogen, - *m.*

raincoat, *n.* Regenmantel, - *m.*

rainy, *adj.* regnerisch.

raise, 1. *n.* (*pay*) Gehaltserhöhung, -en *f.* **2.** *vb.* (*increase*) erhö'hen; (*lift*) heben*; (*erect*) auf·stellen; (*collect*) auf·treiben*; (*bring up*) groß·ziehen*.

raisin, *n.* Rosi'ne, -n *f.*

rake, 1. *n.* (*tool*) Harke, -n *f.,* Rechen, - *m.;* (*person*) Roué', -s *m.* **2.** *vb.* harken.

rally, 1. *n.* (*recovery*) Erho'lung, -en *f.;* (*meeting*) Kundgebung, -en *f.,* Massenversammlung, -en *f.* **2.** *vb.* sich erho'len; sich sammeln.

ram, 1. *n.* Widder, - *m.* **2.** *vb.* rammen.

ramble, *vb.* umher'·schweifen.

..ap, n. Rampe, -n f.
..apart, n. Burgwall, ⸗e m.
..ch, n. Ranch, -es f.
..cid, adj. ranzig.
..cor, n. Groll m.
..dom, n. (at r.) aufs ...ratewohl'.
..ge, 1. n. (distance) ...atfer'nung, -en f.; (scope) ...ielraum, ⸗e m.; (mountains) Bergkette, -n f.; (stove) ...h erstre'cken. 2. vb. (extend)
..k, 1. n. Rang, ⸗e m. 2. vb. ein-reihen.
..sack, vb. durchwüh'len.
..som, n. Lösegeld, -er nt.
.., vb. schlagen*, klopfen.
..e, 1. n. Vergewal'tigung, ...n f. 2. vb. vergewal'tigen.
..id, adj. schnell.
..e, adj. selten.
..cal, n. Schlingel, - m.
..h, adj. übereilt, waghal-

..pberry, n. Himbeere, -n

.., n. Ratte, -n f.
..e, 1. n. (proportion) Maß ...ab, ⸗e m.; (price) Preis, -e ...; (exchange r.) Kurs, ⸗e ...; (speed) Geschwin'dig- ...it, -en f. 2. vb. ein-schät- ...n.
..her, adv. (preferably) lie- ...r; (on the other hand) ...elmehr.
..ify, vb. ratifizie'ren.
..io, n. Verhält'nis, -se nt.
..ion, 1. n. Ration, -en f. 2. vb. rationie'ren.
..ional, adj. vernünft'- ...mäß.
..tle, vb. klappern.
..age, 1. n. Verwüs'tung, ...n f. 2. vb. verwüs'ten.
..e, vb. (fury) toben; (enthusiasm) schwärmen.
..en, 1. n. Rabe, -n, -n m. 2. ...dj. rabenschwarz.
..w, adj. rauh; (uncooked) ...h.
..y, n. Strahl, -en m.
..on, n. Kunstseide, -n f.
..zor, n. (straight) Rasier'- ...esser, - nt.; (safety) Ra- ...esser'apparat, -e m.

reach, 1. n. Reichweite f. 2. vb. (tr.) errei'chen; (intr.) reichen.
react, vb. reagie'ren.
reaction, n. Wirkung, -en f., Reaktion', -en f.
reactionary, 1. n. Reaktionär', -e m. 2. adj. reaktionär'.
reactor, n. Reak'tor, -o'ren m.
read, vb. lesen*.
reader, n. (person) Leser, - m.; (book) Lesebuch, ⸗er nt.
readily, adv. gern; (easily) leicht.
reading, n. Lesen nt.
ready, adj. (prepared) bereit'; (finished) fertig.
real, adj. wirklich, tatsäch'lich; (genuine) echt.
realist, n. Realist', -en m.
reality, n. Wirklichkeit f.
realization, n. (understanding) Erkennt'nis, -se f.; (making real) Verwirk'lichung, -en f., Realisie'rung, -en f.
realize, vb. (understand) erken'nen, begrei'fen; (I r. it) ich bin mir darüber im klaren; (make real, attain) verwirk'lichen, realisie'ren.
realm, n. Reich, -e nt.; (fig.) Bereich', -e m.
reap, vb. ernten.
rear, 1. n. (back) Rückseite, -n f.; (r.-guard) Nachhut, -en f. 2. vb. (bring up) erzie'hen*; (erect) errich'ten; (of horses) sich bäumen.
rear-view mirror, n. Rückspiegel, - m.
reason, 1. n. Vernunft' f.; (cause) Grund, ⸗e m. 2. vb. überle'gen, denken*; (r. with) vernünf'tig reden mit.
reasonable, adj. vernünf'tig.
reassure, vb. versi'chern; beru'higen.
rebate, n. Rabatt', -e m.
rebel, 1. n. Rebell', -en, -en m. 2. vb. rebellie'ren.
rebellion, n. Aufstand, ⸗e m., Rebellion', -en f.
rebellious, adj. rebel'lisch.

rebound, *vb.* zurück'prallen.

rebuild, *vb.* wieder auf‑
bauen.

rebuke, 1. *n.* Tadel, - *m.* **2.**
vb. tadeln.

rebuttal, *n.* Widerle'gung,
-en *f.*

recalcitrant, *adj.* starrköp‑
fig.

recall, *vb.* zurück'rufen*;
(*remember*) sich erin'nern an,
(*revoke*) widerru'fen*.

recapitulate, *vb.* zusam'‑
men·fassen.

recede, *vb.* zurück'weichen*.

receipt, *n.* Quittung, -en *f.;*
(*recipe*) Rezept', -e *nt.*

receive, *vb.* empfan'gen*.

receiver, *n.* Empfän'ger,
m.; (*telephone*) Hörer, - *m.*

recent, *adj.* neu.

recently, *adv.* neulich, kürz‑
lich.

receptacle, *n.* Behäl'ter, -
m.

reception, *n.* Aufnahme, -n
f.; (*ceremony*) Empfang', ‑e
m.

receptive, *adj.* empfäng'lich.

recess, *n.* (*in wall*) Nische, -n
f.; (*intermission*) Pause, -n *f.*

recipe, *n.* Rezept', -e *nt.*

recipient, *n.* Empfän'ger
m.

reciprocate, *vb.* aus·tau‑
schen; erwi'dern.

recitation, *n.* Rezitation',
-en *f.*

recite, *vb.* auf·sagen, vor·
tragen*.

reckless, *adj.* rücksichtslos;
leichtsinnig.

reclaim, *vb.* ein·fordern;
(*land*) urbar machen; (*waste
product*) aus·werten.

reclamation, *n.* (*land*) Ur‑
barmachung *f.*

recline, *vb.* sich zurück'·leh‑
nen.

recognition, *n.* (*acknowledg‑
ment*) Anerkennung, -en *f.;*
(*know again*) Wiedererken‑
nung, -en *f.*

recognize, *vb.* (*acknowledge*)
an·erkennen*; (*know again*)
wieder·erkennen*.

recoil, *vb.* zurück'·prallen.

recollect, *vb.* sich erin'n
an.

recommend, *vb.* empf
len*.

recommendation, *n.* E
fehʻlung, -en *f.*

recompense, 1. *n.* Erst
tung, -en *f.* **2.** *vb.* wied
erstatten.

reconcile, *vb.* versöh'nen.

reconsider, *vb.* wieder erw
gen.

reconstruct, *vb.* rekonstru
ren.

record, 1. *n.* (*docume
Urkunde, -n *f.;* (*top achie
ment*) Rekord', -e *m.;* (*
nograph*) Schallplatte, -n
(**r. player**) Plattenspiele
m. **2.** *vb.* ein·tragen*; a
zeichnen; (*phonograph, ta
auf·nehmen*.

recording, *n.* (*phonogra
tape*) Aufnahme, -n *f.*

recourse, *n.* Zuflucht *f.*

recover, *vb.* wieder·gew
nen*; (*health*) sich erho
gene'sen.

recovery, *n.* Wiedergew
nung, -en *f.;* (*health*) Erh
lung, -en *f.*, Gene'sung,
f.

recruit, 1. *n.* Rekrut', ‑
-en *m.* **2.** *vb.* an·werben*.

rectangle, *n.* Rechteck, -e

rectifier, *n.* Gleichrichte
m.

rectify, *vb.* berich'tigen.

recuperate, *vb.* sich erh
len.

recur, *vb.* wieder·komme
zurück'·kommen*.

red, *adj.* rot(‑).

Red Cross, *n.* Rotes Kre
nt.

redeem, *vb.* ein·lösen; (
cles.) erlö'sen.

redeemer, (*eccles.*) *n.* Erl
ser *m.*, Heiland *m.*

redemption, *n.* Einlösu
-en *f.;* (*eccles.*) Erlö'sung *
*

reduce, *vb.* verrin'ge
mindern, reduzie'ren; (*pri
herab'·setzen*; (*weight*) a
nehmen*.

reduction, *n.* Vermin'

evelation, n. Offenba'rung, -en f.

evelry, n. Schwelgerei', -en f.

evenge. 1. n. Rache f. **2.** vb. rächen.

evenue, n. Einkommen, - nt.

everberate, vb. wider- hallen.

evere, vb. vereh'ren.

everence, n. Vereh'rung, -en f.; Ehrfurcht f.

everend, adj. ehrwürdig.

everent, adj. ehrerbietig.

everie, n. Träumerei', -en f.

everse, 1. n. (opposite) Gegenteil nt.; (back) Rück- seite, -n f.; (misfortune) Rückschlag, -e m.; (auto) Rückwärtsgang, =e m. **2.** vb. um·drehen; (auto) rück- wärts·fahren*; (tech.) um- steuern.

evert, vb. zurück'·kehren.

eview, 1. n. nochmalige Durchsicht, -en f.; Über- blick, -e m.; (book r.) Kritik', -en f.; Bespre'chung, -en f. **2.** vb. überbli'cken; revidie'ren; bespre'chen*.

evise, vb. ab·ändern, re- vidie'ren.

evision, n. Revision', -en f.

evival, n. Wiederbelebung, -en f., Neubelebung, -en f.

evive, vb. (person) wieder zu Bewußt'sein bringen* (fash- ion) wieder auf·leben las- sen*.

evocation, n. Aufhebung, -en f.

evoke, vb. widerru'fen*, auf·heben*.

evolt, 1. n. Aufstand, =e m. **2.** vb. revoltie'ren.

evolution, n. Revolution', -en f.; (turn) Umdre'hung, -en f.

evolutionary, adj. revolu- tionär'.

evolve, vb. sich drehen.

evolver, n. Revol'ver, - m.

eward. 1. n. Beloh'nung, -en f. **2.** vb. beloh'nen.

hetorical, adj. rheto'risch.

rheumatic, adj. rheuma'- tisch.

rheumatism, n. Rheumatis'- mus m.

rhinoceros, n. Nashorn, =er nt.

rhubarb, n. Rhabar'ber m.

rhyme, n. Reim, -e m.

rhythm, n. Rhythmus, -men m.

rhythmical, adj. rhyth- misch.

rib, n. Rippe, -n f.

ribbon, n. Band, =er nt.

rice, n. Reis m.

rich, adj. reich.

rid, vb. los·werden*; sich los·machen.

riddle, n. Rätsel, - nt.

ride, 1. n. (horse) Ritt, -e m.; (vehicles) Fahrt, -en f. **2.** vb. reiten*; fahren*.

rider, n. Reiter, - m.

ridge, n. (mountain) Grat, -e m.; (mountain range) Berg- rücken, - m.

ridicule, 1. n. Spott m. **2.** vb. lächerlich machen, be- spöt'teln.

ridiculous, adj. lächerlich.

rifle, n. Gewehr', -e nt.

rig, 1. n. (gear) Ausrüstung, -en f.; (ship) Takela'ge, -n f.; (oil) Ölbohrer, - m. **2.** vb. auf·takeln.

right, 1. n. Recht, -e nt., **2.** adj. (side) recht-; (just) gerecht'; (be r.) recht ha- ben*. **3.** adv. rechts. **4.** vb. (set upright) auf·richten; (correct) wiedergut'·machen.

righteous, adj. rechtschaffen; (smug) selbstgerecht.

righteousness, n. Recht- schaffenheit f.; Selbst- gerechtheit f.

right of way, n. Vorfahrts- recht, -e nt.

rigid, adj. steif; starr.

rigidity, n. Starrheit f.

rigor, n. Härte, -n f.

rigorous, adj. hart(=), streng.

rim, n. Rand, =er m.

ring, 1. n. Ring, -e m.; (cir- cle) Kreis, -e m.; (of bell) Klingeln nt. **2.** vb. klingeln.

rinse, *vb.* spülen.

riot, 1. *n.* Aufruhr, -e *m.* **2.** *vb.* in Aufruhr gera'ten*.

rip, *vb.* reißen*; auf·trennen.

ripe, *adj.* reif.

ripen, *vb.* reifen.

ripple, 1. *n.* leichte Welle, -n *f.* **2.** *vb.* leichte Wellen schlagen*.

rise, 1. *n.* (*increase*) Zuwachs *m.*; (*emergence*) Aufgang, *e *m.*; (*advance*) Aufstieg, -e *m.* **2.** *vb.* an·steigen*; auf·gehen*; (*get up*) auf·stehen*.

risk, 1. *n.* Risiko, -s *nt.* **2.** *vb.* wagen.

rite, 1. *n.* Ritus, -ten *m.*

ritual, 1. *n.* Rituell', -e *nt.* **2.** *adj.* rituell'.

rival, 1. *n.* Riva'le, -n, -n *m.*, Konkurrent', -en *f.* **2.** *adj.* Konkurrenz- (*cpds.*). **3.** *vb.* wetteifern, rivalisie'ren.

rivalry, *n.* Konkurrenz', -en *f.*, Wettstreit *m.*

river, *n.* Fluß, *sse *m.*

rivet, 1. *n.* Niete, -n *f.* **2.** *vb.* nieten.

road, *n.* Straße, -n *f.*, Landstraße, -n *f.*

roam, *vb.* umher'·schweifen.

roar, 1. *n.* Gebrüll' *nt.* **2.** *vb.* brüllen; brausen.

roast, 1. *n.* Braten, - *m.* **2.** *vb.* braten*; rösten.

rob, *vb.* rauben; berau'ben.

robber, *n.* Räuber, - *m.*; Dieb, -e *m.*

robbery, *n.* Raub *m.*

robe, *n.* Gewand', *er *nt.*

robin, *n.* Rotkehlchen, - *nt.*

robot, *n.* Roboter, - *m.*

robust, *adj.* robust'.

rock, 1. *n.* Stein, -e *m.*; Felsen, - *m.* **2.** *vb.* schaukeln.

rocker, *n.* Schaukelstuhl, *e *m.*

rocket, *n.* Rake'te, -n *f.*

rocky, *adj.* felsig; (*shaky*) wackelig.

rod, *n.* Stab, *e *m.*, Stange, -n *f.*

rodent, *n.* Nagetier, -e *nt.*

roe, *n.* Rogen, - *m.*; (*deer*) Reh, -e *nt.*

role, *n.* Rolle, -n *f.*

roll, 1. *n.* Rolle, -n *f.*; Walze,

-n *f.*; (*bread*) Brötchen, - *nt.* **2.** *vb.* rollen; (*ship*) schlingern.

roller, *n.* Rolle, -n *f.*; Walze, -n *f.*

Roman, 1. *n.* Römer, - *m.* **2.** *adj.* römisch.

romance, *n.* Roman'ze, -n *f.*; Liebesaffäre, -n *f.*

Romance, *adj.* roma'nisch.

romantic, *adj.* roman'tisch.

romanticism, *n.* Roman'tik *f.*

Rome, *n.* Rom *nt.*

roof, *n.* Dach, *er *nt.*

room, *n.* Zimmer, - *nt.*, Raum, *e *m.*; (*space*) Raum *m.*

roommate, *n.* Zimmergenosse, -n, -n *m.*

rooster, *n.* Hahn, *e *m.*

root, 1. *n.* Wurzel, -n *f.* **2.** *vb.* (*be rooted*) wurzeln.

rope, *n.* Tau, -e *nt.*, Seil, -e *nt.*, Strick, -e *m.*

rosary, *n.* Rosenkranz, *e *m.*

rose, *n.* Rose, -n *f.*

rosy, *adj.* rosig.

rot, *vb.* verfau'len, verwe·sen.

rotate, *vb.* rotie'ren; sich ab·wechseln.

rotation, *n.* Umdre'hung, -en *f.*, Rotation', -en *f.*; Wechsel, - *m.*

rotten, *adj.* faul; (*base*) niederträchtig.

rouge, *n.* Rouge *nt.*

rough, *adj.* rauh; (*coarse*) grob(*); (*sea*) stürmisch.

round, 1. *n.* Runde, -n *f.* **2.** *adj.* rund. **3.** *prep.* um um ... herum'.

rout, 1. *n.* Wilde Flucht *f.* **2.** *vb.* in die Flucht schlagen*.

route, *n.* Weg, -e *m.*, Route -n *f.*

routine, 1. *n.* Routi'ne, -n *f.* **2.** *adj.* alltäg'lich.

rove, *vb.* umher'·streifen.

row, 1. *n.* (*line, series*) Reihe -n *f.*; (*fight*) krach *m.* **2.** *vb.* rudern.

rowboat, *n.* Ruderboot, -e *nt.*

royal, *adj.* königlich.

royalty, *n.* Königtum *nt.*

Mitglied eines Königshauses;
(*share of profit*) Gewinn'-
anteil, -e *m.*

rub, *vb.* reiben*.

rubber, *n.* Gummi *nt.*

rubbish, *n.* Abfall, ˝e *m.*;
(*nonsense*) Quatsch *m.*

ruby, *n.* Rubin', -e *m.*

rudder, *n.* Steuerruder, - *nt.*

rude, *adj.* rauh, unhöflich.

rudiment, *n.* erster Anfang,
˝e *m.*; Anfangsgrund, ˝e *m.*

ruffle, *n.* Rüsche, -n *f.* 2.
vb. kräuseln.

rug, *n.* Teppich, -e *m.*

rugged, *adj.* rauh, hart(˝).

ruin, 1. *n.* Untergang *m.;*
Rui'ne, -n *f.;* **(r.s)** Trümmer
pl. 2. *vb.* ruinie'ren.

ruinous, *adj.* verderb'lich,
katastrophal'.

rule, 1. *n.* (*reign*) Herrschaft
f.; (*regulation*) Regel, -n *f.*
2. *vb.* herrschen; entschei-
den*.

ruler, *n.* Herrscher, - *m.;*
(*measuring stick*) Lineal', -e
nt.

rum, *n.* Rum *m.*

rumor, 1. *n.* Gerücht', -e *nt.*
2. *vb.* munkeln.

run, 1. *n.* Lauf *m.;* (*stocking*)
Laufmasche, -n *f.* 2. *vb.*
laufen*; (*flow*) fließen*.

rung, *n.* Sprosse, -n *f.*

runner, *n.* Läufer, - *m.*

runway, *n.* Startbahn, -en *f.*

rupture, 1. *n.* Bruch, ˝e *m.*
2. *vb.* brechen*; reißen*.

rural, *adj.* ländlich.

rush, 1. *n.* Andrange *m.;*
(*hurry*) Eile *f.* 2. *vb.* drängen; eilen, sich stürzen.

Russia, *n.* Rußland *nt.*

Russian, 1. *n.* Russe, -n, -n
m. 2. *adj.* russisch.

rust, 1. *n.* Rost *m.* 2. *vb.*
rosten.

rustic, *adj.* bäurisch.

rustle, *vb.* rascheln.

rusty, *adj.* rostig.

rut, *n.* Rinne, -n *f.;* Radspur, -en *f.*

ruthless, *adj.* erbar'mungslos, rücksichtslos.

rye, *n.* Roggen *m.*

S

Sabbath, *n.* Sabbat, -e *m.*

saber, *n.* Säbel, - *m.*

sable, *n.* Zobel *m.*

sabotage, 1. *n.* Sabota'ge *f.*
2. *vb.* sabotie'ren.

saboteur, *n.* Saboteur', -e *m.*

saccharine, *n.* Sacharin' *nt.*

sack, 1. *n.* Sack, ˝e *m.* 2. *vb.*
(*plunder*) plündern; (*discharge*) auf der Stelle entlas'-
sen*.

sacrament, *n.* Sakrament',
-e *nt.*

sacred, *adj.* heilig.

sacrifice, 1. *n.* Opfer, - *nt.* 2.
vb. opfern.

sacrilege, *n.* Sakrileg', -e *nt.*

sacrilegious, *adj.* gottes-
lästerlich.

sad, *adj.* traurig.

sadden, *vb.* betrü'ben.

saddle, 1. *n.* Sattel, - *m.* 2.
vb. satteln.

sadism, *n.* Sadis'mus *m.*

safe, 1. *n.* Geldschrank, ˝e *m.*
2. *adj.* sicher.

safeguard, 1. *n.* Schutz *m.*
2. *vb.* schützen; sichern.

safety, *n.* Sicherheit *f.*

safety-pin, *n.* Sicherheitsnadel, -n *f.*

sage, *adj.* weise.

sail, 1. *n.* Segel, - *nt.* 2. *vb.*
segeln.

sailboat, *n.* Segelboot, -e *nt.*

sailor, *n.* Matro'se, -n, -n *m.*

saint, 1. *n.* Heilig- *m.&f.* 2.
adj. heilig.

sake, *n.* **(for the s. of)** um
. . . willen.

salad, *n.* Salat', -e *m.*

salary, *n.* Gehalt', ˝er *nt.*

sale, *n.* Verkauf' *m.;* **(bargain s.)** Ausverkauf *m.*

salesman, *n.* Verkäu'fer, -
m.; **(traveling s.)** Handels-
reisend- *m.*

saliva, *n.* Speichel *m.*

salmon, *n.* Lachs *m.*

salon, *n.* Salon', -s *m.*

salt, 1. *n.* Salz, -e *nt.* 2. *vb.*
salzen.

salty, adj. salzig.
salutation, n. Gruß, ⸗e m.; Begrü'ßung, -en f.
salute, 1. n. Gruß, ⸗e m. **2.** vb. salutie'ren.
salvage, 1. n. (act) Bergung f.; (material) Bergegut nt. **2.** vb. bergen*, retten.
salvation, n. Rettung f.; Heil nt.
salve, n. Salbe, -n f.
same, adj. selb-; **(the s.)** derselbe, dasselbe, dieselbe.
sample, 1. n. Probe, -n f.; Muster, - nt. **2.** vb. probie'ren.
sanatorium, n. Sanato'rium, -rien nt.
sanctify, vb. heiligen.
sanction, 1. n. Sanktion', -en f. **2.** vb. sanktionie'ren.
sanctity, n. Heiligkeit f.
sanctuary, n. Heiligtum, ⸗er nt.; (refuge) Zufluchtsort, -e m.
sand, n. Sand, -e m.
sandal, n. Sanda'le, -n f.
sandwich, n. belegtes Brot, -e nt.
sandy, adj. sandig.
sane, adj. vernünf'tig; geistig gesund'.
sanitary, adj. Gesund'heits- (cpds.); hygie'nisch.
sanitation, n. Gesund'heits-wesen nt.
sanity, n. geistige Gesund'heit f.
Santa Claus, n. Weihnachts-mann, ⸗er m.
sap, 1. n. Saft, ⸗e m. **2.** vb. schwächen.
sapphire, n. Saphir', -e m.
sarcasm, n. Sarkas'mus m.
sarcastic, adj. sarkas'tisch.
sardine, n. Sardi'ne, -n f.
sash, n. Schär'pe, -n f.; (window) Fensterrahmen, - m.
satellite, n. Satellit', -en, -en m.
satin, n. Satin', -s m.
satire, n. Sati're, -n f.
satirize, vb. verspot'ten.
satisfaction, n. Genug'-tuung, -en f.; Befrie'digung, -en f.

satisfactory, adj. befrie'-digend, genü'gend.
satisfy, vb. befrie'digen, genü'gen.
saturate, vb. sättigen.
saturation, n. Sättigung f.
Saturday, n. Sonnabend, -e m., Samstag, -e m.
sauce, n. Soße, -n f.
saucer, n. Untertasse, -n f.
sausage, n. Wurst, ⸗e f.
savage, 1. n. Wild- m.&f. **2.** adj. wild.
save, 1. vb. (preserve) bewah'-ren; (rescue) retten; (econo-mize) sparen. **2.** prep. außer.
savings, n.pl. Erspar'nisse pl.
savior, n. Retter, - m.; (eccles.) Heiland m.
savor, 1. n. Geschmack', ⸗e m. **2.** vb. aus'kosten.
saw, 1. n. Säge, -n f.; (prov-erb) Sprichwort, ⸗er nt. **2.** vb. sägen.
say, vb. sagen.
saying, n. Redensart, -en f.
scab, n. Schorf m.; (strike breaker) Streikbrecher, - m.
scaffold, n. Gerüst', -e nt.; (execution) Schafott', -e nt.
scald, vb. brühen; verbrü'-hen.
scale, 1. n. Maßstab, ⸗e m., Skala, -len f.; (music) Ton-leiter, -n f.; (weight measur-ing) Waage, -n f.; (fish) Schuppe, -n f. **2.** vb. (climb) erklet'tern.
scalp, n. Kopfhaut, ⸗e f.; (Indian) Skalp, -e m.
scan, vb. überflie'gen*; (verse) skandie'ren.
scandal, n. Skandal', -e m.
scandalous, adj. schimpf-lich, unerhört'.
scant, adj. knapp.
scar, n. Narbe, -n f.
scarce, adj. selten; knapp.
scarcely, adv. kaum.
scarcity, n. Knappheit f., Mangel m.
scare, 1. n. Schreck m. **2.** vb. erschre'cken; **(be s.d)** erschre'cken*.

scarf, *n.* Schal, -s *m.*; Halstuch, ⸗er *nt.*

scarlet, *adj.* scharlachrot.

scarlet fever, *n.* Scharlach *m.*

scatter, *vb.* zerstreu'en.

scene, *n.* Szene, -n *f.*

scenery, *n.* Landschaft, -en *f.*; (*stage*) Bühnenausstattung, -en *f.*

scent, *n.* Geruch', ⸗e *m.*; (*track*) Spur, -en *f.*

schedule, 1. *n.* Liste, -n *f.*; Programm', -e *nt.*; (*timetable*) Fahrplan, ⸗e *m.*; (*school*) Stundenplan, ⸗e *m.* 2. *vb.* an'setzen.

scheme, 1. *n.* Plan, ⸗e *m.*; Schema, -s *nt.* 2. *vb.* intrigie'ren.

scholar, *n.* Gelehrt'- *m.&f.*

scholarship, *n.* (*knowledge*) Gelehr'samkeit *f.*; (*stipend*) Stipen'dium, -dien *nt.*

school, *n.* Schule, -n *f.*

science, *n.* Wissenschaft, -en *f.*

scientific, *adj.* wissenschaftlich.

scientist, *n.* Natur'wissenschaftler, - *m.*

scissors, *n.pl.* Schere, -n *f.*

scold, *vb.* schelten*.

scolding, *n.* Schelte *f.*

scoop, *n.* (*ladle*) Schöpfkelle, -n *f.*; (*newspaper*) Erstmeldung, -en *f.*

scope, *n.* Reichweite *f.*, Bereich', -e *m.*

scorch, *vb.* sengen, brennen*.

score, 1. *n.* (*points*) Punktzahl, -en *f.*; (**what's the s.?**) wie steht das Spiel?; (*music*) Partitur', -en *f.* 2. *vb.* an'schreiben*; (*mark*) markie'ren.

scorn, 1. *n.* Verach'tung *f.* 2. *vb.* verach'ten.

scornful, *adj.* verächt'lich.

Scotland, *n.* Schottland *nt.*

Scotsman, *n.* Schotte, -n, -n *f.*

Scottish, *adj.* schottisch.

scour, *vb.* scheuern.

scout, 1. *n.* Kundschafter, - *m.*; (**boy s.**) Pfadfinder, - *m.* 2. *vb.* erkun'den.

scowl, *vb.* finster blicken.

scramble, *vb.* (*tr.*) durcheinan'der·wer'fen*; (*intr.*) klettern; (**s. for**) sich reißen* um.

scrambled eggs, *n.* Rührei, -er *nt.*

scrap, 1. *n.* Fetzen, - *m.*; (*fight*) Streit *m.* 2. *vb.* ausrangieren; (*fight*) streiten*.

scrape, *vb.* kratzen.

scratch, 1. *n.* Schramme, -n *f.* 2. *vb.* kratzen; streichen*; (**start from s.**) von Anfang an begin'nen*.

scream, 1. *n.* Schrei, -e *m.* 2. *vb.* schreien*, brüllen.

screen, 1. *n.* (*furniture*) Wandschirm, -e *m.*; (*window*) Fliegengitter, - *nt.*; (*movie*) Leinwand, ⸗e *f.*; (*TV, radar*) schirm, -e *m.*; (*camouflage*) Tarnung, -en *f.* 2. *vb.* (*sift*) sieben; (*hide*) tarnen.

screw, 1. *n.* Schraube, -n *f.* 2. *vb.* schrauben.

scribble, *vb.* kritzeln, schmieren.

scripture, *n.* (*eccles.*) Heilige Schrift, -en *f.*

scroll, *n.* Schriftrolle, -n *f.*

scrub, *vb.* schrubbern.

scruple, *n.* Skrupel, - *m.*, Beden'ken, - *nt.*

scrupulous, *adj.* gewis'senhaft.

scrutinize, *vb.* genau'betrach'ten.

sculptor, *n.* Bildhauer, - *m.*

sculpture, 1. *n.* Skulptur', -en *f.* 2. *vb.* bildhauern.

scythe, *n.* Sense, -n *f.*

sea, *n.* See, Se'en *f.*, Meer, -e *nt.*; (*waves*) Seegang *m.*

seal, 1. *n.* Siegel, - *nt.*; (*animal*) Seehund, -e *m.*, Robbe, -n *f.* 2. *vb.* siegeln, versie'geln.

seam, 1. *n.* Saum, ⸗e *m.* 2. *vb.* säumen.

seaport, *n.* Hafen, ⸗ *m.*

search, 1. *n.* Suche *f.*; Durchsu'chung, -en *f.* 2. *vb.* su'chen; durch·su'chen.

seasick, *adj.* seekrank(⸗).

seasickness, n. Seekrankheit f.

season, 1. n. Jahreszeit, -en f.; Saison', -s f. **2.** vb. würzen.

seasoning, n. Gewürz', -e nt.

seat, 1. n. Platz, ⸗e m., Sitzplatz, ⸗e m.; (headquarters) Sitz, -e m. **2.** vb. Sitzplätze haben für.

second, 1. n. Sekun'de, -n f. **2.** adj. zweit-. **3.** vb. (s. a motion) einen Antrag unterstüt'zen.

secondary, adj. sekundär'.

secret, 1. n. Geheim'nis, -se nt. **2.** adj. geheim', heimlich.

secretary, n. Sekretär', -e m.; Sekretä'rin, -nen f.; (organization) Schriftführer, - m.

sect, n. Sekte, -n f.

section, n. Schnitt, -e m.; Teil, -e m.; Abschnitt, -e m.; Abtei'lung, -en f.

secular, adj. weltlich.

secure, 1. adj. sicher. **2.** vb. sichern.

security, n. Sicherheit, -en f.

sedative, n. Beru'higungsmittel, - nt.

seduce, vb. verfüh'ren.

seductive, adj. verführe'risch.

see, vb. sehen*, schauen.

seed, n. (individual) Samen, - m.; (collective & fig.) Saat, -en f.

seek, vb. suchen.

seem, vb. scheinen*.

seep, vb. sickern.

seesaw, n. Wippe, -n f.

segment, n. Segment', -e nt.

segregate, vb. ab'sondern.

seize, vb. fassen, ergrei'fen*; (confiscate) beschlag'nahmen.

seldom, adv. selten.

select, 1. adj. ausgesucht. **2.** vb. aus'wählen, aus'suchen.

selection, n. Auswahl, -en f.

selective, adj. auswählend.

self, adv. selbst, selber.

selfish, adj. selbstsüchtig.

selfishness, n. Selbstsucht f.

sell, vb. verkau'fen.

semantic, adj. seman'tisch.

semantics, n. Seman'tik f.

semester, n. Semes'ter, - nt.

semicircle, n. Halbkreis, -e m.

semicolon, n. Strichpunkt, -e m., Semiko'lon nt.

seminary, n. Seminar', -e nt.

senate, n. Senat', -e m.

senator, n. Sena'tor, -o'ren m.

send, vb. senden*, schicken.

senile, adj. senil'.

senior, adj. älter-.

sensation, n. Sensation', -en f.; (feeling) Gefühl', -e nt.

sensational, adj. sensationell'.

sense, 1. n. Sinn, -e m.; (feeling) Gefühl', -e nt.; (meaning) Bedeu'tung, -en f. **2.** vb. fühlen, empfin'den*.

sensible, adj. vernün'ftig.

sensitive, adj. empf·.nd'lich; sensitiv'.

sensual, adj. sinnlich.

sentence, 1. n. Satz, ⸗e m.; (judgment) Urteil, -e nt. **2.** vb. verur'teilen.

sentiment, n. Gefühl', -e nt., Empfin'dung, -en f.

sentimental, adj. gefühl'voll, sentimental'.

separate, 1. adj. getrennt'. **2.** vb. trennen.

separation, n. Trennung, -en f.

September, n. Septem'ber, - m.

sequence, n. Reihenfolge, -n f.

serenade, n. Ständchen, -nt.

serene, adj. klar, ruhig.

sergeant, n. Unteroffizier, - m.; (police) Wachtmeister, - m.

serial, 1. n. fortlaufende Erzäh'lung, -en f. **2.** adj. Reihen- (cpds.).

series, n. Reihe, -n f.

serious, adj. ernst.

seriousness, n. Ernst m.

sermon, n. Predigt, -en f.

serpent, n. Schlange, -n f.

serum, n. Serum, -ra nt.

servant, n. Diener, - m.;

(domestic) Hausangestellt-m.&f.

serve, vb. dienen; *(offer food)* servie'ren.

service, n. Dienst, -e m.; *(hotel, etc.)* Bedie'nung f.; *(china, etc.)* Servi'ce nt.; *(church)* Gottesdienst, -e m.

session, n. Sitzung, -en f.

set, 1. n. *(dishes, tennis)* Satz, -e m.; *(articles belonging together)* Garnitur', -en f. **2.** adj. bestimmt'. **3.** vb. setzen; stellen; legen; *(sun)* unter·gehen*.

settle, vb. *(dwell)* sich nieder-lassen*; *(conclude)* erle'digen; *(decide)* entschei'den*.

settlement, n. Niederlassung, -en f.; Siedlung, -en f.; *(decision)* Überein'kommen, - nt.

settler, n. Siedler, - m.

seven, num. sieben.

seventeen, num. siebzehn.

seventeenth, 1. adj. siebzehnt-. **2.** n. Siebzehntel, nt.

seventh, 1. adj. sieb(en)t-. **2.** n. Sieb(en)tel, - nt.

seventieth, 1. adj. siebzigst-. **2.** n. Siebzigstel, - nt.

seventy, num. siebzig.

sever, vb. ab·trennen, ab·brechen*.

several, adj. mehrer-.

severe, adj. streng; hart(-); ernst.

severity, n. Strenge f.; Härte f.; Ernst m.

sew, vb. nähen.

sewer, n. Kanalization' f.

sex, n. Geschlecht', -er nt.; Sexus m.

sexton, n. Küster, - m.

sexual, adj. geschlecht'lich, sexuell'.

shabby, adj. schäbig.

shack, n. Bretterbude, -n f.

shade, 1. n. Schatten, - m.; *(color)* Farbton, -e m. **2.** vb. beschat'ten; schattie'ren.

shadow, n. Schatten, - m.

shady, adj. schattig; *(dubious)* zwielichtig.

shaft, n. Schaft, -e m.; *(mine)* Schacht, -e m.; *(transmis-*

sion) Welle, -n f.; *(wagon)* Deichsel, -n f.

shaggy, adj. zottig.

shake, vb. schütteln.

shall, vb. **(we s. do it)** wir werden* es tun; **(what s. we do?)** was sollen* wir tun?

shallow, adj. flach.

shame, 1. n. Schande f.; **(what a s.)** wie schade. **2.** vb. beschä'men.

shameful, adj. schandbar.

shameless, adj. schamlos.

shampoo, 1. n. Schampun', -s nt. **2.** vb. die Haare waschen*.

shape, 1. n. Form, -en f., Gestalt', -en f. **2.** vb. formen, gestal'ten.

share, 1. n. Anteil, -e m.; *(stock)* Aktie, -n f. **2.** vb. teilen; teil·haben*.

shark, n. Haifisch, -e m.

sharp, 1. n. *(music)* Kreuz, -e nt. **2.** adj. scharf(-); *(clever)* schlau.

sharpen, vb. schärfen.

sharpness, n. Schärfe f.

shatter, vb. zerbre'chen*.

shave, 1. vb. rasie'ren. **2.** n. Rasie'ren nt.; **(get a s.)** sich rasie'ren lassen.

shawl, n. Schal, -s m.

she, pron. sie.

shear, vb. scheren*.

shears, n.pl. Schere, -n f.

sheath, n. Scheide, -n f.; *(dress)* körperenges Kleid, -er nt.

shed, 1. n. Schuppen, - m. **2.** vb. ab·werfen*; *(tears, blood)* vergie'ßen*.

sheep, n. Schaf, -e nt.

sheet, n. *(bed)* Laken, - nt.; *(paper)* Bogen, - m.; *(metal)* Platte, -n f.

shelf, n. Bord, -e nt.

shell, 1. n. Schale, -n f.; *(conch)* Muschel, -n f.; *(explosive)* Grana'te, -n f. **2.** vb. beschie'ßen*.

shellac, n. Schellack, -e m.

shelter, 1. n. Schutz m., Obdach nt. **2.** vb. beschir'men; beher'bergen.

shepherd, *n.* Schäfer, - *m.*; Hirt, -en, -en *m.*

sherbet, *n.* Sorbett, -e *nt.*

sherry, *n.* Sherry, -s *m.*

shield, 1. *n.* Schild, -e *m.* 2. *vb.* schützen.

shift, 1. *n.* Wechsel, - *m.*; (*workers*) Schicht, -en *f.*; (*auto*) Schalthebel, - *m.* 2. *vb.* wechseln; schalten; verschie'ben*.

shin, *n.* Schienbein, -e *nt.*

shine, *vb.* scheinen*, glänzen; (*shoes*) putzen.

shingle, *n.* Schindel, -n *f.*; Dachschindel, -n *f.*

shiny, *adj.* glänzend.

ship, 1. *n.* Schiff, -e *nt.* 2. *vb.* senden*.

shipment, *n.* Ladung, -en *f.*, Sendung, -en *f.*

shipper, *n.* Verfrach'ter, - *m.*, Verla'der, - *m.*

shipping agent, *n.* Spediteur', -e *m.*

shipwreck, *n.* Schiffbruch, ⸗e *m.*

shirk, *vb.* sich drücken vor.

shirt, *n.* Hemd, -en *nt.*

shiver, *vb.* zittern.

shock, 1. *n.* Schock, -s *m.* 2. *vb.* schockie'ren.

shoe, *n.* Schuh, -e *m.*

shoelace, *n.* Schnürsenkel, - *m.*

shoemaker, *n.* Schuhmacher, - *m.*, Schuster, - *m.*

shoot, 1. *n.* (*sprout*) Schößling, -e *m.* 2. *vb.* (*gun*) schießen*; (*person*) erschie'ßen*.

shop, 1. *n.* Laden, ⸗ *m.*, Geschäft', -e *nt.*; (*factory*) Werkstatt, ⸗en *f.* 2. *vb.* Einkäufe machen.

shopping, *n.* Einkaufen *nt.*

shore, *n.* Küste, -n *f.*; (*beach*) Strand, ⸗e *m.*

short, *adj.* kurz(⸗); (*scarce*) knapp.

shortage, *n.* Knappheit, -en *f.*

shorthand, *n.* Stenographie' *f.*

shortly, *adv.* bald(⸗).

shorten, *vb.* kürzen.

shorts, *n.pl.* Shorts *pl.*

shot, *n.* Schuß,⸗sse *m.*; (*photo*) Aufnahme, -n *f.*

should, *vb.* sollte; (**s. have**) hätte ... sollen.

shoulder, 1. *n.* Schulter, -n *f.* 2. *vb.* schultern.

shout, *vb.* schreien*.

shovel, *n.* Schaufel, -n *f.*

show, 1. *n.* (*theater, film*) Vorstellung, -en *f.*; (*spectacle*) Thea'ter, - *nt.*; (*exhibit*) Ausstellung, -en *f.* 2. *vb.* zeigen; vor'führen; ausstellen.

shower, *n.* (*rain*) Schauer, - *m.*; (*bath*) Dusche, -n *f.*

shrapnel, *n.* Schrapnell', -s *nt.*

shrewd, *adj.* scharfsinnig; (*derogatory*) geris'sen.

shriek, *vb.* kreischen.

shrill, *adj.* schrill, gellend.

shrimp, *n.* Garne'le, -n *f.*, Krabbe, -n *f.*; (*small person*) Dreikä'sehoch, -s *m.*

shrine, *n.* Schrein, -e *m.*

shrink, *vb.* schrumpfen; (*cloth*) ein'laufen*.

shroud, *n.* Leichentuch, ⸗er *nt.*

shrub, *n.* Strauch, ⸗er *m.*, Busch, ⸗e *m.*

shudder, *vb.* schaudern.

shun, *vb.* vermei'den*.

shut, 1. *vb.* schließen*, zumachen. 2. *adj.* geschlossen. 3. *adv.* zu.

shutter, *n.* Fensterladen, ⸗ *m.*; (*camera*) Verschluß', ⸗sse *m.*

shy, 1. *adj.* scheu, schüchtern. 2. *vb.* scheuen.

Sicily, *n.* Sizi'lien *nt.*

sick, *adj.* krank(⸗); (**be s. of**) satt'haben*.

sickness, *n.* Krankheit, -en *f.*

side, *n.* Seite, -n *f.*; (*edge*) Rand, ⸗er *m.*

sidewalk, *n.* Bürgersteig, -e *m.*

siege, *n.* Bela'gerung, -en *f.*

sieve, *n.* Sieb, -e *nt.*

sift, *vb.* sieben; sichten.

sigh, 1. *n.* Seufzer, - *m.* 2. *vb.* seufzen.

sight, 1. *n.* Sicht *f.*; (*vision*)

Sehkraft f.; (view) Anblick, -e m.; (sights) Sehenswürdigkeit, -en f. 2. vb. sichten.

sightseeing, n. Besich'tigung (f.) von Sehenswürdigkeiten.

sign, 1. n. Zeichen, - nt.; Schild, -er nt. 2. vb. unterzeich'nen, unterschrei'ben*.

signal, 1. n. Signal', -e nt. 2. vb. signalisie'ren.

signature, n. Unterschrift, -en f.

significance, n. Bedeu'tung, -en f., Wichtigkeit, f.

significant, adj. bezeich'nend, bedeu'tend.

signify, vb. bezeich'nen, bedeu'ten.

silence. 1. n. Schweigen nt., Ruhe f. 2. vb. zum Schweigen bringen*.

silent, adj. still, schweigsam.

silk, 1. n. Seide f. 2. adj. seiden.

silken, **silky**, adj. seidig.

sill, n. (door) Schwelle, -n f.; (window) Fensterbrett, -er nt.

silly, adj. albern.

silo, n. Silo, -s m.

silver, 1. n. Silber nt. 2. adj. silbern.

silverware, n. (silbernes) Besteck', -e nt.

similar, adj. ähnlich.

similarity, n. Ähnlichkeit, -en f.

simple, adj. einfach, schlicht; (ignorant) einfältig.

simplicity, n. Einfachheit f., Schlichtheit f.

simplify, vb. verein'fachen.

simulate, vb. vor'geben*, nach'ahmen.

simultaneous, adj. gleichzeitig.

sin, 1. n. Sünde, -n f. 2. vb. sündigen.

since, 1. prep. seit. 2. conj. seit, seitdem'; (because) da. 3. adv. seitdem'.

sincere, adj. aufrichtig, ehrlich.

sincerely, adv. (s. yours) Ihr erge'bener, Ihre erge'bene.

sincerity, n. Aufrichtigkeit f.

sinful, adj. sündhaft.

sing, vb. singen*.

singe, vb. sengen.

singer, n. Sänger, - m.

single, adj. einzeln; (unmarried) ledig.

singular, 1. n. (gram.) Einzahl f., Singular m. 2. adj. einzig; (unusual) eigentümlich.

sinister, adj. düster, unheimlich.

sink, 1. n. Ausguß, ⸗sse m., Spülstein -e m. 2. vb. (tr.) versen'ken; (intr.) sinken*.

sinner, n. Sünder, - m.

sinus, n. Stirnhöhle, -n f.

sinusitis, n. Stirnhöhlenentzündung, -en f.

sip, 1. n. Schluck, -e m. 2. vb. schlürfen.

siphon, n. Siphon, -s m.

sir, n. (yes s.) Jawohl'.

siren, n. Sire'ne, -n f.

sirloin, n. Lendenstück, -e nt.

sister, n. Schwester, -n f.

sister-in-law, n. Schwägerin, -nen f.

sit, vb. sitzen*; (s. down) sich (hin⸳) setzen.

site, n. Lage, -n f.

sitting, n. Sitzung, -en f.

situated, adj. gele'gen.

situation, n. Lage, -n f., Situation', -en f.

six, num. sechs.

sixteen, num. sechzehn.

sixteenth, 1. adj. sechzehnt-. 2. n. Sechzehntel, - nt.

sixth, 1. adj. sechst-. 2. n. Sechstel, - nt.

sixtieth, 1. adj. sechzigst-. 2. n. Sechzigstel, - nt.

sixty, num. sechzig.

size, n. Größe, -n f., Ausmaß, -e nt.

skate, 1. n. Schlittschuh, -e m. 2. vb. Schlittschuh laufen*.

skeleton, n. Skelett', -e nt.

skeptic, n. Skeptiker, - m.

skeptical, adj. skeptisch.

sketch, 1. n. Skizze, -n f.;

Sketch, -e *m.* **2.** *vb.* skizzie'-ren.

ski, 1. *n.* Schi, -er *m.* **2.** *vb.* Schi'laufen*.

skid, 1. *n.* Hemmschuh, -e *m.* **2.** *vb.* rutschen.

skill, *n.* Geschick', *nt.,* Fertigkeit, -en *f.*

skillful, *adj.* geschickt'.

skim, *vb.* (remove cream) entrah'men; (go over lightly) flüchtig lesen*.

skim milk, *n.* Magermilch *f.*

skin, 1. *n.* Haut, "e *f.;* (fur) Fell, -e *nt.;* (of fruit) Schale, -n *f.* **2.** *vb.* häuten.

skip, *vb.* springen*; (omit) überschla'gen*.

skirt, 1. *n.* Rock, "e *m.* **2.** *vb.* umge'hen*.

skull, *n.* Schädel, - *m.*

skunk, *n.* Stinktier, -e *nt.;* (person) Schuft, -e *m.*

sky, *n.* Himmel, - *m.*

skyscraper, *n.* Wolkenkratzer, - *m.*

slab, *n.* Platte, -n *f.*

slack, *adj.* schlaff, flau.

slacken, *vb.* nach·lassen*.

slacks, *n.pl.* Slacks *pl.*

slam, *vb.* knallen, zu·knallen.

slander, 1. *n.* Verleum'dung, -en *f.* **2.** *vb.* verleum'den.

slang, *n.* Slang *m.,* Jargon', -s *m.*

slant, 1. *n.* Neigung, -en *f.;* schiefe Ebene, -n *f.;* Aspekt', -e *m.* **2.** *vb.* neigen.

slap, 1. *n.* Klaps, -e *m.* **2.** *vb.* schlagen*.

slash, 1. *n.* Schlitz, -e *m.;* Schnittwunde, -n *f.* **2.** *vb.* schlitzen.

slat, *n.* Latte, -n *f.*

slate, *n.* Schiefer *m.;* (list) Liste, -n *f.*

slaughter, 1. *n.* Schlachten *nt.;* Gemet'zel, - *nt.* **2.** *vb.* schlachten; nieder·metzeln.

Slav, *n.* Slawe, -n, -n *m.*

slave, *n.* Sklave, -n, -n *m.*

slavery, *n.* Sklaverei' *f.*

Slavic, *adj.* slawisch.

slay, *vb.* erschla'gen*.

sled, *n.* Schlitten, - *m.;* (go sleigh-ing) Schlitten fahren*, rodeln.

sleek, *adj.* glatt(", -); geschniegelt.

sleep, 1. *n.* Schlaf *m.* **2.** *vb.* schlafen*. (go to s.) einschlafen*.

sleeper, sleeping car, *n.* Schlafwagen, - *m.*

sleepy, *adj.* schläfrig, müde.

sleet, *n.* Eisregen *m.*

sleeve, *n.* Ärmel, - *m.*

sleigh, *n.* Schlitten, - *m.*

slender, *adj.* schlank; (slight) schwach(").

slice, 1. *n.* Scheibe, -n *f.* **2.** *vb.* in Scheiben schneiden*.

slide, *vb.* gleiten*, rutschen.

slight, *adj.* leicht, gering'; (thin) schmächtig.

slim, *adj.* schlank; gering'.

slime, *n.* Schlamm *m.;* Schleim *m.*

slip, 1. *n.* (plant) Steckling, -e *m.;* (error) Verse'hen, - *nt.;* (underwear) Unterrock, "e *m.;* (paper) Zettel, - *m.;* (bedding) Bezug' "e *m.* **2.** *vb.* gleiten*, aus·-leiten*.

slipper, *n.* Hausschuh, -e *m.,* Pantof'fel. -n *m.*

slippery, *adj.* glatt(", -), schlüpfrig.

slit, 1. *n.* Schlitz, -e *m.* **2.** *vb.* schlitzen.

slogan, *n.* Schlagwort, -e or "er *nt.;* (election s.) Wahlspruch, "e *m.*

slope, 1. *n.* Abhang, "e *m.;* Neigung, -en *f.*

sloppy, *adj.* schlampig.

slot, *n.* Schlitz, -e *m.*

slovenly, *adj.* liederlich.

slow, *adj.* langsam; (be s., of a clock) nach·gehen*.

slowness, *n.* Langsamkeit *f.*

sluggish, *adj.* träge.

slum, *n.* Elendsviertel, - *nt.*

slur, 1. *n.* Anwurf, "e, *m.* **2.** *vb.* nuscheln.

slush, *n.* Matsch *m.*

sly, *adj.* schlau, verschla'gen.

small, *adj.* klein.

small pox, *n.* Blattern *pl.*

smart, *adj.* intelligent'; elegant'.

smash, *vb.* zerschla'gen*, zerschmei'ßen*.

smear, vb. schmieren, beschmie'ren.

smell, 1. n. Geruch', ⁻e m. **2.** vb. riechen*.

smelt, 1. n. Stint, -e m. **2.** vb. schmelzen, ein'schmelzen.

smile, 1. n. Lächeln nt. **2.** vb. lächeln.

smock, n. Kittel, - m.

smoke, 1. n. Rauch m. **2.** vb. rauchen; (meat, fish) räuchern.

smooth, 1. adj. glatt(⁻, -). **2.** vb. glätten.

smother, vb. ersti'cken.

smug, adj. selbstgefällig; blasiert'.

smuggle, vb. schmuggeln.

snack, n. Imbiß, -sse m.

snag, 1. n. (stocking) Zugmasche, -n f.; (obstacle) Hindernis, -se nt.

snail, n. Schnecke, -n f.

snake, n. Schlange, -n f.

snap, 1. n. Druckknopf, ⁻e m. **2.** vb. schnappen; (break) zerrei'ßen*.

snapshot, n. Schnappschuß, ⁻sse m.

snare, n. Falle, -n f.

snarl, 1. n. Verhed'derung, -en f. **2.** vb. verhed'dern; (growl) drohend knurren.

snatch, vb. erha'schen, weg'schnappen.

sneak, vb. schleichen*.

sneer, vb. höhnisch grinsen.

sneeze, vb. niesen.

snob, n. Snob, -s m.

snore, vb. schnarchen.

snow, 1. n. Schnee m. **2.** vb. schneien.

snub, 1. n. Affront', -s m. **2.** vb. schneiden*.

snug, adj. eng; (fig.) mollig.

so, adv. so.

soak, vb. durchnäs'sen; ein'weichen.

soap, n. Seife, -n f.

soar, vb. sich empor'schwingen*.

sob, vb. schluchzen.

sober, adj. nüchtern.

sociable, adj. gesel'lig.

social, adj. gesell'schaftlich, sozial'.

socialism, n. Sozialis'mus m.

socialist, n. Sozialist', -en, -en m.

society, n. Gesell'schaft, -en f.

sociology, n. Soziologie' f.

sock, 1. n. Socke, -n f. **2.** vb. schlagen*.

socket, n. (eye) Augenhöhle, -n f.; (elec.) Steckdose, -n f.

sod, n. Sode, -n f.

soda, n. Soda nt.

sofa, n. Sofa, -s nt.

soft, adj. (not hard) weich; (not loud) leise; (not rough) sanft, sacht.

soft drink, n. alkoholfreies Getränk', -e nt.

soften, vb. weich machen*; (fig.) mildern.

soil, 1. n. Boden, ⁻ m. **2.** vb. beschmut'zen.

soiled, adj. schmutzig.

sojourn, 1. n. Aufenthalt, -e m. **2.** vb. sich auf'halten*.

solace, n. Trost m.

solar, adj. Sonnen- (cpds.).

soldier, n. Soldat', -en, -en m.

sole, 1. n. Sohle, -n f.; (fish) Seezunge, -n f. **2.** adj. allei'nig, einzig.

solemn, adj. feierlich.

solicit, vb. an'halten* um.

solicitous, adj. besorgt'; eifrig.

solid, adj. fest; solid', kompakt'.

solidify, vb. festigen; verdich'ten.

solitary, adj. einzeln.

solitude, n. Einsamkeit, -en f.

solo, n. Solo, -s nt.

soloist, n. Solist', -en, -en m.

so long, interj. Wiedersehen.

solution, n. Lösung, -en f.

solve, vb. lösen.

solvent, 1. n. Lösungsmittel, - nt. **2.** adj. (financially capable) zahlungsfähig.

somber, adj. düster.

some, pron.&adj. (with singulars) etwas; (with plurals) einig-, ein paar.

somebody, pron. jemand.

somehow, adv. irgendwie.

someone, pron. jemand.

somersault, n. Purzelbaum, =e m.

something, pron. etwas.

sometime, adv. irgendwann.

sometimes, adv. manchmal.

somewhat, adv. etwas.

somewhere, adv. irgendwo.

son, n. Sohn, =e m.

song, n. Lied, -er nt.

son-in-law, n. Schwiegersohn, =e m.

soon, adv. bald.

soot, n. Ruß m.

soothe, vb. beschwich'tigen.

soothing, adj. wohltuend.

sophisticated, adj. anspruchsvoll verfei'nert, lebenserfahren, weltgewandt.

soprano, n. Sopran', -e m.

sorcery, n. Zauberei' f.

sordid, adj. dreckig; gemein'.

sore, 1. n. wunde Stelle, -n f., offene Wunde, -n f. 2. adj. wund; schmerzhaft; (angry) eingeschnappt; (be s.) weh·tun*.

sorrow, n. Kummer, - m.

sorrowful, adj. kummervoll.

sorry, adj. traurig, betrübt'; (I am s.) es tut* mir leid.

sort, 1. n. Sorte, -n f., Art, -en f. 2. vb. sortie'ren.

soul, n. Seele, -n f.

sound, 1. n. Ton,=e m., Laut, -e m., Klang, =e m. 2. adj. gesund(=, -); (valid) einwandfrei. 3. vb. Klingen*; (take soundings) loten.

soup, n. Suppe, -n f.

sour, adj. sauer.

source, n. Quelle, -n f.

south, 1. n. Süden m. 2. adj. südlich; Süd- (cpds.).

southeast, 1. n. Südos'ten m. 2. adj. südöst'lich; Südost' - (cpds.).

southeastern, adj. südöst'lich.

southern, adj. südlich.

South Pole, n. Südpol m.

southwest, 1. n. Südwes'ten m. 2. adj. südwest'lich; Südwest' - (cpds.).

southwestern, adj. südwest'lich.

souvenir, n. Andenken, - nt.; Reiseandenken, - nt.

Soviet, 1. n. Sowjet, -s m. 2. adj. sowje'tisch.

sow, 1. n. Sau, =e f. 2. vb. säen.

space, n. Raum, =e m.

spacious, adj. geräu'mig.

spade, n. Spaten, - m.; (cards) Pik nt.

spaghetti, n. Spaghet'ti pl.

Spain, n. Spanien nt.

span, 1. n. Spanne, -n f. 2. vb. überspan'nen.

Spaniard, n. Spanier, - m.

Spanish, adj. spanisch.

spank, vb. hauen*.

spanking, n. Haue f.

spar, 1. n. Sparren, - m. 2. vb. boxen.

spare, 1. adj. Ersatz'-, Reser've- (cpds.). 2. vb. sparen, scheuen.

spark, n. Funke(n), - m.

sparkle, vb. funkeln.

spark-plug, n. Zündkerze, -n f.

sparrow, n. Sperling, -e m.

sparse, adj. spärlich.

spasm, n. Krampf, =e m.

spasmodic, adj. krampfhaft; sprunghaft.

spatter, vb. spritzen, bespritz'zen.

speak, vb. sprechen*, reden.

speaker, n. Redner, - m.; (presiding officer) Präsident', -en, -en m.

spear, 1. n. Speer, -e m.; Spieß, -e m. 2. vb. auf·spießen.

special, adj. beson'der.

specialist, n. Spezialist', -en, -en m.

specially, adv. beson'ders.

specialty, n. Spezialität', -en f.

species, n. Art, -en f.; Gattung, -en f.

specific, adj. spezi'fisch.

specify, vb. spezifizie'ren; (stipulate) bestim'men.

specimen, n. Muster, - nt., Exemplar', -e nt., Probe, -n f.

spectacle, n. Schauspiel, -e nt.; Anblick, -e m.; (s.s) Brille, -n f.

spectacular, *adj.* aufsehenerregend.

spectator, *n.* Zuschauer, - *m.*

spectrum, *n.* Spektrum, -tren *nt.*

speculate, *vb.* spekulie'ren.

speculation, *n.* Spekulation', -en *f.*

speech, *n.* Sprache, -n *f.;* (*address*) Rede, -n.

speechless, *adj.* sprachlos.

speed, 1. *n.* Geschwin'digkeit, -en *f.;* Tempo *nt.* 2. *vb.* hasten; (**s. up**) beschleu'nigt erle'digen; (*auto*) die Geschwin'digkeitsgrenze überschrei'ten*.

speedometer, *n.* Geschwin'digkeitsmesser, - *m.*

speedy, *adj.* schnell; unverzüglich.

spell, 1. *n.* Zauber, - *m.* 2. *vb.* buchstabie'ren.

spelling, *n.* Rechtschreibung *f.*

spend, *vb.* (*money*) ausgeben*; (*time*) verwen'den*, verbrin'gen*.

sphere, *n.* Kugel, -n *f.,* Sphäre, -n *f.*

spice, *n.* Gewürz', -e *nt.*

spider, *n.* Spinne, -n *f.*

spike, *n.* langer Nagel, *⸗ m.;* (*thorn*) Dorn, -en *m.,* Stachel, -n *m.*

spill, *vb.* verschüt'ten; (*make a spot*) kleckern.

spin, *vb.* spinnen*.

spinach, *n.* Spinat' *m.*

spine, *n.* Rückgrat, -e *nt.*

spiral, 1. *n.* Spira'le, -n *f.* 2. *adj.* spiral'förmig.

spire, *n.* spitzer Turm, *⸗e m.*

spirit, *n.* Geist *m.;* (*ghost*) Gespenst', -er *nt.;* (*vivacity*) Schwung *m.;* (**s.s**) Spirituo'sen *pl.*

spiritual, 1. *n.* geistliches Negerlied, -er *nt.* 2. *adj.* geistig, seelisch.

spiritualism, *n.* Spiritualis'mus *m.;* Spiritis'mus *m.*

spit, 1. *n.* (*saliva*) Speichel *m.;* (*roasting*) Spieß, -e *m.* 2. *vb.* spucken.

spite, 1. *n.* Trotz *m.;* (**in s. of**) trotz. 2. *vb.* ärgern.

splash, *vb.* spritzen; planschen.

splendid, *adj.* prächtig.

splendor, *n.* Pracht *f.*

splice, *vb.* spleißen.

splint, *n.* Schiene, -n *f.*

splinter, *n.* Splitter, - *m.*

split, 1. *n.* Spalt, -e *m.* 2. *vb.* spalten.

spoil, *vb.* verder'ben*; schlecht werden*; (*child*) verwöh'nen, verzie'hen*.

spoke, *n.* Speiche, -n *f.*

spokesman, *n.* Sprecher, - *m.*

sponge, 1. *n.* Schwamm, *⸗e m.* 2. *vb.* (*live off*) nassauern.

sponsor, 1. *n.* Bürge, -n, -n *m.;* Förderer, - *m.;* (*radio, TV, etc.*) Rekla'meauftraggeber, - *m.* 2. *vb.* fördern; (*advertising*) in Auftrag geben*.

spontaneity, *n.* Impulsivität' *f.*

spontaneous, *adj.* spontan'.

spool, *n.* Spule, -n *f.*

spoon, *n.* Löffel, - *m.*

sport, *n.* Sport *m.;* Vergnügen, - *nt.*

spot, *n.* (*place*) Stelle, -n *f.;* (*blot*) Fleck, -en *m.*

spouse, *n.* Gatte, -n, -n *m.;* Gattin, -nen *f.*

spout, 1. *n.* Tülle, -n *f.;* (*water*) Strahl, -en *m.* 2. *vb.* hervor'sprudeln; speien*.

sprain, 1. *n.* Verren'kung, -en *f.,* Verstau'chung, -en *f.* 2. *vb.* verren'ken, verstau'chen.

sprawl, *vb.* sich aus·breiten; alle Viere aus·strecken.

spray, *vb.* spritzen; zerstäu'ben.

spread, 1. *n.* Spanne, -n *f.;* Umfang, *⸗e m.* 2. *vb.* aus·breiten.

spree, *n.* Bummel, - *m.* Ausflug, *⸗e m.*

sprightly, *adj.* munter.

spring, 1. *n.* (*season*) Frühling, -e *m.,* Frühjahr, -e *nt.;* (*source*) Quelle, -n *f.;* (*leap*) Sprung, *⸗e m.;* (*metal*) Feder, -n *f.* 2. *vb.* springen*.

sprinkle, vb. sprengen; streuen.

sprint, 1. n. Kurzstreckenlauf, ⸗e m. **2.** vb. sprinten.

sprout, 1. n. Sproß, ⸗e m. **2.** vb. sprießen*.

spry, adj. flink.

spur, 1. n. Sporn, Sporen m. **2.** vb. an·spornen.

spurn, vb. verschmä'hen.

spurt, vb. hervor'·schießen*.

spy, 1. n. Spion', ⸗e m. **2.** vb. spionie'ren.

squabble, 1. n. Zank m. **2.** vb. zanken.

squad, n. Trupp, ⸗s m.; (sport) Mannschaft, ⸗en f.

squadron, n. (air) Staffel, ⸗n f.; (navy) Geschwa'der, ⸗ nt.

squall, n. Bö, ⸗en f.

squalor, n. Schmutz m.

squander, vb. vergeu'den.

square, 1. n. Viereck, ⸗e nt., Quadrat', ⸗e nt.; (open place) Platz, ⸗e m. **2.** adj. viereckig, quadra'tisch. **3.** vb. quadrie'ren.

squash, 1. n. Kürbis, ⸗se m. **2.** vb. quetschen, zerquet'schen.

squat, 1. adj. kurz und dick. **2.** vb. hocken, kauern.

squeak, vb. quietschen.

squeamish, adj. zimperlich.

squeeze, vb. drücken; (juice) aus·pressen.

squirrel, n. Eichhörnchen, ⸗ nt.

squirt, vb. spritzen.

stab, 1. n. Stich, ⸗e m. **2.** vb. stechen*; erste'chen*.

stability, n. Bestän'digkeit f., Stabilität' f.

stabilize, vb. stabilisie'ren.

stable, 1. n. Stall, ⸗e m. **2.** adj. bestän'dig; stabil'.

stack, 1. n. Haufen, ⸗ m. **2.** vb. auf·stapeln.

stadium, n. Stadion, ⸗dien nt.

staff, n. Stab, ⸗e m.; (personnel) Personal' nt.; (music) Notenlinien pl.

stag, n. Hirsch, ⸗e m.

stage, 1. n. (theater) Bühne, ⸗n f.; (phase) Stadium, ⸗dien nt. **2.** vb. inszenie'ren.

stagger, vb. taumeln; (amaze) verblüf'fen; (alternate) staffeln.

stagnant, adj. stagnie'rend.

stagnate, vb. stagnie'ren.

stain, 1. n. Fleck, ⸗e m.; (color) Färbstoff, ⸗e m.; (paint) Beize f. **2.** vb. befle'cken, färben; beizen.

staircase, stairs, n. Treppe, ⸗n f.

stake, 1. n. (post) Pfahl, ⸗e m.; (sum, bet) Einsatz, ⸗e m. **2.** vb. aufs Spiel setzen.

stale, adj. alt(·), schal.

stalk, n. Stiel, ⸗e m., Halm, ⸗e m.

stall, 1. n. Stall, ⸗e m.; (vendor's) Bude, ⸗n f. **2.** vb. (hesitate) Zeit schinden*; (engine) ab·würgen.

stamina, n. Energie' f., Ausdauer f.

stammer, vb. stammeln.

stamp, 1. n. Stempel, ⸗ m.; (mark) Gepräge nt.; (postal) Freimarke, ⸗n f.; Briefmarke, ⸗n f. **2.** vb. stempeln; prägen.

stand, 1. n. Stellung, ⸗en f.; (vendor's) Bude, ⸗n f.; (grandstand) Tribü'ne, ⸗n f. **2.** vb. stehen*; (endure) extra'gen*.

standard, 1. n. Norm, ⸗en f., Standard, ⸗s m. **2.** adj. Standard- (cpds.).

standardize, vb. standardisie'ren.

standing, n. Bestand' m.; (reputation) Ruf m.

standpoint, n. Standpunkt, ⸗e m.

star, n. Stern, ⸗e m.; (movie) Star, ⸗s m.

starch, 1. n. Stärke f. **2.** vb. stärken.

stare, vb. starren, glotzen.

stark, adj. kraß; (bare) kahl.

start, 1. n. Anfang, ⸗e m., Start, ⸗s m. **2.** vb. an·fangen*, starten.

startle, vb. erschre'cken, auf·schrecken.

starvation, n. Verhun'gern nt.; Hungertod m.

starve, vb. hungern; **(s. to death)** verhun'gern.

state. 1. n. Staat, -en m.; (condition) Zustand, ⸚e m. **2.** vb. dar·legen, erklä'ren.

statement, n. Erklä'rung, -en f.; Behaup'tung, -en f.

stateroom, n. Kabi'ne, -n f.

statesman, n. Staatsmann, ⸚er m.

static. 1. n. atmosphä'rische Störung, -en f. **2.** adj. statisch.

station, n. Station', -en f.; (position) Stellung, -en f.; (R.R.) Bahnhof, ⸚e m.

stationary, adj. feststehend, stationär'.

stationer, n. Shreibwaren-händler, - m.

stationery, n. Schreibwaren pl.; Briefpapier nt.

station wagon, n. Kombi-wagen, - m.

statistics, n.pl. Statis'tik f.

statue, n. Statue, -n f.

stature, n. Wuchs m., Statur' f.; (fig.) Format', ⸚e nt.

status, n. Stand, ⸚e m.

statute, n. Statut', ⸚e nt. Satzung, -en f.

staunch, adj. treu, wacker.

stay. 1. n. (sojourn) Aufent-halt m; (delay) Einstellung, -en f. **2.** vb. bleiben*; (hold back) zurück·halten*.

steady, adj. fest; sicher; bestän'dig.

steak, n. Beefsteak, -s nt.

steal, vb. stehlen*.

stealth, n. Verstoh'lenheit f.

stealthy, adj. verstoh'len.

steam. 1. n. Dampf, ⸚e m. **2.** vb. dampfen.

steamboat, n. Dampfboot, -e nt.

steamship, n. Dampfer, - m.

steel. 1. n. Stahl, -e m. **2.** adj. stählern; Stahl- (cpds.).

steep, adj. steil; (price) hoch (hoh-, höher, höchst-).

steeple, n. Kirchturm, ⸚e m.

steer. 1. n. Stier, -e m. **2.** vb. steuern.

stellar, adj. Sternen- (cpds.).

stem. 1. n. Stiel, -e m. **2.** vb. stammen.

stenographer, n. Steno-typis'tin, -nen f.

stenography, n. Kurzschrift, -en f.; Stenographie', -i'en f.

step. 1. n. Schritt, -e m.; (stair) Stufe, -n f. **2.** vb. treten*.

stepfather, n. Stiefvater, ⸚ m.

stepmother, n. Stiefmutter, ⸚ f.

stepladder, n. Trittleiter, -n f.

sterile, adj. unfruchtbar, steril'.

sterility, n. Sterilität' f.

sterilize, vb. sterilisie'ren.

sterling, adj. unecht; (silver) echt; **(pound s.)** Pfund Sterling nt.

stern, adj. streng.

stethoscope, n. Stethoskop', -e nt.

stew. 1. n. Stew, -s nt. **2.** vb. dämpfen.

steward, n. Steward, -s m.

stewardess, n. Stewardess', -en f.

stick. 1. n. Stock, ⸚e m. **2.** vb. (adhere) kleben; (pin) stecken.

sticker, n. Etiket'te, -n f.

sticky, adj. klebrig.

stiff, adj. steif.

stiffen, vb. steif werden*; (fig.) verhär'ten.

stiffness, n. Steifheit, -en f.

stifle, vb. ersti'cken.

stigma, n. Stigma, -men nt., Schandfleck, -e m.

still. 1. n. Destillier'apparat, -e m. **2.** adj. still. **3.** vb. stillen. **4.** adv. noch; doch; dennoch.

stillness, n. Stille f.

stimulant, n. Reizmittel, - nt.

stimulate, vb. an·regen.

stimulus, n. Anreiz, -e m.

sting. 1. n. Stachel, - m.; (bite) Stich, -e m. **2.** vb. stechen*; (burn) brennen*.

stingy, adj. geizig.

stink, vb. stinken*.

stipulate, vb. bestim'men.

stir. 1. n. Aufregung, -en f. **2.** vb. rühren; erre'gen.

stitch, 1. n. Stich, -e m.; (knitting) Masche, -n f. **2.** vb. steppen.

stock, 1. n. (supply) Vorrat, =e m., Lager, - nt.; (lineage) Fami'lie, -n f.; (livestock) Viehbestand, =e m.; (gun) Schaft, =e m. **2.** vb. versor'gen; auf Lager haben*.

stockbroker, n. Börsenmakler, - m.

stock exchange, n. Börse, -n f.

stocking, n. Strumpf, =e m.

stodgy, adj. schwerfällig; untersetzt'.

stole, n. Stola, -len f.

stomach, 1. n. Magen, = m. **2.** vb. (fig.) schlucken.

stone, 1. n. Stein, -e m.; (fruit) Kern, -e m. **2.** vb. steinigen.

stool, n. Schemel, - m.

stoop, vb. sich bücken; (demean oneself) sich erniedrigen.

stop, 1. n. Haltestelle, -n f. **2.** vb. halten*; stoppen; (cease) auf·hören.

stop-over, n. Fahrtunterbrechung, -en f.

storage, n. Lagern nt.; Lagerhaus, =er nt.

store, 1. n. Laden, = m., Geschäft', -e nt.; (supplies) Vorräte pl. **2.** vb. lagern.

storehouse, n. Lagerhaus, =er nt.

storm, 1. n. Sturm, =e m. **2.** vb. stürmen.

stormy, adj. stürmisch.

story, n. Erzäh'lung, -en f., Geschich'te, -n f.

stout, adj. dick; (strong) wacker.

stove, n. (cooking) Herd, -e m.; (heating) Ofen, = m.

straight, adj. gera'de; (honest) ehrlich.

straighten, vb. gera'de machen; in Ordnung bringen*.

straightforward, adj. offen.

strain, 1. n. Anstrengung, -en f.; Belas'tung, -en f. **2.** vb. an·strengen; belas'ten; (filter) seihen.

strait, n. Meerenge, -n f.

strand, 1. n. Strähne, -n **2.** vb. stranden.

strange, adj. merkwürdi; (foreign) fremd.

stranger, n. Fremd- m.&f.

strangle, vb. erwür'gen.

strap, n. Riemen, - m.

stratagem, n. Kriegslist, -e f.

strategic, adj. strate'gisch.

strategy, n. Strategie' f.

stratosphere, n. Stratosphä re f.

stratum, n. Schicht. -en f.

straw, n. Stroh nt.; (f drinking) Strohalm, -e m.

strawberry, n. Erdbeere, -

stray, 1. adj. verein'zelt. 2 vb. ab·weichen, ab·schweifer

streak, n. Strähne, -n f.

stream, 1. n. Strom, =e m (small) Bach, =e m.

streamlined, adj. strom linienförmig.

street, n. Straße, -n f.

streetcar, n. Straßenbahr -en f.

strength, n. Kraft, =e f Stärke, -n f.

strengthen, vb. stärken.

strenuous, adj. anstrengenc

stress, 1. n. Belas'tung, -e f.; (accent) Beto'nung, -en j **2.** vb. belas'ten; beto'nen.

stretch, 1. n. Strecke, -n f. Spanne, -n f. **2.** vb. strecken spannen.

stretcher, n. Tragbahre, - f.

strew, vb. streuen.

stricken, adj. getrof'fen.

strict, adj. streng.

stride, 1. n. Schritt, -e m. 2 vb. schreiten*.

strife, n. Streit m.

strike, 1. n. (workers') Streik, -s m. **2.** vb. streiken (hit) schlagen*.

string, 1. n. Bindfaden, = m. Schnur, =e f.; (music) Saite -n f. **2.** vb. auf·reihen.

string bean, n. grüne Bohne -n f.

strip, 1. n. Streifen, - m. 2 vb. ab·streifen; entklei den.

stripe, n. Streifen, - m.

strive, vb. streben.

stroke, 1. n. Schlag, ꞏe m.; (pen, brush, etc.) Strich, ꞏe m.; (med.) Schlaganfall, ꞏe m. **2.** vb. streicheln.

stroll, 1. n. kleiner Spazierꞏgang, ꞏe m. **2.** vb. spazieꞏrenꞏgehen*.

ᴜroller, n. Spazierꞏgänger, - m.; (baby-carriage) Kindersportwagen, - m.

strong, adj. stark(ꞏ), kräftig.

stronghold, n. Feste, -n f.

structure, n. Struktur′, -en f.

struggle, 1. n. Ringen nt. **2.** vb. ringen*.

strut, vb. stolzie′ren.

stub, 1. n. Kontroll′abꞏschnitt, -e m. **2.** vb. anꞏstoßen*.

stubborn, adj. hartnäckig; (person) dickköpfig.

student, n. Student′, -en, -en m.

studio, n. Atelier′, -s nt.

studious, adj. eifrig.

study, 1. n. Studium, -dien nt.; (room) Arbeitszimmer - nt. **2.** vb. studie′ren; (do homework) arbeiten.

stuff, 1. n. Zeug nt. **2.** vb. stopfen.

stuffing, n. Füllung, -en f.

stumble, vb. stolpern.

stump, n. Stumpf, ꞏe m.

stun, vb. betäu′ben; verblüffen.

stunt, n. Kunststück, -e nt.

stupid, adj. dumm(ꞏ), blöde.

stupidity, n. Dummheit, -en f.

stupor, n. Betäu′bungszustand m.

sturdy, adj. stark(ꞏ), stämmig.

stutter, vb. stottern.

sty, n. Schweinestall, ꞏe m.; (eye) Gerstenkorn, ꞏer nt.

style, n. Stil, -e m.

stylish, adj. elegant′.

suave, adj. verbind′lich.

subconscious, adj. unterbewußt.

subdue, vb. unterdrü′cken.

subject, 1. n. (gram.) Subjekt, -e nt.; (topic) Thema, -men nt.; (of king) Untertan,

-en, -en m. **2.** adj. unterwor′fen. **3.** vb. unterwer′fen*; ausꞏsetzen.

subjugate, vb. unterjo′chen.

subjunctive, n. Konjunktiv, -e m.

sublime, adj. erha′ben.

submarine, n. Unterseeboot, -e nt., U-Boot, -e nt.

submerge, vb. unterꞏtauchen.

submission, n. Unterwer′fung, -en f.

submit, vb. (lay before) unterbrei′ten; (offer opinion) anheim′stellen; (yield) sich fügen; (surrender) sich unterwer′fen*.

subnormal, adj. unternormal.

subordinate, 1. n. Untergeꞏben- m. **2.** adj. untergeordnet; **(s. clause)** Nebensatz, ꞏe m.

subscribe. vb. (underwrite) zeichnen; (take regularly) abonnie′ren; (approve) billigen.

subscription, n. Abonnement′, -s nt.; Zeichnung, -en f.

subsequent, adj. folgend.

subside, vb. nachꞏlassen*.

subsidy, n. Zuschuß, ꞏsse m.

substance, n. Substanz′, -en f.

substantial, adj. wesentlich; beträcht′lich.

substitute, 1. n. Ersatz′ m.; Vertre′tung, -en f. **2.** vb. erset′zen; als Ersatz′ geben*; die Vertre′tung überneh′men*.

substitution, n. Erset′zung, -en f.

subtle, adj. subtil′, fein.

subtract, vb. abꞏziehen*.

suburb, n. Vorort, -e m.

subversive, adj. zerset′zend, staatsfeindlich.

subway, n. Untergrundbahn, -en f., U-Bahn, -en f.

succeed, vb. erfolg′reich sein*; (come after) folgen.

success, n. Erfolg′, -e m.

successful, adj. erfolg′reich.

succession, n. (to throne)

Erbfolge, -n f.; (sequence) Reihenfolge, -n f.

successive, adj. aufeinan'-derfolgend.

successor, n. Nachfolger, - m.

succumb, vb. erlie'gen*.

such, adj. solch.

suck, vb. saugen, lutschen.

suction, n. Saugen nt.; Saug-(cpds.).

sudden, adj. plötzlich, jäh.

sue, vb. verkla'gen, gericht'-lich belan'gen.

suffer, vb. leiden*.

suffice, vb. genü'gen, aus-reichen.

sufficient, adj. genü'gend.

suffocate, vb. ersti'cken.

sugar, n. Zucker m.

suggest, vb. vor'schlagen*.

suggestion, n. Vorschlag, -e m.

suicide, n. Selbstmord, -e m.

suit, 1. n. (man's clothing) Anzug, -e m.; (woman's clothing) Kostüm', -e nt.; (cards) Farbe, -n f.; (law) Prozeß', -sse m. 2. vb. passen; (be becoming) ste-hen*.

suitable, adj. passend; ange-messen.

suitcase, n. Koffer, - m.

suitor, n. Freier, - m.

sullen, adj. griesgrämig.

sum, n. Summe, -n f.

summarize, vb. zusam'men-fassen.

summary, 1. n. Übersicht, -en f. 2. adj. summa'risch.

summer, n. Sommer, - m.

summit, n. Gipfel, - m.

summon, vb. zusam'men-rufen*, ein'berufen*; (law) vor'laden*.

sun, n. Sonne, -n f.

sunburn, n. Sonnenbrand, -e m.

sunburned, adj. sonnenver-brannt.

Sunday, n. Sonntag, -e m.

sunken, adj. versun'ken.

sunny, adj. sonnig.

sunshine, n. Sonnenschein m.

superb, adj. hervor'ragend.

superficial, adj. oberfläch-lich.

superfluous, adj. überflüssig.

super-highway, n. Auto-bahn en f.

superior, 1. n. Vorgesetzt-m.&f. 2. adj. höher; überle'-gen.

superiority, n. Überle'gen-heit f.

superlative, 1. n. Super-lativ, -e m. 2. adj. überra'-gend.

supernatural, adj. über-natürlich.

supersede, vb. verdrän'gen; erset'zen.

supersonic, adj. Überschall-(cpds.).

superstition, n. Aberglaube (n), - m.

superstitious, adj. aber-gläubisch.

supervise, vb. beauf'sichti-gen.

supper, n. Abendbrot, -e nt.; Abendessen, - nt.; (Lord's S.) Abendmahl, -e nt.

supplement, n. Ergän'zung, -en f., Nachtrag, -e m.

supply, 1. n. Versor'gung f.; Vorrat, -e m.; (s. and de-mand) Angebot (nt.) und Nachfrage (f.). 2. vb. ver-sor'gen, liefern.

suppose, vb. an'nehmen*, vermu'ten.

support, 1. n. Stütze, -n f.; Unterstüt'zung, -en f. 2. vb. stützen; unterstüt'zen.

suppress, vb. unterdrü'cken.

suppression, n. Unter-drü'ckung, -en f.

supreme, adj. oberst-, höchst-; Ober- (cpds.).

sure, adj. sicher.

surely, adv. sicherlich, gewiß.

surf, n. Brandung, -en f.

surface, n. Oberfläche, -n f.

surge, vb. wogen, branden.

surgeon, n. Chirurg', -en, -en m.

surgery, n. Chirurgie' f.; Operation', -en f.

surmise, 1. n. Vermu'tung, -en f. 2. vb. vermu'ten.

surmount, vb. überwin'den*.

surname, n. Zuname(n), - m., Fami'lienname(n), - m.

surpass, vb. überstei'gen*, übertref'fen*.

surplus, 1. n. Überschuß, ·sse m. **2.** adj. überschüs-sig; Über- (cpds.).

surprise, 1. n. Überra'-schung, -en f. **2.** vb. überra'-schen.

surrender, 1. n. Übergabe f., Erge'bung, -en f.

surround, vb. umge'ben*; umzin'geln.

surroundings, n.pl. Umge'-bung, -en f.

survey, 1. n. Überblick, -e m.; (measuring) Vermes'-sung, -en f. **2.** vb. über-bli'cken; vermes'sen*.

survival, n. Überle'ben nt.

survive, vb. überle'ben.

susceptible, adj. empfäng'-lich, zugänglich.

suspend, vb. (debar) sus-pendie'ren; (stop tempo-rarily) zeitweilig auf·heben*; (payment) ein·stellen; (sen-tence) aus·setzen; (hang) auf·hängen.

suspense, n. Schwebe f.; Spannung, -en f.

suspension, n. Schwebe f.; Suspen'sion, -en f.

suspicion, n. Verdacht' m., Argwohn m.

suspicious, adj. (doubting) misstrauisch; (doubtful look-ing) verdäch'tig.

sustain, vb. aufrecht·er-halten*; (suffer) erlei'den*.

swallow, 1. n. (bird) Schwal-be, -n f.; (gulp) Schluck, -e m. **2.** vb. schlucken.

swamp, 1. n. Sumpf, ·e m. **2.** vb. überschwem'men.

swan, n. Schwan, ·e m.

swarm, 1. n. Schwarm, ·e m. **2.** vb. schwärmen; (fig.) wimmeln.

sway, vb. schwingen*; schwan-ken.

swear, vb. schwören; (curse) fluchen.

sweat, 1. n. Schweiß m. **2.** vb. schwitzen.

sweater, n. Pullo'ver, - m., Strickjacke, -n f.

Swede, n. Schwede, -n, -n m.

Sweden, n. Schweden nt.

Swedish, adj. schwedisch.

sweet, adj. süß.

sweetheart, n. Liebst- m.&f.

sweetness, n. Süße f.; (fig.) Anmut f.

swell, 1. adj. prima. **2.** vb. schwellen*.

swift, adj. rasch, geschwind'.

swim, vb. schwimmen*.

swindle, vb. schwindeln.

swindler, n. Schwindler, - m.

swine, n. Schwein, -e nt.

swing, 1. n. Schaukel, -n f. **2.** vb. schwingen*, schaukeln.

Swiss, 1. n. Schweizer, - m. **2.** adj. schweizerisch; Schwei-zer- (cpds.).

switch, 1. n. (whip) Gerte, -n f.; (railway) Weiche, -n f.; (elec.) Schalter, - m. **2.** vb. (railway) rangie'ren; um·schalten; (exchange) ver-tau'schen.

Switzerland, n. die Schweiz f.

sword, n. Schwert, -er nt.

syllabic, adj. silbisch.

syllable, n. Silbe, -n f.

symbol, n. Symbol', -e nt.

symbolic, adj. symbo'lisch.

sympathetic, adj. mitfühl-end; (med.) sympa'thisch.

sympathize, vb. mit·fühlen.

sympathy, n. Sympathie', -i'en f.

symphonic, adj. sympho'-nisch.

symphony, n. Symphonie', -i'en f.

symptom, n. Anzeichen, - nt., Symptom', -e nt.

symptomatic, adj. sympto-toma'tisch; charakteris'-tisch.

syndicate, n. Syndikat', -e nt.

synonym, n. Synonym', -e nt.

synonymous, adj. sinnver-wandt, synonym'.

synthetic, adj. synthe'tisch; künstlich; Kunst- (cpds.).

syphilis, n. Syphilis f.

syringe, *n.* Spritze, -n *f.*

syrup, *n.* Sirup *m.*

system, *n.* System', -e *nt.*

systematic, *adj.* systema'-tisch.

T

table, *n.* Tisch, -e *m.*; (*list*) Verzeich'nis, -se *nt.*

tablecloth, *n.* Tischdecke, -n *f.*; Tischtuch, ·er *nt.*

tablespoon, *n.* Eßlöffel, - *m.*

tablet, *n.* Tafel, -n *f.*; (*pill*) Tablet'te, -n *f.*

tack, **1.** *n.* Stift, -e *m.* (thumb t.) Heftzwecke, -n *f.* **2.** *vb.* (*sew*) heften; (*sail*) kreuzen.

tact, *n.* Takt *m.*

tag, *n.* Etikett, -e *nt.*; (**play t.**) Fangen spielen.

tail, *n.* Schwanz, ·e *m.*

tailor, *n.* Schneider, - *m.*

take, *vb.* nehmen*; (*carry*) bringen*; (*need*) erfor'dern.

tale, *n.* Geschich'te, -n *f.*; Erzäh'lung, -en *f.*

talent, *n.* Bega'bung, -en *f.*, Talent', -e *nt.*

talk, **1.** *n.* Gespräch', -e *nt.*; (*lecture*) Vortrag, ·e *m.* **2.** *vb.* reden, sprechen*.

talkative, *adj.* gesprä'chig.

tall, *adj.* groß(·); hoch (hoh-, höher, höchst-); lang(·).

tame, **1.** *adj.* zahm. **2.** *vb.* zähmen.

tamper, *vb.* herum'pfuschen.

tan, **1.** *n.* (*sun*) Sonnen-bräune *f.* **2.** *adj.* gelbbraun. **3.** *vb.* bräunen; (*leather*) gerben.

tangle, **1.** *n.* Gewirr', *nt.* **2.** *vb.* sich zu schaffen machen mit.

tank, *n.* Tank, -s *m.*; (*mil.*) Panzer, - *m.*

tap, **1.** *n.* (*blow*) Taps, -e *m.*; (*faucet*) Hahn, ·e *m.* **2.** *vb.* leicht schlagen*; an'zapfen.

tape, *n.* Band, ·er *m.*

tape recorder, *n.* Tonband-gerät, -e *nt.*, Magnetophon', -e *nt.*

tapestry, *n.* Wandteppich, -e *m.*; Tapisserie', -i'en *f.*

tar, **1.** *n.* Teer *m.* **2.** *vb.* teeren.

target, *n.* Ziel, -e *nt.*; Ziel-scheibe, -n *f.*

tariff, *n.* Zolltarif, -e *m.*

tarnish, *vb.* (*fig.*) befle'cken; (*silver*) sich beschla'gen*.

tart, **1.** *n.* Törtchen, - *nt.* **2.** *adj.* sauer, herb.

task, *n.* Aufgabe, -n *f.*

taste, **1.** *n.* Geschmack', ·e *m.* **2.** *vb.* schmecken, kosten.

tasty, *adj.* schmackhaft.

taut, *adj.* straff.

tavern, *n.* Bierlokal, -e *nt.*

tax, **1.** *n.* Steuer, -n *f.* **2.** *vb.* besteu'ern, belas'ten.

taxi, *n.* Taxe, -n *f.*, Taxi, -s *nt.*

taxpayer, *n.* Steuerzahler, - *m.*

tea, *n.* Tee, -s *m.*

teach, *vb.* lehren, unterrich'-ten.

teacher, *n.* Lehrer, - *m.*

team, *n.* Mannschaft, -en *f.*

tea-pot, *n.* Teekanne, -n *f.*

tear, **1.** *n.* Träne, -n *f.*; (*rip*) Riß, -sse *m.* **2.** *vb.* reißen*.

tease, *vb.* necken.

teaspoon, *n.* Teelöffel, - *m.*

technical, *adj.* technisch.

technique, *n.* Technik, -en *f.*, Kunstfertigkeit *f.*

tedious, *adj.* langweilig, mühsam.

telegram, *n.* Telegramm', -e *nt.*

telegraph, **1.** *n.* Telegraph', -en, -en *m.* **2.** *vb.* tele-graphie'ren.

telephone, **1.** *n.* Telephon', -e *nt.*, Fernsprecher, - *m.* **2.** *vb.* telephonie'ren.

telescope, *n.* Fernrohr, -e *nt.*

televise, *vb.* im Fernsehen übertra'gen*.

television, *n.* Fernsehen *nt.*

television set, *n.* Fernseh-apparat, -e *m.*

tell, *vb.* erzäh'len, berich'ten, sagen.

teller, n. Kassie'rer, - m.

temper. 1. n. Laune, -n f.; Temperament' nt.; (anger) Zorn m. **2.** vb. mäßigen; (steel) härten.

temperament, n. Gemüts'art, -en f.

temperamental, adj. Gemüts'- (cpds.); temperament'voll.

temperate, adj. mäßig.

temperature, n. Temperatur', -en f.

tempest, n. Sturm, ⸚e m.

temple, n. Tempel, - m.

temporary, adj. zeitweilig, vorü'bergehend, proviso'risch.

tempt, vb. versu'chen; reizen.

temptation, n. Versu'chung, -en f.

ten, num. zehn.

tenant, n. Mieter, - m.; Pächter, - m.

tend, vb. pflegen, hüten; (incline) neigen zu.

tendency, n. Neigung, -en f., Tendenz', -en f.

tender. 1. n. (money) Zahlungsmittel, - nt.; (train, boat) Tender, - m. **2.** adj. zart; zärtlich. **3.** vb. anbieten*.

tenderness, n. Zartheit, -en f.; Zärtlichkeit, -en f.

tendon, n. Sehne, -n f.

tennis, n. Tennis nt.

tenor, n. Tenor', -e m.

tense, adj. gespannt'; kribbelig.

tension, n. Spannung, -en f.

tent, n. Zelt, -e nt.

tentative, adj. probeweise.

tenth. 1. adj. zehnt-. **2.** n. Zehntel, - nt.

term, n. Perio'de, -n f.; (of office) Amtszeit, -en f.; (college) Semes'ter, - nt.; (expression) Ausdruck, ⸚e m.; (condition) Bedin'gung, -en f.

terminate, vb. been'den; begren'zen.

terrace, n. Terras'se, -n f.

terrible, adj. schrecklich, furchtbar.

territory, n. Gebiet', -e nt.

terror, n. Schrecken, - m.

test. 1. n. Prüfung, -en f.; Probe, -n f.; Test, -s m.; Versuch', -e m. **2.** vb. prüfen.

testify, vb. bezeu'gen; (court) aus·sagen.

testimony, n. Zeugnis, -se nt.; Zeugenaussage, -n f.

text, n. Text, -e m.

textile, 1. n. Textil'ware, -n f. **2.** adj. Textil'- (cpds.).

texture, n. Gewe'be, - nt.; Aufbau m.; Beschaf'fenheit, -en f.

than, conj. als.

thank, vb. danken.

thankful, adj. dankbar.

that. 1. pron.&adj. der, das, die; jener, -es, -e. **2.** conj. daß.

the, art. der, das, die.

theater, n. Thea'ter, - nt.; (fig.) Schauplatz, ⸚e m.

thee, pron. dich; dir.

theft, n. Diebstahl, ⸚e m.

their, adj. ihr, -, -e.

theirs, pron. ihrer, -es, -e.

them, pron. sie; ihnen.

theme, n. Thema, -men nt.

then, adv. (after that) dann; (at that time) damals; (therefore) dann, also.

thence, adv. von da, von dort.

theology, n. Theologie' f.

theoretical, adj. theore'tisch.

theory, n. Theorie', -i'en f.

therapy, n. Therapie' f.

there, adv. (in that place) da, dort; (to that place) dahin', dorthin'; (from t.) daher', dorther'.

therefore, adv. daher, darum, deshalb, deswegen, also.

thermometer, n. Thermome'ter, - nt.

thermonuclear, adj. kernphysikalisch.

these, adj. diese.

they, pron. sie.

thick, adj. dick; (dense) dicht.

thicken, *vb.* dicken, verdi'cken; verdich'ten.

thickness, *n.* Dicke *f.*; Dichtheit *f.*; (*layer*) Schicht, -en *f.*

thief, *n.* Dieb, -e *m.*

thigh, *n.* Schenkel, - *m.*

thimble, *n.* Fingerhut, ᵉᵉ *m.*

thin, *adj.* dünn; mager.

thing, *n.* Ding, -e *nt.*; Sache, -n *f.*

think, *vb.* meinen, glauben; denken*, nach·denken*.

thinker, *n.* Denker, - *m.*

third, **1.** *adj.* dritt-. **2.** *n.* Drittel, - *nt.*

thirst, **1.** *n.* Durst *m.* **2.** *vb.* dürsten.

thirsty, *adj.* durstig.

thirteen, *num.* dreizehn.

thirteenth, **1.** *adj.* dreizehnt-. **2.** *n.* Dreizehntel, - *nt.*

thirtieth, **1.** *adj.* dreißigst-. **2.** *n.* Dreißigstel, - *nt.*

thirty, *num.* dreißig.

this, *pron.&adj.* dieser, -es, -e.

thorough, *adj.* gründlich.

thou, *pron.* du.

though, **1.** *adv.* doch. **2.** *conj.* obwohl', obgleich'.

thought, *n.* Gedan'ke(n), - *m.*

thoughtful, *adj.* gedan'kenvoll; (*considerate*) rücksichtsvoll.

thousand, *num.* tausend.

thousandth, **1.** *adj.* tausendst-. **2.** Tausendstel, - *nt.*

thread, *n.* Faden, ᵉ *m.*; Garn, -e *nt.*

threat, *n.* Drohung, -en *f.*

threaten, *vb.* drohen.

three, *num.* drei.

thrift, *n.* Sparsamkeit *f.*

thrill, **1.** *n.* Aufregung, -en *f.*; Sensation', -en *f.*; Nervenkitzel, - *m.* **2.** *vb.* erre'gen, packen.

throat, *n.* Hals, ᵉᵉ *m.*; Kehle, -n *f.*

throb, *vb.* pochen, pulsie'ren.

throne, *n.* Thron, -e *m.*

through, **1.** *prep.* durch. **2.** *adj.* fertig.

throughout, **1.** *adv.* überall; völlig. **2.** *prep.* durch.

throw, **1.** *n.* Wurf, ᵉe *m.* **2.** *vb.* werfen*, schleudern.

thrust, **1.** *n.* Stoß, ᵉe *m.*; (*tech.*) Schub *m.* **2.** *vb.* stoßen*.

thumb, *n.* Daumen, - *m.*

thunder, **1.** *n.* Donner, - *m.* **2.** *vb.* donnern.

thunderstorm, *n.* Gewit'ter, - *nt.*

Thursday, *n.* Donnerstag, -e *m.*

thus, *adv.* so.

ticket, *n.* Karte, -n *f.*, Billett', -s *or* -e *nt.*; (*admission*) Eintrittskarte, -n *f.*; (*travel*) Fahrkarte, -n *f.*, Fahrschein, -e *m.*; (*traffic*) Strafmandat, -e *nt.*

tickle, *vb.* kitzeln.

ticklish, *adj.* kitzlig; (*delicate,risky*) heikel.

tide, *n.* Gezei'ten *pl.*; (*low t.*) Ebbe *f.*; (*high t.*) Flut *f.*

tidy, *adj.* sauber, ordentlich.

tie, **1.** *n.* (*bond*) Band, -e *nt.*; (*necktie*) Krawat'te, -n *f.*, Schlips, -e *m.*; (*equal score*) Punktgleichheit *f.*, Stimmengleichheit *f.* **2.** *vb.* binden*, knüpfen.

tiger, *n.* Tiger, - *m.*

tight, *adj.* eng; (*taut*) straff; (*firm*) fest; (*drunk*) beschwipst'.

tighten, *vb.* straffen, enger machen.

tile, *n.* (*wall, stove*) Kachel, - *f.*; (*floor*) Fliese, -n *f.*; (*roof*) Ziegel, - *m.*

till, **1.** *n.* Ladenkasse, -n *f.* **2.** *vb.* bebau'en, bestel'len. **3.** *adv., conj.* bis.

tilt, **1.** *n.* Neigung, -en *f.* **2.** *vb.* neigen, kippen.

timber, *n.* Holz *nt.*

time, **1.** *n.* Zeit, -en *f.*; (*o'clock*) Uhr *f.* **2.** *vb.* die Zeit nehmen*.

timetable, *n.* Fahrplan, ᵉe *m.*; Kursbuch, ᵉer *nt.*

timid, *adj.* ängstlich, schüchtern.

timidity, n. Ängstlichkeit f., Schüchternheit f.

tin, n. (metal) Zinn nt.; (t. plate) Blech nt.; (t. can) Konser'vendose, -n f.

tint, n. Farbtönung, -en f.

tiny, adj. winzig.

tip, 1. n. (end) Spitze, -n f.; (gratuity) Trinkgeld, -er nt. 2. vb. (tilt) kippen; (give gratuity) ein Trinkgeld geben*.

tire, 1. n. Reifen, - m. 2. vb. ermü'den.

tired, adj. müde.

tissue, n. Gewe'be, - nt.; (facial t.) Papier'taschentuch, *er nt.

title, n. Titel, - m.; (heading) Überschrift, -en f.

to, prep. zu.

toast, 1. n. Toast m.; (drink to health) Trinkspruch, *e m. 2. vb. rösten; auf jemandes Wohl trinken*.

tobacco, n. Tabak m.

today, adv. heute.

toe, n. Zehe, -n f.

together, adv. zusam'men.

toil, 1. n. Arbeit, -en f., Mühe, -n f. 2. vb. arbeiten, sich ab-mühen.

toilet, n. Toilet'te, -n f.

token, n. Zeichen, - nt.; Symbol', -e nt.

tolerance, n. Duldsamkeit f., Toleranz' f.

tolerant, adj. duldsam, tolerant'.

tolerate, vb. dulden.

tomato, n. Toma'te, -n f.

tomb, n. Grab, *er nt., Grabmal, *er nt.

tomorrow, adv. morgen.

ton, n. Tonne, -n f.

tone, n. Ton, *e m.

tongue, n. Zunge, -n f.

tonic, 1. n. Stärkungsmittel, nt. 2. adj. tonisch.

tonight, adv. heute abend.

tonsil, n. Mandel, -n f.

too, adv. zu; (also) auch.

tool, n. Werkzeug, -e nt.

tooth, n. Zahn, *e m.

toothache, n. Zahnschmerzen pl.

toothbrush, n. Zahnbürste, -n f.

toothpaste, n. Zahnpaste, -n f.

top, 1. n. Spitze, -n f., oberstes Ende, -n nt.; (surface) Oberfläche, -n f.; (on t. of) auf. 2. vb. (fig.) krönen.

topcoat, n. Mantel, * m.

topic, n. Thema, -men nt.

torch, n. Fackel, -n f.

torment, 1. n. Qual, -en f. 2. vb. quälen.

torrent, n. reißender Strom, *e m.

torture, 1. n. Folter, -n f., Qual, -en f. 2. vb. foltern, quälen.

toss, vb. werfen*, schleudern.

total, 1. n. Summe, -n f. 2. adj. gesamt'; total'.

totalitarian, adj. totalitär'.

touch, 1. n. Berüh'rung, -en f.; (sense of t.) Tastsinn m.; (final t.) letzter Schliff, -e m.; (t. of fever, etc.) An'lug m. 2. vb. berüh'ren.

touching, adj. rührend.

tough, 1. n. Rabau'ke, -n, -n m. 2. adj. zäh; (hard) hart(*).

tour, 1. n. Reise, -n f., Tour, -en f. 2. vb. berei'sen.

tourist, n. Tourist', -en, -en m.

tow, vb. schleppen.

toward, prep. nach; gegen; zu.

towel, n. Handtuch, *er nt.

tower, n. Turm, *e m.

town, n. Stadt, *e f., Ort, -e m.

toy, 1. n. Spielzeug, -e nt. 2. vb. spielen.

trace, 1. n. Spur, -en f. 2. vb. (delineate) nach-zeichnen; (track) zurück'-verfolgen.

track, 1. n. Spur, -en f., Fährte, -n f.; (sports) Leichtathletik f.; (R.R.) Gelei'se, - nt., Gleis, -e nt. 2. vb. (t. down) nach-spüren.

tract, n. (land) Gebiet', -e

nt.; (*pamphlet*) Traktat', -e *nt.*

tractor, *n.* Trecker, - *m.*

trade. 1. *n.* Handel *m.*; (*exchange*) Tausch *m.*; **2.** *vb.* Handel treiben*; aus·tauschen.

trader, *n.* Händler, - *m.*

tradition, *n.* Tradition', -en *f.*

traditional, *adj.* traditionell'.

traffic, *n.* Verkehr' *m.*; (*trade*) Handel *m.*

traffic light, *n.* Verkehrs'licht, -er *nt.*, Verkehrs'ampel, -n *f.*

tragedy, *n.* Tragö'die, -n *f.*

tragic, *adj.* tragisch.

trail, *n.* Fährte, -n *f.*

trailer, *n.* Anhänger, - *m.*; (*for living*) Wohnwagen, - *m.*

train. 1. *n.* Zug, "e *m.*; (*of dress*) Schleppe, -n *f.* **2.** *vb.* aus·bilden.

traitor, *n.* Verrä'ter, - *m.*

tramp, *n.* Landstreicher, - *m.*

tranquil, *adj.* ruhig.

tranquillity, *n.* Ruhe *f.*

transaction, *n.* Transaktion', -en *f.*

transfer. 1. *n.* (*ticket*) Umsteigefahrschein, -e *m.* **2.** *vb.* (*change cars*) um·steigen*; (*money*) überwei'sen*; (*ownership*) übertra'gen*; (*move to new location*) verset'zen.

transfix, *vb.* durchboh'ren.

transform, *vb.* um·wandeln, um·formen.

transfusion, *n.* Transfusion', -en *f.*

transition, *n.* Übergang, "e *m.*

translate, *vb.* überset'zen.

translation, *n.* Überset'zung, -en *f.*

transmit, *vb.* übertra'gen*; übersen'den.

transparent, *adj.* durchsichtig.

transport. 1. *n.* Beför'derung, -en *f.*; Transport', -e *m.* **2.** *vb.* beför'dern, transportie'ren.

transportation, *n.* Beför'derung, -en *f.*

trap, *n.* Falle, -n *f.*

trash, *n.* Abfall, "e *m.*; (*fig.*) Kitsch *m.*

travel. 1. *n.* Reise, -n *f.* **2.** *vb.* reisen.

travel agency, *n.* Reisebüro, -s *nt.*

traveler, *n.* Reisend·e *m.&f.*

tray, *n.* Tablett', -e *nt.*

treacherous, *adj.* verrä'terisch; tückisch.

tread. 1. *n.* Schritt, -e *m.* **2.** *vb.* treten*.

treason, *n.* Verrat' *m.*

treasure. 1. *n.* Schatz, "e *m.* **2.** *vb.* hoch·schätzen.

treasurer, *n.* Schatzmeister, - *m.*

treasury, *n.* Finanz'ministerium, -rien *nt.*

treat. 1. *n.* Extragenuß, "sse *m.* **2.** *vb.* gehandeln; (*pay for*) frei·halten*.

treatment, *n.* Behand'lung, -en *f.*

treaty, *n.* Vertrag', "e *m.*

tree, *n.* Baum, "e *m.*

tremble, *vb.* zittern.

tremendous, *adj.* ungeheuer.

trench, *n.* Graben, " *m.*

trend, *n.* Trend, -s *m.*

trespass, *vb.* widerrechtlich betre'ten*; übertre'ten*.

trial, *n.* Versuch', -e *m.*; (*law*) Prozeß', -sse *m.*

triangle, *n.* Dreieck, -e *nt.*

tribute, *n.* Tribut', -e *m.*; (*fig.*) Ehrung, -en *f.*

trick. 1. *n.* Kniff, -e *m.*, Trick, -s *m.* **2.** *vb.* rein·legen.

tricky, *adj.* kniflig; heikel.

trifle, *n.* Kleinigkeit, -en *f.*, Lappa'lie, -n *f.*

trigger, *n.* (*gun*) Abzug, "e *m.*

trim. 1. *adj.* adrett'. **2.** *vb.* (*clip*) stutzen; (*adorn*) besetzen.

trip. 1. *n.* Reise, -n *f.* **2.** *vb.* stolpern; (*tr.*) einem ein Bein stellen.

triple. 1. *adj.* dreifach. **2.** *vb.* verdrei'fachen.

trite, *adj.* abgedroschen.

triumph, 1. *n.* Triumph', -e *m.* **2.** *vb.* triumphie'ren.

triumphant, *adj.* triumphie'rend.

trivial, *adj.* trivial'.

trolley-bus, *n.* Obus, -se *m.*

trolley-car, *n.* Strassenbahn, -en *f.*

troop, *n.* Trupp, -s *m.*

troops, *n.pl.* Truppen *pl.*

trophy, *n.* Trophä'e, -n *f.*

tropic, *n.* Wendekreis, -e *m.*

tropical, *adj.* tropisch.

tropics, *n.pl.* Tropen *pl.*

trot, 1. *n.* Trab *m.* **2.** *vb.* traben.

trouble, 1. *n.* Mühe, -n *f.;* (*difficulty*) Schwierigkeit, -en *f.;* (*unpleasantness*) Unannehmlichkeit, -en *f.;* (*jam*) Klemme, -n *f.* **2.** *vb.* bemühen; beun'ruhigen.

troublesome, *adj.* lästig.

trough, *n.* Trog, ⁼e *m.*

trousers, *n.pl.* Hose, -n *f.*

trousseau, *n.* Aussteuer, -n *f.*

trout, *n.* Forel'le -n *f.*

truce, *n.* Waffenstillstand, ⁼e *m.*

truck, *n.* Lastauto, -s *nt.,* Lastwagen, - *m.,* Lastkraftwagen, - *m.*

true, *adj.* wahr; wahrhaf'tig; (*faithful*) treu.

truly, *adv.* wahrhaf'tig; (**yours t.**) Ihr erge'bener, Ihre erge'bene.

trumpet, *n.* Trompe'te, -n *f.*

trunk, 1. *n.* (*tree*) Stamm, ⁼e *m.;* (*luggage*) Koffer, - *m.*

trust, 1. *n.* Zuversicht *f.,* Vertrau'en *nt.;* (*comm.*) Trust, -s *m.;* (**in t.**) zu treuen Händen. **2.** *vb.* vertrau'en.

trustworthy, *adj.* zuverlässig.

truth, *n.* Wahrheit, -en *f.*

truthful, *adj.* wahr; ehrlich.

try, 1. *n.* Versuch', -e *m.* **2.** *vb.* versu'chen, probie'ren.

tub, *n.* Wanne, -n *f.*

tube, *n.* Röhre, -n *f.;* (*container*) Tube, -n *f.*

tuberculosis, *n.* Tuberkulo'se *f.*

tuck, 1. *n.* Falte, -n *f.* **2.** *vb.* falten.

Tuesday, *n.* Dienstag, -e *m.*

tuft, *n.* Büschel, - *nt.,* Quaste, -n *f.*

tug, *vb.* ziehen*.

tuition, *n.* Schulgeld -er *nt.;* (*university*) Studiengeld, -er *nt.*

tulip, *n.* Tulpe, -n *f.*

tumor, *n.* Tumor, -o'ren *m.*

tumult, *n.* Tumult', -e *m.*

tuna, *n.* Thunfisch, -e *m.*

tune, 1. *n.* Melodie', -i'en *f.* **2.** *vb.* stimmen.

tuneful, *adj.* melo'disch.

tunnel, *n.* Tunnel, - *m.*

turbine, *n.* Turbi'ne, -n *f.*

turbo-jet, *n.* (*plane*) Turbi'nenjäger, - *m.*

turbo-prop, *n.* Turbi'nenpropellertriebwerk, -e *nt.*

Turk, *n.* Türke, -n, -n *m.*

turkey, *n.* Truthahn, ⁼e *m.,* Puter, - *m.*

Turkey, *n.* die Türkei' *f.*

Turkish, *adj.* türkisch.

turmoil, *n.* Durcheinan'der *nt.*

turn, 1. *n.* Umdre'hung, -en *f.;* Wendung, -en *f.,* Kurve, -n *f.;* (**to take t.s**) sich abwechseln; (**it's my t.**) ich bin dran. **2.** *vb.* drehen, wenden*; (**t. around**) umdrehen.

turnip, *n.* Steckrübe, -n *f.*

turret, *n.* Turm, ⁼e *m.*

turtle, *n.* Schildkröte, -n *f.*

tutor, 1. *n.* Lehrer, - *m.,* Nachhilfelehrer, - *m.* **2.** *vb.* Nachhilfeunterricht geben*.

twelfth, 1. *adj.* zwölft-. **2.** *n.* Zwölftel, - *nt.*

twelve, *num.* zwölf.

twentieth, 1. *adj.* zwanzigst-. **2.** *n.* Zwanzigstel, - *nt.*

twenty, *num.* zwanzig.

twice, *adv.* zweimal.

twig, *n.* Zweig, -e *m.*

twilight, *n.* Dämmerung, -en *f.,* Zwielicht *nt.*

twin, *n.* Zwilling, -e *m.*

twine, 1. *n.* (*thread*) Zwirn, -e *m.;* (*rope*) Tau, -e *nt.* **2.** *vb.* winden*.

twist, 1. *n.* Drehung, -en *f.;*

(distortion) Verdre'hung, -en *f.* **2.** *vb.* drehen; verdre'hen.

two, *num.* zwei.

type, 1. *n.* Typ, -en *m.*; Typus, -pen *m.*; *(printing)* Schriftsatz, ¨e *m.*; *(letter)* Type, -n *f.* **2.** *vb.* kennzeichnen; *(write on typewriter)* tippen.

typewriter, *n.* Schreibmaschine, -n *f.*

typhoid fever, *n.* Typhus *m.*

typical, *adj.* typisch.

typist, *n.* Schreibdame, -n *f.*

tyranny, *n.* Tyrannei' *f.*

tyrant, *n.* Tyrann', -en, -en *m.*

U

ugliness, *n.* Häßlichkeit *f.*

ugly, *adj.* häßlich.

ulcer, *n.* Geschwür', -e *nt.*

ulterior, *adj.* höher; weiter; **(u. motives)** Hintergedanken *pl.*

ultimate, *adj.* äußerst-.

umbrella, *n.* Regenschirm, -e *m.*

umpire, *n.* Schiedsrichter, - *m.*

un-, *prefix* un-.

unable, *adj.* unfähig.

unanimous, *adj.* einstimmig.

unbecoming, *adj.* unschicklich; *(of clothes)* unkleidsam.

uncertain, *adj.* ungewiß.

uncertainty, *n.* Ungewißheit, -en *f.*

uncle, *n.* Onkel, - *m.*

unconscious, *adj.* bewußtlos; *(unaware)* unbewußt.

uncover, *vb.* auf·decken; entblö'ßen.

under, *prep.* unter.

underground, 1. *n.* Untergrundbahn, -en *f.* **2.** *adj.* unter der Erde gelegen; Untergrund- *(cpds.)*.

underline, *vb.* unterstrei'chen*.

underneath, 1. *adv.* unter, drunter. **2.** *prep.* unter.

undershirt, *n.* Unterhemd, -en *nt.*

undersign, *vb.* unterzeich'nen.

understand, *vb.* verste'hen*, begrei'fen*.

understanding, *n.* Verständ'nis *nt.*; *(agreement)* Einvernehmen, - *nt.*

undertake, *vb.* unterneh'men*.

undertaker, *n.* Leichenbestatter, - *m.*

underwear, *n.* Unterwäsche *f.*

underworld, *n.* Unterwelt *f.*

undo, *vb.* auf·machen, lösen; ungeschehen machen.

undress, *vb.* entklei'den, (sich) aus·ziehen*.

uneasy, *adj.* unruhig, unbehaglich.

unemployed, *adj.* arbeitslos.

unemployment, *n.* Arbeitslosigkeit *f.*

unequal, *adj.* ungleich.

uneven, *adj.* uneben; ungleich; *(numbers)* ungerade.

unexpected, *adj.* unerwartet.

unfair, *adj.* ungerecht.

unfamiliar, *adj.* unbekannt; ungeläufig.

unfavorable, *adj.* ungünstig.

unfit, *adj.* untauglich.

unfold, *vb.* entfal'ten.

unforgettable, *adj.* unvergeßlich.

unfortunate, *adj.* unglücklich; bedau'erlich.

unhappy, *adj.* unglücklich.

uniform, 1. *n.* Uniform', -en *f.* **2.** *adj.* einheitlich.

unify, *vb.* verei'nen; verein'heitlichen.

union, *n.* Verei'nigung, -en *f.*; **(labor u.)** Gewerk'schaft, -en *f.*

unique, *adj.* einzigartig.

unit, *n.* Einheit, -en *f.*

unite, *vb.* verei'nigen.

United Nations, *n.* die Verein'ten Natio'nen *pl.*

United States, *n.* die Verei'nigten Staaten *pl.*

unity, *n.* Einigkeit *f.*

universal, *adj.* universal'.

universe, *n.* Weltall *nt.*

university, *n.* Universität', -en *f.*

unjust, *adj.* ungerecht.

unknown, *adj.* unbekannt.

unless, *conj.* wenn nicht; es sei denn, daß.

unlike, *adj.* ungleich.

unlikely, *adj.* unwahrscheinlich.

unload, *vb.* ab·laden*, aus·laden*.

unlock, *vb.* auf·schließen*.

unlucky, *adj.* **(be u.)** kein Glück haben*, Pech haben*.

unmarried, *adj.* unverheiratet.

unpack, *vb.* aus·packen.

unpleasant, *adj.* unangenehm.

unqualified, *adj.* (*unfit*) ungeeignet; (*unreserved*) uneingeschränkt.

unsettled, *adj.* unsicher, in der Schwebe.

unsteady, *adj.* unstet.

unsuccessful, *adj.* erfolglos.

untie, *vb.* auf·knüpfen.

until, **1.** *prep.* bis; **(not u.)** erst. **2.** *conj.* bis; **(not u.)** erst wenn; erst als.

untruth, *n.* Unwahrheit, -en *f.*

untruthful, *adj.* unwahr.

unusual, *adj.* ungewöhnlich.

unwell, *adj.* unpäßlich, nicht wohl.

up, **1.** *prep.* auf. **2.** *adv.* auf, hinauf', herauf'.

upbraid, *vb.* schelten*.

uphill, **1.** *adj.* (*fig.*) mühsam. **2.** *adv.* bergan', bergauf'.

uphold, *vb.* aufrecht·erhalten*.

upholster, *vb.* bezie'hen*.

upholsterer, *n.* Tapezie'rer, - *m.*

upon, *prep.* auf.

upper, *adj.* ober-.

upright, *adj.* aufrecht.

uprising, *n.* Aufstand, ⸚e *m.*

uproar, *n.* Getö'se *nt.*

uproot, *vb.* entwur'zeln.

upset, **1.** *n.* Rückschlag, ⸚e *m.*; **(stomach u.)** Magenverstimmung, -en *f.* **2.** *vb.* (*overturn*) um·werfen*; (*disturb*) über den Haufen werfen, verstim'men; (*discompose*) aus der Fassung bringen*.

upside down, *adv.* umgekehrt, verkehrt' herum'.

upstairs, *adv.* oben; nach oben.

urban, *adj.* städtisch.

urge, **1.** *n.* Drang, ⸚e *m.*; (*sex*) Trieb, -e *m.* **2.** *vb.* drängen, nötigen.

urgency, *n.* Dringlichkeit *f.*

urgent, *adj.* dringend.

urinal, *n.* Harnglas, ⸚er *nt.*; (*public*) öffentliche Bedürf'nisanstalt, -en *f.*

urinate, *vb.* urinie'ren.

urine, *n.* Urin', -e *nt.*

urn, *n.* Urne, -n *f.*

us, *pron.* uns.

usage, *n.* Gebrauch' ⸚e *m.*

use, **1.** *n.* Gebrauch', ⸚e *m.*, Benut'zung, -en *f.* **2.** *vb.* gebrau'chen, verwen'den, benut'zen.

useful, *adj.* nützlich.

useless, *adj.* nutzlos.

user, *n.* Benut'zer, - *m.*

usher, *n.* (*theater, etc.*) Platzanweiser, - *m.*; (*wedding*) Brautführer, - *m.*

usual, *adj.* gewöhn'lich.

usury, *n.* Wucher *m.*

utensil, *n.* Gerät', -e *nt.*

uterus, *n.* Gebär'mutter, ⸚ *f.*

utility, *n.* Nutzbarkeit *f.*

utilize, *vb.* aus·nutzen.

utmost, *adj.* äusserst.

utter, **1.** *adj.* völlig. **2.** *vb.* äußern.

utterance, *n.* Äußerung, -en *f.*

V

vacancy, *n.* (*position*) freie Stellung, -en *f.*; (*hotel, etc.*) unvermietetes Zimmer, -*nt.*

vacant, adj. frei; (empty) leer.

vacate, vb. räumen.

vacation, n. Ferien pl.

vaccinate, vb. impfen.

vaccination, n. Impfung, -en f.

vaccine, n. Impfstoff, -e m.

vacuum, n. Vakuum, -kua nt.

vagrant, 1. n. Landstreicher, m.; (worker) Saison'arbeiter, - m. **2.** adj. vagabundie'rend.

vague, adj. unbestimmt, vage.

vain, 1. adj. (conceited) eitel; (useless) vergeb'lich. **2.** n. (in v.) umsonst', verge'bens.

valet, n. Diener, - m.

valiant, adj. tapfer.

valid, adj. gültig.

valise, n. Reisetasche, -n f.

valley, n. Tal, ⸗er nt.

valor, n. Tapferkeit f.

valuable, adj. wertvoll.

value, n. Wert, -e m.

valve, n. Ventil', -e nt.; (med.) Klappe, -n f.

van, n. (delivery truck) Lieferwagen, - m.; (moving v.) Möbelwagen, - m.

vandal, n. Vanda'le, -n, -n m.

vanguard, n. Vorhut f.; (person) Vorkämpfer, - m.

vanilla, n. Vanil'le f.

vanish, vb. verschwin'den*.

vanity, n. Eitelkeit f.

vanquish, vb. besie'gen.

vapor, n. Dampf, ⸗e m.

variance, n. Widerstreit m.

variation, n. Abwechslung, -en f.; Abänderung, -en f., Variation', -en f.

varied, adj. verschie'den; mannigfaltig.

variety, n. Mannigfaltigkeit f.; (choice) Auswahl f.; (theater) Varieté' nt.

various, adj. verschie'den.

varnish, 1. n. Firnis, -se m. **2.** vb. firnissen.

vary, vb. variie'ren, verän'dern.

vase, n. Vase, -n f.

vast, adj. riesig.

vat, n. Faß, ⸗sser nt.

vaudeville, n. Varieté' nt.

vault, n. Gewöl'be, - nt.; (burial chamber) Gruft, ⸗e f.; (bank) Tresor', -e m.; (jump) Sprung, ⸗e m. **2.** vb. springen*.

veal, n. Kalbfleisch nt.

vegetable, n. Gemü'se, - nt.

vehement, adj. heftig.

vehicle, n. Fahrzeug, -e nt.

veil, 1. n. Schleier, - m. **2.** vb. verschlei'ern.

vein, n. Vene, -n f., Ader, -n f.

velocity, n. Geschwin'digkeit, -en f.

velvet, n. Samt m.

veneer, n. Furnier', -e nt.

vengeance, n. Rache f.

venom, n. Gift, -e nt.

vent, n. Öffnung, -en f.; (escape passage) Abzugsröhre, -n f. **2.** vb. freien Lauf lassen*.

ventilate, vb. lüften, ventilie'ren.

ventilation, n. Lüftung f., Ventilation' f.

venture, 1. n. Wagnis, -se nt. **2.** vb. wagen.

verb, n. Verb, -en nt., Zeitwort, ⸗er nt.

verbal, adj. verbal'; (oral) mündlich.

verdict, n. Urteil, -e nt.

verge, 1. n. (fig.) Rand, ⸗er m. **2.** vb. (v. on) grenzen an.

verification, n. Bestä'tigung, -en f.

verify, vb. bestä'tigen.

vernacular, 1. n. Umgangssprache, -n f. **2.** adj. umgangssprachlich.

versatile, adj. vielseitig.

verse, n. Vers, -e m.

versify, vb. in Verse bringen*.

version, n. Fassung, -en f., Version', -en f.

versus, prep. gegen.

vertebrate, 1. n. Wirbeltier, -e nt. **2.** adj. Wirbel- (cpds.).

vertical, adj. senkrecht.

very, adv. sehr.

vespers, n. Vesper, -n f.

vessel, n. Schiff, -e nt.; (container) Gefäß', -e nt.

vest, n. Weste, -n f.

vestige, n. Spur, -en f.
veteran, n. Veteran', -en, -en m.
veterinary, 1. n. Tierarzt, ⹀e m. **2.** adj. tierärztlich.
veto, 1. n. Veto, -s m. **2.** vb. das Veto ein·legen.
vex, vb. ärgern; verblüf'fen.
via, prep. über.
viaduct, n. Viadukt', -e m.
vibrate, vb. vibrie'ren, schwingen*.
vibration, n. Vibration', -en f., Schwingung, -en f.; (tremor) Erschüt'terung, -en f.
vice, n. Laster, - nt.
vicinity, n. Nähe f., Umge'bung, -en f.
vicious, adj. gemein', heimtückisch.
victim, n. Opfer, - nt.
victor, n. Sieger, - m.
victorious, adj. siegreich.
victory, n. Sieg, -e m.
Vienna, n. Wien, nt.
view, 1. n. Aussicht, -en f. **2.** vb. bese'hen*, betrach'ten.
vigil, n. Nachtwache, -n f.
vigilant, adj. wachsam.
vigor, n. Kraft, ⹀e f., Energie', -i'en f.
vigorous, adj. kräftig, kraftstrozend.
vile, adj. gemein', niederträchtig.
village, n. Dorf, ⹀er nt.
villain, n. Bösewicht, -e m., Schurke, -n, -n m.
vindicate, vb. rechtfertigen.
vine, n. Rebstock, ⹀e m.; (creeper) Ranke, -n f.
vinegar, n. Essig m.
vineyard, n. Weingarten, ⹀ m., Weinberg, -e m.
vintage, n. (gathering) Weinlese f.; (year) Jahrgang, ⹀e m.
viol, viola, n. Bratsche, -n f.
violate, vb. verlet'zen; (oath) brechen*; (law, territory) übertre'ten*.
violation, n. Verlet'zung, -en f.; Bruch, ⹀e m.; Übertre'tung, -en f.
violator, n. Verlet'zer, - m.; Übertre'ter, - m.
violence, n. Gewalt'tätig-keit, -en f.; (vehemence) Gewalt'samkeit f., Heftigkeit f.
violent, adj. gewalt'tätig; gewalt'sam, heftig.
violet, 1. n. Veilchen, - nt. **2.** adj. violett', veilchenblau.
violin, n. Geige, -n f.
virgin, n. Jungfrau, -en f.
virile, adj. männlich.
virtue, n. Tugend, -en f.
virtuous, adj. tugendhaft, tugendsam.
virus, n. Virus, -ren m.
visa, n. Visum, -sa nt.
vise, n. Schraubstock, ⹀e m.
visible, adj. sichtbar.
vision, n. Sehkraft, ⹀e f.; (visual image) Vision', -en f.
visit, 1. n. Besuch', -e m. **2.** vb. besu'chen.
visitor, n. Besu'cher, - m.
visual, adj. visuell'.
vital, adj. (essential) wesentlich; (strong) vital'.
vitality, n. Lebenskraft f., Vitalität' f.
vitamin, n. Vitamin', -e nt.
vivacious, adj. lebhaft, temperament'voll.
vivid, adj. leben'dig, lebhaft.
vocabulary, n. Wortschatz, ⹀e m.; (list of words) Wörterverzeichnis, -se nt.
vocal, adj. Stimm-, Gesang'- (cpds.); lautstark.
vogue, n. Mode, -n f.
voice, n. Stimme, -n f.
void, adj. ungültig.
volcano, n. Vulkan', -e m.
volt, n. Volt, - f.
voltage, n. Stromspannung, -en f.
volume, n. Volu'men, - nt.; (book) Band, ⹀e m.; (quantity) Umfang, ⹀e m.
voluntary, adj. freiwillig.
volunteer, 1. n. Freiwillige m.&f. **2.** vb. sich freiwillig melden.
vomit, vb. erbre'chen*.
vote, 1. n. (individual ballot) Wahlstimme, -n f.; (casting) Stimmabgabe, -n f.; (v. of confidence) Vertrau'ensvotum nt. **2.** vb. wählen, stimmen, ab·stimmen.

voter, *n.* Wähler, - *m.*

vouch for, *vb.* verbür'gen für.

vow, 1. *n.* Gelüb'de - *nt.* **2.** *vb.* gelo'ben.

vowel, *n.* Vokal', - *e m.*

voyage, *n.* Reise, -n *f.*

vulgar, *adj.* vulgär', ordinär'.

vulgarity, *n.* Ordinär'heit, -en *f.*

vulnerable, *adj.* verletz'bar; angreifbar.

W

wad, *n.* Bündel, - *nt.*; *(of cotton)* Wattebausch, *e m.*; *(roll)* Rolle, -n *f.*

wade, *vb.* waten.

wag, 1. *n.* Spaßvogel, * m.* **2.** *vb.* wedeln.

wage, 1. *n.* Lohn, *e m.* **2.** *vb.* **(w. war)** Krieg führen.

wager, 1. *n.* Wette, -n *f.* **2.** *vb.* wetten.

wagon, *n.* Wagen - *m.*

wail, *vb.* wehklagen.

waist, *n.* Taille, -n *f.*

waistcoat, *n.* Weste, -n *f.*

wait, 1. *n.* Wartezeit, -en *f.* **2.** *vb.* warten; **(w. for)** warten auf.

waiter, *n.* Kellner, - *m.*

waitress, *n.* Kellnerin, -nen *f.*

waiver, *n.* Verzicht'leistung, -en *f.*

wake, 1. *n.* *(vigil)* Totenwache, -n *f.*; *(of boat)* Kielwasser *nt.* **2.** *vb.* *(tr.)* wecken; *(intr.)* erwa'chen.

walk, 1. *n.* Spazier'gang, *e m.* **2.** *vb.* gehen*, laufen*.

wall, *n.* Wand, *e f.*; *(of stone or brick)* Mauer, -n *f.*

wallet, *n.* Brieftasche, -n *f.*

walnu:, *n.* Walnuß, *sse *f.*

walrus, *n.* Walross, -sse *nt.*

waltz, 1. *n.* Walzer, - *m.* **2.** *vb.* Walzer tanzen.

wander, *vb.* wandern; **(w. around)** umher'wandern.

want, 1. *n.* Mangel, * *m.*;

(needs) Bedarf' *m.*; *(poverty)* Armut *f.* **2.** *vb.* wollen, wünschen.

war, *n.* Krieg, -e *m.*

ward, *n.* Mündel, - *nt.*; *(city)* Bezirk', -e *m.*; *(hospital, prison)* Abtei'lung, -en *f.*

ware, *n.* Ware, -n *f.*

warlike, *adj.* kriegerisch.

warm, 1. *adj.* warm(*). **2.** *vb.* wärmen.

warmth, *n.* Wärme *f.*

warn, *vb.* warnen.

warning, *n.* Warnung, -en *f.*

warp, *vb.* krümmen; *(fig.)* verdre'hen, entstel'len.

warrant, 1. *n.* *(authorization)* Vollmacht, -en *f.*; *(writ of arrest)* Haftbefehl, -e *m.* **2.** *vb.* gewähr'leisten, garantie'ren.

warrior, *n.* Krieger, - *m.*

warship, *n.* Kriegsschiff, -e *nt.*

wash, 1. *n.* Wäsche, -n *f.* **2.** *vb.* waschen*.

wash-basin, *n.* Waschbecken, - *nt.*

washroom, *n.* Waschraum, *e m.*

wasp, *n.* Wespe, -n *f.*

waste, 1. *n.* Abfall, *e m.* **2.** *adj.* *(superfluous)* überflüssig; *(bare)* öde. **3.** *vb.* verschwen'den, vergeu'den.

watch, 1. *n.* *(guard)* Wache, -n *f.*; *(timepiece)* Uhr, -en *f.*; *(wrist w.)* Armbanduhr, -en *f.*; *(pocket w.)* Taschenuhr, -en *f.* **2.** *vb.* *(guard)* bewa'chen, passen auf; *(observe)* beob'achten, acht·geben; **(w. out)** auf·passen; **(w. out!)** Vorsicht!

watchful, *adj.* wachsam.

watchmaker, *n.* Uhrmacher, - *m.*

water, 1. *n.* Wasser, - *nt.* **2.** *vb.* wässern, begie'ßen*.

waterfall, *n.* Wasserfall, *e m.*

waterproof, *adj.* wasserdicht.

wave, 1. *n.* Welle, -n *f.* **2.** *vb.* wellen, wogen; *(flag)* wehen; *(hand)* winken.

waver, *vb.* schwanken.

wax, 1. *n.* Wachs, -e *nt.* **2.** *vb.* wachsen; (*moon*) zunehmen*.

way, *n.* Weg, -e *m.*

we, *pron.* wir.

weak, *adj.* schwach(·).

weaken, 1. *vb.* (*tr.*) schwächen; (*intr.*) schwach werden*.

weakness, *n.* Schwäche, -n *f.*

wealth, *n.* Reichtum, ∘er *m.*; (*possessions*) Vermö'gen, -nt.; (*abundance*) Fülle *f.*

wealthy, *adj.* reich, vermö'gend.

weapon, *n.* Waffe, -n *f.*

wear, *vb.* tragen*, an·haben*, (*hat*) auf·haben*, (*fig.*) ab·tragen*, (*fig.*) erschöp'fen; (**w. out**) aus·höhlen.

weary, *adj.* müde, erschöpft*.

weasel, *n.* Wiesel, - *nt.*

weather, 1. *n.* Wetter *nt.* **2.** *vb.* (*fig.*) durch·stehen*.

weave, *vb.* weben*(*).

weaver, *n.* Weber, - *m.*

web, *n.* Netz, -e *nt.*, Gewe'be *nt.*; (*spider w.*) Spinnennetz, -e *nt.*, Spinngewebe *nt.*

wedding, *n.* Hochzeit, -en *f.*

wedge, 1. *n.* Keil, -e *m.* **2.** *vb.* ein·klemmen.

Wednesday, *n.* Mittwoch, -e *m.*

weed, 1. *n.* Unkraut *nt.* **2.** *vb.* jäten.

week, *n.* Woche, -n *f.*

weekday, *n.* Wochentag, -e *m.*

week end, *n.* Wochenende, -n *nt.*

weekly, 1. *n.* Wochenschrift, -en *f.* **2.** *adj.* wöchentlich.

weep, *vb.* weinen.

weigh, *vb.* wiegen*; (*ponder*) wägen.

weight, *n.* Gewicht', -e *nt.*; (*burden*) Last, -en *f.*

weird, *adj.* unheimlich.

welcome, 1. *n.* Willkom'men *nt.* **2.** *vb.* bewill'kommnen, begrü'ßen. **3.** *adj.* willkom'men; (**you're w.**) bitten.

welfare, *n.* Wohlergehen *nt.*; (*social*) Wohlfahrt *f.*

well, 1. *n.* Brunnen, - *m.* **2.** *vb.* quellen*. **3.** *adv.* gut; (*health*) gesund'(*, -). wohl.

well-known, *adj.* bekannt'.

west, 1. *n.* Westen *m.* **2.** *adj.* westlich; West- (*cpds.*).

western, *adj.* westlich.

westward, *adv.* nach Westen.

wet, 1. *adj.* naß(*, -). **2.** *vb.* nässen, naß machen.

whale, *n.* Walfisch, -e *m.*

what, 1. *pron.* was. **2.** *adj.* welcher, -es, -e.

whatever, 1. *pron.* was . . . auch. **2.** *adj.* welcher, -es, -e . . . auch.

wheat, *n.* Weizen *m.*

wheel, 1. *n.* Rad, ∘er *nt.* **2.** *vb.* rollen.

when, 1. *adv.* (*question*) wann. **2.** *conj.* (*once in the past*) als; (*future; whenever*) wenn; (*indirect question*) wann.

whence, *adv.* woher', von wo.

whenever, 1. *conj.* wenn. **2.** *adv.* wann . . . auch.

where, *adv.* (*in what place*) wo; (*to what place*) wohin'; (**w. . . . from**) woher'.

wherever, *adv.* wo(hin) . . . auch.

whether, *conj.* ob.

which, *pron.&adj.* welcher, -es, -e.

whichever, *pron.&adj.* welcher, -es, -e . . . auch.

while, 1. *n.* Weile *f.* **2.** *conj.* während.

whim, *n.* Laune, -n *f.*

whip, 1. *n.* Peitsche, -n *f.* **2.** *vb.* peitschen, schlagen*.

whirl, *vb.* wirbeln.

whirlpool, *n.* Strudel, - *m.*

whirlwind, *n.* Wirbelwind, -e *m.*

whisker, *n.* Barthaar, -e *nt.*

whiskey, *n.* Whisky, -s *m.*

whisper, *vb.* flüstern.

whistle, 1. *n.* Flöte, -n *f.*, Pfeife, -n *f.* **2.** *vb.* flöten, pfeifen*.

white, *adj.* weiß.

who, *pron.* (*interrogative*) wer; (*relative*) der, das, die.

whoever, *pron.* wer . . . auch.

whole, 1. *n.* Ganz- *nt.* **2.** *adj.* ganz; (*unbroken*) heil.

wholesale, 1. *n.* Großhandel *m.* **2.** *adv.* en gros.

wholesome, *adj.* gesund'(". -).

why, *adv.* warum', wieso', weshalb.

wicked, *adj.* böse, verrucht'.

wickedness, *n.* Verrucht'heit *f.*

wide, *adj.* weit; breit.

widen, *vb.* erwei'tern.

widespread, *adj.* weit verbrei'tet.

widow, *n.* Witwe, -n *f.*

widower, *n.* Witwer, - *m.*

width, *n.* Weite, -n *f.*; Breite, -n *f.*

wield, *vb.* handhaben*; (*fig.*) aus·üben.

wife, *n.* Frau, -en *f.*

wig, *n.* Perü'cke, -n *f.*

wild, *adj.* wild.

wilderness, *n.* Wildnis, -se *f.*

wilful, *adj.* eigensinnig; (*intentional*) vorsätzlich.

will, 1. *n.* Wille(n) *m.*; (*testament*) Testament', -e *nt.* **2.** *vb.* (*future*) werden*; (*want to*) wollen*; (*bequeath*) verma'chen.

willing, *adj.* willig; gewillt'; (**be w.**) wollen*.

willow, *n.* Weide, -n *f.*

wilt, *vb.* welken, verwel'ken.

wilted, *adj.* welk.

win, *vb.* gewin'nen*.

wind, 1. *n.* Wind, -e *m.* **2.** *vb.* winden*, wickeln; (*watch*) auf·ziehen*.

window, *n.* Fenster, - *nt.*

windy, *adj.* windig.

wine, *n.* Wein, -e *m.*

wing, *n.* Flügel, - *m.*

wink, *vb.* blinzeln.

winner, *n.* Gewin'ner, - *m.*, Sieger, - *m.*

winter, *n.* Winter, - *m.*

wintry, *adj.* winterlich.

wipe, *vb.* wischen.

wire, 1. *n.* Draht, "e *m.*; (*telegram*) Telegramm', -e *nt.* **2.** *vb.* telegrafie'ren.

wire recorder, *n.* Drahtaufnahmegerät, -e *nt.*

wisdom, *n.* Weisheit, -en *f.*

wise, *adj.* weise, klug(").

wish, 1. *n.* Wunsch, "e *m.*; (**make a w.**) sich etwas wünschen. **2.** *vb.* wünschen.

wit, *n.* Verstand' *m.*; (*humor*) Humor' *m.*

witch, *n.* Hexe, -n *f.*

with, *prep.* mit.

withdraw, *vb.* 'zurück'·ziehen*.

wither, *vb.* verdor'ren.

withhold, *vb.* zurück'·halten*; ein·behalten*.

within, 1. *adv.* drinnen. **2.** *prep.* innerhalb.

without, 1. *adv.* draußen. **2.** *prep.* ohne.

witness, 1. *n.* Zeuge, -n, -n *m.* **2.** *vb.* Zeuge sein* von.

witty, *adj.* witzig; geistreich.

woe, *n.* Leid *nt.*

wolf, *n.* Wolf, "e *m.*

woman, *n.* Frau, -en *f.*

womb, *n.* Mutterleib *m.*

wonder, 1. *n.* Wunder, - *nt.* **2.** *vb.* (**I w.**) ich möchte gern wissen.

wonderful, *adj.* wunderbar, herrlich.

woo, *vb.* umwer'ben*.

wood, *n.* Holz, "er *nt.*; (*forest*) Wald, "er *m.*

wooden, *adj.* hölzern.

wool, *n.* Wolle *f.*

woolen, *adj.* wollen.

word, *n.* (*single*) Wort, "er *nt.*; (*connected*) Wort, -e *nt.*

wordy, *adj.* (*fig.*) langatmig.

work, 1. *n.* (*labor*) Arbeit, -en *f.*; (*thing produced*) Werk, -e *nt.*; (*gas w.s*) Gaswerke *pl.* **2.** *vb.* arbeiten; (*function*) gehen*, funktionie'ren.

worker, *n.* Arbeiter, - *m.*

workman, *n.* Arbeiter, - *m.*

world, *n.* Welt, -en *f.*

worldly, *adj.* weltlich.

worm, *n.* Wurm, "er *m.*

worn-out, *adj.* abgenutzt.

worry, 1. *n.* Sorge, -n *f.* **2.** *vb.* sich sorgen.

worse, *adj.* schlimmer, schlechter.

worship, 1. *n.* Vereh'rung, -en *f.*; (*church*) Gottesdienst, -e *m.* **2.** *vb.* vereh'ren, an·beten.

worst, *adj.* schlimmst-, schlechtest-.
worth, 1. *n.* Wert, -e *m.* **2.** *adj.* wert.
worthless, *adj.* wertlos.
worthy, *adj.* würdig, ehren- wert.
wound, 1. *n.* Wunde, -n *f.* **2.** *vb.* verwun'den.
wrap, 1. *n.* Umhang, ⁻e *m.* **2.** *vb.* wickeln.
wrapping, *n.* Verpa'ckung, -en *f.*
wrath, *n.* Zorn *m.*
wreath, *n.* Kranz, ⁻e *m.*
wreck, 1. *n.* Wrack, -s *nt.* **2.** *vb.* demolie'ren, kaputt'- machen.
wrench, 1. *n.* Ruck *m.*; *(tool)* Schraubenschlüssel, - *m.* **2.** *vb.* verren'ken.
wrestle, *vb.* ringen*.
wretched, *adj.* erbärm'lich.
wring, *vb.* *(hands)* ringen*; *(laundry)* wringen*; *(neck)* ab·drehen.
wrinkle, 1. *n.* Falte, -n *f.*, Runzel, -n *f.* **2.** *vb.* runzeln; *(cloth)* knittern.
wrist, *n.* Handgelenk, -e *nt.*
wrist-watch, *n.* Armband- uhr, -en *f.*
write, *vb.* schreiben*.
writer, *n.* Schreiber, - *m.*; *(by profession)* Schriftsteller, - *m.*; *(author)* Verfas'ser, - *m.*
writing, *n.* Schrift, -en *f.*; **(in w.)** schriftlich.
wrong, 1. *n.* Unrecht *nt.* *adj.* falsch; unrecht; **(be w.)** unrecht haben*, sich irren. **3.** *vb.* Unrecht tun*.

X

x-ray, 1. *n.* Röntgenauf- nahme, -n *f.* **2.** *vb.* röntgen.
x-rays, *n.pl.* Röntgenstrah- len *pl.*
xylophone, *n.* Xylophon', -e *nt.*

Y

yacht, *n.* Jacht, -en *f.*
yard, *n.* *(garden)* Garten, ⁻ *m.*; *(railroad)* Verschie'be- bahnhof, ⁻e *m.*; *(measure)* Yard, -s *nt.*
yarn, *n.* Garn, -e *nt.*; *(story)* Geschich'te, -n *f.*
yawn, *vb.* gähnen.
year, *n.* Jahr, -e *nt.*
yearly, *adj.* jährlich.
yearn, *vb.* sich sehnen.
yell, 1. *n.* Schrei, -e *m.* **2.** *vb.* schreien*, brüllen.
yellow, *adj.* gelb.
yes, *interj.* ja.
yesterday, *adv.* gestern.
yet, 1. *adv.* *(still)* noch; *(al- ready)* schon; **(not y.)** noch nicht. **2.** *conj.* doch.
yield, 1. *n.* Ertrag', ⁻e *m.* **2.** *vb.* ein·bringen*; *(cede)* nach·geben*.
yoke, *n.* Joch, -e *nt.*
yolk, *n.* Eigelb, - *nt.*
you, *pron.* du, Sie.
young, *adj.* jung(⁻).
youth, *n.* junger Mann, ⁻e *m.*, Jüngling, -e *m.*; *(young people; time of life)* Jugend, -en *f.*
youthful, *adj.* jugendlich.
Yugoslav, *n.* Jugosla'we -n, -n *m.*
Yugoslavia, *n.* Jugosla'wien *nt.*
Yugoslavian, 1. *n.* Jugosla'- we, -n, -n *m.* **2.** *adj.* jugo- sla'wisch.

Z

zeal, *n.* Eifer *m.*
zebra, *n.* Zebra, -s *nt.*
zero, *n.* Null, -en *f.*
zest, *n.* *(zeal)* Eifer *m.*; *(rel- ish)* Genuß' *m.*

zinc, *n.* Zink *nt.*

zipper, *n.* Reißverschluß, ⹁sse *m.*

zone, *n.* Zone, -n *f.*

zoo, *n.* Zoo, -s *m.*

zoological, *adj.* zoolo′gisch.

zoology, *n.* Zoologie′ *f.*

Numerals

CARDINAL		ORDINAL	
1	eins	1st	erst-
2	zwei	2nd	zweit-
3	drei	3rd	dritt-
4	vier	4th	viert-
5	fünf	5th	fünft-
6	sechs	6th	sechst-
7	sieben	7th	sieb(en)t-
8	acht	8th	acht-
9	neun	9th	neunt-
10	zehn	10th	zehnt-
11	elf	11th	elft-
12	zwölf	12th	zwölft-
13	dreizehn	13th	dreizehnt-
14	vierzehn	14th	vierzehnt-
15	fünfzehn	15th	fünfzehnt-
16	sechzehn	16th	sechzehnt-
17	siebzehn	17th	siebzehnt-
18	achtzehn	18th	achtzehnt-
19	neunzehn	19th	neunzehnt-
20	zwanzig	20th	zwanzigst-
21	einundzwanzig	21st	einundzwanzigst-
30	dreißig	30th	dreißigst-
32	zweiunddreißig	32nd	zweiunddreißigst-
40	vierzig	40th	vierzigst-
43	dreiundvierzig	43rd	
			dreiundvierzigst-
50	fünfzig	50th	fünfzigst-
54	vierundfünfzig	54th	vierundfünfzigst-
60	sechzig	60th	sechzigst-
65	fünfundsechzig	65th	
			fünfundsechzigst-
70	siebzig	70th	siebzigst-
76	sechsundsiebzig	76th	
			sechsundsiebzigst-
80	achtzig	80th	achtzigst-
87	siebenundachtzig	87th	
			siebenundachtzigst-
90	neunzig	90th	neunzigst-